Marine Corps Deaths

1917–1921

Craig R. Scott, CG

HERITAGE BOOKS
2013

HERITAGE BOOKS
AN IMPRINT OF HERITAGE BOOKS, INC.

Books, CDs, and more—Worldwide

For our listing of thousands of titles see our website
at
www.HeritageBooks.com

Published 2013 by
HERITAGE BOOKS, INC.
Publishing Division
5810 Ruatan Street
Berwyn Heights, Md. 20740

Copyright © 2013 Craig R. Scott, CG

All rights reserved. No part of this book may be reproduced or transmitted in any form or by any means, electronic or mechanical, including photocopying, recording or by any information storage and retrieval system without written permission from the author, except for the inclusion of brief quotations in a review.

International Standard Book Numbers
Paperbound: 978-0-7884-5487-5
Clothbound: 978-0-7884-6863-6

Marine Corps Deaths, 1917-1929

Preface

The combination of a tour of duty with the First Battalion, Eighth Marines, Second Marine Division as a young hospital corpsman, and one following that at the Naval Hospital, Camp Lejeune changed me immeasurably. Wearing green also had something to do with it I am sure. Changes that would be helpful throughout my twenty years and the years following.

Being a genealogist with a consummate interest in military records made this work a passion for me. Several years ago Peter Linder handed me a set of documents that are the basis for this work. I have added to it where possible. Without Peter's gift this journey would not have begun.

Craig R. Scott
Holly Springs, NC
28 January 2013

Marine Corps Deaths, 1917-1921

Marine Corps Deaths, 1917-1929

An Entry

Each entry gives the name of the Marine, rank, company, regiment, cause of death, date and place of death, and name and address of next of kin. Source information follows. Source codes are identified in the Abbreviations.

Marine Corps Deaths, 1917-1921

Marine Corps Deaths, 1917-1929

Abbreviations

[ANC] – burial in Arlington National Cemetery

Bn.   Battalion

DOA – Died of Accident (AEF)

DOC – Died of Other Causes (AEF)

DOD – Died of Disease (AEF)

DOS – Died of Other Causes (CONUS)

DOW – Died of Wounds

DDS – Died of Disease (CONUS)

DDU - Died of Disease (non-AEF, Overseas)

[FAG] – entry found in Find A Grave (www.FindAGrave.com); this only means that a likely entry was found. In some instances the search criteria does not match what is actually on the tombstone. Those are identified by how they are indexed, not by what is on the tombstone to facilitate locating the information. In some cases the date of death does not match the official records. Where the date of death is close to the date is it is ignored. When the difference is longer it is noted. The lack of a Find a Grave notation does not mean that there is not a Find a Grave entry. The database grows everyday. Recognize that a tombstone does not mean a burial, it may be a memorial. This is especially true of individuals lost at sea (like on the U.S.S. *Cyclops*) or found also on Tablets of the Missing at ABMC cemeteries.

FAGM – memorial entry found in Find A Grave (www.FindAGrave.com); in some cases there is no information concerning what cemetery a Marine is buried in, but there is an entry. In some cases there are memorial stones in cemeteries where is is know that the Marine is buried or on a Tablet of the Missing overseas. These are also included under this source.

Marine Corps Deaths, 1917-1921

KIA - Killed in Action

KOA – Accidentally Killed (AEF)

MAF

MCR – Marine Corps Reserve

MG   Machine Gun

[MOH] – Medal of Honor recipient

Regt.   Regiment

[S1] Record Group 127, Records of the United States Marine Corps, Entry 107, Register of Deaths of Marine Corps Personnel During World War I, 1918 – 19, National Archives, Washington, D.C., Officer List

[S2] Record Group 127, Records of the United States Marine Corps, Entry 107, Register of Deaths of Marine Corps Personnel During World War I, 1918 – 19, National Archives, Washington, D.C., Enlisted List

[S3] A list of the Officers and Enlisted Men of the U.S. Marine Corps Who Lost Their Lives While Serving in the United States and Posessions between the period From April 6, 1917 to November 11, 1918, original source has not been located in the National Archives, this copy in the personal possession of Peter Linder.

[S4] Officers and Enlisted Men of the United States Marine Corps (except Overseas Dead) Who Died Between November 12, 1918 and November 17, 1921, Inclusive, original source has not been located in the National Archives, this copy in the personal possession of Peter Linder.

[S5] Other deaths not yet sourced properly, but found among the papers in the personal possession of Peter Linder.

[TOM] - Tablet of the Missing or ABMC-at Sea

[SW] Marine Corps Roll of Honor, Annual Report of the Secretary of the Navy for 1918

Marine Corps Deaths, 1917-1929

[SW1] Marine Corps Roll of Honor, Annual Report of the Secretary of the Navy for 1919

[VA -] – burial found in VA Locator system at identified cemetery

Marine Corps Deaths, 1917-1921

Summary of Overseas Deaths, by Organizatons, for
The World War

Officers and Elisted Men

Organizaton

Unit	KIA	DOW	DOD	Other	Total
5th Regiment	736	406	46	12	1200
6th Regiment	615	546	60	10	1231
6th M.G. Bn.	92	52	3	1	148
Miscellaneous (see note)	5	2	40	11	58
1st Mar-Av. Force	2	1	24	1	28
1st Mar-Aero. Co.	0	0	3	1	4
8th Av. Training Center	0	0	0	1	1
11th Regiment	0	0	17	4	21
13th Regiment	0	0	111	5	116
Totals	1450	1007	304	46	2807

Total Number of officers 101
Total Number of enlisted men 2706
Grand Total 2807

(note: Replacements pressed into action before records officially transferred and names placed on the roster of 4th Brigade.)

Marine Corps Deaths, 1917-1929

Notes about this work

Dates of death vary from the official reports to the date found on the tombstone. This is not uncommon. Usually the discrepancy between the dates is at most a few days. In cases where the discrepancy is longer it is indicated.

Find A Grave is an interesting source of information about deaths. It can not be assumed that if there is an entry or even a photograph of a tombstone that the entry describes the actual burial of an individual. Many of these tombstones are memorial stones. A good example is that of the Marines who died on the U.S.S. *Cyclops*. All were lost at sea, yet several have tombstones.

In some cases there is a memorial in one cemetery and a tombstone in another. Many times the memorial is a town or county effort to identify the ultimate service of its citizens and is not the burial site. Sometimes is appears that the individual is buried in two places and these instances are identified as [FAGx2]

Sometimes official records do not identify the middle name of an individual. Find a Grave is a source for middle names.

U.S. Marine Corps Muster Rolls, 1798 – 1958 are available on Ancestry.com. The information on these muster rolls include Name, Service Number, Date of Enlistment and further information about death and character of service. The information on these muster rolls is not included in this work, but should be consulted.

Marine Corps Deaths, 1917-1929

Aanes, Arne John, Pvt., Extra Duty Detachment, DDS, November 4, 1918 at Parris Island, South Carolina. Mrs. Louise C. Aanes (Mother), Clarkfield, Minnesota [S3] [FAG]

Abbott, James Francis, Pvt., M.G. Co., 13th Regt., DOD, September 25, 1918 enroute to France. Mrs. Eva Simpson (Mother), 1179 S. Orleans St., Memphis, Tennessee [S2]

Abbott, Roy Simpson, Pvt., 51st Co., 5th Regt., KIA, November 10, 1918 in the Meuse Argonne. Fred S. Abbott (Father), 6402 S. Puget Sound Ave., Tacoma, Washington [S2] [SW1]

Abel, Ray F., 1st Sgt., USS *Mississippi*, DDU, January 18, 1919 aboard the USS *Mississippi*. Mrs. D. O. Abel (Mother), Seymour, Indiana [S4] [FAGM]

Abercrombie, Lewis Felton, Cpl., 8th Co., 5th Regt., DOW, June 8, 1918 in the Chateau Thierry sector. J. C. Abercrombie (Father), R #1, Gray Court, South Carolina [S2] [SW]

Abrams, Edward Belfrage, Cpl., 43rd Co., 5th Regt., KIA, June 12, 1918 in the Chateau Thierry sector. George Abrams (Father), 121 Highland Ave., Middletown, New York [ABMC-Belleau TOM] [S2] [SW]

Acker, Francis Frederick, Pvt., 45th Co., 5th Regt., KIA, October 4, 1918 in the Meuse Argonne. Mrs. Louis Mong (Sister), 160 Concord Ave., Detroit, Michigan [ABMC-Romagne TOM] [S2] [SW1]

Acuff, Norman Douglas, Pvt., 75th Co., 6th Regt., DOW, November 20, 1918 in the Meuse Argonne. Prentiss L. Acuff (Brother), Goodrich, Texas [ANC] [S2]

Marine Corps Deaths, 1917-1921

Acuff, Robert E., Cpl., 67th Co., 5th Regt., DOW, June 10, 1918 in the Chateau Thierry sector. Prentiss L. Acuff (Brother), Goodrich, Texas [ANC] [S2] [SW]

Adams, Eli, Pvt., 20th Co., 5th Regt., DOW, November 3, 1918 in the Meuse Argonne. Wesley Adams (Father), 100 Peachtree St., East Macon, Georgia [S2] [SW1]

Adams, Herbert C., Pvt., Marine Barracks, Navy Yard, Puget Sound, Washington, DAS March 19, 1919 downed at Puget Sound, Washington. Mrs. Martha Adams (Mother), Gen. Del., Sedro Woolley, Washington [S4] [FAG as March 9, 1919]

Adams, John Ralph, Pvt., 95th Co., 6th Regt., KIA, June 13, 1918 in the Chateau Thierry sector. David Adams (Father) R.F.D. #1, Salineville, Ohio [S2] [SW]

Adams, Randell Willie, Pvt., Recruiting, Chicago, Illinois, DDS, September 24, 1918 at Milwaukee, Wisconsin. Mrs. Anie L. Cohn (Mother), Box 251, RFD#1, Memphis, Tennessee [S3] [FAGM]

Adams, Waldo Dakota, Pvt., 1st Division, Squadron D, MAF, DDS, January 7, 1921 at Santo Domingo, Dominican Republic, Mrs. Margaret Adams (Mother), Gen. Del., Romeo, Michigan [S4]

Addante, Frank William, Pvt., 16th Co., 5th Regt., KIA, June 7, 1918 in the Chateau Thierry sector. Vincenzo Addante (not stated), Largo del Mercato, Triggiano, Italy [VA-Rock Island] [S2] [SW]

Addison, George Leslie, Pvt., 97th Co., 6th Regt., DOW, July 19, 1918 in the Aisne Marne offensive. Annie F. Addison (Mother), R.R. #1, Bridgman, Michigan [ABMC-Fere] [S2] [SW1]

Adkins, Kellie, Pvt., MD, Navy Det. Cmp., DDS, April 21, 1919 at Deer Island, Massachusetts. William R. Adkins (Father), Tygarts Valley, Kentucky [S4]

Marine Corps Deaths, 1917-1929

Adwell, Palmer Alexander, Pvt., 79th Co., 6th Regt., KIA, June 6, 1918 in the Chateau Thierry sector. William Adwell (Father), Renville, Minnesota [ABMC-Belleau] [S2] [SW]

Ahl, Max Henry, Cpl., 95th Co., 6th Regt., DOW, July 19, 1918 in the Aisne-Marne offensive (Soissons). Rev. W.D. Ahl (Father), 530 – 9th St., Oshkosh, Wisconsin [ABMC-Fere] [S2] [SW1 says KIA]

Ahlstrand, Ernest Leonard, Pvt., 4h Squardron, FMAF, Miami, Floriada, DAS in an aeroplane on June 24, 1918 at Miami, Florida. Gust Ahlstrand (Father), Monmouth, Illionis [S3]

Ailing, Amil O. M., Pvt., 24th Co., 4th Prov. Regt., DDS, January 4, 1919 at Santo Domingo, Dominican Republic. Mrs. Carolina Ailing (Mother), 39 Saratoga St., Buffalo, New York [S4]

Akins, Thomas Edward, Pvt., 83rd Co., 6th Regt., DOW, June 6, 1918 in the Chateau Thierry sector. Emma Compton (Mother), Richton, Mississippi [FAG] [S2] [SW1 says KIA]

Albert, Oren Harold, Pvt., 148th Co., 8th Regt., DDS, September 18, 1921 at Port au Prince, Haiti, Mrs. Catherine Albert (Mother), 3111 F. 13th St., Kansas City, Missouri [S4]

Albert, Philip Leonard, Pvt., 18th Co., 5th Regt., KIA, June 6, 1918 in the Chateau Thierry sector. Noah L. Albert (Father), 154 S. 2nd St., Brooklyn, New York [S2] [SW says 134th Co.]

Albright, Ebenezer, Pvt., Barracks Detachment, Norfolk, Virginia, DDS, August 21, 1918 at Norfolk, Virginia. Anna Albright (Mother), 220 Williams St., Waukegan, Illionois [FAG] [S3]

Alcock, Harold J., Cpl., MB, Navy Yard, Philadelphia, Pennsylvania, DDS, November 27, 1918 at Philadelphia, Pennsylvania. Mrs. Elizabeth Alcock (Mother), Gen. Del., Lindenwood, Illinois [FAG] [S4]

Marine Corps Deaths, 1917-1921

Aldrich, Edward Joseph, Pvt., 74th Co., 6th Regt., DOW, July 19, 1918 in the Aisne-Marne offensive. Henry and Mary Aldrich (parents), 17 Blake St., Westboro, Massachusetts [ABMC-Fere] [S2] [SW1]

Alexander, Mearl Charles, Cpl., Hdqtrs. Co., 5th Regt., KIA, June 5, 1918 in the Aisne defensive. Anna S. Dean (sister), RFD #3, North Side Station, Youngstown, Ohio [S2] [SW]

Alexander, Sterling Livingston, Pvt., 8th Co., 5th Regt., KIA, July 20, 1918 in the Aisne-Marne (Soissons)., Mrs. L.E. Alexander (Mother), 110 Atlantic Ave., Franklin, Pennsylvania [ABMC-Fere] [S2] [SW1]

Alford, Jimmie Lesslie, Pvt., 19th Co., Quantico, Virginia, DDS, November 11, 1920 at Quantico, Virginia. Andrew J. Alford (Father), Route 1, Box 93a, Osyka, Mississippi [S4]

Allegaert, Pierre Francis, Pvt., Co. I, 11th Regt., DDS, October 6, 1918 at Quantico, Virginia. Mrs. Lonore Allegaert (Mother), 217 N. 9th St., Newark, New Jersey [S3]

Allen, Bernard Diggs, Pvt., 20th Co., 5th Regt., KIA, June 6, 1918 in the Chateau Thierry sector. Roland D. Allen (Father), King & Queen Court House, Virginia [S2] [SW1]

Allen, Charles Carroll, Cpl., 75th Co., 6th Regt., KIA, October 9, 1918 in the Meuse Argonne. Mrs. A.A. Allen (Mother), Bremond, Texas [S2] [SW1]

Allen, James Nelson, Pvt., 20th Co., 5th Regt., KIA, June 6, 1918 in the Chateau Thierry sector. Malinda C. Morgan (Mother), R #6, Alder St., Walla Walla, Washington [ABMC-Belleau] [S2] [SW]

Allen, Lester William, Pvt., 49th Co., 5th Regt., DOW, October 3, 1918 in the Meuse Argonne. Mrs. Catherine Allen (Mother), 2310 Sunnyside Ave., Chicago, Illinois, [ABMC-Belleau] [S2] [SW1]

Marine Corps Deaths, 1917-1929

Allen, Milton S., Pvt., Co. E, MB, Mare Island, California, DDS, November 23, 1918 at Mare Island, California. Mrs. Christiana Allen (Step-mother), Saratoga, California [S4]

Alley, Leaurence Elbridge, Pvt., 95th Co., 6th Regt., KIA, November 2, 1918 in the Meuse Argonne. McClellan Alley (Father), Searcy, Arkansas [VA-Little Rock] [S2] [SW1]

Allmacher, Paul Henry, Jr., Pvt., 53rd Co., Cape Haitien, Haiti, DDS, December 2, 1920 at Cape Haitien, Haiti. Mrs. Laura Allmacher (Mother), 650 Garland Ave., Detroit, Michigan [S4]

Allman, Walter Kenneth, Pvt., "F" Co., 11th Regt., KOA July 5, 1919 in France. Eva Allman (Mother), 1816 N. 4th St., Sheboygan, Wisconsin [S2] [SW1]

Alsobrook, James Alander, Pvt., 74th Co., 6th Regt., KIA, July 19, 1918 in the Aisne-Marne offensive. William J. Alsobrook (Father), Box 103, Chafee, Missouri [VA-Jefferson Barracks] [S2] [SW says HQ Co.]

Althoff, Paul Jacob, Sgt., 51st Co., 5th Regt., DOW, June 11, 1918 in the Chateau Thierry sector. Annie C. Althoff (Mother), 544 W. Clark Ave, York, Pennsylvania [FAG] [S2] [SW]

Altman, John, Sgt., 3129766, 49th Co., 5th Regt., DOW, November 1, 1918 in the Meuse Argonne. Louise Altman (Mother), 4907 Post St., Spokane, Washington [S2] [SW1]

Altman, Theodore W., Cpl., 20th Co., 5th Regt., DOD, October 12, 1918. Wounded in the Chateau Thierry sector. Louise Altman (Mother), 4907 Post St., Spokane, Washington [S2]

Ames, Bert Evert, Cpl., 47th Co., 5th Regt., DOW, June 25, 1918 in the Chateau Thierry sector. Louis H. Ames (Father), Americus, Kansas, [ABMC-Belleau] [S2] [SW]

Anagnos, Peter Konstantain, Pvt., 77th Co., 6th M.G. Bn., DOW, October 5, 1918 in the Meuse Argonne. Mrs. Irene P.

Marine Corps Deaths, 1917-1921

Dramante (Mother), Vrissia Island of Milylene, Greece [ABMC-Belleau] [S2]

Anderson, Allyn Taber, Pvt., 83rd Co., 6th Regt., DOW, June 23, 1918 in the Chateau Thierry sector. Mr. Ernest W. Anderson (Father), 831 Forest Ave., Wilmette, Illinois [FAG] [S2] [SW]

Anderson, Arthur Walter, Cpl., 80th Co., 6th Regt., DOW, July 19, 1918 in the Aisne Marne offensive. Augusta Anderson (Mother), Valparaiso, Nebraska [FAG] [S2] [SW1]

Anderson, Charles Lorimer, Pvt., 82nd Co., 6th Regt., DOD, February 16, 1919 in the Meuse Argonne. Sophia Anderson (sister), Milan, Tennessee [FAG] [S2]

Anderson, Emanuel, Sgt., 80th Co., 6th Regt., KIA, September 15, 1918 in St. Mihiel offensive. Michael Anderson (Father), 1152 Washington Ave., Racine, Wisconsin [ABMC-Romagne] [FAGM] [S2] [SW says 139th Co.]

Anderson, Frank Edward, Pvt., Co. F, 11th Regt., Quantico, Virginia, DDS, October 5, 1918 at Quantico, Virginia. Mr. J. W. Anderson (Father), c/o Mills Brothers, Springfield, Ohio [FAG] [S3]

Anderson, Fred William, Pvt., 67th Co., 5th Regt., DOD, November 18, 1918 in the Meuse Argonne. John Leonard Anderson (Father), Gen. Del., Hadlock, Washington [FAG] [S2]

Anderson, Frederick Lewis, Pvt., Mar. Det. USN Base #13, Azores. DOD, November 2, 1918 in Azores. Mrs. Martha Anderson (Mother), Irwin, Ohio [FAGM] [S2]

Anderson, Harry William, Sgt., 96th Co., 6th Regt., DOW, June 20, 1918 in the Chateau Thierry sector. Hilda Anderson (Mother), 110 W. 11th Pl., Chicago, Illinois [S2] [SW]

Anderson, Henry Dewey, Cpl., "C" Co., 13th Regt., DOD, September 23, 1918 on board the Von Steuben. Calvin Anderson (Father), Pleasant Lake, Indiana [S2]

Marine Corps Deaths, 1917-1929

Anderson, James Walter, Pvt., Co. A, Mare Island, California, DDS, June 2, 1917 at Mare Island, California. Mrs. Mary J. Anderson (Mother), Gen. Del., Surgionsville, Tennesse [FAG] [S3]

Anderson, John Albert, Cpl., 18th Co., 5th Regt., DOW, July 25, 1918 in Aisne Marne offensive. Charlotte Anderson (Mother), 526 S.University St., Blackfoot, Idaho [S2] [SW]

Anderson, John William, Pvt., 20th Co., 5th Regt., KIA, June 6, 1918 in the Chateau Thierry sector. Annie Johnson (Mother), 384 Freeport St., Dorchester, Massachusetts [ANC] [S2] [SW]

Anderson, Jonathan Ervin, Pvt., 96th Co., 6th Regt., KIA, September 15, 1918 in the St. Mihiel offensive. Maggie Anderson (Mother), RFD #2, Hernando, Mississippi [FAG] [S2] [SW1]

Anderson, Joseph Leslie, Pvt., 66th Co., 5th Regt., DOW, June 6, 1918 in the Chateau Thierry sector. Mary Anderson (aunt), 317 Cabell St., Lynchburg, Virginia, [ABMC-Belleau] [S2] [SW1 says KIA]

Anderson, Laverne Watters, Pvt., 95th Co., 6th Regt., KIA, June 13, 1918 in the Chateau Thierry sector. V. L. Anderson (Father), Sheridan, Illinois [FAG] [S2] [SW]

Anderson, Leonard Emanuel, Pvt. Co. B, Mare Island, California, DDS, March 3, 1920 at Mare Island, California. William Anderson (Father), Box 359, Motar, California [FAG] [S4]

Anderson, Otmer Orvell, Cpl., 67th Co., 5th Regt., KIA, June 6, 1918 in the Chateau Thierry sector. Charles W. Anderson (Father), Sta. B. Box 145, Charleston, West Virginia [FAG] [S2] [SW]

Anderson, Ray, Sgt., 84th Co., 6th Regt., KIA, June 6, 1918 in the Chateau Thierry sector. Mrs. Jennie Triplett (Mother), Box 239, Rome City, Indiana [S2] [SW]

Marine Corps Deaths, 1917-1921

Anderson, Roscoe Urbannis, Pvt., Co. F, MB, Navy Yard, Mare Island, California, DDS, November 13, 1918 at Mare Island, California. Mrs. Leota Anderson (Wife), 55th and Cloverdale, South Seattle, Washington [VA-San Francisco] [S4]

Anderson, Thomas Brit, Pvt., 75th Co., 6th Regt., DOW, November 2, 1918 in the Meuse Argonne. James C. Anderson (Brother), RFD #2, Tunnel Hill, Georgia [S2]

Andreasen, Ivar George, Pvt., 82nd Co., 6th Regt., KIA, October 8, 1918 in the Meuse Argonne. Mathilda Andreasen (Mother), 205 Grand Ave., Billings, Montana [ABMC-Romagne] [S2] [SW1]

Andrews, Edwin Arthur, Pvt., Co. B, 10th Separate Battalion, DDS, November 8, 1918 at Quantico, Virginia. William H. Andrews (Father), 58 Kenmore Rd., Medford, Massachusetts [S3]

Angle, Taylor J., Pvt., Balloon Det. Sept. BN, HAF, Quantico, Virginia, DAS, DAS, January 2, 1919 at Portsmouth, Ohio. Mrs. Francie Angle (Mother), Wheelersburg, Ohio [S4]

Anthony, William Donald, Pvt., 82nd Co., 6th Regt., KIA, June 6, 1918 in the Chateau Thierry sector. Isaac M. Anthony (Father), Centerville, Maryland [FAG] [S2] [SW1]

Antoine, Harold Mayberry, Pvt., 97th Co., 6th Regt., DOD, March 21, 1919 in the Meuse Argonne. Francis Antoine (Father), Doe Run, Missouri [VA-Jefferson Barracks] [S2]

Apple, Felix, Pvt., Hdqrs. Co., 5th Regt., KIA, November 1, 1918 in the Meuse Argonne. Herman Apple (Father), 605 W. 181st St., New York, New York [S2] [SW1]

Applebee, Edward George, Pvt., 51st Co., 5th Regt., KIA, June 11, 1918 in the Chateau Thierry sector. Leora L. Applegate (Mother), 1708 Crerck Ave., Detroit, Michigan [FAG] [S2] [SW1]

Marine Corps Deaths, 1917-1929

Arbuckle, Angus, Pvt., 83rd Co., 6th Regt., KIA, October 4, 1918 in the Meuse Argonne. Andrew Arbuckle (Father), Manor, Pennsylvania [S2] [SW1 says DOW]

Archer, Jerry O., Pvt., 114th Co., 3rd Prov. Regt., DDS, February 10, 1919 at San Domingo, Dominican Republic. Mrs. Mattie Archer (Mother), Ennis, Texas [FAG] [S4]

Armbrister, Henry, Sgt., Hdqtrs. Det., MB, DDS, May 30, 1919 at Brooklyn, New York. John Armbrister (Father), RFD#2, Zurich, Kansas [S4]

Armer, Sieber James, Pvt., MCR, Co. C., Mare Island, California, DDS, February 16, 1918 at Mare Island, California. James B. Armer (Father), 1502 W. Monroe St., Phoenix, Arizona [S3]

Armstrong, Eldon Leroy, Cpl., 66th Co., 5th Regt., KIA, October 1918 in the Meuse Argonne. Mrs. Dora Lovejoy (Mother) Box 943, Newark, Ohio [ABMC-Romagne] [S2] [SW says Hdqrs. O. S. Dept.]

Armstrong, Fred Edwood, Cpl., Barracks Det., New York, New York, DDS, January 17, 1918 at New York, New York. Mrs. A. O. Freeland (Mother), Corning, Tehama County, California [S3]

Arneson, Ludwig Oscar, Pvt., 55th Co., 5th Regt., DOW, September 15, 1918 in the St. Mihiel offensive. Albert Arneson (Brother), Almira, Washington [ABMC-Thiaucort] [S2] [SW says Co. C, 4th Sep. Btln.]

Arnett, Thomas Pinckey, Sgt., 66th Co., 5th Regt., KIA, June 6, 1918 in the Chateau Thierry sector. Grace Arnett (wife), Christopher, Illinois, [ABMC-Belleau] [S2] [SW]

Arnold, Otis Zephaniah, Pvt., 65th Co., Haiti, DAS, May 18, 1919 drowned at Haiti. Mrs. Dolly Arnold (Mother), Bogalusa, Louisiana [FAG] [S4]

Arnott, James Barnes, Pvt., 8th Co., 5th Regt., KIA, October 4, 1918 in the Meuse Argonne. Archibald Arnott (Father),

Marine Corps Deaths, 1917-1921

5331 Greenway Ave., Philadelphia, Pennsylvania [S2] [SW1]

Arnquist, Otto Clemence, Pvt., 23rd Co., 6th MGBn, KIA, November 5, 1918 in the Meuse Argonne. J. M. Arnquist (Father), New Richmond, Wisconsin, [ABMC-Romagne] [S2] [SW1]

Arnstein, Joseph, Sgt., Bks. Det., Navy Yard, Brooklyn, New York, DDS, February 6, 1920 at Brooklyn, New York. Mrs. Joseph Arnstein (Wife), 347 Harris St., Plymouth, Pennsylvania [S4]

Arps, Benjamin William, Pvt., 78th Co., 6th Regt., KIA, July 19, 1918 in the Aisne Marne. Junius W. Arps (Brother), Gen. Del., Augusta, Montana [ANC] [S2] [SW says Co. B, Repl. Btln.]

Arthur, Leslie Herndon, Pvt., 74th Co., 6th Regt., DOW, April 16, 1918 (gassed) Toulon Sector, Verdun. Mrs. C. C. Arthur (Mother), 420 E. 2nd St., Maysville, Kentucky [R] [S2] [SW]

Arthur, Romeo, Pvt., 78th Co., 6th Regt., DOW, October 4, 1918 in the Meuse Argonne. David D. Arthur (Father), Vienna, West Virginia [VA-Grafton] [S2] [SW1 says KIA]

Asbury, William Thomas, Pvt., 83rd Co., 6th Regt., DOW, June 8, 1918 in the Chateau Thierry sector. Susan Asbury (Mother), Dunow, Wayne Co., West Virginia [ABMC-Belleau TOM] [S2] [SW1]

Aselton, Ernest Kilbert, Pvt., 76th Co., 6th Regt., KIA, October 8, 1918 in the Meuse Argonne. Isaac Aselton (Father), Chesaning, Michigan [FAG] [S2] [SW1]

Ashby, Harry Bufford, Pfc., USS *Albany*, DDS, February 8, 1920 at Puget Sound, Washington. Mrs. Henrietta Ashmun (Mother), Lewis Hall, University of Washington, Seattle, Washington [S4]

Marine Corps Deaths, 1917-1929

Ashe, Arthur James, Pvt., 51st Co., 5th Regt., KIA, June 11, 1918 in the Chateau Thierry sector. Alfred M. Ashe (Father), R #2, Kittanning, Pennsylvania [FAG] [S2] [SW]

Ashley, Thomas W., 2nd Lieut., 67th Co., 5th Regt., KIA, June 6, 1918 in the Chateau Thierry sector; Charles H. Ashley (Father), Deerfield, Massachusetts [ABMC-Belleau] [S1] [SW]

Ashley, William H., Cpl., 79th Co., 6th Regt., KIA, November 1, 1918 in the Meuse Argonne. Pauline Ashley (Mother), P O Box 51, Dundas, Minnesota [S2] [SW1]

Ashmun, Donald, Pvt., 129th Co., Puget Sound, Washington, DDS, February 8, 1920 at Puget Sound, Washington. Mrs. Henrietta Ashmun (Mother) Lewis Hall, University of Washington, Seattle, Washington [S4]

Ashton, Jack, Pvt., Hdqtrs. Det., 2nd Br., DOS, September 8, 1919 at Santo Domingo City. Edward Ashton (Brother), 305 Independence Ave., Kansas City, Missouri [FAG] [S4]

Ashworth, John Denham, Cpl., 45th Co., 5th Regt., KIA, June 23, 1918 in the Chateau Thierry sector. Nancy A. Ashworth (Mother), P O Box 471, Pasadena, California [VA-San Fransico] [S2] [SW1 says DOW]

Asprooth, Oscar Maurice, Pvt., 66th Co., 5th Regt., KIA, November 5, 1918 in the Meuse Argonne. Selma Asprooth (Mother), 918 Third Ave., Rockford, Illinois [FAGM] [S2] [SW1]

Atchison, John Calvin, Pvt., 95th Co., 6th Regt., DOW, June 14, 1918 in the Chateau Thierry sector. Mary Atchison (Mother), Marissa, Illinois [FAG] [S2] [SW says 1st Repl. Btln.]

Atha, Thomas R., Cpl., "D" Co., 5th Regt., KIA, November 4, 1918 in the Meuse Argonne. Jacob S. Atha (Father), 306 Merchant St., Fairmont, West Virginia [S2] [SW1]

Atkins, Harold Dewey, Pvt., 8th Co., 5th Regt., DOW, June 9, 1918 in the Chateau Thierry sector. Lillian A. Kirk

Marine Corps Deaths, 1917-1921

(Mother), 304 N 41st St., Philadelphia, Pennsylvania [R] [S2] [SW says M.G.B.]

Atkins, Lonzele, Pvt., 66th Co., 5th Regt., KIA, June 6, 1918 in the Chateau Thierry sector. Anges Pendergraph (sister), Hartshorn, Oklahoma [ABMC-Belleau] [S2] [SW1]

Attaway, William Joseph, Pvt., 49th Co., 5th Regt., DOW, June 6, 1918 in the Chateau Thierry sector. Joseph Attaway (Father), 1006 N. 2nd Ave., Rome, Georgia [FAG] [S2] [SW]

Atwater, Ray L., Pvt., Central Recruiting Division, DDS, May 13, 1920 at Las Animas, Colorado. Mrs. Della Atwater (Mother), RFD#4, Ipava, Illinois [S4]

Auer, Charles, Cpl., 20th Co., 5th Regt., KIA, June 6, 1918 in the Chateau Thierry sector. John F. Auer (Father), R #6, Box 117-B, Salem, Oregon [VA-ANC say June 7, 1918] [S2] [SW]

Ault, Thomas Wesley, Pvt., "A" Co., 13th Regt., DOD, October 6, 1918 in France. Mrs. Vesta Ault (Mother), Pikeville, Tennessee [ABMC-Fere] [S2]

Ausborn, Sylvanus, Pvt., 74th Co., 6th Regt., KIA, November 1, 1918 in the Meuse Argonne. Thomas N. Ausborn (Father), Baldwin, Georgia [ABMC-Romagne] [S2] [SW1]

Austin, Robert Edgar, Pvt., 17th Co., 5th Regt., DOW, July 23, 1918 in the Aisne-Marne. Dr. David Austin (Father), Newbern, Tennessee [VA-Memphis] [S2] [SW1]

Austin, Walter Stanley, Pvt., 15th Co., 6th MGBn, DOW, July 15, 1918 in the Aisne Defensive. Charles P. Austin (Father), 365 Drexel Ave., Detroit, Michigan [ANC] [S2] [SW]

Austin, Wayne Gordon, Pvt., 45th Co., 5th Regt., KIA, June 7, 1918 in the Chateau-Thierry. Mary J. Austin (Mother), Burton, Kansas [FAG] [S2] [SW1]

Auten, Curtis R., Pvt., QM Dept., Hdqtrs. USMC, Washington D.C., DDS, January 24, 1919 at Washington, D.C. Mrs.

Marine Corps Deaths, 1917-1921

Cecelia O. Auten (Wife), 417 Eye St., S.E., Washington, D.C. [S4]

Auten, Lawrence Leslie, Pvt., 55th Co., 5th Regt., KIA, October 4, 1918 in the Meuse Argonne. George Butler (friend), 406 Terry Ave., Seatte, Washington, [ABMC- Romagne] [S2] [SW1]

Au Werter, Andrew Louis, Pvt., 51st Co., 5th Regt., KIA, November 4, 1918 in the Meuse Argonne. I. L. AuWerter (Father), 705 Walnut St., Columbia, Pennsylvania [ABMC-Romagne] [S2] [SW1]

Avis, John, Pvt., 76th Co., 6th Regt., DOW, November 1, 1918 in the Meuse Argonne. Mrs. John Avis (widow), Brighton, Michigan [S2] [SW1]

Axline, Ralph Cartan, Pvt., 80th Co., 6th Regt., KIA, July 19, 1918, in the Aisne-Marne. Luther M. Axline (Father), Medicine Lodge, Kansas, [ABMC-Fere] [S2] [SW1 says DOW]

Axton, Andrew Kramer, Pvt., 82nd Co., 6th Regt., KIA, June 6, 1918 in the Chateau Thierry sector. Nel P. Axton (Mother), 5510 Stanton Ave., Pittsburgh, Pennsylvania [S2] [SW] [SW1]

Ayars, Charles Wesley, Pvt. 74th Co., 6th Regt., KIA, September 15, 1918 in the St. Mihiel offensive. Charles Ayars (Father), 622 Ohio St., Neodesha, Kansas [FAG] [S2] [SW]

Babb, Claud Augustus, Pvt., 17th Co., 5th Regt., KIA, June 15, 1918 in the Chateau Thierry sector. Mrs. Ola Brown (sister), Hampton, Georgia [FAG] [S2] [SW]

Babbitt, Lawson McVey, Pvt., 51st Co., 5th Regt., KIA, June 11, 1918 in the Chateau Thierry sector. Christina C. Babbitt (Mother), P. O. Box 55, Youngstown, Illinois [ABMC-Belleau TOM] [S2] [SW]

Babcock, Robert C., 2nd Lieut., 20th Co., 5th Regt., KIA, November 1, 1918 in the Meuse Argonne, Fred D.

Marine Corps Deaths, 1917-1921

Babcock (Father), Box 126, Santa Rosa, California [FAG] [S1] [SW1]

Backes, Leslie P., Pvt., Co. A, 3rd Sep. BN, Quantico, Virginia, DDS, November 19, 1918 at Quantico, Virginia. Mrs. Barbara Backes (Mother), 3000 Palmer Ave., New Orleans, Louisana [S4]

Bacon, Lonnie Joseph, Pvt., 20th Co., 5th Regt., KIA, November 1, 1918 in the Meuse Argonne. Richard C. Bacon (Brother), 119 Cabelle St., Lynchburg, Virginia [S2] [SW1]

Bagby, Richard Coleman, Jr., Pvt., 3rd Co., Philadelphia, Pennsylvania, DDS, September 27, 1918 at Philadelphia. Richard C. Bagby (Father), 503 West Main St., Louisville, Kentucky [FAG] [S3]

Bahr, David Francis, 1st Sgt., 129th Co., MB, Navy Yard, Puget Sound, Washington, DOS, April 17, 1919 at Puget Sound, Washington. William Bahr (Father), 239 Rutledge Ave., Charleston, South Carolina [S4]

Baier, Ernest Hubert, Pvt., 47th Co., 5th Regt., KIA, June 24, 1918 in the Chateau Thierry sector. Margarette Baier (Mother), Mason Co., West Virginia, [ABMC-Belleau] [S2] [SW1]

Bailey, Alfred Lowe, Pfc., 158th Co., Quantico, Virginia, DDS, September 25, 1918 at Quanitco, Virginia. Mary F. Bailey (Wife), 5223 Stiles St., Philadelphia, Pennsylvania [S3]

Bailey, Ralph Loudenback, Pvt., 97th Co., 6th Regt., DOW, November 2, 1918 in the Meuse Argonne. Jennie L. Bailey (Mother), R.F.D. #5, St. Parris, Ohio [FAG] [S2] [SW1]

Bailey, Walter, Pvt., 26th Co., San Diego, California, DAS, November 30, 1918 drowned at San Diego, California. Mrs. Annie H. Bailey (Mother), Box 323, Cheney, Washington [VA-Ft. George Wright] [S4]

Marine Corps Deaths, 1917-1921

Baird, Guy Ralph, Pvt., 76th Co., 6th Regt., KIA, July 19, 1918 in the Aisne Marne. William T. Baird (Father), Carlinville, Illinois [ABMC-Fere] [S2] [SW]

Baker, Clay, Pvt., USNH, Fort Lyons, Colorado, DDS, November 2, 1918 at Fort Lyons, Colorado. Haryy Baker (Father), Crockettsville, Kentucky [VA-Ft. Lyon] [S3]

Baker, Elward James, Trumpeter, Naval Proving Grounds, Indian Head, Maryland, DDS, October 14, 1918 at Indian Head, Maryland. Agnes B. Heckel (Mother), Gardenville, Maryland [S3]

Baker, Erasmus Roy, Pvt., MG Co., 11th Regt., Quantico, Virginia, DDS, October 2, 1918 at Quantico, Virginia. William F. Baker (Father), Jelks, Arkansas [FAG] [S3]

Baker, Robert Fitz, Cpl., 81st Co., 6th MGBn, KIA, October 7, 1918 in France. Edward H. Baker (Father), 4 Rensselear St., Troy, New York [ANC] [FAGM] [S2] [SW1]

Baker, Walter Zemeri, Pvt., "D" Co., 13th Regt., DOD, October 7, 1918 in France. Gertrude I. Baker (wife), Durango, Colorado [S2]

Baldwin, Raymond Hiram, Pvt., 67th Co., 5th Regt., KIA, November 2, 1918 in the Meuse Argonne. Victoria Baldwin (Mother), 10532 Earle Ave., Cleveland, Ohio [S2] [SW1]

Ballard, Arthur Roland, Cpl., 96th Co., 6th Regt., KIA, October 3, 1918 in the Meuse Argonne. Mrs. M.V. Ballard (Mother), R.F.D. #1, Milner, Georgia [FAG] [S2] [SW]

Ballard, Virgil Ray, Pvt., Nav. Amm. Depot, Hingham, Massachusetts, DOS, March 11, 1921 of a skull fracture at Chelsea, Massachusetts. Jasper N. Ballard (Father), Beloit, Kansas [S4]

Balzer, Eugene Ingatius, Pvt., Hdqrs. Co., 5th Regt., KIA, November 1, 1918 in the Meuse Argonne. Catherine A. Bazer (Mother), 1402 Guerrero St., San Francisco, California [S2] [SW1]

Marine Corps Deaths, 1917-1921

Bamforth, Jack, Pvt., 51st Co., 5th Regt., DOW, June 15, 1918 in the Chateau Thierry sector. H. Baumforth (Father), Box 95, Mohegan Lake, New York [FAG] [S2] [SW1]

Bandes, Harry, Pvt., 74th Co., 6th Regt., DOW, September 13, 1918 in the Aisne Marne (Soissons). Mrs. A. Sonin (Mother), 102 W. 114th St., New York, New York [R] [S2] [SW]

Bangs, Theodore Edward, Pvt., 51st Co., 5th Regt., KIA, June 11, 1918 in the Chateau Thierry sector. Laura V. Bangs (Mother), Stemmers Run, Rossville, Maryland [ABMC-Belleau] [S2] [SW]

Banister, Ira Hill, Pvt., 18th Co., 5th Regt., DOW, June 6, 1918 in the Chateau Thierry sector. Ada Banister (Mother), RFD, Dryden, Michigan [S2] [SW]

Baranski, Frank, Pvt., Naval Prison Det., Parris Island, South Carolina, DAS, June 16, 1919 drowned at Parris Island, South Carolina. Mrs. Stella Baranski (Mother), Kinde, Michigan [FAG] [S4]

Barber, Gordon Curtis, Pvt., 18th Co., 5th Regt., KIA, June 10, 1918 in the Chateau Thierry sector. Delia Barber (Mother), Mosinee, Wisconsin [R] [S2] [SW]

Barber, Simon David, 1st Sgt., 79th Co., 6th Regt., DOW, June 27, 1918 in the Chateau Thierry sector. Margaret Barber (Mother), Arkansas Pass, Texas [R] [S2] [SW]

Barden, Leon Thomas, Pvt., USS *Arizona*, DDS, July 30, 1919 at Brooklyn, New York. Thomas Barden (Father), 143 Fremont St., Jersey City, New Jersey [S4]

Barkell, James, Pvt., 97th Co., 6th Regt., KIA, November 1, 1918 in the Meuse Argonne. Christina Barkell (Mother), Lake Linden, Michigan [S2] [SW1]

Barker, Floyd, Sgt., 66th Co., 5th Regt., KIA, September 14, 1918 in the St. Mihiel offensive. Sarah Barker (wife), 1026 Bladensburg Rd., N.E., Washington, D.C. [ABMC-Thiaucourt] [S2] [SW says Casualty Co.]

Marine Corps Deaths, 1917-1921

Barley, Garrie Elmore, Pvt., R.R. Det., Mare Island, California, DDS, January 31, 1921 at Mare Island, California. William O. Barley (Father), Troy, New York [S4]

Barlow, Joel Clifton, Pvt., 45th Co., 5th Regt., DOW, November 9, 1918 in the Meuse Argonne. Euphemia Barlow (Mother), 74 S. Temple, Salt Lake City, Utah [ABMC-Romagne] [S2] [SW1]

Barnes, Bruno, Pvt., 79th Co., 6th Regt., DOW, June 27, 1918 in the Chateau Thierry sector. Boleslow Tirksles (cousin), 2153 W. 4th St., Chicago, Illinois [ABMC-Belleau] [S2] [SW]

Barnes, Robert DeWitt, Pvt., 20th Co., 5th Regt., KIA, October 4, 1918 in the Meuse Argonne. Charles Barnes (Father), R.F.D. #4, Oxford, New York [R] [S2] [SW says Co. D, 4th Sep. Btln.]

Barnett, Cecil Monroe, Pvt., "F" Co., 13th Co., DOD, September 28, 1918 in France. Alice Barnett (Mother), 5th and Main Sts., Durant, Oklahoma [S2]

Barnett, Maurice F., Jr., 2nd Lieut., 79th Co., 6th Regt., DOW, November 1, 1918 in the Meuse Argonne, Maurice f. Barnett (Father), 112 Franklin Ave, Neenah, Wisconsin, [ABMC-Romagne says M. E.] [S1] [SW1 says KIA]

Barnett, Robert S., Cpl., Co. Z, NCO School, Parris Island, South Carolina, DDS, December 21, 1918 at Parris Island, South Carolina. Mrs. Lily Barnett (Mother), 1143 S. Ardmore Ave., Los Angeles, California [S4]

Barnett, William Michael, Cpl., 84th Co., 6th Regt., KIA, July 19, 1918 in the Aisne Marne offensive. James Barnett (Father), 124 Erie St., Oswego, New York, [ABMC-Belleau TOM] [S2] [SW says 115th Co.]

Baroch, Joseph, Pvt., USNH, Fort Lyons, Colorado, DDS, December 12, 1917 at Fort Lyons, Colorado Mary Wieland (Sister), 1017 Forest St., Baltimore, Maryland [VA-Ft. Lyon] [S3]

Marine Corps Deaths, 1917-1921

Barr, Chapin C., 2nd Lieut., MCR N. B. Gr., FMAF, DOW, September 29, 1918, in the St. Mihiel offensive. Sam F. Barr (Father), 50 Church St., New York, New York, [ABMC-Bony] [S1] [SW]

Barr, John A., Jr., Cpl., Bks. Det., Philadephia, Pennsylvania, DDS, December 7,. 1918 at Philadelphia, Pennsylvania. John A. Barr (Father), 63 Cleveland St., Arlington, Massachusetts [S4]

Barr, John Watson, Pvt., 78th Co., 6th Regt., KIA, July 19, 1918 in the Aisne Marne (Soissons). Elizabeth B. Wood (Mother), C/o Hunter Wood, Hopkinsville, Kentucky, [ABMC-Belleau TOM] [S2] [SW1]

Barrett, Floyd Elvis, Pvt., 43rd Co., 5th Regt., KIA, October 7, 1918 in the Meuse Argonne. Ruby Barrett (widow), 2107 Bluff St., Boulder, Colorado [ANC] [SW says Co. C, 4th Sep. Btln.]

Barron, William Lawrence, Pvt., 2488385, MCR, 16th Co., 5th Regt., DOD, August 29, 1918 in the Chateau Thierry sector. Mrs. Ella Wires (Mother), R.F.D. #4, Holley, New York [FAG] [S2]

Barry, Clyde Loren, Pvt., RDD, Mare Island, California, DOS, December 12, 1917 at San Francisco, California. Mrs. Ida Guthrie (Mother), Blue Springs, Missouri [S3]

Barry, Lewis Walter, Pvt., 18th Co., 5th Regt., KIA, June 10, 1918 in the Chateau Thierry sector. Catherine Barry (Mother), 1005 Philadelphia Ave., West Detroit, Michigan [ABMC-Belleau] [S2] [SW]

Bartee, Thomas R., Pvt., Co. A, MB, Mare Island, California, DDS, February 2, 1920 at Mare Island, California. Mrs. Grace L. Bartee (Mother), Elk Point, Alberta, Canada [S4]

Bartelt, Albert Emil, Cpl., 75th Co., 6th Regt., KIA, June 18, 1918 in the Chateau Thierry sector. Gottlieb Bartelt (Father), Berlin, Wisconsin [R] [S2] [SW]

Marine Corps Deaths, 1917-1921

Bartle, Marcia, Pvt. (female), MCR, Department of Supply, Philadelphia, Pennsylvania, DDS, October 15, 1918 at Philadelphia, Pennsylvania. Elizabeth Bartle (Mother), 6820 Chew St., Philadelphia, Pennsylvania [S3]

Bartlett, Emery Augustus, Pvt., 20th Co., 5th Regt., DOW, June 12, 1918 in the Chateau Thierry sector. Arthur W. Bartlett (Father), R.F.D. #2 Rickreall, Oregon [ABMC-Suresnes] [S2] [SW]

Bartlett, James, Pvt., 76th Co., 6th Regt., KIA, September 15, 1918 in the St. Mihiel offensive. Amanda Bartlett (Mother), R.D. #2, Wellston, Ohio [S2] [SW says Co. A, 3rd Sep. Btln.]

Bartley, Oscar Henry, Pvt., 82nd Co., 6th Regt., DOW, July 19, 1918 in the Aisne Marne (Scissons). Charles H. Bartley (Father), Box 325, Anita, Iowa [R] [S2] [SW1]

Bassani, John Angelo, Cpl., 74th Co., 6th Regt., DOW, July 24, 1918 in the Aisne Marne (Scissons). Charles Bassani (Father), 15 Bradford Ave., Haverhill, Massachusetts, [ABMC-Belleau] [S2] [SW1]

Bates, Arthur T., Pvt., Co. F, Mare Island, California, DDS, November 14, 1918 at Mare Island, California. Mrs. Ethel Bates (Mother), Montpelier, Ohio [FAG] [S4]

Bates, George Cleveland, Pvt., 96th Co., 6th Regt., KIA, October 3, 1918 in the Meuse Argonne. David P. Bates (Brother), Marietta, South Carolina [FAG] [S2] [SW1]

Batterton, Bishop Smith, Pvt., 76th Co., 6th Regt., DOW, July 20, 1918 in the Aisne Marne (Scissons). Benjamin A. Batterton (Father), Paris, Kentucky [R] [S2] [SW] [SW1]

Batton, Julius Edward, Pvt, 55th Co., 5th Regt., DOD, January 16, 1918 in France. Maggie E. Batton (Mother), R.F.D. #2, Danville, Virginia [ABMC-Romagne] [S2]

Baude, Carl Frederick, Pvt., 77th Co., 6th MGBn, DOW, June 19, 1918 in the Chateau Thierry sector. Emma H. Baude

Marine Corps Deaths, 1917-1921

(Mother), 1049 Cherokee Rd., Louisville, Kentucky [S2] [SW]

Baudis, Thomas James, Pvt., MCR, 75th Co., 6th Regt., KIA, July 19, 1918 in the Aisne Marne (Soissons). Florence Slagle (sister), R.F.D. #1, State College, Pennsylvania [ABMC-Fere] [S2] [SW says Co. A, Repl. Btln.]

Bauer, Chester Bernett, Pvt., 23rd Co., 6th MG Bn, KIA, November 5, 1918 in the Meuse-Argonne. Ruth Bauer (Mother), 6923 Minnesota Ave., St. Louis, Missouri [VA-Jefferson Barracks] [S2] [SW1]

Bauer, George Franklin, Pvt., 79th Co., 6th Regt., KIA, September 7, 1918 in the Aisne-Marne. Mary Bauer (Mother), 436 No. Main St., Bethlehem, Pennsylvania, [ABMC-Fere] [S2] [SW1]

Baughman, Frank M., Pvt., USNH, Las Animas, Colorado, DDS, October 6, 1919 at West Newton, Pennsylvania. Mrs. Lily Baughman (Mother), Railroad St., West Newton, Pennsylvania [FAG] [S4]

Baughman, Victor Kenan, Pvt. 51st Co., 5th Regt., DOW, October 6, 1918 in the Meuse-Argonne Ella Shuman (Mother), Gen. Del., Mt. Etna, Indiana [R] [S2] [SW1]

Bayless, William Thomas, Sgt., 82nd Co., 6th Regt., KIA, July 19, 1918 in the Aisne-Marne. Elizabeth O. Bayless (Mother), Box #7, RFD #1, Heiskell, Tennessee [ABMC-Belleau TOM] [S2] [SW1]

Bayne, Russell C., 1st Lieut., 15th Co., 6th MGBn., DOW, October 26, 1918 in the Meuse Argonne. Albert J. Bayne (Father), Mulberry, Indiana [ABMC-Thiaucourt] [S1] [SW1]

Beabout, Lawrence Clem, Pvt., 74th Co., 6th Regt., DOW, April 21, 1918 at the Toulon Sector, Verdun. Wm.O. Beabout (Father), R.R. #1, Shelburn, Indiana [FAG] [S2] [SW]

Beach, Joseph Mansfield, Pvt., 45th Co., 5th Regt., DOW, July 9, 1918 in the Chateau-Thierry Sector. Zora Ruggiero

Marine Corps Deaths, 1917-1921

(Sister), 320 Arden Ave., Glendale, California [ABMC-Belleau] [S2] [SW]

Beach, Newton Lewis, Pvt., 96th Co., 6th Regt., KIA, October 9, 1918 in the Meuse-Argonne. John W. Williams (Brother), Morganton, North Carolina [R2] [S2] [SW1]

Beal, Marion Milton, Pvt., Bks. Det., Portsmouth, New Hampshire, DDS, October 5, 1918 at Portsmouth, New Hampshire, Jennie Beal (Mother), Moline, Kansas [FAG] [S3]

Beals, Myron Hobart, Sgt., 97th Co., 6th Regt., DOW, July 31, 1918 in the Aisne-Marne Offensive. Marion Beals (Mother), Plymouth, Michigan [FAG] [S2] [SW]

Bean, Lawrence Henry, Pvt., Hdqtrs. 13th Regt., DOD, September 26, 1918 in France. Mrs. Ione Beane (Wife), Box 85, Riviera, Texas [R] [S2]

Beard, Lynn Lincoln, Pvt., 153rd Co., 2nd Regt., Port au Prince, Haiti, DDS, March 12, 1920 at Port au Prince, Haiti. Mrs. Wells M. Beard (Mother), Box 67, Pompey, New York [S4]

Beardin, Paul, Pvt., MB, Chaleston, South Carolina, DDS, July 14, 1920 at Charleston, South Carolina. Mrs. W. D. Beardin (Mother), Kirkwood, Georgia [S4]

Beasman, Carl William, Pvt., 15th Co., 6th MG Bn., DOW, October 7, 1918 in the Meuse-Argonne. Anna Beasman (Mother), Finksburg, Maryland [FAG] [S2] [SW]

Beatty, Harry Pond, Pvt., 97th Co., 6th Regt., DOW, June 11, 1918 in the Chateau-Thierry Sector. Lilly Beatty (Mother), Clearwater, Minnesota [ABMC-Belleau] [S2] [SW]

Beauman, Louis C., 2nd Lieut., DAS, March 23, 1918 at Miami, Florida. L. Beapman (Father), Garfield, Utah. [S3] [SW1]

Beavers, Albert Alexander, Pvt., 18th Co., 5th Regt., KIA, November 11, 1918 in the Meuse-Argonne. William Beavers (Father), Blackville, Georgia [ABMC-Romagne] [S2] [SW1]

Marine Corps Deaths, 1917-1921

Bechtel, Russel R., Pvt., B. Det., MB, Navy Yard, Marel Island, California, DDS, September 26, 19120 at Fort Lyon, Colorado. Mrs. Marion Baumstark (Sister), 1058 Fifth St., San Diego, California [S4]

Beck, Edward J., Pvt., MB, Boston, Massachusetts, DDS, January 24, 1919 at Chelsea, Massachusetts. Fred T. Beck (Father), 966 Berry St., Toledo, Ohio [S4]

Beck, Marcus Wailand, Jr., Cpl., 78th Co., 6th Regt., KIA, June 14, 1918 in the Chateau-Thierry Sector. M. W. Beck (Father), 26 Columbia Ave., Atlanta, Georgia [FAG] [S2] [SW]

Becker, Floyd, Pvt., 17th Co., 5th Regt., KIA, August 3, 1918 in the Marbache Sector. Agartha F. Nichols (Sister), 207 East Ave., Bridgeton, New Jersey [R] [S2] [SW1]

Becker, Otto, Jr., Major, 4th Prov. Regt., Santiago, Dominican Republic, DDS, January 9, 1919 at Santiago, Dominican Republic. Lt. Col. Otto Becker, USA (Ret'd) (Father), 3835 Cleveland Ave., St. Louis, Missouri [S4]

Becker, Vernon P., Trumpter, 79th Co., 6th Regt., DOW, June 7, 1919 of wound received in France at Washington, D.C. Mrs. Janey M. Becker (Mother), 53 N. Union St., Akron, Ohio [ANC] [S4]

Becking, Alvin Frank, Pvt., 18th Co., 5th Regt., KIA, June 12, 1918 in the Chateau-Thierry Sector. Charles Becking (Father), 3652 Hermitage Ave., Chicago, Illinois [FAG] [S2] [SW]

Bedell, Charles Russell, Pvt., "I" Co., 13th Regt., DOD, September 24, 1918 enroute to France. Mrs. Sarah Bedell (Mother), 97 Mt. Carmel Way, Ocean Grove, New Jersey [R] [S2]

Bedford, George Carry, Pvt., "D" Co., 2nd Tr. Batt., DOD, November 26, 1918 in France. Serena Bedford (Mother), C/o W. A. Owen, Neola, Iowa [R] [S2]

Marine Corps Deaths, 1917-1921

Bedker, Wesley George, Pvt., 80th Co., 6th Regt., DOW, July 20, 1918 in the Aisne-Marne. Alma Becker Ogden (Mother), Stronghurst, Illinois [ANC] [S2] [SW]

Beebe, John, Pvt., 20th Co., 5th Regt., KIA, October 4, 1918 in the Meuse-Argonne. Alice Beebe (Mother), 6 Kinloch Ave., Troy, New York [FAG] [S2] [SW1]

Beevers, Frank Allen, Pvt., 49th Co., 5th Regt., DOW, June 8, 1918 in the Chateau-Thierry Sector. Alfred E. Beevers (Father), U.S. Coast Guard Station #19, Salisbury Beach, Massachusetts [R] [S2] [SW]

Behan, Raymond Alloyois, Pvt., 80th Co., 6th Regt., KIA, June 8, 1918 in the Chateau-Thierry Sector. Michael Behan (Father), 2705 Wyoming St., St. Louis, Missouri [FAG] [S2] [SW1]

Behr, Frederick Charles, Pvt., 55th Co., 5th Regt., DOW, June 8, 1918 in the Chateau-Thierry Sector. Therasa Behr (Mother), 552 ½ W. 52nd St., New York, New York [ABMC-Belleau] [S2] [SW]

Belcher, Bert, Pvt., 74th Co., 6th Regt., KIA, June 5, 1918 in the Aisne Defensive. Minnie Belcher (Mother), RFD #2, Walworth, New York [FAG] [S2] [SW says 71st Co.]

Belcher, Charles Melvin, Pvt., 78th Co., 6th Regt., DOW, October 1, 1918 in the Chateau-Thierry Sector. Mrs. Margaret Belcher (Mother), 3109 Peavey St., Port Huron, Michigan [FAG] [S2] [SW1]

Belcher, Fred, Cpl., 20th Co., 5th Regt., DOW, June 26, 1918 in the Chateau-Thierry Sector. Mrs. Minerva Belcher Weller (Mother), RFD #4, Box 216, Tacoma, Washington [FAG] [S2] [SW]

Belfry, Earl, Sgt., 96th Co., 6th Regt., DOW, June 8, 1918 in the Chateau-Thierry Sector. Mrs. Marguerite Belfry White (Widow), 2359 Farragut Ave., Chicago, Illinois [R] [S2] [SW]

Marine Corps Deaths, 1917-1921

Belk, Charles, Pvt., 18th Co., 5th Regt., KIA, June 10, 1918 in the Chateau-Thierry Sector. Mrs. Sarah Belk (Mother), 25 Halket St., Pittsburgh, Pennsylvania [ABMC-Belleau] [S2] [SW]

Bell, Arthur Blaylock, Pvt., 78th Co., 6th Regt., DOD, September 20, 1918 in France. Frank D. Bell (Father), 12 Orange St., Charleston, South Carolina [FAG] [S2]

Bell, Elmer Jefferson, Pvt., 22nd Co., Philadelphia, Pennsylvania, DDS, October 2, 1918 at Philadelphia, Pennsylvania. Mrs. Mary Bell (Mother), Gen. Del., Austin, Nevada [S3]

Bell, Jesse James, GySgt., 66th Co., 5th Regt., KIA, November 5, 1918 in the Meuse Argonne. Mrs. Jesse J. Bell (Wife), 939 W. 52nd St., Seattle, Washington [FAG] [S2] [SW1]

Bell, Thomas Henry, Pvt., 43rd Co., 5th Regt., KIA, June 14, 1918 in Chateau-Thierry Sector. Mary Bell (Mother), 1335 Laketon Rd., Wilkinsburg, Pennsylvania [FAG] [S2] [SW] [SW1]

Bellinger, Harold Henry, Pvt., 95th Co., 6th Regt., KIA, July 19, 1918 in the Aisne-Marne. Frank E. Bellinger (Father), 415 Henry St., Herkimer, New York [FAG] [S2] [SW1 says DOW]

Beltman, Harold William, Pvt., 79th Co., 6th Regt., KIA, June 14, 1918 in the Chateau Thierry sector. A. A. Beltman (Father), Tower City, North Dakota [FAG] [S2] [SW]

Bemberg, Henry, Pvt., 16th Co., 5th Regt., KIA, June 23, 1918 in the Chateau Thierry sector. William Bemberg (Father), 1324 Barber Ave., Little Rock, Arkansas [VA-Little Rock] [S2] [SW]

Bemusdaffer, Claude Conrad, Pvt., 96th Co., 6th Regt., DOW, June 16, 1918 in the Chateau Thierry sector. Joseph F. Bemusdaffer (Father), 810 West Main St., Oklahoma City, Oklahoma [VA-Ft. Gibson] [S2] [SW]

Benners, Archibald Bartleson, Pvt., 80th Co., 6th Regt., DOW, July 3, 1918 in the Chateau Thierry sector. George B. Benners

Marine Corps Deaths, 1917-1921

(Father), 2418 Spruce St., Philadelphia, Pennsylvania [ABMC-Belleau] [S2] [SW]

Bennett, Artie, Pvt., 82nd Co., 6th Regt., KIA, June 8, 1918 in the Chateau Thierry sector. Susan A. Bennett (Mother), R.R. #2, Clinton, Illinois [FAG] [S2] [SW]

Bennett, Elwood Allen, Pvt., 18th Co., 5th Regt., DOW, June 13, 1918 in the Chateau Thierry sector. Kathryne Siner (Sister), Reiglesville, Pennsylvania [ABMC-Belleau] [S2] [SW says 138th to Repl.]

Bennett, Eugene Joseph, Pvt., 75th Co., 6th Regt., DOW, October 8, 1918 in the Meuse Argonne. Fillmore Benett (Father), 1537Light St., Baltimore, Maryland [ABMC-Romagne] [S2] [SW]

Bennett, Frederick Strassenbargh, Cpl., 43rd Co., 5th Regt., KIA, June 10, 1918 in the Chateau Thierry sector. Mary Bennett (Mother), North Blommfield, New York [FAG] [S2] [SW]

Bennett, Thomas, Pvt., 47th Co., 5th Regt., KIA, June 25, 1918 in the Chateau Thierry sector. Susie Miller (Sister), Route #1, Dallas, Oregon [R] [S2] [SW1]

Bennett, Walter Lee, Pvt., 20th Co., 5th Regt., KIA, June 6, 1918 in the Chateau Thierry sector. Cora A. Bennett (Mother), Salem, Missouri [FAG] [S2] [SW1 says DOW]

Bennett, William Edward, Pvt., 43rd Co., 5th Regt., KIA, June 13, 1918 in the Chateau Thierry sector. Mary Bennett (Mother), 4 Wolf St., Rochester, New York [ABMC-Belleau TOM] [S2] [SW]

Benson, Edwin Bernard, Pvt., Co. "C" Co., 3rd September Bn., DOD, September 19, 1918 in France. Mrs. August Benson (Mother), 116 S. Green Bay Rd., Highland Park, Illinois [ABMC-Romagne] [S2]

Benson, Francis Edwin, Pvt., USS *Prometheus*, DAS, December 9, 1919 drowned at Santo Domingo. Jesse L. Savage (Friend), Sherman, New York [S4]

Marine Corps Deaths, 1917-1921

Benson, John Bryon, Pvt., 23rd Co., 6th MG Bn, DOW, November 5, 1918 in the Meuse Argonne. Robert Benson (Father), Ava, Illinois [ABMC-Romagne] [S2] [SW1]

Benson, Raymond Reuben, Pvt., 51st Co., 5th Regt., DOW, June 11, 1918 in the Chateau Thierry sector. Anna V. Hicks (Mother), North Woodstock, Connecticut [FAG] [S2] [SW]

Benton, William Allen, Pvt., 51st Co., 5th Regt., KIA, June 11, 1918 in the Chateau Thierry sector. Eliza Penton (Mother), Mayodan, North Carolina [S2] [SW]

Benz, George Edward, Pvt., 51st Co., 5th Regt., KIA, October 4, 1918 in the Meuse Argonne. Amelia Benz (Mother), Gen. Del., Grandvew, Wisconsin [FAG] [S2] [SW]

Berg, Edwin, Pvt., "E" Co., 13th Regt., DOD, September 22, 1918 enroute to France. Ole J. Berg (Father), Brandon, Minnesota [FAG] [S2]

Berg, Gustav, Pvt., 96th Co., 6th Regt., DOW, July 19, 1918 in the Aisne-Marne. Clara Berg (Sister), Gen. Del., Harmony, Minnesota [R] [S2]

Berg, Louis Arthur, Pvt., 17th Co., 5th Regt., DOW, October 12, 1918 in the Meuse Argonne. Louis F. Berg (Father), R #3, Wadena, Minnesota [FAG] [S2] [SW]

Bergdahl, Carl Frithiof, Cpl., 55th Co., 5th Regt., KIA, October 4, 1918 in the Meuse Argonne. Arthur Boden (Cousin) 735 31st Ave., N. Minneapolis, Minnesota, [ABMC-Romagne] [S2] [SW]

Berger, Alex. Tindolph, Pvt., 78th Co., 6th Regt., KIA, July 19, 1918 in the Aisne-Marne Offensive. Eva Berger (Mother), 190 South Ardmore Ave., Los Angeles, California [FAG] [S2] [SW1]

Berger, Walter Howard, Pvt., 95th Co., 6th Regt., KIA, June 13, 1918 in the Chateau-Thierry Sector. Dora Berger (Mother), Maderia, Ohio [FAG] [S2] [SW]

Marine Corps Deaths, 1917-1921

Bergerom, Calvin, Cpl., 66th Co., 5th Regt., KIA, October 4, 1918 in the Meuse Argonne. Willie Bergerom (Father), Houma, Louisiana [ABMC-Romagne] [S2] [SW1]

Bergman, Arthur Samuel, Pvt., 141st Co., Portsmouth, New Hampshire, DDS, October 13, 1918 at Portsmouth, New Hampshire. Samuel M. Bergman (Father), Arnold, Nebraska [S3]

Berman, Benjamin, Pvt., 97th Co., 6th Regt., KIA, September 15, 1918 in the St. Mihiel Offensive. Jacob Berman (Father), 548 W. Pike St., Philadelphia, Pennsylvania [ABMC-Thiaucourt TOM] [S2] [SW says 134th Co.]

Bernauer, William G., Pvt., 186th Co., 15th Regt., Domincan Republic, DOS, February 16, 1920 at San Domingo, Dominican Republic. Mrs. Beroinica Bernauer (Mother), 613 S. 19th St., Newark, New Jersey [S4]

Berner, William Fred, Pvt., 54th Co., 2nd Regt., Haiti, DAS, August 12, 1921 of a broken neck diving in shallow water at Hinche, Haiti. Minnie Berner (Mother), 420 W. 44th St., New York, New York [S4]

Berry, John Edward, Pvt., 81st Co., 6th MG Bn., DOW, September 14, 1918 in the St. Mihiel Offensive. Robert Berry (Father), Madison, Arkansas [ANC] [S2] [SW]

Bertram, Clyde Russell, Pvt., Co. F., Parris Island, South Carolina, DDS, April 20, 1918 at Parris Island, South Carolina. Alma L. Bertram (Wife), Gen. Del., Muskego Center, Wisconsin [FG] [S3]

Betcher, Ervin Clarence, Pvt., 79th Co., 6th Regt., KIA, July 19, 1918 in the Aisne-Marne. Emil Betcher (Father), Ada, Minnesota [FAG] [S2] [SW]

Betts, Gregg William, Pvt., Interior Guard Co. #1, Cl. Camp. DOA, May 31, 1919 in France. Elijah Betts (Father), Quaker City, Ohio [R] [S2] [SW1 says KOA]

Marine Corps Deaths, 1917-1921

Betz, Glenn Dale, Pvt., Co. C., Mare Island, California, DOS, July 19, 1917 at Sacramento, California. Mary Jane Betz (Mother), 219 North Grand, Los Angeles, California [S3]

Bicker, Carl Frederick, Pvt., 132nd Co., Quantico, Virginia, DDS, September 29, 1918 at Quantico, Virginia. Dorothy Bicker (Sister), 1710 Springwells Ave., Detroit, Michigan [FAG] [S3]

Bielenberg, Henry Joseph, Pvt., 78th Co., 6th Regt., DOW, October 4, 1918 in the Meuse Argonne. Mary Bielenberg (Mother), R#3, Genosoe, Idaho [ANC] [S2] [SW]

Bierce, Jerome Arthur, Pvt., 97th Co., 6th Regt., DOW, June 11, 1918 in the Chateau-Thierry Sector. Mrs. Eva Bierce (Mother), 4 Hickory Ave, Takoma Park, Washington, D.C. [ANC] [S2] [SW]

Bigley, Walter Stanley, Pvt., 20th Co., 5th Regt., KIA, June 8, 1918 in the Chateau-Thierry Sector. William Bigley (Father), 4103 St. Johns St., Pittsburgh, Pennsylvania [ABMC-Belleau] [S2] [SW says 137th Co.]

Biglow, Leslie, Pvt., 55th Co., 5th Regt., KIA, June 10, 1918 in the Chateau-Thierry Sector. Susan Gunderson (Guardian), 100 W. 99th St., New York, New York [ABMC-Belleau] [S2] [SW]

Bilderback, Oscar Otto, Pvt., 23rd Co., 6th MG Bn., DOW, November 2, 1918 in the Meuse Argonne. Downcy Bilderback (Father), Owensville, Indiana [ABMC-Romagne] [S2]

Bingham, Arnold Archibald, Pvt., Co. "I", 11th Regt., DOD, November 21, 1918 in France. George H. Bingham (Father), Redford, Missouri [FAG] [S2]

Bingham, Merle Campbell, Pvt., 76th Co., 6th Regt., KIA, October 4, 1918 in the Meuse Argonne. Lillian R. Axford (Mother), Route #, Box 86, Oregon City, Oregon [VA-Custer Battlefield] [S2] [SW1]

Marine Corps Deaths, 1917-1921

Binkley, Herbert Joseph., Pvt., 18th Co., 5th Regt., DOW, July 19, 1918 in the Aisne Marne Offensive. Mrs. Anna Binkley (Mother), C/o Mrs. R.E. Cuthrie, 4101 Adams St., Chicago, Illinois [ABMC-Belleau says Binckley] [S2] [SW says Binckley]

Biondi, Philip, Pvt., 75th Co., 6th Regt., DOW, October 14, 1918 in the Meuse Argonne. Philemina Biondi (Mother), Lincoln, New Jersey, [ABMC-Suresnes] [S2] [SW]

Bird, Eugene, Pvt., MCR, Ft. Lyons, Colorado, DDS, January 29, 1918 at Colorado Springs, Colorado. Henry Bird (Brother), 4416 Campbell Ave., Chicago, Illinois [S3]

Bisbee, Earl Brunson, Sgt., 76th Co., 6th Regt., KIA, September 15, 1918 in the St. Mihiel Offensive. Mrs. Earl B. Bisbee (Wife), 3909 S. Hill St., Los Angeles, California [ABMC-Thiaucourt] [S2] [SW says Co. A., 3rd Sep. Btln.]

Bischoff, Bernhard Philip, Pvt., 34th Co., 1st Replacement Bn., DOC, March 13, 1918 in France. Lena Bischoff (Mother), 185 Ley St., N.S., Pittsburgh, Pennsylvania [ABMC-Fere] [S2] [SW1 says DOW]

Bissell, William Sidney, Pvt., Co. C, 15th Sep. Bn, DOS, December 19, 1919 at Philadelphia at Philadelphia, Pennsylvania. Orlando H. Bissell (Father), Pomeroy, Ohio [S4]

Bixler, Ancel Hall, Pvt., 78th Co., 6th Regt., KIA, September 15, 1918 in the St. Mihiel Offensive. Jacob Bixler (Father), Forgan, Oklahoma [ABMC-Thiaucourt] [S2] [SW says Co. B, 5th Sep. Btln.]

Black, Louis, Pvt., USNH, Fort Lyon, Colorado, DDS, May 19, 1920 at Herrick, Ohio. Mrs. Mary Flix (Mother), Herrick, Ohio [S4]

Black, William B., Capt., 95th Co., 6th Regt., KIA, September 12, 1918 in the St. Mihiel offensive. Edgar N. Black (Father), 4901 Cedar St., Philadelphia, Pennsylvania [FAG] [S1] [SW]

Marine Corps Deaths, 1917-1921

Black, William W., Pvt., 1st Casual Det., MB, Navy Yard, Philadelphia, Pennsylvania, DDS, March 12, 1919 at Philadelphia, Pennsylvania. Wm. H. Black (Father), 115 W. 4th St., Lewistown, Pennsylvania [S4]

Blackburn, William Prenn, Cpl., 18th Co., 5th Regt., DOW, June 12, 1918in the Chateau-Thierry Sector. Charles Blackburn (Mother), 3726 Borden St., Cincinnati, Ohio [ABMC-Belleau] [S2] [SW1]

Blackden, Earl Benjamin, Cpl., 20th Co., 5th Regt., KIA, June 7, 1918 in the Chateau-Thierry Sector. Perry D. Blackden (Father), 3623 Sacramento Blvd., Sacramento, California [R] [S2] [SW1 says DOW]

Blackham, Russell Porter, Pvt., 80th Co., 6th Regt., DOW, October 6, 1918 in the Meuse Argonne. Mrs. Anna Blackham (Mother), 3726 Borden St., Cincinnati, Ohio [FAG] [S2] [SW1]

Blackwood, Harold Fred, Pvt., 17th Co., 5th Regt., DOW, June 8, 1918 in the Chateau-Thierry Sector. George W. Blackwood (Father), Winchester, Tennessee [ABMC-Belleau] [S2] [SW says 136th Co.]

Blackwood, William Donald, Pvt., 67th Co., 5th Regt., KIA, November 4, 1918 in the Meuse Argonne. Kittie E. Blackwood (Mother), 62 State St., Pontiac, Michigan [R] [S2] [SW1]

Blair, Howard, Pvt., 8th Co., 5th Regt., DOW, June 10, 1918 in the Chateau-Thierry Sector. William Blair (Father), 113 Montgomery Ave., Jackson, Michigan [ABMC-Belleau] [S2] [SW says M.G.C.]

Blake, John Rennie, Pvt., 67th Co., 5th Regt., KIA, November 6, 1918 in the Meuse Argonne. Cora L. Blake (Mother), Mansfield, Newton Co., Georgia [ABMC-Romagne] [S2] [SW1]

Blalock, John Franklin, Pvt., 49th Co., 5th Regt., KIA, June 6, 1918 in the Chateau-Thierry Sector. Julius H. Blalock

Marine Corps Deaths, 1917-1921

(Father), 211 West Ave., Hamlet, North Carolina [ABMC-Belleau] [S2] [SW]

Blanchett, Lawrence Joseph, Pvt., MG Bn., 13th Regt., DOD, September 24, 1918 enroute to France. Alice Blanchett (Wife), Elk River, Minnesota [FAG] [S2]

Blanchfield, John, Capt., 55th Co., 5th Regt., DOW, June 8, 1918 in the ChateauThierry sector. Mrs. John Blanchfield (widow), 108 Ryerson St., Brooklyn, New York [R] [S1] [SW]

Blandin, Paul Gilbert, Pvt., 23rd Co., 6th MG Bn., KIA, June 13, 1918 in the Chateau-Thierry Sector. Harvey C. Blandin (Father), Pittsfield, Maine [FAG] [S2] [SW]

Blankinship, Dan Moser, Pvt., 83rd Co., 6th Regt., DOW, June 12, 1918 in the Chateau-Thierry Sector. Mellie Blankinship (Mother), Higgins, Texas [ANC] [S2] [SW]

Bledsoe, Elwood Lloyd, Pvt., Supply Co., 5th Regt., Quantico, Virginia, DDS, April 9, 19121 at Quantico, Virginia. Mrs. Mary F. Bledsoe (Mother), 114 Ohio St., French Lick, Indiana [FAG] [S4]

Bledsoe, Roscoe, Sgt., 74th Co., 6th Regt., DOW, April 18, 1918 in the Tenlon Sector, Verdun. Dalphas Bledsoe (Father), RFD #3, French Lick, Indiana [ABMC-Romagne] [S2] [SW says Gy. Sgt.]

Blenkinsop, Marcus William, Cpl., 75th Co., 6th Regt., DOW, October 10, 1918 in the Meuse Argonne. Mary Blankinsop (Mother), 320 Walnut St., Chicago, Illinois [ABMC-Romagne] [S2] [SW1]

Bliven, Raymond E., Cpl., 16th Co., 5th Regt., KIA, June 23, 1918 in the Chateau-Thierry Sector. Marvin F. Bliven (Mother), 73 Constitution St., Bristol, Rhode Island [ABMC-Belleau TOM] [S2] [SW]

Blodget, Lewis Jefferson, Pvt., 74th Co., 6th Regt., KIA, October 4, 1918 in the Meuse Argonne. Moses Blodget (Father), Folsom City, California [R] [S2] [SW1]

Marine Corps Deaths, 1917-1921

Bloom, Harry Melvin, Pvt., Bks. Detch., Quantico, Virginia, DDS, November 7, 1918 at Quantico, Virginia. Katherine Bloom (Mother), P. O., Oak Harbor, Ohio [S3]

Bloomquist, John William, Cpl., 55th Co., 5th Regt., DOW, June 8, 1918 in the Chateau-Thierry Sector. Gust Bloomquist (Father), Gen. Del., Cheney, Washington [ABMC-Belleau TOM] [S2] [SW]

Blough, Herbert Benjamin, Cpl., 97th Co., 6th Regt., DOD, October 7, 1918. Mrs. Blanche Blough (Wife), 203 Case St., Portsmouth, New Hampshire [ABMC-Fere] [S2]

Blount, William Edgar, Pvt., 69th Co., Santo Domingo, Dominican Republic, DDS, December 7, 1918 at Santo Domingo, Domincan Republic. Miss Eula Blount (Sister), Bethel, North Carolina [S4]

Boardman, Fred William, Pvt., 49th Co., 5th Regt., DOW, November 4, 1918 in the Meuse Argonne. Jennie Boardman (Mother), 41 Pine Grove, Pontiac, Michigan [ABMC-Romagne] [S2] [SW1]

Bobick, Michael, Pvt., 16th Co., 5th Regt., DOW, June 23, 1918 in the Chateau-Thierry Sector. Mary Kraynevick (Mother), 11205 Continental Ave., Cleveland, Ohio [ABMC-Belleau] [S2] [SW1]

Bock, Fred Eugene, Pvt., 51st Co., 5th Regt., KIA, June 11, 1918 in the Chateau-Thierry Sector. Mrs. Amanda Bock (Mother), 310 McKinney Ave., Houston, Texas [ABMC-Belleau] [S2] [SW1]

Boettcher, Charles Henry, Pvt., 23rd Co., 6th MG Bn., KIA, June 18, 1918 in the Chateau-Thierry Sector. Johanna Boettcher (Mother), 1352 Spring St., Cincinnati, Ohio [R] [S2] [SW]

Boggess, Rolley Edward, Pvt., 78th Co., 6th Regt., KIA, June 14, 1918 in the Chateau-Thierry Sector. John B. Boggess (Father), 1516 Pecos St., Dallas, Texas [FAG] [S2] [SW]

Marine Corps Deaths, 1917-1921

Bohanan, Harry Raymond, Pvt., 67th Co., 5th Regt., KIA, June 6, 1918 in the Chateau-Thierry Sector. Eli R. Bonanan (Father), Fountain City, Tennessee [ABMC-Belleau] [S2] [SW]

Boies, Carlton Reed, Pvt., Co. E, 11th Regt., DOD, January 23, 1919 in France. William R. Boies (Father), Leicester, New York [R] [S2]

Bokosky, Frank Joseph, Pvt., 67th Co., 5th Regt., KIA, June 17, 1918 in the Chateau-Thierry Sector. William Bokosky (Father), 11 Glinko St., Scranton, Pennsylvania [R] [S2] [SW]

Bolding, Paul Elbert, Cpl., 75th Co., 6th Regt., DOW, October 3, 1918 in the Meuse Argonne. Mrs. W. E. Bolding (Mother), 37 Park St., Gainsville, Georgia [ABMC-Belleau] [S2] [SW]

Bolender, Hugh Everett, Cpl., 16th Co., 5th Regt., KIA, June 23, 1918 in the Chateau-Thierry Sector. Henry T. Bolender (Father), RFD #2, Maysville, Kentucky [R] [S2] [SW]

Boley, Charles Dewitt, Cpl., Bks. Det., Navy Yard, Washington, D.C., DDS, November 29, 1918 at Washington, D.C. Mrs. Myrtie Boley (Mother), Quincy, Michigan [FAG] [S4]

Boll, Robert Ambrose, Pvt., Bks. Detach., Quantico, Virginia, DDS, September 27, 1918 at Quantico, Virginia. Mary Boas Boll (Wife), 239 Woodbine St., Harrisburg, Virginia [S3]

Bollack, Edmond Carll, Pvt., 74th Co., 6th Regt., DOW, April 15, 1918 in the Toulon Sector, Verdun. Mrs. Max Bollack (Mother), 712 ½ Kearney St., Portland, Oregon [ABMC-Romagne] [S2] [SW says 120th Co.]

Bonczar, Michael, Pvt., 23rd Co., 6th MG Bn., KIA, November 10, 1918 in the Meuse Argonne. Frank Bonczar (Father), 260 Barnard St., Buffalo, New York [ABMC-Romagne] [S2] [SW1]

Marine Corps Deaths, 1917-1921

Boniewell, Lawrence Denis, Pvt., 54th Co., 2nd Regt., Hinche, Haiti, DDS, May 23, 1921 at Thomonde, Haiti. John Boniewell (Father), Spencer, Indiana [S4]

Bonnell, Ellsworth Max, Pvt., Co. A, 11th Regt., DOD, July 9, 1919 in France. Mrs. Amy Gordon (Mother), 70 Woodside Ave., Essexville, Michigan [R] [S2]

Bonner, Edison Endicott, Pvt., MCR, 36th Co., Mare Island, California, DDS, June 7, 1917 at Mare Island, California. Mrs. Mary MacVicar (Sister), 4422 Van Ness Ave., Los Angeles, California [S3]

Bonner, Guy Leslie, Pfc., Hdqtrs. Co., 5th Regt., DOW, October 2, 1918 in the Meuse Argonne. Martin Bonner (Father), Martinsburg, Pennsylvania [FAG] [S2] [SW] [SW1]

Bontemps, Clement Robert, Pvt., 78th Co., 6th Regt., DOW, June 15, 1918 in the Chateau-Thierry Sector. Mary Gager (Sister), P O Box 93, Bay St. Louis, Mississippi [FAG] [S2] [SW]

Bonvillain, Ernest Henry, Pvt., 82nd Co., 6th Regt., KIA, July 19, 1918 in the Aisne Marne. Eliska Bonvillain (Mother), Houma, Louisiana [R] [S2] [SW]

Boomer, Solon Terence, Pvt., 23rd Co., 6th MG Bn., KIA, November 5, 1918 in the Meuse Argonne. Anna Boomer (Mother), Sabetha, Kansas [FAG] [S2] [SW1]

Boone, Isaac Neal, Pvt., 51st Co., 5th Regt., KIA, June 4, 1918 in the Aisne Defensive. Dela Boone (Mother), RFD #2, Stocksdale, North Carolina [FAG] [S2] [SW]

Booth, Carl G., Pvt., 15th Co., 6th MG Bn., KIA, October 4, 1918 in the Meuse Argonne. Samuel Booth (Father), Eolian, Texas [FAG] [S2] [SW says 1st Corps Repl. Btln.]

Booth, Douglas H., Pay Clerk, Haiti, DAS, February 17, 1921 in an airplane crash at Mirebalais, Republic of Haiti. Mrs. Ruth Madaline Booth (Wife), 514 Francis St., Key West, Florida [S4]

Marine Corps Deaths, 1917-1921

Booth, Earl Ellis, Pvt., Hdqtrs. Co., 5th Regt., DOD, November 7, 1918 enroute to France. Pauline Alice Booth (Wife), 1633 Lula St., Wichita, Kansas [FAG] [S2]

Booth, John Frederick, Pvt., MD, Nav. Radio Station, New Brunswick, New Jersey, DAS, June 9, 1919 drowned at New Brunswick, New Jersey. Mrs. Louise Booth (not given), 189 Hunnewell St., Needham, Massachusetts [S4]

Booth, Lawrence Duncan, Pvt., 8th Co., 5th Regt., DOW, October 4, 1918 in the Meuse Argonne. I. T. Booth (Father), 1015 E. 8th St., Dallas, Texas [R] [S2] [SW1]

Boothe, William Horace, Jr., Pvt., 97th Co., 6th Regt., KIA, October 4, 1918 in the Meuse Argonne. William E. Boothe (Father), Box 30, Alcoa, Tennessee [ABMC-Romagne] [S2]

Boots, Wade A., Pvt., 43rd Co., 5th Regt., DOW, November 4, 1918 in the Meuse Argonne. Mary Boots (Mother), Palmyra, Missouri [FAG] [S2] [SW1]

Borden, William J., Captain, DDS, October 16, 1918 at Quantico, Virginia Mrs. Lillian Nilsson (Sister), Box 101, Sheridan, Wyoming [S3]

Borghesani, Martin L., Pvt., Co. B, MB, Mare Island, California, DDS, February 7, 1920 at Mare Island, California. Ceasar Borghesani (Father), P O Box 304, Martinez, California [S4]

Bork, Joseph George, Cpl., Dominican Republic, DAS, May 24, 1917 while riding in a box car at Santiago, Dominican Republic. Josephine Bork (Mother), 64 Brandle Ave., Lancaster, New York [S3]

Bornemann, Alfred Hugo, Pvt., 18th Co., 5th Regt., DOD, February 20, 1919 in France. Alexander R. Bornemann (Father), 929 Lumber Exchange, Minnesota [ANC] [S2]

Bosch, Frank, Pvt., 74th Co., 6th Regt., DOW, November 9, 1918 in the Meuse Argonne. Mrs. Peter Bosch (Mother), Vineburg, Sonoma, California [S2] [SW1]

Marine Corps Deaths, 1917-1921

Bourdette, Vernon, 1st Lieut., Hdqtrs., Washington, D.C., DDS, August 2, 1921 at Washington, D.C. Mrs. Margaret R. Bourdette (Wife), 2055 Park Rd., Washington, D.C. [VA-ANC as September 2, 1921] [S4]

Bourn, George Winthrop, Jr., Pvt., 18th Co., 5th Regt., KIA, July 21, 1918 in the Aisne Marne Offensive. George W. Bourn, Sr. (Father), Templeton, Massachusetts [R] [S2] [SW1]

Bovee, Samuel Arthur, Pvt., 66th Co., 5th Regt., DOW, July 26, 1918 in the Aisne Marne. Meredith Bovee (Brother), Munnsville, New York [FAG] [S2] [SW]

Bowen, James G., 2nd Lieutenant, 1st Brigade, Haiti. DAS, August 9, 1920 in an aeroplane accident at Haiti. Mrs. Margarete C. Bowen (Mother), 2361 McCullough St., Baltimore, Maryland [S4]

Bower, Ollis Gilbert, Pvt., 142nd Co., New London, Connecticut, DDS, October 9, 1918 at New London, Connecticut Samuel Bower (Father), Shelbyville, Missouri [S3]

Bowers, Perry Franklin, Pvt., 96th Co., 6th Regt., KIA, October 3, 1918 in the Meuse Argonne. Frank Bowers (Father), P O Box 166, Montfort, Wisconsin [S2] [SW1]

Bowlby, George Marcus, Pvt., 78th Co., 6th Regt., DOW, October 5, 1918 in the Meuse Argonne. Elmer A. Bowlby (Father), Ovid, Michigan [ABMC- Romagne] [S2] [SW]

Bowman, Joseph S., Pvt., Extra Duty Det., MB, Parris Island, South Carolina, DDS, February 4, 1919 at Parris Island, South Carolina. Mrs. Mary Bowman (Mother), 17 Mathias St., Leipsic, Ohio [S4]

Bowness, Harry, Sgt., 49th Co., 5th Regt., KIA, July 18, 1918 in the Aisne Marne. Annie Bowness (Mother), Gen. Del., Montrose, Prince Edward Island, Canada [ANC] [S2] [SW says Casualty Btln.]

Bowyer, Robert Clinton, Cpl., 43rd Co., 5th Regt., DOW, June 13, 1918 in the Chateau-Thierry Sector. Charles W. Boyer,

Marine Corps Deaths, 1917-1921

(Father), 4468 E. 126th St., Cleveland, Ohio [FAG] [S2] [SW]

Boyce, John C., Pvt., Co. A, Parris Island, South Carolina, DDS, January 16, 1919 at Parris Island, South Carolina. Mrs. Betty H. Boyce (Mother), Lutherville, Maryland [FAG] [S4]

Boyd, Foy, Pvt., 82nd Co., 6th Regt., DOW, June 24, 1918 in the Chateau-Thierry Sector. Lou Boyd (Mother), Abbott, Texas [R] [S2] [SW]

Boydston, Richard, 1st Lieut., Hdqrs. Co., 13th Regt., DOD, September 22, 1918 enroute to France. Mrs. Caraline Boydston (Mother), 412 Willard Ave., Bloomington, Illinois [FAG] [S1]

Boylan, James Francis, Pvt., 96th Co., 6th Regt., KIA, October 3, 1918 in the Meuse Argonne. Margaret Boyland (Mother), 177 1st St., Troy, New York [FAG] [S2] [SW1]

Boyle, William Henry, Pvt., 76th Co., 6th Regt., KIA, June 2, 1918 in the Aisne Defensive. A. J. Boyle (Brother), 2311 Sumpter St., Houston, Texas [FAG] [S2] [SW]

Boynton, Rheuna Louis, Pvt., MCR, Hdqtrs. Det., Philadelphia, Pennsylvania, DDS, October 6, 1918 at League Island, Philadelphia, Pennsylvania. Katherine Boynton (Mother), RR#39, Pleasant Plains, Illinois [FAG] [S3]

Brabon, Elmer A., Pvt., Supply Co., Parris Island, South Carolina, DDS, November 13, 1918 at Parris Island, South Carolina. Mrs. Mina Brabon (Mother), 733 Mary St., Flint, Michigan [FAG] [S4]

Bracken, Harry, Pvt., 43rd Co., 5th Regt., DOW, June 13, 1918 in the Chateau-Thierry Sector. Edward Bracken (Brother), 334 9th Ave., New Brighton, Pennsylvania [FAG] [S2] [SW1 says Sgt.]

Bradbury, Eben Jr., Pvt., 55th Co., 5th Regt., KIA, June 12, 1918 in the Chateau-Thierry Sector. Eben Bradbury, Sr. (Father),

Marine Corps Deaths, 1917-1921

    67 Bromfield St., Newburyport, Massachusetts [ABMC-Belleau] [S2] [SW]

Bradigan, Karl, Pvt., 98th Co., Newport, Rhode Island, DDS, September 26, 1918 at Providence, Rhode Island. Jennie Bradigan (Mother), 2566 East Church St., Stockton, California [FAG] [S3]

Bradley, Fred, Pvt., 84th Co., 6th Regt., KIA, November 1, 1918 in the Meuse Argonne. William H. Bradley (Brother), 3407 Archwood Ave., Cleveland, Ohio [S2] [SW1]

Bradley, William A., 2nd Lieut., 18th Co., 5th Regt., DOW, October 4, 1918 in the Meuse Argonne. Mrs Elizabeth Bradley (Mother), 346 Lenox Ave., New York, New York [R] [S1] [SW]

Brady, Vincent A., 2nd Lieut., 55th Co., 5th Regt., DOW, November 14, 1918 in the Meuse Argonne. Thomas J. Brady (Father), 71 Radford St., Yonkers, New York [R] [S1] [SW1]

Bragg, Ray Turner, Sgt, Co. H, 13th Regt., DOD, September 24, 1918 enroute to France. Ethel Bragg (Wife), 1168 10th St., San Diego, California [R] [S2]

Brailsford, Thomas R., 2nd Lieut., 96th Co., 6th Regt., DOW, July 29, 1918 in the Chateau Thierry sector. Mrs. Thomas R. Brailsford (widow), Apt. 4, 1202 Smith and Dallas, Houston, Texas [ABMC-Belleau] [S1] [SW]

Brainerd, Robert Leslie, Pvt., Hdqtrs. Co., 5th Regt., DOW, June 13, 1918 in the Chateau-Thierry Sector. Mrs. Russell Brainerd (Mother), 2223 Broadview Rd., Cleveland, Ohio [S2] [SW]

Brandes, Eddie Otto, Pvt., 78th Co., 6th Regt., DOW, July 29, 1918 in the Chateau-Thierry Sector. Addie Brandes (Mother), Star Route 15, Tillamock, Oregon [ANC] [S2] [SW]

Brandon, Ian, Pvt., 49th Co., 5th Regt., KIA, June 6, 1918 in the Chateau-Thierry Sector. Mrs. Mary Brandon (Mother), Clearwater, Florida [ABMC-Belleau TOM] [S2] [SW]

Marine Corps Deaths, 1917-1921

Brandt, Clair Edward, Pvt., Co. D, RD, Mare Island, California, DDS, February 11, 1921 at Mare Island, California. Edward Brandt (Father), Bridgeport, Washington [FAG] [S4]

Branson, Emulous, Pvt., Supply Co., Parris Island, South Carolina, DAS, March 6, 1921 drowned at Parris Island, South Carolina. Emulous Branson (Father), 601 Sixth St., Peoria, Illinois [S4]

Brant, Orville John., Cpl., 55th Co., 5th Regt., KIA, October 4, 1918 in the Meuse Argonne. Mary F. Brant (Mother), Box 195, Bonners Ferry, Idaho [FAG] [S2] [SW says 140th Co.]

Brantley, Dudley Boyd, Pvt., 75th Co., 6th Regt., KIA, June 10, 1918 in the Chateau-Thierry Sector. Mrs. Cassie A. Brantley (Mother), Route #2, Box 82, Middlesex, North Carolina [FAG] [S2] [SW]

Brashears, James H. B., 1st Lieut., Georgia School of Technology, DDS, January 10, 1919 at Annapolis, Maryland. Mrs. Eleanor O. Brashears (Widow), Annapolis, Maryland [FAG] [S4]

Brassel, Frank Joseph, Pvt., 73rd Co., 6th Regt., DOW, November 2, 1918 in the Meuse Argonne. Bertha Brassel (Mother), Gen. Del., Gervis, Oregon [S2] [SW1]

Braswell, Louis Benjamin, Jr., Pvt., 20th Co., 5th Regt., DOW, November 6, 1918 in the Meuse Argonne. Mary M. Braswell (Mother), Demopolis, Alabama [R] [S2] [SW1 says KIA]

Bray, William Kenneth., Pvt., 51st Co., 5th Regt., KIA, June 11, 1918 in the Chateau-Thierry Sector. Oscar E. Bray (Father), 199 Northland Ave., Buffalo, New York [ABMC-Belleau] [S2] [SW]

Breaux, Leon Chester, 1st Sgt., 118th Co., Pearl Harbor, Territory Hawaii, DAS, March 18, 1918 of a compound skull fracture at Pearl Harbor. James F. Breaux (Brother), Silver City, New Mexico [S3]

Marine Corps Deaths, 1917-1921

Breeden, Easseme, Cpl., 44th Co., Dominican Republic, DAS, August 13, 1918 in the Macho action near Hato Mahor. Ella Breeden (Mother), Archville, Tennessee [S3]

Breen, Kryn, Pvt., 17th Co., 5th Regt., KIA, October 4, 1918 in the Meuse Argonne. Susan Breen (Mother), 716 Dykema St., Grand Rapids, Michigan [ABMC-Romagne] [S2] [SW1]

Bremer, Frank F., Pvt., Nav. Amm. Depot, St. Julien's Creek, Virginia, DDS, July 31, 1919 at St. Julien's Creek, Virginia. Joseph Bremer (Father), 1710 S. 10th St., St. Louis, Missouri [FAG] [S4]

Brennan, Francis Joseph, Pvt., 67th Co., 5th Regt., DOW, November 2, 1918 in the Meuse Argonne. Mrs. T F. Brennan (Mother), 10410 Baltic Rd., Cleveland, Ohio [S2] [SW1]

Brennan, John Joseph, Pvt., St. Juliens Creek, Virginia, DDS, October 7, 1918 at Norfolk, Virginia. Mrs. Helen Brennan (Mother), 47 McChesney St.,Orange, New Jersey [S3]

Brennan, John Patrick, Gy. Sgt., Hdqtrs. Detch., Peking, China, DDS, May 14, 1918 on a train between Mukdenand Antung. William James Brennan (Brother), Muirdale Sanitorium, Wauwatosa, Wisconsin [S3]

Brennan, William Norman, Pvt., 66th Co., 5th Regt., KIA, November 1, 1918 in the Meuse Argonne. William Brennan (Father), Hockessin, Delaware [FAG] [S2] [SW1 says William Morman]

Brewer, Benjamin, Pvt., MB, Pensacola, Florida, DAS, accidentally killed at Pensacola, Florida. Mrs. Nina L. Brewer (Mother), Route 3, Box 96, Edison, Georgia [S4]

Brewer, Nathan, Pfc., 17th Co., 5th Regt., DOW, December, 1, 1918 in the Meuse Argonne. Betty Brewer (Mother), 1410 E. 12th St., Highland Park, Chattanooga, Tennessee [ABMC-Belleau] [S2] [SW1 says Pvt.]

Marine Corps Deaths, 1917-1921

Brickley, Wilmer Henry, GySgt., MCR, Miami, Florida, DAS, October 31, 1918 in an aeroplane accident at Marine Flying Field, Miami, Florida. Quince Brickley (Father), RR#2, Ebensburg, Pennsylvania [FAG] [S3]

Bridge, Alansen Frank, Cpl., 180th Co., San Domingo, Dominican Republic, DAS, drowned September 5, 1921 in Saco River, San Domingo, Dominican Republic. Mrs. Lydia J. Backus (Mother), Adams St., Vermillion, California [S4]

Bridges, Thomas Terrell, Pvt., Co. G, 13th Regt., DOD, September 22, 1918 enroute to France. Mattie B. C. Bridges (Mother), Inverness, Mississippi [FAG] [S2]

Bridwell, Bruce H., Pvt., Co. Y, Parris Island, South Carolina, DDS, December 4, 1918 at Parris Island, South Carolina. Mrs. Susan Holtz Bridwell (Mother), Route #3, Shepherdsville, Kentucky [S4]

Briere, Alphonse, Pvt., 13th Co., 10th Regt., Quanitco, Virginia, DDS, October 2, 1918 at Quanitco, Virginia. Julie Briere (Sister), 19 Orchard St., Cohoes, New York [S3]

Briggs, Leon F., Cpl., RR Det., Parris Island, South Carolina, DDS, January 13, 1919 at Parris Island, South Carolina. Frank P. Briggs (Father), Pleasant St., Ayer, Massachusetts [S4]

Briggs, Willard W., Pvt., 49th Co., 5th Regt., DOD, September 12, 1918 in France. James Briggs (Father), RFD #6, Jackson, Michigan [FAG] [S2]

Brighton, James Roy, Pvt., Hdqtrs. Co., 13th Regt., DOD, September 23, 1918 enroute to France. Ellen Brighton (Mother), 528 S. 13th St., E. Salt Lake City, Utah [R] [S2]

Bristol, Homer E., Pvt., Co. L, Charleston, South Carolina, DDS, November 18, 1918 at Charleston, South Carolina. Mrs. Luella Bristol (Mother), 32 Aurelius Ave., Auburn, New York [FAG] [S4]

Marine Corps Deaths, 1917-1921

Britton, Paul Wood, Sgu., 55th Co., 5th Regt., KIA, October 6, 1918 in the Meuse Argonne. Fred H. Britton (Brother), 10 N. Ford St., Hutchinson, Kansas [ANC] [S2] [SW]

Brock, Joe McKinley, Pvt., 18th Co., 5th Regt., KIA, June 8, 1918 in the Chateau-Thierry Sector. Geo. Milton Brock (Father), 803 Grant St., LaGrange, Georgia [FAG] [S2] [SW]

Brock, Warren, Pvt., 79th Co., 6th Regt., KIA, July 19, 1918 in the Aisne Marne. J. M. Brock (Father), 1622 E. St., Bedford, Indiana [FAG] [S2] [SW]

Brockway, Clifford Leslie, Sgu., 84th Co., 6th Regt., KIA, June 6, 1918 in the Chateau-Thierry Sector. Elbert S. Brockway (Brother), 1657 Elm St., Utica, New York, [ABMC-Belleau] [S2] [SW] [SW1 says Brookway]

Brodstrom, Brer Gustaf, Captain, USNH, Washington, D.C., DDS, November 21, 1921 at Washington, D.C. Mathilda M. Broadstrom (Mother), Stromsdal Brosttsta, Eskilstuna, Sweden [S4]

Brolander, Peter Raymond, Pvt., 78th Co., 6th Regt., DOW, June 22, 1918 in the Chateau-Thierry Sector. Mrs. R. E. Sprau (Mother), Hopkins, Michigan [S2] [SW] [SW]

Brommer, Eisse, Pvt., 25th Co., 4th Regt., Monte Christie, Dominican Republic, DDS, September 27, 1921 at Monte Christie, Dominican Republic. Lambert Brommer (Father), Ellsworth, Nobles Co., Minnesota [FAG] [S4]

Brooke, Arthur Edward, Pvt., Co. F., Philadelphia, Pennsylvania, DDS, June 5, 1917 at Philadephia, Pennsylvania. Edward F. Brooke (Father), Vineland, New Jersey [S3]

Brookes, William, Cpl., Marine Barracks, Navy Yard, Washington, D.C., DDS, June 26, 1917 at Washington, D.C. No next of kin given. [ANC] [S3]

Brooks, Harold Alfred, Pvt., 76th Co., 6th Regt., KIA, June 3, 1918 in the Aisne Defensive. Nettie Schuldt (Foster-Mother), RFD#5, Sterling, Illinois [S2] [SW]

Marine Corps Deaths, 1917-1921

Brooks, Harry Vernon, Pvt., 49th Co., 5th Regt., DOW, June 17, 1918 in the Chateau-Thierry Sector. Mrs. Elizbeth O'Neal (Aunt), 1026 Cross St., West Baltimore, Maryland [R] [S2] [SW]

Brooks, John Wood, Pvt., 47th Co., 5th Regt., KIA, June 6, 1918 in the Chateau-Thierry Sector. Mrs.Henry Books (Mother), 123 S. 15th St., Sebring, Ohio [S2] [SW]

Brooks, Prosper Roscoe, Pvt., 18th Co., 5th Regt., KIA, June 10, 1918 in the Chateau-Thierry Sector. Grace Brooks-McFarland (Mother), Georgetown, Illinois [R] [S2] [SW]

Brooks, Russell Roy, Pvt., 4th Sq., FMAF, DOD, (Pneumonia), September 30, 1918 in England. Elizabeth C. Brooks (Wife), 701 S. Chesnut St., Kowanee, Illinois [ABMC-Brookwood] [S2]

Broome, Lawrence Edwin, Pvt., 75th Co., 6th Regt., KIA, October 9, 1918 in the Meuse Argonne. Florence Broome (Mother), 260 E. Main St., New London, Ohio [S2] [SW1]

Brosius, Lloyd, Sgu., 81st Co., 6th MG Bn., DOW, July 19, 1918 in the Aisne Marne. John Brosius (Father), Gen. Del., Carthage, Missouri [ABMC-Belleau] [S2] [SW]

Brosseau, Paul Alfred, Pvt., 66th Co., 5th Regt., DOW, July 18, 1918 in the Aisne Marne. William Brosseau (Father), 30 Mead St., Everett, Massachusetts [ABMC-Belleau TOM] [S2] [SW1 says KIA]

Brough, Frank Cristopher, Pvt., 82nd Co., 6th Regt., DOW, July 23, 1918 in the Aisne Marne. Dr. Frank T. Brough (Father), 150 E. 127th St., New York, New York [ABMC-Belleau] [S2] [SW says Repl. Co.]

Brown, Aden, Pvt., 17th Co., 5th Regt., DOW, June 9, 1918 in the Chateau-Thierry Sector. Mrs. Hannah Brown (Mother), P. O. Box 38, Clyde, New York [ABMC-Suresnes] [S2] [SW]

Marine Corps Deaths, 1917-1921

Brown, Charles Francis, Pvt., 77th Co., 6th MG Bn., KIA, June 2, 1918 in the Aisne Defensive. Gabriel H. Brown (Father), 389 Dayton Ave., St. Paul, Minnesota [R] [S2] [SW]

Brown, Charles Vernon, Pvt., 47th Co., 5th Regt., DOW, October 24, 1918 in the Meuse Argonne. Lena Mm. Brown (Mother), 1202 Duncan St., Massillon, Ohio [S2] [SW1]

Brown, Dilmus, Pvt., 55th Co., 5th Regt., KIA, June 12, 1918 in the Chateau-Thierry Sector. John W. Brown (Father), Watkinsville, Georgia [FAG] [S2] [SW]

Brown, Dudley Leicester, Sgt., 83rd Co., 6th Regt., KIA, October 8, 1918 in the Meuse Argonne. Marie L. Gibson (Mother), 2510 Beachwood Dr., Hollywood, California [ANC] [S2] [SW1]

Brown, Francis Woodbury, Pvt., 45th Co., 5th Regt., KIA, June 6, 1918 in the Chateau-Thierry Sector. Mrs. Frank E. Cole (Aunt), 2 Orange St., Newburyport, Massachusetts [S2] [SW]

Brown, Gilbert, Pvt., Supply Co., 13th Regt., DOD, October 18, 1918 in France. Henry J. Brown (Father), Franklinville, New York [R] [S2]

Brown, Henry James, Pvt., 82nd Co., 6th Regt., DOW, July 21, 1918 in the Aisne Marne. Catherine Brown (Mother), 79 Clinton Ave., Albany, New York [ABMC-Belleau] [S2] [SW1]

Brown, Hogey, Pvt., 17th Co., 5th Regt., DOW, June 16, 1918 in the Chateau-Thierry Sector. Mrs. Joe Brown (Mother), RFD #3, Box 198, Waco, Texas [R] [S2] [SW]

Brown, Joseph Benjimin, Pvt., 47th Co., 5th Regt., KIA, June 25, 1918 in the Chateau-Thierry Sector. George B. Brown (Father), 1813 Forest St., Lynchburg, Virginia [R] [S2]

Brown, Leo Herbert, Pvt., 83rd Co., 6th Regt., DOW, July 19, 1918 in the Aisne Marne. Herbert F. Brown (Father), 304 N. Main St., Canastota, New York [ABMC-Belleau TOM] [S2] [SW1]

Marine Corps Deaths, 1917-1921

Brown, Norman Branson, Pvt., 8th Co., 5th Regt., DOD, March 2, 1919 in France. Alexander Brown (Father), Ardmore, Pennsylvania [R] [S2]

Brown, Robert Jefferson, Sgt, Co. H, 13th Regt., DOD, September 26, 1918 in France. Mrs. Margaret O'Mara (Aunt), Morrison, Washington [R] [S2]

Brown, Thomas, Pvt., 49th Co., 5th Regt., DOW, June 2, 1918 in the Aisne Defensive. Thomas Nugent (Uncle), Massachusetts Ave. and Washington Streets, Boston, Massachusetts [ABMC-Belleau] [S2]

Brow, Walter Vernon, 2nd Lieutenant, Flying Field, Quantico, Virginia, DAS, June 9, 1921 in an aeroplane crash near Colonial Beach, Virginia. Mrs. Clara M. Brown (Mother), 1314 State St., Boise, Idaho [S4]

Brown, Willard Leighton, Pvt., 67th Co., 5th Regt., KIA, October 5, 1918 in the Meuse Argonne. Jessie Brown (Mother), Yampa, Colorado [R] [S2] [SW says 134th Co.]

Brown, William Henry, Pvt., 79th Co., 6th Regt., KIA, June 2, 1918 in the Aisne Defensive. Mrs. Mary T. Ruenbuhl (Mother), 1102 33rd St., Galveston, Texas [R] [S2] [SW says Hdqrs. Co., 2nd Repl. Btln.]

Brown, Willie Leslie, Pvt., 78th Co., 6th Regt., DOW, October 4, 1918 in the Meuse Argonne. Mrs. Verta Brown (Mother), C/o Stillwater Lumber Co., Vader, Washington [R] [S2] [SW1 says KIA]

Browning, Porter, Pvt., 75th Co., 6th Regt., KIA, July 19, 1918 in the Chateau-Thierry Sector. William R. Browning (Father), Verona, Missouri [R] [S2][SW1]

Browning, Virgil A., Pfc, BD, MB, Washington, D.C., DDS, January 22, 1920 at Washington, D.C. Will Browning (Father), Piedmont, South Carolina [S4]

Brownlee, Estey Harold, Pvt., Co. D, 11th Regt., DOD, October 5, 1918 enroute to France. Harry S. Brownlee (Father), RFD #3, Villisca, Iowa [R] [S2]

Marine Corps Deaths, 1917-1921

Broxup, John, Cpl., 49th Co., 5th Regt., KIA, November 5, 1918 in the Meuse Argonne. Grace Broxup (Wife), 62 College St., Buffalo, New York [ABMC-Romagne] [S2] [SW1]

Bruce, Christopher, Cpl., Co. A, 2nd Casualty Replacement Battalion. [SW]

Bruer, Frederick Marion, Pvt., Co. A, 2nd MG Replacement Bn, DDS, at Quanitco, Virginia. Wm. Bruer (Father), 119 South Broadway St., Joliet, Illinois [S3]

Brush, Izaak Walton, Pvt., 45th Co., 5th Regt., KIA, October 4, 1918 in the Meuse Argonne. E. F. Brush (Father), 320 S. 5th Ave., Mt. Vernon, New York [ABMC-Romagne] [S2][SW1 says DOW]

Bryan, John Victor, Pvt., 76th Co., 6th Regt., DOW, July 19, 1918 in the Aisne Marne. John W. Bryan (Father), Box 90, Bowners Grove, Illinois [ABMC-Belleau TOM] [S2] [SW1]

Bryant, Glenwin Elliott, Pvt., 47th Co., 5th Regt., DOW, November 2, 1918 in the Meuse Argonne. Alta Bryant (Mother), Drake, Colorado [ANC] [S2] [SW1 says Elliott Glenwin Bryant]

Bryant, Malcome Eugene, Pvt., Co. F, 13th Regt., DOD, September 26, 1918 in France. James H. Bryant (Father), Groveland, Florida [R] [S2]

Bryce, Clarence Archibald J Jr., Pvt., 82nd Co., 6th Regt., KIA, November 2, 1918 in the Meuse Argonne. Dr. Clarence A. Bryce (Father), 516 N. 10th St., Richmond, Virginia [ABMC-Romagne] [S2] [SW1]

Buchanan, Albert William, Pvt., Marine Detachment, NPG, Indian Head, Maryland, DDS, October 20, 1918 at Indian Head, Maryland. Mrs. George Harvey (Sister), Bakersfield, California [S3]

Buchanan, Robert L., Pvt., Co. B, 10th Sep. Bn, Quantico, Virginia, DDS, November 12, 1918 at Quantico, Virginia.

Marine Corps Deaths, 1917-1921

Robert L. Buchanan (Father), Route #6, Bryan, Texas [S4]

Buchheister, Ernest Louis, Pvt., 16th Co., 5th Regt., KIA, June 23, 1918 in the Chateau-Thierry Sector. Oscar Buchheister (Father), 910 Fullerton Ave., Chicago, Illinois [ABMC-Belleau TOM] [S2] [SW]

Buchlein, Edward Raymond, Pvt., 55th Co., 5th Regt., DOW, June 5, 1918 in the Chateau-Thierry Sector. Christian Buchlein (Father), 4668 Hudson Blvd., Union Hill, New Jersey [R] [S2] [SW]

Buchman, Herbert John Philip, Cpl., Co. B, OSD, Quanitco, Virginia, DDS, October 15, 1918 at Quanitco, Virginia. Robert Buchman (Father), Springbrook, Wisconsin [S3]

Buck, Kinsley Clark, Pvt., 67th Co., 5th Regt., KIA, June 6, 1918 in the Chateau-Thierry Sector. Mary F. Buck (Mother), 304 North Elm Ave., Elmhurst, Illinois [ABMC-Belleau] [S2] [SW]

Buckley, Raymond, Pvt., 75th Co., 6th Regt., DOW, November 12, 1918 in the Meuse Argonne. Mrs. Josephine Buckley (Mother), 1246 Bush St., Apt. #17, San Francisco, California [R] [S2] [SW1]

Buckman, Jewell, Pvt., 17th Co., 5th Regt., KIA, June 7, 1918 in the Chateau-Thierry Sector. Albert S. Buckman (Father), Holley, New York [R] [S2] [SW]

Budde, George William, Pvt., 17th Co., 5th Regt., KIA, November 11, 1918 in the Meuse Argonne. Elizabeth Budde (Mother), 655 Hawthorne Ave., Cincinnati, Ohio [S2] [SW1]

Budlong, William Theodore Roosevelt, Pvt., 43rd Co., 5th Regt., DOW, June 8, 1918 in the Chateau-Thierry Sector. Charles A. Budlong (Father), 2628 Park Ridge Ave., Marinetta, Wisconsin [R] [S2] [SW1]

Budman, Judson Eugene, Pvt., 83rd Co., 6th Regt., DOW, June 14, 1918 in the Chateau-Thierry Sector. Isaac W.Budman

Marine Corps Deaths, 1917-1921

(Father), 104 South Market St., Muncey, Pennsylvania [S2] [SW1]

Buechele, Robert Laurence, 1st Sgt., Marine Detachment, USS *Nevada*, DOD, October 24, 1918 at Bantry Bay, Ireland. Mary B. Buechele (Mother), 825 Ontario Ave., Sheboygan, Wisconsin [S2]

Buford, David Lambert, Gy. Sgt., 55th Co., 5th Regt., KIA, June 13, 1918 in the Chateau-Thierry Sector. Decatur J. Buford (Father), Frankston, Texas [S2] [SW1]

Buford, Nelson Milton, Cpl., Hdqtrs. Co., 2nd Replacement Bn., KIA, June 9, 1918 in the Chateau-Thierry Sector. William Buford (Father), Guymon, Oklahoma [R] [S2] [SW1 says DOW]

Buli, Albert Noren, Pvt., 20th Co., 5th Regt., KIA, November 6, 1918 in the Meuse Argonne. Margaret Buli (Mother), RFD #2, E. Stanwood, Washington [ABMC-Romagne] [S2] [SW1]

Bullard, Arthur Lee, Sgt., 75th Co., 6th Regt., KIA, October 9, 1918 in the Meuse Argonne. Mrs. Arthur L. Bullard (Wife), 40 Harrison St., Newton Highlands, Massachusetts [ANC] [S2] [SW1]

Bullis, Ward Elon, Pvt., 75th Co., 6th Regt., DOW, October 13, 1918 in the Meuse Argonne. H. B. Bullis (Father), Lidgerwood, North Dakota [R] [S2] [SW1]

Bulman, William Henry, Sgt., 18th Co., 5th Regt., DOW, July 30, 1918 in the Aisne Marne. Mrs. Annie Bulan Aminoto (former wife), 2310 Grays Ferry Ave., Philadelphia, Pennsylvania [R] [S2] [SW1 says Cpl.]

Bunn, Frederick Jethro, Pvt., 97th Co., 6th Regt., DOW, July 21, 1918 in the Aisne Marne. Ida Bunn (Mother), 21 Lincoln St., Columbus, Ohio [ABMC-Belleau] [S2] [SW1]

Burch, Mark, Pvt., MBks, New Orleans, Lousiana, DOS, March 4, 1921 at New Orleans, Louisiana. Luther L. Burch (Brother), Route #1, Easterly, Texas [S4]

Marine Corps Deaths, 1917-1921

Burch, Ralph William, Pvt., 95th Co., 6th Regt., KIA, October 5, 1918 in the Meuse Argonne. W. H. Burch (Father), Marietta, Oklahoma [ABMC-Romagne] [S2] [SW1]

Burchardi, Adolph Christian, Pvt., 51st Co., 5th Regt., DOW, November 7, 1918 in the Meuse Argonne. Margaret Burchardi (Mother), Gen. Del., Solvang, California [R] [S2] [SW1]

*Burchele, Robert Laurence, 1stSgt., Med, USMC, DOD, October 24, 1918, Sheboygan, Wisconsin [R] [check S3]

Burd, Vern Vance, Pvt., 67th Co., 5th Regt., DOW, October 8, 1918 in the Meuse Argonne. Leonard Burd (Father), Manterville, Minnesota [R] [S2] [SW1]

Burdick, Edward Michael, Pvt., 18th Co., 5th Regt., DOW, October 12, 1918 in the Meuse Argonne. Mary Brannick (Foster-mother), Renville, Minnesota, [ABMC-Suresnes] [S2] [SW says Co. C, 4th Sep. Btln.]

Burgess, Wilbert F. M., Sgt., BD, New York, DDS, May 29, 1919 at Brooklyn, New York. Mr. Edwin J. Burgess (Brother), 416 E. 65th St., Los Angeles, California [S4]

Burhans, Robert Almon, Cpl., 47th Co., 5th Regt., KIA, June 25, 1918 in the Chateau-Thierry Sector. William D. Burhans (Father), RFD #5, Harbor Beach, Michigan [ABMC-Belleau] [S2] [SW says Burnhams]

Burhart, Frank Pierce, Pvt., Co. B, 13th Regt., DOD, October 4, 1918in France. Mrs. J. J. Murbach (Mother), 1119 Patterson St., Houston, Texas [R] [S2]

Burke, Chester Arthur, Pvt., 17th Co., 5th Regt., KIA, June 9, 1918 in the Chateau-Thierry Sector. George Wade (Step-father), 68 New St., Shelton, Connecticut [ABMC-Belleau] [S2] [SW1]

Burke, Clifford T., Pvt., Co. A, 10th Sep. Bn., Quantico, Virginia, DDS, November 23, 1918 at Quantico, Virginia. Thomas Frank Burke (Father), 3013 Avenue P, Galveston, Texas [S4]

Marine Corps Deaths, 1917-1921

Burke, Leo Thomas, Pvt., Hdqtrs. Co., 6th Regt., KIA, July 19, 1918 in the Aisne Marne. Sarah Burke (Mother), 460 Pleasant St., Gardner, Massachusetts [ABMC-Belleau TOM] [S2] [SW1]

Burke, Philip Joseph, Pvt., 55th Co., 5th Regt., DOD, September 19, 1918 in France. Mrs. Ellen Ryan (Aunt), 310 Madison St., Troy, New York [R] [S2]

Burkett, Homer Wells, Pvt., Co. L, 13th Regt., DOD, October 1, 1918 in France. Laura Burkett (Mother), 19th and Beach Sts. Abilene, Texas [R] [S2]

Burleson, Van Parson, Pvt., M.G. Co., 13th Regt., DOD, September 24, 1918 enroute to France. Mrs. Mary F. Barleson (Mother), Canisteo, New York [R] [S2]

Burnes, John F., Capt., 74th Co., 6th Regt., DOW, June 14, 1918 in the Chateau Thierry sector. Mrs. Margaret Keigler (sister), 126 Pulteny St., Corning, New York [ANC] [S1] [SW]

Burnett, John Thomas, 1st Sgt., 55th Co., 5th Regt., KIA, June 13, 1918 in the Chateau-Thierry Sector. Mr. O. O. Burnett (Brother), Grovetown, Georgia [ABMC-Belleau TOM] [S2] [SW]

Burnhams *see* Burhans

Burns, Charles Raymond, Pvt., 47th Co., 5th Regt., KIA, June 25, 1918 in the Chateau-Thierry Sector. Mrs. Mary Burns (Mother), 56 N. Second St., Duquesne, Pennsylvania [R] [S2] [SW]

Burns, Hubert Hyrum, Pvt., 23rd Co., 6th MG Bn., KIA, June 4, 1918 in the Aisne Defensive. Fannie Burns (Mother), Randlett, Utah [ABMC-Belleau] [S2] [SW]

Burns, John Irving, Pvt., 10th Sq., FMAF, DOD, October 24, 1918 in England. Mary E. Hannan (Aunt), 2418 Pennsylvania Ave., N.W., Washington, D.C. [S2]

Burns, Robert Samuel, Pvt., 51st Co., 5th Regt., DOW, June 10, 1918 in the Chateau-Thierry Sector. Arthur Burns

Marine Corps Deaths, 1917-1921

(Brother), 334 N. 5th St., Hamilton, Ohio [ABMC-Suresnes] [S2] [SW]

Burns, Ruble Francis, Pvt., N.P. Det, Parris Island, South Carolina, DDS, December 3, 1918 at Parris Island, South Carolina. Mrs. Sallie Burns (Mother), Folsom, Louisiana [S4]

Burnside, George Monroe, Sgt., Co. F, 13th Regt., DOD, October 28, 1918 in France. Mrs. Jennie Burnside (Mother), Sand Springs, Oklahoma [R] [S2]

Burnside, William Louis, Pvt., 19th Co., HAF, DDS, March 28, 1918 at Quanitco, Virginia. Robert Burnside (Father), 111 West End Ave., Carthage, New York [S3]

Burr, Carleton, 2nd Lieut., 74th Co., 6th Regt., KIA, July 19, 1918 in the Aisne Marne. I. Tucker Barr (Father), 53 State St., Boston, Massachusetts [ABMC-Belleau] [S1] [SW]

Burroughs, John Edward, 1st Sgt., Bks. Det., Quanitco, Virginia, DDS, April 11, 1918 at Quanitco, Virginia. Dent E. Burroughs (Father), 730 St. Louis Ave., Edwardsville, Illinois [S3]

Burrows, Carl Austin, Cpl., MD USNH, Fort Lyon, Colorado, DDS, October 24, 1920 at Fort Lyon, Colorado. Mrs. Mathilda Burrows (Mother), 253 Belgrade Ave., Roslindale, Massachusetts [S4]

Burstan, Rupert M., Capt., Det. Duty with Hdqtrs. Co., 1st Casual Regt., DOD, September 19, 1918 in France. Mrs. Sarah B. Burstan (Mother), 201 S. Victoria Ave., Atlantic City, New Jersey [R] [S1]

Burt, Claire Nile, Pvt., 82nd Co., 6th Regt., KIA, October 6, 1918 in the Meuse Argonne. Eliza Burt (Mother), Laingsburg, Michigan [R] [S2] [SW1]

Burtner, Winton Paul, Pvt., 67th Co., 5th Regt., KIA, June 14, 1918 in the Chateau-Thierry Sector. William H. Burtner (Father), RR#2, Box #8, Harrisonburg, Virginia [ANC] [S2] [SW]

Marine Corps Deaths, 1917-1921

Burton, Alvin F., Pvt., MD, NRR, Caldwell, New Jersey, DAS, July 27, 1919 accidently drowned near Singac, New Jersey. Mrs. Robert Burton (Mother), 1624 Laurel St., Wilmington, Delaware [S4]

Burton, William Eugene, Pvt., 80th Co., 6th Regt., KIA, June 27, 1918 in the Chateau-Thierry Sector. Emma Burton (Mother), 4807 E. 7th St., Kansas City, Missouri [ABMC-Belleau TOM] [S2] [SW]

Busby, William Henshaw, 2nd Lieut., 75th Co., 6th Regt., DOW, November 1, 1918 in the Meuse Argonne. Mrs. Anna L. Busby (Mother), R.R. #2, Catlin, Illinois [S1] [SW1 syas KIA]

Busch, Roy Headrick, Sgt., 47th Co., 5th Regt., DOW, August 16, 1918 in the Chateau-Thierry Sector. A. J. Busch (Father), Box 273, Covington, Virginia [ABMC-Fere] [S2] [SW]

Buschman, William C., Pvt., MD, USNH, Fort Lyon, Colorado, DDS, February 22, 1919 at Fort Lyon, Colorado. Mrs. Henry Mark (Sister), 1091 16th Ave., N.E., Minneapolis, Minnesota [FAG] [S4]

Bush, Charles G., Sgt., Hdqtrs., 4th Regt., DAS, July 31, 1920 at Santo Domingo City, Dominican Republic. Maynard Bush (Father), 3406 Euclid Ave., Kansas City, Missouri [S4]

Bush, Francis Henshaw, Pvt., 43rd Co., 5th Regt., DOW, October 7, 1918 in the Meuse Argonne. Jord Bush (Father), Tonkawa, Oklahoma [S2] [SW1]

Bush, John Joseph, Pvt., 47th Co., 5th Regt., KIA, October 4, 1918 in the Meuse Argonne. Mary Bush (Mother), 5806 E. 10th St., Kansas City, Missouri [R] [S2]

Bush, Joseph Edward, Cpl., 80th Co., 6th Regt., DOW, July 13, 1918 in the Meuse Argonne. Mary C. Bush (Mother), Farrplay, Missouri [S2] [SW]

Marine Corps Deaths, 1917-1921

Bush, Willard Edward, Pvt., Co. Z, Parris Island, S.C., DOS August 7, 1918 at Parris Island, South Carolina. Clarence Bush (Brother), 92 Park Way, Rochester, New York [S3]

Bushman, Henry F., Pvt., Co. A, Mare Island, California, DDS, February 6, 1920 at Mare Island, California. John Bushman (Father), Catawba, Wisconsin [S4]

Busse, Harry Frederic, Pvt., 84th Co., 6th Regt., KIA, November 1, 1918 in the Meuse Argonne. Caroline Busse (Mother), 327 Hartwell St., Waukesha, Wisconsin [ABMC-Romagne] [S2] [SW1]

Butler, Edmund Arthur, Pvt., 79th Co., 6th Regt., DOW, June 7, 1918 in the Chateau-Thierry Sector. Elizabeth Butler (Mother), 1401 17th Ave., N. Minneapolis, Minnesota [R] [S2] [SW1]

Butler, Jesse Fayette, Pvt., 79th Co., 6th Regt., DOW, July 24, 1918 in the Aisne Marne. John Ackerson (Father), Box #72, Lewistown, Illinois [R] [S2] [SW says Repl. Btln.]

Button, William Robert, Sgt., Cape Haitien, Haiti, DDS, April 5, 1921 at Cape Haitien, Haiti. William P. Button (Father), 4323 Manchester Ave., St. Louis, Missouri [S4]

Byergo, Meldon, Pvt., Navy Yard, Washington, D.C., DDS, January 31, 19120 at Washington, D.C. Andrew T. Byergo (Father), Epharin, Utah [S4]

Byrne, John Waldron., Pvt., Co. G, MFF, Miami, Florida, DAS, December 27, 1918 of a skull injury from an aeroplane propeller at Miami, Florida. Mrs. Nora Bryne (Mother), 2412 N. 26th St., Philadelphia, Pennsylvania [S4]

Byron, Walter Anthony, Pvt., Co. H, 13th Regt., DOD, October 1, 1918 in France. Mrs. Rose A. B. Babock (Sister), 2306 Morris Ave., New York, New York [ABMC-Fere] [S2]

Cabell, Edward Elvin, Cpl., 55th Co., 5th Regt., DOW, August 20, 1918 in the Chateau-Thierry Sector. Mrs. Ollie Robey (Mother), 1536 S. Lindenwood St., Philadelphia, Pennsylvania [R] [S2] [SW]

Marine Corps Deaths, 1917-1921

Cahill, Raymond Joseph, Pvt., 82nd Co., 6th Regt., KIA, June 14, 1918 in the Chateau-Thierry Sector. James J. Cahill (Father), 243 Hermitage St., Manayunk, Pennsylvania [S2] [SW says 144th Co., Repl. Btln.]

Cain, Edward, 2nd Lieutenant, MCR, MFF, Miami, Florida, DAS, February 15, 1919 of multiple injuries in an aeroplane crash at Miami, Florida. Dr. James W. Cain (Father), Washington College, Chestertown, Maryland [S4]

Cain, Olna Young, Pvt., 67th Co., 5th Regt., KIA, November 1, 1918 in the Meuse Argonne. Lillie Miller Cain (Mother), Medora, Illinois [ABMC-Romagne] [S2] [SW1]

Caldwell, Joseph Richard, Jr., Pvt., 67th Co., 5th Regt., KIA, October 4, 1918 in the Meuse Argonne. Joseph R. Caldwell, Sr. (Father), 335 So. Linden Ave., Pittsburgh, Pennsylvania [FAG] [S2] [SW1]

Call, Darrell Harcourt, Pvt., 81st Co., 6th MG Bn., DOW, August 4, 1918 in the Aisne Marne. Clifford N. Call (Brother), 4919 Fulton St., Chicago, Illinois [S2] [SW]

Call, George, Sgt., 96th Co., 6th Regt., KIA, October 3, 1918 in the Meuse Argonne. Joseph W. Call (Father), RFD#4, Box 245, Joplin, Missouri [ABMC- Romagne] [S2] [SW says Replacement]

Callahan, John James, Pvt., 55th Co., 5th Regt., KIA, June 11, 1918 in the Chateau-Thierry Sector. Elizabeth Callahan (Mother), 7 Bank St., Troy, New York [FAG] [S2] [SW]

Cameron, Duncan H., 2nd Lieut., 1st Mar. Avia. Force, DAS, June 24, 1918 at Miami, Florida. Duncan Cameron (Father), 204 Hawthorne St., Edgewood, Pennsylvania [FAG] [S3] [SW1]

Cameron, Robert Cutber, Pvt., 18th Co., 5th Regt., DOW, July 21, 1918 in the Aisne Marne. Niel Cameron (Father), 2125 W. Monroe St., Chicago, Illinois [ABMC- Fere] [S2] [SW1 says KIA]

Marine Corps Deaths, 1917-1921

Campbell, Carl Hamilton, Pvt., MD, Naval Operating Base, Hampton Roads, Virginia, DDS, November 28, 1920 at Hampton Roads, Virginia. Benjamin N. Campbell (Father), RFD#1, Winterset, Iowa [S4]

Campbell, Charles Gordon, Cpl., 80th Co., 6th Regt., KIA, July 19, 1918 in the Aisne Marne. Ch H. Campbell (Father), 3209 Bryant Ave., Minneapolis, Minnesota [ABMC- Suresnes] [S2]

Campbell, John Louis, Pvt., Co. H, Quanitco, Virginiam, DDS, October 2, 1918 at Quanitco, Virginia. X. L. Campbell (Mother), Marthaville, Louisiana [FAG] [S3]

Campbell, John William, Cpl., Sup Co., 6th Regt., DOD, February 8, 1919 in France. Anna Campbell (Mother), 1160 Riopelle St., Detriot, Michigan [ANC] [S2]

Campbell, Richard Creswell, Cpl., 80th Co., 6th Regt., DOD, November 1, 1918 [S2]

Campbell, Roe Ellsworth, Pvt., 20th Co., 5th Regt., DOW, November 19, 1918 in the Meuse Argonne. Mrs. Opal C. Meyer (Sister), 80 "R" St., Fairbury, Nebraska [S2] [SW1]

Campf, Russell James, Pvt., Co. L, 13th Regt., DOD, October 1, 1918 in France. James B. Campf (Father), RFD #3, Salem, Ohio [FAG] [S2]

Candito, Vincent John, Pvt., 20th Co., 5th Regt., KIA, November 1, 1918 in the Meuse Argonne. Frank Candito (Father), 306 East 34th St., New York, New York [S2] [SW1]

Candlin, Victor Gladstone, Pvt., 74th Co., 6th Regt., DOW, October 12, 1918 in the Meuse Argonne. Henry Candlin (Father), 1111 10th St., Greeley, Colorado [ABMC-Romagne] [S2] [SW1]

Canedy, Joseph John, Pvt., 50th Co., 3rd Regt., 2nd Brigade, Santo Domingo, Dominican Republic, DOS, April 15, 1917 at Santo Domingo, Dominican Republic. Raffel Canedy (Father), 402 Chestnut St., Newark, New Jersey [S3]

Marine Corps Deaths, 1917-1921

Canfield, John Raymond, Pvt., 43rd Co., 5th Regt., KIA, June 12, 1918 in the Chateau-Thierry Sector. Benjamin Canfield (Father), Cedar Grove, New Jersey [S2] [SW]

Cannon, Rollin Mariner, Pvt., 18th Co., 5th Regt., DOW, June 8, 1918 in the Chateau-Thierry Sector. Fletcher B. Cannon (Father), Damon Hill, Westminister, Massachusetts [ABMC-Belleau] [S2] [SW]

Capehart, Lawrence Homer, Pvt., 84th Co., 6th Regt., DOW, August 5, 1918 in the Aisne Marne Offensive. Sara Capehart (Mother), 304 E. Court, Jeffersonville, Indiana [S2] [SW says 145th Co.]

Capps, Walter Eugene, Pvt., 82nd Co., 6th Regt., DOW, June 8, 1918 in the Chateau-Thierry Sector. George Capps (Father), 342 Western Ave., Chicago, Illinois [FAG] [S2] [SW1]

Card, Arthur, Pvt., 18th Co., 5th Regt., DOW, July 6, 1918 in the Chateau-Thierry Sector. Anna Card (Mother), 40 Alexander Ave., Madison, New Jersey [S2] [SW]

Carey, Boyd W., Pvt., Bks. Det., Brooklyn, New York, DDS, April 4, 1919 at Brooklyn, New York. Mrs. Joicy O. Mickey (Mother), 3321 Davenport St., Omaha, Nebraska [S4]

Carey, Charles Herbert, Pvt., 15th Co., 6th MG Bn., DOW, June 13, 1918 in the Chateau-Thierry Sector. Charles M. Carey (Father), RFD #5, Goshen Rd., Salem, Ohio [FAG] [S2] [SW]

Carey, Rudy Daniel, Sgt., 104th Co., 9th Regt., Galveston, Texas, DDS, December 17, 1918 at Galveston, Texas. Mrs. Ellen Carey (Mother), Gen. Del., Somerset, Colorado [S4]

Carey, Theo Thurman, Pvt., 97th Co., 6th Regt., DOW, July 19, 1918 in the Aisne Marne. Sadie Carey (Mother), Walnut, Iowa [S2] [SW1]

Cargill, Myrtis Beverly, Pvt., 74th Co., 6th Regt., DOW, April 24, 1918 in the Toulon Sector, Verdun. Elzar Cornelious

Marine Corps Deaths, 1917-1921

Cargill (Father), So. Ward St., Italy, Texas [ABMC- Romagne as Myatis] [S2] [SW]

Carletti, Joseph, Pvt., MB, Pensacola, Florida, DDS, January 17, 1919 at Pensacola, Florida. Mrs. Jennie Carletti (Stepmother), 2242 Curtis St., Denver, Colorado [S4] [FAG]

Carlson, Ernest Ludwig, Sgt., Earster Recruiting Division, DDS, September 19, 1918 at Chelsea, Massachusetts. Mrs. Marcia D. Carlson (Wife), 40 Wellington St., Worcester, Massachusetts [S3]

Carlson, Frank Shurtleff, Pvt., 84th Co., 6th Regt., KIA, June 5, 1918 in the Aisne Defensive. Magnus Carlson (Father), 313 W. Exchange St., Sycamore, Illinois [ABMC- Belleau] [S2] [SW]

Carlson, James Francis John, Pvt., 75th Co., 6th Regt., DOW, October 5, 1918 in the Meuse Argonne. Bertha Carlson Manning (Sister), Box 96, Duke Center, Pennsylvania [FAG] [S2] [SW]

Carman, Harold, Sgt., 80th Co., 6th Regt., KIA, June 10, 1918 in the Chateau-Thierry Sector. Cecelia Carman (Mother), 32 Puntine St., Jamaica, L.I., New York [R] [S2] [SW]

Carnegie, David, Pvt., 15th Co., 6th MG Bn., KIA, October 6, 1918 in the Meuse Argonne. David Carnegie (Father), Stephen, Minnesota [ABMC- Romagne] [S2] [SW1]

Carpenter, Charles B., Pvt., 83rd Co., 6th Regt., KIA, November 2, 1918 in the Meuse Argonne. Marion and Margaret Carpenter (Parents), RFD #1, Dorsey, Mississippi [ABMC- Romagne as Charlie] [S2] [SW1]

Carpenter, Oates, Pvt., 23rd Co., 6th MG Bn., KIA, November 5, 1919 in the Meuse Argonne. Glendora Carpenter (Mother), P O Box 281, Forest Grove, Oregon [R] [S2] [SW1]

Carpenter, Stanley Diem, Pvt., 66th Co., 5th Regt., DOW, June 6, 1918 in the Chateau-Thierry Sector. Caroline Carpenter

Marine Corps Deaths, 1917-1921

(Mother), 516 Orchard Ave., Bellevue, Pennsylvania [FAG] [S2] [SW]

Carr, John Richard, Pvt., Bks. Detch., Quanitco, Virginia, DDS, October 15, 1918 at Quanitco, Virginia. Mrs. Mattie Clark (Mother), Clark, Missouri [FAG] [S3]

Carr, Joseph Frederick, Pvt., 51st Co., 5th Regt., KIA, November 10, 1918 in the Meuse Argonne. Mrs. Joseph F. Carr (Mother), 1012 Mohawk St., Utica, New York [R] [S2] [SW1]

Carrigan, William, Pvt., MD, American Legation, Managua, Nicaragua, DDS, October 8, 1917 at Managua, Nicaragua. Miss Mary A. Carrigan (Sister), 1624 N. Dover St., Philidelphia, Pennsylvania [ANC] [S3]

Carroll, James Patrick, Pvt., 78th Co., 6th Regt., KIA, September 15, 1918 in the St. Mihiel Offensive. John Carroll (Father), 56 Monmouth St., Red Bank, New Jersey [FAG] [S2] [SW]

Carson, Nathan Bryan Jr., Pvt., 45th Co., 5th Regt., KIA, November 1, 1918 in the Meuse Argonne. Nathan B. Carson (Father), 403 Broadway, Kissimmee, Florida [FAG] [S2] [SW1]

Carson, Renick Harry, Pvt., 132th Co., Quanitco, Virginia, DDS, September 30, 1918 at Quanitco, Virginia. Essie Carson (Mother), 405 S. Brighton St., Kansas City, Missouri [FAG] [S3]

Carson, Steve Pearson, Pvt., Co. G., 11th Regt., Quanitco, Virginia, DDS, October 4, 1918 at Quanitco, Virginia. Mildred Tainter Carson (Wife), Johnson City, Tennessee [S3]

Carson, William Arthur, Pvt., 75th Co., 6th Regt., DOW, July 19, 1918 in the Aisne Marne. Mrs. Mary E. Carson (Mother), 952 E. Central Ave., Relands, California [ABMC- Fere] [S2] [SW1]

Marine Corps Deaths, 1917-1921

Carstedt, Albert Bertie, Pvt., 80th Co., 6th Regt., KIA, July 19, 1918 in the Aisne Marne Offensive. Fredericka E. Carstedt (Mother), Cherryale, Kansas [ANC] [S2] [SW1 says DOW]

Carswell, Elroy E., Sgt., U.S. Naval Training Camp, San Diego, California, DDS, December 10, 1918 at San Diego, California. Mrs. Elizabeth Carswell (Mother), 3451 E. 104th St., S.E., Cleveland, Ohio [S4]

Carter, Gilbert LeRoy, Pvt., 18th Co., 5th Regt., KIA, July 21, 1918 in the Aisne Marne. John H. Carter (Father), Gen. Del., Elmer, Missouri [ABMC- Belleau as G. Carter] [S2] [SW1]

Carter, Joe Winlock, Pfc, MD, USNH, Fort Lyon, Colorado, DDS, October 7, 1920 at Fort Lyon, Colorado. Mrs. May Richardson (Aunt), 118 North 3rd Ave., Franklin, Tennessee [S4]

Carter, Omer Ralph, Pvt., 45th Co., 5th Regt., KIA, October 6, 1918 in the Meuse Argonne. John H. Carter (Father), Gen. Del., Elmer, Missouri [ABMC- Romagne] [S2] [SW1]

Carver, Rock, Pvt., MCR Co. A, 9th Sep. Batt., DOD, November 5, 1918 in France. Ettie J. Carver (Mother), Huntington, Tennessee [FAG] [S2]

Case, Marvin, 2nd Lieutenant, MCR, MB, Quantico, Virginia, DDS, January 7, 1919 at Chicago, Illinois. Mr. Elmer G. Case (Father), Blackstone Hotel, Chicago, Illinois [S4]

Casey, Dennis Patrick, Cpl., 75th Co., 6th Regt., DOW, October 12, 1918 in the Meuse Argonne. Mrs. Nora Casey (Mother), 1049 Tod Ave., Girard, Ohio [R] [S2] [SW1]

Casey, James, Pvt., Marine Barracks, Navy Yard, Washington, D.C., DDS, December 18, 1917 at Washington, D.C. No next of kin given. [ANC] [S3]

Marine Corps Deaths, 1917-1921

Casey, Theodore Roosvelt, Pvt., 79th Co., 6th Regt., KIA, July 19, 1918 in the Aisne Marne. George L. Casey (Father), RFD #2, Mechanicstown, Ohio [R] [S2] [SW1]

Casey, Walter Bernard, 2nd Lieutenant, 2nd Brigade, Dominican Republic, DAS, September 23, 1921 drowned enroute to Bayaguana, Dominican Republic. Mrs. Frances Casey (Mother), 480 Grove St., Columbus, Ohio [S4]

Cash, Roy Alfred, Pvt., 79th Co., 6th Regt., DOW, July 19, 1918 in the Aisne Marne. Ella Cash (Mother), 643½ Pearl St., Beaumont, Texas [ANC] [S2] [SW1]

Casner, Earl Parker, Cpl., Hdqtrs. Co., 6th MG Bn., KIA, July 5, 1918 in the Chateau-Thierry Sector. Adolphus Casner (Father), 933 North St., R#2, Box 8, Boulder, Colorado [S2] [SW]

Casperson, Carl Frederick, Pvt., Marine Detachment, NAD, St. Julien's Creek, Virginia, DDS, November 9, 1918 at Norfolk, Va. Mrs. Anna Casperson (Mother), 2221 Rainer Ave., Everett, Washington [FAG] [S3]

Cassady, Howard W., Pvt., Marine Detachment, Annapolis, Maryland, DDS, October 19, 1918 at Annapolis, Maryland. Della Cassady (Mother), 420 Webster St., Camden, New Jersey [S3]

Casteel, John Lon, Pvt., 15th Co., 6th MG Bn., KIA, October 3, 1918 in the Meuse Argonne. Mary Casteel (Mother), Gen. Del., Ukiah, Oregon [ANC] [S2] [SW]

Caster, Walter Franklin, Pfc, Depot of Supplies, Philadephia, Pennsylvania, DDS, September 25, 1918 at his home in Philadelphia, Pennsylvania. Mrs. Laura F. Moran (Mother), 214 South Stanton St., El Paso, Texas [FAG] [S3]

Cathers, Joseph, 1st Sgt., MD, USNH, Fort Lyon, Colorado, DDS, November 15, 1919 at Fort Lyon, Colorado. Mrs. Rose Vanarder (not given), Rushville, Illinois [S4]

Marine Corps Deaths, 1917-1921

Catlett, James Calvin, Cpl., 52nd Co., 3rd Regt., Domincan Republic, DDS, January 17, 1921 at Santo Domingo, Dominican Republic. Mrs. Elizabeth Catlett (Mother), 710 Cleveland St., Tampa, Florida [S4]

Caylor, Joseph Byers, Pvt., 47th Co., 5th Regt., KIA, June 15, 1918 in the Chateau-Thierry Sector. Mrs. J.b.Caylor (Mother), R#2, Box 331, Houston, Texas [FAG] [S2] [SW]

Cecil, Edwin Francis, Pvt., MCR, 95th Co., 6th Regt., DOW, July 3, 1918 in the Aisne Marne. Verna G. Tyler (Mother), North Ben, Oregon [S2] [SW1 says KIA]

Chadwick, James Russell, Pvt., 20th Co., 5th Regt., DOW, June 7, 1918 in the Chateau-Thierry Sector. Mrs. Maggie Dixon (Mother), Swifts, Ohio [ABMC- Belleau] [S2] [SW1]

Chaffee, Wallace Hyde, Pvt., 23rd Co., 6th MG Bn., KIA, November 10, 1918 in the Meuse Argonne. Lorena Chaffee (Mother), Ventura, California [FAG] [S2] [SW1]

Chalk, Frank Burton, Pvt., 73rd Co., 6th Regt., KIA, June 12, 1918 in the Chateau-Thierry Sector. Anna Clark (Mother), 622 E. 13th St., Wichita, Kansas [R] [S2] [SW1]

Chamberlain, Earle Holmes, Cpl., 55th Co., 5th Regt., DOW, October 9, 1918 in the Meuse Argonne. Harry Chamberlain (Father), 150 Norton St., New Haven, Connecticut [S2] [SW1]

Chamberlain, Maxwell Eugene, Pvt., MCR, 4th Sq, FMAF, DOD, September 28, 1918 in Liverpool, England. Eugene A. Chamberlain (Father), 150 Norton St., New Haven, Connecticut [S2]

Champlin, Curtis Miles C., Pvt., Depot of Supplies, Philadephia, Pennsylvania, DDS, March 26, 1918 at Philadelphia, Pennsylvania. Mrs. Fred Wack (Sister), 104 Illinois St., Battle Creek, Michigan [S3]

Chandler, George Isaac, Pvt., 43rd Co., 5th Regt., KIA, June 11, 1918 in the Chateau-Thierry Sector. Mrs. Sidney

Marine Corps Deaths, 1917-1921

Chandler (Mother), Gen. Del., Waverly Hall, Georgia [ABMC-Belleau] [S2] [SW] [SW1]

Chandler, Henry F., Capt., 75th Co., 6th Regt., KIA, October 9, 1918 in the Meuse Argonne. Mrs. Irene M.Chandler (widow), 1745 California St., N.W., Washington, D.C. [ABMC-Romagne] [S1] [SW]

Chaney, Henry L., Pvt., MD, USNH, Fort Lyon, Colorado, DDS, January 10, 1919 at Fort Lyon, Colorado. Mrs. Jennie D. Chaney (Mother), 500 Josephine St., Dallas, Texas [FAG] [S4]

Chaney, Ralph Vergil, Cpl., 83rd Co., 6th Regt., KIA, June 6, 1918 in the Chateau-Thierry Sector. Cordelia Chaney (Mother), Oakland, Iowa [ABMC- Belleau TOM] [S2] [SW]

Channell, Lovette Leo, Pvt., Co. H, 11th Regt., DOD, November 30, 1918 in France. Mrs. Rose Channell (Mother), RR#1, Blue Ash, Ohio [R] [S2]

Chanski, Joseph Bruny, Pvt., Hdqtrs. Co., 3rd Regt., Dominican Republic, DDS, October 11, 1921 at San Domingo, Dominican Republic. Mike Chanski (Father), 466 Hall St., Perth Amboy, New Jersey [S4]

Chapin, Clarence Basil, Cpl., 96th Co., 6th Regt., DOW, October 4, 1918 in the Meuse Argonne. Albert B. Chapin (Father), 791 Worthington St., Springfield, Massachusetts [FAG] [S2] [SW1]

Chapman, George Clem, Pvt., 43rd Co., 5th Regt., KIA, June 11, 1918 in the Chateau-Thierry Sector. Christine Chapman (Mother), RFD#1, House 49, Wynantskill, New York [FAG] [S2] [SW]

Chapman, Henry Washington, Pvt., 74th Co., 6th Regt., DOW, July 4, 1918 in the Chateau-Thierry Sector. Mary D. Chapman (Mother), 914 N. 8th St., Paducah, Kentucky [FAG] [S2] [SW1]

Chapman, Wyatt McNeil, Pvt., 83rd Co., 6th Regt., KIA, June 6, 1918 in the Chateau-Thierry Sector. Adau Williamson

Marine Corps Deaths, 1917-1921

(Mother), 230 S. Jackson St., Americus, Georgia [ABMC- Belleau] [S2] [SW]

Chard, Elliott Francis, Pvt., 49th Co., 5th Regt., DOW, November 1, 1918 in the Meuse Argonne. Alice Chard (Mother), 29 Winter St., Winchendon, Massachusetts [S2] [SW1]

Chartier, Louis Ernest, Pvt., 66th Co., 5th Regt., KIA, [R] [SW] [this may be Louis Ernest Chartier, Pvt., USMC, World War I who died on March 3, 1973 and is buried in VA-Rock Island]

Chase, Bruce Gilbert, Pvt., 20th Co., 5th Regt., KIA, June 6, 1918 in the Chateau-Thierry Sector. Mrs. Margaret Mosser (Mother), c/o Standish Hotel, Denver, Colorado [ABMC-Belleau] [S2] [SW1 says DOW]

Chase, Carleton B., Marine Gunner, MB, Parris Island, South Carolina, DDS, January 18, 1919 at Parris Island, South Carolina. Mr. Frederick P. Chase (Father), 50 Parrott Ave., Bridgeport, Connecticut [S4]

Chatfield, Isaac Raines, Pvt., 158th Co., Philadelphia, Pennsylvania, DDS, September 28, 1918 at Philadelphia, Pennsylvania. Mrs. Mollie F. Chatfield (Mother), Culloden, Georgia [FAG] [S3]

Chefetz, Harry, Cpl., 55th Co., 5th Regt., KIA, July 18, 1918 in the Aisne Marne. Nelson Chefetz (Father), 23 Mulberry St., Fall River, Massachusetts [ABMC- Belleau TOM as H.] [S2] [SW1]

Cherry, William Richard, Pvt., 97th Co., 6th Regt., DOD, February 13, 1919 in France. Hellen Cherry (Mother), Eagle Lake, Texas [R] [S2]

Chism, James Herbert, Pvt., 18th Co., 5th Regt., DOW, July 18, 1918 in the Aisne Marne. Trootwood K. Chism (Father), Tompkinsville, Kentucky [ABMC- Belleau TOM] [S2] [SW1]

Chodupski, Phillip Charles, Pvt., 74th Co., 6th Regt., DOW, November 1, 1918 in the Meuse Argonne. Josephine

Marine Corps Deaths, 1917-1921

Chodupski (Mother), 3137 Warren E, Detroit, Michigan [S2] [SW1]

Chord, Alton Leeonn, Pvt., 81st Co., 6th MG Bn., KIA, July 19, 1918 in the Aisne Marne. Ida Aldrich (Mother), 1137 N. Second St., Memphis, Tennessee [ANC] [S2] [SW]

Christ, James Franklin, Pvt., 67th Co., 5th Regt., KIA, June 6, 1918 in the Chateau-Thierry Sector. Charles Christ (Father), RFD#24, South Akron, Ohio [S2] [SW]

Christensen, George Gurney, Cpl., 96th Co., 6th Regt., DOW, June 16, 1918 in the Chateau-Thierry Sector. Emma Gurney Christensen (Mother), RFD #1, Santa Anna, California, [ABMC- Suresnes] [S2]

Christian, Victor Trim, Pvt., Hdqtrs. Co., 13th Regt., DOD, October 3, 1918 in France. Sarah Christian (Mother), La Ryor, Texas [FAG] [S2]

Christian, Wesley John, Pvt., 67th Co., 5th Regt., KIA, June 6, 1918 in the Chateau-Thierry Sector. George D. Christian (Father), Barnard, New York [S2] [SW1]

Christiansen, Frank Daniel, Pvt., Hdqtrs. Co., 6th Regt., DOW, July 19, 1918 in the Aisne Marne. Hans. Christiansen (Father), 1806 James Ave. No., Minneapolis, Minnesota [ABMC-Fere] [S2] [SW] [SW1 says Christianson]

Christie, Harold Jay, Cpl., 67th Co., 5th Regt., KIA, June 6, 1918 in the Chateau-Thierry Sector. Frank A. Christie (Father), 509 Sheldon St., Grand Rapids, Michigan [ABMC-Belleau] [S2] [SW]

Christie, Irving Peter, Pvt., Naval Academy, Annapolis, Maryland, DAS, November 15, 1918 drowned at Annapolis, Maryland. Mrs. Ingerborgh Christie (Mother), RFD#4, Box 75, Petaluma, California [S4]

Christman, Joseph Elbert, Pvt., 67th Co., 5th Regt., KIA, October 4, 1918 in the Meuse Argonne. Mary H. Christman (Mother), Route #1, Colville, Washington [FAG] [S2] [SW says 134th Co.] [SW1]

Marine Corps Deaths, 1917-1921

Christoffersen, Axel Peter, Sgt., 45th Co., 5th Regt., KIA, June 13, 1918 in the Chateau-Thierry Sector. Peter Christoffersen (Father), Elko, Virginia [VA-Seven Pines] [S2] [SW]

Christopher, John Kenneth, Cpl., 20th Co., 5th Regt., KIA, November 1, 1918 in the Meuse Argonne. Flora S. Christopher (Mother), 808 Quincy Hill, Parkersburg, W. Virginia [S2] [SW1]

Church, Lorin Jasper, Pvt., 140th Co., 3rd Repl. Batt., DOW, June 13, 1918 in the Chateau-Thierry Sector. Helen Holtz (Former wife), 329 E. 16th St., Oakland, California [ABMC- Belleau] [S2] [SW]

Chute, Joseph W., Pvt., Co. B, 3rd Sep. MG Bn, Quantico, Virginia, DDS, November 20, 1918 at Quantico, Virginia. Miss Eva Chute (Sister), Shelton Sanitarium, Shelton, Connecticut [VA-ANC as November 23, 1918] [S4]

Cilley, George Ewart, Sgt., 76th Co., 6th Regt., KIA, November 1, 1918 in the Meuse Argonne. George Cilley (Father), Harmony, Maine [FAG] [S2] [SW1]

Clardy, William L., Pvt., Hdqtrs., USMC, Washington, D.C., DDS, January 18, 1920 at Washington, D.C. Mrs. Martha Clardy (Mother), Maben, Mississippi [S4]

Clark, Charles F., Sgt., Supply Co., Parris Island, South Carolina, DOS, September 4, 1920 at Beaufort, South Carolina. Mrs. Mary Tresa Clark (Mother), 3775 Kessuth St., Baltimore, Maryland [S4]

Clark, Clarence Lee, Pvt., 23rd Co., 6th Regt., KIA, November 2, 1918 in the Meuse Argonne. Fred R. Clark (Brother), 18 Logan St., Auburn, New York [ABMC- Romagne] [S2] [SW1]

Clark, Clifford Stewart, Pvt., 84th Co., 6th Regt., KIA, November 4, 1918 in the Meuse Argonne. Jesse G. Clark (Father), Burwell, Nebraska [FAG] [S2] [SW1]

Marine Corps Deaths, 1917-1921

Clark, Dean Clinton, Cpl., 45th Co., 5th Regt., KIA, October 4, 1918 in the Meuse Argonne. Mrs. Olive Clark (Mother), 471 Beaumont St., St. Paul, Minnesota [S2] [SW1]

Clark, Ernest Clyde, Pvt., 51st Co., 5th Regt., KIA, November 10, 1918 in the Meuse Argonne. Fred N. Clark (Father), Gen. Del., Mariposa, California [FAG] [S2] [SW1]

Clark, Frank Arthur, Pvt., 67th Co., 5th Regt., KIA, June 6, 1918 in the Chateau-Thierry Sector. Sylvester Clark (Father), 16084 George St., Highland Park, Michigan [S2] [SW]

Clark, Harry Elton, Pvt., Hdqtrs. Co., 6th Regt., DOW, April 26, 1918 in the Toulon Sector, Verdun. Othelia Adams (Mother), Box 667, Spokane, Washington [S2] [SW]

Clark, Horace Cobb, Pvt., Bks. Det., Philadelphia, Pennsylvania, DDS, October 8, 1918 at Philadelphia, Pennsylvania. Lord B. Clark (Father), 759 Poplar St., Macon, Georgia [S3]

Clark, Joseph Charles, Pvt., 79th Co., 6th Regt., KIA, June 8, 1918 in the Chateau-Thierry Sector. Delia Jane Clark (Mother), 1315 Roe Ave., Alexandria, Indiana [FAG] [ABMC-Belleau] [S2] [SW]

Clark, Joseph King, Pvt., 82nd Co., 6th Regt., DOW, May 24, 1918 in France. Mable Clark (Sister), Walton, Indiana [FAG] [S2]

Clark, Newell Gustavus, Pvt., Naval Prison, Portsmouth, New Hampshire, DDS, October 1, 1918 at Portsmouth, New Hampshire. Newell Clark (Father), 5030 Emerson Ave., South, Mineapolis, Minnesota [FAG] [S3]

Clark, Robert Burney, Cpl., Co. E, Parris Island, South Carolina, DOS, December 15, 1917 at Oberlin, Kansas. James P. Clark (Father), Oberlin, Kansas [S3]

Clark, Willard Franklin, Pvt., 96th Co., 6th Regt., KIA, April 28, 1918 in the Toulon Secor, Verdun. Celesta Clark (Mother), 71 E. Eagle St., Buffalo, New York [FAG] [S2] [SW]

Marine Corps Deaths, 1917-1921

Clark, William Audrey, Pvt., 96th Co., 6th Regt., DOW, June 28, 1918 in the Chateau-Thierry Sector. Kitty Clark (Mother), 3849-A Flad Ave., St. Louis, Missouri [R] [S2] [SW]

Clary, Ralph Emerson, Pvt., 23rd Co., 6th MG Bn., DOW, November 5, 1918 in the Meuse Argonne. Emery C. Clary (Father), 133 S. 5th Ave., Mt. Vernon, New York [ABMC- Romagne] [S2] [SW1]

Clausen, Clyde Lawrence, Pvt., 97th Co., 6th Regt., KIA, October 4, 1918 in the Meuse Argonne. Anna Jensen (Mother), Aromas, California [R] [S2] [SW say 74th Co.]

Clausen, Harry Elmer, Pvt., 83rd Co., 6th Regt., DOW, June 12, 1918 in the Chateau-Thierry Sector. Peter Clausen (Father), 1851 N. Kimball Ave., Chicago, Illinois [ABMC- Suresnes] [S2] [SW]

Clay, Firmin Earl, Pvt., Co. G., 11th Regt., at Quanitco, Virginia, DDS, October 8, 1918 at Quanitco, Virginia. Mrs. Reva L. Clay (Wife), Fordham Hospital, New York [S3]

Clayton, James Arthur, Pvt., 51st Co., 5th Regt., DOW, June 7, 1918 in the Chateau-Thierry Sector. Jacob Clayton (Father), Box 77, Dayton, Virginia [ANC] [S2] [SW]

Clem, Elmer Dewey, Cpl., Hdqtrs. Co., 3rd Regt., Dominican Republic, DDS, April 30, 1921 at Santo Domingo City, Dominican Republic. Mrs.Emma J. Clem (Mother), Spruce St., Westernport, Maryland [FAG] [S4]

Clements, Ernest Gerald, Pvt., 83rd Co., 6th Regt., DOW, October 10, 1918 in the Meuse Argonne. Mrs. H. E. Bidlack (Mother), % Mrs. J. T. Miller, 820 W. High St., Lima, Ohio [ANC] [S2] [SW1]

Clements, George H., Pvt., 7th Co., Quantico, Virginia, DDS, January 12, 1920 at Quantico, Virginia. Mrs. Eva Kundie (Sister), Superior, Wyoming [S4]

Clementson, Carl J., Mar. Gun., Hdqrs. Co., 13th Regt., DOD, September 25, 1918 aboard the *Von Steuben*. Mres.

Marine Corps Deaths, 1917-1921

Louisa Clementson (Mother), 1102 N. 5th St., Grand Forks, North Dakota [FAG] [S1]

Cleveland, George Emery, Pvt., 16th Co., 5th Regt., KIA, June 23, 1918 in the Chateau-Thierry Sector. Mary Cleveland (Mother), East Greenwich, Rhode Island [ABMC-Belleau TOM as G. E.] [S2] [SW]

Cleveland, William Robert, Sgt., 51st Co., 5th Regt., DOW, June 11, 1918 in the Chateau-Thierry Sector. William C. Cleveland (Father), Crosby, McKeen County, Pennsylvania [FAG] [S2] [SW says KIA]

Clifford, James Henry, Pvt., Co. C, Repl. Btln., KIA, [R] [SW]

Clifford, Leonard Adolph, Cpl., 15th Co., 6th MG Bn., DOW, July 19, 1918 in the Aisne Marne. Rose L. Clifford (Mother), R#1, Box 72, Cairo, Illinois [S2] [SW1]

Clingan, Darrel Dale, Pvt., 74th Co., 6th Regt., KIA, June 13, 1918 in the Chateau-Thierry Sector. Dora Clingan (Mother), Willow Springs, Missouri [FAG] [S2] [SW]

Clocke, Charles B., Pvt., USNAD, Iona Island, New York, DAS, July 20, 1920 at Iona Island, New York. Emm Skapce (Sister), 2328 South Kedzie Ave., Chicago, Illinois [S4]

Clohesy, Philip Michael, Pvt., Co. G., 11th Regt., at Quanitco, Virginia, DDS, October 4, 1918 at Quanitco, Virginia. Margarett Clohesy (Mother), 3255 Douglass Blvd., Chicago, Illinois [S3]

Clopton, George Izzard, Pvt., 96th Co., 6th Regt., DOW, June 27, 1918 in the Chateau-Thierry Sector. Mrs. Mary E. Watt (Sister), 1708 Grove Ave., Richmond, Virginia [ABMC-Belleau] [S2] [SW1]

Clore, Robert Leminel, Pvt., 17th Co., 5th Regt., KIA, June 6, 1918 in the Chateau-Thierry Sector. Bell Clore (Mother), Lees Summit, Missouri [FAG as Robert Lemuel Clore] [S2] [SW]

Cloud, James A., Pvt., Supply Co., Mare Island, California, DDS, February 6, 1920 at Mare Island, California. Mrs. Nanchy

Marine Corps Deaths, 1917-1921

Cloud (Mother), Rural Route #2, Willard, Missouri [FAG] [S4]

Clough, Charles Leslie, Cpl., 74th Co., 6th Regt., KIA, October 31, 1918 in the Meuse Argonne. Kate Clough (Mother), East Aurora, New York [ABMC- Romagne] [S2] [SW1]

Cobb, Fred Walter, Cpl., 49th Co., 5th Regt., DOW, November 3, 1918 in the Meuse Argonne. Sara R. Reid (Mother), 220 York St., Vallejo, California [ABMC- Romagne] [S2] [SW1]

Cobb, Howell, Captain, MB, Quantico, Virginia, DDS, October 17, 1921 at Fredericksburg, Virginia. Mrs. Mamie B. Cobb (Wife), Nashville, North Carolina [S4]

Cobeldick, John Henry, Sgt., 8th Co., 5th Regt., KIA, July 19, 1918 in the Aisne Marne. Frank J. Cobeldick (Brother), Forgan, Beaver County, Oklahoma [ABMC- Fere] [S2] [S check]

Cocanour, Joseph Edgar, Pvt., 96th Co., 6th Regt., DOD, November 2, 1918 in the Meuse Argonne. Relda Cocanour (Mother), RFD#1, Newark, Ohio [FAG] [S2]

Cockburn, Guy R., QM Sgt., Constable Det., Haiti, DDS, February 10, 1920 at Capt Haitien, Haiti. Mrs. Miriam Cockburn (Wife), 1932 South Hick St., Philadelphia, Pennsylvania [S4]

Cochran, Harry K., Capt., 67th Co., 5th Regt., KIA, November 2, 1918 in the Meuse Argonne. Mrs. Bertha W. Cochran (widow), 1823 Houston Ave, Kansas City, Missouri [ANC] [S1]

Cochran, Harry King, Pvt., 82nd Co., 6th Regt., KIA, June 3, 1918 in the Aisne Defensive. Theresa Bragg (Mother), So. Tenth St., Martins Ferry, Ohio [S2] [SW]

Cody, Emmett Thomas, Pvt., 8th Co., 5th Regt., KIA, July 20, 1918 in the Aisne Marne. Mrs. Mary Kennedy (Guardian), 6317 S. Laflin St., Chicago, Illinois [ABMC- Fere] [S2] [SW1]

Marine Corps Deaths, 1917-1921

Coe, Charles Clarence, Trumpeter, 96th Co., 6th Regt., DOW, June 13, 1918 in the Chateau-Thierry Sector. Lelia Coe (Mother), Box 544, Miami, Florida [S2] [SW says Pvt.]

Coffee, Leon, Gy. Sgt., Squadron E, MAF, Haiti, DDS, May 23, 1920 at Haiti. Mrs. Juanita Coffee (Mother), P O B ox 203, Georgetown, Texas [FAG] [S4]

Coffey, Charles Wallace, Pvt., Co. C, 13th Regt., DOD, September 22, 1918 enroute to France. Sally Coffey (Mother), 1706 W. Main St., Staunton, Virginia [FAG] [S2]

Coffin, Charles Ignatius, Jr., Pvt., Hdqtrs. Co., 6th Regt., KIA, July 19, 1918 in the Aisne Marne. Charles I. Coffin, Sr., (Father), Itasca, Texas [ABMC- Belleau] [S2] [SW]

Cohee, Donald Rhinehart, Trumpeter, 182nd Co., 15th Regt., DDS, December 21, 1920 aboard the *Kittery* enrout to U.S. Mrs. Bessie Cohee (Mother), 151 Baker St., Dayton, Ohio [S4]

Cohen, Erwin Alfred, Pvt., 75th Co., 6th Regt., KIA, October 9, 1918 in the Meuse Argonne. Barnard Cohen (Father), 62 Spring St., Norwich, Connecticut [S2] [SW1]

Colby, Elwood Loring, Cpl., 51st Co., 5th Regt., KIA, June 12, 1918 in the Chateau-Thierry Sector. Charles L. Colby (Father), 65 West 70th St., New York, New York [ABMC- Belleau] [S2] [SW says Elwood Loring] [SW1]

Colby, Homer Rolandus, Pvt., 78th Co., 6th Regt., DOW, November 15, 1918 in the St. Mihiel Offensive. William H. Colby (Father), RFD #1, Houston, Ohio [R] [S2] [SW1]

Colby, Irl, Pvt., 79th Co., 6th Regt., KIA, October 3, 1918 in the Meuse Argonne. Mina Colby (Mother), Delta, Utah [FAG] [S2] [SW1]

Coldwell, Elijah Harris, Cpl., 49th Co., 5th Regt., KIA, June 13, 1918 in the Chateau-Thierry Sector. Jessie Coldwell (Mother), Medway, Massachusetts [S2] [SW]

Marine Corps Deaths, 1917-1921

Cole, Edward B., Major, Hdqrs., 6th MGBn., DOW, June 18, 1918 in the Chateau Thierry sector. Mrs. Mary Elizabeth Cole (widow), 231 Rawson Rd., Brookline, Massachusetts [ABMC-Belleau as E. B.] [S1] [SW]

Cole, George D., Pvt., Nav. Air Station, Pensacola, Florida, DDS, March 6, 1920 at Pensacola, Florida. Mrs. Marie Cole (Mother), Route #2, Zumbro Falls, Minnesota [S4]

Cole, Holland Joseph, Pvt., 75th Co., 6th Regt., KIA, October 9, 1918 in the Meuse Argonne. John Cole (Father), Murray, Kentucky [FAG] [S2] [SW]

Cole, Howard Walter, Pvt., Hdqtrs. Co., 5th Regt., KIA, November 11, 1918 in the Meuse Argonne. Peter F. Cole (Father), 244 W. Oak St., Kankakee, Illinois [S2] [SW1]

Coleman, Arnet Brown, Pvt., 20th Co., 5th Regt., KIA, June 14, 1918 in the Chateau-Thierry Sector. Lily M. Coleman (Mother), Route #5, Mart, Texas [S2] [SW says 119th Co.]

Coleman, John Edward, Pvt., 136th Anti-Aircraft Batt., DOD, October 2, 1918 in France. Patrick F. Coleman (Father), #6 Pearl St., Natick, Massachusetts [S2]

Coleman, John K., Pvt., 153rd Co., 2nd Regt., Port au Prince, Haiti, DDS, March 7, 1920 at Port au Prince, Haiti. Mrs. Stacey T. Keesee (Grandmother), Luxora, Arkansas [S4]

Coley, Walter M., Pvt., Bks. Det., Fort Lyon, Colorado, DDS, November 15, 1919 at Fort Lyon, Colorado. Edward Coley (Father), LaFayette, Georgia [VA-Fort Lyon] [S4]

Colley, Milford Raymond, Pvt., 73rd Co., 6th Regt., KIA, June 8, 1918 in the Chateau-Thierry Sector. Charles H. Colley (Father), Waynesville, Missouri [ABMC- Fere] [S2] [SW]

Collier, Earl Milton, Pvt., 84th Co., 6th Regt., KIA, June 6, 1918 in the Chateau-Thierry Sector. Inez Collier (Mother), Gen. Del., Olathe, Kansas [FAG] [S2] [SW]

Marine Corps Deaths, 1917-1921

Collier, Frank, Pvt., 97th Co., 6th Regt., DOW, July 29, 1918 in the Aisne Marne. Fred Collier (Father), 1220 Pool St., Springfield, Illinois [FAG] [S2] [SW]

Collier, Marion Maxey, Cpl., 83rd Co., 6th Regt., KIA, June 6, 1918 in the Chateau-Thierry Sector. Boyd T. Collier (Brother), 1804 Austin St., Houston, Texas [ABMC- Belleau] [S2] [SW]

Collins, Harry Francis, Pvt., 82nd Co., 6th Regt., KIA, October 3, 1918 in the Meuse Argonne. Cora Collins (Mother), 802 Poplar St., Nelsonville, Ohio [FAG] [S2] [SW says Co. I]

Collins, Isaac Jefferson, Cpl., Hdqtrs. Co., 5th Brigade MG Battn., DOD, November 7, 1918 enroute to France. John W. Collins (Father), Jena, Louisiana [FAG] [S2]

Collins, John, Cpl., Bks. Det., Philadelphia, Pennsylvania, DDS, January 3, 1919 at Parris Island, South Carolina. Mrs. Helle Collins (Mother), 717 East Independence St., Shamokin, Pennsylvania [FAG] [S4]

Collins, John William, Pvt., 83rd Co., 6th Regt., KIA, June 2, 1918 in the Aisne Defensive. Mae Pounds (Mother), Clarksburg, W. Virginia [ABMC- Belleau as J.W.] [S2] [SW says 67th Co., 5th Regt.]

Collins, William Peter, Pvt., Bks. Detch., Quanitco, Virginia, DDS, November 2, 1918 at Grove City, Pennsylvania. Sarah Dahn (Mother), 2181 W. 45th St., Cleveland, Ohio [S3]

Colon, George Oren, Sgt., 18th Co., 5th Regt., DOW, July 21, 1918 in the Aisne Marne. Mary Lalonde (Mother), Clayton, New York [ABMC- Fere] [S2] [SW1]

Colvin, David Park, 2nd Lieut., 18th Co., 5th Regt., KIA, July 18, 1918 in the Aisne Marne. Mrs. Catherine Quigley, 405 Foster St., Grensburg, Pennsylvania [FAG] [S1] [SW] [SW1 says Pvt.]

Marine Corps Deaths, 1917-1921

Colwell, Frank Lowery, Pvt., 97th Co., 6th Regt., KIA, July 19, 1918 in the Aisne Marne. Cora Colwell (Mother), RFD#2, Vinton, Ohio [R] [S2] [SW]

Combs, Charles C., Pfc, 44th Co., 2nd Brigade, Dominican Republic, DDS, February 24, 1919 at Santo Domingo, Dominican Republic. Elmer Combs (Father), 1054 Superior Ave., Middletown, Ohio [FAG] [S4]

Combs, Lencil, Pvt., 63rd Co., 2nd Regt., Haiti, DOW, January 15, 1920 of wounds received in action at Port au Prince, Haiti. Mrs. Arti Combs (Mother), Route #2, Wheelersburg, Ohio [S4]

Comfort, William John, Pvt., Co. C, 10th Sep. Bn, Quanitco, Virginia, DDS, November 11, 1918 at Quantico, Virginia. Mrs. Ellen Comfort (Mother), 1416 S. Bloomington St., Streator, Illinois [FAG] [S3]

Cone, Ben, Cpl., 82nd Co., 6th Regt., KIA, June 6, 1918 in the Chateau-Thierry Sector. Bertha Cone (Mother), 324 McGraw St., Detroit, Michigan [S2] [SW]

Conklin, Alonzo Herman, Pvt., 8th Co., 5th Regt., DOW, June 28, 1918 in the Chateau-Thierry Sector. Charles Conklin (Father), Box 188, Kimberly, Idaho [FAG] [S2] [SW]

Conley, Patrick L., Sgt. Major [1st Sgt.], Navy Yard, Washington, D.C, DDS, December 31, 1917 at Washington, D.C. John J. Conley (Brother), 72 Dimock St., Somerville, Massachusetts [S3]

Conn, Kenneth William, Pvt., 9th Co., 1st FAB, Quantico, Virginia, DDS, December 10, 1917 at Quantico, Virginia. Le Grande Conn (Brother), Dryden, Michigan [S3]

Connaughton, Joe, Pvt., 77th Co., 6th MG Bn., KIA, October 4, 1918 in the Meuse Argonne. Frances Connaughton (Mother), Norge, Virginia [ABMC- Romagne] [S2] [SW]

Connell, Joseph Michael, Pvt., Supply Detch, Quantico, Virginia, DDS, September 27, 1918 at Quantico, Virginia. William

Marine Corps Deaths, 1917-1921

    J. Connell (Father), 147 Western Ave., Cambridge, Massachusetts [S3]

Connelly, Raymond Francis, Cpl., 51st Co., 5th Regt., DOW, June 20, 1918 in the Chateau-Thierry Sector. Mrs. Marion Connelly Wright (former wife), 1022 16th St., Rock Island, Illinois [ANC] [S2] [SW]

Conner, Robert F., 2nd Lieut., 49th Co., 5th Regt., KIA, October 3, 1918 in the Meuse Argonne. Mrs. Gertrude Hineline (sister), 936 Quincy Ave., Scranton, Pennsylvania [ABMC-Romagne] [S1] [SW]

Connery, John Henry, Pvt., 95th Co., 6th Regt., KIA, October 4, 1918 in the Meuse Argonne. Joseph M. Connery (Father), Enfield, Illinois [ABMC- Romagne] [S2] [SW1]

Connolly, George William, Pvt., 45th Co., 5th Regt., KIA, June 6, 1918 in the Chateau-Thierry Sector. Emma Connolly (Mother), 16 Chestnut Pl., Nutley, New Jersey [S2] [SW1]

Connolly, Michael John, Cpl., NAS Rockaway, New York, DAS, February 24, 1921 drowned at Rockaway Beach, Long Island, New York. Anna and Francis Connolly (Parents), 523 East 16th St., New York, New York [S4]

Connor, George Thomas, Pvt., 73rd Co., 6th Regt., DOW, October 4, 1918 in the Meuse Argonne. John L. Connor (Father), 35 Pleasant St., Speneer, Massachusetts [S2] [SW1 says Conner]

Connor, Lawrence James, Pvt., Co. H, 13th Regt., DOD, September 30, 1918 in France. Simon Connor (Father), Waseca, Minnesota [FAG] [S2]

Connors, Thomas, Sgt., Hdqtrs. A & I, Washington, D.C., DDS, November 5, 1920 at Washington, D.C. Michael Connors (Brother), 4 Green St., Stamford, Connecticut [S4]

Conover, Kenneth Sayles, Pvt., 43rd Co., 5th Regt., DOW, November 1, 1918 in the Meuse Argonne. Catherine

Marine Corps Deaths, 1917-1921

Conover (Mother), 123 Church St., Keyport, New Jersey [ABMC- Romagne] [S2] [SW1]

Conrad, Amos Adelbert, Pvt., 18th Co., 5th Regt., DOW, July 19, 1918 in the Aisne Marne. Mrs. Badie Burgner (Widow-remarried), 708 N. 19th St., Philadelphia, Pennsylvania [R] [S2] [SW says Amon]

Conroy, Frank, Gy. Sgt., 8th Co., 5th Regt., DAO, April 27, 1918 in France. Wounds received in stone quarry. Avita Koceja (Mother), 922 8th Ave., Milwaukee, Wisconsin [S2] [SW says DOW]

Conway, Peter, Sgt., 49th Co., 5th Regt., KIA, June 6, 1918 in the Chateau-Thierry Sector. Mrs. P. J. Conway (Mother), 4511 North Whipple St., Chicago, Illinois [FAG] [S2] [SW]

Conwell, George Barrett, Pvt., 96th Co., 6th Regt., DOD, March 3, 1919 in France. Mrs. Sallie M. Dean (Sister), 352 W. 46th St., New York, New York [R] [S2]

Conyer, Daniel J., Cpl., 36th Co., 2nd Regt., DAS, August 9, 1919 while on furlough at St. Louis, Missouri. Mrs. Bertie Bourn (Sister), Rockwall, Texas [S4]

Cook, Claud Thompson, Cpl., Hdqtrs. Co., 6th Regt., DOW, July 19, 1918 in the Aisne Marne. Walter Cook (Father), 309 N. Maple, Hutchinson, Kansas [ABMC- Fere] [S2] [SW1]

Cook, Floyd W., Pvt., Co. A, Mare Island, California, DDS, February 1, 1920 at Mare Island, California. Mrs. Olive Stenerson (Mother), Oaks Ave., Anacortes, Skagit Co., Washington [S4]

Cook, George Fuson, Pvt., 67th Co., 5th Regt., KIA, November 6, 1918 in the Meuse Argonne. Florence Cook (Mother), 507 E. Sherman St., Portland, Oregon [R] [S2] [SW1 says DOW and George A. Cook]

Marine Corps Deaths, 1917-1921

Cook, Herbert, Pvt., 95th Co., 6th Regt., Quantico, Virginia, DDS, September 2, 1917 at Akron, Ohio. Emma Cook (Mother), Seville, Medina Co., Ohio [FAG] [S3]

Cook, James Asbury, Pvt., 76th Co., 6th Regt., DOW, July 19, 1918 in the Aisne Marne. John A. Cook (Father), 109 Poplar St., Winston-Salem, North Carolina [R] [S2] [SW1]

Cook, Lester W., Pvt., USNH, Fort Lyon, Colorado, DDS, August 3, 1920 at Fort Lyon, Colorado. Mr. Fred Cook (Father), Enterprise, Oregon [S4]

Cook, Murvill Jessie Jr., Pvt., 17th Co., 5th Regt., DOW, October 10, 1918 in the Meuse Argonne. Murville J. Cook (Father), 120 Temple St., Hinton, West Virginia [ANC] [S2] [SW1 says Marvill Jessie Cook]

Cooke, Ralph, Pvt., 16th Co., 5th Regt., DOW, June 12, 1918 in the Chateau-Thierry Sector. Margaret Cooke (Mother), 38 West Cedar St., Boston, Massachusetts [ABMC-Suresnes] [S2] [SW]

Coon, Charles H., Pvt., Bks. Det., Puget Sound, Washington, DDS, January 27, 1920 at Puget Sound, Washington. Mrs. Mary H. Coon (Mother), Route #3, West Plains, Missouri [VA-San Francisco] [S4]

Cooney, John Thomas, Pvt., 95th Co., 6th Regt., DOW, July 19, 1918 in the Aisne Marne. Marie Conney (Mother), 1738 W. 31st., Cleveland, Ohio [ABMC- Belleau TOM] [S2] [SW1]

Cooper, Frank Horace, Cpl., 74th Co., 6th Regt., KIA, September 16, 1918 in the St. Mihiel Offensive. Elizabeth Cooper (Mother), 605 Tillman Ave., Detroit, Michigan [FAG] [S2] [SW]

Cooper, Gus Adolph, Pvt., 82nd Co., 6th Regt., DOW, November 2, 1918 in the Meuse Argonne. Lilly May Cooper (Wife), 1021 Warren St., Nashville, Tennessee [ABMC-Romagne] [S2] [SW1]

Marine Corps Deaths, 1917-1921

Cooper, William H., Sgt., NNV, 75th Co., 6th Regt., KIA, July 19, 1918 in the Aisne Marne. Mildred Cooper Louden (Sister), 135 Bryan St., Rochester, New York [ABMC- Fere] [S2] [SW]

Coor, Sandy Alfred, Pvt., Co. L, 13th Regt., DOD, February 1, 1919 in France. Dempsey P. Coor (Father), RFD #2, Glendale, Arizona [FAG] [S2]

Copeland, Samuel Laffette, Sgt., Hdqtrs. Co., 6th Regt., KIA, July 19, 1918 in the Aisne Marne. Julia Schmidt (Mother), 1250 Minnesota Ave., Wichita, Kansas [ABMC- Belleau TOM] [S2] [SW]

Coppinger, William J., Pvt., Co. B, 3rd Sep. Bltn., KIA, [R] [SW] [SW1 reported of have been found alive]

Corbet, John Franklin Jr., Pvt., 80th Co., 6th Regt., KIA, June 8, 1918 in the Chateau-Thierry Sector. John F. Corbet, Sr. (Father), 5551 Glenwood Ave., Chicago, Illinois [ABMC- Belleau] [S2] [SW]

Corbett, Benjamin Harrison, 1st Sgt., Eastern Reserve Division, DDS, October 20, 1918 at Washington, D.C. Margaret Crawford Corbett (Wife), 408 N. 38th St., West Philadelphia, Pennsylvania [VA-ANC][S3]

Corbin, Francis Bernard, Pvt., 17th Co., 5th Regt., KIA, July 18, 1918 in the Aisne Marne. Bernard J. Corbin (Father), 1823 South 4th St., Philadelphia, Pennsylvania [ABMC- Belleau] [S2] [SW says Corp.]

Corey, James Lowell, Pvt., 83rd Co., 6th Regt., KIA, July 19, 1918 in the Aisne Marne. Melvin L. Corey (Father), Argos, Indiana [ABMC- Belleau TOM] [S2] [SW]

Corn, David Peabody, Pvt., 95th Co., 6th Regt., DOW, July 19, 1918 in the Aisne Marne. Anna D. Corn (Mother), RFD#1, Outlook, Washington [FAG] [S2] [SW1 says KIA]

Corn, Leslie E., Pvt., 95th Co., 6th Regt., DOW, June 12, 1918 in the Chateau-Thierry Sector. Mrs Bettie Garrison

Marine Corps Deaths, 1917-1921

(Mother), Box 205, Okmulgee, Oklahoma [FAG] [S2] [SW says KIA]

Cornell, Walter R., Mar. Gun., Hdqrs. Co., 6th Regt., DOW, June 7, 1918 in the Chateau Thierry sector. Henry M. Cornell (Father), Eustis, Florida [ABMC-Belleau] [S1][SW]

Cornet, Henry Albert, Pvt., MCR, 1st Res. Co., Philadelphia, Pennsylvania, DDS, September 22, 1918 at Great Lakes, Illinois. Mrs. Martha C. J. Cornet (Wife), 45 South Gore Ave., Webster Groves, Missouri [S3]

Cornwall, Norman James, Pvt., 76th Co., 6th Regt., DOW, November 3, 1918 in the Meuse Argonne. John Cornwall (Father), 3107 W. Polk St., Chicago, Illinois [R] [S2] [SW1]

Cornwell, John, QM Sgt., DQM, Philadelphia, Pennsylvania, DDS, March 20, 1920 at League Island, Pennsylvania. Mrs. Mary V. Cornwell (Mother), 8613 Superior Ave., Cleveland, Ohio [S4]

Corriveau, Paul E., 1st Lieut., 55th Co., 5th Regt., KIA, October 6, 1918 in the Meuse Argonne. Paul Carriveau (Father), 27 Charter St., Concord, New Hampshire [R] [S1] [SW]

Costello, Frank Martin, Pvt., 67th Co., 5th Regt., KIA, June 16, 1918 in the Chateau-Thierry Sector. Margaret Costello (Mother), 2820 E. Baltimore St., Baltimore, Maryland [R] [S2] [SW]

Costigan, James Wallace, Pvt., 96th Co., 6th Regt., DOW, July 31, 1918 in the Aisne Marne. Michael J. Costigan (Father), 415 E. 4th St., Newort, Kentucky [ABMC- Belleau] [S2] [SW says Co. H, 5th Regt.]

Cotter, James Thomas, Pvt., 49th Co., 5th Regt., KIA, June 6, 1918 in the Chateau-Thierry Sector. Mary Cotter (Mother), 1822 Elston Ave., Chicago, Illinois [ABMC- Belleau] [S2] [SW1]

Cotter, Myron Timothy, Pvt., 52nd Co., 3rd Regt., Dominican Republic, DOW, December 27, 1919 of a gunshot wound

Marine Corps Deaths, 1917-1921

at Santo Domingo, Dominican Republic. Mrs. Mary Cotter (Mother), 8613 Superior Ave., Cleveland, Ohio [S4]

Cottrell, Oscar, Pvt., 16th Co., 5th Regt., KIA, June 23, 1918 in the Chateau-Thierry Sector. George Cottrell (Father), Tuscaloosa, Alabama [ANC] [S2] [SW]

Couch, William, Cpl., 4 Sq, FMAF, DOD, September 29, 1918 in Harbor, Liverpool, England. Rachel Couch (Mother), 657 Webster St., Palo Alto, California [S2]

Coughlin, James Patrick, Gy. Sgt., Bks. Det., Philadelphia, Pennsylvania, DDS, February 17, 1921 at Philadelphia, Pennsylvania. Katie Powers (Sister), 9 Franklin Ave., Phoenixville, Pennsylvania [S4]

Coughlin, William Harold, Pvt., 49th Co., 5th Regt., KIA, June 6, 1918 in the Chateau-Thierry Sector. Mrs. John J. Coughlin (Mother), 832 Pershing Rd., E. Chicago, Illinois [S2] [SW]

Coulter, Edwin Clark, Pvt., 16th Co., 5th Regt., KIA, October 4, 1918 in the Meuse Argonne. John Coulter (Father), Box 26, Oxford, Ohio [ABMC- Romagne] [S2] [SW says Co. D, 4th Sep. Btln.]

Counts, Ole Edward, Pvt., 20th Co., 5th Regt., KIA, June 6, 1918 in the Chateau-Thierry Sector. James Gilbert (Stepfather), Gen. Del., Toppenish, Washington [FAG] [S2] [SW]

Courier, Alva, Pvt., 84th Co., 6th Regt., DOD, February 20, 1919 in France. Stella Pratt (Mother), Chester, Illinois [R] [S2]

Courtney, Daniel George, Pvt., 79th Co., 6th Regt., KIA, September 26, 1918 in the St. Mihiel Offensive. Dan J. Courtney (Father), 626 S. 5th St. West, Missoula, Montana [FAG] [S2] [SW says Replacement]

Cowdrey, Robert Hall Jr., Pvt., 97th Co., 6th Regt., KIA, July 19, 1918 in the Aisne Marne. Robert H. Cowdrey (Father), 17 N. LaSalle St., Chicago, Illinois [ANC] [S2] [SW1]

Marine Corps Deaths, 1917-1921

Cowl, John Officer, Pvt., 83rd Co., 6th Regt., DOW, July 16, 1918 in the Chateau-Thierry Sector. Grace Steward (Sister), Leon, Iowa [FAG] [S2] [SW1 says KIA]

Cowles, Donald B., 1st Lieut., Sq. "D", FMAF, DOD, October 1, 1918 in England. Walter G. Cowles (Father), 545 Prospect Ave., c/o Travelers' Ins. Co., Hartford, Connecticut [FAG] [S1]

Cox, Fred Nicholson, Pvt., Hdqtrs. Co., 6th Regt., DOW, September 15, 1918 in the St. Mihiel offensive. Cora Kirk (Mother), Sharon, Maryland [ANC] [S2] [SW1]

Cox, Walter Judson, Pvt., 83rd Co., 6th Regt., KIA, July 19, 1918 in the Aisne Marne. James B. Cox (Father), 1521 Gentilly Ave., New Orleans, Louisiana [ABMC- Belleau TOM] [S2] [SW says 140th Co.]

Coxe, Harold James, Sgt., 97th Co., 6th Regt., DOW, June 12, 1918 in the Chateau-Thierry Sector. Fanny Coxe (Mother), 512 Knollwood Ave., Cedar Rapids, Iowa [ABMC- Belleau] [S2] [SW1]

Coyne, James Edward, Pvt., 82nd Co., 6th Regt., KIA, October 4, 1918 in the Meuse Argonne. Theresa Coyne (Mother), 117 Lawrence St., Rensselaer, New York [FAG] [S2] [SW1]

Coyne, William J., Pvt., 102nd Co., Charleston, South Carolina, DDS, January 25, 1919 at Charleston, South Carolina. Hannah Coyne (Mother), Inmate State Hospital, Albany, New York [S4]

Craig, Edward R., Pvt., Co. A, Parris Island, South Carolina, DDS, December 30, 1918 at Parris Island, South Carolina. Calvin D. Craig (Brother), Alton, Illinois [FAG] [S4]

Crancer, Walter Aronson, Pvt., 79th Co., 6th Regt., KIA, July 19, 1918 in the Aisne Marne. Valentine & Anna Crancer (Parents), 6447 W. Chester Rd., West Chester, Pennsylvania [ANC] [S2] [SW1]

Marine Corps Deaths, 1917-1921

Crandall, James Page, Pvt., Marine Barracks, New Orleans, Lousiana, DDS, October 10, 1918 at New Orleans, Louisana. William P. Crandall (Father), Box 28, Willow Route #1, Kirkland, Texas [S3]

Crane, William Ezra, Pvt., Nav. Amm. Dep., St. Julien's Creek, DDS, October 28, 1921 at Norfolk, Virginia. George H. Crane (Father), 726 Palmwood Ave., Toledo, Ohio [FAG] [S4]

Cranford, Reid Davis, Pvt., 83rd Co., 6th Regt., DOW, July 19, 1918 in the Aisne Marne. Manley W. Cranford (Father), Davidson, North Carolina [FAG] [S2] [SW1 says KIA]

Craze, Ezra Edward, Pvt., 95th Co., 6th Regt., DOW, June 14, 1918 in the Chateau-Thierry Sector. Thomas B. Craze (Father), Dixie, West Virginia [S2] [SW says 34th Co.]

Creed, Carlos Dickson, Cpl., 96th Co., 6th Regt., KIA, September 15, 1918 in the St. Mihiel Offensive. Mrs. D. N. Moore (Sister), 551 North High St., Columbus, Ohio [FAG] [S2] [SW1]

Creighton, Joseph Vincent, Pvt., 80th Co., 6th Regt., DOW, July 30, 1918 in the Aisne Marne. Margaret Creighton (Mother), 770 E. 160th St., New York, New York [ABMC-Suresnes] [S2] [SW says 2nd Repl. Btln.]

Creighton, William Frank, Pvt., Co. C, 7 Sep. Batt., DOD, November 21, 1918 in France. Margaret Creighton (Mother), 222 N. Lombard Ave., Oak Park, Illinois [S2]

Crippen, William Henry, Pvt., 17th Co., 5th Regt., KIA, October 4, 1918 in the Meuse Argonne. Daniel Wilks Crippen (Father), Humboldt, South Dakota [S2] [SW1]

Crishock, Edward Anthony, Pvt., Hdqtrs. Det., Parris Island, South Carolina, DOS, March 20, 1918 at Parris Island, South Carolina. Mrs. Andrew Crishock (Mother), 342 South West St., Shenandoah, Pennsylvania [S3]

Crollay, William H., Cpl., Supply Co., Parris Island, South Carolina, DDS, March 11, 1919 at Camp Taylor,

Marine Corps Deaths, 1917-1921

Kentucky. Mrs. Desta M. Crollay (Mother), St. James, Missouri [S4]

Cron, Arthur F., Pvt., Bks. Det., Washington, D.C., DDS, November 29, 1918 at Washington, D.C. Mrs. Lena Cron (Mother), 513 W. Willis Ave, Detroit, Michigan [S4]

Cronenberg, Albert Louis, Pvt., 75th Co., 6th Regt., KIA, June 13, 1918 in the Chateau-Thierry Sector. Marie Cronenberg (Mother), 3810 Campt St., New Orleans, Louisiana [S2] [SW]

Cronin, Raymond Paul, Sgt., 49th Co., 5th Regt., KIA, June 6, 1918 in the Chateau-Thierry Sector. Edna A. Cronin (Mother), 1503 Berkshire Ave., Pittsburgh, Pennsylvania [S2] [SW]

Cronk, Calvin Emilio, Pvt., 1st Mar. Av. Force., Miami, Florida, DAS in an areoplane May 7, 1918 at Miami, Florida. Mrs. Lottie Cronk (Mother), 1798 Alik Ave., Seattle, Washington [S3]

Crooks, Lloyd McKinley, Pvt., 79th Co., 6th Regt., KIA, September 15, 1918 in the St. Mihiel offensive. Mattie Crooks (Mother), Bashaw, Alberta, Canada [FAG] [S2] [SW]

Crosby, Henry Melvin, Pvt., 68th Guard Co., USMC, DOD, April 17, 1919 in France. Nancy Crosby (Mother), RFD #1, Norman Park, Georgia [FAG] [S2]

Cross, Robert W., Pvt., Squadron C, MAF, Great Lakes, Illinois, DDS, January 23, 1920 at Great Lakes, Illinois. George Cross (Father), RFD#2, Oneida, New York [S4]

Cross, William McKinley, Pvt., 75th Co., 6th Regt., DOW, July 5, 1918 in the Chateau-Thierry Sector. Minnie B. Cross (Mother), Halliday Hotel, Spokane, Washington [ABMC-Belleau] [S2] [SW]

Crossen, Vernon John, Sgt., 18th Co., 5th Regt., KIA, November 4, 1918 in the Meuse Argonne. John Crossen (Father), Hotel

Marine Corps Deaths, 1917-1921

Essex, 684 Ellis St., San Francisco, California [ABMC- Romagne] [S2] [SW1]

Crotty, Edward James, Pvt., Co. M, Parris Island, South Carolina, DDS, September 26, 1918,of surgical shock after an operation at Parris Island, South Carolina. Mrs. Crotty (Mother), 144 Main St., Great Barrington, Massachusetts [S3]

Crouch, Harvey Ellery, Pvt., Hdqtrs. Co., 6th Regt., DOW, July 19, 1918 in the Aisne Marne. A. W. Crouch (Father), #1, Box 6, Fresno, California [ABMC- Belleau] [S2] [SW1]

Crouter, George Auld, Pvt., Co. I, Parris Island, DDS, September 12, 1918 at Parris Island, South Carolina. Mrs. George A. Crouter (Wife), Charlevoix, Michigan [S3]

Crow, Arthur Jennings, Pvt., 55th Co., 5th Regt., DOW, July 27, 1918 in the Aisne Marne. Helen Jennings Crow (Mother), 5208 Davenport St., Omaha, Nebraska [ABMC- Belleau] [S2] [SW1 says KIA]

Crow, Harvey Isaac, Pvt., 12th Guard Co., USMC, DOD, December, 1, 1918 in France. Minnie Crow (Mother), Hutchinson, Kansas [FAG] [S2]

Crow, Raymond Franklin, Pvt., 78th Co., 6th Regt., KIA, April 26, 1918 in Toulon Sector, Verdun. Mr. Franklin Crow (Father), 421 Ramona Ave., Salt Lake City, Utah [FAG] [S2] [SW]

Crowder, William Arthur, Pvt., 45th Co., 5th Regt., KIA, June 6, 1918 in the Chateau-Thierry Sector. Lillian Crowder (Mother), 68 Isabella St., Ogdensburg, New York [ANC] [S2] [SW]

Crowther, Orlando G., 1st Lieut., 67th Co., 5th Regt. KIA, June 6, 1918 in the Chateau Thierry sector. Mrs. Lou Crowther (step-mother), 361 Hipie St., Cantan, Illinois [ABMC- Belleau] [S1] [SW]

Marine Corps Deaths, 1917-1921

Crozman, James Elmer, Pvt., 78th Co., 6th Regt., DOD, April 13, 1919 in France. Mrs. Evelyn Crozman Lancaster (Sister), Overlea Ave., South Peabody, Massachusetts [FAG] [S2]

Cruger, Russell C., Pvt., Hdqtrs. Co., 16th Regt., Pensacola, Florida, DAS, May 31, 1920 drowned at Pensacola, Florida. Silas Cruger (Father), 420 Reading Rd., Cincinnati, Ohio [S4]

Crum, William Jr., Pvt., 73rd Co., 6th Regt., KIA, October 5, 1918 in the Meuse Argonne. Maud Crum (Cousin), Crum, West Virginia [R] [S2] [SW1 says Gy. Sgt.]

Crutcher, Felix G., Pvt., Co. A, Mare Island, California, DDS, November 26, 1919 at Mare Island, California. Herbert P. Crutcher (Father), Gen. Del., Cherryville, Clackamas Co., Oregon [S4]

Crygier, Howard Peter, Pvt., Co. L, 13th Regt., DOD, September February 1918 enroute to France. May H. Crygier (Wife), 535 45th St., Brooklyn, New York [R] [S2]

Cuff, Edward Charles, Cpl., Navy Yard, Washington, D.C., DDS, July 11, 1918 at Washington, D.C. Mary Cuff (Sister), East Hartford, Connecticut [ANC] [S3]

Culbert, Kenneth P., 2d Lieut., 74th Co., 6th Regt., KOA, May 23, 1918 in France. Mrs. Mariam F. Culbert (widow) 318 S. Euclid Ave., Westfield, New Jersey [S1] [SW1 says 1st Aero Squadron, A.E.F.]

Culbertson, Rudolph H., Pvt., Bks. Det., Mare Island, Calfornia, DDS, April 3, 1920 at Mare Island, California. Mrs. Susan Culbertson (Mother), Date, Virginia [S4]

Cullen, Howard Preston, Pvt., Co. F, 13th Regt., DOD, September 30, 1918 in France. Perry C. Cullen (Father), Linn Creek, Missouri [VA-Springfield] [S2]

Cullerot, Stanis Joseph, Pvt., 96th Co., 6th Regt., DOW, April 23, 1918 in the Toulon Sector, Verdun. Eugene P. Cullerot (Brother), 389 Thornton St., Manchester, New Hampshire [R] [S2] [SW]

Marine Corps Deaths, 1917-1921

Cumings, Wells Bradley, Pvt., 80th Co., 6th Regt., DOW, June 30, 1918 in the Chateau-Thierry Sector. Florence Cumings (Mother), 987 Madison Ave., New York, New York [S2] [SW says Repl. Btln.]

Cummings, Alonzo Bernard, Pvt., 82nd Co., 6th Regt., DOD, October 22, 1918 in France. Henry H. Cummings (Father), % D. E. Wright, Traverse City, Michigan [S2]

Cummings, Brinton Smith, Pvt., 74th Co., 6th Regt., DOW, October 12, 1918 in the Meuse Argonne. George Cummings (Father), 24 W. Logan St., Philadelphia, Pennsylvania [FAG] [S2] [SW1]

Cummings, Francis Patrick, Pvt., 74th Co., 6th Regt., DOW, October 5, 1918 in the Meuse Argonne. Maria Cummings (Mother), 295 9th St., Troy, New York [R] [S2] [SW] [SW1]

Cummings, Frank Albert, Pvt., 96th Co., 6th Regt., KIA, June 19, 1918 in the Chateau-Thierry Sector. Anna Brown (Sister), California, Washington County, Pennsylvania [S2] [SW]

Cummins, Hubert Hue, Pvt., 97th Co., 6th Regt., DOW, November 2, 1918 in the Meuse Argonne. Hatty Dodge (Mother), Gen. Del., Reichle, Montana [S2] [SW1]

Cunningham, Arthur, Pvt., 73rd Co., 6th Regt., DOW, June 10, 1918 in the Chateau-Thierry Sector. Clara Cunningham (Mother), Fife Lake, Michigan [S2] [SW]

Cunningham, Charles Francis, Pvt., 55th Co., 5th Regt., KIA, July 21, 1918 in the Aisne Marne. John Cunningham (Father), 13 Summit St., Cohoes, New York [ABMC- Belleau as C.F.] [S2] [SW]

Cunningham, Fred Martin, Pfc, Bks. Det., Mare Island, California, DDS, October 24, 1918 at Eureka, California. Margaret Cunningham (Aunt), Dyersville, Iowa [S3]

Cunningham, Robert, Pvt., 96th Co., 6th Regt., DOW, June 10, 1918 in the Chateau-Thierry Sector. Mary J. Cunningham

Marine Corps Deaths, 1917-1921

(Mother), 420 N. Cedar St., Sturgeon Bay, Wisconsin [S2] [SW]

Curnan, Michael, Sgt., 153rd Co., 2nd Regt., Haiti, DOS, December 3, 1920 at Maissade, Haiti. Miss Kate A. Curnan (Sister), 41 Cedar St., Worcester, Massachusetts [S4]

Curtice, Rex, Pvt., 67th Co., 5th Regt., DOW, June 6, 1918 in the Chateau-Thierry Sector. Cora M. Bell (Mother), R. D. #2, Thorn Hill, Orchards, Thompsonville, Michigan [FAG] [S2] [SW1 says KIA]

Curtis, Clarence Anthony, Pvt., 11th Co., Quantico, Virginia, DDS, March 29, 1918 at Quantico, Virginia. Chrles Curtis (Brother), Groton, Massachusetts [S3]

Curtis, Horace Hartson, Pvt., Co. G, 13th Regt., DOD, September 22, 1918 enroute to France. Ira Curtis (Father), 51 Chestnut Ave., Danville, New York [FAG] [S2]

Curtis, Leal, Cpl., 74th Co., 6th Regt., DOW, May 26, 1918 in France. Cora Curtis (Mother), 9838 S. Robey St., Chicago, Illinois [FAG] [S2]

Cushman, Clifford Snider, Cpl., 45th Co., 5th Regt., KIA, June 6, 1918 in the Chateau-Thierry Sector. Marietta Cushman (Mother), 535 Hudson Rd., Toledo, Ohio [ABMC-Belleau TOM as C.S.] [S2] [SW]

Cutting, Benjamin Gates, Pvt., 96th Co., 6th Regt., DOW, August 7, 1918 in the Aisne Marne. Oscar B. Cutting (Father), Gen. Del., Glasgow, Montana [ANC] [S2] [SW says Co. B, Repl. Btln.]

Dahl, Gunnar, Pvt., 73rd Co., 6th Regt., KIA, June 10, 1918 in the Chateau-Thierry Sector. Harold Dahl (Father), 130 Augusta St., Oak Park, Illinois [S2] [SW]

Dailey, Donald Harold, Pvt., MB, New Orleans, Louisana, DDS, October 9, 1918 at New Orleans, Louisiana. Ivie Dailey (Mother), 513 S. Beach St., Bryan, Ohio [S3]

Marine Corps Deaths, 1917-1921

Dalby, William Jennings Bryan, Pvt., Bks. Det., Norfolk, Virginia, DDS, November 10, 1918 at Norfolk, Virgnia. John F. Dalby (Father), Banner, Kansas [S3]

Daley, Arthur James, Cpl., 51st Co., 5th Regt., DOD, October 19, 1918 in France. Edward Daley (Father), Gen. Del. Wauconda, Illinois [S2]

Daley, Joseph Michael, Cpl., 18th Co., 5th Regt., KIA, June 10, 1918 in the Chateau-Thierry Sector. Michael Daley (Father), 60½ Garrow St., Auburn, New York [ABMC- Belleau] [S2] [SW]

Dalquist, Oscar Edward, Pvt., 80th Co., 6th Regt., KIA, July 19, 1918 in the Aisne Marne. Peter Dalquist (Father), Randall, Minnesota [ABMC- Fere] [S2] [SW1]

Dalton, Eugene, Pvt., 7th Co., Quantico, Virginia, DDS, January 16, 1920 at Quantico, Virginia. Brigham Dalton (Father), Rockville, Utah [S4]

Dalton, Francis, Pvt., 78th Co., 6th Regt., DOW, October 4, 1918 in the Meuse Argonne. Mary L. Dalton (Mother), Elm St., Lima, New York [ABMC- Belleau] [S2] [SW say KIA] [SW1]

Dalton, Jeremiah J., 2nd Lieut., 75th Co., 6th Regt., DOW, October 21, 1918 in the Meuse Argonne. Mrs. Anna Dalton (Mother), 563 59th St., Brooklyn, New York [S1] [SW1 says KIA]

Dalton, Thomas James, Pvt., Co. H, 11th Regt., Quantico, Virginia, DDS, October 7, 1918 at Quantico, Virginia. Ellen D. Dalton (Wife), Mauston, Wisconsin [S3]

Dana, Charles Loomis Jr., Pvt., Co. B, 13th Regt., DOD, October 12, 1918 in France. Dr. C. L. Dana (Father), 53 W. 53rd St., New York, New York [S2]

Dance, Powhatan Richardson, Pvt., 45th Co., 5th Regt., KIA, November 1, 1918 in the Meuse Argonne. William F. Dance (Father), 1832 Park Ave., Richmond, Virginia

Marine Corps Deaths, 1917-1921

[S2] [SW1] [SW1 also lists a Richardson Powhatan as KIA]

Danford, Erwin I., Sgt., 47th Co., 5th Regt., DOW, July 23, 1918 in the Chateau-Thierry Sector. Isaac Danford (Father), 242 E. 12th Ave., Columbus, Ohio [ABMC- Fere] [S2] [SW]

Daniel, Frank W., Pvt., M. Per. Det., 3rd Naval District, New York, DDS, January 16, 1920 at Quantico, Virginia. Mrs. Aline Daniel (Mother), RFD#13, Box 40, Nashville, Tennessee [S4]

Daniels, Luke, Pvt., 28th Co., 4th Regt., Dominican Republic, DDS, December 18, 1918 at Santo Domingo, Dominican Republic. Mrs. Lucy B. Daniels (Mother), Calais, Vermont [S4]

Daniels, Roy Lee, Pvt., 75th Co., 6th Regt., DOW, July 19, 1918 in the Aisne Marne. Amanda Pate (Mother), Booth Point, Tennessee [ABMC- Belleau TOM] [S2] [SW1 says KIA]

Danielson, Joseph, Pvt., 82nd Co., 6th Regt., DOW, July 4, 1918 in the Chateau-Thierry Sector. Johanna Danielson (Mother), 4315 N. Central Park Ave., Chicago, Illinois [ABMC- Suresnes] [S2] [SW]

Danley, John Robert, Cpl., 78th Co., 6th Regt., KIA, June 13, 1918 in the Chateau-Thierry Sector. Miss Daisy Danley (Sister), 2621 Reid Ave., Lorain, Ohio [FAG] [S2] [SW]

Danz, Walter, Pvt., 84th Co., 6th Regt., KIA, July 19, 1918 in the Aisne Marne. Mollie Danz (Mother), Creve Coeur, Missouri [ABMC- Fere] [S2] [SW1]

Darling, James Roland, Pvt., Co. C, 13th Regt., DOD, September 28, 1918 in France. Mrs. Eliza Darling (Mother), R.R. #39, Mukwonago, Wisconsin [S2]

Daugherty, John Louis, Pvt., 78th Co., 6th Regt., DOW, October 4, 1918 in the Meuse Argonne. Elizabeth Daugherty (Mother), Bellevue, Iowa [FAG] [S2] [SW says Co. B, 5th Sep. Bltn.]

Marine Corps Deaths, 1917-1921

Daugherty, Philip Joseph, Pvt., 82nd Co., 6th Regt., KIA, October 9, 1918 in the Meuse Argonne. John Flanigan (Uncle), 193 N. 4th St., Newark, Ohio [ANC] [S2] [SW1]

Davenport, Clarence Lee, Pvt., 78th Co., 6th Regt., DOW, July 19, 1918 in the Aisne Marne. Mrs. Anna Davenport (Mother), Hampton, Georgia [S2] [SW1 says KIA]

Davey, Gregory MacPherson, Pvt., Supply Det., San Francisco, DDS, May 14, 1919 at San Francisco, California. W. H. K. Davey (Father), 154 Nassau St., New York, New York [FAG] [S4]

Davidian, Dickran Theodore, Cpl., 49th Co., 5th Regt., KIA, November 2, 1918 in the Meuse Argonne. Mesrope Davidian (Father), R. A. Box 388, Reedley, California [ABMC- Romagne] [S2] [SW1]

Davidson, Charles Joseph, Pvt., 23rd Co., 6th MG Bn., DOW, November 17, 1918 in the Meuse Argonne. Carrie Ingalls (Mother), Morris Plains, New Jersey [ABMC-Thiaucort] [S2] [SW1]

Davidson, Fred Cyrel (Cyril), Pvt., 75th Co., 6th Regt., KIA, November 4, 1918 in the Meuse Argonne. Mrs. F. C. Meis (Sister), 565 E. Adams Ave., Detroit, Michigan [ANC] [S2] [SW1]

Davidson, John Edgar, Pvt., 83rd Co., 6th Regt., DOW, October 6, 1918 in the Meuse Argonne. John Davidson (Father), 509 McKinstree St., Detroit, Michigan [ABMC- Romagne] [S2] [SW]

Davidson, Johnnie Eugine, Pvt., Co. H., 11th Regt., Quantico, Virginia, DDS, October 4, 1918 at Quantico, Virginia. Estella B. James (Mother), RR#1, Tolbert, Texas [S3]

Davies, John Roscoe, Pvt., 84th Co., 6th Regt., KIA, July 19, 1918 in the Aisne Marne. Minnie L. Davies (Mother), 833 Wndsor Ave., Chicago, Illinois [ABMC- Belleau TOM] [S2] [SW]

Marine Corps Deaths, 1917-1921

Davis, Charles Moreau, Pvt., Hdqtrs. Co., 6th Regt., KIA, September 12, 1918 in the St. Mihiel. Elizabeth Davis (Wife), 265 Berkeley Ave., Bloomfield, New Jersey [ABMC- Thiaucourt] [S2] [SW1]

Davis, Chuck Bert, Sgt., 73rd Co., 6th Regt., DOW, July 19, 1918 in the Aisne Marne. Mrs. Nola Stepp (Aunt), 92 Jefferson Drive, Ashville, North Carolina [S2] [SW1]

Davis, Claude E., Pvt., 49th Co., 5th Regt., DOW, June 7, 1918 in the Chateau-Thierry Sector. Mrs. Hazel Foster (Sister), P. O. Box 217, Battle Creek, Michigan [S2] [SW]

Davis, Cleo Baxter, Sgt., 66th Co., 5th Regt., KIA, June 5, 1918 in the Chateau-Thierry Sector. Mrs. Mattie Davis (Mother), 1177 Kentucky St., Bowling Green, Kentucky [FAG] [S2] [SW]

Davis, Cloyd Kocher, Pvt., 67th Co., 5th Regt., KIA, October 4, 1918 in the Meuse Argonne. Elmer Davis (Father), Petersburg, Pennsylvania [FAG] [S2] [SW1 says Lloyd]

Davis, Ernest Webster, Pvt., 20th Co., 5th Regt., DOW, November 2, 1918 in the Meuse Argonne. Mrs. Ida Davis (Mother), Gen. Del., Nevada, Missouri [S2] [SW1]

Davis, Eugene Calve, Pvt., 74th Co., 6th Regt., DOW, April 21, 1918 in the Toulon Sector, Verdun. Dorcas Davis (Mother), Walnut, Mississppi [FAG] [S2] [SW] [SW1]

Davis, John Ward, Cpl., 95th Co., 6th Regt., KIA, September 15, 1918 in the St. Mihiel. Amanda E. Davis (Mother), Perry, Missiouri [ANC] [S2] [SW 133rd Co.]

Davis, Joseph Marion, Pvt., 67th Co., 5th Regt., KIA [SW] [SW1 reported to have been found alive]

Davis, Joseph Meadow, Pvt., 97th Co., 6th Regt., KIA, October 4, 1918 in the Meuse Argonne. Amanda Davis (Wife), 122 Hendricks Ave., New Brighton, New York [R] [S2] [SW1]

Marine Corps Deaths, 1917-1921

Davis, Karl King, Pvt., Bks. Det., Indain Head, Maryland, DDS, October 18, 1918 at Indian Head, Maryland. Bascom Davis (Father), Petersburg, Tennessee [S3]

Davis, Lawrence A., Pvt., Co. N, Parris Island, Tennessee, DDS, November 11, 1918 at Parris Island, South Carolina. Edna S Davis (Wife), 375 Canton Ave., Detroit, Michigan [S3]

Davis, Patrick Haralson, Pvt., 51st Co., 5th Regt., DOW, June 11, 1918 in the Chateau-Thierry Sector. Ernest S. Davis (Father), 2434 4th Ave., West Seattle, Washington [S2] [SW1]

Davis, Teasley, Pvt., 96th Co., 6th Regt., DOW, July 19, 1918 in the Aisne Marne. F. M. Davis (Father), Ellijay, Georgia [FAG] [S2] [SW says Co. B, Repl. Btln.]

Davis, Walter Lee, Pvt., 84th Co., 6th Regt., DOW, November 6, 1918 in the Meuse Argonne. Mrs. Anna F. Davis (Mother), R. R.#3, Munda, Texas [ABMC- Romagne] [S2] [SW1]

Davis, William Loyd, Pvt., 23rd Co., 6th MG Bn., DOW, December, 8, 1918 in the Meuse Argonne. Clara Davis (Mother), Box 442, Sonora, California [VA-San Francisco] [S2] [SW1]

Davis, William Lloyd, Pvt., Co. D, Mare Island, California, DAS, May 22, 1918 at Mare Island, California. Fannie R. Davis (Mother), 821 South 15th St., Lincoln, Nebraska [FAG] [S3]

Day, Clarence Eugene, Pvt., 74th Co., 6th Regt., KIA, November 5, 1918 in the Meuse Argonne. Myra Day (Mother), 672 van Buren St., Milwaukee, Wisconsin [ABMC-Romagne] [S2] [SW1]

Day, Richard, Sgt., Hdqtrs., 4th Regt., Santo Domingo, Domincan Republic, DOS, August 10, 1919 at Santo Domingo, Domincan Republic. Charles H. Day (Uncle), Bartow, Florida [VA-Cypress Hills] [S4]

Marine Corps Deaths, 1917-1921

Deal, Oscar, Sgt., Bks. Det., Norfolk, Virginia, DDS, November 9, 1918 at Norfolk, Virginia. Winford D. Boland (Brother), Horton's Hotel, South and Pacific Sts., Norfolk, Virginia [S3]

Dean, James Leonard, Pvt., 96th Co., 6th Regt., KIA, June 12, 1918 in the Chateau-Thierry Sector. Alma Kittrell (Mother), Flatwoods, Tennessee [ABMC- Belleau] [S2] [SW]

Dean, John, 1st Sgt., Rhine River Patrol, DAO, May 18, 1919 in France. No next of kin. [VA-ANC says May 19,1919] [S2] [SW1 say KOA]

Dean, William Franklin, Pvt., 18th Co., 5th Regt., KIA, October 4, 1918 in the Meuse Argonne. DOW, I. Dean (Father), RFD #4, Box 64, Buckhannon, West Virginia [ABMC- Romagne] [S2] [SW1]

Deans, James Benjamin, Pvt., 49th Co., 5th Regt., KIA, October 4, 1918 in the Meuse Argonne. Ella Deans (Sister), Middlesex, North Carolina [ABMC- Romagne] [S2] [SW1]

Deaton, McKinley, Pvt., 96th Co., 6th Regt., DOW, June 19, 1918 in the Chateau-Thierry Sector. Dan Deaton (Father), Barbersville, Kentucky [S2] [SW]

DeBuhr, Ray John, Pvt., MB, NS, Cavite, Philippine Islands, DAS, February 19, 1921 drowned at Olongapo, Philippine Islands. Mr. Ray J. DeBuhr (Father), RFD#1, Canby, Clackamas Co., Oregon [FAG] [S4]

Decatur, Robert Bateman, Pvt., 76th Co., 6th Regt., KIA, June 3, 1918 in the Aisne Defensive. Effie Fitzwater (Mother), Plainville, Ohio [ABMC- Belleau] [S2] [SW]

Decker, Emil Francis Jr., Pvt., 43rd Co., 5th Regt., DOW, October 4, 1918 in the Meuse Argonne. Elizabeth Decker (Mother), 298 Cleveland St., Orange, New Jersey [FAG] [S2] [SW1]

Marine Corps Deaths, 1917-1921

Decker, Tracey Kilpatrick, Pvt., 84th Co., 6th Regt., KIA, June 6, 1918 in the Chateau-Thierry Sector. Mrs. Margaret McCusker (Sister), Gen. Del., Parkers Glen, Pennsylvania [S2] [SW]

Deckro, Floyd Henry, Pvt., 81st Co., 6th MG Bn., KIA, June 3, 1918 in the Aisne Defensive. Elizabeth R. Deckro (Wife), 39 Sloane Ave., Amsterdam, New York [S2] [SW]

Dederick, Ellsworth William, Pvt., Hdqtrs., OSD, Quantico, Virginia, DDS, November 8, 1918 at Quantico, Virginia. Carrie G. Dederick (Mother), Sun Inn, Bethleham, Pennsylvania [S3]

Deeks, Henry G., Pay Clerk, DDS, August 5, 1918 at Washington, D.C. Chalres H. Deeks (Father), Tiverton, Devonshire, England [S3]

Deemer, Crockett, Pvt., MD, USNH, Fort Lyon, Colorado, DDS, December 14, 1918 at Fort Lyon, Colorado. Jimmie Deemer (Brother), Calvert, Texas [S4]

Degnan, James Francis, Cpl., 51st Co., 5th Regt., KIA, November 10, 1918 in the Meuse Argonne. John E. Degnan (Father), 906 Second Ave., New York, New York [ABMC-Romagne] [S2] [SW1]

Degnan, John, Pvt., 66th Co., 5th Regt., KIA, June 6, 1918 in the Chateau-Thierry Sector. John Degnan (Father), 110 Ninth Ave., New York, New York [S2] [SW]

DeHaven, John Franklin, Pvt., 16th Co., 5th Regt., KIA, June 23, 1918 in the Chateau-Thierry Sector. Anna. DeHaven (Mother), 605 Ford St., Conshohocken, Pennsylvania [ABMC- Belleau TOM as J.F. De Haven] [S2] [SW]

Deishl, Edward Joseph, Pvt., 23rd Co., 6th MG Bn., KIA, November 10, 1918 in the Meuse Argonne. Barbara Deishl (Mother), Otis Orchards, Washington [ABMC-Romagne] [S2] [SW1]

Delaney, LeRoy Harry, Pvt., 95th Co., 6th Regt., KIA, July 19, 1918 in the Aisne Marne. John W. Delaney (Father), R.

Marine Corps Deaths, 1917-1921

R. 17, Mt. Washington, Cincinnati, Ohio [S2] [SW1 says DOW]

De La Mater, Seth C., Pvt., Bks. Det., Cavite, Philippine Islands, DDS, February 5, 1920 at Canacao, Philippine Islands. Mrs. Lillian De La Mater (Mother), 6424 Fife St., South Tacoma, Washington [S4]

Deloach, Edwin, Pvt., Supply Co., Parris Island, South Carolina, DAS, July 10, 1920 of fractured skull at Parris Island, South Carolina. Eli W. Deloach (Father), Brooklet, Georgia [FAG] [S4]

Demeter, Theodore Fredrick, Pvt., 75th Co., 6th Regt., KIA, September 16, 1918 in the St. Mihiel. Mr. and Mrs. Charles Demeter (Parents), 19 Garfield Ave., Freeport, Illinois [ABMC- Thiaucourt] [S2] [SW1]

Deming, Edgar Joseph, Pvt., 76th Co., 6th Regt., KIA, June 12, 1918 in the Chateau-Thierry Sector. Isabelle Deming (Mother), 1258 Stevens Ave., Flint, Michigan [S2] [SW]

Denlinger, Clinton Ellsworth., Pvt., 20th Co., 5th Regt., DOW, June 19, 1918 in the Chateau-Thierry Sector. Tillie Denlinger (Mother), Pierson, Iowa [FAG] [S2] [SW says 140th Co.]

Denman, Henry Elmer, Pvt., 67th Co., 5th Regt., KIA, June 6, 1918 in the Chateau-Thierry Sector. Mrs. Elfa Denman (Mother), 305 Williams Ave., Hamilton, Ohio [S2] [SW]

Denn, Alexander, Pvt., 55th Co., 5th Regt., KIA, June 12, 1918 in the Chateau-Thierry Sector. Richard Dean (Father), 72 Loomis St., Wilkes Barre, Pennsylvania [ABMC-Belleau] [S2] [SW1]

Denney, Leslie Gilbert, Pfc, MAD, Puget Sound, Washington, DAS, June 30, 1921 drowned at Puget Sound, Washington. Delena Weber (Mother), 713 Milwaukee St., Milwaukee, Wisconsin [S4]

Dennis, Clarence A., 2nd Lieut., 80th Co., 6th Regt., KIA, June 8, 1918 in the Chateau Thierry sector. W.H. Dennis

Marine Corps Deaths, 1917-1921

(Father), 87 Nassau St., New York, New York [FAG] [S1] [SW]

Dennis, France Edmunds, Pvt., 82nd Co., 6th Regt., KIA, June 6, 1918 in the Chateau-Thierry Sector. Frrressa Dennis (Mother), 424 Woodland Ave., Wooster, Ohio [S2] [SW]

Dennis, Raymond Laverette, Pvt., 74th Co., 6th Regt., DOD, January 12, 1918 James E. Dennis (Father), 651 Collins St, Fresno, California [FAG] [S2]

Dentel, Martin Anspach, Pvt., 43rd Co., 5th Regt., DOW, November 11, 1918 in the Meuse Argonne. John Dentel (Father), Lulu, Michigan [FAG] [S2] [SW1]

Deppler, Abraham, Pvt., 78th Co., 6th Regt., KIA, July 19, 1918 in the Aisne Marne. Mrs. Liddy Deppler (Mother), R. R. #1, Columbus Grove, Ohio [ABMC- Belleau TOM] [S2] [SW1 says DOW]

Depue, David Travis, Pvt., 76th Co., 6th Regt., KIA, November 1, 1918 in the Meuse Argonne. James Depue (Father), Gen. Del., Whitehall, Michigan [ABMC- Romagne] [S2] [SW1]

De Riso, Maurice N., Pvt., 153rd Co., 1st Regt., Cuba, DAS, December 22, 1918 at Guantanamo, Cuba. Dominick De Riso (Father), 322 Fifth St., Union, New Jersey [S4]

Dermody, James Patrick, Pvt., 20th Co., 5th Regt., KIA, October 4, 1918 in the Meuse Argonne. Bertha Dermody (Mother), 1379 15th St., Detroit, Michigan [S2] [SW Co. B, 2nd Cas. Btln.]

Derome, Herbert [S.], Cpl., 74th Co., 6th Regt., KIA, October 8, 1918 in the Meuse Argonne. Jules A. Derome (Father), 516 W. 10th St., Souix Falls, South Dakota [FAG] [S2] [SW1]

Derrick, John Leon, Pvt., 80th Co., 6th Regt., KIA, October 5, 1918 in the Meuse Argonne. John H. Derrick (Father), P. O. Box 4, Clayton, Georgia [S2] [SW1]

Marine Corps Deaths, 1917-1921

De Souza, Louis Edward, Pvt., 96th Regt., DOW, June 6, 1918 in the Chateau-Thierry Sector. Louis De Souza (Father), 928 N. 12th St., Springfield, Illinois [ABMC-Belleau TOM] [S2]

Des Ruisseaux, Charles Lucas, Sgt., Chief Paymaster's Office, USMC, DOD, November 19, 1918 in France. Myra Des Ruisseaux (Mother), Twin Falls, Idaho [ABMC-Suresnes] [S2]

Desmond, James D., 1st Lieutenant, DDS, September 21, 1818 at Quantico, Virginia. John D. Desmond (Father), 1015 Sycamore St., Milwaukee, Wisconsin [FAG] [S3]

Detmer, Crockett, Pvt., DDS, Calvert, Texas [S5]

Devaney, Thomas Francis, Pvt., 18th Co., 5th Regt., KIA, June 12, 1918 in the Chateau-Thierry Sector. Katherine Devaney (Mother), 759 Sherbourne Ave., St. Paul, Minnesota [S2] [SW]

Deveney, John Francis, Pvt., 45th Co., 5th Regt., DOW, November 1, 1918 in the Meuse Argonne. Mrs. Mary DeVeney (Mother), 130 W. Broadway, San Diego, California [ANC] [S2] [SW1 says KIA]

Devine, Ralph, Pfc, 98th Co., Newport, Rhode Island, DDS, September 24, 1918 at Newport, Rhode Island. Emma Devine (Mother), 5867 Wall St., Los Angeles, California [FAG] [S3]

Devlin, Bernard Joseph, Pfc, 67th Co., 5th Regt., KIA, November 4, 1918 in the Meuse Argonne. Mrs. Josephine Heinbacker (Sister), 613 W. Tioga St., Philadelphia, Pennsylvania [ABMC-Romagne] [S2] [SW1]

Dewey, Rupert Carthalo, Lt. Col., DDS, January 13, 1920 at home in Oakland, California. Mrs. Alice P. Dewey (Wife), 6435 Hillgrass Ave., Oakland, California [FAG] [S4]

Marine Corps Deaths, 1917-1921

Dewitt, Sylvester, Pvt., Co. D, Pvt., DOD, September 8, 1918 in France. Stephen D. DeWitt (Father), Summersville, Kentucky [ANC] [S2]

Dey, Claude Monroe, Cpl., 49th Co., 5th Regt., DOW, June 16, 1918 in the Chateau-Thierry Sector. Richard H. Dey (Father), RFD #4, Youngstown, Ohio [R] [S2] [SW]

Deyon, Joseph Royal, Pvt., 95th Co., 6th Regt., KIA, June 15, 1918 in the Chateau-Thierry Sector. John B. Deyon (Father), Tuolome, California [ABMC- Romagne TOM] [S2] [SW]

Dial, Harvey Grady, Pvt., 83rd Co., 6th Regt., KIA, June 13, 1918 in the Chateau-Thierry Sector. Mary Dial (Mother), 237 Whiteford Ave. South, Atlanta, Georgia [FAG] [S2] [SW]

Diamond, Sam, Sgt., Bks. Det., Philadelphia, Pennsylvania, DDS, October 29, 1918 at Philadelphia, Pennsylvania. Fanny Diamond (Wife), 125 Wolf St., Philadephia, Pennsylvania [S3]

Dibble, Elbie A., Pvt., MB, USNH, Fort Lyon, Colorado, DDS, July 29, 1919 at Fort Lyon, Colorado. Mrs. Sarah Dibble (Mother), 703 Meldrum Ave., Detroit, Michigan [S4]

Dick, George Franklin, Pvt., 66th Co., 5th Regt., DOW, November 13, 1918 in the Meuse Argonne. George Dick (Father), 7326 26th Ave. N.W., Seattle, Washington [ANC] [S2] [SW1]

Dickinson, Howard Henry, Pvt., 45th Co., 5th Regt., KIA, June 6, 1918 in the Chateau-Thierry Sector. W. W. Dickinson (Father), 119 Allen Blvd., Kalamazoo, Michigan [ABMC- Belleau] [S2] [SW]

Dickson, Robert Glen, Pvt., 82nd Co., 6th Regt., DOW, June 8, 1918 in the Chateau-Thierry Sector. John Dickson (Father), RR #2, Waukegan, Illinois [S2] [SW1]

Dietrich, Reinhard, Sgt., Bks. Det. Philadelphia, Pennsylvania, DDS, May 16, 1917 at Philadelphia, Pennsylvania. Mrs.

Marine Corps Deaths, 1917-1921

Katie Dietrich (Wife), 2132 Satona St., Philadelphia, Pennsylvania [FAG] [S3]

Digby, Russell Beach, Pvt., 20th Co., 5th Regt., DOW, June 28, 1918 in the Chateau-Thierry Sector. John H. Digby (Father), Kirkand, Washington [ANC] [S2] [SW]

Dille, Paul Ferdinand, Pvt., 51st Co., 5th Regt., KIA, July 18, 1918 in the Aisne Marne. Peter O. Dille (Father), Dassel, Minnesota [FAG] [S2] [SW Casualty Co., 4th Rep.Btln.]

Dillon, William G., Quartermaster Clerk, DDS, October 6, 1918 at Whitewright, Texas. Anna Lucile Dillon (Wife), 132 3rd St., S.E., Washington, D.C. [S3]

Dines, Donald Corprew, Pvt., 84th Co., 6th Regt., KIA, October 5, 1918 in the Meuse Argonne. Tyson S. Dines (Father), 195 High St., Denver, Colorado [ABMC- Romagne] [S2] [SW1 says KOA]

Dingle, Richard Wallace, Pvt., 20th Co., 5th Regt., KIA, June 6, 1918 in the Chateau-Thierry Sector. Joseph Dingle (Father), St. Paul Park, Minnesota [ABMC- Belleau] [S2] [SW]

Dingle, William, Pvt., 79th Co., 6th Regt., DOW, June 2, 1918 in the Aisne Defensive. Mary Dingle (Mother), 817 N. Lombard Ave., Oak Park, Illinois [ANC] [S2] [SW]

Di Noto, Salvatore, Drm, 51st Co., 5th Regt., KIA, June 11, 1918 in the Chateau-Thierry Sector. Mrs. Carmela Albo Vedora Di Noto (Mother), #9 Via Manin, Palermo, Italy [ANC] [S2] [SW]

Dion, Harold Seward, Pvt., 88th Co., Philadelphia, Pennsylvania, DDS, March 11, 1918 at Philadelphia, Pennsylvania. Mary F. Dion (Mother), RR#1, North St. Paul, Minnesota [S3]

Dippold, Lawrence John, Cpl., Co. E, 13th Regt., DOD, January 5, 1919 in France. Joseph Dippold (Father), 624 Fisher Ave., No. Bergen, New Jersey [FAG] [S2]

Marine Corps Deaths, 1917-1921

Dirkson, Chester W., Trumpeter, 2nd Co., Philadelphia, Pennsylvania, DDS, February 6, 1920 at League Island,Pennsylvania. Joseph C. Dirkson (Father), 2118 Standaed Ave., Louisville, Kentucky [S4]

Disbennett, Curtis Edward, Pvt., 74th Co., 6th Regt., DOW, June 16, 1918 in the Chateau-Thierry Sector. Edward C. Disbennett (Father), 307 East Wood Ave., Caruthersville, Missouri [VA-Memphis] [S2] [SW]

Dittman, Carl Joseph, Pvt., 74th Co., 6th Regt., KIA, June 13, 1918 in the Chateau-Thierry Sector. Mary Dittman (Mother), RFD#1, Woodstock, Illinois [ABMC- Belleau] [S2] [SW]

Divine, Louis Sharp, Cpl., Hdqtrs. Co., 5th Regt., KIA, June 3, 1918 in the Aisne Defensive. Isaac Devine (Father), 3507 W. Heroy St., Spokane, Washington [S2] [SW] [SW1]

Dobovitz, Abe, Pvt., 55th Co., 5th Regt., KIA, June 12, 1918 in the Chateau-Thierry Sector. Julius Dobovitz (Father), 619 19th St., Newark, New Jersey [S2] [SW]

Dockx, Francis Joseph, Cpl., 55th Co., 5th Regt., KIA, June 5, 1918 in the Aisne Defensive. Joseph Dockx (Father), 8 Dunham St., South Boston, Massachusetts [R] [S2] [SW]

Dodd, James Irving, Pvt., 51st Co., 5th Regt., KIA, June 6, 1918 in the Chateau-Thierry Sector. Anna Dodd (Mother), 503 Wells St., Sistersville, West Virginia [ABMC- Belleau] [S2] [SW]

Dodge, Miles Harrison, Sgt., 18th Co., 5th Regt., KIA, June 1, 1918 in the Chateau-Thierry Sector. James L. Dodge (Father), Isle au Haut, Maine [ABMC- Belleau] [S2]

Dodson, Earl, Pvt., MBks., Boston, Massachusetts, DDS, December 29, 1918 at Chelsea, Massachusetts. John C. Dodson (Father), Clifty, Tennessee [FAG] [S4]

Dodson, Ray Richard, Cpl., 95th Co., 6th Regt., DOW [SW] [SW1 reported to have been found alive]

Dollard, Harry Theodore, Pvt., 80th Co., 6th Regt., DOW, November 24, 1918 in the Meuse Argonne. Margaret

Marine Corps Deaths, 1917-1921

Dollard (Mother), 1023 21st St., Bay City, Michigan [R] [S2] [SW1]

Donahue, Daniel Edward, Sgt., 81st Co., 6th MG Bn., KIA, June 15, 1918 in the Chateau-Thierry Sector. John F. Donahue (Brother), 61 Templeton St., Dorchester, Massachusetts [ABMC- Belleau] [S2] [SW]

Donalds, John Howard, Pvt., 2nd Squadron, FMAF, DOD, November 1, 1918 in France. Jerry Donalds (Father), Turtle Lake, Wisconsin [ANC] [S2]

Donaldson, Jack Meredith, Pvt., 78th Co., 6th Regt., DOD, March 2, 1918 in France. Mrs. Ella M. Webb (Mother), 106 Crescent Ave., Atlanta, Georgia [R] [S2]

Dondanville, Carl J., Pvt., USAT *Madawaska*, DDS, July 8, 1920 aboard the USAT *Madawaska* enroute to the United States. Emil Dondanville (Father), Gen. Del., San Gabriel, California [FAG] [S4]

Donnelly, William Edgar Joseph, Trumpeter, Naval Prison, Portsmouth, New Hampshire, DDS, September 29, 1918 at Portsmouth, New Hampshire. William F. Donnelly (Father), 444 W. 164th St., New York, New York [S3]

Donohoe, Charles Everett, Sgt., 18th Co., 5th Regt., DOW, October 5, 1918 in the Meuse Argonne. Elira E. Hyde (Mother), P. O. Box 235, Anita, Iowa [FAG] [S2] [SW1]

Donohue, William Alfred, Pfc, 49th Co., 5th Regt., KIA, November 1, 1918 in the Meuse Argonne. Maude A. Donohue (Wife), c/o Cokato Enterprise, Cokato, Minnesota [ABMC- Romagne] [S2] [SW1 says DOW]

Doody, Lawrence R., Pvt., 61st Co., Brooklyn, New York, DDS, February 3, 1920 at Brooklyn, New York. Maurice Doddy (Father), 119 Walnut St., Lebanon, Kentucky [S4]

Dopp, Daniel Gifford, Pvt., 81st Co., 6th Regt., KIA, June 9, 1918 in the Chateau-Thierry Sector. Frank E. Dopp (Father), Wild Rose, Wisconsin [FAG] [S2] [SW]

Marine Corps Deaths, 1917-1921

Dorbandt, Justin Davis, Pvt., 4th Squadron, FMAF, DOD, October 3, 1918 in France. Daisy D. Dorbandt (Wife), 1203½ Capitol Ave., Houston, Texas [FAG] [S2]

Dorian, Gregory Alan, Pvt., 83rd Co., 6th Regt., DOW, April 30, 1918 in the Toulon Sector, Verdun. Annie G. Dorian (Mother), 1226 E. 63rd St., Chicago, Illinois [ABMC-Romagne] [S2] [SW]

Doris, John Joseph, Jr., Pvt., 80th Co., 6th Regt., DOW, July 20, 1918 in the Aisne Marne. John J. Doris (Father), 1650 Park Ave., New York, New York [R] [S2] [SW]

Dornblaser, Paul Logan, Cpl., 82nd Co., 6th Regt., DOW, October 10, 1918 in the Meuse Argonne. Thomas F. Dornblaster (Father), 3743 Wilton Ave., Chicago, Illinois [ABMC-Romagne] [S2] [SW1]

Dornblaser, Ray Edison, Pvt., 95th Co., 6th Regt., DOW, June 17, 1918 in the Chateau-Thierry Sector. Mary Dornblaser (Mother), Georgetown, Illinois [ABMC- Belleau] [S2] [SW]

Dorr, Cyrus T., Pvt., MA Det., Miami, Florida, DOS, December 2, 1918 enroute to Nashville, Tennessee. Mrs. Margaret P. Dorr (Wife), 714 Gloyd Bldg., Kansas City, Missouri [FAG] [S4]

Dorr, Thomas Ripley, Pvt., MCR, 46th Co., Norfolk, Virginia, DDS, August 14, 1917 at Norfolk, Virginia. Janet Dorr (Mother), Williamston, Massachusetts [S3]

Dorrell, John Lee, Cpl., 96th Co., 6th Regt., KIA, October 3, 1918 in the Meuse Argonne. Mrs. Louie Dorrell (Mother), Heyworth, Illinois [S2] [SW1]

Dorris, Frank Parks, Pvt., 83rd Co., 6th Regt., KIA, June 6, 1918 in the Chateau-Thierry Sector. Mrs. John B. Dorris (Mother), Douglasville, Georgia [FAG] [S2] [SW]

Dorsey, Edward, Pvt., 51st Co., 5th Regt., KIA, October 5, 1918 in the Meuse Argonne. Emma Dorsey (Mother), 4246

Marine Corps Deaths, 1917-1921

Wyalusing Ave., Philadelphia, Pennsylvania [ABMC-Romagne] [S2]

Dorsey, Howard Swier, Cpl., 51st Co., 5th Regt., KIA, October 5, 1918 in the Meuse Argonne. . Emma Dorsey (Mother), 4246 Wyalusing Ave., Philadelphia, Pennsylvania [ABMC- Romagne] [S2] [SW1]

Dorsey, William Joseph, Pvt., 10th Co., Dominican Republic, DDS, July 29, 1917 at Monte Cristi, Dominican Republic. Kate Gore (Sister), 41 Grand St., Trenton, New Jersey [S3]

Dosch, Frank Bernard, Pvt., 84th Co., 6th Regt., DOW, November 9, 1918 in the Aisne Marne. Adam Dosch (Father), 5711 S. Wood St., Chicago, Illinois [S2] [SW1]

Dosch, Frank Peter, Pvt., 78th Co., 6th Regt., DOD, December, 17, 1918 in the Meuse Argonne. Samuel Dosch (Foster-father), Finlayson, Minnesota [R] [S2]

Dost, Franklin Leon, Sgt., 45th Co., 5th Regt., KIA, June 6, 1918 in the Chateau-Thierry Sector. Mrs. F. L. Dost (Wife), 435 Melville St., Rochester, New York [FAG] [S2] [SW1]

Dougherty, James David, Jr., Pvt., 16th Co., 5th Regt., KIA, June 25, 1918 in the Chateau-Thierry Sector. Mary D. Dougherty (Mother), 114 South 4th St., St. Louis, Missouri [S2] [SW]

Dougherty, James William, Pvt., MB, New London, Connecticut, DOS, August 14, 1921 at New London, Connecticut Mrs. Cara Daugherty (Mother), Pine Grove, Wetzel Co., West Virginia [S4]

Douglas, Henry Hampton, Pvt., 79th Co., 6th Regt., KIA, October 5, 1918 in the Meuse Argonne. Mr. J. S. Douglas (Father), Slaughter, Louisiana [ANC] [S2] [SW1 says DOW]

Douglass, Ora James, Pvt., 20th Co., 5th Regt., DOW, June 24, 1918 in the Chateau-Thierry Sector. Amy E. Douglas

Marine Corps Deaths, 1917-1921

(Mother), 608 Central Ave., Greenville, Ohio [R] [S2] [SW]

Douthitt, Raymond Edwin, Gy. Sgt., MD, NAD, Cambridge, Massachusetts, DDS, September 21, 1918 at Boston, Massachusetts. Dora F. Douthitt (Mother), 219 S. Crowder St., Sullivan, Indiana [FAG as September 12, 1918] [S3]

Dowd, John Joseph, Pvt., 55th Co., 5th Regt., DOW, June 12, 1918 in the Chateau-Thierry Sector. James Murray (Foster-father), R#3, Montrose, Pennsylvania [S2] [SW1]

Dowdle, Henry Lawrence, Cpl., 49th Co., 5th Regt., KIA, June 6, 1918 in the Chateau-Thierry Sector. Mary Dowdle (Mother), 1739 W. Adams St., Chicago, Illinois [S2] [SW]

Dowdy, James Arthur, Jr., Pvt., Co. F, 11th Regt., Quantico, Virginia, DDS, October 11, 1918 at Quantico, Virginia. James A. Dowdy (Father), 611 West Sevier St., Clarksville, Arkansas [FAG] [S3]

Dowling, Joseph Edward, Pvt., 47th Co., 5th Regt., KIA, June 25, 1918 in the Chateau-Thierry Sector. Joseph P. Dowling (Father), 1601 Hunting Park Ave., Philadelphia, Pennsylvania [VA-Philiadelphia] [S2] [SW]

Downard, Louis Joseph, Pvt., 43rd Co., 5th Regt., DOW, June 12, 1918 in the Chateau-Thierry Sector. Minnie Downard (Mother), 1401 14th St., Arnold, Pennsylvania [S2] [SW]

Doyen, Charles A., Brig. Gen., DDS, October 6, 1918 at Quantico, Virginia. Mrs. Claude Ray Doyen (Wife), Wardour, Anapolis, Maryland [FAG] [VA-ANC, but not in database, see Claude F. Doyen in ANC database] [S3]

Drake, Alonzo, Pvt., 74th Co., 6th Regt., DOW, July 19, 1918 in the Aisne Marne. Alonzo A. Drake (Father), Wilmot, South Dakota [S2] [SW1]

Marine Corps Deaths, 1917-1921

Drummond, John Joseph, Pvt., Co. D, 13th Regt., DOD, October 2, 1918 in France. Mrs. Mary Drummond (Mother), 14 Prospect St., Summit, New Jersey [R] [S2]

Duck, Henry, Pvt., USS *Constitution*, DDU, DDS, December 23, 1918 at Newport, Rhode Island. Mr. Clynt Duck (Brother), RFD#8, Greenville, Tennessee [S4]

Duclo, George Eber, Pvt., 15th Co., 6th MG Bn., KIA, June 15, 1918 in the Chateau-Thierry Sector. John Duclo (Father), Gen. Del., Colorado Springs, Colorado [FAG] [S2] [SW1]

Duda, Walter Frank, Sgt., 20th Co., 5th Regt., DOW, June 22, 1918 in the Chateau-Thierry Sector. Frank Duda (Father), 1836 North Wood St., Chicago, Illinois [ABMC- Suresnes] [S2] [SW]

Dudley, Earl Bouton, Pvt., 55th Co., 5th Regt., KIA, June 12, 1918 in the Chateau-Thierry Sector. Clara Dudley (Mother), 306 Bryant Ave., Ithaca, New York [S2] [SW]

Duffer, Wilfred Osborne, Pvt., 74th Co., 6th Regt., KIA, July 19, 1918 in the Aisne Marne. Mrs. Mamie Duffer (Stepmother), Shannon, Mississippi [ABMC- Belleau TOM as W.O.] [S2] [SW says 34th Co.]

Duffin, Arthur Thomas, Pvt., 95th Co., 6th Regt., KIA, July 19, 1918 in the Aisne Marne. Henry Duffin (Father), 332 18th St., Oregon, Utah [ABMC- Belleau TOM as A.T.] [S2] [SW says Co. A, Rep. Btln.]

Duffy, James Harold, Pvt., Co. C., Navy Yard Guard, Philadelphia, Pennsylvania, DDS, January 27, 1920 at Philadelphia, Pennsylvania. Mrs. Ellan Duffy (Mother), 36 Campt St., Waterbury, Connecticut [S4]

Duke, Jimmie Lewis, Pvt., 49th Co., 5th Regt., KIA, July 18, 1918 in the Aisne Marne. L. B. Duke (Father), Santa Rosa, California [ABMC- Belleau TOM] [S2] [SW as Jimmie Lewis 134th Co.] [SW1]

Marine Corps Deaths, 1917-1921

Duley, Henry George, Pvt., 81st Co., 6th MG Bn., KIA, July 19, 1918 in the Aisne Marne. George A. Duley (Father), South Royalston, Massachusetts [ABMC- Belleau TOM as H.G.] [S2] [SW1]

Dulgar, James Harry, Pvt., 83rd Co., 6th Regt., KIA, November 3, 1918 in the Meuse Argonne. Harvey Dulgar (Brother), Mt. Sterling, Ohio [R] [S2] [SW1]

Dulin, William Carlton, Pvt., Co. A, MG Bn, Quantico, Virginia, DDS, October 5, 1918 Quantico, Virginia. William R. Dulin (Father), Preston, Maryland [S3]

DuMars, William Wilbur, Pvt., 17th Co., 5th Regt., KIA, June 6, 1918 in the Chateau-Thierry Sector. John T. DuMars (Father), National Military Home, Kansas [ABMC- Belleau as Du Mars] [S2] [SW]

Dunbar, Lewis Edward, Pvt., 16th Co., 5th Regt., KIA, October 4, 1918 in the Meuse Argonne. Mrs. Ethel Dunbar Chase (Sister), 4048 Walnut St., Philadelphia, Pennsylvania [ABMC- Romagne] [S2] [SW Co. B, 4th Sep. Btln.]

Duncan, Baxter Carlisle, Cpl., 78th Co., 6th Regt., KIA, September 15, 1918 in the St. Mihiel. Thomas W. Duncan (Father), Nacogdoches, Texas [S2] [SW1]

Duncan, Claud Frank, Pvt., 17th Co., 5th Regt., DOW, November 11, 1918 in the Meuse Argonne. Miss Bonnie Duncan and Miss Viva Duncan (Sisters), 312 Duke St., Norfolk, Virginia [ANC] [S3] [SW1 says Frank Duncan and KIA] [SW1 also has listed as DOW]

Duncan, David Theodore, Pvt., 74th Co., 6th Regt., KIA, July 2, 1918 in the Chateau-Thierry Sector. James Duncan (Father), 629 Cathlem St., Bloomsburg, Pennsylvania [ABMC- Belleau] [S2] [SW1 says Davis T.]

Duncan, Donald F., Capt., 96th Co., 6th Regt., KIA, June 6, 1918 in the Chateau Thierry sector. Mrs. Josephine A. Duncan (Mother), 1027 Meanie St., St. Joseph, Missouri [ANC] [S1] [SW]

Marine Corps Deaths, 1917-1921

Duncan, Erwin Hubert, Pvt., 58th Co., Norfolk, Virginia, DDS, February 9, 1918 at Norfolk, Virginia. Addie Duncan (Mother), RR#1, Aetna, Tennessee [S3]

Duncan, Frank, Cpl., 17th Co., 5th Regt., DOW, October 6, 1918 in the Meuse Argonne. G. W. Duncan (Father), Duxbury, Minnesota [ABMC- Romagne] [S2]

Duncan, James F., Pvt., 27th Co., 4th Prov. Regt., Dominican Republic, DDS, January 10, 1919 at Santo Domingo, Dominican Republic. Mrs. Laura Duncan (Mother), 713 Freeman Ave., Cincinnati, Ohio [S4]

Duncan, William Oran, Pvt., Hdqtrs. Co., 13th Regt., DOD, September 28, 1918 in France. Mrs. Amy Duncan (Mother), Ripley, Mississippi [VA-Cornith] [S2]

Dunfee, Alton Laforest, Pvt., 55th Co., 5th Regt., DOW, June 11, 1918 in the Chateau-Thierry Sector. Mrs. Emma F. Dunfee (Mother), RFD #4, Morses Pond Grove, Wellesley, Massachusetts [S2] [SW]

Dunham, Charles H., Gy. Sgt., 3rd District, New York, DDS, February 18, 1919 aboard the USS *Louisville*. Mrs. Mamie M. Dunham (Mother), Lake Odessa, Michigan [FAG] [S4]

Dunlap, Roscoe Lincoln, Sgt., 84th Co., 6th Regt., KIA, October 3, 1918 in the Meuse Argonne. Mrs. Mary D. Dunlap (Sister), 302 Virginia Ave., Effingham, Illinois [ABMC- Romagne TOM] [S2] [SW1]

Dunlavy, Herbert D., Pvt., 96th Co., 6th Regt., KIA, June 8, 1918 in the Chateau-Thierry Sector. Mrs. George H. Perry (Mother), Box 95, West Columbus, Texas [ANC] [S2] [SW]

Dunleavy, Thomas Richard, Pvt., 76th Co., 6th Regt., DOW, November 1, 1918 in the Meuse Argonne. Celia F. Dune (Mother), 1737 Clements St., San Francisco, California [ABMC- Romagne] [S2] [SW1]

Marine Corps Deaths, 1917-1921

Dunn, Allen Levi, Cpl., 83rd Co., 6th Regt., KIA, June 8, 1918 in the Chateau-Thierry Sector. Mrs. Nancy P. Dunn (Mother), Georgetown, Brown County, Ohio [ABMC- Belleau] [S2] [SW1]

Dunn, William Frederick, Pvt., 1st MAF, Dominican Republic, DAS, May 21, 1917 of drowning at Chevon River, Seybo Province, Dominican Republic. Patrick Dunn (Father), RFD#3, Eldrid, Pennsylvania [FAG] [S3]

Dupree, Albert David, Pvt., 17th Co., 5th Regt., DOC, June 3, 1919 in France. Mitchell Dupree (Father), 215 Grove St., St. Paul, Minnesota [ANC] [S2] [SW1 has DOW]

Durand, Riley Eugene, Pvt., Supply Co., 13th Regt., DOD, September 26, 1918 in France. Charlotte Durand (Mother), Bristow, Iowa [S2]

Durbin, Lester Delno, Gy. Sgt., Hdqtrs. Co., 6th Regt., KIA, July 19, 1918 in the Aisne Marne. Elizabeth Durbin (Mother), Cameron, West Virginia [ANC] [S2] [SW]

Durkin, John J., Pvt., 27th Co., 4th Prov. Regt., Dominican Republic, DAS, March 29, 1919 of an electric shock at Santo Domingo, Dominican Republic. Mrs. Anna Durkin (Mother), 909 Walnut St., Elmira, New York [S4]

Durkin, William P., Pvt., Parris Island, South Carolina, DDS, January 12, 1919 at Parris Island, South Carolina. William Durkin (Father), RR#2, Atchison, Kansas [ABMC- Fere] [S4]

Durocher, Sidney Harry, Pvt., 61st Co., 35th St. Pier, New York, New York, DDS, October 17, 1918 at Brooklyn, New York. Emile J. Burocher (Father), Thibodaux, Louisiana [FAG] [S3]

Durrell, Lester Harry, Cpl., Co. L, 13th Regt., DOD, September 29, 1918 in France. Harry E. Durrell (Father), 536 Park Ave., Dunkirk, New York [FAG] [S2]

Dutcher, Allan Van Rensselear, Pvt., 43rd Co., 5th Regt., DOW, November 18, 1918 in the Meuse Argonne. Belle Dutcher

Marine Corps Deaths, 1917-1921

(Mother), 138 E. 38th St., New York, New York [ABMC-Belleau] [S2] [SW1]

Dutro, Robert Lincoln, Pvt., 76th Co., 6th Regt., KIA, July 19, 1918 in the Aisne Marne. Clarence S. Dutro (Father), Groveport, Ohio [S2] [SW1]

Dutton, Dwight Paul, Sgt., 18th Co., 5th Regt., DOW, August 30, 1918 in the Aisne Marne. Mrs. Esther Dutton (Mother), 84 W. Rutland Ave., Boston, Massachusetts [FAG] [S2] [SW says Co. C]

Duvall, Robert G., Pvt., 191st Co., Puget Sound, Washington, DDS, January 25, 1919 at Puget Sound, Washington. Mrs. Ruth Duvall (Mother), Freeman, Missouri [S4]

Dye, William Earl, Pvt., 80th Co., 6th Regt., KIA, July 19, 1918 in the Aisne Marne. Susan V. Dye (Mother), 2007 Maine Ave., Kenmore, Ohio [FAG] [S2] [SW1]

Dysart, Edwin, Pvt., Supply Co., 10th Regt., Philadelphia, Pennsylvana, DDS, February 11, 1919 at Philadelphia, Pennsylvania. Mrs. Minnie Dysart (Mother), 1392 East 53rd St., Cleveland, Ohio [FAG] [S4]

Eager, George W., Pvt., DAS, Nashville, Tennessee. [S5]

Eames, Raymond Rexford, Pvt., 96th Co., 6th Regt., DOW, June 29, 1918 in the Chateau-Thierry Sector. Joseph P. Eames (Father), 237 Burr Oak Ave., Blue Island, Illinois [ABMC- Suresnes] [S2] [SW]

Earl, Charles Harcourt, Cpl., 78th Co., 6th Regt., DOW, June 15, 1918 in the Chateau-Thierry Sector. Rosa Earl (Mother), 400 W. Winona St., Austin, Minnesota [S2] [SW]

Earley, Deyo, Cpl., 80th Co., 6th Regt., DOD, February 23, 1919 in France. Clara Earley (Mother), RD#2, Avoca, New York [R] [S2]

Early, George Thomas, Sgt., 45th Co., 5th Regt., KIA, November 6, 1918 in the Meuse Argonne. Anna Early (Mother), 327 Hillside Ave., Newark, New Jersey [R] [S2] [SW1]

Marine Corps Deaths, 1917-1921

Early, Hobart Evans, Pvt., Co. S, Parris Island, South Carolina, DDS, November 1, 1918 at Parris Island, South Carolina. Thomas M. Early (Father), 130 Winthrop St., Medford, Massachusetts [S3]

East, Cheetle Burch, Pvt., 96th Co., 6th Regt., DOW, July 23, 1918 in the Aisne Marne. Mary L. East (Mother), 629 Maple Ave., St. Louis, Missouri [ANC] [S2] [SW1]

East, Walter William, Pvt., Batt. C., Parris Island, South Carolina. DAS, June 24, 1921 drowned at Hampton Roads, Virginia. Charles W. East (Father), 69 Addison St., Chelsea, Massachusetts [S4]

Easter, James Wheeler, Pvt., 49th Co., 5th Regt., KIA, July 15, 1918 in the Aisne Marne. Florence Easter (Mother), 1205 W. 7th St., Cincinnati, Ohio [ABMC- Belleau TOM] [S2] [SW1]

Eaton, John Patchill, Pvt., 80th Co., 6th Regt., KIA, June 6, 1918 in the Chateau-Thierry Sector. Jemima Eaton (Mother), 152 E. 2nd St., Corning, New York [S2] [SW]

Eaton, Robert Price, Pvt., 78th Co., 6th Regt., DOW, July 19, 1918 in the Aisne Marne. Robert L. Eaton (Father), Enid, Okalahoma [FAG] [S2] [SW1]

Eaton, William V., Cpl., 100th Co., 8th Regt., Haiti, DAS, June 24, 1920 drowned at Haiti. James W. Eaton (Father), 36 McKinley St., Franklin, Pennsylvania [S4]

Eckerlen, Ernest Theodore, Pvt., 23rd Co., 6th MG Bn., KIA, November 5, 1918 in the Meuse Argonne. Alice Eckerlen (Mother), 605 Liberty St., Salem, Oregon [ABMC-Romagne] [S2] [SW1]

Eckert, Louis Lloyd, Pvt., Hdqtrs. Co., 10th Regt., Quantico, Virginia, DDS, February 21, 1918 at Quantico, Virginia. Henry M. Edkert (Father), Greenfield, Ohio [S3]

Eckhardt, Charles Francis, Pvt., USS *Vermont*, DAU, September 11, 1917 when he accidently drowned when he fell overboard at sea. Mary Eckhardt (Mother), Donohue St., Inwood, Long Island, New York [S3]

Edgar, Ernest Draper, Pvt., 79th Co., 6th Regt., KIA, July 19, 1918 in the Aisne Marne. Roy A. Edgar (Father), 1005 King St. E., Bakersfield, California [ABMC- Fere] [S2]

Edge, Edward Thomas, Pvt., 51st Co., 5th Regt., DOW, June 11, 1918 in the Chateau-Thierry Sector. Mrs. Mary Wheller (Sister), Ridgely, Maryland [ABMC- Belleau] [S2] [SW1]

Edge, Floyd, Pvt., 67th Co., 5th Regt., KIA, June 14, 1918 in the Chateau-Thierry Sector. Mrs. J. B. Sutton (Friend), RFD#3, E. Chattanooga, Tennessee [ABMC- Belleau] [S2] [SW]

Edge, Jess R., Pvt., Nav. Amm. Depot, St. Julien's Creek, Virginia, DAS, June 3, 1920 of an accidental gunshot wound at Norfolk, Virginia. Mrs. Fannie Edge (Mother), 1114 San Pedro Ave., San Antonio, Texas [S4]

Edmondson, Marvin Eugene, Pvt., 79th Co., 6th Regt., KIA, October 3, 1918 in the Meuse Argonne. Mary Edmondson (Mother), R#2, NE Station, Nashville, Tennessee [R] [S2] [SW1 says DOW]

Edward, Wesley O., Pvt., DDS, Evansville, Indiana [S5]

Edwards, Alvin Leroy, Cpl., 83rd Co., 6th Regt., DOW, October 16, 1918 in the Meuse Argonne. Mary Edwards (Mother), Gen. Del. McFarland, Wisconsin [ABMC- Thiaucourt] [S2] [SW]

Edwards, Calvin Jefferson, Jr., Pvt., Bks. Detch., Norfolk, Virginia, DDS, March 13, 1918 at Norfolk, Virginia. Calvin J. Edwards, Sr., (not given), Crawford, Texas [FAG] [S3]

Edwards, Henry G., Pvt., Replacement, KIA [SW] [SW1 reported to have been found alive]

Edwards, Herschel Vernon, Jr., Pvt., 83rd Co., 6th Regt., DOW, October 7, 1918 in the Meuse Argonne. Mr. and Mrs. H.

Marine Corps Deaths, 1917-1921

V. Edwards (Parents), P O Box 225, Wallace, Idaho [ABMC- Romagne] [S2] [SW1 says KIA]

Edwards, Oran, Pvt., Co. A, MG Bn, Quantico, Virginia, DDS, October 5, 1918 at Quantico, Virginia. Mrs. West Edwards (Mother), Gen. Del., Merkel, Texas [FAG] [S3]

Edwards, Thomas L., Captain, 1st Brigade, Haiti, DAS, August 10, 1920 of injuries received in an aeroplane crash in Haiti. Mrs. Martha Edwards (Mother), 2405 Estes St., Baker, Oregon [FAG] [S4]

Edwards, Wesley Orville, Pvt., Supply Co., Quantico, Virginia, DDS, September 25, 1918 at Quantico, Virginia. Joshua R. Edwards (Father), 1909 Division St., Evansville, Indiana [FAG] [S3]

Edwords, Thomas Franklin, Pvt., 158 Co., Philadelphia, Pennsylvania, DDS, October 5, 1918 at League Island, Philadelphia, Pennsylvania. Edna Boudreau (Sister), Crandall, South Dakota [S3]

Efinger, Joseph Fred, Pvt., 76th Co., 6th Regt., DOW, July 19, 1918 in the Aisne Marne. Mary Efinger (Mother), 320 Broad St., Newark, New Jersey [S2] [SW1]

Eggleston, Claude L., Cpl., Supply Co., 3rd Regt., San Domingo, Domincan Republic, DAS, March 27, 1920 drowned at San Domingo, Dominican Republic. Mahlon C. Eggleston (Father), Terry Island, Florida [S4]

Ehrenhofer, Frank Joseph, Pvt., 82nd Co., 6th Regt., DOW, November 9, 1918 of wounds received in the Aisne Marne at U.S. Naval Hospital, Fort McHenry, Maryland. Joseph Ehrenhofer (Father), 4003 Forest Ave., Kansas City, Missouri [FAG] [S2]

Ehret, Henry S., Jr., 2nd Lt., MCR, Squadron D, FMAF, Miami, Florida, DAS, December 31, 1918 of injuries sustained in an automobile accident at Miami, Florida [S4]

Ehrhardt, Raymond, Pvt., 74th Co., 6th Regt., KIA, June 23, 1918 in the Chateau-Thierry Sector. Charles Scherrer (Uncle),

Marine Corps Deaths, 1917-1921

3300 Walworth Ave., Cincinnnati, Ohio [ABMC-Belleau] [S2] [SW]

Ehrstine, Ohmer Cleveland, Pvt., 79th Co., 6th Regt., DOW, June 6, 1918 in the Chateau-Thierry Sector. Louis C. Ehrstine (Father), 15 Woodward Ave., Dayton, Ohio [ABMC-Belleau TOM] [S2] [SW1 says KIA]

Eigelbach, Martin, Pvt., 76th Co., 6th Regt., DOW, July 20, 1918 in the Aisne Marne. Peter J. Eigelbach (Father), 536 Daxter Ave., Louisville, Kentucky [R] [S2] [SW1]

Eilers, Henry Herman, Gy. Sgt., 67th Co., 5th Regt., KIA, October 6, 1918 in the Aisne Marne. No net of kin given. [ABMC- Romagne] [S2] [SW]

Elastad, Clarence W., Pvt., 16th Co., 5th Regt. KIA [R] [SW1]

Elder, John Oreal, Pvt., NS, Pensacola, Florida, DAS, March 25, 1921 drowned at Pensacola, Florida. Clara Strong Elder (Mother), Lebanon, New York [S4]

Elderson, William Frank, Pvt., 49th Co., 5th Regt., KIA, June 6, 1918 in the Chateau-Thierry Sector. Mary Metzger (Mother), 9515 Fuller Ave., Cleveland, Ohio [ABMC-Belleau TOM] [S2] [SW]

Elgesheiser, William, Pvt., 97th Co., 6th Regt., KIA, July 19, 1918 in the Aisne Marne. Julia Elgesheiser (Mother), 206 Grove St., Brooklyn, New York [S2] [SW]

Ellington, Clifford Henry, Cpl., 75th Co., 6th Regt., KIA, September 13, 1918 in the St. Mihiel Offensive. John M. Rowe (Uncle), R#3, Munford, Alabama [R] [S2] [SW]

Elliott, Barton Wilkinson, Pvt., 8th Co., 5th Regt., DOW, November 4, 1918 in the Meuse Argonne. James Elliott (Father), Elliott Nursery Co., Pittsburgh, Pennsylvania [ABMC-Romagne] [S2] [SW1]

Elliott, Harry William, Cpl., 84th Co., 6th Regt., KIA, June 6, 1918 in the Chateau-Thierry Sector. Betty Elliott (Mother), 312 Hennepin Ave., Minneapolis, Minnesota [ANC] [S2] [SW]

Marine Corps Deaths, 1917-1921

Elliott, Leonard John, Pvt., 78th Co., 6th Regt., DOD, October 20, 1918 in France. Isabell Elliott (Mother), Gen. Delivery, Selma, California [VA-Fort Levenworth] [S2]

Elliott, Seaton Samuel, Pvt., 79th Co., 6th Regt., DOW, October 5, 1918 in the Meuse Argonne. Mrs. Lily Dargan Smith (Sister), 28 Pine St., Petersburg, Virginia [S2] [SW1]

Ellis, Alton Bradford, Pvt., 18th Co., 5th Regt., KIA, June 10, 1918 in the Chateau-Thierry Sector. Albert J. Ellis (Father), North Harwich, Massachusetts [S2] [SW]

Ellis, Joseph Elmer, Pvt., 82nd Co., 6th Regt., KIA, October 4, 1918 in the Meuse Argonne. Della Ellis (Mother), 419 3rd St., Cameron, Missouri [R] [S2] [SW]

Ellsworth, Buster Andrew, Pvt., 43rd Co., 5th Regt., KIA, June 11, 1918 in the Chateau-Thierry Sector. Mrs. Rosa Ellsworth (Mother), 3720 Downing St., Denver, Colorado [S2] [SW]

Elmore, Arthur T., 1st Lieut., 20th Co., 5th Regt., DOW, July 13, 1918 in the Chateau Thierry sector. F. H. Elmore (Father), 425 Walnut St., Philadelphia, Pennsylvania [ANC] [S1] [SW]

Elrod, Robert Gipsy, Pvt., 91st Co., 10th Regt., Quantico, Virginia, DDS, October 14, 1918 at Quantico, Virginia. Mrs. Martha Elrod (Mother), RFD#2, Athens, Georgia [FAG as September 14, 1918] [S3]

Elstad, Clarence Wilhelm, Pvt., 16th Co., 5th Regt., KIA, June 6, 1918 in the Chateau-Thierry Sector. Hans M. Elstad (Father), 916 College Ave., Red Wing, Minnesota [ABMC- Belleau] [S2]

Ely, Robert Lee, Pvt., 49th Co., 5th Regt., DOW, June 20, 1918 in the Chateau-Thierry Sector. J. E. Ely (Father), 1005 Kirby Ave., Chattanooga, Tennessee [ABMC-Belleau TOM] [S2] [SW1 says KIA]

Marine Corps Deaths, 1917-1921

Emerson, William F., Pvt., Co. D, Parris Island, South Carolina, DDS, December 7, 1918 at Parris Island, South Carolina. William M. Emerson (Father), Alvin, Texas [FAG] [S4]

Empey, Hollis Edward, Cpl., 20th Co., 5th Regt., KIA, November 10, 1918 in the Meuse Argonne. Charles Empey (Father), RR#1, Idaho Falls, Idaho [ABMC- Romagne] [S2] [SW1]

Enderle, Charles Edward, Pvt., 79th Co., 6th Regt., KIA, July 19, 1918 in the Aisne Marne. Charles B. Enderle (Father), Dutchtown, Missouri [VA-Jefferson Barracks] [S2] [SW1]

Engel, Orley W., Pvt., Bks. Det., Charleston, South Carolina. DDS, April 12, 1920 at Charleston, South Carolina. Mrs.Minnie Engel (Mother), 2540 6th Ave., Council Bluffs, Iowa [FAG] [S4]

England, John Rollin, Trumpeter, Bks. Det., Norfolk, Virginia, DDS, December 25, 1917 at Norfolk, Virginia. Clarence M. England (Brother), Medina, Ohio [S3]

English, Edgar Harmony, Pvt., 73rd Co., 6th Regt., KIA, November 1, 1918 in the Meuse Argonne. Anna M. English (Mother), RFD#1, bo 87, Greeley, Colorado [S2] [SW1]

Enos, Ray Frederick, Sgt., Co. E, 13th Regt., DOD, September 30, 1918 in France. Christian Enos (Mother), 119½ Brand Blvd., Glendale, California [VA-Fort Rosecrans] [S2]

Enright, George J., Gy. Sgt., MD, Yorktown, Virginia, DOS, July 5, 1920 at Yorktown, Virginia. No next of kin given. [S4]

Eplin, Frank Leiberg, Pvt., 66th Co., 5th Regt., DOW, November 11, 1918 in the Meuse Argonne. Nora E. Eplin (Mother), Box 145, Larchwood, Montana [ABMC- Romagne says Frank Leiber Eplin] [S2] [SW1 says Frank Heiberg Eplin]

Erdman, Ford Eaton, Pvt., 96th Co., 6th Regt., DOW, July 19, 1918 in the Aisne Marne. Joseph W. Erdman (Brother), 1334 Regent Ave., Bond Hill, Cincinnati, Ohio [ABMC- Fere] [S2] [SW1]

Marine Corps Deaths, 1917-1921

Erickson, Donald Edward, Pvt., 20th Co., 5th Regt., DOW, June 13, 1918 in the Chateau-Thierry Sector. Lula A Erickson (Mother), Box 242, Long Beach, California [FAG] [S2] [SW says Daold]

Erickson, Ernest Arnold, Pvt., 78th Co., 6th Regt., KIA, June 14, 1918 in the Chateau-Thierry Sector. Mrs. Clara Lancaster (Mother), Box 33, Curlew, Washington [S2] [SW]

Erickson, Walter E., Cpl., 90th Co., Cuba, DDS, November 20, 1918 at Santiago de Cuba. Mrs. Margaret Erickson (Mother), 722a Fifth Ave., Oakland, California [S4]

Erlando, George Needham, Pvt., 43rd Co., 5th Regt., KIA, June 14, 1918 in the Chateau-Thierry Sector. Arvid G. Erlando (Father), Mt. Vernon, New Hampshire [FAG] [S2] [SW]

Erlandson, Alfred, Cpl., 96th Co., 6th Regt., KIA, October 3, 1918 in the Meuse Argonne. Mrs. Alex LeClaire (Sister), Flat #9, Munger Bldg., 53rd Ave., West Duluth, Minnesota [S2] [SW]

Ernst, Henry A., Pvt., 184th Co., 15th Regt., Quantico, Virginia, DDS, January 16, 1919 at Quantico, Virginia. Charles H. Ernst (Father), Henderson, Colorado [S4]

Ernst, Lawrence Fredinand, Pvt., 67th Co., 5th Regt., KIA, June 14, 1918 in the Chateau-Thierry Sector. Helen Ernst (Mother), East Aurora, New York [S2] [SW says 138th Co.]

Erwin, James Clayton, Pvt., MD, NAD, St. Julien's Creek, Virginia, DDS, October 5, 1918 at Norfolk, Virginia. James Erwin (Father), 1301 Burdette Ave., Cincinnati, Ohio [FAG] [S3]

Erwin, Joseph A., Pvt., 17th Co., 5th Regt., DOW, October 4, 1918 in the Meuse Argonne. Andrew Erwin (Father), 2239 Carter Ave., St. Paul, Minnesota [ABMC- Romagne] [S2] [SW1]

Esslin, Lionel Harold, Pvt., 79th Co., 6th Regt., KIA, June 14, 1918 in the Chateau-Thierry Sector. Frances L. Esslin (Father),

Marine Corps Deaths, 1917-1921

912 Seminole Ave., Detroit, Michigan [ABMC- Belleau] [S2] [SW]

Estes, Jasper Norten, Pvt., 49th Co., 5th Regt., DOW, November 1, 1918 in the Meuse Argonne. Mary L. Estes (Mother), Box 216, Arbuckle, California [S2] [SW1]

Evans, Edward Newton, Cpl., Aero Co., Adv Base, Azores, DOD, October 24, 1918 in the Azores. Mrs. Emma Evans (Mother), Rock Rapids, Iowa [FAG] [S2]

Evans, Lloyd Vincent, Pvt., 73rd Co., 6th Regt., DOW, June 15, 1918 in the Chateau-Thierry Sector. Dexa Evans (Mother), Hamilton, New York [FAG] [S2] [SW]

Evans, Raymond Charles John, Pvt., Co., Q, Parris Island, South Carolina, DDS, November 4, 1918 at Parris Island, South Carolina. Agnes C. Evans (Wife), 554 Hermn St., Philadelphia, Pennsylvania [FAG] [S3]

Evans, Richard Allen, Sgt., 76th Co., 6th Regt., DOW, July 22, 1918 in the Aisne Marne. Etta Evans (Mother), 922 Louisiana St., Richmond, Virginia [R] [S2] [SW]

Evans, Robert Henry, Pvt., 45th Co., 5th Regt., DOW, November 2, 1918 in the Meuse Argonne. Ellen Evans (Mother), 1683 Broadway West, Vancouver, British Columbia, Canada [ANC] [S2] [SW1]

Evans, Walter, Pvt., Supply Co., 4th Regt., Dominican Republic, DAS, May 6, 1921 drowned in the Yaque River, Santiago, Dominican Republic. Elizabeth Evans (Mother), Gen. Del., Wales, Wisconsin [S4]

Evans, William, Pvt., 2109430, 55th Co., 5th Regt., KIA, November 4, 1918 in the Meuse Argonne. Thomas Evans (Father), 514 Emerson Ave, Farrell, Pennsylvania [R] [S2] [SW1]

Evans, William, Pvt., Co. G, Parris Island, South Carolina, DAS, April 17, 1917 drowned at Parris Island, South Carolina. Mrs. Hattie Smith (Aunt), Mark-Center, Ohio [S3]

Marine Corps Deaths, 1917-1921

Evers, Wallace Arthur, Sgt., 45th Co., 5th Regt., DOD, December, 7, 1918 in the Meuse Argonne. Mrs. Helen Breitwisch (Wife), 309½ 25th Ave., Milwaukee, Wisconsin [R] [S2] [SW1 says DOW]

Ewin, Charles W., Gy. Sgt., 10th Squadron, Northern Bombing Group, DOD, October 7, 1918 in England. Clara B. Ewin (Mother), Piasa, Illinois [S2]

Exner, William Paul, Pvt., 49th Co., 5th Regt., DOW, June 17, 1918 in the Chateau-Thierry Sector. Otto E. Exner (Father), 463 Michigan Ave., Buffalo, New York [R] [S2] [SW]

Eynson, Walter Merl, Pvt., 96th Co., 6th Regt., DOW, July 19, 1918 in the Aisne Marne. Stanley M. Eynson (Brother), 929 "N" St., Fresno, California [ANC] [S2] [SW1 says KIA]

Fackrell, Hugh, Pvt., 16th Co., 5th Regt., KIA, June 23, 1918 in the Chateau-Thierry Sector. Eliza Fackrell (Mother), Blackfoot, Idaho [ABMC- Belleau TOM] [S2] [SW1]

Fagan, Joseph Francis, Cpl., 45th Co., 5th Regt., KIA, June 13, 1918 in the Chateau-Thierry Sector. William Fagan (Father), 55 Spencer St., Albany, New York [ABMC-Belleau] [S2] [SW says Eagan]

Fahey, Martin Patrick, Pvt., 47th Co., 5th Regt., DOW, January 1, 1919 in the Meuse Argonne. Mrs. P. Fahey (Mother), 703 Broadway, Louisville, Kentucky [FAG] [S2] [SW1]

Fairchild, Ezra Acle, Pvt., 99th Co., NTS, Newport, Rhode Island, DDS, October 11, 1918 at Newport, Rhode Island. Ruby B. Petteys (Mother), Gen. Del., Tygh Valley, Oregon [FAG] [S3]

Fairclough, Frank Dagnal, Pvt., 49th Co., 5th Regt., KIA, June 6, 1918 in the Chateau-Thierry Sector. Elizabeth Fairclough (Sister), 14 River St., Beacon, New York [ABMC-Belleau] [S2] [SW]

Marine Corps Deaths, 1917-1921

Falkenburg, Albert John, Pvt., Co. E, Parris Island, South Carolina, DDS, May 19, 1917 at Parris Island, South Carolina. Emma Finn (Mother), 1630 Sycamore St., Cincinnati, Ohio [FAG] [S3]

Falling, Carl Valdimer, Pvt., 3rd Regt., 113th Co., 2nd Brigade, Domincan Republic, DOS, January 8, 1918 at Santo Domingo, Domincan Republic. Carl G. Falling (Father), 4 Lund St., Worcester, Massachusetts [S3]

Famea, Patsey, Pvt., 119133, Hdqtrs. Co., 5th Regt., DOD, December, 25, 1918 in France. George Famea (Father), Gioiosa Ionica, Reggio Calabria, Italy [ANC] [S2]

Fankhauser, Adolf, Pvt., Supply Co., 13th Regt., DOD, September 27, 1918 in France. Mrs. Anna Gottlier (Mother), Rushville, Nebraska [R] [S2]

Fanning, William, Pvt., 67th Co., 5th Regt., KIA, June 6, 1918 in the Chateau-Thierry Sector. Patrick Fanning (Brother), 347 Cherry St., New York, New York [S2] [SW]

Fant, Joseph T., Sgt., MB, Puget Sound, Washington, DOS, May 18, 1920 at Puget Sound, Washington. Ebb H. Ogletree (Uncle), Talladega, Alabama [S4]

Farley, Fletcher Lawrence, Pvt., MCR, 51st Co., 5th Regt., KIA, June 27, 1918 in the Chateau-Thierry Sector. Edward Farley (Father), Bancroft, Nebraska [FAG] [S2] [SW says Co. C]

Farley, Leonard Guy, Pvt., 8th Co., 5th Regt., KIA, October 4, 1918 in the Meuse Argonne. Kate Sobel (Mother), 715 7th St., Ogden, Utah [VA-San Francisco] [S2] [SW says 150 Co.]

Farmer, Houston Burleson, Cpl., 17th Co., 5th Regt., DOW, October 4, 1918 in the Meuse Argonne. Maggie Weaver (Mother), 2011 Spencer St., Dallas, Texas [ABMC-Romagne] [S2] [SW1 says KIA]

Marine Corps Deaths, 1917-1921

Farmer, Walter Grant, Pvt., 78th Co., 6th Regt., DOD, October 22, 1918 in the Meuse Argonne. Mollie Farmer (Mother), 427 Crescent St., Walla Walla, Washington [FAG] [S2]

Farmer, William Henry, Pvt., 75th Co., 6th Regt., KIA, July 19, 1918 in the Aisne Marne. John Farmer (Brother), Mason City, Iowa [ABMC- Belleau TOM as W.H.] [S2] [SW]

Farnham, Waldo Harvey, Pvt., 16th Co., 5th Regt., KIA, October 4, 1918 in the Meuse Argonne. Clarissa A. Farnham (Mother), Gen. Del., Waterville, Oregon [R] [S2] [SW says Co. I, 5th Regt.]

Farrant, Oliver Chapman, Sgt., 95th Co., 6th Regt., KIA, July 22, 1918 in the Aisne Marne. Alfred A. Frarrant (Father), 433 Washington St., Dorcester, Massachusetts [ABMC- Suresnes as O.C.] [S2] [SW]

Farrell, Joseph, Pvt., 67th Co., 5th Regt., KIA, June 6, 1918 in the Chateau-Thierry Sector. Andrew Farrell (Father), 2029 S. 66th St., Philadelphia, Pennsylvania [ABMC- Belleau] [S2] [SW]

Farrell, Raymond Francis, Pvt., 55th Co., 5th Regt., DOW, August 8, 1918 in France. Mrs. Carrie Farrell (Aunt), 38 Halstead St., Newton, New Jersey [FAG] [S2] [SW1]

Fasano, Joseph, Pvt., 43rd Co., 5th Regt., KIA, June 11, 1918 in the Chateau-Thierry Sector. Anthony Frasano (Father), 609 E. Second St., Boston, Massachusetts [ABMC- Belleau] [S2] [SW]

Fauble, Arthur Newton, Pvt., 83rd Co., 6th Regt., KIA, June 6, 1918 in the Chateau-Thierry Sector. William Fauble, Jr., (Brother), 912 Broadway, Bedford, Ohio [ABMC- Belleau TOM] [S2] [SW]

Faul, George Alfred, Cpl., Marine Barracks, Washington, D.C., DDS, October 1, 1918 at Washington, D.C. William H. Paul (Father), 850 Sheridan Rd., Wilmette, Illinois [S3]

Marine Corps Deaths, 1917-1921

Fawcette, Allen, Pvt., 102nd Co., New York, New York, DDS, February 2, 1918 at New York, New York. Harry E. King (Uncle), Gen. Del., Carmel, Indiana [FAG] [S3]

Fay, Christopher Ernest, Cpl., 81st Co., 6th MG Bn., KIA, October 3, 1918 in the Meuse Argonne. Christ H. Fay (Father), Stephen, Minnesota [FAG] [S2] [SW says Co. C., 3rd Rep. Btln.]

Fehr, John Dave, Pvt., 20th Co., 5th Regt., DOW, June 26, 1918 in the Chateau-Thierry Sector. Florian Fehr (Brother), 6733 Palatin Ave., Seattle, Washington [ANC] [S2] [SW]

Felker, Charles Leroy, Pvt., 55th Co., 5th Regt., DOW, July 20, 1918 in the Aisne Marne. Rev. Daniel G. Felker (Father), Lincoln Way., Fayetteville, Pennsylvania [R] [S2] [SW1]

Felmet, Ralph, Pvt., 84th Co., 6th Regt., DOW, October 9, 1918 in the Meuse Argonne. William Felmet (Father), 158 Penn Ave., Asheville, North Carolina [FAG] [S2] [SW says 139th Co., 2nd Repl. Btln.]

Fenley, Roscoe Conklin, Pvt., USS *Pittsburg*, DDU, October 25, 1918 on aboard the USS *Pittsburg*. John Fenley (Father), Louisburg, Wisconsin. [S3]

Fennen, Timothy Francis, Pvt., 49th Co., 5th Regt., KIA, November 2, 1918 in the Meuse Argonne. Johanna Fennen (Mother), 6 Garner St., Cohoes, New York [S2] [SW1]

Ferch, Aaron J., 1st Lieut., MCR, 67th Co., 5th Regt., KIA, November 1, 1918 in the Meuse Argonne. George C. Ferch (Brother), 1045 16th Ave., S.E., Minneapolis, Minnesota [ABMC-Romagne] [S1] [SW1]

Ferguson, Cleasant William, Pvt., Co. L, 11th Regt., DOD, February 3, 1919 in France. Racheal E. Freguson (Mother), Naponee, Nebraska [R] [S2]

Ferguson, Thomas John [James], Pvt., Naval Prison, Portsmouth, New Hampshire, DDS, October 2, 1918 at Portsmouth,

Marine Corps Deaths, 1917-1921

New Hampshire. Thomas J. Ferguson (Uncle), Cheyenne, Wyoming [FAG as Thomas James Ferguson] [S3]

Ferguson, Willard F., Pvt., Co. V, Parris Island, South Carolina, DDS, December 10, 1918 at Parris Island, South Carolina. Mrs. Emma Ferguson (Mother), 4918 Aspen St., Philadelphia, Pennsylvania [FAG] [S4]

Ferranti, Ernest Joseph, Pvt., 51st Co., 5th Regt., KIA, June 11, 1918 in the Chateau-Thierry Sector. Frank Ferranti (Father), 30 Copeland St., West Bridgewater, Massachusetts [ABMC- Belleau] [S2] [SW]

Ferrara, Louis Joseph, Pvt., 82nd Co., 6th Regt., DOW, September 21, 1918 in the St. Mihiel. Leano M. Ferrara (Mother), 1834 Dauphine St., New Orleans, Louisiana [ABMC- Thiaucourt] [S2] [SW says Co. C, 3rd Sep. Btln.]

Ferrell, Richard Howard, Pvt., 171st Co., 14th Regt., Quantico, Virginia, DDS, May 27, 1919 at Quantico, Virginia. Mrs. Anna Ferrell (Mother), Little Falls, Minnesota [S4]

Ferris, James, Sgt., MCR, 67th Co., 5th Regt., KIA, November 1, 1918 in the Meuse Argonne. Fannie Ferris (Mother), 181 Earl St., Troy, New York [ABMC- Romagne] [S2] [SW1]

Ferris, Stephen Philip, Cpl., 80th Co., 6th Regt., KIA, October 4, 1918 in the Meuse Argonne. Mrs. Ellen Ferris (Mother), R.R.#23, LaSalle, Illinois [ABMC- Romagne TOM] [S2] [SW says 133rd Repl. Btln.]

Ferris, William Caswell, Cpl., 95th Co., 6th Regt., KIA, June 4, 1918 in the Aisne Defensive. Abraham Ferris (Father), Box 208, New Baltimore, Michigan [R] [S2] [SW]

Ferson, Matthew, Cpl., 93rd Co., 7th Regt., Cuba, DDS, November 20, 1918 at Santiago de Cuba. Mrs. Mary Ferson (Mother), 70 Bigelow St., Pittsburgh, Pennsylvania [S4]

Fiander, Robert, Pvt., MB, Pearl Harbor, Hawaii, DAS, August 4, 1921 of a compound fracture at the base of the skull at Pearl Harbor, Hawaii [S4]

Marine Corps Deaths, 1917-1921

Fichter, Charles Edward, Cpl., 95th Co., 6th Regt., DOW, July 19, 1918 in the Aisne Marne. George Fichter (Father), 711 9th St., Niagara Falls, New York [ABMC- Fere] [S2] [SW1]

Field, Harry James White, Pvt., 49th Co., 5th Regt., KIA, June 6, 1918 in the Chateau-Thierry Sector. Charles W. Field (Father), Hatfield, Pennsylvania [ABMC- Belleau TOM as H.J.W.] [S2] [SW]

Fields, Howard Halestead, Pvt., 97th Co., 6th Regt., DOW, July 19, 1918 in the Aisne Marne. James M. Fields (Father), 1113 Church St., Indianapolis, Indiana [ABMC- Fere] [S2] [SW1]

Fien, Wigbert Anthoy, Pvt., 47th Co., 5th Regt., KIA, June 25, 1918 in the Chateau-Thierry Sector. Mary Fien (Mother), 1094 Lyell Ave., Rochester, New York [R] [S2] [SW]

Fierera, John M., Sgt., Constable Detachment, Haiti, DDS, July 30, 1920 at Cape Haitien, Haiti. Miss Julia Fierera (Sister), 725 N. 17th St., San Jose, California [S4]

Figgins, John Anderson, Pvt., 75th Co., 6th Regt., KIA, July 19, 1918 in the Aisne Marne. Alonzo P. Figgins (Father), 229 Meyers St., Nelsonville, Ohio [ABMC- Fere] [S2] [SW1 says DOW]

Filek, George Edward, Sgt., 75th Co., 6th Regt., DOW, July 19, 1918 in the Aisne Marne. Mary Filek (Mother), 4804 W. Jackson Blvd., Chicago, Illinois [S2] [SW1]

Finch, Earl Atlas, Pvt., Co. B, 2nd Tr. Batt., DOD, October 4, 1918 in France. Mr. Edward Finch (Father), FRD #1, Hume, Michigan [FAG] [S2]

Fine, Correll Leroy, Cpl., Bks. Det., Mare Island, California, DOS, December 10, 1919 of exhaustion from over exposure rescuing two marines from drowning at Mare Island, California. James M. Fine (Father), Gilman, Montana [S4]

Marine Corps Deaths, 1917-1921

Fink, Charles Allen, Pvt., Co. L, 11th Regt., DOD, February 2, 1919 in France. Mr. W. H. Fink (Father), Route #2, Quinter, Kansas [R] [S2]

Finn, James Monroe, Sgt., 96th Co., 6th Regt., DOW, June 19, 1918 in the Chateau-Thierry Sector. James F. Finn (Father), Elmwood, Beaver Co., Oklahoma [FAG] [S2] [SW1]

Finnegan, Gerald Robert, Gy. Sgt., 49th Co., 5th Regt., KIA, June 6, 1918 in the Chateau-Thierry Sector. Mrs. Ellen F. Finnegan (Wife), Suite #1, 60 E. Springfield St., Boston, Massachusetts [ABMC- Belleau] [S2] [SW]

Finney, Emmert Owen, Pvt., 18th Co., 5th Regt., KIA, June 13, 1918 in the Chateau-Thierry Sector. Anna Sparks (Mother), Shelbina, Missouri [S2] [SW]

Finzer, Emanuel R., Cpl., Bks. Det., Philadelphia, Pennsylvania, DDS, December 28, 1918 at Philadelphia, Pennsylvania. Mrs. Esther L. Finzer (Wife), Post Office, Sugar Creek, Ohio [S4]

Fischer, Herman Edward, Pvt., 81st Co., 6th MG Bn., KIA, June 15, 1918 in the Chateau-Thierry Sector. George A. Fischer (Father), O'Fallon, Illinois [R] [S2] [SW]

Fischer, Robert McCaughlin, Cpl., 20th Co., 5th Regt., KIA, June 6, 1918 in the Chateau-Thierry Sector. Minna Fischer (Aunt), 2113 Harriet Ave., Minneapolis, Minnesota [ABMC- Belleau] [S2] [SW]

Fish, Clarence Edgar, Pvt., Co. F, 11th Regt., DOD, November 25, 1918 in France. Harvey Fish (Father), 56 E. 8th Ave., Gloversville, New York [ABMC- Thiaucourt] [S2]

Fish, Gerald Ellison, Pvt., 67th Co., 5th Regt., KIA, July 18, 1918 in the Aisne Marne. Edith Fish (Mother), RD#1, Pittsford, Michigan [ABMC- Fere] [S2] [SW says Casualty Co., 4th Repl. Btln.]

Marine Corps Deaths, 1917-1921

Fisher, Arthur J., Cpl., 29th Co., 4th Prov. Regt., San Domingo, DDS, December 31, 1918 at San Domingo. Mrs. Sarah Fisher (Mother), Arapahoe, Nebraska [S4]

Fisher, James Edward, Pvt., 67th Co., 5th Regt., KIA, June 6, 1918 in the Chateau-Thierry Sector. William Fisher (Father), 2396 Louden Ave., Columbus, Ohio [ABMC- Belleau] [S2] [SW]

Fisher, James Owen, Pvt., 79th Co., 6th Regt., DOD, March 2, 1919 in France. John Fischer (Father), 770 Elmwood Ave., Buffalo, New York [R] [S2]

Fisher, John Eli, Pvt., 75th Co., 6th Regt., KIA, June 10, 1918 in the Chateau-Thierry Sector. Loetta Fisher (Mother), Gen. Del., Carrollton, Illinois [FAG] [S2] [SW]

Fisher, Roland, Cpl., 51st Co., 5th Regt., DOD, February 23, 1919 in France. Henry Fisher (Father), Ingleside, Nebraska [ANC] [S2]

Fisher, Terry Leonard, Pvt., 20th Co., 5th Regt., KIA, April 22, 1918 in the Toulon Sector, Verdun. W. J. Fisher (Father), Royce City, Texas [ANC] [S2] [SW]

Fisher, Thomas L., Cpl., Navy Yard, Puget Sound, Washington, DDS, November 16, 1918 at Puget Sound, Washington. Mrs. Nina Spangler (Sister), Lometa, Texas [FAG] [S4]

Fitzgerald, Thomas John, Cpl., 47th Co., 5th Regt., KIA, November 1, 1918 in the Meuse Argonne. John J. Fitzgerald (Father), 4 W. 104th St., New York, New York [ABMC- Romagne TOM as T.J.] [S2] [SW1]

Fitzpatrick, Melvin Reinsford, Pvt., 85th Co., Arty. Batt., Quantico, Virginia, DDS, September 26, 1918 at Quantico, Virginia. Samuel Fitzpatrick (Father), Yellsville, Arkansas [S3]

Fitzsimmons, Walter J., Pvt., MD,. USS *New York*, DAS, September 17, 1920 of electric shock at Pearl Harbor, Hawaii. Mrs. May Fitzsimmons (Mother), 804 Ridgely St., Baltimore, Maryland [S4]

Marine Corps Deaths, 1917-1921

Flagler, Clifton, Pvt., 55th Co., 5th Regt., KIA, June 8, 1918 in the Chateau-Thierry Sector. Mrs. Irene Flagler (Mother), Berne, New York [R] [S2] [SW]

Flaherty, John Vincent, Pvt., 67th Co., 5th Regt., KIA, July 18, 1918 in the Aisne Marne. Catherine Flaherty (Mother), 216 12th St., N. Great Falls, Montana [FAG] [S2] [SW1]

Flaherty, William Joseph, Cpl., 67th Co., 5th Regt., KIA, June 6, 1918 in the Chateau-Thierry Sector. Bridget Flaherty (Mother), 4241 Desoto Ave., St. Louis, Missouri [S2] [SW]

Flanagan, James Daniel, Pvt., 79th Co., 6th Regt., DOD, December, 22, 1918 in France. Mrs. Emma Flanagan (Mother), 336 Dean St., Brooklyn, New York [FAG] [S2]

Flanagan, James Patrick, Pvt., 2473306, Co. H, 335inf, DOW, September 16, 1918 in the St. Mihiel Offensive. Mrs. Mary Smithhisler (Sister), 1302 Edmonton Rd., Cleveland, Ohio [ANC] [S2] [SW says 134th Co., 2nd Repl. Btln.]

Flanagan, Joseph Martin, Pvt., 83rd Co., 6th Regt., DOW, June 4, 1918 in the Aisne Defensive. Mary Flanagan (Mother), Bellewood Ave., Bellewood, Illinois [R] [S2] [SW]

Flanagan, William Bryan, Pvt., 75th Co., 6th Regt., DOW, June 30, 1918 in the Chateau-Thierry Sector. Nancy Tannehill (Mother), Gilford, Missouri [FAG] [S2] [SW]

Fleet, Frederick William, Pvt., 76th Co., 6th Regt., DOW, November 1, 1918 in the Meuse Argonne. Mrs. Margaret Fleet (Mother), 425 Pasedena Ave., Youngstown, Ohio [S2] [SW1]

Flegal, Russell Cole, Pvt., 74th Co., 6th Regt., KIA, October 7, 1918 in the Meuse Argonne. Harvey J. Flegal (Father), Clearfield, Pennsylvania [FAG] [S2] [SW]

Flemming, Arthur William, Pvt., 43rd Co., 5th Regt., KIA, June 12, 1918 in the Chateau-Thierry Sector. William F.

Marine Corps Deaths, 1917-1921

Fleming (Father), 1115 Chateau St., N.S., Pittsburgh, Pennsylvania [ANC] [S2] [SW]

Flick, Frederick Sherman, Pvt., 95th Co., 6th Regt., KIA, June 12, 1918 in the Chateau-Thierry Sector. Marie A. Flick (Widow), 2504 N. Opal St., Philadelphia, Pennsylvania [ABMC- Belleau] [S2] [SW says 139th Co.]

Flinn, John Evan, Sgt., 47th Co., 5th Regt., KIA, October 4, 1918 in the Meuse Argonne. John W. Flinn (Father), Corpus Christi, Texas [FAG] [S2] [SW] [SW1 says Flynn]

Florence, Tullie, Pvt., 95th Co., 6th Regt., DOD, February 16, 1919 in France. M. Florence (Father), RFD #3, Fate, Rockwell, Texas [FAG] [S2]

Florian, Frederick William, Jr., Pvt., 45th Co., 5th Regt., KIA, June 6, 1918 in the Chateau-Thierry Sector. Madame F. W. Florian (Widow), Avenue de Neuily, 140 bis, Neuilly-sur-Seine, France [ABMC- Belleau] [S2] [SW]

Flowers, John, Pvt., 43rd Co., 5th Regt., KIA, June 11, 1918 in the Chateau-Thierry Sector. Mrs. Anna Flowers (Mother), Olive Branch, Mississippi [R] [S2] [SW]

Floyd, Louie, Pvt., 95th Co., 6th Regt., DOD, September 23, 1918 in France. Elizabeth Floyd (Mother), Kerrville, Texas [FAG] [S2]

Flynn, Francis Joseph, Gy. Sgt., 20th Co., 5th Regt., KIA, June 6, 1918 in the Chateau-Thierry Sector. Elizabeth Flynn (Mother), 512 Chenango St., Binghampton, New York [S2] [SW]

Flynn, Harry, Pvt., 67th Co., 5th Regt., KIA, June 6, 1918 in the Chateau-Thierry Sector. Leo Flynn (Brother), c/o Postmaster, San Francisco, California USS *New Mexico*, Box 10 [FAG] [S2] [SW]

Fogelstad, Elmer, Pvt., 79th Co., 6th Regt., KIA, June 6, 1918 in the Chateau-Thierry Sector. John Fogelstad (Father), 3745 Palmer St., Chicago, Illniois [ABMC- Fere] [S2] [SW]

Marine Corps Deaths, 1917-1921

Fogle, Lester Alvin, Pvt., USS *New York*, DDS, February 9, 1920 at Puget Sound, Washington. Harry M. Fogle (Father), Daphna, Virginia [VA-San Francisco] [S4]

Fogt, Robert Comer, Pvt., MCR, MB, Key West, Florida, DDS, August 27, 1918 at Key West, Florida. Beulah Fogt (Mother), Box 16, Anna, Shelby Co., Ohio [FAG] [S3]

Forbach, Richard Frank, Pvt., 67th Co., 5th Regt., KIA, October 4, 1918 in the Meuse Argonne. Christ Forbach (Father), 204 French St., Buffalo, New York [ABMC- Romagne] [S2] [SW]

Forbes, Edward Paul, Pvt., 20th Co., 5th Regt., KIA, June 25, 1918 in the Chateau-Thierry Sector. Jesse R. Forbes (Father), 317 N. Division Ave., Sterling, Colorado [FAG] [S2] [SW]

Ford, Charles Louis, Pvt., MCR, Co. D, Mare Island, California, DDS, November 21, 1917 at Mare Island, California. Sidney E. Mayer (Nephew), 3796 Hugo Ave., San Diego, California [FAG] [S3]

Ford, Daniel, Pvt., 8th Co., 5th Regt., KIA, October 4, 1918 in the Meuse Argonne. Mary Ford (Mother), 327 N. Hoback St., Helena, Montana [ABMC- Romagne] [S2] [SW1]

Ford, Roy Joshua, Pvt., 49th Co., 5th Regt., KIA, June 6, 1918 in the Chateau-Thierry Sector. Mrs. Mary J. Ford (Mother), 1320 Lafayette St., Kansas City, Kansas [ABMC-Belleau] [S2] [SW]

Ford, William Lawrence, Pvt., 55th Co., 5th Regt., KIA, November 10, 1918 in the Meuse Argonne. Mrs. Adelaide Ford (Mother), c/o E. J. Ford, 51 Broadway, New York, New York [R] [S2] [SW1]

Fore, Birdo, Pvt., Co. A, 11th Regt., DOD, February 8, 1919 in France. Sara H. Fore (Mother), 104 B. St., Bemis, Tennessee [FAG] [S2]

Fore, Wiley David, Pvt., 47th Co., 5th Regt., KIA, June 6, 1918 in the Chateau-Thierry Sector. Warren S. Fore (Brother),

Marine Corps Deaths, 1917-1921

229 N. Church St., Brockhave, Mississippi [ABMC-Belleau] [S2] [SW]

Foren, Irving Walter, Pvt., 20th Co., 5th Regt., KIA, June 6, 1918 in the Chateau-Thierry Sector. Mrs. Laura Thomas (Mother), 2942 Madeline St., Oakland, California [VA-San Fransisco] [S2] [SW1]

Formall, John, Cpl., 74th Co., 6th Regt., DOW, April 18, 1918 in the Toulon Sector, Verdun. Jennie Formall (Sister), 19 Sylvan St., Detroit, Michigan [ABMC- Romagne] [S2] [SW]

Forrest, Michael Dinan, Pvt., 84th Co., 6th Regt., KIA, July 19, 1918 in the Aisne Marne. Rose Forrest (Mother), 3644 Blaine Ave., St. Louis, Missouri [R] [S2] [SW1]

Forristall, Early Orlando, Pvt., Co. A, 13th Regt., DOD, September 24, 1918 enroute to France. Olando Forristall (Father), Box 161, Sulphur Springs, Arkansas [R] [S2]

Forse, Floyd Arthur, Cpl., 97th Co., 6th Regt., DOW, October 3, 1918 in the Meuse Argonne. Thomas B. Forse (Brother), Chireno, Texas [FAG] [S2] [SW]

Forsythe, Jasper Paul, Pvt., 132nd Co., Quantico, Virginia, DDS, September 24, 1918 at Quantico, Virginia. Martha Clay (Mother), 315 Lee St., Garrett, Indiana [S3]

Fossett, Edward Alexander, Cpl., Hdqtrs. Det., 1st Regt., Philadelphia, Pennsylvania, DDS, March 9, 1918 at Philadelphia, Pennsylvania. Edna Fossett (Wife), 436 N. Vermont Ave., Atlantic City, New Jersey [FAG] [S3]

Foster, David Burton, Cpl., 43rd Co., 5th Regt., KIA, June 12, 1918 in the Chateau-Thierry Sector. Mr. J. D. Foster (Father), 227 6th Ave., McKeesport, Pennsylvania [S2] [SW]

Foster, Floyd Abraham, Pvt., 66th Co., 5th Regt., DOW, July 18, 1918 in the Aisne Marne. Marous C. Foster (Father), R#4, Belle rive, Illinois [ANC] [S2] [SW1 says KIA]

Marine Corps Deaths, 1917-1921

Foster, Sylvan L., Pvt, Co. B, Mare Island, California, DDS, November 27, 1919 at Mare Island, California. S. L. Marney (Friend), Gen. Del., Drummond, Oklahoma [S4]

Foster, Thomas Patrick, Pvt., Gd. Det., MB, Navy Yard, Philadelphia, Pennsylvania, DDS, October 28, 1920 at League Island, Pennsylvania. Lollota M. Foster (Wife), 614 Edwards St., Portsmouth, Virginia [FAG] [S4]

Fournier, Emile Alfred, Pvt., MB, New Orleans, Louisana, DOS, February 12, 1921 at New Orleans, Louisana. Mrs. Marie Fournier (Mother), 111 Cypress St., Manistee, Michigan [S4]

Fountain, James Merle, Pvt., 55th Co., 5th Regt., DOW, October 5, 1918 in the Meuse Argonne. Mrs. Georgia E. Fountain (Mother), c/o D. H. Foutain, Walterville, Oregon [FAG] [S2] [SW]

Fowler, Mark Perrin, Pvt., 51st Co., 5th Regt., KIA, November 4, 1918 in the Meuse Argonne. Emma J. Fowler (Mother), Blue Mountain, Mississippi [ANC] [S2] [SW1]

Fowler, Robert Carl, Pvt., 45th Co., 5th Regt., DOW, June 29, 1918 in the Chateau-Thierry Sector. Robert L. Fowler (Father), Route No. 2, Woodbury, Georgia [ANC] [S2] [SW1 says KIA]

Fox, Frederick Hamilton, Cpl., 67th Co., 5th Regt., KIA, June 6, 1918 in the Chateau-Thierry Sector. Esther E. Fox (Mother), 1155 W. Kensington Rd., Los Angeles, California [ANC] [S2] [SW]

Fox, Julius Joseph, Pvt., 80th Co., 6th Regt., KIA, July 19, 1918 in the Aisne Marne. Caroline Fox (Mother), 1220 Missouri Ave., St. Louis, Missouri [S2] [SW1]

Fox, William McKinley, Pvt., 84th Co., 6th Regt., KIA, July 22, 1918 in the Aisne Marne. Mrs. Fannie Fox (Mother), 2705 Arlington Ave., St. Louis, Missouri [VA-Jefferson Barracks] [S2] [SW]

Marine Corps Deaths, 1917-1921

Fradette, Edward Arthur, Pvt., 158th Co., Philadelphia, Pennsylvania, DDS, October 5, 1918 at Philadelphia, Pennsylvania. Donald Fradette (Father), 77 Erb St., Buffalo, New York [S3]

Fralick, Leslie William, Pvt., 84th Co., 6th Regt., DOD, March 21, 1919 in France. Mrs. Flora Garron (Mother), 16 Willow Ave., Somerille, Massachusetts [S2]

Francois, Joseph Christopher, Pvt., 23rd Co., 6th MG Bn., KIA, November 5, 1918 in the Meuse Argonne. Katherine Francois (Mother), 422 Blair St., St. Paul, Minnesota [R] [S2] [SW1]

Franczek, Frank William, Cpl., 43rd Co., 5th Regt., DOW, June 10, 1918 in the Chateau-Thierry Sector. William F. Franczek (Father), P. O. Box 105, Chicopee, Massachusetts [S2] [SW]

Franko, John Andrew, Pvt., 45th Co., 5th Regt., DOW, October 4, 1918 in the Meuse Argonne. John Franko (Father), Train Ave., 91 Poprad, Spiska Zupa, Slovakia, Europe [ANC] [S2] [SW1]

Frankum, Dale Evans, Pvt., Co. A, OSD, Quantico, Virginia, DDS, October 29, 1918 at Utica, New York. Belle Frankum (Mother), Quitman, Missouri [S3]

Frantz, Glenn, Pvt., 67th Co., 5th Regt., DOW, July 18, 1918 in the Aisne Marne. Kate Frantz (Mother), 109 Livingston St., Peoria, Illinois [FAG] [S2] [SW]

Fraser, Gilbert Duncan, Pvt., 18th Co., 5th Regt., DOW, June 12, 1918 in the Chateau-Thierry Sector. John D. Fraser (Not stated), Box 691, New London, Connecticut [ABMC-Belleau] [S2] [SW1 says KIA]

Fraser, Gordon McK., Pvt., Co. B, 2nd Sep. Batt., Quantico, Virginia, DDS, November 19, 1918 at Quantico, Virginia. Robert L. Fraser (Father), 58 Sidney St., Dorchester, Massachusetts [S4]

Marine Corps Deaths, 1917-1921

Fravell, Guy, Pvt., 67th Co., 5th Regt., KIA, June 6, 1918 in the Chateau-Thierry Sector. Edward Fravell (Father), Orient, Illinois [S2] [SW]

Frazer, Homer Campbell, Trp, 34th Replacement Bn., DOD, February 16, 1918 on the *Von Steuben* enroute to France. John H. Frazer (Father), 733 South Ave., Rochester, New York [FAGM] [S2]

Frazer, James Noble, Pvt., Hdqtrs. Co., 6th Regt., DOW, July 19, 1918 in the Aisne Marne. Annabelle Frazer (Mother), RFD#5, Grand Ledge, Michigan [S2] [SW1]

Frazer, Rollo Houston, Sgt., 78th Co., 6th Regt., KIA, October 4, 1918 in the Meuse Argonne. Hough Nickel Frazer (Father), 403 Marquerite Ave., Portland, Oregon [ABMC- Romagne] [S2] [SW]

Frazier, Walter D., 2nd Lieut., 49th Co., 5th Regt., KIA, June 5, 1918 in the Aisne defensive. W.A. Frazier (Father), 6414 Dean St., Pittsburgh, Pennsylvania [ANC] [S1] [SW]

Frazier, Walter Elmer, Pvt., R.R., Wakefield, Massachusetts, DAS, August 15, 1921 killed in an automobile accident at Reading, Wakefield Rd., Massachusetts. Mrs. Ruth Frazier (Mother), Dana, Indiana [S4]

Fredenburg, Clarence Kenneth, Pvt., 79th Co., 6th Regt., DOW, October 4, 1918 in the Meuse Argonne. Frank Fredenburg (Father), 122 Main St., Groveland, New York [R] [S2] [SW1]

Frederick, Harvey, Pvt., MB, Navy Yard, Washington, D.C., DDS, April 12, 1918 at Washington, D.C. Otto Frederick (Father), 119 15th St., South Side, Pittsburg, Pennsylvania [S3]

Freeman, Clare Lawrence, Pvt., 84th Co., 6th Regt., KIA, October 9, 1918 in the Meuse Argonne. Nellie Freeman (Mother), RFD#2, Corning, New York [ABMC- Romagne] [S2] [SW1]

Marine Corps Deaths, 1917-1921

Freeman, Morse, Pvt., Co. B, 11th Regt., Quantico, Virginia, DDS, October 4, 1918 at Quantico, Virginia. Franklin Freeman (Father), 79 Orchard St., Leominster, Massachusetts [FAG as August 4, 1918] [S3]

Freer, Milton Glen, Pvt., Co. L, 13th Regt., DOD, September 25, 1918 enroute to France. George F. Freer (Father), RFD#1, Lockport, New York [FAG] [S2]

Frehse, Charles John, Pvt., 45th Co., 5th Regt., KIA, June 6, 1918 in the Chateau-Thierry Sector. Lillian Morris (Mother), Saugatuck, Michigan [ABMC- Belleau] [S2] [SW]

French, Andy S., Pvt., NP, Portsmouth, New Hampshire, DDS, February 25, 1919 at Portsmouth, New Hampshire. Mrs. Doshie French (Mother), Fitzhugh, Arkansas [FAG] [S4]

French, Herbert Roy, Pvt., 15th Co., 6th MG Bn., KIA, October 7, 1918 in the Meuse Argonne. Mrs. Anna B. Porter (Mother), 2417 E. 7th Ave., Spokane, Washington [VA- San Fransisco] [S2] [SW1]

Frick, Roy Victor, Pvt., Bks. Det., New York, N.Y., DDS, April 1, 1918 in the U.S. Naval Hospital, New York, New York. Ethel Frick (Sister), Gen. Del., Medford, Oregon [VA-Cypress Hills] [S3]

Friedman, Harry Samuel, Sgt., 97th Co., 6th Regt., KIA, October 4, 1918 in the Meuse Argonne. Celia Friedman (Mother), 54 Broadway, Arlington, Boston, Massachusetts [ABMC-Romagne] [S2] [SW]

Fritz, Charles Louis, Cpl., 43rd Co., 5th Regt., DOW, November 5, 1918 in the Meuse Argonne. John F. Fritz (Father), 658 Poplar St., Lancaster, Pennsylvania [ABMC- Romagne] [S2] [SW1]

Fritz, Louis Henry, Cpl., 76th Co., 6th Regt., DOW, November 4, 1918 in the Meuse Argonne. Helen F. Fritz (Wife), 415 Front St., Barea, Ohio [ABMC-Romagne] [S2] [SW1]

Frock, Maurice Edward, Pvt., 43rd Co., 5th Regt., KIA, June 12, 1918 in the Chateau-Thierry Sector. Jacob B. Frock

Marine Corps Deaths, 1917-1921

(Father), 64 Bellevue Ave., Hagerstown, Maryland [ABMC- Romagne TOM] [S2] [SW]

Frost, George Lee, Sgt., 75th Co., 6th Regt., DOW, November 1, 1918 in the Meuse Argonne. Mrs. Caroline F. Lyman (Sister), 600 Broadway, Hastings-on-Hudson, New York [ABMC- Romagne] [S2] [SW1]

Fry, Edwin Emerson, Pvt., Co. L, 13th Regt., DOD, September 24, 1918 enroute to France. Rose Fry (Mother), 1435 Third St., S.E., Canton, Ohio [R] [S2]

Fry, Lee Lincoln, Pvt., 20th Co., 5th Regt., KIA, June 6, 1918 in the Chateau-Thierry Sector. Mrs. John J. Fry (Mother), 1172 Boise St., New E. 39th St., Portland, Oregon [ANC] [S2] [SW]

Frye, Charles Loring, Pvt., 82nd Co., 6th Regt., KIA, November 6, 1918 in the Meuse Argonne. Levina R. Frye (Mother), 1119 W. 32nd St., Minneapolis, Minnesota [R] [S2] [SW1]

Fugate, Jesse H., Jr., Captain, 4th Prov. Regt., Domincan Republic, DDS, January 9, 1919 at Santo Domingo, Dominican Republic. Mr. Jesse H. Fugate (Father), Radford, Virginia [ANC] [S4]

Fuhrman, Charles R., Cpl., Squardron D, Aviation, Domincan Republic, DAS, May 30, 1920 drowned in the Ozama River, Dominican Republic. Grant M. Fuhrman (Father), RFD#2, Columbia, Ohio [S4]

Fuller, Edward C., Capt., 75th Co., 6th Regt., KIA, June 13, 1918 in the Chateau Thierry sector. Colonel B. H. Fuller, USMC (Father), First Brigade, Port au Prince, Republic of Haiti [USNA Annapolis] [S1] [SW] [Note: USS Fuller (DD-297) was named for Captain Fuller]

Fullerton, Daniel, Gy. Sgt., Flying Field, Quantico, Virginia, DAS, February 20, 1920 accidentally drowned at Quantico, Virginia. Miss Mary Hoch (Friend), 128 Montague St., Brooklyn, New York [VA-ANC as February 28, 1920] [S4]

Marine Corps Deaths, 1917-1921

Fullerton, Oren, Pvt., Co. A, Mare Island, California, DDS, June 2, 1918 at Mare Island, California. Alice C. Fullerton (Mother), RFD#4, Dayton, Washington [S3]

Fulmer, Clifford John, Pvt., 67th Co., 5th Regt., KIA, June 6, 1918 in the Chateau-Thierry Sector. May Fulmer (Mother), Sanger St., Oneida County, Waterville, New York [S2] [SW]

Fulton, John Hugh, Pvt., Co. B, MB, Navy Yard, Mare Island, DAS, March 6, 1921 of a fractured skull at Mare Island, California. Mira L. Fulton (Mother), RFD#3, Wenatchee, Washington [FAG] [S4]

Fulwiler, John Linton, Pvt., 82nd Co., 6th Regt., DOW, October 7, 1918 in the Meuse Argonne. Fannie Fulwiler (Mother), 01624 Ash St., Spokane, Washington [S2] [SW1]

Funkhouser, Edward R., Pvt., Co. B, OSD, Quantico, Virginia, DDS, March 7 1919 at Quantico, Virginia. Mrs. Caroline Funkhouser (Mother), 4610 Hazel Ave., Chicago, Illinois [S4]

Fuqua, Claude, Cpl., 66th Co., 5th Regt., KIA, June 6, 1918 in the Chateau-Thierry Sector. John Smith (Grandfather) Burlington, North Carolina [ABMC- Belleau] [S2] [SW]

Fussinger, Arthur, Pvt., Mar. Det., Azores, DOO, June 16, 1919 at Ponta del Gada, Azores. Joseph Fussinger (Father), 46 McCracken Ave., Clifton, Newport, Kentucky [S4]

Gabel, Philip Garfield, Pvt., 79th Co., 6th Regt., KIA, July 19, 1918 in the Aisne Marne. George Cabel (Father), 1099 Eighth St., N. Portland, Oregon [ABMC-Belleau TOM] [S2] [SW1]

Gaddis, George Dewey, Pvt., 49th Co., 5th Regt., DOW, June 20, 1918 in the Chateau-Thierry Sector. Mrs. Esther Gaddis (Mother), RFD#5, Dahlonego, Georgia [ANC] [S2] [SW1 says KIA]

Marine Corps Deaths, 1917-1921

Gaden, Alexander, Pvt., Bks. Det., Norfolk, Virginia, DDS, March 24, 1918 at Norfolk, Virginia. Benedict Gaden (Father), 1 Walter St., Schenectady, New York [S3]

Gaffey, Frank Patrick, Pvt., 78th Co., 6th Regt., DOW, July 19, 1918 in the Aisne Marne. Wiliam H. Gaffey (Father), Easton, Minnesota [FAG] [S2] [SW1]

Gahr, Albert Leroy, Pvt., 47th Co., 5th Regt., DOW, June 7, 1918 in the Chateau-Thierry Sector. Mrs. LaBelle L. Gahr (Mother), 308 Ninth Ave., Dayton, Kentucky [S2] [SW1]

Gall, Paul William, Pvt., 17th Co., 5th Regt., KIA, June 15, 1918 in the Chateau-Thierry Sector. Mr. J. Gall (Father), 519 Lincoln Ave., Dolton, Illinois [ABMC- Belleau TOM] [S2] [SW]

Galland, Ernest Abijah, Cpl., 84th Co., 6th Regt., KIA, November 1, 1918 in the Meuse Argonne. Cora Galland (Mother), Salix, Iowa [FAG] [S2] [SW1]

Gallant, Alfred James, Pfc, 19th Co., HAF, Quantico, Virginia, DDS, September 25, 1918 at Quantico, Virginia. Mrs. Jessie Gallant (Mother), 23 Key St., Eastport, Maine [S3]

Galloway, T. Z., 1st Sgt., Bks., Quantico, Virginia, DDS, January 28, 1919 at Quantico, Virginia. Mrs. Susan Galloway (Mother), RFD#1, Mayfield, Kentucky [FAG as T. A.] [S4]

Gallup, Harley Berton, Pvt., 49th Co., 5th Regt., KIA, October 4, 1918 in the Meuse Argonne. William Gallup (Father), New England, North Dakota [ABMC- Romagne] [S2] [SW1]

Galusha, Ivan H., Drumer, Bks. Det., Fort Lyon, Colorado, DDS, December 3, 1918 at Fort Lyon, Colorado. Mr. Luman F. Galusha (Father), 290 East Market St., Corning, New York [FAG] [S4]

Gandy, Tony Louis, Pvt., 75th Co., 6th Regt., DOW, September 14, 1918 in the St. Mihiel Offensive. Rose G. Williams (Mother), Albion, Indiana [FAG] [S2] [SW1]

Marine Corps Deaths, 1917-1921

Gann, Birt D., Sgt., 67th Co., 5th Regt., DOW, November 4, 1918 in the Meuse Argonne. Nancy M. Gann (Mother), 2506 N. Central Ave., Knoxville, Tennessee [ABMC-Romagne] [S2] [SW1]

Gardner, John Martin, Cpl., 74th Co., 6th Regt., DOW, April 30, 1918 in the Toulon Sector, Verdun. Rufus Gardner (Father), Dunn, North Carolina [ABMC- Romagne] [S2] [SW]

Gardner, Verne Wilson, Pvt., 47th Co., 5th Regt., KIA, June 6, 1918 in the Chateau-Thierry Sector. John N. Gardner (Father), 315 Machesa Bldg., New Orleans, Louisana [ABMC- Belleau] [S2] [SW]

Garity, Joseph Bernard, Jr., Pvt., 78th Co., 6th Regt., DOW, September 16, 1918 in the St. Mihiel Offensive. Barbara M. Garity (Mother), Mt. Olivet Ave., Maspeth, New York [S2] [SW]

Garner, Harvey Edward, Pvt., 76th Co., 6th Regt., KIA, November 1, 1918 in the Meuse Argonne. Mrs. Delia B. Garner (Mother), 27 E. Montgomery St., Baltimore, Maryland [FAG] [S2] [SW1]

Garnier, Earle W., Pvt., Bks. Det., Pearl Harbor, Territory of Hawaii, DDS, January 27, 1920 at Pearl Harbor, Territory of Hawaii. Mrs. Clara Lucy Garnier (Mother), 119 North 13th St., Colorado Springs, Colorado [S4]

Garrett, Claude C., Pvt., Bks. Det., Quantico, Virginia, DDS, December 2, 1918 at Quantico, Virginia. Mrs. Oria W. Garrett (Mother), 317 West Third St., Garnett, Kansas [FAG] [S4]

Garrett, Thomas Earl, Jr., Pvt., 96th Co., 6th Regt., KIA, July 19, 1918 in the Aisne Marne. T. E. Garrett (Father), Box 751, Teague, Texas [FAG] [S2] [SW says 144th Co., 3rd Repl. Btln.]

Garrett, William Marvin, Pvt., 74th Co., 6th Regt., KIA, June 14, 1918 in the Chateau-Thierry Sector. Thomas Garrett (Father), RFD#4, Ripley, Tennessee [S2] [SW]

Marine Corps Deaths, 1917-1921

Garrison, Ed Theron, Pvt., 74th Co., 6th Regt., KIA, July 19, 1918 in the Aisne Marne. Zeb V. Garrison (Father), Route #2, Keener, Alabama [ABMC- Belleau TOM] [S2] [SW]

Garrison, John Newton, Pvt., 49th Co., 5th Regt., KIA, November 1, 1918 in the Meuse Argonne. Samantha Garrison (Mother), Castle Rock, Colorado [ABMC- Romagne] [S2] [SW1]

Garvey, Claude Revere, Pvt., 49th Co., 5th Regt., DOW, June 16, 1918 in the Chateau-Thierry Sector. William F. Garvey (Father), 4041 Humboldt Ave., Minneapolis, Minnesota [R] [S2] [SW1]

Garvey, Edward Joseph, Pvt., 84th Co., 6th Regt., DOW, July 19, 1918 in the Aisne Marne. James F. Garvey (Father), 78 Libert St., Binghampton, New York [ABMC- Belleau TOM] [S2] [SW1 says KIA]

Gary, Marion, Pvt., 73rd Co., 6th Regt., DOW, June 15, 1918 in the Chateau-Thierry Sector. Fannie Gary (Mother), Tahoka, Texas [ABMC- Belleau] [S2] [SW]

Gassert, Howell A., 2nd Lieut., 18th Co., 5th Regt., DOC, May 16, 1918 in France. Mrs. Phebe J. Lynch (Mother), Port Jefferson, New York [R] [S1]

Gates, Walter W., Pvt., 44th Co., 3rd Regt., Dominican Republic, DOS, June 12, 1919 at Lapuja, Dominican Republic. Silas Gates (Father), 413 West Maryland Ave., Evansville, Indiana [FAG] [S4]

Gault, Edwin LeRoy, Sgt., 95th Co., 6th Regt., KIA [SW] [SW1 reported to have been found alive]

Gaume, Victor, Pvt., Hdqtrs. Co., 5th Regt., DOW, November 1, 1918 in the Meuse Argonne. Martha Hayes Gaume (Mother), Gen. Del., Winlock, Washington [VA-Custer] [S2] [SW1]

Geary, William Joseph, Sgt Maj., Hdqtrs. Co., 4th Brigade, KIA, June 25, 1918 in the Chateau-Thierry Sector. Mrs.

Marine Corps Deaths, 1917-1921

Claudia E. Geary (Mother), 49 T St., N.W., Washington, D.C. [FAG] [S2] [SW]

Gee, David Casper, Drm, 51st Co., 5th Regt., DOW, June 11, 1918 in the Chateau-Thierry Sector. J. H. Gee (Father), RFD#3, Tampa, Florida [ANC] [S2] [SW1]

Gehlert, Edward Clarence, Pvt., 45th Co., 5th Regt., KIA, April 20, 1918 in the Toulon Sector, Verdun. Marion E. Gehlert (Mother), 5703 Tompkins Ave., Madisonville, Ohio [FAG] [S2] [SW]

Geho, David William, Pvt., 97th Co., 6th Regt., KIA, November 5, 1918 in the Meuse Argonne. Thomas Geho (Father), Bellton, West Virginia [FAG] [S2] [SW1]

Gehrke, Emil Henry, Pvt., 82nd Co., 6th Regt., KIA, April 1, 1918 in the Toulon Sector, Verdun. William Gehrke (Father), Arbor Vitae, Wisconsin [FAG] [S2] [SW]

Geiger, Harold Clifford, Pvt., 47th Co., 5th Regt., DOW, June 16, 1918 in the Chateau-Thierry Sector. Mrs. J. B. Geiger (Mother), Mt. Vernon, Georgia [FAG] [S2] [SW] [Note: Brother of Judson Carlton Geiger]

Geiger, Judson Carlton, Pvt., Bks. Det., Philadelphia, Pennsylvania, DDS, March 12, 1918 at Philadelphia, Pennsylvania. Clifford E. Geiger (Mother), Mt. Vernon, Georgia [FAG] [S3] [Note: Brother of Harold Clifford Geiger]

Gendreau, Byron M., Gy. Sgt., Nav. Air Sta., Miami, Florida, DAS, March 29, 1919 in a flying boat accident. Mrs. Lillian Gendreau (Mother), 5498 University Ave., Chicago, Illinois [FAG] [S4]

Gerard, George Robert, Pvt., 23rd Co., 6th MG Bn., DOW, June 13, 1918 in the Chateau-Thierry Sector. Louis Gerard (Brother), 155 5th Ave., N. Nashville, Tennessee [VA-Nashville] [S2] [SW1]

Marine Corps Deaths, 1917-1921

Gerhard, Ernest John, Pvt., 96th Co., 6th Regt., DOD, January 29, 1919 in France. Mrs. Ernest J. Gerhard (Wife), 1404 Glasgow Ave., St. Louis, Missouri [ANC] [S2]

Gerwig, Percy McGrew, Gy. Sgt., MCR, Marine Aviation Detachment, Miami, Florida, DAS, October 22, 1918 in an aeroplane, at Marine Flying Field, Miami, Florida. George W. Gerwig (Father), 1105 Davis Ave., N.S., Pittsburgh, Pennsylvania [FAG] [S3]

Gibbes, Lacy Willmott, Cpl., MCR, Hdqtrs. OSD, Quantico, Virginia, DDS, October 7, 1918 at Quantico, Virginia. Samuel J. Gibbes (Brother), 1922 Spring St., Little Rock, Arkansas [FAG] [S3]

Gibbons, James Joseph, Sgt., 45th Co., 5th Regt., KIA, June 6, 1918 in the Chateau-Thierry Sector. Evelyn Gibbons (Sister), 2559 Creston Ave., Bronx, New York [VA-Cypress Hills] [S2] [SW]

Gibbs, Rufus Montgomery, Pvt., 81st Co., 6th Regt., DOW, June 10, 1918 in the Chateau-Thierry Sector. Charles D. Gibbs (Brother), 207 Lawton St., Atlanta, Georgia [ABMC-Belleau] [S2] [SW]

Gibson, Abner L., Pvt., MB, Navy Yard, Norfolk, Virginia, DOS, January 17, 1919 at Ottawa, Kansas. Mrs. Mary V. Gibson (Mother), 409 West 8th St., Ottawa, Kansas [FAG] [S4]

Gibson, John Wesley, Pvt., 20th Co., 5th Regt., KIA, June 6, 1918 in the Chateau-Thierry Sector. Jennie M. Sherman (Mother), 342 W. 8th St., Eugene, Oregon [FAG] [S2] [SW]

Giek, Robert John, Pvt., 76th Co., 6th Regt., KIA, July 19, 1918 in the Aisne Marne. Stephen Giek (Father), 2954 Glenwood Park Ave., Erie, Pennsylvania [S2] [SW]

Gilbert, Howard Franklin, Pvt., 79th Co., 6th Regt., DOD, September 29, 1918 in the St. Mihiel Offensive. Frank B. Gilbert (Father), 204 Boston Block, Minneapolis, Minnesota [R] [S2] [SW1 says DOW]

Marine Corps Deaths, 1917-1921

Gildemeister, Alfred W., Pvt., Bks. Det., Puget Sound, Washington, DDS, December 12, 1918 at Puget Sound, Washington. Mrs. Margaret Gildemeister (Mother), 1745 E. 16th St., Portland, Oregon [S4]

Giles, William Edgar, Pvt., 74th Co., 6th Regt., DOW, April 18, 1918 in the Toulon Sector, Verdun. George Giles (Father), Kizer, Tennessee [R] [S2] [SW]

Giles, William Noel, Pvt., 17th Co., 5th Regt., KIA, October 5, 1918 in the Meuse Argonne. Carolena Giles (Wife), 923 Huron St., Toledo, Ohio [ABMC- Romagne] [S2] [SW1]

Gill, Homer Edward, Pvt., Hdqtrs. Co., 5th Regt., KIA, October 31, 1918 in the Meuse Argonne. Robert I. Gill (Brother), 214 W. Anderson St., Savannah, Georgia [R] [S2] [SW1]

Gillen, Arthur Andrew, Pvt., 16th Co., 5th Regt., DOD, November 28, 1918 in the Meuse Argonne. Joseph Gillen (Father), 2430 S. 10th St., Ironton, Ohio [R] [S2]

Gillespie, John Wilford, Cpl., Bks. Det., New York, New York, DDS, October 16, 1918 at New York, New York. Mary A. Gillespie (Mother), Salt Lake City, Utah [FAG] [S3]

Gilman, Frederick S., Pvt., Nav. Ammo. Dep., Mare Island, California, DDS, November 19, 1918 at Mare Island, California. Mrs. Beatrice I. Gilman (Wife), 1006 W. 22nd St., Los Angeles, California [FAG] [S4]

Gilmore, James R., Pvt., 97th Co., 6th Regt., KIA, November 2, 1918 in the Meuse Argonne. Sanford Gilmore (Father), Cottonwood, Alabama [FAG as November 7, 1918] [S2] [SW1]

Ginsburg, Samuel S., Cpl., MB, Navy Yard, Puget Sound, Washington, DAS, February 29, 1919 of a severe gunshot wound at Puget Sound, Washington. David Ginsburg (Father), 1548 S. Trumbull Ave., Chicago, Illinois [S4]

Given, Raymond Newlin, Pvt., 66th Co., 5th Regt., KIA, October 4, 1918 in the Meuse Argonne. John W. Given (Father),

Marine Corps Deaths, 1917-1921

606 Hermitage St., Philadelphia, Pennsylvania [FAG] [S2] [SW1]

Givens, Arch Zibouth, Pvt., Co. F, 13th Regt., DOD, October 3, 1918 in France. Jeff Davis (Father), Route #2, Slocomb, Alabama [FAG] [S2]

Glantz, George Robinson, Pvt., Supply Co., 13th Regt., DOD, September 25, 1918 on the *Von Steuben* enroute to France. Ida May Glantz (Mother), 35 White Ave., Baltimore, Maryland [R] [S2]

Gleason, John William Jr., Pvt., 96th Co., 6th Regt., DOW, July 18, 1918 in the Aisne Marne. John W. Gleason (Father), Box 633, Kingman, Kansas [ABMC- Fere] [S2] [SW1]

Glen, Fred Beck, Pvt., 43rd Co., 5th Regt., DOW, June 12, 1918 in the Chateau-Thierry Sector. Nellie Glen (Mother), c/o Cecelia Glen, RFD#5, Atlanta, Georgia [S2] [SW]

Glen, Thomas Dawson Jr., Pvt., 76th Co., 6th Regt., KIA, June 11, 1918 in the Chateau-Thierry Sector. Thomas D. Glen (Father), c/o Nellie Glen, RFD#5, Box 76, Atlanta, Georgia [S2] [SW says Gleb] [SW1]

Glenn, Leslie Paret, Pvt., Co. Z, Parris Island, South Carolina, DDS, November 11, 1918 at Parris Island, South Carolina. William H. Glenn (Father), Forrest Hill, Maryland [FAG] [S3]

Glick, Frank Lewis, 1st Sgt., 80th Co., 6th Regt., KIA, June 3, 1918 in the Aisne Defensive. Helen Glick (Mother), 2554 Jefferson Ave., Ogden, Utah [ABMC- Belleau] [S2] [SW]

Glidden, Clinton Rosette, Pvt., 84th Co., 6th Regt., DOW, July 19, 1918 in the Aisne Marne. Missie Glidden (Mother), 523 South 2nd St., DeKalb, Illinois [S2] [SW1]

Glover, Harry Lester, Pvt., 55th Co., 5th Regt., DOW, June 7, 1918 in the Chateau-Thierry Sector. Richard Glover (Father), RFD#4, Arkport, New York [S2] [SW]

Marine Corps Deaths, 1917-1921

Goad, Leonard Carl, Pvt., 78th Co., 6th Regt., DOW, July 19, 1918 in the Aisne Marne. William Goad (Brother), San Benito, Texas [ANC] [S2] [SW1 says KIA]

Godshaw, Samuel Grazier, Pvt., 55th Co., 5th Regt., KIA, June 13, 1918 in the Chateau-Thierry Sector. Emil Godshaw (Father), 103 West Woodlawn Ave., Louisville, Kentucky [S2] [SW]

Goelkel, Julius Fred, Pvt., 160th Co., Norfolk, Virginia, DDS, April 22, 1919 at Norfolk, Virginia. Mrs. Lena Goelkel (Mother), 1954 Sedgewick St., Chicago, Illinois [S4]

Goetz, Gustav Herman, Pvt., 83rd Co., 6th Regt., KIA, November 6, 1918 in the Meuse Argonne. Mrs. Augusta Goetz (Mother), 258 W. 37th St., New York, New York [VA-Cypress Hills] [S2] [SW1]

Goetze, Arthur Clarence, Gy. Sgt., 79th Co., 6th Regt., KIA, July 19, 1918 in the Aisne Marne. Herman G. Goetze (Father), Hudson, Staford County, Kansas [ANC] [S2] [SW1]

Gohrband, Emil Paul, Pvt., MB, New York, New York, DDS, October 11, 1918 at New York, New York. Anna Gohrband (Mother), Box 6A, Raspeburg, Maryland [FAG] [S3]

Goldbeck, Eric Albert, Pvt., 67th Co., 5th Regt., KIA, June 6, 1918 in the Chateau-Thierry Sector. Mrs. G. R. Goldbeck (Mother), c/o Palmer School of Chriopady, Davenport, Iowa [FAG] [S2] [SW]

Goldberg, David, Pvt., 82nd Co., 6th Regt., KIA, June 6, 1918 in the Chateau-Thierry Sector. Carrie Goldberg (Mother), 412 West 115th St., New York, New York [ABMC-Belleau] [S2]

Goldsberry, John Vernon, Pvt., 67th Co., 5th Regt., KIA, June 6, 1918 in the Chateau-Thierry Sector. Mrs. A. B. Goldsberry (Mother), 2562 N. Summit St., Columbus, Ohio [ANC] [S2] [SW says 137th Co.]

Marine Corps Deaths, 1917-1921

Goldsmith, Arthur Ray, Pvt., Bks. Det., Quantico, Virginia, DDS, Ocotober 18, 1918 at Quantico, Virginia. Charles Wagman (Grandfather), 402 Green St., Parkersburg, West Virginia [S3]

Gonsalves, Joseph A., Pvt., Hdqtrs., USMC, A & I, Washington, D.C., DDS, October 6, 1919 at Washington, D.C. Mrs. Clara Gonsalves (Mother), Beechwood, Cohasset, Massachusetts [S4]

Good, Dwight Bushnell, Pvt., 73rd Co., 6th Regt., KIA, November 1, 1918 in the Meuse Argonne. Davis Jay Good (Father), 216 Lowes St., Dayton, Ohio [FAG] [S2] [SW1]

Goode, Morris Farris, Pvt., 64th Co., 2nd Regt., Haiti, DAS by drowning November 12, 1917 at Cape Haitien, Haiti. Mr. Samuel G. Goode (Father), Danville, Kentucky [VA-Danville, Ky.] [S3]

Goodeve, Frederick Weaver, Pvt., 74th Co., 6th Regt., KIA, October 8, 1918 in the Meuse Argonne. Mrs. Mildred A. Wesp (Sister), Lincoln Ave., Grantwood, New Jersey [ABMC- Romagne] [S2] [SW1]

Goolsby, Eulie Thurston, Pvt., 76th Co., 6th Regt., KIA, November 5, 1918 in the Meuse Argonne. William Goolsby (Father), Blythe, Georgia [ABMC- Romagne] [S2] [SW1]

Gordon, Bert, Pvt., 95th Co., 6th Regt., DOW, June 4, 1918 in the Aisne Defensive. E. B. Gordon (Mother), RFD#1, Joaquin, Texas [VA-San Antonio] [S2] [SW]

Gordon, Charles Russel, Cpl., 45th Co., 5th Regt., DOW, October 4, 1918 in the Meuse Argonne. Louise R. Gordon (Mother), 505 E. Chestnut St., Robinson, Illinois [ABMC- Belleau] [S2] [SW1]

Gordon, Donald Smith, 2nd Lieut., 95th Co., 6th Regt., DOW, July 24, 1918 in the Aisne Marne. Mrs. B.G. Smith (Brother), 924 West End Ave., New York, New York [ABMC- Belleau] [S1] [SW]

Marine Corps Deaths, 1917-1921

Gordon, James Monroe, Pvt., 78th Co., 6th Regt., DOW, July 19, 1918 in the Aisne Marne. Harry Spencer (Friend), Honeycreek, Iowa [ABMC- Belleau] [S2] [SW1]

Gorman, Edwin Mobley, Pvt., 55th Co., 5th Regt., KIA, July 18, 1918 in the Aisne Marne. William C. Gorman (Father), Oakwood, Texas [ABMC- Fere] [S2] [SW]

Gorshel(l), David Herman, Pvt., 55th Co., 5th Regt., KIA, June 13, 1918 in the Chateau-Thierry Sector. Fannie T. Gorshel (Mother), 131 Homestead St., Roxbury, Massachusetts [S2] [SW]

Gorsky, Casimier A., Pvt., Co. T, Parris Island, South Carolina, DDS, November 14, 1918 at Parris Island, South Carolina. John Gorsky (Father), 286 Maine St., Springville, New York [S4]

Gorth, Harry Jacob, Pvt., 79th Co., 6th Regt., KIA, July 17, 1918 in the Aisne Marne. Kate Gutmann (Sister), 3025 W. 6th St., Cincinnati, Ohio [ABMC- Belleau TOM] [S2] [SW1]

Gosney, Terrence Ivan, Pvt., 66th Co., 6th Regt., KIA, September 14, 1918 in the St. Mihiel Offensive. Ella Gosney (Mother), Chrisman, Illinois [R] [S2] [SW]

Gossage, Thomas Embry, Pvt., 14th Co., Quantico, Virginia, DDS, December 14, 1917 at Quantico, Virginia. William Gossage (Father), Estill Springs, Tennessee [S3]

Gostylla, Leo Pearl, Cpl., 24th Co., Guantanamo Bay, Cuba, DOS, September 16, 1917 at Caimanera, Cuba. Stella Ruszozewka (Wife), 253 South Dalls St., Baltimore, Maryland [USN – Guantanamo] [S3]

Goth, Louis Eugene, Pvt., 83rd Co., 6th Regt., KIA, October 6, 1918 in the Meuse Argonne. Michael Goth (Father), 111 Berry St., Fredonia, New York [R] [S2] [SW1]

Gotham, Edward W., Pvt., 11th Sep. Batt., Quantico, Virginia, DDS, November 19, 1918 at Quantico, Virginia. Mrs. Nellie Koester (Mother), Gen. Del., Springston, Idaho [FAG] [S4]

Marine Corps Deaths, 1917-1921

Gottlieb, William, Cpl., MCR, Co. A, Mare Island, California, DDS, August 12, 1918 at Mare Island, California. Anna Gottlieb (Mother), Route #1, Box 16, Hillsboro, Oregon [FAG] [S3]

Goudy, Francis Boyd, Pvt., Co. E, 13th Regt., DOD, September 28, 1918 in France. Helen Goudy (Wife), Box 488, Strandquist, Minnesota [ABMC- Fere] [S2]

Goudy, George Ray, Pvt., 49th Co., 5th Regt., KIA, September 15, 1918 in the St. Mihiel Offensive. Estella Goudy (Mother), 320 East Broadway, Kokoma, Indiana [FAG] [S2] [SW located in the "C" section of report]

Gould, Harold Allen, Pvt., 97th Co., 6th Regt., KIA, October 6, 1918 in the Meuse Argonne. Ruth F. Gould (Wife), 510 Plymouth Ave, N. Minneapolis, Minnesota [ABMC- Romagne] [S2] [SW1]

Gould, Louis Van Buren, Sgt., 44th Co., 3rd Prov. Regt., Dominican Republic, DDS, January 17, 1919 at Santo Domingo, Dominican Republic. Mrs. Nora Gould (Mother), Poultney, Virginia [FAG as May 17, 1919] [S4]

Gourley, Robert Clark, Pvt., 66th Co., 5th Regt., DOW, June 8, 1918 in the Chateau-Thierry Sector. Ella V. Fischer (Mother), RFD#2, Waterville, Ohio [ABMC- Belleau] [S2] [SW1]

Gower, Frank Nelson, Pvt., 45th Co., 5th Regt., DOW, November 1, 1918 in the Meuse Argonne. William A. Gower (Father), Baring, Maine [S2] [SW1]

Grady, James Wilbert, Pvt., 17th Co., 5th Regt., DOW, October 4, 1918 in the Meuse Argonne. Nora Grady (not stated), 2623 Scranton Rd., Cleveland, Ohio [ABMC- Romagne] [S2] [SW1]

Gragard, Thomas Armistead, Cpl., 79th Co., 6th Regt., KIA, June 6, 1918 in the Chateau-Thierry Sector. George R. Gragard (Father), 331 Carondelet St., New Orleans, Louisana [ABMC- Belleau] [S2] [SW]

Marine Corps Deaths, 1917-1921

Graham, Alvin Myron, Pvt., 73rd Co., 6th Regt., KIA, June 20, 1918 in the Chateau-Thierry Sector. Mrs. Mary E. Graham (Mother), Gen. Del. Oxford, Kansas [FAG] [S2] [SW1]

Graham, Charles Dewey, Pvt., 96th Co., 6th Regt., DAO, April 17, 1918 in the Toulon Sector, Verdun. Mrs. Carolina M. Graham (Mother), Manning, South Carolina [S2] [SW1 says KOA]

Graham, Charles Duane, Pvt., Hdqtrs. Co., 5th Regt., KIA, November 5, 1918 in the Meuse Argonne. John Hunter Graham (Father), RFD#1, Carrollton, Ohio [ABMC-Romagne] [S2] [SW1]

Graham, David Sloan, Pvt., 8th Co., 5th Regt., KIA, June 6, 1918 in the Chateau-Thierry Sector. Mrs. Kate B. Graham (Mother), 1001 S. Brevard St., Charlotte, North Carolina [ABMC- Belleau] [S2] [SW]

Graham, Leon Roy, Sgt., Co. A, 11th Regt., Quantico, Virginia, DDS, September 22, 1918 at Quantico, Virginia. Willialm G. Graham (Father), 1104 Iowa Ave., Butte, Montana [FAG] [S3]

Graham, Ross Quinn, Cpl., 78th Co., 6th Regt., DOW, June 16, 1918 in the Chateau-Thierry Sector. John A. Graham (Father), RFD#1, LaFayette, Georgia [FAG] [S2] [SW]

Graham, Roy Barnie, Pvt., 75th Co., 6th Regt., DOW, July 19, 1918 in the Aisne Marne. Lucille Graham (Mother), Snyder, Texas [ABMC- Fere] [S2] [SW1]

Graham, Stafford, Cpl., 82nd Co., 6th Regt., KIA, October 7, 1918 in the Meuse Argonne. Mattie Graham (Mother), 2118 Ave. F., Ennsley, Alabama [FAG] [S2] [SW1]

Granlund, Axel, Pvt., OSD, Quantico, Virginia, DDS, November 15, 1918 at Norfolk, Virginia. Mrs.Annie Granlund (Mother), Garfield, Minnesota [S4]

Grant, John, 1st Sgt., 3538604, 20th Co., 5th Regt., KIA, June 6, 1918 in the Chateau-Thierry Sector. Mrs. Rosie Brown

Marine Corps Deaths, 1917-1921

(Friend), 2115 E. North Ave., Baltimore, Maryland [FAG] [S2] [SW]

Grant, Theodore Charles, Pvt., 84th Co., 6th Regt., KIA, June 6, 1918 in the Chateau-Thierry Sector. Charles G. Grant (Father), 2104 Obear Ave., St. Louis, Missouri [VA-Jefferson Barracks] [S2] [SW]

Grant, William Frederick, Pvt., 2nd Co., Philadelphia, Pennsylvania, DDS, September 17, 1918 at Philadelphia, Pennsylvania. Mary J. Grant (Mother), Nelson, British Columbia, Canada [FAG] [S3]

Grassie, Walter Geoffrey, Pvt., Supply Co., 11th Regt., DOD, January 4, 1919 in France. Charlotte Grassie (Mother), Glendale, Arizona [ANC] [S2]

Gratehouse, John William, Pvt., 79th Co., 6th Regt., DOD, September 30, 1918 in France. Mr. W. H. Gratehouse (Father), Box 194, Conroe, Texas [FAG] [S2]

Grath, Patrick D., 2nd Lieutenant, MCR, MB, Philadelphia, Pennsylvania, DDS, Mrs. Julia L. Grath (Widow), 426 North 37th St., Camden, New Jersey [S4]

Gratton, Edward Robbins, Pvt., Bks. Det., Philadelphia, Pennsylvania, DDS, March 21, 1918 at Philadelphia, Pennsylvania. Rose Gratton (Mother), RFD#2, Andover, New Jersey [FAG] [S3]

Graven, James John, Pvt., Bks. Det., New York, New York, DDS, June 26, 1917 at New York, New York. James J. O'Donnel (Step-father), 2222 8th Ave., Seattle, Washington [S3]

Gravener, John Nelson, Cpl., 55th Co., 5th Regt., KIA, June 12, 1918 in the Chateau-Thierry Sector. Mrs. Ada Gravener (Mother), 68 Naomi Ave., Philadelphia, Pennsylvania [ABMC- Belleau] [S2] [SW1]

Graves, Justus W., Pvt., Co. W, Parris Island, South Carolina, DDS, June 7, 1919 at Parris Island, South Carolina. Mrs. Myrtie Graves (Mother), Clarence, New York [S4]

Marine Corps Deaths, 1917-1921

Graves, Richard N., 1st Sgt., 64th Co., 2nd Prov. Regt., Haiti, DDS, March 22, 1919 at Capt Haitien, Haiti. Henry B. Graves (Father), 448 Castle Heights, Geneva, New York [S4]

Graves, Walter Philip, Pvt., 16th Co., 5th Regt., KIA, November 4, 1918 in the Meuse Argonne. Frank E. Graves (Father), 2760 Thomas Ave., S. Minneapolis, Minnesota [ANC] [S2] [SW1]

Gray, Austin Ellsworth, Cpl., 95th Co., 6th Regt., KIA, November 1, 1918 in the Meuse Argonne. Jasper B. Gray (Father), 58 Oak Ave., Moundsville, West Virginia [FAG] [S2] [SW1]

Gray, Charles Henry, Pvt., Co. B, Field T.D., Quantico, Virginia, DDS, March 22, 1919 at Quantico, Virginia. Mrs. Lewisa Mae Gray (Wife), 7511 Ranken Blvd., Maplewood, Missouri [VA-Jefferson Barracks] [S4]

Gray, Donald D., Pvt., Squadron C, MAF, MB, Quantico, Virginia, DDS, July 29, 1920 at Great Lakes, Illinois. Grace A. Gray (Mother), RR#3, Excelsior, Minnesota [FAG] [S4]

Gray, Frank Harold, Sgt., 43rd Co., 5th Regt., KIA, June 12, 1918 in the Chateau-Thierry Sector. Delia L. Gray (Mother), Fitzgerald, Georgia [ANC] [S2] [SW]

Gray, George Pease, Pvt., 51st Co., 5th Regt., KIA, September 16, 1918 in the St. Mihiel Offensive. Harrison F. Gray (Father), Elkin, North Carolina [S2] [SW says Co. C, 4th Sep. Btln.]

Gray, Joe Hallard, Pvt., BD, MB, Navy Yard, Mare Island, DDS, January 19, 1920 at Mare Island, California. Mrs. Gertrude Swabby (Mother), 139 East 82nd St., Los Angeles, California [S4]

Green, Charles Naylor, Pvt., 55th Co., 5th Regt., KIA, June 12, 1918 in the Chateau-Thierry Sector. Alice Parkhill (Mother), 3217 N. Carlisle St., Philadelphia, Pennsylvania [ABMC- Belleau] [S2] [SW1 says Charles Maylor Green]

Marine Corps Deaths, 1917-1921

Green, Fred G., Pvt., 78th Co., 6th Regt., KIA, July 19, 1918 in the Aisne Marne. Bessie Green (Mother), 920 Liberty St., Bellingham, Washington [FAG] [S2] [SW says Co. A, Repl. Btln.]

Green, Herbert Erwin, Sgt., 20th Co., 5th Regt., DOW, June 16, 1918 in the Chateau-Thierry Sector. Herbert W. Green (Father), 650 E. 58th St., Indianapolis, Indiana [R] [S2] [SW says 134th Co.]

Green, Kirt, Capt., 80th Co., 6th Regt., KIA, November 1, 1918 in the Meuse Argonne. Mrs. Linda Green (widow), 739 12th St., S.E., Washington, D.C. [S1] [SW1]

Green, Lloyd Chandler, Cpl., 38th Co., Peking, China, DDS, November 7, 1917 aboard the *USAT Merritt*. Travis L. Green (Uncle), 1175 10th St., Des Moines, Iowa [S3]

Green, Oval Harlan, Pvt., 51st Co., 5th Regt., KIA, July 18, 1918 in the Aisne Marne. Joseph Green (Father), Milray, Rush County, Indiana [R] [S2] [SW1]

Green, William, Cpl., , 2134782, 67th Co., 5th Regt., DOD, December 24, 1918 in France. Mrs. Lena Green (Mother), Box 331, Midleboro, Massachusetts [FAG] [S2]

Greene, Arch, Pvt., 76th Co., 6th Regt., DOW, July 24, 1918 in the Aisne Marne. Mrs. G. N. Alice Greene (Mother), 3234 St. Marys Ave., Hannibal, Missouri [ABMC- Belleau] [S2] [SW1]

Greene, Edgar Carl, Pvt., Military Police Detachment, Base Section #4, AEF, DOD, July 16, 1918 in France. Ana Greene (Mother), 654 Second St., Macon, Georgia [FAG] [S2]

Greenfield, Alec, Pvt., Bks. Det., Quantico, Virginia, DOS, December 4, 1918 at Quantico, Virginia. Mr. Hyman Greenfield (Brother), 1322 W. Claremont Ave., Chicago, Illinois [S4]

Greenlee, George Anthony, Cpl., 18th Co., 5th Regt., DOW, July 20, 1918 in the Aisne Marne. Edward Parr (Friend), Idaho

Marine Corps Deaths, 1917-1921

Falls, Idaho [ABMC- Belleau] [S2] [SW says Co. C, Repl. Btln.]

Greenspan, Harry, Pvt., 79th Co., 6th Regt., KIA, September 15, 1918 in the St. Mihiel Offensive. Mollie Greenspan (Mother), 180 Riverdale Ave., Yonkers, New York [ABMC-Thiaucourt] [S2] [SW1]

Greenup, Leo Charles, Cpl., 84th Co., 6th Regt., KIA, October 8, 1918 in the Meuse Argonne. George Greenup (Father), 881 Newport Ave., Detroit, Michigan [ABMC- Romagne TOM] [S2] [SW1]

Greenwood, Herschel, Pvt., MCR, Co. F, Mare Island, California, DOS, May 2, 1918 at Mare Island, California. John W. Greenwood (Father), Route #2, Cabool, Missouri [FAG] [S3]

Greer, Orman Powell, Cpl., 74th Co., 6th Regt., KIA, October 8, 1918 in the Meuse Argonne. X. U. Greer (Brother), 1041 Bailey Ave., Nashville, Tennessee [R] [S2] [SW1]

Gregg, Thomas Joseph, Pvt., 55th Co., 5th Regt., KIA, July 19, 1918 in the Aisne Marne. Catharine Gregg (Mother), 76 Hill St., Troy, New York [ABMC- Belleau TOM] [S2] [SW1]

Gregory, George, Gy. Sgt., 84th Co., 6th Regt., KIA, September 15, 1918 in the St. Mihiel Offensive. Miss Louise Gallagher (Sister), 21 Castle St., Devonshire, Plymouth, England [ABMC- Thiaucourt] [S2] [SW]

Grennan, John Francis, Pvt., 79th Co., 6th Regt., DOW, June 6, 1918 in the Chateau-Thierry Sector. Mary Grennan (Mother), Ge. Del., Sequim, Washington [ABMC- Belleau TOM] [S2] [SW1]

Gresham, Bert William, Pvt., 73rd Co., 6th Regt., DOW, November 4, 1918 in the Meuse Argonne. Elva Gresham (Mother), Atlanta, Illinois [FAG] [S2] [SW1]

Grey, William Denton, Pvt., MCR, Radio Station, Tuckertown, New Jersey, DDS, October 9, 1918 at Tuckerton, New

Marine Corps Deaths, 1917-1921

Jersey. Ella Chilton (Mother), Bartlesville, Oklahoma [S3]

Grieve, William Earl, Cpl., 84th Co., 6th Regt., KIA, September 15, 1918 in the St. Mihiel Offensive. William R. Grieve (Father), Box 273, Bloomington, Indiana [ABMC- Thiaucourt TOM] [S2] [SW]

Griffin, John, Pvt., 49th Co., 5th Regt., DOW, November 4, 1918, in the Meuse Argonne. Mrs. P. J. Riley (Sister), 116 Winchester St., Grass Valley, California [R] [S2] [SW1]

Griffin, William Lawrence, Cpl., 45th Co., 5th Regt., KIA, June 6, 1918 in the Chateau-Thierry Sector. Mrs. E. M. McConnell (Sister), 1310 Avery St., Parkersburg, West Virginia [ABMC- Belleau] [S2] [SW]

Grimes, Cecil, Sgt., 74th Co., 6th Regt., DOW, April 20, 1918 in the Toulon Sector, Verdun. James E. Grimes (Father), RR#1, Salem, Indiana [FAG] [S2] [SW]

Grinnell, David Johnson, Pvt., 82nd Co., 6th Regt., DOW, June 29, 1918 in the Chateau-Thierry Sector. Alice Porter (Mother), 5250 Hecla Ave., Detroit, Michigan [FAG] [S2] [SW]

Grissom, Curtis Farris, Pvt., 8th Co., 5th Regt., KIA, October 4, 1918 in the Meuse Argonne. Nettie I. Grissom (Mother), 1430 7th St., San Diego, California [ABMC- Romagne] [S2] [SW1]

Grober, Edward Adolph, Pvt., 96th Co., 6th Regt., KIA, April 5, 1918 in the Toulon Sector, Verdun. Rosie M. Hillyer (Mother), 215 College St., Peoria, Illinois [R] [S2] [SW]

Groff, Ira Hipple, Pfc, Bks. Det., Philadelphia, Pennsylvania, DDS, October 8, 1918 at Philadelphia, Pennsylvania. Mary E. Groff (Wife), 633 Rockland St., Lancaster, Pennsylvania [S3]

Grollman, Herman, Cpl., 16th Co., 5th Regt., KIA, June 23, 1918 in the Chateau-Thierry Sector. Marie Grollman (Mother),

Marine Corps Deaths, 1917-1921

79 Madison Ave., Newark, New Jersey [ABMC- Belleau TOM] [S2] [SW]

Grooms, Arvi M., Pvt., 59th Co., 7th Regt., Cuba, DAS, March 11, 1919 as a result of an automobile accident at Santiago, Cuba. Mr. F. H. Grooms (Father), Worthington, Ohio [FAG] [S4]

Grosskurth, Carl, Cpl., Hdqtrs. Co., 13th Regt., DOD, September 27, 1918 in France. Irene K. Grosskurth (Wife), 785 North St., New Durham, New Jersey [ABMC- Fere] [S2]

Grossman, Homer, Cpl., 76th Co., 6th Regt., KIA, June 11, 1918 in the Chateau-Thierry Sector. Jenette Vogel (Mother), 20 Forbes Terrace, Pittsburgh, Pennsylvania [ABMC-Belleau] [S2] [SW]

Grow, Paul Victor, Pvt., MB, NAD, Dover, New Jersey, DOS, December 31, 1917 at New York, New York. Edith Grow (Mother), 02 Lexington Ave., Lawrenceville, Illinois [FAG] [S3]

Growe, Harold M., Pvt., 20th Co., 5th Regt., KIA, June 6, 1918 in the Chateau-Thierry Sector. Leonora Grove (Mother), 219 N. Gibson St., Canandaigua, New York [ABMC-Belleau] [S2] [SW]

Grucza, Michael, Pvt., Hdqtrs. Co., 13th Regt., DOC, August 29, 1919 in France. Frank Grucza (Father), 5805 Howard Ave., Cleveland, Ohio [R] [S2]

Gruhn, Dewey Admiral, Pvt., 134th Co., 2nd Replacement Batt., DOW, June 14, 1918 in the Chateau-Thierry Sector. Minnie Gruhn (Mother), Malcom, Iowa [FAG] [S2] [SW says 140th Co.]

Grunow, Richard Riehold, Pfc., USS *Pittsburgh*, DDU, October 23, 1918 aboard the USS *Pittsburgh*. Caroline Grunow (Mother), 1412 New York Ave., Sheboygan, Wisconsin [S3]

Marine Corps Deaths, 1917-1921

Gruver, Fred Byron, Pvt., 18th Co., 5th Regt., DOW, July 21, 1918 in the Aisne Marne. Henry Gruver (Father), Box 14, Asoton, Washington [ABMC- Belleau TOM] [S2] [SW1]

Guerry, Theodore LeGrande, Pvt., 96th Co., 6th Regt., KIA, June 16, 1918 in the Chateau-Thierry Sector. Sam Guerry (Father), Montezuma, Georgia [ABMC- Belleau] [S2] [SW]

Guibault, Adelard, Pvt., MB, New York, New York, DDS, October 8, 1918 at New York, New York. Joseph Guibault (Father), Box 104, Warroad, Minnesota [FAG] [FAGM] [S3]

Guile, Noble Eric, Cpl., 76th Co., 6th Regt., KIA, July 19, 1918 in the Aisne Marne. Hilma Guile (Mother), 1905 Crystal Lake Ave., Minneapolis, Minnesota [FAG] [S2] [SW1]

Guillod, Frank Leo, Sgt., 51st Co., 5th Regt., DOW, June 11, 1918 in the Chateau-Thierry Sector. Clara MacKenna (Sister), 180 Latta Rd., Rochester, New York [S2] [SW1]

Guja, Theodore, Cpl., Hdqtrs. Det., Guam, DDS, November 14, 1921 at Guam. nrich Guja (Brother), 352 Adelphia St., Brooklyn, New York [VA-Cypress Hills] [S4]

Gulbrandsen, Erling Eugene, Pvt., 43rd Co., 5th Regt., KIA, June 13, 1918 in the Chateau-Thierry Sector. Ole Svendsen (Cousin), 845 N. Montford Ave., Baltimore, Maryland [ABMC- Belleau TOM as E.E.] [S2] [SW]

Gunn, John Louis, Pvt., 97th Co., 6th Regt., DOW, October 7, 1918 in the Meuse Argonne. Mary K. Gunn (Mother), 211 Third Ave., E., Cordele, Georgia [FAG] [S2] [SW says KIA, and 115th Co.]

Gustafson, Fritz Albert, Cpl., Bks. Det., Quantico, Virginia, DDS, November 2, 1918 at Quantico, Virginia. Albert Gustafson (Father), 1187 Edgerton St., St. Paul, Minnesota [S3]

Gustafson, George Albert, Pvt., 15th Co., 6th MG Bn., KIA, June 5, 1918 in the Aisne Defensive. G. E. Gustafson

Marine Corps Deaths, 1917-1921

(Brother), 944 N. Parkside Ave., Chicago, Illinois [ABMC- Belleau as G.A.] [S2] [SW]

Gustafson, Lorne Nathaniel, Pvt., 17th Co., 5th Regt., KIA, November 1, 1918 in the Meuse Argonne. S. N. Gustafson (Father), 4048 Greenview Ave., Chicago, Illinois [FAG] [S2] [SW1]

Haas, Eugene Frederick Francis, Pvt., 67th Co., 5th Regt., KIA, June 6, 1918 in the Chateau-Thierry Sector. Roy Haas (Brother), Normandy, Illinois [ABMC- Belleau] [S2] [SW]

Haase, Eugene, 1st Sgt., Eastern Recruiting Division, DDS, October 20, 1918 at Syracuse, New York. Liebchen Bloomenthal (Sister), 172 Ralph Ave., Brooklyn, New York [S3]

Haberland, Franklin William, Pvt., 79th Co., 6th Regt., DOW, July 19, 1918 in the Aisne Marne. Lena Haberland (Mother), Gen. Del., Middleton, Wisconsin [S2] [SW1]

Hackenyos, Julius Francis, Pvt., 95th Co., 6th Regt., KIA, July 19, 1918 in the Aisne Marne. Julia Hackenyos (Mother), 3932 Sullinvan Ave., St. Louis, Missouri [S2] [SW]

Haegele, Leo John, Pvt., 26th Co., 7th Regt., San Diego, California, DAS, July 5, 1921 drowned at La Jolla, California. Ida Miller (Mother), Route #2, Forestville, Wisconsin [S4]

Haessler, Carl Gustave, Pvt., 76th Co., 6th Regt., DOD, October 23, 1918 in the Aisne Marne. Mary D. Haessler (Mother), 169 Sharon Ave., Zanesville, Ohio [R] [S2] [SW1 says DOW]

Hagan, Harvey Joseph, Pvt., 15th Co., 6th MG Bn., KIA, June 22, 1918 in the Chateau-Thierry Sector. Christina Hagan (Mother), 3432 N. 9th St., St. Louis, Missouri [FAG] [S2] [SW says 15th Co., 5th Regt.] [SW1 says Joseph Hagen Harvey]

Marine Corps Deaths, 1917-1921

Hageman, Warren Robert, Pvt., 78th Co., 6th Regt., KIA, October 3, 1918 in the Meuse Argonne. Benjamin S. Hageman (Father), RFD#6, Bakersfield, California [ANC] [S2] [SW1]

Hager, George William, Pvt., 114th Co., Santo Domingo, Dominican Republic, DDS, on September 4, 1918 of sun stroke at Monte Plata, Dominican Republic. Celia Ann Hager (Mother), 940 Fatherland St., Nashville, Tennessee [S3]

Halblaub, Steve, Pvt., 80th Co., 6th Regt., DOW, June 10, 1918 in the Chateau-Thierry Sector. John Halblaub (Father), 2719 N. Jefferson St., St. Louis, Missouri [S2] [SW]

Hale, Charles Cunningham, Pvt., 77th Co., 6th MG Bn., KIA, June 11, 1918 in the Chateau-Thierry Sector. Samuel Hale (Father), RFD#4, McConnelsville, Ohio [ABMC-Belleau] [S2] [SW says 77th Co., 6th Regt.]

Hale, Enoch Roth, Pvt., 67th Co., 5th Regt., KIA, June 6, 1918 in the Chateau-Thierry Sector. R. O. Hale (Father), Gorrigan, Texas [S2] [SW1]

Hall, Edward Maurice, Pvt., Naval Prisoner, Portsmouth, New Hampshire, DDS, September 24, 1918 at Portsmouth, New Hampshire. Stella Brueckber (Mother), 223 Odeon St., Cincinnati, Ohio [S3]

Hall, John Edwin, Pvt., 74th Co., 6th Regt., DOW, July 25, 1918 in the Aisne Marne. John F. Hall (Father), 401 W. 9th St., Newton, Kansas [FAG] [S2] [SW]

Hall, Milton Frederick, Pvt., 79th Co., 6th Regt., KIA, October 3, 1918 in the Meuse Argonne. Phoebe Hall (Mother), 540 Davis Ave., Arlington, New Jersey [ABMC- Romagne] [S2] [SW says Co. C, 2nd Casualty Btln.]

Hall, Ralph Milton, Cpl., 8th Co., 5th Regt., DOW, October 6, 1918 in the Meuse Argonne. C. G. Hall (Mother), 34 Ormwood Ave., Atlanta, Georgia [ANC] [S2] [SW]

Marine Corps Deaths, 1917-1921

Hall, Raymond Spencer, Pvt., 66th Co., 5th Regt., DOW, October 4, 1918 in the Meuse Argonne. Nellie G. Hall (Mother), 308 Church St., Herkimer, New York [ABMC- Romagne] [S2] [SW1]

Hall, William, Pvt., 66th Co., 5th Regt., DOD, June 8, 1918 in the Chateau-Thierry Sector. 46 Eustus St., Cambridge, Massachusetts [R] [S2] [SW says DOW]

Hall, Willie Bennie, Apprentice [Pvt.], Fld. Music Det., Parris Island, South Carolina, DOS, September 8, 1918 at Parris Island, South Carolina. Mrs. Lou Hall (Mother), Houston Harbor, Houston, Texas [FAG] [S3]

Halpain, Alexander, Pvt., 80th Co., 6th Regt., KIA, June 3, 1918 in the Aisne Defensive. N. M. Halpain (Father), 329 Exposition Ave., Dallas, Texas [FAG] [S2] [SW]

Halperin, Louis, Pvt., Co. G, 13th Regt., DOD, September 21, 1918 enroute to France. Helen and Max Halperin (Parents), 375 Johnston Ave., Jersey City, New Jersey [S2]

Halverson, Henry Nathaniel, Pvt., 76th Co., 6th Regt., DOW, November 1, 1918 in the Meuse Argonne. Blanda Halverson (Wife), 2405 29th Ave., S. Minneapolis, Minnesota [FAG] [S2] [SW1]

Halvorsen, Henry Oscar, Pvt., 75th Co., 6th Regt., KIA, June 10, 1918 in the Chateau-Thierry Sector. Elsie Halversen (Mother), 4345 McLean Ave., Chicago, Illinois [S2] [SW]

Hamberry, Joseph Henry, Pvt., 80th Co., 6th Regt., DOW, September 15, 1918 in the St. Mihiel Offensive. Mrs. Leah Haberry (Wife), 1733 Ridge Ave., Philadelphia, Pennsylvania [ABMC- Romagne] [S2] [SW1]

Hamilton, Frank Leo, Pvt., 75th Co., 6th Regt., KIA, July 19, 1918 in the Aisne Marne. Elmira Hamilton (Mother), 915 State St., Port Huron, Michigan [ABMC- Romagne] [S2] [SW1]

Marine Corps Deaths, 1917-1921

Hamilton, Richard James, Pvt., 43rd Co., 5th Regt., KIA, October 4, 1918 in the Meuse Argonne. Mrs. Frank S. Leonard (Mother), Gen. Del., Andover, Maine [R] [S2] [SW says 137th Co.]

Hamilton, William Walter, Sgt., 49th Co., 5th Regt., KIA, November 1, 1918 in the Meuse Argonne. William J. Hamilton (Father), South Rd., Bedford, Massachusetts [S2] [SW1]

Hamlet, George Oren, Pvt., 49th Co., 5th Regt., KIA, June 6, 1918 in the Chateau-Thierry Sector. Robert L. Hamlet (Father), c/o Police Department, Birmingham, Alabama [FAG] [S2] [SW]

Hamlink, Clarence Albert, Pvt., 95th Co., 6th Regt., DOW, October 6, 1918 in the Meuse Argonne. Abraham A. Hamlink (Father), Demster, New York [R] [S2] [SW1]

Hammett, Marcus Collins, Pvt., 97th Co., 6th Regt., KIA, October 8, 1918 in the Meuse Argonne. Mrs. Alberta G. Ford (Sister), 605 McDonough St., Helena, Arkansas [FAG] [ABMC- Romagne] [S2] [SW says Co. C, 3rd Sep. Btln.]

Hammill, Edward M., Pvt., Bks. Det., Mare Island, California, DDS, January 9, 1919 at Mare Island, California. Mrs. Lillian Hamill (Mother), 220 London St., San Francisco, California [S4]

Hammer, John Alphonsus, Pvt., 95th Co., 6th Regt. KIA, [R] [SW]

Hammon, Aubry Almer, Cpl., 96th Co., 6th Regt., DOW, October 7, 1918 in the Meuse Argonne. Joseph H. Hammon (Father), Maben, Mississippi [ANC] [S2] [SW]

Hammond, Frederick Albert, Pvt., 91st Co., 1st F.A. Regt., Quantico, Virginia, DOS, July 21, 1918 at Quantico, Virginia. Emma Hammond (Mother), Medina, Texas [FAG] [S3]

Hamrick, James Calvin, Pvt., 84th Co., 6th Regt., KIA, November 1, 1918 in the Meuse Argonne. Luisa Hamrick (Mother), Barksdale, Texas [FAG] [S2] [SW1]

Marine Corps Deaths, 1917-1921

Handley, Clarence M., Pvt., MB, Parris Island, South Carolina, DDS, January 12, 1919 at Parris Island, South Carolina. Charles D. Handley (Father), RFD#1, Marion, Missouri [S4]

Handsley, Sydney J., 1st Lieutenant, 2nd Brigade, Domincan Republic, DDS, August 25, 1921 at Santo Domingo, Domincan Republic. Mrs. Sydney J. Handsley (Wife), c/o H. F. Hess, Marysville, Pennsylvania [ANC] [S4]

Haney, Charley Luck, Pvt., 67th Co., 5th Regt., DOW, August 1, 1918 in the Chateau-Thierry Sector. Homer L. Haney (Father), 718 Frankford Rd., Louisana, Missouri [R] [S2] [SW1]

Hanks, Alvarious, Pvt., Co. D, Mare Island, California, DDS, April 8, 1919 at Mare Island, California. Mrs. Lottie Hanks (Mother), Box 410, Shelley, Idaho [S4]

Hanlon, Paul L., Pvt., MB, Navy Yard, New York, DAS, June 15, 1920 drowned at Port Washington Lake. John F. Hanlon (Father), 61 Clement Ave., West Roxbury, Massachusetts [S4]

Hanmer, John Alphonsus, Pvt., 95th Co., 6th Regt., KIA, June 12, 1918 in the Chateau-Thierry Sector. Mrs. Mary Alice Hanmer Malloy (Sister), 4117 St. Peter St., New Orleans, Louisana [ANC] [S2]

Hansen, Delisle Ward, Pvt., Supply Co., 11th Regt., Quantico, Virginia, DDS, October 2, 1918 at Quantico, Virginia. Sophia Hansen (Mother), Preston, Idaho [FAG] [S3]

Hansen, Rueben Edwin, Pvt., 23rd Co., 6th MG Bn., DOW, November 1, 1918 in the Meuse Argonne. Hans C. Hansen (Father), Hendricks, Minnesota [ABMC-Romagne] [S2] [SW1]

Hansen, William, Cpl., 4062226, 20th Co., 5th Regt., KIA, June 6, 1918 in the Chateau-Thierry Sector. Benhard Hansen (Father), 1731 Portsmouth Ave., Portland, Oregon [ABMC- Belleau TOM] [S2] [SW]

Marine Corps Deaths, 1917-1921

Hanson, Arvid Henry, Pvt., 76th Co., 6th Regt., DOW, July 19, 1918 in the Aisne Marne. Ida Marie Hanson (Mother), RFD, Coulterville, Illinois [VA- ANC undated] [S2] [SW1]

Hanson, Eugene Otto, Pvt., Marine Barracks, Washington, D.C., DDS, October 25, 1918 at Washington, D.C. Kristina Hanson (Mother), 607 44th St., Rock Island, Illinois [S3]

Harbulak, Andrew Steve, Pvt., Hdqtrs. Co., 5th Regt., KIA, July 17, 1918 in the Aisne Marne. Susan Maskell (Mother), 777 Newcastle St., Sharon, Pennsylvania [FAG] [S2] [SW says Habulak]

Hardwick, Hendon Hazard, Pvt., 20th Co., 5th Regt., DOW, June 7, 1918 in the Chateau-Thierry Sector. Mr. Henry Hill (Uncle), Aquilla, Texas [VA-San Antonio] [S2] [SW]

Hargan, Norman, Pvt., 43rd Co., 5th Regt., DOW, June 13, 1918 in the Chateau-Thierry Sector. Mattie L. Hargan (Mother), Vine Grove, Kentucky [S2] [SW says Replacement]

Hargrove, Albert McRae, Cpl., 97th Co., 6th Regt., KIA, June 6, 1918 in the Chateau-Thierry Sector. Mrs. John H. Hargrave (Mother), Eastman, Georgia [S2] [SW]

Harlow, Albert Lincoln, Pvt., 16th Co., 5th Regt., KIA, November 2, 1918 in the Meuse Argonne. Enoch S. Harlow (Father), 192 Simpson St., Portland, Oregon [S2] [SW1]

Harms, John G., Pvt., MBks., Parris Island, South Carolina, DDS, January 14, 1919 at Parris Island, South Carolina. Mrs. Mary M. Harms (Mother), 4652 Nebraska Ave., St. Louis, Missouri [FAG] [S4]

Harper, Milton James, Pvt., 96th Co., 6th Regt., KIA, October 3, 1918 in the Meuse Argonne. Dora Harper (Mother), Gen. Del., Glendale, Oregon [ABMC- Romagne] [S2] [SW1]

Harper, William Ralph, Pvt., 75th Co., 6th Regt., KIA, June 13, 1918 in the Chateau-Thierry Sector. Mrs. William R. Harper (Wife), 370 21st St., East Moline, Illinois [VA-Rock Island] [S2] [SW]

Marine Corps Deaths, 1917-1921

Harralson, Aymard Collins, Pvt., 55th Co., 5th Regt., KIA, October 4, 1918 in the Meuse Argonne. Logan . Harralson (Father), Ruffin, North Carolina [FAG] [S2] [SW1]

Harrington, Allen W., Captain, DDS, October 19, 1918 at Key West, Florida. A. W. Harrington (Father), Stockbridge, Massachusetts [ANC] [S3]

Harrington, Karl G., Cpl., Co. H, Parris Island, South Carolina, DDS, February 1, 1919 at Parris Island, South Carolina. Mrs. Mary F. Harrington (Mother), Orchard Park, New York [S4]

Harrington, Thomas W., Cpl., 74th Co., 6th Regt., DOW, September 16, 1918 in the St. Mihiel Offensive. Margaret F. Harrington (Mother), #2 Middagh St., Brooklyn, New York [S2] [SW1]

Harris, Alvin Hugh, Pvt., Hdqtrs. Co., 6th Regt., DOW, June 9, 1918 in the Chateau-Thierry Sector. Alvin D. Harris (Father), Route #5, Newman, Georgia [FAG] [S2] [SW]

Harris, Frank James, Pvt., Depot Det., Haiti, DAS, November 10, 1920 of injuries received in an automobile accident at Haiti. Anna Harris (Mother), 3912 Melville Ave., East Chicago, Illinois [S4]

Harris, George Newman, Sgt., MB, San Diego, California, DDS, June 20, 1921 at San Diego, California. William D. Harris (Father), 478 Milwaukee St., Denver, Colorado [S4]

Harris, Joseph Jabonic(k), Pvt., 82nd Co., 6th Regt., KIA, June 12, 1918 in the Chateau-Thierry Sector. Moses H. Harris (Brother), 5233 Calumet St., Chicago, Illinois [FAG] [S2] [SW]

Harris, Nay B., Pvt., 8th Co., 5th Regt., KIA, November 7, 1918 in the Meuse Argonne. Samuel B. Harris (Father), Rutledge, Missouri [R] [S2] [SW1]

Marine Corps Deaths, 1917-1921

Harris, Robert Elmer, Pvt., 40th Co., Guam, M.I., DOS, July 22, 1918 at Guam. Susie E. Harris (Mother), Plaza, Washington [S3]

Harris, Wesley Ernest, Pvt., 43rd Co., 5th Regt., DOD, September 16, 1918 in France. Rev. and Mrs. Ernest O. Harris (Parents), Seattle Heights, Washington [S2] [SW1 says DOW]

Harrisburg, John Archibald, Pvt., 82nd Co., 6th Regt., KIA, July 19, 1918 in the Aisne Marne. Abraham Harrisburg (Father), 9 3rd St., Auburn, Maine [S2] [SW]

Harrison, Bertie, Pvt., 95th Co., 6th Regt., DAO, January 13, 1919 in France. Robert Harrison (Father), Hazelhurst, Georgia [FAG] [S2] [SW1 says DOW]

Harrison, Carl Ervin, Pvt., 142nd Co., NDB, New London, Connecticut, DDS, September 29, 1918 at New London, Connecticut Jim Harrison (Father), RFD#1, Hixson, Tennessee [VA-Chattanooga] [S3]

Harrison, George Dewey, Pvt., 80th Co., 6th Regt., DOW, September 17, 1918 in the St. Mihiel Offensive. Mrs. Ellen G. Harrision (Mother), RR#1,Box 111, Springfield, Illinois [FAG] [S2] [SW]

Harrison, Leo, Pvt., Hdqtrs., 4th Brigade, Chelsea, Massachusetts, DDS, September 16, 1919 at Chelsea, Massachusetts. Mrs. Elizabeth Harrison (Mother), Glifty, Kentucky [S4]

Harrison, Milo Hendrix, Pvt., 167th Co., Norfolk, Virginia, DDS, February 2, 1919 at Portsmouth, Virginia. Mrs. Daisy C. Hall (Mother), Whitefield, Oklahoma [FAG] [S4]

Harsch, Joseph John, Pvt., 66th Co., 5th Regt., KIA, October 5, 1918 in the Meuse Argonne. John Harsch (Uncle), Berea, Ohio [S2] [SW1]

Hart, Herbert LeRoy, Pvt., 96th Co., 6th Regt., KIA, October 3, 1918 in the Meuse Argonne. Chase D. Hart (Father), Ranneby, Minnesota [ABMC- Romagne] [S2] [SW]

Marine Corps Deaths, 1917-1921

Hart, Ronald Henry, Cpl., MD, Hingham, Massachusetts, DDS, September 18, 1918 at Chelsea, Massachusetts. Jane Hart (Mother), 68 Circuit St., Roxbury, Massachusetts [S3]

Hartenbower, Marian Francis, Pvt., 84th Co., 6th Regt., DOW, July 19, 1918 in the Aisne Marne. Henry Hartenbower (Father), Gen. Del., Cladwell, Idaho [ABMC- Belleau TOM as M.F.] [S2] [SW1]

Harter, Francis L., Cpl., Co. H, MBks., Parris Island, South Carolina, DDS, January 8, 1919 at Parris Island, South Carolina. Mrs. Alverna Harter (Mother), Wadsworth, Ohio [S4]

Hartley, Paul Francis, Pvt., 45th Co., 5th Regt., DOW, June 24, 1918 in the Chateau-Thierry Sector. Pauline Hartley (Mother), 645 N. Frazier St., W. Philadelphia, Pennsylvania [VA-Philadelphia] [S2] [SW]

Hartley, Milo Evertt, Pvt., Co. A, Mare Island, California, DDS, January 30, 1920 at Mare Island, California. John W. Hartley (Father), Earlham, Iowa [S4]

Hartley, Oscar D., Pvt., Nav. Amm. Depot, DAS, August 23, 1919 at Dover, New Jersey.James Hartley (Father), RFD#1, Bentley, Michigan [FAG] [S4]

Hartt, Paul Mathew, Cpl., 18th Co., 5th Regt., KIA, July 21, 1918 in the Aisne Marne. Sanford Hartt (Father), Sunny Crest Plantation, Aven Park, Florida [ANC] [S2] [SW1]

Hartzell, Phillip William, Pvt., 79th Co., 6th Regt., DOW, September 15, 1918 in the St. Mihiel Offensive. William Hartzell (Father), 302 N. Madison St., Carthage, Illinois [FAGM] [S2] [SW says Co. B, 5th Sep. Btln.]

Harvey, Clair Dewey, Pvt., Co. D, 13th Regt., DOD, September 23, 1918 aboard the USS *Von Steuben* enroute to France. Anna Harvey (Mother), Nashville, Michigan [FAG] [S2]

Hash, Kyle C., 1st Lieut., MCR, 16th Co., 5th Regt., DOW, October 19, 1918 in the Meuse Argonne. Mrs. Nellie Hash (Mother), Independence, Virginia [ANC] [S1] [SW]

Marine Corps Deaths, 1917-1921

Hatch, Robert Augustus, Pvt., 47th Co., 5th Regt., DOW, October 5, 1918 in the Meuse Argonne. Henry L. Hatch (Father), 26 Randolph Ave., Randolph, Vermont [S2] [SW says Co. B, 2nd Cas. Btln.]

Hatfield, Harry Stuart, Pvt., 8th Co., 5th Regt., KIA, November 2, 1918 in the Meuse Argonne. Samuel R. Hatfield (Father), 503 W. 3rd St., Faribault, Minnesota [ABMC- Romagne] [S2] [SW1]

Hathaway, Harry Franklin, Pvt., 47th Co., 5th Regt., DOW, June 26, 1918 in the Chateau-Thierry Sector. Set Hathaway (Father), 64 Court St., Geneseo, New York [ABMC-Romagne] [S2] [SW]

Hathaway, Sanger Allen, Pvt., Quantico, Virginia, DAS, October 17, 1917 from a fractured skull resulting from a blow from a falling tree at Quantico, Virginia. Anna D Hathaway (Wife), Newton, Massachusetts [S3]

Haught, Arlie, Pvt., 83rd Co., 6th Regt., DOW, June 7, 1918 in the Chateau-Thierry Sector. Nimrod Haught (Father), RFD#3, Fairview, West Virginia [FAG] [S2] [SW says 138th Co., Repl. Btln.]

Haugsten, Nils Olaf, Pvt., 78th Co., 6th Regt., DOW, July 19, 1918 in the Aisne Marne. Christian Haughsten (Father), Two Harbors, Minnesota [ABMC- Fere] [S2] [SW1]

Haukland, Arthur Olive, Pvt., 79th Co., 6th Regt., KIA, October 4, 1918 in the Meuse Argonne. Minnie Haukland (Mother), North St. Paul, Minnesota [FAG] [S2] [SW1]

Hausler, Walter Anthony, Cpl., 45th Co., 5th Regt., KIA, June 6, 1918 in the Chateau-Thierry Sector. Frederick Hausler (Father), 918 Wagoner Ave., Logan, Philadelphia, Pennsylvania [S2] [SW]

Havlicek, Louis F., Pvt., PM, Hdqtrs., USMC, DAS, July 23, 1919 of an accidental gunshot wound at Washington, D.C. Mrs. Stella Havlicek (Mother), 2628 S. Harding Ave., Chicago, Illinois [S4]

Marine Corps Deaths, 1917-1921

Hawk, Eldon George, Pvt., MD, NPG, Indian Head, Maryland, DDS, October 21, 1918 at Indian Head, Maryland. Julie Hawk (Mother), 513 Main St., Charleston, West Virginia [S3]

Hawk, Russell Simon, Pvt., 79th Co., 6th Regt., KIA, July 19, 1918 in the Aisne Marne. S. M. Hawk (Father), 1810 Tydall St., Portland, Oregon [FAG] [S2] [SW says 134th Co., 2nd Repl. Btln.]

Hawthorne, Harry, Pvt., 75th Co., 6th Regt., KIA, July 19, 1918 in the Aisne Marne. Irene Zentz (Fiancee), 659 Wabash Ave., Detroit, Michigan [R] [S2] [SW1]

Haybeck, Charles Jr., Pvt., 55th Co., 5th Regt., KIA, June 12, 1918 in the Chateau-Thierry Sector. Charles Haybeck, Sr. (Father), 756 Jay St., Elmira, New York [S2] [SW]

Haydel, Henry Joseph, Pvt., 44th Co., Santa Domingo, Dominican Republic, DAS, August 13, 918 at Mancho, Dominican Republic. Stanislaus Haydel (Father), 1325 Carondelet St., New Orleans, Louisana [S3]

Hayes, Frank Bryan, Pvt., 75th Co., 6th Regt., DOW, October 5, 1918 in the Meuse Argonne. Mollie Hayes (Mother), Shelby, North Carolina [ABMC- Romagne] [S2] [SW1]

Hayes, Henry, Sgt., RRD, Parris Island, South Carolina, DDS, November 15, 1918 at Parris Island, South Carolina. Mrs. Henry Hayes (Wife), Parris Island, South Carolina [S4]

Haynes, Walter Lee, Pvt., 67th Co., 5th Regt., KIA, June 6, 1918 in the Chateau-Thierry Sector. Thomas and Fannie Haynes (Parents), Hambleton, West Virginia [ANC] [S2] [SW]

Hays, Earl E., Pvt., Co. D, 11th Regt., DAO, June 11, 1919 in France. John B. Hayes (Father), 401 S. River St., Austin, Minnesota [ABMC- Fere] [S2]

Hays, Geoffrey Baxter, Pvt., Co. B, OSD, Quantico, Virginia, DDS, October 14, 1918 at Quantico, Virginia. Thelma Hays (Wife), Lyman, Utah [FAG] [S3]

Marine Corps Deaths, 1917-1921

Hayward, Don Lynch, Pvt., 97th Co., 6th Regt., KIA, June 23, 1918 in the Chateau-Thierry Sector. Mrs. Vergiline Hayward Bauer (Sister), 516 East Main St., Sparta, Illinois [S2] [SW]

Hazzard, John Cosby, Pvt., 23rd Co., 6th MG Bn., KIA, November 11, 1918 in the Meuse Argonne. W. J. Hazzard (Father), Riddleton, Tennessee [VA-Nashville] [S2] [SW1]

Head, Harris James, Pvt., 97th Co., 6th Regt., DOD, September 23, 1918 in France. Harry W. Head (Father), 230 Genesee St., Utica, New York [ABMC- Thiaucourt] [S2]

Healy, John Francis, Cpl., 84th Co., 6th Regt., DOD, February 12, 1919 in France. Mrs. Ellen Healy (Mother), 26 Sixth St., Ansonia, Connecticut [R] [S2]

Heard, Walter Levi, Pvt., Co. B, Mare Island, California, DDS, February 10, 1920 at Mare Island, California. Mrs. Emma Beech (Sister), 1118 Sherman St., Boise, Idaho [FAG] [S4]

Heckman, Harry George, Sgt., 89th Co., 1st Regt., Philadelphia, Pennsylvania, DDS, February 17, 1918 at Pennsylvania Hospital, Philadelphia, Pennsylvania. Wm. Heckman (Brother), 1338 Armansas Ave., Pittsburgh, Pennsylvania [S3]

Hedden, Harvey Putnam, Pvt., 67th Co., 5th Regt., KIA, November 1, 1918 in the Meuse Argonne. Alice P. Hedden (Mother), 18 Newton St., Brighton, Massachusetts [S2] [SW1]

Hedrick, Burt Newton, Pvt., 76th Co., 6th Regt., KIA, October 8, 1918 in the Meuse Argonne. Lydia J. Hedrick (Mother), Wiliamsburg, Greenbrier County, West Virginia [R] [S2] [SW1]

Hedrick, Ora Loyd, Pvt., 79th Co., 6th Regt., KIA, September 15, 1918 in the St. Mihiel Offensive. John Hedrick (Father), RFD#2, Ado, Indiana [ABMC- Romagne] [S2] [SW1]

Marine Corps Deaths, 1917-1921

Heffernan, Austin Francis, Pvt., MCR, MD, Hingham, Massachusetts, DAS, August 8, 1918 of electric shock at Hingham, Massachusetts. Delia Heffernan (Mother), 17 E. Dedhaw St., Boston, Massachusetts [FAG] [S3]

Heffley, Jake Loren, Pvt., 55th Co., 5th Regt., KIA, June 12, 1918 in the Chateau-Thierry Sector. Mary Heffley (Mother), Elbert, Colorado [FAG] [S2] [SW]

Hefron, Frederick, Pvt., 95th Co., 6th Regt., DOW, July 30, 1918 in the Aisne Marne. William Hefron (Father), 23 Queen St., Niagara Falls, New York [ABMC- Fere] [S2] [SW1]

Hegewald, Edward Thomas, Sgt., 82nd Co., 6th Regt., KIA, November 2, 1918 in the Meuse Argonne. Herman Hegewald (Father), 600 Grand Ave., Laramie, Wyoming [ANC] [S2] [SW1]

Heil, Howard Allison, Pvt., 79th Co., 6th Regt., KIA, September 15, 1918 in the St. Mihiel Offensive. Charles H. Heil (Father), Clairton, Pennsylvania [ABMC- Thiaucourt] [S2] [SW1]

Hein, Frank George, Pvt., 80th Co., 6th Regt., DOW, July 19, 1918 in the Aisne Marne. Hugo Hein (Father), 1113 S. 11th St., Springfield, Illiniois [ABMC- Fere] [S2] [SW1]

Heinrich, Richard Herman, Pvt., 17th Co., 5th Regt., KIA, June 26, 1918 in the Chateau-Thierry Sector. G. A. Heinrich (Brother), 1417 Waveland Ave., Chicago, Illinois [ABMC- Belleau TOM] [S2] [SW1]

Heinz, Edward Lewis, Pvt., 76th Co., 6th Regt., DOW, June 3, 1918 in the Aisne Defensive. C. P. Heinz (Father), 218 S. 38th St., Louisville, Kentucky [S2] [SW]

Heinz, Lionel Ridel, Pvt., 22nd Co., 1st Regt., Philadelphia, Pennsylvania, DDS, October 2, 1918 at Philadelphia, Pennsylvania. Mildred Rathbone (Mother), 514 Argyle St., Waterloo, Iowa [FAG] [S3]

Heisel, James Emmitt, Pvt., 16th Co., 5th Regt., KIA, June 23, 1918 in the Chateau-Thierry Sector. Mrs. Florence

Marine Corps Deaths, 1917-1921

    Condiff (Mother), 1815 W. New York St., Indianapolis, Indiana [ABMC- Belleau] [S2] [SW]

Heiser, Jacob, Pvt., Co. A, Canacao, Philippine Islands, DDS, February 16, 1920 at Canacao, Philippine Islands. Frank Heiser (Brother), Gen. Del., Bellfield, North Dakota [S4]

Helgeson, Axel Arnold, Pvt., USS *Brooklyn*, DDS, April 13, 1918 at Vladivostock, Siberia. Carl G. Helgeson (Father), Forest Lake, Minnesota [S3]

Hellams, Elias Ball, Pvt., Hdqtrs. Co., OSD, Quantico, Virginia, DDS, January 21, 1919 at Quantico, Virginia. Mrs. Catherine Hellams (Sister), 19 Arnold St., Atlanta, Georgia [FAG] [S4]

Hellman, Simon, Cpl., 83rd Co., 6th Regt., KIA, June 8, 1918 in the Chateau-Thierry Sector. Fannie Hellman (Mother), 1004 Broadway, New Orleans, Louisana [R] [S2] [SW]

Helm, Lester Ray, Pvt., Co. F, 13th Regt., DOD, September 26, 1918 in France. Jonas S. Helm (Father), Witmer, Pennsylvania [R] [S2]

Helms, John H., Pvt., 48th Co., 4th Regt., Domincan Republic, DDS, February 17, 1919 at Santo Domingo, Dominican Republic. James H. Helms (Father), 224 N. Evergreen Ave., Kankakee, Illinois [FAG] [S4]

Hemmerling, Loren Alexander, Pvt., 18th Co., 5th Regt., DOW, November 4, 1918 in the Meuse Argonne. Mary Gasser (Mother), 2327 Orleans St., New Orleans, Louisana [ABMC-Romagne] [S2] [SW1]

Henderson, Aetna C., Pvt., Bks. Det., Quantico, Virginia, DDS, December 21, 1918 at Quantico, Virginia. Mrs. Lucy E. Henderson (Mother), RFD#3, Oxford, Iowa [FAG] [S4]

Henderson, Benjamin Everhart, Pvt., 49th Co., 5th Regt., KIA, June 6, 1918 in the Chateau-Thierry Sector. Charles Henderson (Father), 6404 Parnell Ave., Chicago, Illinois [ABMC- Belleau] [S2] [SW1]

Marine Corps Deaths, 1917-1921

Hendricks, Charles Aloysious, Pvt., 84th Co., 6th Regt., KIA, November 1, 1918 in the Meuse Argonne. Mary Hendricks (Mother), 1828 4th St, Moline, Illinois [S2] [SW1]

Hendricks, John, Cpl., 18th Co., 5th Regt., KIA, October 4, 1918 in the Meuse Argonne. Mrs.Lou Zook (Mother), Mooresille, Indiana [R] [S2] [SW1 says DOW]

Heningar, Henry Authur, Pvt., 18th Co., 5th Regt., DOW, July 18, 1918 in the Aisne Marne. Mrs. Margaret E. Heningar (Wife), 133 Hendricks Ave., Stapleton, New York [R] [S2] [SW1]

Henkhaus, Henry Edward, Pvt., 66th Co., 5th Regt., DOW, July 19, 1918 in the Aisne Marne. Mrs. Julia Henkhaus (Mother), 1006 Elliot Ave., Alton, Illinois [S2] [SW]

Hennessee, William Clayton, Pvt., 17th Co., 5th Regt., DOW, September 22, 1918 in the St. Mihiel Offensive. James R. Hennessee (Father), Sparta, Tennessee [FAG] [S2] [SW says Casualty Co.]

Henry, Cecil Ewert Gladston(e), Pvt., 96th Co., 6th Regt., KIA, October 3, 1918 in the Meuse Argonne. Thomas N. Henry (Father), 12 Pearl St., Asheville, North Carolina [ABMC- Romagne] [S2] [SW1]

Henry, Curtis Lafayette, Pvt., 66th Co., 5th Regt., DOW, July 18, 1918 in the Aisne Marne. Sylvia Henry (Mother), Wallerville, Mississippi [ABMC- Belleau TOM] [S2] [SW1]

Henry, William D., Gy. Sgt., 52nd Co., 3rd Regt., Dominican Republic, DDS, January 19, 1920 at Santo Domingo, Dominican Republic. Rose Edwards (Sister), Westfield, New Jersey [S4]

Hensiek, Alonzo Charles, Cpl., 51st Co., 5th Regt., KIA, June 11, 1918 in the Chateau-Thierry Sector. Fritz Hensiek (Father), Janesburg, Ohio [FAG] [S2] [SW1]

Marine Corps Deaths, 1917-1921

Hensley, Willard Edgar, Sgt., 97th Co., 6th Regt., KIA, June 6, 1918 in the Chateau-Thierry Sector. Mrs. Prudence Hensley (Mother), Morristown, Indiana [S2] [SW]

Herdle, Albert Ernest, Pvt., 96th Co., 6th Regt., DOD, January 28, 1919 in France. Jacob Herdle (Father), North Evans, New York [R] [S2]

Heslop, Guy Douglas, Pvt., 130th Co., Quantico, Virginia, DDS, September 27, 1918 at Quantico, Virginia. Florence Heslop (Mother), 136 Warner St., Marietta, Ohio [FAG] [S3]

Hesner, Andrew F., Pvt., Co. A, 3rd Sep. MG Bn, Quantico, Virginia, DDS, November 20, 1918 at Quantico, Virginia. Charles A. Hesner (Father), Edgewood, Iowa [FAG] [S4]

Hess, Harry Edison, Pvt., 17th Co., 5th Regt., DOW, June 11, 1918 in the Chateau-Thierry Sector. May Dillon (Mother), Box 746, New Augustine, Florida [FAG] [S2] [SW]

Hess, Harry Joseph, Pvt., 96th Co., 6th Regt., DOW, July 19, 1918 in the Aisne Marne. Hattie Bates (Mother), 440 N. Expositon Ave., Wichita, Kansas [FAG] [S2] [SW1]

Hess, Raymond James, Pvt., 66th Co., 5th Regt., KIA, July 3, 1918 in the Chateau-Thierry Sector. James Hess (Father), 310 N. Mulberry St., Marshall, Michigan [FAG] [S2] [SW]

Hess, Robert Burns, Cpl., 20th Co., 5th Regt., DOW, June 15, 1918 in the Chateau-Thierry Sector. Mrs. Sarah Hess (Mother), 415 Jenks St., St. Paul, Minnesota [R] [S2] [SW]

Hession, Andrew J., Pvt., OSD, Quantico, Virginia, DDS, November 13, 1918 at Quantico, Virginia. Miss Anna Hession (Sister), 108 W. 109th St., New York, New York [S4]

Hetzner, George John, Cpl., 74th Co., 6th Regt., DOW, June 3, 1918 in the Aisne Defensive. John Hetzner (Father), 1901 Denison Ave., Cleveland, Ohio [S2] [SW]

Heurich, Elmer Valentine, Cpl., Field and Staff, 13th Regt., DAO, April 23, 1919 in the Chateau-Thierry Sector by reason of a German shell accidentally exploding. Valentine Heurich (Father), 1031 W. Liberty St., Cincinnati, Ohio [R] [S2]

Hewitt, Charles Wilmer Jr., Cpl., 45th Co., 5th Regt., KIA, June 6, 1918 in the Chateau-Thierry Sector. Charles W. Hewitt (Father), 5127 N. 12th St., Philadelphia, Pennsylvania [FAG] [S2] [SW]

Heymann, Henry Peter, Sgt., 20th Co., 5th Regt., KIA, June 25, 1918 in the Chateau-Thierry Sector. Anna Heymann (not stated), 523 S. West St., Bellevue, Ohio [ABMC-Belleau] [S2] [SW]

Hibbard, Harrell Harris, 1st Sgt., MB, Navy Yard, Boston, Massachusetts, DDS, March 17, 1918 at Chelsea, Massachusetts. Matie T. Hibbard (Mother), 727 N. Ewing St., Helena, Montana [S3]

Hickey, Joseph William, Pvt., 15th Co., 6th MG Bn., KIA, October 6, 1918 in the Meuse Argonne. Mary Hickey (Sister), 1207 Santa Clara Ave., Alameda, Calfornia [R] [S2]

Hicks, John William, Pvt., 44th Co., 3rd Regt., 2nd Brigade, Dominican Republic, DAS, May 22, 1921 accidently drowned in the Ozama River, Santo Domingo City, Dominican Republic. Charles Hicks (Brother), 15 Saunder St., Salem, Massachusetts [S4] [SW]

Hiddleson, Alfred Heaton, Pvt., 95th Co., 6th Regt., KIA, November 2, 1918 in the Meuse Argonne. Margaret Hiddleson (Mother), 508 N. Orange St., Morrison, Illinois [FAG] [S2] [SW1]

Higginbotham, John Wesley, Cpl., 74th Co., 6th Regt., KIA, June 11, 1918 in the Chateau-Thierry Sector. Willis F. Higginbotham (Father), Box 394, Blocton, Alabama [ANC] [S2] [SW]

Higgins, Andrew Jackson, Pvt., 16th Co., 5th Regt., KIA, June 3, 1918 in the Aisne Defensive. Bettie Higgins (Mother), Ennice, North Carolina [ABMC- Belleau TOM] [S2]

Marine Corps Deaths, 1917-1921

Higgins, Francis George, Cpl., 75th Co., 6th Regt., DOW, November 1, 1918 in the Meuse Argonne. Mrs. George Higgins (Mother), 519 N. Pine St., Lansing, Michigan [ANC] [S2] [SW1 says George Francis Higgins]

Higgins, Henry Edward, Pvt., 47th Co., 5th Regt., DOW, June 25, 1918 in the Chateau-Thierry Sector. Elizabeth Higgins (Mother), 1328 Blaisdells, Rockford, Illinois [ABMC-Belleau] [S2] [SW1]

Higgins, Ralph Seymour, Pvt., 97th Co., 6th Regt., DOW, November 1, 1918 in the Meuse Argonne. Rachel Higgins (Mother), 177 Clinton St., Salamanca, New York [FAG] [S2] [SW1]

Higginson, William Paul, 1st Sgt., 45th Co., 5th Regt., KIA, June 6, 1918 in the Chateau-Thierry Sector. Bridget Higginson (Mother), 986 Harvard St., Rochester, New York [FAG] [S2] [SW]

Highams, John William, Pvt., 97th Co., 6th Regt., KIA, October 6, 1918 in the Meuse Argonne. Mrs. Lucy E. Highams (Mother), 300 Bethel Ave., Memphis, Tennessee [FAG] [S2] [SW]

Hilbert, James Roswell, Pvt., 82nd Co., 6th Regt., DOW, July 19, 1918 in the Aisne Marne. Mary A. Alford (Mother), 509 Second St., Loagostee, Indiana [FAG] [S2] [SW1]

Hiles, Earle Clifton, Pvt., 79th Co., 6th Regt., KIA, July 19, 1918 in the Aisne Marne. Mrs. Dorothy Hiles (Mother), 2986 Beals Ave., Detriot, Michigan [FAG] [S2] [SW1]

Hill, Glayron Earl, Pvt., 67th Co., 5th Regt., DOW, July 28, 1918 in the Aisne Marne. Della M. Deckard (Mother), 126 W. 9th St., Mt. Carmel, Illinois [R] [S2] [SW says 134th Repl. Co.]

Hill, Herbert Lee, Pvt., 49th Co., 5th Regt., DOW, June 7, 1918 in the Chateau-Thierry Sector. Myrtle Hill (Mother), 604 Campbell St., Florence, Alabama [ABMC- Suresnes] [S2][SW]

Marine Corps Deaths, 1917-1921

Hill, Jewell Tallmadge, Pvt., 49th Co., 5th Regt., KIA, June 6, 1918 in the Chateau-Thierry Sector. Mrs. M. V. Hill (Mother), Jefferson, Georgia [FAG] [S2] [SW]

Hill, Leo John, Cpl., 74th Co., 6th Regt., KIA, July 19, 1918 in the Aisne Marne. Charles F. Hill (Father), Steamboat Springs, Colorado [ANC] [S2] [SW]

Hill, Louis, Pvt., 18th Co., 5th Regt., DOW, September 15, 1918 in the St. Mihiel Offensive. Mrs. Carrie McKay (Sister), Libby, Minnesota [FAG] [S2] [SW1]

Hill, Ralph Harmon, Pvt., 76th Co., 6th Regt., KIA, November 1, 1918 in the Meuse Argonne. Mrs. Madge Brehm (Mother), 28 S. Plum St., Springfield, Ohio [S2] [SW1 says DOW]

Hill, Ralph Orion, Pvt., 47th Co., 5th Regt., KIA, June 6, 1918 in the Chateau-Thierry Sector. Susan Hill (Mother), 28 Pierpont Ave., Potsdam, New York [S2] [SW1]

Hill, Robert Alyn, Pvt., MBks., Quantico, Virginia, DDS, January 5, 1919 at Holly, Michigan. MRs. Anna G. Hill (Mother), Box 451, Holly, Michigan [FAG] [S4]

Hill, Theodore Boyd, Cpl., 75th Co., 6th Regt., DOW, October 8, 1918 in the Meuse Argonne. minie Hill (Mother), 1236 E. Beach St, Gulfport, Mississippi [FAGM] [S2] [SW1]

Hill, Thornton Winders, Pvt., Cyclops (Navy Collier), DAU, June 14, 1918 aboard Cyclops which was lost at sea. Mrs Charles Morris (Sister), 317 E. Center St., Fostoria, Ohio [FAG] [S3]

Hillery, David Joseph, Pvt., 43rd Co., 5th Regt., KIA, June 11, 1918 in the Chateau-Thierry Sector. Dennis J. Hillery (Father), 2046 Seneca St., Buffalo, New York [S2] [SW]

Hillery, Dwight R., Cpl., 58th Co., Norfolk, Virginia, DOS, DOS, December 2, 1918 at Norfolk, Virginia. Mrs. Leah Hillery (Mother), 2823 Stickney Ave., Toledo, Ohio [S4]

Hilliard, Howard Gates, Cpl., 16th Co., 5th Regt., KIA, November 9, 1918 in the Meuse Argonne. Fannie Hilliard (Mother),

Marine Corps Deaths, 1917-1921

Waterside Ave., Clinton, Connecticut [ABMC- Romagne] [S2] [SW1 says DOW]

Hillix, Harry, Cpl., 16th Co., 5th Regt., KIA, June 23, 1918 in the Chateau-Thierry Sector. Jeanette Branson (Mother), 522 Harrison St., Fredonia, Kansas [ABMC- Belleau TOM] [S2] [SW]

Hilton, Frank Henry, Pvt., 22nd Co., Philadelphia, Pennsylvania, DDS, October 2, 1918 at Philadelphia, Pennsylvania. Mrs. Frank H. Hilton (Wife), Orchard Park, New York [S3]

Hinchman, Clarence Benjiman, Pvt., 49th Co., 5th Regt., DOW, November 1, 1918 in the Meuse Argonne. Mrs. J. W. Crews (Sister), RR #2, Lawrenceville, Illinois [S2] [SW1]

Hinckley, Joel Carr, Pvt., 51st Co., 5th Regt., KIA, November 2, 1918 in the Meuse Argonne. Jaides Hinckley (Mother), RFD #1, Bear Lake, Pennsylvania [S2] [SW1]

Hindeily, John Simon, Pvt., 97th Co., 6th Regt., DOW, July 20, 1918 in the Aisne Marne. Ida M. Hindeily (Wife), 34 Baltimore Lane, Wilkes Barre, Pennsylvania [ABMC- Belleau] [S2] [SW says Hdqtrs. Co., 3rd Repl. Btln.]

Hindman, Thomas Jehu, Sgt., 95th Co., 6th Regt., KIA, July 19, 1918 in the Aisne Marne. Julia Hindman (Aunt), Indpendent Bldg., Nashville, Tennessee [ABMC- Belleau TOM] [S2] [SW1 says Thomas John Hindman]

Hinds, Frederick Campbell, Pvt., 81st Co., 6th MG Bn., KIA, July 19, 1918 in the Aisne Marne. Edward Hinds (Father), Gen. Del., Dutton, Montana [ABMC- Belleau] [S2] [SW]

Hines, John, Jr., Pvt., 97th Co., 6th Regt., DOD, September 29, 1918 in France. Mrs. John Hines (Mother), Box 113, Radner, Ohio [FAG as September 9, 1918] [S2]

Hinton, Gibson, Pvt., Co. F, 11th Regt., Quantico, Virginia, DDS, October 10, 1918 at Quantico, Virginia. William T. Hinton (Brother), Sadieville, Kentucky [S3]

Marine Corps Deaths, 1917-1921

Hinz, Otto George, 1st Sgt., Quantico, Virginia, DAS, September 26, 1921 in an automobile accident at Quantico, Virginia. Mrs. Florence Hinz (Wife), 1253 Ship Yard, Quantico, Virginia [ANC] [S4]

Hires, Fred Elmer, Pvt., Co. Z, Parris Island, South Carolina, DDS, September 13, 1918 at Parris Island, South Carolina. Negley Hires (Brother), 415 Floyd St., Toledo, Ohio [S3]

Hitchcock, John Hutchinson, Pvt., Co. Y, Parris Island, South Carolina, DDS, October 24, 1918 at Parris Island, South Carolina. H. L. Hitchcock (Father), c/o C. E. Arndt, Washington St., Michigan City, Indiana [S3]

Hitter, Leonard Augustus, Pvt., 18th Co., 5th Regt., KIA, October 4, 1918 in the Meuse Argonne. Mrs. Ida Mae Gibson (Mother), 1309½ Commerce St., Tacoma, Washington [FAG] [S2] [SW1]

Hitzel, Walter Henry, Pvt., Co. O, Parris Island, South Carolina, DDS, October 29, 1918 at Parris Island, South Carolina. Dora H. Dittman (Mother), Foot of Gull St., Buffalo, New York [S3]

Hixson, Clarence R., Pfc, MD, USNH, Fort Lyon, Colorado, DDS, January 27, 1920 at Fort Lyon, Colorado. Mr. F. Hixson, Hixson Station, Tennessee [FAG] [S4]

Hixson, Frederick Hieford, Pvt., 79th Co., 6th Regt., KIA, June 14, 1918 in the Chateau-Thierry Sector. Carolyn L. Hixson (Mother), 126 Wilson St., Syracuse, New York [S2] [SW says Repl. Btln.]

Hloucal, Joseph H., Pvt., 79th Co., 6th Regt., DOW, November 1, 1918 in the Meuse Argonne. Anna Hloucal (Mother), Ellsworth, Kansas [FAG] [S2] [SW1]

Hoagland, Floyd F., Pvt., 92nd Co., Nav. Sta., Pearl Harbor, Territory of Hawaii, DAS, December 25, 1918 of a fractured skull at Pearl Harbor, Territory of Hawaii. Mrs. Josephine Hoagland (Mother), 313 Belleu Ave., Walla Walla, Washington [S4]

Marine Corps Deaths, 1917-1921

Hobson, Harold V., Pvt., 152nd Co., San Diego, California, DDS, December 2, 1918 at San Diego, California. Mrs. Eliza C. Hobson (Mother), Richmond, Cache Co., Utah [FAG] [S4]

Hockenberry, Cecil Claud, Pvt., 17th Co., 5th Regt., KIA, October 4, 1918 in the Meuse Argonne. Charles Hockenberry (Father), Sully, West Virginia [ANC] [S2] [SW1]

Hockett, Harley B., QM Clerk, Supply Co., 13th Regt., DOD, September 24, 1918 aboard the *Henderson*. Mrs. Harley B. Hockett (widow), P. O. Box 509, Fresno, California [S1]

Hodges, James Simpson, Pvt., 43rd Co., 5th Regt., KIA, June 3, 1918 in the Aisne Defensive. Amy Sgtryker (Sister), Overton, Nebraska [ABMC- Belleau] [S2] [SW]

Hodges, Robert Raymond, Cpl., 96th Co., 6th Regt., KIA, June 18, 1918 in the Chateau-Thierry Sector. Priscilla Hodges (Mother), 836 N. Washington Ave., Saginaw, Michigan [FAG] [S2] [SW1]

Hodgkinson, Chester B., Sgt. Major, Brigade Hdqtrs. Det., Dominican Republic, DOS, April 29, 1921 at Santo Domingo, Dominican Republic. Arnold Hodgkinson (Father), 6616 Clearlot Rd., Oakland, California [S4]

Hoesch, Joseph Jacob, Pvt., Co. E, 13th Regt., DOD, September 26, 1918 in France. Emma Dewey (Sister), R#3, Milford, Iowa [R] [S2]

Hofelt, Fred Charles, Gy. Sgt., 42nd Co., Guam, DOS, February 12, 1920 at Guam. Mrs. Louis Hug (Sister), 7613 Lowe Ave., Chicago, Illinois [S4]

Hoffman, Charles Schaefer, Sgt., Pub Bur, New York, DDS, January 14, 1921 at New York, New York. Mrs. Henrietta Hoffman (Wife), 202 Amherst St., E. Orange, New Jersey [FAG] [S4]

Hoffman, Clarence Nicholas, Pvt., 51st Co., 5th Regt., KIA, September 15, 1918 in the St. Mihiel Offensive. Fred

Marine Corps Deaths, 1917-1921

Hoffman (Father), 111-119 Dearborn St., Buffalo, New York [ABMC- Thiaucourt] [S2] [SW]

Hoffman, Harry, Cpl., 73rd Co., 6th Regt., DOW, June 8, 1918 in the Chateau-Thierry Sector. Mrs. Mary Hoffman (Mother), RR#9, Lancaster, Ohio [R] [S2] [SW1]

Hoffman, Tom Brown, Pvt., 95th Co., 6th Regt., KIA, July 19, 1918 in the Aisne Marne. Gussie Hoffman (Mother), Box 67, N. Pleasanton, Texas [ANC] [S2] [SW1]

Hoffman, William, Sgt., 43rd Co., 5th Regt., DOW, June 24, 1918 in the Chateau-Thierry Sector. Margaret N. O'Brien (Mother), 713 State St., Milwaukee, Wisconsin [R] [S2] [SW1]

Hoffmeister, William McK., Pvt., Co. H, MB, Navy Yard, Mare Island, California, DDS, November 18, 1918 at Mare Island, California. Fred Hoffmeister (Father), RFD#1, Eagle Creek, Clackamas Co., Oregon [FAG] [S4]

Hogan, John Arthur, Pvt., 3rd Co., Paoli, Pennsylvania, DDS, September 26, 1918 at Philadelphia, Pennsylvania. J. F. Hogan (Father), Tooele, Utah [FAG] [S3]

Hogan, Thomas, Gy. Sgt., MD, Point Isabel, Texas, DOS, November 9, 1920 at Brownsville, Texas. Mrs. John Haley (Sister), 824 Baker St., Flint, Michigan [S4]

Hogarth, Frank William, Pvt., 147th Signal Co., Camp Ed C. Fuller, Paoli, Pennsylvania, DDS, October 2, 1918 at Philadlephia, Pennsylvania. Frances Hogarth (Mother), 1135 Cedar Ave., Long Beach, California [S3]

Hoggatt, Harry, Pvt., 79th Co., 6th Regt., KIA, October 5, 1918 in the Meuse Argonne. Lelia E. Hoggartt (Mother), 2627 E. 29th St., Kansas City, Missouri [FAG] [S2] [SW1 has Hogatt]

Hogue, Oliver Farfield, Sgt., 84th Co., 6th Regt., DOW, October 8, 1918 in the Meuse Argonne. Mrs. Sarah J. Hogue (Mother), Cottonwood, Idaho [ANC] [S2] [SW1 says Oliver Garfield Hogue]

Marine Corps Deaths, 1917-1921

Hoke, John Clarence, Pvt., 140th, 3rd Replacement Battalion, KIA, June 6, 1918 in the Chateau-Thierry Sector. John D. Hoke (Father), Green Sulphur Springs, West Virginia [S2] [SW1]

Holder, Arthur, Sgt., 51st Co., 5th Regt., DOW, November 29, 1918 in the Meuse Argonne. William Holder (Father), N. Wilkesboro, North Carolina [FAG] [S2] [SW1]

Holdman, John, Gy. Sgt., 96th Co., 6th Regt., DOW, November 18, 1918 in the Meuse Argonne. Docia Holdman (Mother), Ramsey, Illinois [FAG] [S2] [SW1]

Holland, Timothy Joseph, Captain, MB, Quantico, Virginia, DDS, June 2, 1921 at Quantico, Virginia. John Holland (Father), 10 Carpenter St., Northfield, Vermont [S4]

Holland, William Everette, Pvt., Supply Co., 6th Regt., DOD, October 3, 1918 in France. Nettie Holland (Sister), 415 W. 30th St., Norfolk, Virginia [ANC] [S2]

Holliday, Charles P., Capt., Supply Co., 5th Regt., DOD, August 5, 1918 aboard the *Henderson*. Mrs. Ethel F. Holliday (widow), Box 251, Rockland, Maine [ABMC-Suresnes] [S1]

Hollingshead, Charles, Sgt., 20th Co., 5th Regt., DOW, June 29, 1918 in the Chateau-Thierry Sector. Annie Hollingshead (Mother), #3 Mt. Pleasant St., Derry, New Hampshire [FAG] [S2] [SW]

Hollinshed, Percy Lincoln, Pvt., 17th Co., 5th Regt., DOW, June 7, 1918 in the Chateau-Thierry Sector. Mary E. Hollinshed (Mother), Deair, New Jersey [S2] [SW]

Hollister, Marloyne Vincent, III, Pvt., MCR, MAD, Miami, Florida, DDS, September 22, 1918 at Miami, Florida. Mrs. M. V. Hollister (Wife), 11 B Crossan Apartments, Atlantic City, New Jersey [S3]

Hollow, Emil John, Pvt., Mar. Det., Fort Lyon, Colorado, DDS, October 7, 1920 at Fort Lyon, Colorado. Leander J. Parce

Marine Corps Deaths, 1917-1921

(Stepfather), 339 K St., Salt Lake City, Utah [VA-Fort Lyon] [S4]

Holly, Wenceslow Burt, Pvt., Co. B, Mare Island, California DDS, May 2, 1921 at Mare Island, California. Joseph Holly (Father), 1854 S. Hayne Ave., Chicago, Illinois [S4]

Holman, Charlie Jackson, Pvt., 47th Co., 5th Regt., KIA, October 4, 1918 in the Meuse Argonne. Lena Holman (Mother), 950 W. Eastland Ave., Nashville, Tennessee [R] [S2] [SW1]

Holmes, Lewis Anderson, Pvt., 49th Co., 5th Regt., KIA [SW] [SW1 reported to have been found alive]

Holmes, Roy Samuel, Pvt., Co. H, 13th Regt., DOD, January 13, 1919 in France. Mary L. Holmes (Wife), 4830 LeDuc St., St. Louis, Missouri [VA-Jefferson Barracks] [S2]

Holmgren, Henry, Pvt., Nav. Sta., Great Lakes, Illinois, DOS, May 4, 1920 at Great Falls, Montana. Mrs. Annie Holmgren (Mother), 505 5th St., S.W., Great Falls, Montana [S4]

Holt, James William, Pvt., 66th Guard Co., USMC, DAO, January 25, 1919 in France. J. Cal Holt (Father), RR#5, Franklin, Tennessee [ABMC- Fere] [S2] [SW1 says KOA]

Holtman, George, Cpl., 47th Co., 5th Regt., DOW, June 25, 1918 in the Chateau-Thierry Sector. John Holtman (Father), Shoshone, Idaho [FAG] [S2] [SW1]

Holtz, John Walter, Pvt., 66th Co., 5th Regt., KIA, October 4, 1918 in the Meuse Argonne. Pauline H. Holtz (Mother), 19 Norway Park, Buffalo, New York [ABMC- Romagne TOM] [S2] [SW1]

Homesley, Lloyd C., Pvt., MB, Navy Yard, Brooklyn, New York, DDS, January 30, 1919 at Brooklyn, New York. Mrs. Mattie Homesley (Mother), c/o Confederate Soldiers Home, Higginsville, Missouri [FAG] [FAGM] [S4]

Marine Corps Deaths, 1917-1921

Hoopes, Harlow Red Field, Pvt., 17th Co., 5th Regt., DOW, October 10, 1918 in the Meuse Argonne. Lavina Hoopes (Mother), Rupert, Idaho [FAG] [S2] [SW1]

Hoover, Phillip Herbert, Pvt., 67th Co., 5th Regt., DOW, June 17, 1918 in the Chateau-Thierry Sector. Manson M. Hoower (Father), R#2, Box 64, Oklahoma City, Oklahoma [R] [S2] [SW]

Hope, Martin Luther, Gy. Sgt., MCR, MAD, Miami, Florida, DAS, October 22, 1918 in an aeroplane accident at Miami, Florida. Martha L. Hope (Mother), West DePere, Wisconsin [S3]

Hoppel, Charles John, Jr., Pvt., Co. Y, Parris Island, South Carolina, DDS, November 7, 1918 at Parris Island, South Carolina. Charles J. Hoppel (Father), 96 Hawley St., Buffalo, New York [FAG] [S3]

Hopta, Joseph Leo, Sgt., 55th Co., 5th Regt., KIA, November 4, 1918 in the Meuse Argonne. John Hopta (Father), 491 Mulberry St., Newark, New Jersey [ABMC-Romagne] [S2] [SW1]

Horgan, Roy Lawrence, Pvt., 66th Co., 5th Regt., DOW, June 22, 1918 in the Chateau-Thierry Sector. Katherine Horgan (Mother), Langdon, North Dakota [FAG] [S2] [SW]

Horstmann, Paul Fred, Cpl., 55th Co., 5th Regt., KIA, July 21, 1918 in the Aisne Marne. Dorothy Horstmann (Mother), Glennburne, Maryland [ABMC- Belleau TOM] [S2] [SW says Hortsmann]

Horton, Carle Harvie, Gy. Sgt., 15th Co., 6th MG Bn., DOW, June 30, 1918 in the Aisne Defensive. Jennie Horton (Mother), RR 29, Box 40, Macy, Indiana [R] [S2] [SW]

Horton, Donald Constantine, Pvt., 20th Co., 5th Regt., KIA, June 23, 1918 in the Chateau-Thierry Sector. Gilbert L. Horton (Father), Litchfield, Minnesota [ANC] [S2] [SW]

Marine Corps Deaths, 1917-1921

Hosack, Clarence Frank, Pvt., 17th Co., 5th Regt., DOD, May 10, 1919 in France. Mrs. Charles F. Jindrich (Aunt), 5401 McBride St., Cleveland, Ohio [ABMC- Fere] [S2]

Houchins, Lyle C., Pvt., 73rd Co., 6th Regt., DOW, November 1, 1918 in the Meuse Argonne. Robert Lee Houchins (Father), RR #10, Box 38, Station M, Cincinnati, Ohio [ABMC- Romagne] [S2] [SW1]

Hourigan, Richard Edward, Pvt., 79th Co., 6th Regt., KIA, October 5, 1918 in the Meuse Argonne. Michael H. Hourigan (Brother), 66 Main St., Norwich, Connecticut [S2] [SW says Co. B, 5th Rep. Bltn.]

House, John Orator, Pvt., 47th Co., 5th Regt., KIA, October 4, 1918 in the Meuse Argonne. Thomas G. House (Father), Ness City, Kansas [R] [S2] [SW1]

House, Lisle Sherman, Pvt., 47th Co., 5th Regt., DOW, October 16, 1918 in the Meuse Argonne. Harvey J. House (Father), 531 Williams St., Rome, New York [ABMC-Thiaucourt] [FAG] [S2] [SW1]

Houston, Harry Martin, Pvt., 8th Co., 5th Regt., KIA, October 4, 1918 in the Meuse Argonne. Jennie Houston (Mother), 1100 Charlotte St., Pekin, Illinois [R] [S2] [SW says 16th Co.]

Howard, Richard G., 2nd Lieutenant, 183rd Co., 15th Regt., 2nd Prov. Brigade, Dominican Republic, KIA, August 13, 1919 by bandits at Santo Domingo, Dominican Repubic. Mr. A. J. Howard (Father), RFD#3, Darlington, South Carolina [FAG] [S4]

Howe, Allen Hawkes, Pvt., 97th Co., 6th Regt., KIA, June 8, 1918 in the Chateau-Thierry Sector. Sumner L. Howe (Father), 184 Pleasant St., Marlboro, Massachusetts [FAG] [S2]

Hoxie, Guy De Lamater, Pvt., 97th Co., 6th Regt., KIA, July 19, 1918 in the Aisne Marne. Joseph B. Hoxie (Father), 4164 Drexel Blvd., Chicago, Illinois [FAG] [S2] [SW]

Marine Corps Deaths, 1917-1921

Hoyle, Warren F., Pvt., 75th Co., 6th Regt., KIA [ABMC-Belleau [SW]

Hoyt, Wesley Allen, Pvt., 83rd Co., 6th Regt., KIA, June 6, 1918 in the Chateau-Thierry Sector. Miss Loretta H. Hoyt (Sister), 94 E. Main St., Middletown, New York [ABMC-Belleau] [S2] [SW]

Hubbartt, Charles Edward, Pvt., 67th Co., 5th Regt., KIA, June 6, 1918 in the Chateau-Thierry Sector. Mary Hubbartt (Mother), Beecher City, Illinois [FAG] [S2] [SW]

Hubner, William Louis, Cpl., 95th Co., 6th Regt., KIA, June 12, 1918 in the Chateau-Thierry Sector. Frida Hubner (Mother), 1326 Washington St., La Porte, Indiana [ABMC- Belleau TOM] [S2] [SW]

Hudgings, Clay Thomas, Cpl., 18th Co., 5th Regt., KIA, July 18, 1918 in the Aisne Marne. Mrs. Minnie B.Hudgings (Wife), 204 E. 3rd St., Caruthersville, Missouri [FAG] [S2] [SW1]

Hudson, Eugene, Pvt., 33rd Co., 15th Regt., Domincan Republic, DAS, December 11, 1919 at Conseulo, Dominican Republic. Mrs. Fannie L. Morgan (Sister), Opp, Covington Co., Alabama [FAG] [S4]

Hudson, Otis Lee, Cpl., 45th Co., 5th Regt., DOD, February 25, 1919 in the Chateau-Thierry Sector. Sam Hudson (Father), Mt. Creek, Alabama [ABMC- Suresnes] [S2]

Huey, Wellman Hazlett, Pvt., 80th Co., 6th Regt., KIA, June 11, 1918 in the Chateau-Thierry Sector. Charles H. Huey (Father), 115 Maplewood St., Detroit, Michigan [ABMC-Belleau] [S2] [SW]

Huff, John Burnett, Pvt., Bks. Det., Norfolk, Virginia, DDS, October 27, 1917 at Norfolk, Virginia. Hiram Huff (Father), Clermont, Indiana [FAG] [S3]

Huff, William Nile, Pvt., 96th Co., 6th Regt., DOW, June 15, 1918 in the Chateau-Thierry Sector. Viloa Huff (Mother), 206

N. Third St., Ponca City, Oklahoma [ANC] [S2] [SW says Replacement]

Huffstater, Leon David, Pvt., 97th Co., 6th Regt., KIA, October 11, 1918 in the Meuse Argonne. Belle Haines (Mother), RFD#3, Oswego, New York [R] [S2] [SW]

Hufstedler, Erie, Cpl., So. Rec. Div., Memphis, Tennessee, DAS, September 1, 1919 at Memphis, Tennessee. Mrs. Beatrice Hufstedler (Mother), Imboden, Arkansas [FAG as Clyde Eric Hufstedler] [S4]

Huggard, George S., 2nd Lieut., M Co., 13th Regt., DOD, September 27, 1918 aboard the *Von Steuben*. Mrs. R. J. Huggard (Mother), 58 Everett St., Newton Centre, Massachusetts [R] [S1]

Hughes, Ambrose, Cpl., 49th Co., 5th Regt., KIA, June 6, 1918 in the Chateau-Thierry Sector. Mrs. Margarete Hughes (Mother), Madrid, New York [ANC] [FAG lists VA-Alexandria] [S2] [SW]

Hughes, Elmer Herbert, Pvt., 74th Co., 6th Regt., KIA, October 4, 1918 in the Meuse Argonne. Elizabeth Hughes (Mother), 823 Livingston St., Cincinnati, Ohio [ABMC- Romagne] [S2] [SW1]

Hughes, Wert, Pvt., USNH, Las Animas, Colorado, DDS, February 8, 1921 at Las Animas, Colorado. Thomas Hughes (Father), Defeated, Tennessee [S4]

Hulbert, Henry L., 1st Lieut., 66th Co., 5th Regt., KIA, October 4, 1918 in the Meuse Argonne. Mrs. H. L. Hulbert (widow), C/o Mr. Akelitys, Washington Park, Halethrope, Maryland [ANC] [S1] [SW]

Humber, Paul, Pvt., Dominican Republic, DOS, March 10, 1918 at Santo Domingo, Domincan Republic. Katie E. Dickroeger (Sister), Wright City, Missouri [FAG] [S3]

Humler, Joe McFarland, Pvt., 97th Co., 6th Regt., DOW, July 20, 1918 in the Aisne Marne. Bert Humler (Father), 1818 S. Third St., Louisville, Kentucky [R] [S2] [SW1]

Marine Corps Deaths, 1917-1921

Hummelsheim, Herbert Rowland, Pvt., 15th Co., 6th MG Bn., DOW, July 18, 1918 in the Chateau-Thierry Sector. Mrs. Charles Hummelsheim (Mother), 1107 Bates St., St. Louis, Missouri [R] [S2] [SW says 138th Co., 2nd Repl. Btln.]

Humpal, Joseph John, Sgt., 74th Co., 6th Regt., KIA, September 15, 1918 in the St. Mihiel Offensive. Nettie . Semrad (Mother), 13210 Ferris ve., Cleveland, Ohio [S2] [SW]

Humphrey, George Henry, 1st Sgt., 96th Co., 6th Regt., KIA, September 15, 1918 in the St. Mihiel Offensive. Winifred W. Humphrey (Mother), 1223 Seymour Ave., Utica, New York [ABMC- Thiaucourt TOM] [S2] [SW says Co. B, 5th Sep. Btln.] [VA-ANC remains recovered in 2010 and interred at ANC]

Humphrey, John Thomas, Sgt., 73rd Co., 6th Regt., KIA, November 1, 1918 in the Meuse Argonne. Mrs. J. T. Humphrey (Wife), 2025 Male St., Louisville, Kentucky [ABMC- Romagne] [S2] [SW1]

Humphries, Lewis Grady, Pvt., 79th Co., 6th Regt., DOW, June 27, 1918 in the Chateau-Thierry Sector. Ida Keller (Mother), 517 Woodlawn Ave., Indianapolis, Indiana [R] [S2] [SW]

Hungate, Shelby, Cpl., MD, USNH, Fort Lyon, Colorado, DDS, March 3, 1919 at Woodman, Colorado. Mrs. Maud Moss (Sister), Blandinsville, Illinois [FAG] [S4]

Hunker, Jacob John, QM Sgt. [Sgt.], MCR, Bks. Det., Norfolk, Virginia, DDS, October 17, 1918 at Norfolk, Virginia. Anna H. Hunker (Mother), 3132 Kimball Ave., Toledo, Ohio [FAG] [S3]

Hunt, Charles John, Pvt., Bks. Det., Quantico, Virginia, DDS, September 26, 1918 at Quantico, Virginia. Thomas J. Hunt (Father), 133 E. 10th St., Covington, Kentucky [S3]

Hunt, Herbert, Pvt., Co. B, Mare Island, California, DDS, April 19, 1920 at Mare Island, California. Thomas and Ellen Hunt (Parents), P O Box 74, Laner, Saskatchewan, Canada [S4]

Marine Corps Deaths, 1917-1921

Hunt, John Robert, Pvt., 79th Co., 6th Regt., DOW, September 20, 1918 in the St. Mihiel Offensive. John Hunt (Father), 57 Clair St., Buffalo, New York [FAG] [S2] [SW say Co. C, 2nd Cas. Btln.]

Hunt, Leon Wesley, Pvt., 76th Co., 6th Regt., KIA, June 2, 1918 in the Aisne Defensive. Hattie Hunt (Mother), Route 2, Box 11, Tyre, Michigan [FAG] [S2] [SW]

Hunt, William Calvin Jr., Pvt., Co. D Co., 5th MG Bn., DOD, November 10, 1918 in France. Love Hunt (Mother), 1497 Peabody Ave., Memphis, Tennessee [R] [S2]

Hunter, Daniel Amos, 1st Sgt., 67th Co., 5th Regt., KIA, June 6, 1918 in the Chateau-Thierry Sector. Ida May Hunter (Wife), 32 Greenman Ave., Westerly, Rhode Island [S2] [SW]

Hunter, George Playford, Cpl., 79th Co., 6th Regt., KIA, October 3, 1918 in the Meuse Argonne. Maranda E. Hunter (Mother), Charlevoi, Pennsylvania [S2] [SW]

Hunter, William Andrew, Pvt., 96th Co., 6th Regt., DOW, July 21, 1918 in the Aisne Marne. Lenora Sloan (Mother), Centreville, Missouri [R] [S2] [SW says 137th to Replacement]

Huntowski, Leon, Pvt., M.G. Co., 13th Regt., DOD, September 24, 1918 in France. Hattie Huntowski (Mother), 5455 Parkside Ave., Chicago, Illinois [R] [S2]

Hurley, James Patrick, Cpl., NNV, RRD, Quantico, Virginia, DDS, April 1, 1918 at Quantico, Virginia. Ada Carfrey (Sister), 571 Hawk Ave., Columbus, Ohio [FAG] [S3]

Hurley, William Francis, Pvt., Bks. Det., Quantico, Virginia, DDS, July 12, 1921 at Brooklyn, New York. Jerry and Helen Hurley (Parents), 889 Franklin Ave., Brooklyn, New York [S4]

Hursey, Thomas L., Cpl., Hdqtrs. Det., 4th Prov. Regt., Domincan Republic, DDS, January 18, 1919 at Santo Domingo,

Marine Corps Deaths, 1917-1921

Dominican Republic. Mrs. Ana Winnie Morgan (Not given), 1711 Habersham St., Savannah, Georgia [S4]

Hurst, John, Pvt., 73rd Co., 6th Regt., KIA, October 8, 1918 in the Meuse Argonne. Lula Tuttle (Sister), 1027 Poe St., New Orleans, Louisiana [FAG] [S2] [SW1]

Hussey, John Patrick, Pvt., Supply Co., Parris Island, South Carolina, DAS, July 9, 1918 in a train wreck near Nashville, Tennessee. Mary E. Hussey (Wife), Lawrenceville, Illinois [S3]

Husted, Chester S., Pvt., 81st Co., 6th MG Bn., KIA, October 5, 1918 in the Meuse Argonne. Mrs. Emma M. Husted (Mother), 611 E. 8th St., Corona, California [S2] [SW]

Hutchins, Walter, Pvt., 49th Co., 5th Regt., KIA, October 4, 1918 in the Meuse Argonne. Mrs. J. Hutchins (Mother), Yadkinville, North Carolina [R] [S2] [SW1]

Hutchinson, Fryer Patrick, Pvt., 75th Co., 6th Regt., KIA, October 10, 1918 in the Meuse Argonne. Mrs. Anie Hutchinson (Mother), 1351 E. 56th St.,Chicago, Illinois [VA-ANC as Fryar] [S2] [SW1 says Fryar Patrick Hutchinson]

Hutchinson, Norman Douglas, Pvt., 78th Co., 6th Regt., DOW, June 17, 1918 in the Chateau-Thierry Sector. Roswell Hutchinson (Father), Eaton, Colorado [FAG] [S2] [SW says Horman]

Hymel, Edgar Josph, Pvt., 66th Co., 5th Regt., DOW, November 3, 1918 in the Meuse Argonne. Rosa Hymel (Mother), 4409 Annunciation St., New Orleans, Louisana [FAG] [S2] [SW1]

Hynne, Elvin Joseph, Pvt., 75th Co., 6th Regt., DOW, July 19, 1918 in the Aisne Marne. Ida Hynne (Mother), 416 S. 19th St., LaCrosse, Wisconsin [ABMC- Belleau] [S2] [SW1]

Imeson, Thomas H., Cpl., 76th Co., 6th Regt., DOW, July 19, 1918 in the Aisne Marne. Mrs. M. B. Hawkins (Mother), Ridge Road, Barnard, New York [ABMC- Belleau TOM] [S2] [SW1]

Marine Corps Deaths, 1917-1921

Inden, Clarence Edward, Pvt., 45th Co., 5th Regt., KIA, June 6, 1918 in the Chateau-Thierry Sector. Fred J. Inden (Father), 781 Third St., Milwaukee, Wisconsin [ABMC-Belleau] [S2] [SW]

Ingram, Thomas Edgar, Pvt., Hdqtrs. Co., 5th Regt., DDS, March 22, 1919 at Ft. Lyons, Colorado. William T. Land (Friend), 31 W. Evans Ave., Denver, Colorado [R] [S2]

Ipson, William Wallace, Pvt., Co. G, 13th Regt., DOD, September 26, 1918 in France. Mary Jane Ipson (Mother), 169 W. 6th South, Salt Lake City, Utah [FAG] [S2]

Ireland, James K., 1st Sgt., DAS, Pittsfield, Massachusetts [S5]

Ireland, Ralph B., Pvt., Bks. Det., Canacao, Philippine Islands, DDS, February 5, 1920 at Canacao, Philippine Islands. Mrs. Caroline Ireland (Not given), Williamsfield, Illinois [FAG] [S4]

Irminger, James Philip, Pvt., 16th Co., 5th Regt., KIA, June 25, 1918 in the Chateau-Thierry Sector. Marie Irminger (Mother) RFD #5, Liberty, Missouri [ABMC- Belleau TOM] [S2] [SW]

Irwin, Herbert, Cpl., 83rd Co., 6th Regt., DOW, November 14, 1918 in the Meuse Argonne. Laura Irwin (Sister), c/o pat Meloy, Wapato, Washington [R] [S2] [SW says 138th Co., 2nd Repl. Btln.]

Irwin, William, Cpl., 45th Co., 5th Regt., KIA, June 24, 1918 in the Chateau-Thierry Sector. Stewart Irwin (Father), 848 33rd St., Oakland, California [ABMC- Belleau TOM] [S2]

Isaacs, Solomon, Pvt., 96th Co., 6th Regt., KIA, July 19, 1918 in the Aisne Marne. Alma H. Isaacs (Wife), New Ulm, Minnesota [ABMC- Belleau] [S2] [SW says Co. B, Rep. Btln.]

Isaly, Earl William, Pvt., 18th Co., 5th Regt., KIA, October 7, 1918 in the Meuse Argonne. Mrs. Bertha Isaly (Mother), 130 Mithoff St., Columbus, Ohio [FAG] [S2] [SW1 says Islay]

Marine Corps Deaths, 1917-1921

Ish, Rex Whitfield, Sgt., 20th Co., 5th Regt., KIA, June 23, 1918 in the Chateau-Thierry Sector. Rosa Ish (Mother), 1661 Octavia St., San Francisco, California [ABMC- Belleau] [S2] [SW]

Jackson, Frank Edward, Pvt., Constabulary Det., Haiti, DOS, November 15, 1917 at Cayas, Haiti. Richard E. Jackson (Uncle), Gen. Del., Charleston, South Carolina [S3]

Jackson, Joseph, Pvt., 8th Co., 5th Regt., KIA, October 4, 1918 in the Meuse Argonne. Mary Jackson (Mother), Behah Arva, County Cavan, Ireland [ABMC- Belleau] [S2]

Jackson, Norman Richard, Cpl., 74th Co., 6th Regt., DOW, April 15, 1918 in the Toulon Sector, Verdun. Wm. A. Jackson (Father), Bonne Terre, Missouri [ABMC- Romagne] [S2] [SW says Norman A.]

Jackson, Richard G., Pvt., 100th Co., 8th Regt., Haiti, DDs, July 17, 1920 at Haiti. Richard Ivey (Father), 341 Par Dale Ave., Buffalo, New York [S4]

Jacobensky, Stephen, Pvt., 51st Co., 5th Regt., KIA, October 4, 1918 in the Meuse Argonne. John Jacobensky (Father), Park Place, East Brunswick Township, New Brunswick, New Jersey [R] [S2] [SW]

Jacobowitz, Jacob, QM Clerk, Philadelphia, Pennsylvania, Pennsylvania, DDS, April 19, 1920 at Philadelphia, Pennsylvania. Mrs. Dena Jacobowitz (Wife), 2226 N. Natrena St., Philadelphia, Pennsylvania [S4]

Jacobs, Arthur F., Pvt., Co. B, Parris Island, South Carolina, DDS, January 5, 1919 at Parris Island, South Carolina. Mrs Johanna Jacobs (Mother), Route #5, Sterling, Illinois [S4]

Jacobs, Charles Addison Rhet, Pvt., 96th Co., 6th Regt., KIA, October 3, 1918 in the Meuse Argonne. Robertha Jacobs (Mother), The Cairo Hotel, Washington, D.C. [ANC] [S2] [SW1]

Marine Corps Deaths, 1917-1921

Jacobs, Lester Henry, Pvt., 23rd Co., 6th MG Bn., KIA, July 19, 1918 in the Aisne Marne. Mary F. Jacobs (Mother), 409 N. Riverside Ave., Medford, Oregon [FAG] [S2] [SW1]

Jacobson, Kenneth James, Pvt., 49th Co., 5th Regt., DOW, November 1, 1918 in the Meuse Argonne. Mrs. Ruth Jacobson (Wife), Tropic, Utah [S2] [SW1]

Jain, Miles Robert, Pvt., 75th Co., 6th Regt., KIA, September 15, 1918 in the St. Mihiel Offensive. Hattie B. Jain (Mother), 3361 Herman St., San Diego, California [S2] [SW]

James, Charles Henry, Cpl., 47th Co., 5th Regt., DOW, November 21, 1919 in the Chateau-Thierry Sector. Russell S. Moore (Uncle), 29 Rainer St., Rochester, New York [R] [S2] [SW1]

James, Edward J., Pvt., 184th Co., 15th Regt., Dominican Republic, KIA, May 18, 1919 by bandits at Santo Domingo, Dominican Republic. Joseph Daniel James (Father), 8 Valentine St., Roxbury, Massachusetts [ANC] [S4]

James, Ernest, Pvt., Bks. Det., Navy Yard, Washington, D.C., DOS, January 15, 1920 at Washington, D.C. Mrs. Nellie James (Wife), 85 Chapel St., Portsmouth, New Hampshire [Naval – Portsmouth, N.H.] [S4]

James, Isaac Foster, Pvt., 97th Co., 6th Regt., KIA, November 2, 1918 in the Meuse Argonne. Jessie James (Brother), Iranton, Minnesota [FAG] [S2] [SW1]

James, James T., Cpl., 82nd Co., 6th Regt., KIA, October 8, 1918 in the Meuse Argonne. Thomas J. James (Father), Amsterdam, Ohio [ABMC- Romagne] [S2] [SW1]

James, Jesse Rooseelt, Pvt., 153rd Co., 2nd Regt., Haiti, DDS, September 28, 1921 at Haiti. Mr. Alexander James (Father), 436 West Washington St., Hagerstown, Maryland [VA-Fredericksburg] [S4]

Marine Corps Deaths, 1917-1921

James, John Henry, Pvt., 82nd Co., 6th Regt., DOW, October 28, 1918 in the Meuse Argonne. Evan T. Jones (Father), 24 Reese Ct., Philipsburg, New Jersey [R] [S2] [SW1]

James, William Wiley, Pvt., USS *Pittsburgh*, DDU, October 18, 1918 aboard the USS *Pittsburgh*. Tylee H. James (Father), Box 128, Loleta, California [S3]

Jansson, Eric Hjalmar, Pvt., Rec. Dept. Det., Mare Island, California, DAS, December 10, 1919 drowned at Mare Island, California. Anders F. Jansson (Father), Landsberg Elgenas, Lofta, Sweden [S4]

Jaquess, John Robert, Pvt., 45th Co., 5th Regt., KIA, October 4, 1918 in the Meuse Argonne. Fletcher Jaquess (Father), Owensville, Indiana [FAGM] [ABMC- Romagne] [S2] [SW1]

Jarnagin, William Oscar, Pvt., Co. D, 13th Regt., DOD, September 21, 1918 enroute to France. Wm. T. Jarnagin (Father), Bridgeport, Texas [S2]

Jarosik, Jacob Frank, Pvt., 55th Co., 5th Regt., KIA, June 12, 1918 in the Chateau-Thierry Sector. Anna Jarosik (Mother), 1835 Menard St., St. Louis, Missouri [ABMC- Belleau] [S2] [SW1]

Jarrett, Howard, Pvt., 73rd Co., 6th Regt., KIA, November 1, 1918 in the Meuse Argonne. Mrs. Margaret Jarrett (Mother), Box 372, Oakland, Iowa [FAG] [S2] [SW1]

Jarvis, William George, Pvt., Bks. Det., Norfolk, Virginia, DDS, July 31, 1917 at Norfolk, Virginia. Henry Jarvis (Father), South Range, Wisconsin [FAG] [S3]

Jay, Robert W., QM Clerk, 1st Marine Aero Co., DOD, October 27, 1918 in the Azores. Robert W. Jay, Sr. (Father), 420 Frisco Bldg., Springfield, Missouri [R] [S1]

Jeannotte, William Francis, Pvt., 210th Co., 3rd Regt., Dominican Republic, DAS, March 10, 1921 drowned at Santo Domingo City, Dominican Republic. Mrs. Annie

Marine Corps Deaths, 1917-1921

Jeannotte (Mother), 115 Hemenway St., Boston, Massachusetts [S4]

Jeffries, Wilbur Harland, Pvt., 96th Co., 6th Regt., DAO, September February 1918 in France. Rhoda Jeffries (Mother), 3120 Walworth Ave., Cincinnati, Ohio [R] [S2] [SW1 says KIA]

Jenkins, Carl Campbell, Pvt., 74th Co., 6th Regt., DOD, May 23, 1918 in France. Herbert L. Jenkins (Father), Box 39, Lawson, Missouri [FAG] [S2]

Jenkins, Edward, Pvt., 113th Co., 3rd Prov. Regt., Dominican Republic, DAS, August 24, 1919 drowned at Santo Domingo, Dominican Republic. Mrs. Phoebe Jenkins (Mother), 564 South St., Peekskill, New York [S4]

Jenkins, Homer, Sgt., 45th Co., 5th Regt., KIA, October 6, 1818 in the Meuse Argonne. Mary Jenkins (Mother), RFD#3, Riceville, Tennessee [ABMC- Romagne] [S2] [SW1]

Jensen, Andrew, Pvt., 90th Co., 7th Regt., Cuba, DAS, February 8, 1918 accidently killed at Guantanamo, Cuba. Margaret Jensen (not given), 2018 Grand Ave., Everett, Washington [S3]

Jensen, Claude M., Pvt., 210th Co., 3rd Regt., Dominican Republic, DDS, July 11, 1920 at Santo Domingo City, Dominican Republic. James P. Jensen (Father), RFD#4, Box 18, Waupaca, Washington [S4]

Jensen, Earl Emil, Cpl., 80th Co., 6th Regt., DOW, August 12, 1918 in the Aisne Marne. Nelse Jesen (Father), 1003 Jefferson Bldg., Peoria, Illinois [ABMC- Suresnes] [S2] [SW]

Jensen, Jens Jacob, Pvt., Co. B, 13th Regt., DOD, September 20, 1918 aboard the USS *Von Steuben* enroute to France. Jens P. Jensen (Father), Gen. Del. Winside, Nebraska [R] [S2]

Jensen, Laurence George, Pvt., 83rd Co., 6th Regt., KIA, June 4, 1918 in the Aisne Defensive. Elisie Jensen (Mother),

Marine Corps Deaths, 1917-1921

    3509 Clark St., Houston, Texas [FAG] [S2] [SW says Lawrence]

Jensen, Niels Oliver, Pvt., [unit not given], DDS, December 7, 1918 at Fort Douglas, Utah. Hans C. Jensen (Father), Centerfild, Utah [S4]

Jentes, Hubert W., Cpl., 27th Co., 4th Prov. Regt., Dominican Republic, DAS, July 30, 1919 drowned at San Domingo, Dominican Republic. William Jentes (Father), 1017 Walnut St., North Dover, Ohio [S4]

Jeppesen, Henry, Cpl., 78th Co., 6th Regt., KIA, October 3, 1918 in the Meuse Argonne. Willie Jeppesen (Brother), RFD Box 237, Fresno, California [FAG] [S2] [SW1]

Jesperson, Elmer Verdell, Pvt., 43rd Co., 5th Regt., KIA, June 13, 1918 in the Chateau-Thierry Sector. Emma Jesperson (Mother), RFD#2, Box 116, Tucson, Arizona [S2] [SW] [SW]

Jessen, Emil, 1st Sgt., 17th Co., 5th Regt., KIA, November 2, 1918 in the Meuse Argonne. Bertha Jessen (Mother), 71 Denver Ave., Bridgeport, Connecticut [S2] [SW1]

Jewett, Allen Walts, Pvt., 74th Co., 6th Regt., DOW, April 21, 1918 in the Toulon Sector, Verdun. Rosella Jewett (Mother), 806 W. Washington St., Fairfield, Iowa [FAGM] [S2] [SW]

Jewett, Claude Elbert, Pvt., MBks., Boston, Massachusetts, DAS, May 24, 1919 as a result of an auto accident at Northwood, Iowa. Mrs. Mayme Jewett (Mother), Gen. Del., Kensett, Iowa [S4]

Jimerfield, Herbert William, Pvt., 67th Co., 5th Regt., KIA, June 15, 1918 in the Chateau-Thierry Sector. Mary Jimerfield (Mother), 220 Helen Ave., Detroit, Michigan [ABMC-Belleau] [S2] [SW]

Jochum, James Joseph, Pvt., 74th Co., 6th Regt., DOW, June 13, 1918 in the Chateau-Thierry Sector. Peter Jochum

Marine Corps Deaths, 1917-1921

(Father), 125 Bluff St., Dubuque, Iowa [S2] [SW1 says KIA]

Johanningmeier, Ollie Henry, Sgt., 96th Co., 6th Regt., KIA, June 3, 1918 in the Aisne Defensive. August C. Johanningmeier (Brother), 8604 Mora Lane, St. Louis, Missouri [FAG] [S2] [SW]

John, Thomas L., Cpl., Bks. Det., Norfolk, Virginia, DDS, March 31, 1919 at Portsmouth, Virginia. Elijah John (Father), 39 Montgomery St., Shamokin, Pennsylvania [FAG] [S4]

Johns, Henry Arthur, Pvt., Bks. Det., Mare Island, DDS, October 29, 1918 at Eureka, California. Betha Johns (Mother), RR#2, Buhl, Idaho [S3]

Johnsen, Arthur Elmer, Pvt., 78th Co., 6th Regt., KIA, October 4, 1918 in the Meuse Argonne. Minnie Armbuster (Mother), 1904 W. 22nd St., Chicago, Illinois [ABMC- Romagne] [S2] [SW1]

Johnson, Ben C., Pvt., Co. B, 2nd MG Bn, Quantico, Virginia, DDS, November 20, 1918 at Quantico, Virginia. Simon Johnson (Father), Dunseith, North Dakota [FAG] [S4]

Johnson, Carl Albert, Sgt., 43rd Co., 5th Regt., KIA, June 12, 1918 in the Chateau-Thierry Sector. Florence Johnson (Sister), c/o Warner L. Johnson, 10808 Fairchild Ave., Cleveland, Ohio [ANC] [S2] [SW]

Johnson, Cecil David, Cpl., MB, Guam, DAS, September 14, 1921 as a result of a motorcycle accident at Guam. Mrs. Sarah Johnson (Mother), Glendola, New Jersey [FAG] [S4]

Johnson, Clyde Dalton, Pvt., 8th Co., 5th Regt., DOW, October 6, 1918 in the Meuse Argonne. Mrs. Susife M. Johnson (Mother), 821 N. Liberty St., Winston-Salem, North Carolina [FAG] [S2] [SW1]

Johnson, Conrad Leonard, Pvt., 78th Co., 6th Regt., KIA, June 14, 1918 in the Chateau-Thierry Sector. George E. Johnson

Marine Corps Deaths, 1917-1921

(Father), 114 9th Ave., North Fargo, North Dakota [FAG] [S2] [SW1]

Johnson, David Anton, Cpl., 17th Co., 5th Regt., DOW, June 16, 1918 in the Chateau-Thierry Sector. Mary Johnson (Mother), 7311 Cottage Grove Ave., Chicago, Illinois [ABMC- Belleau] [S2] [SW]

Johnson, Edgar Emory, Pvt., 45th Co., 5th Regt., KIA, October 6, 1918 in the Meuse Argonne. John C. Johnson (Father), Fountain City, Tennessesse [VA-Knoxville] [S2] [SW says Edgar H. and Co. D, 4th Sep. Btln.]

Johnson, Emil F., Pvt., Squardron E, FMAF, Haiti, DOS, October 30, 1919 at Port au Prince, Haiti. Mrs. Margaret Johnson (Wife), 1803 West Ohio St., Chicago, Illinois [S4]

Johnson, Floyd Louis, Pvt., MCR, USS *Mercy*, DDU, October 3, 1918 aboard the USS *Mercy*. Josephine Johnson (Mother), 747 South Linden Ave., Alliance, Ohio [S3]

Johnson, Frederick Wayne, Pvt., 16th Co., 5th Regt., KIA, June 25, 1918 in the Chateau-Thierry Sector. Rachel Johnson (Mother), RFD#3, Box 109, Fayetteville, Arkansas [FAGM] [S2] [SW]

Johnson, George Alvin, Pvt., Bks. Det., Quantico, Virginia, DDS, October 9, 1918 at Quantico, Virginia. Gilbert Gulickson (Step-father), Route #1, Clear Lake, Wisconsin [FAG] [S3]

Johnson, George Carl, Pvt., 80th Co., 6th Regt., KIA, June 11, 1918 in the Chateau-Thierry Sector. Eelyn Johnson (Mother), 9 Requa Ave., Muskegon, Michigan [S2] [SW]

Johnson, George W., Jr., Pvt., Co. C, Parris Island, South Carolina, DDS, January 24, 1919 at Parris Island, South Carolina. Mrs. Rose E. Johnson (Mother), 229 Gross St., Pittsburgh, Pennsylvania [S4]

Johnson, Gustaf, Cpl., MB, Washington, D.C., DOS, June 8, 1918 in Washington, D.C. Alice Johnson (Wife), 524 7th St., S.E., Washington, D.C. [S3]

Marine Corps Deaths, 1917-1921

Johnson, Harry Claxton, Sgt., 84th Co. 6th Regt., DOW, October 9, 1918 in the Meuse Argonne. Clara F. Johnson (Mother), Box 363, LaSalle, New York [FAG] [S2] [SW1]

Johnson, Harry John, Pvt., Cent. Rec. Div., Chicago, Illinois, DDS, March 18, 1919 at Great Lakes, Illinois. John E. Johnson (Father), 1529 Van Buren St., St. Paul, Minnesota [FAG] [S4]

Johnson, Henry Edward, Pvt., 74th Co., 6th Regt., September 15, 1918 in the St. Mihiel Offensive. Anna Johnson Elmer (Mother), 1656 Lafand St., St. Paul, Minnesota [S2] [SW says Edward Henry]

Johnson, James Drewry, Cpl., 47th Co., 5th Regt., KIA, June 25, 1918 in the Chateau-Thierry Sector. Beulah Johnson (Wife), 948 W. Main St., Blytheville, Arkansas [ABMC-Belleau] [S2] [SW says 137th Co., Repl.]

Johnson, Jonas, Pvt., 84th Co., 6th Regt., KIA, July 19, 1918 in the Aisne Marne. John Johnson (Father), 3614 Mt. Vernon Ave., Milwaukee, Wisconsin [ABMC- Belleau TOM] [S2] [SW]

Johnson, Leslie Jay, Pvt., Co. D, Mare Island, California, DDS, November 20, 1918 at Mare Island, California. Mrs. Carrie M. Johnson (Mother), Motor Route "A", Box 72, Ceres, California [FAG] [S4]

Johnson, Louis Wint, Cpl., 73rd Co., 6th Regt., KIA, June 13, 1918 in the Aisne Defensive. Jordon W. Johnson (Father), Mountain Grove, Missouri [AMBC-Belleau] [S2] [SW]

Johnson, Manuel, Pvt., 75th Co., 6th Regt., KIA, June 13, 1918 in the Chateau-Thierry Sector. Oscar C. Carlson (Stepfather), 7516 Ethel Ave., St. Louis, Missouri [ANC] [S2] [SW says Mannel]

Johnson, Paul Thorsten, Pvt., 18th Co., 5th Regt., KIA, October 4, 1918 in the Meuse Argonne. John A. Johnson (Father), 37 Arden St., Allston, Massachusetts [ABMC- Romagne] [S2] [SW1]

Marine Corps Deaths, 1917-1921

Johnson, Ralph Clay, Pvt., 74th Co., 6th Regt., DOW, April 29, 1918 in the Toulon Sector, Verdun. Casper C. Johnson (Father), Guthrie, Oklahoma [FAG] [S2]

Johnson, Ralph C., Pvt., 120th Co., 2nd Repl. Btln., DOW [R] [SW]

Johnson, Ralph Winge, Pvt., 55th Co., 5th Regt., DOW, November 11, 1918 in the Meuse Argonne. Edward Johnson (Father), 3429 Schubert Ave., Chicago, Illinois [ABMC-Romagne] [S2] [SW1]

Johnson, Robert Dimmitt, Sgt., 80th Co., 6th Regt., KIA, June 10, 1918 in the Chateau-Thierry Sector. Mrs. Louisa W. Johnson (Mother), 84 Mt. Pleasant Ave., Ft. Thomas, Kentucky [FAG] [S2] [SW]

Johnson, Robert Nelson, Pvt., Extra Duty, Det., Parris Island, South Carolina, DDS, November 4, 1918 at Parris Island, South Carolina. Nelson Johnson (Father), Box 92, W. Newton, Pennsylvania [FAG] [S3] [X]

Johnson, William Mellor, Pvt., 17th Co., 5th Regt., DOW, September 16, 1918 in the St. Mihiel Offensive. Minnie Johnson (Mother), 6120 Greenwood Ave., Chicago, Illinois [ABMC- Thiaucourt] [S2] [SW1]

Johnston, Arthur Havelock, Gy. Sgt., 45th Co., 5th Regt., DOW, August 15, 1918 in the Chateau-Thierry Sector. Mrs. Cora C. Williams (Sister), 23 Francis St., Lindsay, Canada [S2] [SW1]

Johnston, Lemuel Linder, Jr., Pvt., 43rd Co., 5th Regt., DOW, September 16, 1918 in the St. Mihiel Offensive. Beden Johnston (Mother), Bellville, Texas [S2] [SW]

Johnston, Russell Ervin, Pvt., 96th Co., 6th Regt., KIA, June 6, 1918 in the Chateau-Thierry Sector. Mrs. W. V. Mattoon (Mother), 235 S. Marsalis Ave., Dallas, Texas [S2] [SW1]

Johnston, Scott M., 2nd Lieut., 76th Co., 6th Regt., DOW, August 15, 1918 in the Aisne Marne. Mrs. Jennie J. Johnston

Marine Corps Deaths, 1917-1921

(Mother), 1457 Captal Ave., St. Paul, Minnesota [ABMC-Suresnes] [S1] [SW]

Joinville, Victor Edward, Pvt., 43rd Co., 5th Regt., KIA, June 9, 1918 in the Chateau-Thierry Sector. Zachary J. Joinville (Father), 1032 Main St., Bridgeport, Connecticut [ABMC-Belleau] [S2] [SW]

Jolly, Moab, Pvt., Co. H, Parris Island, South Carolina, DDS, November 13, 1918 at Parris Island, South Carolina. George Jolly (Father), Buckeye, Lousiana [FAG] [S4]

Jones, Albert Edward, Pvt., 47th Co., 5th Regt., KIA, June 25, 1918 in the Chateau-Thierry Sector. Ann Jones (Mother), 137 President St., Troy, New York [R] [S2] [SW]

Jones, Ansel Alex, Pvt., 78th Co., 6th Regt., KIA, September 15, 1918 in the St. Mihiel Offensive. Walter P. Jones (Father), 4616 Harriet Ave., Minneapolis, Minnesota [FAG] [S2] [SW1 says DOW]

Jones, Anselm Patrick, Pvt., 18th Co., 5th Regt., DOW, October 7, 1918 in the Meuse Argonne. Sallie Jones (Mother), Raleigh, Mississippi [FAG] [S2] [SW1]

Jones, Cecil James, Pvt., 80th Co., 6th Regt., KIA, July 19, 1918 in the Aisne Marne. Perter M. Jones (Brother), 207 Tallman St., Monroe, Wisconsin [ABMC- Fere] [S2] [SW1]

Jones, Clarence Dockery., Cpl., 7th Co., 6th Regt., KIA, October 3, 1918 in the Meuse Argonne. Walter S. Jones (Father), c/o Carrier Dept., Post Office, St. Louis, Missouri [ABMC-Romagne] [S2] [SW1]

Jones, Dewey Jay, Pvt., 66th Co., 5th Regt., DOW, October 4, 1918 in the Meuse Argonne. Mr. Dewey J. Jones (Wife), c/o Mrs. Calra Jones, 509 S. 6th St., Coshocton, Ohio [R] [S2] [SW1 says KIA]

Jones, Douglas Conrad, Sgt., Const. Det., USMC, Port au Prince, DOS, December 7, 1920 at Pationville, Haiti. W. A. Jones (Father), Victoria, Mississippi [S4]

Marine Corps Deaths, 1917-1921

Jones, Felix William, Sgt., 45th Co., 5th Regt., DOW, October 5, 1918 in the Meuse Argonne. Caroline Jones (Wife), 6 Church St., Bordentown, New Jersey [ABMC- Belleau] [S2] [SW1]

Jones, George, Gy. Sgt., 2134066, 51st Co., 5th Regt., KIA, October 4, 1918 in the Meuse Argonne. Sarah Jones (Mother), RR#3, Kingston, New York [FAG] [S2] [SW]

Jones, George Willie, Pvt., 80th Co., 6th Regt., DOW, November 1, 1918 in the Meuse Argonne. George L. Jones (Father), Box 187, Pine River, Minnesota [FAG] [S2] [SW1]

Jones, Henry, 1st Sgt., 1454444, 97th Co., 6th Regt., KIA, October 8, 1918 in the Meuse Argonne. Inez B. Jones (Wife), 3419 5th St., San Diego, California [FAG] [S2] [SW1]

Jones, Jack Hodge, Pvt., 74th Co., 6th Regt., DOW, October 8, 1918 in the Meuse Argonne. William F. Jones (Father), Moscow., Texas [FAG] [S2] [SW1]

Jones, James Rowlins, Pvt., Athletic Det., Parris Island, South Carolina, DDS, October 18, 1918 at Washington, D.C. Mary B. Jones (Mother), 216 R. St., N.E., Washington, D.C. [ANC] [S3]

Jones, John William, Pvt., 18th Co., 5th Regt., KIA, November 3, 1918 in the Meuse Argonne. Mr. and Mrs. Owen E. Jones (Parents), Camp 89, Copper River and Northwestern Railway, Cordova, Alaska [FAG] [S2] [SW1]

Jones, Leslie Frank, Pvt., 67th Co., 5th Regt., KIA, October 12, 1918 in the Meuse Argonne. W. H. Jones (Father), Fredericktown, Missouri [R] [S2] [SW1]

Jones, Luther Noy, Pvt., 49th Co., 5th Regt., KIA, June 6, 1918 in the Chateau-Thierry Sector. William Johns (Brother), Washington, Oklahoma [FAG] [S2] [SW]

Jones, Lyle Bernard, Pvt., 97th Co., 6th Regt., DOW, November 21, 1918 in the Meuse Argonne. Mrs. Ida M. Jones (Mother), 455 Elliott Ave., Arlington Heights, Cincinnati, Ohio [R] [S2] [SW1]

Marine Corps Deaths, 1917-1921

Jones, Marcus W., Pvt., Naval Prison, Portsmouth, New Hampshire, DAS, May 10, 1920 drowned at Portsmouth, New Hampshire. John Arthur Jones (Father), Locke, New York [S4]

Jones, Paul, Pvt., 181st Co., 15th Regt., Dominican Republic, DOS, May 30, 1920 at Higuey, Dominican Republic. John Jones (Father), 162 James St., Syracuse, New York [ANC] [S4]

Jones, Russel William, Pvt., Dominican Republic, KIA, August 15, 1918 against bandits near Hatamayo, Dominican Republic. Jerry A. Jones (Brother), 2225 7th Ave., Altoona, Pennsylvania [FAG] [S3]

Jones, Samuel Stanhope, Pvt., 66th Co., 5th Regt., KIA, June 6, 1918 in the Chateau-Thierry Sector. Charles Jones (Brother), 1149 Luttrell St., Knoxville, Tennessee [VA-Knoxville] [S2] [SW]

Jones, Theron Oscar, Pvt., Co. C, 1ptr, DOD, September 19, 1918 in France. Gertrude E. Jones (Mother), 534 Franklin St., Whittier, California [FAG] [S2]

Jones, Thomas Henry, Pvt., Hdqtrs. Co., 5th Regt., DOD, March 27, 1918 in France. Lillian Jones (Mother), 349 Franklin St., Bloomfield, New Jersey [R] [S2]

Jones, Victor, Pvt., 47th Co., 5th Regt., DOW, July 20, 1918 in the Chateau-Thierry Sector. Harriet Jones (Mother), 27 Meadow St., Duquesne, Pennsylvania [R] [S2] [SW]

Jordan, Delbert Rutledge, Pvt., 47th Co., 5th Regt., KIA, November 2, 1918 in the Meuse Argonne. Alex Jordan (Father), Enfield, Illinois [ABMC- Romagne] [S2] [SW1] [SW1 also listed as DOW]

Jordan, Harvey O'M., Pvt., Supply Det., MB, Navy Yard, Mare Island, California, DDS, February 11, 1920 at Mare Island, California. Mrs. Julia Jordan (Mother), 626 Medocino Ave., Santa Rosa, California [S4]

Marine Corps Deaths, 1917-1921

Jordan, John Henry, Pvt., 47th Co., 5th Regt., DOW, September 15, 1918 in the St. Mihiel Offensive. George Jordan (Father), 2230 57th Ave., Oakland, California [S2] [SW1]

Jordan, Marcus A., 2nd Lieut., Av. Tr. School, FMAF, DOA, March 27, 1918 at Army Aviation School, Foggia, Italy. Eldridge E. Jordan (Brother), 823 15th St., N.W., Washington, D.C. [ANC] [S1] [SW1]

Jordan, Michael Anthony, Pvt., 84th Co., 6th Regt., DOW, November 9, 1918 in the Meuse Argonne. Mr. and Mrs. Patrick Jordan (Parents), 57 Dove St., Albany, New York [S2] [SW1]

Joseph, Hurtis Raymond, Pvt., USS *Hancock*, DDU, August 11, 1918 aboard the USS *Hancock*. Viola Edwards (Mother), RR#2, Norris City, Illinois [S3]

Josephson, Charles Alfred, Pvt., 51st Co., 5th Regt., KIA, June 11, 1918 in the Chateau-Thierry Sector. Mrs. Marie Josephson (Mother), Drifting, Pennsylvania [FAG] [S2] [SW1]

Joy, John Joseph, Pvt., 51st Co., 5th Regt., DOW, October 4, 1918 in the Meuse Argonne. Elizabeth M. Joy (Mother), 106 Sawyer Ave., Dorchester, Massachusetts [ABMC-Romagne] [S2] [SW1]

Joyce, Daniel, Pvt., 49th Co., 5th Regt., KIA, June 12, 1918 in the Chateau-Thierry Sector. Agnes M. Joyce (Mother), Kansas City, Kansas [fAG] [S2] [SW1]

Joyce, Thomas Henry, Pvt., 47th Co., 5th Regt., KIA, June 24, 1918 in the Chateau-Thierry Sector. John J. Joyce (Father), 208 F. St., South Boston, Massachusetts [ABMC- Belleau TOM] [S2] [SW]

Judge, Willliam Bicknell, Musican 1st Class, Marine Band, Washington, D.C., DOD, November 12, 1920 at Washington, D.C. Sarah R. Judge (Wife), 665 South Carolina Ave., S.E., Washington, D.C. [ANC] [S4]

Marine Corps Deaths, 1917-1921

Judkins, Willie Grey, Pvt., Co. G, 13th Regt., DOD, September 27, 1918 in France. Mrs. Laura V. Judkins (Mother), Krum, Denton County, Texas [VA-San Antonio] [S2]

Juelfs, Allen, Pvt., Co. B, Mare Island, California, DDS, March 20, 1920 at Mare Island, California. Herman Juelfs(Father), Caser, Wyoming [S4]

Julian, William R., Sgt., 3rd Squadron, FMAF, DOD, October 28, 1918 in France. Mrs. Corrie Smith (Mother), Berry, Alabama [R] [S2]

Just, William August Henry, Pvt., 77th Co., 6th MG Bn., DOD, February 8, 1919 in France. Charles F. Just (Father), 4317 Linton Ave., St. Louis, Missouri [R] [S2]

Justice, Charles John, Pvt., 55th Co., 5th Regt., DOD, September 22, 1918 in France. Lena Justice (Mother), 420 Cleveland Ave., Hamilton, Ohio [FAG] [S2]

Kahl, William Franklin, Cpl., 75th Co., 6th Regt., KIA, June 10, 1918 in the Chateau-Thierry Sector. Stella Kahl (Mother), 442 W. James St., Lancaster, Pennsylvania [S2] [SW]

Kahler, Howard Willard, Pvt., 82nd Co., 6th Regt., KIA, June 22, 1918 in the Chateau-Thierry Sector. W. F. Kahler (Father), 342 George St., S. Williamsport, Pennsylvania [FAG] [S2] [SW]

Kaiser, John Hugo, Pvt., 79th Co., 6th Regt., KIA, June 6, 1918 in the Chateau-Thierry Sector. August Kaiser (Father), 313 E. Perry St., Belvidere, Illinois [ABMC- Belleau] [S2] [SW]

Kaliner, David, Pvt., Bks. Det., New York, DDS, October 16, 1918 at New York, New York. Esther Kaliner (Mother), 823Home St., New York, New York [FAG] [S3]

Kanouse, Simon Wightman, Pvt., 20th Co., 5th Regt., KIA, June 6, 1918 in the Chateau-Thierry Sector. Charles Kanouse (Father), 307 N. Gertruda Ave., Rondo Beach, California [S2] [SW]

Marine Corps Deaths, 1917-1921

Kanserske, Otto, Pvt., 83rd Co., 6th Regt., KIA, June 24, 1918 in the Chateau-Thierry Sector. Mrs. Augusta Oehmke (Mother), 3219 Hancock Ave., Cleveland, Ohio [R] [S2] [SW]

Kapalis, John Raphael, Pvt., 82nd Co., 6th Regt., KIA, July 19, 1918 in the Aisne Marne. Anna Kapalis (Mother), 21 Park St., Amsterdam, New York [ABMC- Fere] [S2] [SW]

Karnatz, Henry Joseph, Pvt., 97th Co., 6th Regt., DOW, October 3, 1918 in the Meuse Argonne. John Karnatz (Father), 520 24th St., Niagara Falls, New York [ABMC- Romagne] [S2] [SW1]

Karnes, Fred Jester, Pvt., MB, New Orleans, Louisiana, DDS, October 8, 1918 at New Orleans, Louisiana. Osrow Karnes (Father), 661 Virgninia St., Hillsboro, Illinois [S3]

Karow, Gustav, Captain, MB, Parris Island, South Carolina, DAS, June 25, 1920 as a result of an aeroplane accident at Parris Island, South Carolina. Mrs. Sarah B. Karow (Wife), 228 Oglethorpe Ave., East, Savannah, Georgia [FAG] [S4]

Karr, Adala S., Cpl., Hdqtrs., 2nd Brigade, Brooklyn, New York, DDS, Janauary 28, 1919 at Brooklyn, New York. S. J. Karr (Father), Villa Rica, Georgia [S4]

Kaspryzyk, Louis J., Pvt., MD, USNH, Fort Lyon, Colorado, DDS, July 27, 1919 at Fort Lyon, Colorado. John Kasprysyk (Father), 109 Loepere St., Buffalo, New York [S4]

Kearns, John, Capt., 95th Co., 6th Regt., DOW, July 20, 1918 in the Aisne Marne. Mrs. Ellen MacDonald (sister), 600 Hollins Ave., Helena, Montana [ABMC-Belleau] [S1] [SW1 says KIA]

Keate, Daniel Lester, Pvt., 8th Co., 5th Regt., KIA, October 4, 1918 in the Meuse Argonne. Julius C. Keate (Father), St. George, Utah [FAG] [S2] [SW1]

Marine Corps Deaths, 1917-1921

Keeley, James, Capt., 51st Co., 5th Regt., KIA, October 3, 1918 in Meuse Argonne. Mrs. Kathryn Keeley (widow), 458 11th St., S.W., Washington, D.C. [ABMC-Romagne] [S1] [SW]

Keenan, Joseph, 2nd Lieut., Supply Co., 5th Regt., KIA, November 9, 1918 in the Meuse Argonne. James F. Keenan (Brother), 6306 Penn. Ave., Pittsburgh, Pennsylvania [ABMC-Romagne] [S1] [SW1]

Keene, Thaddaeus David, Pvt., 95th Co., 6th Regt., DOW, October 9, 1918 in the Meuse Argonne. Edgar Keene (Brother), West Alton, Missouri [S2] [SW1]

Keeney, Charles Hobson, Pvt., 43rd Co., 5th Regt., KIA, June 14, 1918 in the Chateau-Thierry Sector. Fannie Kenney (Mother), Eastbank, West Virginia [ABMC- Belleau TOM] [S2] [SW] [SW1]

Keeney, George D., Trumpeter, MBks., New York, New York, DAS, May 10, 1920 of injuries at New York, New York. Theodore A. Keeney (Father), Woodsboro, Maryland [FAG] [S4]

Keep, Gerald F., Pvt., Co. D, Parris Island, South Carolina, DDS, December 6, 1918 at Parris Island, South Carolina. George W. Keep (Father), White Bear Lake, Minnesota [S4]

Keffer, Daniel Webster, Cpl., Hdqtrs. Co., 5th Regt., DOW, June 30, 1918 in the Chateau-Thierry Sector. Mrs. Martha Keffer (Mother), 112 Shaw Ave., Clairton, Pennsylvania [FAG] [S2] [SW] [SW1]

Kehoe, William John, Pvt., 47th Co., 5th Regt., KIA, June 25, 1918 in the Chateau-Thierry Sector. John Kehoe (Father), 2304 Snto Ave., W. Spokane, Washington [R] [S2] [SW]

Keiber, Vernon Everett, Cpl., Hdqtrs. USMC, Washington, D.C., DDS, March 15, 1918 at Washington, D.C. Edward L. Keiber (Father), RR#2, Shelby, Michigan [FAG] [S3]

Marine Corps Deaths, 1917-1921

Keirn, Otha Sylas, Pvt., 16th Co., 5th Regt., KIA, June 6, 1918 in the Chateau-Thierry Sector. Mrs. Mary E. Keirn (Mother), RFD#1, Westover, Pennsylvania [ABMC-Belleau] [S2] [SW1]

Kelley, Charles Leroy, Pvt., 78th Co., 6th Regt., KIA, July 19, 1918 in the Aisne Marne. Said Kelley (Mother), 3212 Pacific Ave., Everett, Washington [S2] [SW says Keley]

Kelley, Douglas Henry, Pvt., Co. C, 2nd Sep. MG Bn, Quantico, Virginia, DDS, November 3, 1918 at Quantico, Virginia. Ivy A. Kelley (Wife), Hill St., Cherokee, Iowa [S3]

Kelley, Garfield William, Pvt., 23rd Co., 6th MG Bn., DOW, October 3, 1918 in the Meuse Argonne. Abbie Perkins (Mother), Kincaid St., South Portland, Maine [S2] [SW1]

Kellner, Jacob John, Pvt., 47th Co., 5th Regt., KIA, October 4, 1918 in the Meuse Argonne. Mrs. Mary Kellner (Mother), 203 Summer Place, Buffalo, New York [ABMC- Romagne] [S2] [SW1]

Kellum, Charles H., Pvt., 20th Co., 5th Regt., KIA, June 24, 1918 in the Chateau-Thierry Sector. Samuel Kellum (Father), 111 So. Humphrey Ave., Oak Park, Illinois [FAGM] [S2] [SW]

Kellum, James Bernard, Pvt., 49th Co., 5th Regt., DOW, June 5, 1918 in the Aisne Defensive. Mrs. Katie McLaughlin (Mother), 219 Lee St., Maysville, Kentucky [R] [S2] [SW]

Kelly, Edward Michael, Sgt., 15th Co., 6th MG Bn., KIA, October 6, 1918 in the Meuse Argonne. Mrs. A. W. Campbell (Sister), 271 S.French Broad, Asheville, North Carolina [ABMC- Romagne] [S2] [SW says Co. A] [SW1]

Kelly, James Jerome, Cpl., 73rd Co., Quantico, Virginia, DOS, October 20, 1921 at Quantico, Virginia. Mrs. Anna Kelly (Mother), 633 Grand Ave., Brooklyn, New York [S4]

Marine Corps Deaths, 1917-1921

Kelly, Joseph Bryan, Pvt., 80th Co., 6th Regt., DOW, June 14, 1918 in the Aisne Defensive. Harry C. Kelly (Brother), RR#2, Carrollton, Illinois [FAG] [S2] [SW]

Kelly, William Stephen, Pvt., 17th Co., 5th Regt., KIA, November 11, 1918 in the Meuse Argonne. Margaret Kelly (Mother), 28 Jefferson St., Albany, New York [S2] [SW1]

Kemble, Frank Wesley, Pvt., 47th Co., 5th Regt., DOW, June 26, 1918 in the Chateau-Thierry Sector. Allen Messler (Uncle), Rutherford, New Jersey [ABMC- Belleau] [S2] [SW]

Kemp, Claud, Cpl., 47th Co., 5th Regt., KIA, October 4, 1918 in the Meuse Argonne. Delbert M. Kemp (Father), Cedarvale, Kansas [FAG] [S2] [SW1]

Kennedy, Patrick Aloysius, Pvt., 23rd Co., 6th MG Bn., DOW, November 11, 1918 in the Meuse Argonne. Mrs. Mary Kennedy (Mother), 2614 E. Grace St., Richmond, Virginia [S2] [SW1]

Kennedy, Walter Marcy, Cpl., 75th Co., 6th Regt., KIA, October 9, 1918 in the Meuse Argonne. Anna B. Kennedy (Mother), 411 Elm Ave., Riverton, New Jersey [S2] [SW1]

Kennedy, William Henry, Pvt., 51st Co., 5th Regt., KIA, November 10, 1918 in the Meuse Argonne. Roy Kennedy (Father), Brookfield, Missouri [ABMC- Romagne] [S2] [SW1]

Kennel, Ralph Scott, Pvt., Co. D, 11th Regt., Quantico, Virginia, DDS, September 23, 1918 at Quantico, Virginia. Mrs. Sarah Kennel (Mother), 338 Loeffler Ave., Columbus, Ohio [FAG] [S3]

Kenney, Thomas Benton, Pvt., 15th Co., 6th MG Bn., DOW, June 4, 1918 in the Aisne Defensive. Nellie Kenney (Mother), 45 Park Hill Place, Milwaukee, Wisconsin [ABMC- Belleau] [S2] [SW]

Marine Corps Deaths, 1917-1921

Kennon, Isham Madison, Sgt., Chief Paymaster's Office, USMC, DOD, March 11, 1918 in France. Mabel B. Kennon (Wife), 504 W. Airy St., Norristown, Pennsylvania [R] [S2]

Kern, William Trevis Hobart, Trumpter, Bks. Det., Philadelphia, Pennsylvania, DDS, February 8, 1918 at Philadelphia, Pennsylvania. Cordelia L. Johnston (Aunt), 129 11th Ave., Newark, New Jersey [S3]

Kerr, Alfred Andrew, Pvt., 97th Co., 6th Regt., DOW, July 19, 1918 in the Aisne Marne. Mrs. L. Gross (Mother), 821 North Main St., Springfield, Missouri [FAG] [S2] [SW1]

Kerr, Harold Root, Cpl., 17th Co., 5th Regt., KIA, June 15, 1918 in the Chateau-Thierry Sector. J. M. Kerr (Father), 441 N. Madriver St., Bellefontaine, Ohio [FAG] [SW]

Kerrigan, Frank Anthony, Pvt., 67th Co., 5th Regt., KIA, June 14, 1918 in the Chateau-Thierry Sector. Margaret Kerrigan (Mother), 1062 Second Ave., South, Nashville, Tennessee [S2] [SW]

Kershaw, Edward Leon, Pvt., NAS, Pensacola, Florida, DAS, March 25, 1921 at Pensacola, Florida. Robert Kershaw (Brother), Rayne, Louisiana [S4]

Ketner, Palmer, Jr., 2nd Lieut., MCR, 75th Co., 6th Regt., DOW, November 2, 1918 in the Meuse Argonne. Mrs. Anna Lee Ketner (Mother), Gallup, New Mexico [ABMC-Romagne] [S1] [SW1 says KIA]

Keyes, Clarence Leroy, Pvt., 76th Co., 6th Regt., DOW, July 23, 1918 in the Aisne Marne. Jennie Keyes (Mother), P. O. Box 1, Auburn, Washington [ANC] [S2] [SW1]

Keyes, George Irving, Pvt., 17th Co., 5th Regt., DOW, October 4, 1918 in the Meuse Argonne. Ana Keyes (Mother), 3051 Montross Ave., Chicago, Illinois [R] [S2] [SW1]

Kidder, Hugh P., 2nd Lieut., MCR, 78th Co., 6th Regt., KIA, October 3, 1918 in the Meuse Argonne. Mrs. Kate Kidder (Mother), Wauken, Iowa [ABMC-Romagne] [S1] [SW1]

Marine Corps Deaths, 1917-1921

Kidwell, Paul McGraph, Pvt., 49th Co., 5th Regt., KIA, June 6, 1918 in the Chateau-Thierry Sector. Mary Kidwell (Mother), 2011 Channing Way, Berkeley, California [ABMC- Belleau] [S2] [SW]

Kildow, Percy Proctor, Cpl., 73rd Co., 6th Regt., KIA, November 1, 1918 in the Meuse Argonne. Delilah Kildow (Mother), Box 103, Oakland, Maryland [ABMC- Romagne] [S2] [SW1]

Kilduff, David R., Capt., 80th Co., 6th Regt., DOW, September 15, 1918 in the St. Mihiel offensive. Mrs. Kathleen Rogers Kilduff (widow), 2525 Durant Ave., Berkeley, California [ABMC-Thiaucourt] [S1] [SW]

Killam, David Chenoweth, Pvt., Co. F, 13th Regt., DOD, September 25, 1918 in France. W. T. Killam (Father), Hamilton Hotel, Laredo, Texas [VA-Jefferson Barracks] [S2]

Killean, Blair, Cpl., Sup Co., 6th Regt., DAO, May 30, 1919 in France. Mrs. Katherine Killean (Mother), Fairbury, Nebraska [R] [S2] [SW1 says KOA]

Killelea, Patrick F., 1st Sgt., USS *Utah*, DDS, March 28, 1920 aboard the USS *Utah*. Mrs. Mary Kilelea (not given), 141 State St., Rutland, Vermont [S4]

Killgrove, Joe Martin, Pvt., Hdqtrs. Det., OSD, Quantico, Virginia, DDS, October 8, 1918 at Quantico, Virginia. Mary A. Killgrove (Mother), El Dorado Springs, Missouri [FAG] [S3]

Killin, Oscar Joseph, Pvt., 8th Co., 5th Regt., DOW, October 2, 1918 in the Meuse Argonne. Mrs. Effie Killin (Mother), 225 Sargent Ave., Glendive, Montana [FAG] [S2] [SW1]

Killoran, James Leo, Pvt., Hdqtrs. Co., 5th Regt., DOW, June 23, 1918 in the Chateau-Thierry Sector. Thomas E. Killoran (Father), 17 Marie Ave., Cambridge, Massachusetts [S2] [SW says 139th Co., 2nd Repl. Btln.]

Marine Corps Deaths, 1917-1921

Kimball, George Alfred Marshal, Pvt., 82nd Co., 6th Regt., KIA, July 19, 1918 in the Aisne Marne. George H. Kimball (Father), P. O. Box 447, Cass Lake, Minnesota [FAG] [S2] [SW says 114th Repl. Btln.]

Kimball, Richard, Pvt., 16th Co., 5th Regt., DOW, June 25, 1918 in the Chateau-Thierry Sector. Emily H. Kimball (Mother), 18 Norman Rd., Newton Highlands, Massachusetts [ABMC- Belleau] [S2] [SW says 134th Co., 2nd Repl. Btln.]

Kimball, Walter Crawford, Pvt., 42nd Co., Guam, DAS, March 19, 1921 in an auto accident at Guam. Edith Kimball (Mother), Route #2, Monte Vista, Colorado [FAG as Walter Catherine Kimball] [S4]

Kimble, Lowell L., Sgt., Prison Det., Mare Island, California, DDS, February 4, 1920 at Mare Island, California. Mrs. Sarah Kimball (Mother), Benton, Pennsylvania [S4]

Kimbrell, Silas Lamar, Pvt., Sea School Det., MB, Norfolk, Virginia, DOS, September 12, 1921 at Norfolk, Virginia. George W. Rentz (Uncle), 116 Albany Ave., Waycross, Georgia [S4]

Kimes, Henry Sylvester, Pvt., 42nd Co., Guam, DAS, March 19, 1921 at Guam, DAS, March 19, 1921 at Guam. Anna Kimes (Mother), 201 5th St., Streator, Illinois [FAG] [S4]

Kimmel, Harry, Pvt., 74th Co., 6th Regt., KIA [SW] [SW1 reported to have been found alive]

Kimmins, Winfield Benjamin, Pvt., 97th Co., 6th Regt., DOW, October 6, 1918 in the Meuse Argonne. William Wallace Kimmins (Father), 57 Warren Ave., Kenmore, New York [R] [S2] [SW says Co. C, 3rd Repl. Btln.]

Kinane, James Robert, Pvt., Bks. Det., Quantico, Virginia, DAS, January 18, 1918 of blood poisoning at Quantico, Virginia. Nora Keefe (God-mother), 95 N. Common St., Lynn, Massachusetts [S3]

Marine Corps Deaths, 1917-1921

Kindig, Lester Harrison, Pvt., 17th Co., 5th Regt., DOW, November 2, 1918 in the Meuse Argonne. Mrs. Lester H. Kindig (Widow), Doniphan, Nebraska [S2] [SW1]

Kindley, Giles E., Cpl., 28th Co., 4th Prov. Regt., Dominican Republic, DDS, December 17, 1918 at Santo Domingo, Dominican Republic. W. A. Kindley (Father), Mt. Pleasant, North Carolina [FAG] [S4]

King, Arthur James, Pvt., 97th Co., 6th Regt., DOW, October 7, 1918 in the Meuse Argonne. Mrs. Effie J. King (Mother), 1221 W. 46th St., Norfolk, Virginia [ANC] [S2] [SW1]

King, Earnest A., Sgt., Hdqtrs. Det., Rec. Dep., Philadelphia, Pennsylvania, DDS, November 28, 1918 at Fort Lyon, Colorado. Mrs. John H. York (Sister), 1437 South 50th St., West Philadelphia, Pennsylvania [S4]

King, Eugene Joseph, Pvt., 96th Co., 6th Regt., DOW, July 19, 1918 in the Aisne Marne. Mary F. King (Mother), 154 Sherwood Ave., Syracuse, New York [ABMC- Fere] [S2] [SW1]

King, Gordon Boecher, Pvt., Naval Prison, Portsmouth, New Hampshire, DDS, May 28, 1918 at Portsmouth, New Hampshire. Winfield King (Father), 84 Main St., Canton, Pennsylvania [FAG] [S3]

King, Homer David, Pvt., 79th Co., 6th Regt., KIA, July 19, 1918 in the Aisne Marne. Mary D. Hill (Mother), 130 Summit St., French Lick, Indiana [FAG] [S2] [SW1]

King, Joseph Elmer, Pvt., 78th Co., 6th Regt., DOW, June 19, 1918 in the Chateau-Thierry Sector. Rose King (Mother), 1257 Union St., San Francisco, California [FAG] [S2] [SW]

Kinney, Barney Ernest, Pvt., 23rd Co., 6th MG Bn., KIA, November 10, 1918 in the Meuse Argonne. Laura Kinney (Mother), Paoli, Oklahoma [FAG] [S2] [SW1]

Kipp, Joseph Harem, Pvt., 79th Co., 6th Regt., DOW, June 14, 1918 in the Chateau-Thierry Sector. Wilson H. Kipp

Marine Corps Deaths, 1917-1921

(Father), 366 Nelson Ave., St. Paul, Minnesota [S2] [SW]

Kirby, James Waldo, Pvt., Mar. Det., USS Chatanooga, DOS, October 18, 1920 at Constantinople, Turkey. Ina Cole (Mother), Ellijay, Georgia [S4]

Kirchner, Henry, Pvt., 76th Co., 6th Regt., KIA, June 3, 1918 in the Aisne Defensive. William L. R. Kirchner (Father), 9 Mine Brook Rd., Bernardsville, New Jersey [ANC] [S2] [SW]

Kirchner, Jacob John, Cpl., 77th Co., 6th MG Bn., DOW, October 4, 1918 in the Meuse Argonne. Jacob Kirchner (Father), 10 Central Ave., Albany, New York [FAG] [S2] [SW1 says KIA]

Kirk, John Severe, Pvt., Co. L, 13th Regt., DOD, November 11, 1918 in France. Mrs. Perlee Kirk (Mother), P.O. Box 639, Dallas, Texas [FAG] [S2]

Kirk, Robert Bruce, Pvt., 80th Co., 6th Regt., KIA, June 11, 1918 in the Chateau-Thierry Sector. Frank Ashby (Friend), 1019 Dearborn St., Chicago, Illinois [ABMC- Belleau TOM] [S2] [SW]

Kirkpatrick, William Edgar, Gy. Sgt., 1st Brigade, Haiti, DDS, October 2, 1921 at Port au Prince, Haiti. Genevive Kirpatrick (Mother), South English, Iowa [FAG] [S4]

Kirscht, Adam Bernard, Pvt., 45th Co., 5th Regt., KIA [SW] [SW1 reported to have been found alive]

Kishler, Edwin Porter, Pvt., 16th Co., 5th Regt., KIA, June 25, 1918 in the Chateau-Thierry Sector. Jennie Kishler (Mother), Greenville, Pennsylvania [FAG] [S2] [SW1]

Kite, Clement Cresson, Gy. Sgt., 81st Co., 6th MG Bn., KIA, June 17, 1918 in the Chateau-Thierry Sector. Frances V. Kite (Wife), 606 Westview St., Mt. Airy, Pennsylvania [ABMC- Belleau] [S2] [SW]

Marine Corps Deaths, 1917-1921

Kivett, John C., QM Sgt., Hdqtrs. Det., American Legion, China, DAS, June 6, 1920 at Peking, China. Sarah Kivett (Mother), RFD#6, Martinsville, Indiana [FAG] [S4]

Kjos, Tillman Arty, Cpl., 80th Co., 6th Regt., DOW, November 2, 1918 in the Meuse Argonne. Mrs. B. Anderson (Sister), Kindred, North Dakota [FAG] [S2] [SW1]

Klapp, Joseph George William, Cpl., 20th Co., 5th Regt., KIA, June 23, 1918 in the Chateau-Thierry Sector. Katherine Klapp (Mother), 199 Chadwick Ave., Newark, New Jersey [S2] [SW]

Klebes, Herbert Gold, Pvt., 75th Co., 6th Regt., KIA, June 15, 1918 in the Chateau-Thierry Sector. William E. Klebes (Father), Sharan, Connecticut [R] [S2] [SW]

Kleinfield, Joseph Lewis, Pvt., MB, NS, Olongapo, Philippine Islands, DAS, September 6, 1918 by drowning in Subic Bay, Philippine Islands. Louhaney Pfeuffer (Mother), Latin Station, California [S3]

Kleinman, Moroni, Pvt., 20th Co., 5th Regt., KIA, June 25, 1918 in the Chateau-Thierry Sector. Lulu Kleinman (Mother), Toqueville, Utah [ABMC- Belleau] [S2] [SW]

Klema, Fred Arthur, 1st Sgt., 34th Co., 1st Replacement Battalion, DOO, March 25, 1918 in France. Amila Klema (Mother), RFD#1, Box 41, Racine, Wisconsin [FAG] [S2] [SW1]

Kline, Orrie Francis, Sgt., 67th Co., 5th Regt., KIA, July 18, 1918 in the Aisne Marne. Norma A. Kline (Wife), 912 S. Cushman Ave., Tacoma, Washington [ANC] [S2] [SW says Casualty Co.]

Klingelhofer, Banhardt, Pvt., Co. R, Parris Island, South Carolina, DDS, September 25, 1918 at Parris Island, South Carolina. Bertha Schler (Sister), 45 Kilhoffer St., Buffalo, New York [S3]

Klingenstein, Herbert W., Drm, 23rd Co., 6th MG Bn., DOW, July 22, 1918 in the Aisne Marne. Lepold Klingenstein

Marine Corps Deaths, 1917-1921

(Father), 300 Snydam St., Brooklyn, New York [ABMC-Belleau] [S2] [SW1 says KIA]

Klotz, Leonard Sebastion, Pvt. [Cpl.], 73rd Co., 6th Regt., DOW, July 22, 1918 in the Aisne Marne. Mrs. Margaret Hickey (Aunt), 1212 Ashland St., Richmond, Virgnia [FAG] [S2] [SW]

Kmiec, Stanislau, Sgt., 51st Co., 5th Regt., DOW, October 8, 1918 in the Meuse Argonne. Mrs. Maria Kowalska (Sister), 635 Grand Ave., NE, Grand Rapids, Michigan [R] [S2] [SW1]

Knapp, Charles Herbert, Trumpeter, Supply Co., 11th Regt., DOW, February 28, 1919 in France. Almer H. Knapp (Father), 34 Groverland St., Haverhill, Massachusetts [FAG] [S2] [SW1 says KOA]

Knapp, Thomas R., Pvt., West Recruiting Division, DDS, November 13, 1918 at Butte, Montana. Mrs. Mary Knapp (Mother), P. O. Box 214, Lewiston, Idaho [FAG] [S4]

Knauss, Walter Houck, Pvt., 23rd Co., 6th MG Bn., KIA, October 4, 1918 in the Meuse Argonne. Mrs. Catherine Knauss (Mother), 364 Raymond St., Milton, Pennsylvania [R] [S2] [SW1]

Knecht, Albert Joseph, Pvt., 43rd Co., 5th Regt., KIA, June 12, 1918 in the Chateau-Thierry Sector. Adam Knecht (Father), 5335 St. Louis Ave., St. Louis, Missouri [S2] [SW1]

Knecht, Harold Van Horn, Pvt., 83rd Co., 6th Regt., KIA, June 8, 1918 in the Chateau-Thierry Sector. Emma Knecht (Mother), 10 N. Main St., Nazareth, Pennsylvania [FAG] [S2] [SW1]

Kneil, Lawrence Henry, Cpl., 55th Co., 5th Regt., DOW, November 12, 1918 in the Meuse Argonne. Charlotte Cain (Sister), 892 Corley St., E. Akron, Ohio [FAG] [S2] [SW1 says KIA]

Marine Corps Deaths, 1917-1921

Knepp, Clarence Carleton, Sgt., 55th Co., 5th Regt., DOW, June 23, 1918 in the Chateau-Thierry Sector. James R. Wilson (Uncle), Route #2, Huntingdon, Pennsylvania [S2] [SW]

Knight, Floyd Charles, Sgt., 66th Co., 5th Regt., DOW, June 16, 1918 in the Chateau-Thierry Sector. Mrs. Hattie Syers (Mother), Muskegon County, Holton, Michigan [R] [S2] [SW]

Knight, Lester Collins, Pvt., 45th Co., 5th Regt., DOW, October 3, 1918 in the Meuse Argonne. John and Margaret Knight (Parents), Cooksburg, Pennsylvania [FAG] [S2] [SW1]

Knisel, Benjamin Chrisotopher, Pvt., Co. F, 13th Regt., DOD, December, 18, 1918 in France. Mrs. Martha Knisel (Mother), Blissfield, Michigan [R] [S2]

Knowlton, James W., Sgt., Hdqrs., 1st M.G. Repl. Btln., September 12, 1918. Texas. [ANC] [SW]

Knorr, George, Pvt., 67th Co., 5th Regt., KIA, June 6, 1918 in the Chateau-Thierry Sector. Julia Knorr (Mother), 840 Lakewood Ave., Youngstown, Ohio [ABMC- Belleau] [S2] [SW]

Knott, George Thomas, Sgt., 17th Co., 5th Regt., KIA, July 18, 1918 in the Aisne Marne. Mrs. Jennie Knott (Mother), Granby, Connecticut [ABMC- Belleau] [S2] [SW]

Knox, Douglas Hamilton, Pvt., 79th Co., 6th Regt., DOW, June 18, 1918 in the Chateau-Thierry Sector. Mrs. Loula B. Knox (Mother), 1013 Prince Edward St., Fredericksburg, Virginia [ANC] [S2] [SW says Replacement]

Knox, William Newton, Pvt., Co. C, Parris Island, South Carolina, DDS, March 4, 1918 at Parris Island, South Carolina. Alice M. Knox (Mother), 1617 Fatherland St., Nashville, Tennessee [FAG] [S3]

Knox, William Robert, Sgt., Hdqtrs. 2nd Brigade, Dominican Republic, KIA, March 24, 1918 killed by bandits at Margarin, Dominican Republic. Anna B., Knox (Mother), Baracher St., Montreal, Canada [VA-Cypress Hills] [S3]

Marine Corps Deaths, 1917-1921

Knuck, Anthony Patrick, Pvt., 8th Co., 5th Regt., KIA, October 3, 1918 in the Meuse Argonne. John J. Knuck (Brother), 1405 Broad St., Augusta, Georgia [FAG] [S2] [SW]

Knutson, Carl Salmer, Cpl., 140th Co., 3rd Repl. Battn., KIA, June 6, 1918 in the Chateau-Thierry Sector. Christ Knutson (Father), Belview, Minnesota [S2] [SW1]

Knutson, Jens Martin, Pvt., Casual Co., Mare Island, California, DDS, June 20, 1921 at Mare Island, California. John Peter Knutson (Father), Gen. Del., Poulsbo, Washington [S4]

Knutson, Joe, Pvt., Dominican Republic, DOS, March 23, 1918 at Santiago, Dominican Republic. Annie Stanbaugh (Sister), Box, 36, Raymond, Montana [S3]

Knutzen, Werner Kickhefel, Cpl., 79th Co., 6th Regt., DOW, October 6, 1918 in the Meuse Argonne. Matilda Knutzen (Mother), 112 N. Plum St., Richmond, Virginia [R] [S2] [SW says 150 Co.]

Kocak, Matej, Sgt., 66th Co., 5th Regt., KIA, October 4, 1918 in the Meuse Argonne. Julia Kocak (Sister-in-law) Binghampton, New York [ABMC- Romagne] [S2] [SW]

Kochis, John, Pvt., 95th Co., 6th Regt., KIA, July 19, 1918 in the Aisne Marne. Elizabeth Kochis (Mother), 346 Melvin St., Barberton, Ohio [FAG] [S2] [SW]

Koehler, George Washington, Pvt., 55th Co., 5th Regt., KIA, October 4, 1918 in the Meuse Argonne. Mrs. Floy Estelle Koehler Rudy (Wife), 3325 Virginia Ave., St. Louis, Missouri [FAG] [S2] [SW1]

Koehler, George Wesley, Pvt., 45th Co., 5th Regt., KIA, June 23, 1918 in the Chateau-Thierry Sector. Steven W. Koehler (Father), Mound, Minnesota [S2] [SW says 138th Co., 2nd Repl. Btln.]

Koehne, Edward Anthony, Pvt., 74th Co., 6th Regt., DOW, October 7, 1918 in the Meuse Argonne. Mrs. Joseph

Koehne (Mother), 2554 Liddell St., Cincinnati, Ohio [FAG] [S2] [SW says Koehn and Co. A]

Kofroth, Reno Joseph, Pvt., 6th Co., Quantico, Virginia, DDS, February 6, 1919 at Lititz, Pennsylvania. Mrs. Ruth B. Kofroth (Wife), 215 Broad St., Lititz, Pennsylvania [S4]

Kolson, Francis Earl, Pvt., 18th Co., 5th Regt., KIA, June 8, 1918 in the Chateau-Thierry Sector. Theodore J. Kolson (Father), 1128 Braddock Ave, Braddock, Pennsylvania [ABMC- Belleau] [S2] [SW]

Kornegay, Sidney Everett, Pvt., 95th Co., 6th Regt., KIA, November 1, 1918 in the Meuse Argonne. Carry F. Kornegay (Mother), Gen. Del. Malone, Texas [FAG] [S2] [SW1]

Koroly, John H., Pvt., 174th Co., 14th Prov. Regt., Quantico, Virginia, DDS, January 15, 1919 at Quantico, Virginia. Joseph Korloy (Father), Smithdale, Allegheny Co., Pennsylvania [FAG] [S4]

Korskey, Joseph William, Cpl., 16th Co., 5th Regt., KIA, June 23, 1918 in the Chateau-Thierry Sector. Mike Korskey (Brother), 1227 Hamilton St., Grand Rapids, Michigan [ABMC- Belleau TOM] [S2] [SW]

Kotalik, George Phillip, Pvt., 84th Co., 6th Regt., KIA, June 7, 1918 in the Chateau-Thierry Sector. Andrew Kotalik (Father), 65 E. Liberty St., Ashley, Pennsylvania [ABMC-Belleau] [S2] [SW1]

Kowalak, Anthony Stanley, Cpl., 49th Co., 5th Regt., KIA, June 20, 1918 in the Chateau-Thierry Sector. Mrs Mary Gielda (Sister), 1124 24th St., Bay City, Michigan [S2] [SW1]

Kowker, Anthony Joseph, Cpl., 43rd Co., 5th Regt., KIA, June 10, 1918 in the Chateau-Thierry Sector. William Kowker (Father), 262 N. Balliet St., Frackville, Pennsylvania [FAG] [S2] [SW]

Kraft, David Foster, Pvt., 67th Co., 5th Regt., KIA, November 1, 1918 in the Meuse Argonne. Mary J. Kraft (Mother), 24

Marine Corps Deaths, 1917-1921

East Church St., Sellerville, Pennsylvania [FAG] [S2] [SW1]

Krakau, Earl E., Pvt., MBks., Norfolk, Virginia, DDS, April 3, 1919 at Norfolk, Virginia. Henry T. Krakau (Father), 13802 Lake Shore Blvd., Cleveland, Ohio [S4]

Krankowski, Anton Frank, Pvt., 157th Co., NTS, Newport, Rhode Island, DAS, September 15, 1918 at Newport, Rhode Island. Linte Krankowski (Mother), 652 Sebert Ave., Cleveland, Ohio [S3]

Krantz, Joris Ernest, Pvt., 79th Co., 6th Regt., Quantico, Virginia, DDS, January 4, 1918 at Quantico, Virginia. Augusta Krantz (Mother), Gen. Del., Minneapolis, Minnesota [ANC] [S3]

Krause, Maurice Samuel, Pvt., 82nd Co., 6th Regt., DOW, July 19, 1918 in the Aisne Marne. Minnie Krause (Mother), 4129 Hartford St., St. Louis, Missouri [S2] [SW1]

Krause, Max, Gy. Sgt. [Sgt.], 80th Co., 6th Regt., DOW, June 4, 1918 in the Aisne Defensive. Aelxander R. Krause (Brother), 159 N. State St., Room 1620, Chicago, Illinois [R] [S2] [SW] [SW1]

Kreiger, Edward Louis, Pvt., 95th Co., 6th Regt., DOW, June 16, 1918 in the Chateau-Thierry Sector. Mrs. Louise Hager (Sister), 44Timon St., Buffalo, New York [R] [S2] [SW]

Krieg, Elmer Michel, Pvt., 84th Co., 6th Regt., KIA, June 6, 1918 1918 in the Chateau-Thierry Sector. Bertha Krieg (Mother), 109 Beals Ave., Detroit, Michigan [S2] [SW]

Krift, George Edward, Pvt., M.G. Co., 13th Regt., DOD, September 24, 1918 enroute to France. Anna Krift (Mother), 1328 LaSalle St., St. Louis, Missouri [R] [S2]

Kripisch, Lewis August, Pfc., 38th Co., Peking, China, DDS, February 25, 1920 at Peking, China. Mrs. Ricka Kripisch (Mother), RFD#3, Box 39, Medaryville, Indiana [FAG] [S4]

Marine Corps Deaths, 1917-1921

Krohn, Edward Maley, Pvt., 67th Co., 5th Regt., KIA, June 6, 1918 in the Chateau-Thierry Sector. Kate Krohn (Mother), 8109 Reilly Ave., St. Louis, Missouri [VA-Jefferson Barracks] [S2] [SW]

Kroll, Fred William, Pvt., 20th Co., 5th Regt., KIA, September 14, 1918 in the St. Mihiel Offensive. Heran Kroll (Father), South Stillwater, Minnesota [ABMC- Romagne] [S2] [SW says Replacement]

Kroll, Walter Frank, Pvt., 127th Co., 7th Regt., Cuba, DAS, July 11, 1918 struck by lightning at Camp La Union, San Luis, Cuba. Frank Kroll (Father), Glenwood City, Wisconsin [FAG] [S3]

Kromeburg, Charles August, Pvt., 42nd Co., Guam, DDS, May 24, 1918 at Guam. Henry Kromeburg, 1121 W. 18th Place, Chicago, Illinois [S3]

Kropf, Adolph, Pvt., Bks. Det., Philadelphia, Pennsylvania, DDS, October 2, 1918 at Philadelphia, Pennsylvania. Carl Kropf (Brother), Tarcey, Minnesota [FAG] [S3]

Kruth, Hugo Walter, Sgt., 19th Co., 1st Regt., Quantico, Virginia, DDS, September 25, 1918 at Quantico, Virginia. Gussie L. L. Tatzke (Sister), Miller, Ave., Meridan, Connecticut [FAG] [S3]

Kryszewski, Charles, Cpl., 74th Co., 6th Regt., DOW, June 4, 1918 in the Aisne Defensive. Stefania Kryszewski (Mother), 733 Newark Ave., Jersey City, New Jersey [FAG] [S2] [SW1]

Kudell, Ernest Charles, Pvt., 75th Co., 6th Regt., DOW, October 12, 1918 in the Meuse Argonne. Emma Konz (Mother), 10th and Monroe Sts., Newport, Kentucky [ABMC-Romagne] [S2] [SW1]

Kuempel, Edward Emil, Pvt., Bks. Det., New York, New York, DDS, October 15, 1918 at New York, New York. Annie Kuempel (Mother), 6 Stevenson Place, Ionia, Michigan [S3]

Marine Corps Deaths, 1917-1921

Kuhn, John Leon, Cpl., 16th Co., 5th Regt., DOW, April 20, 1918 in the Toulon Sector, Verdun. Michael Kuhn (Father), 22 E. Abbott St., Lansford, Pennsylvania [FAGM] [S2] [SW]

Kunkee, Alfred H., Pfc, Co. H, Mare Island, California, DDS, November 17, 1918 at Mare Island, California. Mrs. Julia A. Kunkee (Mother), Atascadero, California [FAG] [S4]

Kunkel, William Richard, Pvt., 97th Co., 6th Regt., KIA [SW] [SW1 reported to have been found alive]

Kurtz, Henry Hobart, Pvt., Co. B, 13th Regt., DOD, September 30, 1918 in France. Alice C. Kurtz (Mother), North Salem, Indiana [FAG] [S2]

Kurzawski, John, Cpl., 51st Co., 5th Regt., KIA, July 21, 1918 in the Aisne Marne. Frank Kurzawski (Father), 17 Brown St., Albion, New York [ABMC- Fere] [S2] [SW1]

Kush, Geroge Edward, Pvt., 76th Co., 6th Regt., KIA [SW] [SW1 reported to have been found alive]

Kusie, Joseph William, Pvt., 80th Co., 6th Regt., DOW, October 4, 1918 in the Meuse Argonne. Mary Kusie (Mother), Dickinson, North Dakota [R] [S2] [SW says Co. B, 5th Sep. Btln.]

La Banta, Dean Deirich Jr., Pvt., Hdqtrs. Co., 6th Regt., DOW, November 3, 1918 in the Meuse Argonne. Dean D. La Banta (Father), 710 Randolph St., Jackson, Michigan [R] [S2] [SW1]

La Barge, Palmer Joseph, Pvt., 97th Co., 6th Regt., DOD, November 24, 1918 in France. Mary E. La Barge (Mother), 943a Beach Ave., St. Louis, Missouri, [ABMC-Suresnes] [S2]

La Belle, Clarence Richard, Pvt., 78th Co., 6th Regt., DOW, October 3, 1918 in the Meuse Argonne. Elleanora La Belle (Mother), 3839 6th St., Minneapolis, Minnesota [ABMC- Romagne] [S2] [SW1 says KIA]

Marine Corps Deaths, 1917-1921

La Bonte, Edmond Joseph, Pvt., 49th Co., 5th Regt., KIA, June 6, 1918 in the Chateau-Thierry Sector. John B. LaBonte (Father), Gen. Del., York Beach, Maine [ANC] [S2] [SW]

La Brash, Charles Edward, Pvt., 79th Co., 6th Regt., KIA, October 3, 1918 in the Meuse Argonne. Henry La Brash (Father), Winbledon, North Dakota [ANC] [S2] [SW]

Lacey, William Joseph, Pvt., 97th Co., 6th Regt., DOW, November 3, 1918 in the Meuse Argonne. Emma Lacey (Mother), 2309 N. Cleveland Ave., Philadelphia, Pennsylvania [R] [S2] [SW1]

Lacy, Harry Neville, Sgt., 76th Co., 6th Regt., KIA, July 19, 1918 in the Aisne Marne. Samuel A. Lacy (Father), Lancaster, Texas [ANC] [S2] [SW]

Laidlaw, Rollin William, Cpl., 74th Co., 6th Regt., KIA, June 9, 1918 in the Chateau-Thierry Sector. Mrs. William Laidlaw (Mother), 1098 Woodycrest Ave., New York, New York [R] [S2] [SW]

Laing, Joe S., Pvt., Co. R, Parris Island, South Carolina, DDS, November 12, 1918 at Parris Island, South Carolina. Joseph Early Laing (Father), 621 Oak Ave., Sanford, Florida [FAG] [S4]

Lake, Archie Lewis, Pvt., 97th Co., 6th Regt., DOW, July 19, 1918 in the Aisne Marne. Jennie N. Lake (Mother), 28 Burlington Ave., LaGrange, Illinois [ABMC- Fere] [S2] [SW1 says KIA]

Lake, William H., Trumpeter, F Music Det., Parris Island, South Carolina, DDS, December 5, 1918 at Parris Island, South Carolina. Mrs. Catherine Lake (Mother), Laredo, Texas [S4]

Lalonde, Richard, Cpl., MD, Fort Lyons, Colorado, DDS, April 30, 1917 at Fort Lyon, Colorado. Frank Lalonde (Father), address unknown. [VA-Fort Lyon] [S3]

Marine Corps Deaths, 1917-1921

Lamb, Eton Stanley, Pvt., USS *New Jersey*, DDS, March 8, 1918 aboard the USS *New Jersey*. Mary Lamb (Mother), 212 Kalamazoo Ave., Marshall, Michigan [S3]

Lamb, Jimmie H., Gy. Sgt., 87th Co., Signal Bn., Philadelphia, Pennsylvania, DDS, March 9, 1919 at Philadelphia, Pennsylvania. Thomas Arthur Lamb (Brother), c/o U.S. Army, Jefferson Barracks, Missouri [S4]

Lancaster, Elmer Nelson, Cpl., 78th Co., 6th Regt., KIA, September 15, 1918 in the St. Mihiel Offensive. Nellie Lancaster (Mother), Alliance, Humboldt County, California [FAG] [S2] [SW1 says DOW]

Land, Robert Priest, Sgt., 79th Co., 6th Regt., DOW, August 2, 1918 in the Aisne Marne. Mr. Allan L. Land (Father), 551 S.W. Blvd., Rosedale, Kansas [R] [S2] [SW]

Landers, Keneston Parker, Pvt., 82nd Co., 6th Regt., DOW, June 6, 1918 in the Aisne Defensive. Wm. Keneston Landers (Father), 106 N. State St., Syracuse, New York [S2] [SW]

Lane, Benjamin Franklin Jr., Pvt., 81st Co., 6th MG Bn., KIA, July 19, 1918 in the Aisne Marne. Benjiman Franklin Lane (Father), 3220 Big Ben Road, Box 405, Maplewood, St. Louis, Missouri [FAG] [S2] [SW]

Lane, James Howard, Pvt., 20th Co., 5th Regt., KIA, June 25, 1918 in the Chateau-Thierry Sector. James F. Lane (Father), 1324 11th Ave., Port Huron, Michigan [R] [S2] [SW says Replacement]

Lane, Stuart Gardener, Pvt., DDS, February 17, 1918 at Chelsea, Massachusetts. Annie Lane (Mother), 20 Lawsen Rd., Winchester, Massachusetts [S3]

Lange, Albert Nicholas, Pvt., Hdqtrs., USMC, Washington, D.C., DDS, May 1, 1921 at Washington, D.C. Julia Elizabeth Lange (Wife), 3 New York Ave., N.W., Washington, D.C. [VA-ANC as June 1, 1921] [S4]

Marine Corps Deaths, 1917-1921

Lange, Roy Bearnard, Pvt., 47th Co., 5th Regt., DOD, October 12, 1918 in France. John B. Lange (Father), 2500 Homon Ave., Waco, Texas [R] [S2]

Langell, George Linwood, Pvt., 97th Co., 6th Regt., KIA, July 19, 1918 in the Aisne Marne. Emma B. McCombie (Mother), 550 Main St., Malden, Massachusetts [S2] [SW]

Langley, Charles Erl., Pvt., 17th Co., 5th Regt., KIA, September 14, 1918 in the St. Mihiel Offensive. John B. Langley (Father), Big Clifty, Kentucky [ABMC- Thiaucourt] [S2] [SW]

Langley, Herbert, Pvt., 115th Co., 2nd Brigade, Dominican Repbulic, DAS, February 24, 1919 at Santo Domingo, Dominican Republic. Dr. John Wesley Langley (Father), Box 240, Granby, Missouri [S4]

Lanham, Robert Roy, Pvt., 80th Co., 6th Regt., KIA, June 3, 1918 in the Chateau-Thierry Sector. Mrs. Mary Lanham (Mother), 3624 Hillger St., Detroit, Michigan [VA-Cave Hill] [S2] [SW]

Lanham, Thomas Raymond, Pvt., Co. A, MG Bn, 5th Brig., Quantico, Virginia, DDS, October 4, 1918 at Quantico, Virginia. Steven C. Lanham (Father), RFD #1, Mitchelville, Maryland [S3]

Lankford, Alexander Cameron, Pvt., Bks. Det., Philadelphia, Pennsylvania, DDS, October 2, 1918 at Philadelphia, Pa. John Lankford (Father), 312 Ann St., Harrison, New Jersey [S3]

Lannigan, John L., Pvt., Co. D, 1st Tr. Bn., Brooklyn, New York, DDS, February 1, 1919 at Brooklyn, New York. Mrs. Mary T. Lannigan (Mother), 26 Plympton St., Waltham, Massachusetts [S4]

Lannom, Altie, Pvt., 23rd Co., 6th MG Bn., KIA, October 4, 1918 in the Meuse Argonne. Bessie Lannom (Sister), Gen. Del., Garevellie, Illinois [ABMC- Romagne] [S2] [SW says 1st Corps Repl. Btln.]

Marine Corps Deaths, 1917-1921

Lannon, John Francis, Pvt., 80th Co., 6th Regt., DOW, July 19, 1918 in the Aisne Marne. Mrs. Annie Lannon (Mother), 1525 Fourth Ave., Sault Ste. Marie, Michigan [S2] [SW1 says KIA]

Lantzy, Dennis Olen, Cpl., 45th Co., 5th Regt., KIA, June 24, 1918 in the Chateau-Thierry Sector. Harriet E. Lantzy (Mother), Coeur d'Alene, Idaho [FAG] [S2] [SW1]

LaPage, George, Sgt., Hdqtrs., USMC (Garage), Washington, D.C., DOS, October 21, 1921 at Twining City, D.C. Mrs. Audrey G. LaPage (Wife), 1329 Belmont St., N.W., Washington, D.C. [ANC] [S4]

Largen, Otis, Pvt., 51st Co., 5th Regt., DOW, November 1, 1918 in the Meuse Argonne. Arthur Largen (Brother), Ritchey, Missouri [VA-Springfield] [S2] [SW1]

Larsen, Edwin John, Cpl., 83rd Co., 6th Regt., KIA, June 6, 1918 in the Chateau-Thierry Sector. Hannah Larsen (Mother), 317 6th St., Manistee, Michigan [S2] [SW] [SW1]

Larson, Clarence Aivid, Pvt., 97th Co., 6th Regt., KIA, June 6, 1918 in the Chateau-Thierry Sector. Charles Larson (Father), Grant St., Lemant, Illinois [S2] [SW]

Larson, Fay, Pvt., MD, NAD, St. Julien's Creek, Virginia, DDS, October 11, 1918 at Norfolk, Virginia. Mrs. Joe Hedkinson (Step-mother), 3653 W. Ohio St., Chicago, Illinois [S3]

Laster, James Lineal, Jr., Pvt., 97th Co., 6th Regt., KIA, September 15, 1918 in the St. Mihiel Offensive. James L. Laster, Sr. (Father), 1420 Morrow St., Waco, Texas [ABMC-Thiaucourt] [S2]

Latscha, Julius Joseph, Pvt., USS *Mercy*, DDS, October 18, 1918 aboard the USS *Mercy*. Julia Latscha (Mother), 3829 Llewellyn St., Cincinnati, Ohio [S3]

Latsko, Martin John, Pvt., 51st Co., 5th Regt., DOW, October 4, 1918 in the Meuse Argonne. Susanna Latsko (Mother),

614 Hamilton Ave., Farrell, Pennsylvania [ABMC-Romagne TOM] [S2] [SW1 says KIA]

Lauchheimer, Charles H., Brig. Gen., Hdqtrs., USMC, Washington, D.C., DDS, January 14, 1920 at Washington, D.C., Mrs. Nathan Schoss (Sister), 2410 Eutaw Place, Baltimore, Maryland [ANC] [S4]

Laurie, Arthur J., Sgt., 62nd Co., 2nd Regt., Haiti, DDS, November 20, 1919 at Haiti. Mrs. Louise Laurie (Mother), Soperton, Wisconsin [S4]

Lawhead, Victor Josephus, Pvt., 80th Co., 6th Regt., DOW, July 19, 1918 in the Aisne Marne. Eta Sweitzer (Mother), 132 N. Grant St., Pocatello, Idaho [ANC] [S2] [SW1]

Lawrence, Harry, Pvt., 100th Co., 8th Regt., Haiti, KIA, November 28, 1919 by bandits at Port au Prince, Haiti. Samuel Lawrence (Father), Mt. Valley, Kansas [S4]

Lawrence, John Richard, Pvt., 51st Co., 5th Regt., KIA, June 11, 1918 in the Chateau-Thierry Sector. David J. Lawrence (Father), 4251 E. 114th St., Cleveland, Ohio [S2] [SW]

Lawrentz, Herbert Francis, Pvt., 79th Co., 6th Regt., DOW, July 24, 1918 in the Aisne Marne. Josephine Lawrentz (Mother), Munroe Falls, Summit County, Ohio [FAG] [S2] [SW says 137th Co., 2nd Repl. Btln.]

Laws, Charles Thomas, Pvt., 84th Co., 6th Regt., KIA, November 1, 1918 in the Meuse Argonne. Emma Laws (Mother), 807 Bainbridge St., South Richmond, Virginia [FAG] [S2] [SW1]

Laws, Cyril Morle, Pvt., Naval Prison, Portsmouth, New Hampshire, DDS, September 2, 1918 at Portsmouth, New Hampshire. Ruby Laws (Wife), 113 W. Mowalk St., Buffalo, N.Y. [FAG] [S3]

Laws, Douglas Kent, Cpl., 75th Co., 6th Regt., KIA, June 14, 1918 in the Chateau-Thierry Sector. Mrs. J. D. Richardson (Mother), Cecilia, Kentucky [ABMC- Belleau] [S2] [SW]

Marine Corps Deaths, 1917-1921

Lawson, Thomas Bell, Pvt., MD, NH, Las Animas, Colorado, DDS, October 28, 1918 at Las Animas, Colorado. William Lawson (Father), Pueblo, Colorado [S3]

Lawson, Valentine, Pvt., 18th Co., 5th Regt., KIA, June 11, 1918 in the Chateau-Thierry Sector. Henry Lawson (Mother), Blanco, Texas [ABMC- Belleau] [S2] [SW1]

Layman, Hollie James, Pvt., 17th Co., 5th Regt., DOW, October 11, 1918 in the Meuse Argonne. James Layman (Mother), R#1, Box 76, Gainesville, Arkansas [FAG] [S2] [SW1]

Layton, Rush, Pvt., 20th Co., 5th Regt., DOW, June 23, 1918 in the Chateau-Thierry Sector. Albert Layton (Father), RFD#6, Everett, Pennsylvania [FAG] [S2] [SW1]

Leach, Everett Oscar, Pvt., 85th Co., Quantico, Virginia, DDS, October 10, 1918 at Quantico, Virginia. Flora M. Leach (Wife), Hiawatha, Kansas [S3]

Leaf, John Frederic, Pvt., 22nd Co., Cuba, DDS, February 23, 1919 at Guantanamo Bay, Cuba. John A. H. Leaf (Father), 18 Woodbury St., New Rochelle, New York [S4]

League, William Clayton, Pvt., 79th Co., 6th Regt., DOW, July 19, 1918 in the Aisne Marne. Mrs. Lethia Smith (Mother), 31 Athens St., Gainesville, Georgia [FAG] [S2] [SW1 says KIA]

Lease, Frank Vernon, Pvt., 79th Co., 6th Regt., DOW, July 17, 1918 in the Aisne Marne. Oliver B. Lease (Father), R#2, Gazette, Missouri [ABMC- Belleau] [S2] [SW]

Leber, Paul Revere, Pvt., 67th Co., 5th Regt., DOW, June 7, 1918 in the Chateau-Thierry Sector. Mrs. Maggie Leber (Mother), 801 Locust St., Columbia, Pennsylvania [S2] [SW]

Le Blanc, Napoleon Joseph, Cpl., 76th Co., 6th Regt., KIA, June 11, 1918 in the Chateau-Thierry Sector. Eva Le Blanc (Mother), 3252 Franklin Blvd., Chicago, Illinois [FAGM] [ABMC- Belleau] [S2] [SW]

Marine Corps Deaths, 1917-1921

Lederberg, Herbert, Pvt., NTS, Alexandria, Virginia, DDS, October 7, 1921 at Washington, D.C. Mrs. Charles Lederberg 513 "L" St., N.W., Washington, D.C. [S4]

Ledoux, Joseph, Pvt., 20th Co., 5th Regt., Brooklyn, New York, DDS, January 31, 1919 at Brooklyn, New York. Mrs. Ursin Ledoux (Mother), Opelousas, Louisiana [S4]

Lee, Harry Willard, Gy. Sgt., 51st Co., 5th Regt., DOD, February 17, 1919 in France. John W. Lee (Father), Mars, Pennsylvania [FAG] [S2]

Lee, Louis Edward, Pvt., 20th Co., 5th Regt., KIA, June 6, 1918 in the Chateau-Thierry Sector. Mrs. W. H. Hamby (Mother), 62 Lindsley Ave., Nashville, Tennessee [S2] [SW says 131st Co., 2nd Repl. Btln.]

Lee, Vernie Duffy, Pvt., Hdqtrs. Det., Parris Island, South Carolina, DDS, June 28, 1917 at Parris Island, South Carolina. Victor R. Lee (Brother), 413 Gifford St., Syracuse, New York [S3]

Leenhouts, Willard George, Pvt., Hdqtrs. Co., 5th Regt., KIA, July 3, 1918 in the Chateau-Thierry Sector. Abram Leenhouts (Father), 284 Maple Ave., Holland, Michigan [ABMC-Belleau] [S2] [SW]

Leftridge, William, Pvt., 37th Co., Cuba, DAS, June 25, 1920 at Camaguey, Cuba. Maggie Leftridge (Mother), Richmond, Missouri [S4]

Legnard, John Bernard, Pvt., 17th Co., 5th Regt., DOW, October 6, 1918 in the Meuse Argonne. John Legnard (Father), 28 Hudson Ave., Greene Island, New York [ABMC-Thiaucourt] [S2] [SW1]

Lehman, Kerlin, Pvt., 97th Co., 6th Regt., KIA, July 19, 1918 in the Aisne Marne. Ida M. Lehman (Mother), c/o St. Albans School, Sycamore, Illinois [ABMC- Fere] [S2] [SW]

Marine Corps Deaths, 1917-1921

Lehr, John Samuel, Pvt., 75th Co., 6th Regt., DOW, October 12, 1918 in the Meuse Argonne. Mrs. Susie Lehr (Mother), 585 Toledo Ave., Detroit, Michigan [R] [S2] [SW1]

Leitner, Aloysi(s)us, Pvt., Hdqtrs. Co., 5th Regt., DOW, June 11, 1918 in the Chateau-Thierry Sector. Joseph Leitner (Father), Route #2, Box 95,Holstein, Wisconsin [ABMC- Belleau] [S2] [SW]

Lemmon, Berrel Andrew, Pvt., 67th Co., 5th Regt., DOW, June 15, 1918 in the Chateau-Thierry Sector. Mrs. Mary E. Lemmon (Mother), Millersburg, Homes County, Ohio [R] [S2] [SW1]

Lemon, Gilbert Williard, Cpl., 51st Co., 5th Regt., KIA, June 11, 1918 in the Chateau-Thierry Sector. Margaret Lemon (Mother), RFD#2, Walker, Wood County, West Virginia [ABMC- Belleau] [S2] [SW]

Lemon, Henry Gurnard, Cpl., Supply Co., Parris Island, South Carolina, DDS, November 9, 1918 at Parris Island, South Carolina. Maud Leman (Mother), White Clouds, Kansas [FAG] [S3]

Lemons, Charles Valentine, Jr., Pvt., 67th Co., 5th Regt., KIA, November 2, 1918 in the Meuse Argonne. Mrs. Harry Lemons (Mother), R#2, Sugar Run, Pennsylvania [VA-Philadelphia] [S2] [SW1]

Lent, Vernon Jefferson, Pvt., 82nd Co., 6th Regt., DOD, October 14, 1918 in France. Cythia Lent (Mother), 53 Harvest St., Salinas, California [R] [S2]

Leonard, Raymond Ross, Pvt., 74th Co., 6th Regt., DOW, October 9, 1918 in the Meuse Argonne. Bella Leonard (Mother), P. O. Box 391, Fort Worth, Texas [ANC] [S2] [SW1 says 17th Co., 5th Regt.]

Le Pere, Walter Henry, Sgt., 75th Co., 6th Regt., KIA, October 9, 1918 in the Meuse Argonne. Salane Le Pere (Mother), Farmington, Missouri [ABMC- Romagne as Lepere] [S2] [SW1]

Marine Corps Deaths, 1917-1921

Le Prell, Ambrose Joseph, Pvt., 17th Co., 5th Regt., KIA, October 4, 1918 in the Meuse Argonne. in the Meuse Argonne. Frank J. Le Prell (Father), 415 Grant St., Buffalo, New York [ANC] [S2] [SW1]

Lerch, Leo Joseph, Sgt., Athletic Det., Parris Island, South Carolina, DDS, October 10, 1918 at Parris Island, South Carolina. John Lerch (Father), 11639 Princeton Ave., Chicago, Illinois [S3]

Lesher, Denver Arnold, Pvt., 76th Co., 6th Regt., DOW, August 20, 1918 in the Aisne Marne. Alice Lasher (Mother), Leitchfield, Kentucky [ABMC- Suresnes] [S2] [SW]

Lessard, John Francis, Pvt., 39th Co., Peking, China, DDS, June 7, 1921 at Peking, China. Mrs. Bridget Fullerton (Grandmother), 3955 Nakomis St., Minneapolis, Minnesota [S4]

Leverson, Bennie Lawrence, Pvt., 77th Co., 6th MG Bn., DOW, October 5, 1918 in the Meuse Argonne. Knute Levarsen (Father), Box 54, Lightfoot, Virginia [S2] [SW1]

Lewis, Albert May, Pvt., 51st Co., 5th Regt., KIA, October 4, 1918 in the Meuse Argonne. Katie Lewis (Mother), Crothersville, Indiana [R] [S2] [SW1]

Lewis, Clayton, Pvt., Co. A, Mare Island, California, DDS, September 9, 1917 at Mare Island, California. W. A. Starey (Cousin), Gen. Del., Walsenburg, Colorado [S3]

Lewis, Edward D., Pvt., 1st Casual Det., Philadelphia, Pennsylvania, DOS, March 15, 1919 at League Island, Philadelphia, Pennsylvania. Mrs. Elizabeth Lewis (Mother), 125 Gertrude St., Syracuse, New York [S4]

Lewis, Guy Melvin, Pvt., Co. M, 13th Regt., DOD, September 29, 1918 in France. Martha C. Lewis (Mother), Golden, Missouri [FAG as Guy Meloin Lewis] [S2]

Lewis, Herbert, Pvt., Co. C, 5th Br.M.G. Bn, DOD, December, 19, 1918 in France. Clifton R. Lewis (Father), RFD#2, Higbee, Missouri [FAG] [S2]

Marine Corps Deaths, 1917-1921

Lewis, Joseph, Pvt., NADD, Mare Island, California, DAS, May 24, 1918 at Mare Island, California. Francis Lewis (Brother), Gen. Del., Namaimo, British Columbia, Canada [S3]

Lewis, Wheatley Dale, Pvt., 55th Co., 5th Regt., KIA, November 4, 1918 in the Meuse Argonne. Alfred Lewis (Father), Chinoateagne Island, Virginia [R] [S2] [SW1] [X]

Lewis, William Theodore, Pvt., 20th Co., 5th Regt., KIA, June 7, 1918 in the Chateau-Thierry Sector. Ernest A. Lewis (Father), Long Prairie, Minnesota [S2] [SW]

Lewter, Perley Giles, Pvt., 8th Co., 5th Regt., DOW, October 9, 1918 in the Meuse Argonne. Eva L. Lewter (Mother), 3315 Stockton St., Richmond, Virginia [S2] [SW1]

Leyden, Leo Thomas, Pvt., 17th Co., 5th Regt., KIA, June 15, 1918 in the Chateau-Thierry Sector. Nellie Leyden (Mother), 240 W. 4th Ave., Denver, Colorado [FAG] [S2] [SW]

Liberty, Frank Alexander, Sgt., 74th Co., 6th Regt., DOD, October 22, 1918 in the Meuse Argonne. Mary Liberty (Mother), 105 4th St., North, Tomahawk, Wisconsin [S2]

Liebrecht, Louis, QM Sgt., Hdqtrs., Washington, D.C., DOS, November 5, 1919 at Washington, D.C. Mrs. Ida H. Hofmeister (Sister), 1405 Temple Place, St. Louis, Missouri [ANC] [S4]

Lietz, William, Pvt., 81st Co., 6th MG Bn., KIA, September 15, 1918 in the St. Mihiel Offensive. Adalea Lietz (Mother), 2028 S. 10th St., East Salt Lake City, Utah [ABMC-Thiaucourt] [S2] [SW] [SW1 says Leitz]

Light, Comer Edward, Cpl., 15th Co., 6th MG Bn., DOW, October 5, 1918 in the Meuse Argonne. Mr. W. R. Light (Father), Stackbridge, Georgia [S2] [SW1]

Ligon, Joe Whitefield, Pvt., 67th Co., 5th Regt., KIA, June 6, 1918 in the Chateau-Thierry Sector. Minty Ligon (Mother), Loving, Texas [FAG] [S2] [SW]

Marine Corps Deaths, 1917-1921

Lile, Roy E., Pvt., Central Records Division, DOW, February 13, 1919 at Great Lakes, Illinois of wounds received in action. Mrs. Anna Lile (Mother), Richmond Heights, St. Louis County, Missouri [S4]

Lilly, Clarence Edwin, Sgt., 47th Co., 5th Regt., KIA, June 25, 1918 in the Chateau-Thierry Sector. Ella V. Lilly (Mother), 1535 Baldwin St., Baltimore, Maryland [ABMC- Belleau] [S2] [SW1]

Limbert, Raymond Winston, Pvt., 67th Co., 5th Regt., KIA, June 6, 1918 in the Chateau-Thierry Sector. George W. Limbert (Father), Route #12, N. Tanawanda, New York [ABMC- Belleau] [S2] [SW]

Lindblad, Edward James, Pvt., 79th Co., 6th Regt., KIA, September 15, 1918 in the St. Mihiel Offensive. Anna Lindblad (Mother), RFD#2, Box 184, Bellingham, Washington [S2] [SW1]

Lindblom, George Leslie, Cpl., 111th Co., 8th Regt., Galveston, Texas, DDS, December 17, 1918 at Galveston, Texas. Mrs. Sarah Lindblom (Mother), Route H, Box 252, Fresno, California [FAG] [S4]

Lindemann, Alvin H., QM Sgt., Hdqtrs., A&I, USMC, Washington, D.C., DDS, January 25, 1919 at Washington, D.C. Mrs. Minnie Lindemann (Mother), 3216 Knapp St., St. Louis, Missouri [FAG] [S4]

Linder, Earl Stanley, Pvt., 49th Co., 5th Regt., DOW, June 14, 1918 in the Chateau-Thierry Sector. John Linder (Father), Dundas, Illinois [ABMC- Belleau TOM] [S2] [SW1]

Linder, Emerson Shannon, Pvt., 74th Co., 6th Regt., KIA, July 19, 1918 in the Aisne Marne. John Linder (Father), Waynesville, Ohio [ANC] [S2] [SW1]

Lindley, David Edgar, Pvt., Bat. C, MB, Parris Island, South Carolina, DDS, June 5, 1920 at Parris Island, South Carolina. William P. Lindley (Father), Wellington, Texas [FAG] [S4]

Marine Corps Deaths, 1917-1921

Lindsey, Clinton Steven, Pvt., 82nd Co., 6th Regt., KIA, June 8, 1918 in the Chateau-Thierry Sector. Felix W. Lindsey (Father), San Marcos, Texas [FAG as Clinton Stephen Lindsey] [S2] [SW]

Lindsey, Raymond F., Sgt., 55th Co., 5th Regt., DDS, February 3, 1919 at New York, New York. Mrs. Alice Lindsey (Mother), 5137 Globe Ave., Norwood, Ohio [S4]

Lindsey, William Floyd, Cpl., 78th Co., 6th Regt., DOW, October 4, 1918 in the Meuse Argonne. Lydia Lindsey (Mother), 1410 Baymiller St., Cincinnati, Ohio [ABMC- Belleau] [S2] [SW]

Lindstrom, Verner, Pvt., 76th Co., 6th Regt., KIA, July 19, 1918 in the Aisne Marne. Emma Lindstrom (Mother), Lemant, Illinois [FAG] [S2] [SW]

Line, William Erskin, Cpl., Co. C, OTC, Quantico, Virginia, DDS, October 11, 1918 at Quantico, Virginia. Mary J. Line (Mother), RR#1, Talbott, Tennessee [FAG] [S3]

Link, Roy, Pvt., 90th Co., 7th Regt., Cuba, DDS, November 7, 1918 at Camp La Union, San Louis, Oriente, Cuba. Andrew Link (Father), 103 Church St., Nanticoke, Pennsyvania [FAG] [S3]

Linnell, Harold Thomas, Pvt., 79th Co., 6th Regt., KIA, June 6, 1918 in the Chateau-Thierry Sector. Susie S. Linnell (Mother), 2545 Harriet Ave., South, East Minneapolis, Minnesota [S2] [SW1]

Linnemann, Leo Peter, Pvt., 76th Co., 6th Regt., DOW, June 16, 1918 in the Chateau-Thierry Sector. Mrs. Minnie Linneann Bley (Sister), 1072 Wilstach St., Cincinnati, Ohio [FAG] [S2] [SW]

Linthicum, Benjamin James, Trumpeter, 76th Co., 6th Regt., DOD, April 23, 1919 in France. Benjamin J. Linthicum (Father), Church Creek, Maryland [FAG] [S2]

Linton, Willie, Pvt., 51st Co., 5th Regt., KIA, October 4, 1918 in the Meuse Argonne. Viola Hillegas (Mother), 6702

Marine Corps Deaths, 1917-1921

Converse Ave., Los Angeles, California [R] [S2] [SW1 says Willey]

Lipinski, Stephen S., Pvt., 153rd Co., 2nd Regt., Haiti, DDS, June 12, 1920 at Haiti. Mary Lipinski (Mother), 20 Clinton Ave., Maspeth, Long Island, New York [S4]

Little, George Lee, Pvt., Co. H, 11th Regt., DOD, February 17, 1919 in France. Eliza J. Little (Mother), Route #6, Box 86, Birmingham, Alabama [FAG] [S2]

Little, Roy Walter, Pvt., 43rd Co., 5th Regt., DOW, November 11, 1918 in the Meuse Argonne. Mrs. Sarah Little (Mother), Corner Hancock and Marene Ave., Colorado Springs, Colorado [FAG] [S2] [SW1]

Livezey, Donald Litzenberger, Pvt., 4th Co., Quantico, Virginia, DDS, September 30, 1918 at Quantico, Virginia. Flavilla L. Hiatt (Mother), 1634 N. "C" St., Elwood, Indiana [S3]

Lloyd, Edgar B., Pvt., MCR, 1st Aviation Squadron, Lake Charles, Louisiana, DAS January 17, 1918 at Lake Charles, Louisana. Florence P. Millispaugh (Mother), Haddenfield, New Jersey [S3]

Lloyd, James Thomas, Jr., Pvt., 75th Co., 6th Regt., KIA, July 19, 1918 in the Aisne Marne. James T. Lloyd (Father), 213 N. Hudson St., Greenville, South Carolina [S2] [SW1 says DOW]

Lloyd, Robert Edmund, Sgt., 20th Co., 5th Regt., DOW, June 7, 1918 in the Chateau-Thierry Sector. Mrs. Henry Sippel (Mother), RR#4, Box 23, Chippewa Falls, Wisconsin [FAG] [S2] [SW]

Loch, Oliver Harold, Pfc., Supply Det., Mare Island, California, DDS, February 15, 1920 at Mare Island, California. Oliver M. Loch (Father), 2237 West Jefferson St., Phoenix, Arizona [S4]

Lock, Henry Lawrence, Pvt., Bks. Det., Philadelphia, Pennsylvania, DAS, May 29, 1919 at Philadelphia,

Marine Corps Deaths, 1917-1921

Pennsylvania. Mrs. Anna Lock (Mother), 671 Meldrum Ave., Detroit, Michigan [S4]

Locke, Karl Wilson, Cpl., 51st Co., 5th Regt., KIA, June 3, 1918 in the Aisne Defensive. Elizabeth Locke (Mother), 353 E. Erie St., Painsville, Ohio [ABMC- Belleau] [S2] [SW]

Lockhart, Dan Alexander, Pvt., 55th Co., 5th Regt., KIA, June 3, 1918 in the Aisne Defensive. Nettie Lockhart (Mother), Wallsburg, Utah [ABMC- Belleau TOM] [S2] [SW]

Lockhart, George William, Pvt., 43rd Co., 5th Regt., KIA, June 11, 1918 in the Chateau-Thierry Sector. Nettie Lockhart (Mother), Wallsburg, Utah [ABMC- Belleau TOM] [S2] [SW]

Lockhart, Tona Lambert, Cpl., 82nd Co., 6th Regt., DOW, July 21, 1918 in the Aisne Marne. John W. Lockhart (Father), Windy, West Virginia [FAG as Tony Lambert Lockhart] [S2] [SW says 141st Co., Repl. Btln.]

Lockwood, Harry Muir, Pvt., 20th Co., 5th Regt., KIA, June 23, 1918 in the Chateau-Thierry Sector. Henry C. Lockwood (Father), Box 90, Puento, California [ABMC- Belleau] [S2] [SW1]

Lodowski, Joseph, Pvt., 55th Co., 5th Regt., KIA, November 1, 1918 in the Meuse Argonne. Simon Lodowski (Father), 503 Walden Ave., Buffalo, New York [S2] [SW1]

Loftus, Michael, Cpl., 465469, 67th Co., 5th Regt., KIA, June 14, 1918 in the Chateau-Thierry Sector. Patrick Loftus (Brother), 1372 West 65th St., Cleveland, Ohio [ANC] [S2] [SW]

Logston, Alvin Wesley, Pvt., Hdqtrs. Co., 5th Regt., DOW, October 20, 1918 in France. Rose Logston (Mother), Benwood Junction, Benwood, West Virginia [R] [S2]

Logue, Frank C., 2nd Lieut., 13th Regt., DOD, September 19, 1918 aboard the USS *Von Steuben*. J. Washington Logue (Father), 1313 Stephen Girard Bldg., Philadelphia, Pennsylvania [R] [S1]

Marine Corps Deaths, 1917-1921

Lohmer, Michael Albert, Pvt., Bks. Det., Norfolk, Virginia, DDS, March 11, 1918 at Norfolk, Virginia. John Lehmer (Father), 629 18th Ave., Altonna, Pennsylvania [FAG] [S3]

Lohr, Wilbur Milon, Pvt., 8th Co., 5th Regt., KIA, October 4, 1918 in the Meuse Argonne. James J. Lohr (Father), 229 Alexander St., Greensburg, Pennsylvania [ANC] [S2] [SW1]

Loiselle, Archie Joseph, Pfc, Bks. Det., Philadelphia, Pennsylvania, DDS, October 13, 1918 at Philadelphia, Pennsylvania. Exilda Loiselle (Mother), 7 Park St., Fitchburg, Massachusetts [S3]

Lomax, Fred Erymn, Pvt., 80th Co., 6th Regt., KIA, June 3, 1918 in the Aisne Defensive. Sally Lomax (Mother), RR#4, Hahenwald, Tennessee [FAG] [S2] [SW]

Long, Albert Willard, Pvt., 49th Co., 5th Regt., DOW, November 17, 1918 in the Meuse Argonne. Luisinana Long (Mother), 562 West Grove St., Ontario, California [ABMC- Romagne] [S2] [SW1]

Long, Alvin Eugene, Pvt., Hdqtrs. Co., 5th Regt., KIA, June 16, 1918 in the Chateau-Thierry Sector. William T. Lang (Father), Hickory Corners, Pennsylvania [FAG] [S2] [SW]

Long, Cordie C., Cpl., Hdqtrs., 4th Prov. Regt., Santo Domingo, Dominican Republic, DDS, January 5, 1919 at Santo Domingo, Dominican Republic. Latimer H. Long (Father), 349 Brichwood St., Louisville, Kentucky [S4]

Long, Ellis William, Pvt., 79th Co., 6th Regt., DOW, September 15, 1918 in the St. Mihiel Offensive. Andrew F. Long (Father), West Point, Illinois [S2] [SW1]

Long, Fred, Pvt., MCR, Co. R, Parris Island, South Carolina, DOS, April 14, 1918 at Dayton, Ohio. Loretta C. Long (Wife), RR#12, Dayton, Ohio [VA-Dayton] [S3]

Marine Corps Deaths, 1917-1921

Long, Lothar R., 1st Lieutenant, Bayonville, France, DOS, September 4, 1920 at Bayonville, France. J. H. Long (Mother), Maple Court Apts., Evanston, Illinois [S4]

Long, Ora, Pvt., 67th Co., 5th Regt., DOW, November 13, 1918 in the Meuse Argonne. Pearl I. Long (Wife), 1422 Gardner Ave., Spokane, Washington [S2] [SW1]

Long, Ray, Pvt., 97th Co., 6th Regt., DOW, October 9, 1918 in the Meuse Argonne. Mrs. Mary Long (Mother), 4546 Park Ave., Chicago, Illinois [S2] [SW]

Looger, Charles David, Cpl., Hdqtrs. Co., 5th Regt., KIA, June 13, 1918 in the Chateau-Thierry Sector. Henry Looger (Father), RFD#3, Glasford, Illinois [FAG] [S2] [SW]

Lookingland, Walter Scott, Pvt., 127th Co., Cuba, DDS, October 24, 1918 at Guantoanomo Bay, Cuba. Betie Muratroyd (Sister), 521 E. 27th St., Baltimore, Maryland [S3]

Loomis, Glenn Shotwell, Pvt., 17th Co., 5th Regt., KIA, June 7, 1918 in the Chateau-Thierry Sector. Charles R. Loomis (Father), 21 Lincoln Ave., Batavia, New York [S2] [SW]

Loper, David William, Pvt., Co. A, 13th Regt., DOD, September 26, 1918 in France. Mrs. Bula Loper (Wife), 2633 Granada St., Los Angeles, California [R] [S2]

Loranger, Ray, Pvt., MD, Fort Lyon, Colorado, DDS, January 11, 1919 at Fort Lyon, Colorado. Henry Loranger (Father), Gen. Del., Havre, Montana [S4]

Losey, Fred Russell, Cpl., Hdqtrs. Co., 10th Sept. Batt., Quantico, Virginia, DDS, October 4, 1918 at Quantico, Virginia. James H. Losey (Father), 1603 Sharp Ave., Ridgedale, Tennessee [S3]

Lott, Wade Barrington, Pvt., Supply Co., Parris Island, South Carolina, DDS, November 8, 1918 at Parris Island, South Carolina. Luther B. Lott (Father), 125 Furlow St., Americus, Georgia [FAG] [S3]

Love, John Dudley, Sgt., 79th Co., 6th Regt., DOW, October 6, 1918 in the Meuse Argonne. Henry D. Love (Father), 297

Marine Corps Deaths, 1917-1921

Mass Ave., Lexington, Massachusetts [ABMC-Romagne] [S2] [SW1]

Lovejoy, Joseph Clinton, Pvt., 10th Sept. Bn, Quantico, Virginia, DDS, November 8, 1918 at Quantico, Virginia. Rena Luca (Mother), Lee Center, New York [S3]

Lowe, John William, Jr., Pvt., 84th Co., 6th Regt., DOD, February 14, 1919 in France. John W. Lowe (Father), 830 N 38th St., Philadelphia, Pennsylvania [R] [S2]

Lowery, Austin Rogers, Cpl., 82nd Co., 6th Regt., DOW, July 19, 1918 in the Aisne Marne. Joseph S. Lowery (Father), 177 S. E. Blvd., Corona, California [ANC] [S2] [SW1 says KIA]

Lowery, William Wade, Pvt., 82nd Co., 6th Regt., KIA, June 8, 1918 in the Chateau-Thierry Sector. Mrs. Alice J. Lowrey (Mother), 1197 Andrews Ave., Lakewood, Ohio [R] [S2] [SW]

Lubers, Harry Lauritz, Jr., Pvt., 18th Co., 5th Regt., DOD, October 16, 1918 in France. Harry L. Lubers (Mother), 4250 Grave St., Denver, Colorado [FAG] [S2] [SW1 says DOW]

Lucas, Deloss, Pvt., 80th Co., 6th Regt., Quantico, Virginia, DDS, December 11, 1917 at Quantico, Virginia. Flora Lucas (Mother), RD#1, Karns City, Pennsylvania [S3]

Lucas, Walter Earl, Cpl., 82nd Co., 6th Regt., KIA, June 6, 1918 in the Chateau-Thierry Sector. Mary Lucas (Mother), Box 1233, Shadyside, Ohio [S2] [SW]

Luce, George Winfield, Pvt., 49th Co., 5th Regt., KIA, June 6, 1918 in the Chateau-Thierry Sector. Dora J. French (Mother), Charlton, Massachusetts [ABMC- Belleau TOM] [S2] [SW]

Lueken, Benjamin Jacob, Pvt., 74th Co., 6th Regt., DOW, April 21, 1918 in the Toulon Sector, Verdun. Bernard C. Lueken (Father), 1545 Mulberry St., Evansville, Indiana [R] [S2] [SW]

Marine Corps Deaths, 1917-1921

Luhman, Hiram George, Pvt., 23rd Co., 6th MG Bn., KIA, June 19, 1918 in the Chateau-Thierry Sector. Mrs. Matamara Lohman (Mother), Oakfield, New York [FAG] [S2] [SW]

Lukins, Fred Theodore, Sgt., 20th Co., 5th Regt., KIA, June 6, 1918 in the Chateau-Thierry Sector. Margaret Lukins (Mother), 274 Holmes Ave., Indianapolis, Indiana [ABMC- Belleau] [S2] [SW]

Lumaree, Leroy Whitmore, Pvt., 45th Co., 5th Regt., KIA, June 26, 1918 in the Chateau-Thierry Sector. Luda L. Lumaree (Mother), 104 W. Sinclair Ave., Wabash, Indiana [ABMC- Belleau] [S2] [SW1]

Lumley, John Robert, Pvt., 82nd Co., 6th Regt., KIA, June 8, 1918 in the Chateau-Thierry Sector. Elizabeth Lumley (Mother), 24 Johnson Park, Utica, New York [ABMC- Belleau TOM] [S2] [SW1]

Lund, Carl W., Pvt., 115th Co., 2nd Brigade, Dominican Republic, DDS, December 30, 1918 at Santo Domingo, Domincan Republic. John P. Lund (Father), Route #2, Ashby, Minnesota [S4]

Lusader, Maurice S., Pvt., 51st Co., 5th Regt., KIA, November 10, 1918 in the Meuse Argonne. Homer H. Lusander (Father), Covington, Indiana [ABMC- Romagne] [S2] [SW1]

Lyman, Grant Herbert, Pvt., 78th Co., 6th Regt., DOW, June 17, 1918 in the Chateau-Thierry Sector. Mrs. Susan D. Lyman (Mother), 111 E. St., Fillmore, Utah [ABMC- Belleau] [S2] [SW]

Lynch, Frank James, Pvt., 47th Co., 5th Regt., KIA, June 6, 1918 in the Chateau-Thierry Sector. Mrs. May Lynch Breeding (Mother), 645 North Main St., Napa, California [S2] [SW]

Lynch, James John, Pvt., 32nd Co., 4th Regt., Sanchez, Domincan Republic, DDS, September 14, 1921 at Sanchez, Dominican Republic. Elizabeth Lynch (Mother), 369 E. 148th St., New York, New York [S4]

Marine Corps Deaths, 1917-1921

Lynch, James Joseph, Cpl., American Legion, Peking, China, DDS, May 15, 1921 at Peking, China. John H. Lynch (Brother), Watertown, South Dakota [FAG] [S4]

Lynch, John Joseph, Pvt., 95th Co., 6th Regt., DOD, June 30, 1918 in France. Mrs. Mary Toshey (Sister), 212 Stewart St., Easton, Pennsylvania [R] [S2]

Lynch, Tom Mitchell, Pvt., Co. G, 11th Regt., Quantico, Virginia, DDS, October 7, 1918 at Quantico, Virginia. Mrs. Charlie L. Lynch (Wife), P O Box 819, Dallas, Texas [S3]

Lynch, William Joseph, Pvt., 82nd Co., 6th Regt., KIA, October 7, 1918 in the Meuse Argonne. William C. Lynch (Father), 16 Davis Road, Waverly, Massachusetts [S2] [SW1]

Lyon, Harry Thomas, Cpl., 49th Co., 5th Regt., KIA, June 6, 1918 in the Chateau-Thierry Sector. Mrs. J. F. Lyon (Mother), Malvern, Arkansas [ABMC- Belleau] [S2] [SW]

Lyon, Marlin Horatio, Pvt., Co. B, Parris Island, South Carolina, DDS, December 24, 1917 at Parris Island, South Carolina. Walter S. Lyon (Father), 512 Bear St., Syracuse, New York [FAG] [S3]

Lyon, Russell Gillson, Pvt., 51st Co., 5th Regt., DOW, November 11, 1918 in the Meuse Argonne. Jane A. Lyon (Mother), 41 N. 6th St., Newark, New Jeresey [ABMC- Romagne] [S2] [SW1]

Lyons, John William, Pvt., Co. H, 11th Regt., Quantico, Virginia, DDS, September 29, 1918 at Quantico, Virginia. Elizabeth Lyons (Mother), Sparta, Illinois [FAG] [S3]

Maas, Otto Carl Herman, Pvt., USS *Pittsburgh*, DDS, October 30, 1918 on board the USS *Pittsburgh*. William Maas (Father), RR#1, Cedarburg, Wisconsin [FAG] [S3]

Mabbott, Douglas C., Pvt., 79th Co., 6th Regt., KIA, September 15, 1918 in the St. Mihiel Offensive. Mrs. Orra R. Mabbott (Mother), Unity, Wisconsin [ANC] [S2] [SW says 138th Repl. Btln.]

Marine Corps Deaths, 1917-1921

Mabee, Arthur Emerson, Pvt., 96th Co., 6th Regt., KIA, June 6, 1918 in the Chateau-Thierry Sector. Launa Mabee (Mother), Gen. Del. Deer Creek, Illinois [FAG] [S2] [SW1]

Mabry, Lawrence G., Pvt., 74th Co., 6th Regt., KIA, September 15, 1918 in the St. Mihiel Offensive. Robert A. Mabry (Father), RFD#25, Roswell, Georgia [ABMC-Thiaucourt] [S2] [SW]

Mabry, Raymond M., Sgt., 76th Co., 6th Regt., KIA, July 19, 1918 in the Aisne Marne. Loella Mabry (Mother), 204 South 9th St., Poplar Bluff, Missouri [S2] [SW]

MacCauley, John Leo, Cpl., 18th Co., 5th Regt., KIA, October 4, 1918 in the Meuse Argonne. Mrs. Annie W. Lowe (Mother), 543 N. San Pedro St., San Jose, California [R] [S2] [SW1]

MacConnell, Charles Franklin, Cpl., 20th Co., 5th Regt., KIA, June 6, 1918 in the Chateau-Thierry Sector. Benjamin S. MacConnell (Father), 702 W. 3rd St., Crown Hotel, Los Angeles, California [ABMC-Belleau as MacConnell] [S2] [SW1]

MacDiarmid, Orvis Ring, Pvt., Bks. Det., Mare Island, California, DDS, October 20, 1918 at 316 South 6th St., Richmond, California. June F. MacDiarmid (Wife), 316 South 6th St., Richmond, California [S3]

MacDonald, Hugh Alexander, Sgt., 97th Co., 6th Regt., DOW, July 19, 1918 in the Aisne Marne. Mrs. J. MacDonald (Mother), Pond and Randolph Ave., Randolph, Massachusetts [ABMC- Fere as Mac Donald] [S2] [SW1]

MacDonald, Lloyd Proctor, Pvt., Co. L, 11th Regt., DOD, January 31, 1919 in France. Frances C. MacDonald (Wife), 582 35th St., Oakland, California [ABMC- Fere as Mac Donald] [S2]

MacGregor, Lewis Archibald, Pvt., 47th Co., 5th Regt., DOW, June 27, 1918 in the Chateau-Thierry Sector. Catharine

Marine Corps Deaths, 1917-1921

MacGregor (Mother), 1335 E. 9th St., Des Moines, Iowa [ABMC- Belleau as Mac Gregor] [S2] [SW]

MacHatton, Joseph Park, Pvt., 18th Co., 5th Regt., DOW, October 5, 1918 in the Meuse Argonne. Rev. B. R. MacHatten (Father), Plymouth Congregational Church, Des Moines, Iowa [S2] [SW1]

Macikowski, John, Gy. Sgt., 84th Co., 6th Regt., DOW, July 19, 1918 in the Aisne Marne. Jacob Macikowski (Father), 179 Coit St., Buffalo, New York [S2] [SW1]

Mack, Donald Lesley, Gy. Sgt., Flight G, 4th Air Squadron, Haiti, DAS, February 17 1921 in an airplane crash at Mirebalais, Haiti. Rebecca Mack (Wife), 1620 13th Ave., Seattle, Washington [S4]

Mack, William H., 2nd Lieut., 20th Co., 5th Regt., KIA, July 19, 1918 in the Aisne Marne. Miss Kitty McNally (sister), 173 Cabot St., Holyoke, Massachusetts [ABMC-Belleau] [S1] [SW]

MacKenzie, Robert Bruce, Cpl., 33th Co., 15th Regt., Domincan Republic, DAS, September 20, 1919 drowned at Santo Domingo, Dominican Republic. Angus McDonald (Cousin), 1310 Oakes Ave., Superior, Wisconsin [ANC] [S4]

Mackler, Isadore Irving, Pvt., 20th Co., 5th Regt., KIA, September 15, 1918 in the St. Mihiel Offensive. Mrs. Sophia Mackler (Mother), 1745 St. Johns Pl., Brooklyn, New York [FAG] [S2] [SW says B Co., 2nd Casualty Btln.]

MacLachlin, Harold Douglas, Major, "C" Co., 13th Regt., DOD, September 27, 1918 in France. Mrs. Dorothy C. MacLachlin (widow), 69 Sin An, P. O. Hutung, Peking, China [ABMC-Fere as Mac Lachlin] [S1]

MacLeod, Charles Raymond, Cpl., MB, Norfolk, Virginia, DDS, April 20, 1918 at Portsmouth, Virginia. Alexander J. MacLeod (Father), Tyler, Pennsylvania [FAG] [S3]

Marine Corps Deaths, 1917-1921

MacLiesch, George A., 2nd Lieutenant, MCR, Marine Detachment, Camaguey, Cuba, DOS, September 21, 1919 at Camaguey, Cuba. Mr. Archibald F. MacLiesch (Stepfather), 116 Lincoln Place, Brooklyn, New York [S4]

MacMillan, Frederick J., Pvt., USNH, Fort Lyon, Colorado, DDS, April 2, 1920 at Las Aimas, Colorado. No next of kin. given. [VA-Fort Lyon] [S4]

MacNeil, Samuel P., 2nd Lieutenant, MB, Quantico, Virginia, DAS, August 18, 1920 in an aeroplane accident at Quantico, Virginia. Samuel M. MacNeil (Father), 243 D Milwaukee Ave., Waueatosa, Wisconsin [S4]

MacSparran, William Thomas, Sgt., 18th Co., 5th Regt., DOD, October 31, 1918 in France. George MacSparran (Brother), 610 W. Johnson St., Germantown, Philadelphia, Pennsylvania [ABMC- Romagne as Mac Sparran] [S2]

Madden, Robert J., Pvt., Hdqtrs., 1st Regt., Philadelphia, Pennsylvania, DDS, July 21, 1919 at Philadelphia, Pennsylvania. Mrs. Charlotte Madden (Mother), 873 North 9th St., Columbus, Ohio [S4]

Madden, Sidney Arthur, Pvt., MD, USS *South Dakota*, DDS, March 4, 1920 at Vladivostok, Russia. Mrs. Lillie Madden (Mother), Bungalow "B", South East Lake Ave., Los Angeles, California [S4]

Mader, Robert, Pvt., 67th Co., 5th Regt., KIA, October 2, 1918 in the Meuse Argonne. George Mader (Father), Tannersville, Pennsylvania [ABMC- Romagne TOM] [S2] [SW says C Co., Overseas Dep.]

Madsen, Carl John George, Pvt., Co. B, OSD, Quantico, Virginia, DDS, October 5, 1918 at Quantico, Virginia. John George Madsen (Father), 7734 Broadway, Cleveland, Ohio [S3]

Madsen, Edmund Terner, 1st Sgt., 47th Co., 5th Regt., KIA, June 6, 1918 in the Chateau-Thierry Sector. Mrs. Johnanne M.

Marine Corps Deaths, 1917-1921

Terner (Mother), No. 25, H.P. Orumsgade, Copenhagen, Denmark [ANC] [S2] [SW]

Magee, Homer Benton, Pvt., 80th Co., 6th Regt., DOW, July 19, 1918 in the Aisne Marne. Willis Magee (Father), Franklinton, Louisana [FAG] [S2] [SW1 says KIA] [SW1 also listed as DOW]

Magill, Gerald Perham, Sgt., 49th Co., 5th Regt., KIA, November 3, 1918 in the Meuse Argonne. Anna Magill (Mother), 221 Greene Ave., Brooklyn, New York [ABMC-Romagne] [S2] [SW1]

Magill, Louis John, Colonel, Navy Yard, Philadelphia, Pennsylvania, DDS, February 20, 1921 at Philadelphia, Pennsylvania. Florence M. Magill (Wife), 315 S. 21st St.,. Philadelphia, Pennsylvania [FAG] [S4]

Maher, Joseph F., 2nd Lieut., 55th Co., 5th Regt., KIA, October 4, 1918 in the Meuse Argonne. James W. Maher (Father), 463 West 159th St., New York, New York [R] [S1] [SW]

Maher, Joseph Francis, Sgt., 95th Co., 6th Regt., September 16, 1918 in the St. Mihiel Offensive. Mrs. William Maher (Mother), 1819 W. Fourth St., Chester, Pennsylvania [S2] [SW]

Maher, William Francis, Pvt., 98th Co., DDS, September 26, 1918 at Newport, Rhode Island. Anna Maher (Mother), 2712 Banfield St., Chicago, Illinois [S3]

Mahoney, Michael Joseph, Pvt., 96th Co., 6th Regt., DOW, October 12, 1918 in the Meuse Argonne. Patrick J. Mahoney (Father), 95 Taft Ave., New Brighton, New York [R] [S2] [SW1]

Mahrer, William John, Pvt., 45th Co., 5th Regt., KIA, July 20, 1918 in the Aisne Marne. William J. Mahrer (Father), 3426 G St., Philadelphia, Pennsylvania [ABMC- Belleau] [S2] [SW says 138th Co., Repl. Btln.]

Marine Corps Deaths, 1917-1921

Main, Cecil Melvin, Pvt., USS *Alert*, DDS, January 21, 1921 at San Pedro, California. J. W. Main (Father), Booneville, California [FAG] [S4]

Major, Dora Earl, Pvt., Co. A, 4th Replacement Batt., DOD, October 10, 1918 in France. Walter D. Major (Father), 510 E. Church St., Sparta, Illinois [FAG] [S2]

Major, Harlan E., Capt., 15th Co., 6th MGBn, KIA, June 15, 1918 in the Chateau Thierry sector. Mrs. Catherine J. Major (Mother), Crescent, Ohio [ANC] [S1] [SW]

Malecki, John Edward, Pvt., 76th Co., 6th Regt., KIA, July 19, 1918 in the Aisne Marne. Jenie Malecki (Mother), 409 Arthur Ave., Milwaukee, Wisconsin [ABMC- Belleau] [S2] [SW]

Mallion, John Alexander, Pvt., 47th Co., 5th Regt., DOW, September 15, 1918 in the St. Mihiel Offensive. Mrs. Elizabet Mallion (Mother), 53 Lockwood Ave., Buffalo, New York [FAG] [S2] [SW1]

Malone, Hugh, Pvt., 186th Co., Quantico, Virginia, DDS, January 15, 1919 at Quantico, Virginia. Mrs. Orlena Wallace Malone (Wife), Beaufort, South Carolina [VA-Beaufort] [S4]

Maloney, Joseph Christopher, Pvt., 45th Co., 5th Regt., KIA, October 5, 1918 in the Meuse Argonne. Ella Maloney (Mother), 411 N. Perrine St., Jackson, Michigan [FAG] [S2] [SW1]

Mangin, Howard, Pvt., 20th Co., 5th Regt., KIA, June 13, 1918 in the Chateau-Thierry Sector. Mrs. Mary Sanford (Mother), 52 Main St., Bradford, Pennsylvania [ANC] [S2] [SW]

Manning, Hiram George, Pvt., Co. M, 11th Regt., Quantico, Virginia, DDS, October 10, 1918 at Quantico, Virginia. George Stattler (Uncle), Armour, South Dakota [FAG] [S3]

Marine Corps Deaths, 1917-1921

Manning, James Beverly, Pvt., Hdqtrs. Co., 6th Regt., DOW, April 27, 1918 in the Toulon Sector, Verdun. W. B. Manning (Father), Huntsville, Alabama [R] [S2] [SW]

Manning, Stephen Arnold, Pvt., 45th Co., 5th Regt., DOW, October 4, 1918 in the Meuse Argonne. Felicia M. Manning (Mother), 287 Williams Ave., Portland, Oregon [FAG] [S2] [SW1]

Mannis, Jesse Rufus, Pvt., 76th Co., 6th Regt., KIA, July 19, 1918 in the Aisne Marne. William A. Mannis (Father), 801 Stockrel St., Nashville, Tennessee [ABMC- Belleau TOM] [S2] [SW]

Mansfield, Gabe, Pvt., 15th Co., 6th MG Bn., DOW, June 3, 1918 in the Aisne Defensive. Elizabeth Mansfield (Mother), RFD#2, Poplar Bluff, Missouri [R2 [S2] [SW] [SW1]

Manwaring, Harold, Pvt., 8th Co., 5th Regt., DOW, October 16, 1918 in the Meuse Argonne. Mrs. E. S. Steiner (Mother), 947 Dresden Ave., Salt Lake City, Utah [R] [S2] [SW]

March, Lester William, Pvt., 78th Co., 6th Regt., DOW, June 8, 1918 in the Chateau-Thierry Sector. Clara March (Mother), Milliken, Colorado [ABMC- Belleau] [S2] [SW]

Marco, James Joseph, Sgt., 55th Co., 5th Regt., DOW, October 6, 1918 in the Meuse Argonne. Alexander Marco (Brother), Haskell, New Jersey [ABMC- Romagne] [S2] [SW]

Marcum, Henley Franklin, Cpl., 45th Co., 5th Regt., DOW, October 4, 1918 in the Meuse Argonne. Mrs. Mary Marcum (Mother), Rose Hill, Virginia [R] [S2] [SW1]

Marcus, Carl Earnest, Pvt., Supply Co., 6th Regt., KIA, June 14, 1918 in the Chateau-Thierry Sector. James A. Marcus (Half-Brother), 5456 Washington St., Denver, Colorado [S2] [SW]

Marcus, Joseph, Pvt., 76th Co., 6th Regt., DOW, July 20, 1918 in the Aisne Marne. Rose Marcus (Mother), 315 Chadwick Ave., Newark, New Jersey [R] [S2] [SW]

Marine Corps Deaths, 1917-1921

Markham, Burt Austin, Pvt., 80th Co., 6th Regt., DOW, September 16, 1918 in the St. Mihiel Offensive. Nellie L. Markham (Mother), Janesville, Minnesota [ABMC- Thiaucourt] [S2] [SW1]

Markley, George W., Sgt., 47th Co., 5th Regt., KIA, October 4, 1918 in the Meuse Argonne. W. B. Markley (Father), RFD #3, Silcam Springs, Arkansas [R] [S2] [SW1]

Marks, Jerome, Pvt., 75th Co., 6th Regt., DOW, October 14, 1918 in the Meuse Argonne. Michel Marks (Father), 1415 Race St., Philadelphia, Pennsylvania [R] [S2] [SW1 says KIA]

Markus, Edward Henry, 1st Sgt., Hdqtrs. Det., Haiti, DOS, July 6, 1921 at Port au Prince, Haiti. Clara Hayes (Sister), 2317 15th St., Chicago, Illinois [S4]

Markusic, Fred, Pvt., 55th Co., 5th Regt., DOW, June 12, 1918 in the Chateau-Thierry Sector. Frank Markusic (Brother), 737 Cassius Ave., Youngstown, Ohio [S2] [SW1]

Marlette, Claude Horace, Pvt., 95th Co., 6th Regt., DOW, June 19, 1918 in the Aisne Defensive. Blanche Hull (Mother), Memphis, Tennessee [FAG as July 6, 1918] [S2] [SW]

Marquardt, Clarence William, Pvt., 83rd Co., 6th Regt., DOW, November 1, 1918 in the Meuse Argonne. Fred Marquardt (Father), 814 Jefferson St., Martins Ferry, Ohio [FAG] [S2] [SW1]

Marsh, Clinton, Pvt., 66th Co., 5th Regt., DOW, November 15, 1918 in the Meuse Argonne. Emma Marsh (Mother), Holt, Missouri [FAG] [S2] [SW1]

Marsh, Douglas Gerald, Pvt., 74th Co., 6th Regt., KIA, June 10, 1918 in the Chateau-Thierry Sector. May D. Marsh (Mother), 340 S. 5th St., W. Missoula, Montana [FAG] [S2] [SW] [SW1]

Marshall, Albert Richard, Pvt., 17th Co., 5th Regt., KIA, June 14, 1918 in the Chateau-Thierry Sector. Catherine Horst (Aunt), 1943 State Ave., Cincinnati, Ohio [FAG] [S2] [SW]

Marine Corps Deaths, 1917-1921

Marshall, James Ashley, Pvt., 80th Co., 6th Regt., DOW, October 25, 1918 in the Meuse Argonne. Mrs. M. J. Marshall (Mother), Sevierville, Tennessee [FAG] [S2] [SW1]

Marston, James R., Pvt., Hdqtrs., A&I, Washington, D.C., DDS, February 6, 1919 at Washington, D.C. Mrs. Alice Marston (Mother), 5900 Woodbine Ave., Overbrook, Pennsylvania [S4]

Marter, Timothy Earl, Pvt., 51st Co., 5th Regt., DOD, June 15, 1919 in France. Mrs. Lenora Caton (Sister), 1369 E. 90th St., Cleveland, Ohio [R] [S2]

Martin, Augburn Dean, Pvt., 55th Co., 5th Regt., KIA, June 12, 1918 in the Chateau-Thierry Sector. Fannie Martin (Mother), East Bend, North Carolina [FAG] [S2] [SW]

Martin, Charles Andrew, Pvt., 79th Co., 6th Regt., DOW, June 8, 1918 in the Chateau-Thierry Sector. James E. Martin (Father), East Davis St., Sullivan, Indiana [FAG] [S2] [SW]

Martin, Everett E., Cpl., MD, USNH, Fort Lyon, Colorado, DDS, June 18, 1919 at Vancouver, Washington. George Louden (Stepfather), RFD#45, Vancouver, Washington [S4]

Martin, Grier Caldwell, Pvt., Hdqtrs. Co., 6th Regt., KIA, October 4, 1918 in the Meuse Argonne. Susie Martin (Mother), Lake Providence, Louisana [R] [S2] [SW1]

Martin, Howard Randall, Pvt., BD, MB, Norfolk, Virginia, DDS, May 13, 1917 at Norfolk, Virginia. William L. Martin (Father), 360 W. 123rd St., New York, New York [S3]

Martin, John R., Captain, DAS December 14, 1917 at Port au Prince, Haiti. Mrs. Mary Raveel (Mother), 147 Nodd St., Charleston, South Carolina [FAG] [S3]

Martin, Louis Nicholas, Pvt., Co. F, Parris Island, South Carolina, DDS, June 9, 1918 at Parris Island, South Carolina. Julia Martin (Mother), 2325 N. Tripp Ave., Chicago, Illinois [S3]

Martin, Paul, Pvt., DDS, Osgood, Indiana [S5]

Marine Corps Deaths, 1917-1921

Martin, Ray William, Pvt., 23rd Co., 6th MG Bn., KIA, October 4, 1918 in the Meuse Argonne. Helen Martin (Sister), Gen. Del., Sheffield, Illinois [R] [S2] [SW1]

Martin, Roland Wordsworth, Pvt., Supply Co., 13th Regt., DOD, October 15, 1918 in France. Tobias B. Martin (Father), RFD, Ijamsville, Maryland [ABMC- Fere] [S2]

Martin, Walker Whitford, Pvt., 97th Co., 6th Regt., KIA, June 7, 1918 in the Chateau-Thierry Sector. George M. Martin (Father), Centenary, South Carolina [FAG] [S2] [SW]

Martin, William Edgar, Pvt., MD, USS *Huntington*, DDU, October 26, 1918 aboard the USS *Huntington*. Pearl Brown (Sister), RFD#2, Dickson, Tennessee [S3]

Martino, Joseph Franklin, Pvt., USNH, Chelsea, Massachusetts, DDS, February 1, 1921 at Chelsea, Massachusetts. Geatino Martino (Father), 24 Sheaf St., Boston, Massachusetts [S4]

Martinson, Charles H., Pvt., Co. A, 11th Regt., DOD, January 29, 1919 in France. William Martinson (Father), 222 East Ohio St., Neodesha, Kansas [FAG] [S2]

Marx, Henry Joseph, Pvt., 49th Co., 5th Regt., KIA, November 4, 1918 in the Meuse Argonne. Miss Christina Marx (Sister), Granville, Iowa [R] [S2] [SW1]

Mason, Max Merril, Cpl., Hdqtrs. Det., MB, Parris Island, South Carolina, DDS, November 5, 1918 at Parris Island, South Carolina. Nellie Mason (Mother), Mt. Morris, Michigan [FAG] [S3]

Mass, August, Pvt., Patient on USS *Solace*, DDU, January 17, 1918 aboard the USS *Solace*. William Mass (Father), Wappingers Falls, New York [FAG] [S3]

Mastin, Roland Godrey, Sgt., 95th Co., 6th Regt., KIA, November 1, 1918 in the Meuse Argonne. Alice C. Mastin (Mother), Statebury, Missouri [FAG] [S2] [SW1]

Marine Corps Deaths, 1917-1921

Mathis, Minlo, Pvt., 79th Co., 6th Regt., DOW, September 15, 1918 in the St. Mihiel Offensive. Florence Mathis (Wife), Clinton, Maryland [ABMC- Thiaucourt] [S2] [SW1]

Matthews, Elburt P., Sgt., BD, MB, San Diego, California, DDS, November 27, 1918 at San Diego, California. Mrs. Mary Matthews (Mother), 927 North Broadway, Decatur, Illinois [FAG] [S4]

Matthews, Norbert Timothy, Cpl., 8th Co., 5th Regt., KIA, October 4, 1918 in the Meuse Argonne. Paul F. Matthews (Brother), 516 McCandless Ave., Pittsburgh, Pennsylvania [R] [S2] [SW]

Mattimore, Earl William, Pvt., 80th Co., 6th Regt., DOW, June 29, 1918 in the Chateau-Thierry Sector. Patrick Mattimore (Father), 3652 Park Blvd., San Diego, California [ABMC- Belleau] [S2] [SW]

Mattingly, James McKinly, Pvt., Co. C, 10th Sep. Batt., Quantico, Virginia, DDS, November 7, 1918 at Quantico, Virginia. Robert L. Matingly (Father), May King, Kentucky [S3]

Mattingly, Randel Augustus, Pvt., 20th Co., 5th Regt., KIA, June 6, 1918 in the Chateau-Thierry Sector. Mrs. Georgia Gray (Sister), West Plains, Howell Co., Missouri [ABMC- Belleau] [S2] [SW says 134th Co., Repl. Btln.]

Mattox, James John, Pvt., Depot of Supplies, Philadelphia, Pennsylvania, DDS, October 1, 1918 at Philadelphia, Pennsylvania [FAG] [S3]

Mattson, James, Sgt., 96th Co., 6th Regt., DOA, August 17, 1918 in France. Elias Mattson (Father), Wintrop, Minnesota [ABMC- Suresnes] [S2] [SW1 says KIA] [SW1 also says KOA]

Mattz, Herman, Pvt., 49th Co., 5th Regt., KIA, June 6, 1918 in the Chateau-Thierry Sector. Charles Mattz (Father), 28 Grape St., Buffalo, New York [ABMC- Belleau TOM] [S2] [SW]

Marine Corps Deaths, 1917-1921

Mauk, Joseph W., Pvt., Co. D, 11th Sep. Bn., Quantico, Virginia, DDS, November 18, 1918 at Quantico, Virginia. Harry W. Mauk (Father), Gen. Del., Rochester Mills, Pennsylvania [S4]

Maulhardt, Alfred H., Pvt., Co. A, Mare Island, California, DDS, March 10, 1920 at Mare Island, California. Mr. Heinrich Maulhardt (Father), Oxnard, California [FAG] [S4]

Maull, Louis F., Sgt., Co. C, Navy Yard Guard, Philadelphia, Pennsylvania, DDS, February 13, 1920 at League Island, Pennsylvania. Edward T. Maull (Father), 5816 Willows St., West Philadelphia, Pennsylvania [S4]

Mautz, Henry Charles, Pvt., Co. C, 13th Regt., DOD, September 25, 1918 enroute to France. Gladys M. Mautz (Wife) 2642 Sepviva St., Philadelphia, Pennsylvania [FAG] [S2]

Maxwell, Howard Stonwall, Pvt., 67th Co., 5th Regt., KIA, June 6, 1918 in the Chateau-Thierry Sector. Bonnie Maxwell (Mother), Troy, Tennessee [FAG] [S2] [SW]

Maxwell, Norman Paul, Pvt., Co. B, 15th Sep. Batt., DOO, September 10, 1919 in France. Minnie Maxwell (Mother), 617 E. Wabash Ave., Crawfordsville, Indiana [FAG] [S2]

May, Charles Hammett, Pvt., 76th Co., 6th Regt., DOW, July 19, 1918 in the Aisne Marne. Susie May (Mother), 420 South Grand Ave., Sedalia, Missouri [ANC] [S2] [SW1]

May, Walter Adolph, Pvt., 74th Co., 6th Regt., KIA, June 11, 1918 in the Chateau-Thierry Sector. Bertha May (Mother), 1221 Lafayette Ave., St. Louis, Missouri [ABMC-Belleau] [S2] [SW says 137th Repl. Btln.]

Mayer, Gordon Charles, Pvt., 8th Co., 5th Regt., KIA, October 3, 1918 in the Meuse Argonne. Sophia Mayer (Mother), 123 Evergreen St., Rochester, New York [ABMC- Romagne] [S2] [SW]

Mayer, John L., Major, 57th Co., 1st Prov. Brigade, Haiti, DAS, KIA, April 4, 1919 in action with bandits at Haiti. Mrs.

Marine Corps Deaths, 1917-1921

Julia I. Mayer (Sister), c/o Grier Hersh, York, Pennsylvania [S4]

Maynard, Charles B., 1st Lieut., 84th Co., 6th Regt., DOW, June 7, 1918 in the Chateau Thierry sector. Charles Maynard (Father), Colten, Washington [FAG] [S1] [SW]

Maynor, John Adile, Pvt., Hdqtrs. Det., Parris Island, South Carolina, DOS, May 30, 1921 at Parris Island, South Carolina. Martha Maynor (Mother), Water Valley, Mississippi [S4]

Mazereeuw, Richard, Pvt., 79th Co., 6th Regt., DOW, July 19, 1918 in the Aisne Marne. Nellie Mazereeuw (Sister), 35 Caroline Place, Grand Rapids, Michigan [S2] [SW]

McAdam(s), Ralph Mott, Pvt., Co. I, 13th Regt., DOD, September 24, 1918 enroute to France. James McAdam (Father), c/o Miss B. McAdam, 340 W. 85th St., New York, New York [R] [S2]

McAdams, Gerals Edward, Pvt., Bks. Det., Quantico, Virginia, DDS, September 22, 1918 at Quantico, Virginia. Margaret McAdams (Mother), Penn Yan, New York [S3]

McAlpin, Douglas I., Pvt., Co. D, Mare Island, California, DDS, December 10, 1918 at Mare Island, California. Mrs. Alice McAplin (Mother), Creston, California [S4]

McAmis, John Joseph, Sgt., 76th Co., 6th Regt., DOW, July 12, 1918 in the Chateau-Thierry Sector. David W. McAmis (Father), 1911 Howell St., Covington, Kentucky [R] [S2] [SW]

McAneny, Orley, Pvt., Hdqtrs. Co., 6th Regt., DOW, October 7, 1918 in the Meuse Argonne. Winifred McAneny (Mother), 400 18th Ave., Milwaukee, Wisconsin [ABMC-Romagne] [S2] [SW says B Co., 2nd Casualty Btln.]

McArthur, Roland Fred, Pvt., Sup Co., 6th Regt., DOD, January 19, 1918 in France. Irene J. McArthur (Mother), Carthage, North Carolina [R] [S2]

Marine Corps Deaths, 1917-1921

McBeth, Padgett Alexander, Pvt., 83rd Co., 6th Regt., DOW, September 13, 1918 in the St. Mihiel Offensive. Mrs. Mary McBeth (Mother), Harper, Texas [FAG] [S2] [SW says C Co., 3rd Sep. Btln.]

McBride, Arthur, Pvt., 49th Co., 5th Regt., KIA, June 6, 1918 in the Chateau-Thierry Sector. Mrs. Carrie Miller (Mother), 301 West Miami St., Paela, Kansas [FAG] [S2] [SW]

McBride, James Thomas, Pvt., 54th Co., 2nd Regt., Haiti, DDS, September 4, 1918 at Haiti. John McBride (Father), 2206 Christian St., Philadelphia, Pennsylvania [FAG] [S3]

McCabe, John Christopher, Sgt., 66th Co., 5th Regt., KIA, October 4, 1918 in the Meuse Argonne. Miss Kittie Kennedy (Friend), 213 E. 40th St., New York, New York [VA-Cypress Hills] [S2] [SW1 says McGabe]

McCahey, John H., 2nd Lt., Quantico, Virginia, DAS, July 16, 1917 at Quantico, Virginia. Mrs. Mary B. McCahey (Mother), 1801 So. Broad St., Philadelphia, Pennsylvania [S3]

McCartan, Leonard J., Sgt., Radio Det., Parris Island, South Carolina, DDS, December 9, 1918 at Parris Island, South Carolina. John J. McCartan (Father), 619 West Weber St., DuBois, Pennsylvania [S4]

McCarthy, James, Pvt., 51st Co., 5th Regt., KIA, October 4, 1918 in the Meuse Argonne. Patrick McCarthy (Father), 173 Campbell Ave., W. New Brighton, Long Island, New York [R] [S2] [SW1]

McCarthy, John Frank, QM Sgt., Bks. Det., Mare Island, California, DAS, June 14, 1917 of a skull fracture at Oakland, California. Ella McCarthy (Mother), Gen. Del., Richmond, Indiana [S3]

McCarthy, John Joseph, Pvt., Bks. Det., Norfolk, Virginia, DDS, March 15, 1918 at Norfolk, Virginia. Owen McCarthy (Father), 1650 5th Ave., Troy, New York [S3]

Marine Corps Deaths, 1917-1921

McCarty, Sylvus Bassett, Cpl., 76th Co., 6th Regt., KIA, November 1, 1918 in the Meuse Argonne. May McCarty (Mother), Lisle, Missouri [S2] [SW1]

McClain, David W., 2nd Lieut., MCR, 66th Co., 5th Regt., DOW, October 5, 1918 in the Meuse Argonne. W.J. McClain (Father), McCune, Kansas [S1] [SW]

McClanahan, Medford Oran, Pvt., 80th Co., 6th Regt., KIA, June 8, 1918 in the Chateau-Thierry Sector. Raymond McClanahan (Brother), RFD#4, Fredericktown, Missouri [ANC] [S2] [SW1]

McClellan, John M., 2nd Lieut., Hdqrs. Co., 5th Regt., KIA, July 18, 1918 in the Aisne Marne. A. L. McClellan (Father), Hampton Gardens, Richmond, Virginia [S1] [SW]

McClure, Charles Percy, Pvt., Co. C, 13th Regt., DOD, September 22, 1918 enroute to France. Etta C. McClure (Mother), Fayette, Mississippi [FAG] [S2]

McClure, William Henry, Cpl., Supply Co., Parris Island, South Carolina, DDS, November 9, 1918 at Parris Island, South Carolina. Mrs. W. H. McClure (Mother), RFD#1, Waynesville, North Carolina [S3]

McColm, Floyd L., Pvt., Co. H, Mare Island, California, DDS, November 14, 1918 at Mare Island, California. Lyman T. McColm (Father), RFD#4, Boise, Idaho [S4]

McColm, William J., Sgt., 51st Co., 5th Regt., KIA, June 6, 1918 in the Chateau-Thierry Sector. Mrs. Lottie D. Tanner (Sister), Lynch, Nebraska [ABMC- Belleau] [S2] [SW]

McConnell, John Edmund, Pvt., 8th Co., 5th Regt., DOD, September 17, 1918 in the St. Mihiel Offensive. Robert W. McConnell (Father), Galata, Toole County, Montana [VA-ANC as September 27, 1918] [S2] [SW says DOW]

McConnell, John Kendall, Pvt., Co. A, Parris Island, South Carolina, DDS, November 5, 1918 at Parris Island, South Carolina. William H. Fowler (Uncle), 285 Van Dyke Ave., Detroit, Michigan [FAG] [S3]

Marine Corps Deaths, 1917-1921

McConnell, John Lawry, Pvt., Co. Y, Parris Island, South Carolina, DDS, November 3, 1918 at Parris Island, South Carolina Lucy McConnell (Mother), RFD#3, Elizabeth, Pennsylvania [S3]

McCook, Martin Joseph, Pvt., 55th Co., 5th Regt., KIA, June 12, 1918 in the Chateau-Thierry Sector. Bridget Conlin (Mother), 280 Nassau Ave., Brooklyn, New York [ABMC- Belleau] [S2] [SW]

McCormack, Leo Glen, Pvt., 78th Co., 6th Regt., DOW, June 21, 1918 in the Chateau-Thierry Sector. Dr. J. L. McCormack (Father), Bone Gap, Illinois [R] [S2] [SW says Replacement]

McCormick, Charles Treadwell, Jr., Pvt., 80th Co., 6th Regt., KIA, July 19, 1918 in the Aisne Marne. Charles F. A. McCormick (Father), 88 Harama, Havana, Cuba [ABMC- Fere as C.T.A.] [S2] [SW]

McCormick, Frank P., Pvt., Bks. Det., Philadelphia, Pennsylvania, DDS, March 10, 1919 at Philadelphia, Pennsylvania. Edward Aide (Uncle), Mineral Point, Wisconsin [S4]

McCormick, Irwin Nile, Pvt., 40th Co., MB, NS, Guam, DAS, December 26, 1917 drowned at Asan, Guam. James N. McCormick (Father), Box 27, Route A, Modesto, California [FAG] [S3]

McCormick, James Albert, Pvt., 43rd Co., 5th Regt., DOW, June 14, 1918 in the Chateau-Thierry Sector. Jenie N. Haddock (Mother), RFD #5, Box 23, Panxsutawney, Pennsylvania [ABMC- Belleau] [S2] [SW1]

McCormick, James Jay, Gy. Sgt., 73rd Co., 6th Regt., KIA, July 19, 1918 in the Aisne Marne. Henry J. McCormick (Brother), St. Marks, Cheltenham, England [ABMC-Fere] [S2] [SW]

McCormick, Oliver R., Pvt., Nav. Ammo. Depot, Dover, New Jersey, DAS, December 18, 1919 by the explosion of a shell at Dover, New Jersey. Mrs. Irene McCormick (Wife), 33 Glenrock Circle, Malden, Massachusetts [S4]

McCormick, Peat, Pvt., MB, Annapolis, Maryland, DDS, October 8, 1918 at Annapolis, Maryland. George W. McCormick (Father), Box 245, Portageville, Missouri [S3]

McCoy, James, Capt., Hdqrs. Co., 5th Regt., KIA, June 4, 1918 in the Aisne defensive. Miss Mabel Davol (niece), 135 Buffington St., Fall River, Massachusetts [R] [S1] [SW]

McCrea, Joseph Henry, Pvt., MB, Navy Yard, Washington, D.C., DDS, November 3, 1917 at Washington, D.C. Robert McCrea (Brother), Depot St., Daltonm Massachusetts [S3]

McCreary, Donald Kennedy, Pvt., 96th Co., 6th Regt., DOW, July 19, 1918 in the Aisne Marne. Charles McCreary (Father), 167 Linden Ave., E. Aurora, New York [ABMC- Fere] [S2] [SW1]

McCreary, Harry C., Pvt., 66th Co., 5th Regt., KIA, November 2, 1918 in the Meuse Argonne. Della L. McCreary (Mother), Ringwood, Oklahoma [S2] [SW1]

McCune, George Dewey, Pvt., 82nd Co., 6th Regt., KIA, October 3, 1918 in the Meuse Argonne. Mary C. McCune (Mother), 1808 Jersey St., Alton, Illinois [S2] [SW]

McCune, Leroy W., Pfc, MB, Navy Yard, Philadelphia, Pennsylvania, DDS, February 17, 1919 at League Island, Pennsylvania. Chauncey W. McCune (Father), Olivet, Kansas [FAG] [S4]

McCurry, Lewis Melton, Pvt., 51st Co., 5th Regt., DOW, June 25, 1918 in the Chateau-Thierry Sector. Mrs. Viola A. McCurry (Mother), Gen. Del., Wheatland, California [R] [S2] [SW says 134th Co., 2nd Repl. Btln.]

McDaniel, Dee Herschell, Pvt., 16th Co., 5th Regt., KIA, November 6, 1918 in the Meuse Argonne. Joel T. McDaniel (Father), Adamsville, Tennessee [VA-Shiloh] [S2] [SW1]

Marine Corps Deaths, 1917-1921

McDermott, Edward John, Pvt., 45th Co., 5th Regt., DOO, August 10, 1918 in France. Anna McDermott (Mother), 2325 W. 9th St., Duluth, Minnesota [ABMC- Thiaucourt] [S2]

McDermott, Joseph James, Pvt., 55th Co., 5th Regt., KIA, October 4, 1918 in the Meuse Argonne. Helen McDermott (Sister), 6202 Greenwood Ave., Chicago, Illinois [R] [S2] [SW1]

McDonald, Cecil Floyd, Pvt., 74th Co., 6th Regt., DOW, September 13, 1918 in the St. Mihiel Offensive. Mrs. James McDonald (Mother), R#2, Box 70, Eddyvillle, Kentucky [FAG] [S2] [SW says Replacement]

McDonald, George Stuart, Cpl., 47th Co., 5th Regt., DOW, September 15, 1918 in the St. Mihiel Offensive. Mrs. Helen McDonald (Mother), 316 N. 6th St., Brainerd, Minnesota [FAG] [S2] [SW says Co. C, Repl. Btln.]

McDonald, Henry Olin, Pvt., Bks. Det., New York, New York, DDS, November 11, 1918 at New York, New York. Daniel P. McDonald (Father), Elk City, Oklahoma [FAG] [S3]

McDonald, John Boone, Pvt., 75th Co., 6th Regt., KIA, June 11, 1918 in the Chateau-Thierry Sector. Mrs. Mary McDonald (Mother), Mortonsville, Kentucky [ABMC-Belleau] [S2] [SW]

McDonald, Thomas Peter, Pvt., 81st Co., 6th MG Bn., KIA, October 3, 1918 in the Meuse Argonne. Edward McDonald (Father), 1249 Third Ave., Cedar Rapids, Iowa [ABMC- Romagne TOM] [S2] [SW says Repl. Btln.]

McDonough, Michael Henry, Sgt., Bks. Det., Quantico, Virginia, DDS, February 2, 1918 at Quantico, Virginia. Michael J. McDonough (Father), 823 5th St., Boston, Massachusetts [S3]

McDowell, Edward Brown, 1st Sgt., 147th Co., Camp Edward C. Fuller, Paoli, Pennsylvania, DDS, October 17, 1918 at Westchester, Pennsylvania. Catherine McDowell

Marine Corps Deaths, 1917-1921

(Mother), 830 North Ave., Braddock, Pennsylvania [FAG] [S3]

McDowell, Irvin Bryan, Sgt., 66th Co., 5th Regt., DOW, November 6, 1918 in the Meuse Argonne. Louis McDowell (Brother), 2923 Bank St., Louisville, Kentucky [ABMC- Romagne] [S2] [SW1]

McElfresh, Edward Lincoln, Pvt., Co., A, 10th Sept. Batt., Quantico, Virginia, DDS, November 10, 1918 at Quantico, Virginia. Sallie Baltz (Mother), 247 Pike St., Cincinnati, Ohio [FAG] [S3]

McElroy, George Comstock, Pvt., 66th Co., 5th Regt., KIA, June 6, 1918 in the Chateau-Thierry Sector. Cathryn McElroy Garrison (Mother), Box 463, Monroe, New York [ABMC- Belleau] [S2] [SW]

McElwain, William E., Pvt., Bks. Det., Philadelphia, Pennsylvania, DDS, December 26, 1918 at Philadelphia, Pennsylvania. Mrs. Francis McElwain (Mother), Blue Mountain, Mississippi [FAG] [S4]

McEntee, Bernard Charles, Sgt., 47th Co., 5th Regt., DOW, June 6, 1918 in the Chateau-Thierry Sector. _____ (Brother), 1438 E. 17th St., Brooklyn, New York [S2] [SW1 says McEntree]

McEntree *see* McEntee

McFarland, Edward Vean, Pvt., MB, NS, Cavite, Philippine Islands, DDS, January 11, 1921 in the Philippine Islands. Ione I. McFarland (Wife), Gen. Del., Great Falls, Montana [S4]

McGabe *see* McCabe

McGartland, Clarence Francis, Pvt., 51st Co., 5th Regt., KIA, June 11, 1918 in the Chateau-Thierry Sector. Sarah J. McGartland (Mother), Monroe City, Missouri [S2] [SW]

McGee, Joe, Pvt., 51st Co., 5th Regt., DOW, June 11, 1918 in the Chateau-Thierry Sector. Ellen McGee (Mother), Slocomb, Arkansas [FAG] [S2] [SW1]

Marine Corps Deaths, 1917-1921

McGentry, Earl J., Pvt., Co. B, Mare Island, California, DDS, February 2, 1920 at Mare Island, California. Steven L. Duffy (Friend), Johnson, Minnesota [S4]

McGettrick, Arthur Clifton, Pvt., Bks. Det., Cavite, Philippine Islands, DDS, December 25, 1919 at Cancao, Cavite, Philippine Islands. Mrs. Olive Ranamel (Mother), Cooke, Montana [S4]

McGinnis, Charles Rosco, Sgt., 55th Co., 5th Regt., KIA, June 12, 1918 in the Chateau-Thierry Sector. Clammie McGinnis (Mother), RFD#4, Parkersburg, West Virginia [S2] [SW]

McGinnis, Charles Samuel, Pvt., Hdqtrs. Co., 5th Regt., KIA, June 13, 1918 in the Chateau-Thierry Sector. Hannah McGinnis (Mother), 227 Columbia Ave., Rochester, New York [ABMC- Belleau] [S2] [SW]

McGough, Robert Emmet, Pvt., Co. L, 13th Regt., DOD, September 25, 1918 enroute to France. John Henry McGough (Brother), 175 Thayer St., Providence, Rhode Island [FAG] [S2]

McGovern, Philip Michael, Pvt., 51st Co., 5th Regt., KIA, June 11, 1918 in the Chateau-Thierry Sector. Mary McGovern (Mother), Irvington-on-Hudson, New York [S2] [SW]

McGrath, James Raymond, Pvt., 79th Co., 6th Regt., KIA, July 19, 1918 in the Aisne Marne. Mary McGrath (Mother), New Richmond, Wisconsin [ANC] [S2] [SW1]

McGrath, John Joseph, Pvt., 96th Co., 6th Regt., DOW, June 17, 1918 in the Chateau-Thierry Sector. Mary McGrath (Mother), 101 Grove Ave., Dayton, Ohio [ABMC- Belleau] [S2] [SW]

McGrath, John Lawrence, Pvt., 79th Co., 6th Regt., DOW, July 19, 1918 in the Aisne Marne. John McGrath (Father), Barnesville, Minnesota [ABMC- Belleau TOM] [S2] [SW1]

McGrath, Joseph James, Pvt., 55th Co., 5th Regt., KIA, June 12, 1918 in the Chateau-Thierry Sector. Eliza McGrath

(Mother), 5 Dorrance St., Worcester, Massachusetts [ABMC- Belleau TOM] [S2] [SW1]

McGraw, Charles Joseph, Pvt., 49th Co., 5th Regt., DOW, December, 12, 1918 in the Meuse Argonne. Mr. Michael McGraw (Father), RFD#2, Harpersville, New York [R] [S2] [SW1]

McGuckin, James Arthur, Pvt., 49th Co., 5th Regt., KIA, October 4, 1918 in the Meuse Argonne. Mary McGuckin (Mother), 1047 Haddon Ave., Camden, New Jersey [FAG as James Anthony McGuckin] [S2] [SW1]

McGuffey, Willie Clarence, Pvt., 90th Co., Cuba, DAS, DAS May 21, 1919 drowned at Cuba. Ethel Greensberg (Sister), 3412 W. Madison St., Louisville, Kentucky [S4]

McHenry, John, Jr., 1st Lieut., 78th Co., 6th Regt., KIA, October 3, 1918 in the Meuse Argonne. John McHenry (Father), Mercantile Trust & Deposit Co., Baltimore, Maryland [FAG] [S1] [SW1]

McIlhenney, George Valentine, Cpl., 81st Co., 6th MG Bn., DOW, October 12, 1918 in the St. Mihiel Offensive. Margaret Gallagher (Aunt), 115 S. 43rd St., Philadelphia, Pennsylvania [ABMC- Thiaucourt as McIllhenney] [S2] [SW1]

McIlhenny, John Edmund, Pvt., 18th Co., 5th Regt., DOW, November 13, 1918 in the Meuse Argonne. Effie McIlhenny (Mother), 943 W. Franklin St., Baltimore, Maryland [ANC] [S2] [SW1]

McIntosh, Sidney, Pvt., 96th Co., 6th Regt., DOW, June 6, 1918 in the Chateau-Thierry Sector. Edith McIntosh (Mother), 206 5th Ave., Council Bluffs, Iowa [ABMC- Belleau] [S2] [SW1 says KIA]

McIntyre, Clifton Neil, Pvt., 66th Co., 5th Regt., KIA, October 4, 1918 in the Meuse Argonne. John McIntyre (Father), Indiana, Pennsylvania [R] [S2] [SW says 116th Co.]

Marine Corps Deaths, 1917-1921

McIntyre, Leslie P., Pvt., 10th Sep. Bn., Quantico, Virginia, DDS, November 15, 1918 at Quantico, Virginia. Mrs. Clara V. McIntyre (Mother), 406A Morris St., Charleston, West Virginia [FAG] [S4]

McIntyre, Oliver Curtis, Pvt., 79th Co., 6th Regt., DOW, October 2, 1918 in the Meuse Argonne. Elmer McIntyre (Brother), 1511 E. Canfield Ave., Detriot, Michigan [ABMC- Romagne TOM] [S2] [SW1 says KIA]

McKay, Leslie Boyd, Sgt., 18th Co., 5th Regt., KIA, June 10, 1918 in the Chateau-Thierry Sector. Lynn B. McKay (Father), 1628 West 45th St., Los Angeles, California [FAG] [S2] [SW1]

McKee, Harry Charles, Pvt., Bks. Det., New York, New York, DDS, October 25, 1918 at New York, New York. Cora Wagner (Mother), 1529 Andrew St., Fort Wayne, Indiana [S3]

McKeehan, Gay John, Pvt., 75th Co., 6th Regt., KIA, October 9, 1918 in the Meuse Argonne. John McKeehan (Father), New Haven, Missouri [ABMC- Romagne] [S2] [SW1 says DOW]

McKenna, James Joseph, Pvt., 51st Co., 5th Regt., KIA, June 7, 1918 in the Chateau-Thierry Sector. Mary O'Keefe (Mother), 965 Carroll St., Brooklyn, New York [ABMC- Belleau] [S2] [SW says 116th Co.]

McKenney, Robert William, Cpl., 95th Co., 6th Regt., DOW, July 26, 1918 in the Aisne Marne. Patrick McKenney (Father), 632 South Main St., Piqua, Ohio [FAG] [S2] [SW1]

McKenzie, James Henry, Pvt., 20th Co., 5th Regt., KIA, June 6, 1918 in the Chateau-Thierry Sector. Isabella McKenzie (Mother), 123 Bay 13th St., Bath Beach, Brooklyn, New York [S2] [SW]

McKenzie, James R., Pvt., Co. A, Mare Island, California, DDS, February 9, 1920 at Mare Island, California. William Alexander McKenzie (Father), Gen. Del., Buens, Oregon [S4]

Marine Corps Deaths, 1917-1921

McKeone, Joseph C., Gy. Sgt., MAD MFF, Miami, Florida, DAS, DAS November 13, 1918 at Miami, Florida. Eugene McKeone (Father), 831 Bryn Mawr Rd., Pittsburgh, Pennsylvania [S4]

McKinney, Grover C., Pvt., 127th Co., Cuba, DOS, DOS, February 26, 1919 at Santiago de Cuba. Mrs. Hazel Eileen McKinney (Wife), 117 East Erie St., Chicago, Illinois [S4]

McKinney, Lee Roy, Pvt., 95th Co., 6th Regt., DOD, September 15, 1918 in the Chateau-Thierry Sector. Rhoda McKinney (Mother), Tango, Washington [ANC] [S2] [SW]

McKinny, Harry William, Pvt., 17th Co., 5th Regt., KIA, July 18, 1918 in the Aisne Marne. Mrs. J. W. Irish (Mother), Pelican Rapids, Michigan [ABMC- Belleau] [S2] [SW1]

McKune, Herbert J., Cpl., 67th Co., 5th Regt., KIA, October 4, 1918 in the Meuse Argonne. Mary E. McKune (Mother), RR#4, Chelsea, Michigan [FAG] [S2] [SW1]

McLaughlin, Cornelius Joseph, Pvt., MD, NAD, St. Julien's Creek, Virginia, DDS, September 30, 1918 at Norfolk, Virginia. Adelia McLaughlin (Mother), RFD#3, Cuba, New York [FAG] [S3]

McLaughlin, William James, Cpl., 77th Co., 6th MG Bn., KIA, November 1, 1918 in the Meuse Argonne. William J. McLaughlin (Father), 512 Savoye St., West Hoboken, New Jersey [FAG] [S2] [SW1]

McLean, John, Pvt., 8th Co., 5th Regt., KIA, June 6, 1918 in the Chateau-Thierry Sector. Catherine McLean (Mother), 1209 E. State St., Boise, Idaho [S2] [SW]

McLemore, Albert Sydney, Colonel, Department of Pacific, Mare Island, DDS, July 13, 1921 at Mare Island, California. Mrs. Albert S. McLemore (Wife), 1859 Vallejo St., San Francisco, California [ANC] [S4]

McLeod, Frederick Dodd, Cpt, 45th Co., 5th Regt., KIA, June 16, 1918 in the Chateau-Thierry Sector. Donal McLeod

Marine Corps Deaths, 1917-1921

(Father), Schuyler, Nebraska [R] [S2] [SW says 134th Co., 2nd Repl. Btln.] [SW1]

McLernon, John, Pvt., 43rd Co., 5th Regt., DOW, July 19, 1918 in the Aisne Marne. Mary A. McLernen (Mother), 247 South Ellwood Ave., Balitimore, Maryland [VA-Loudon Park] [S2] [SW says Trumpeter and 34th Co., 5th Regt.]

McMahon, Ambrose Bernard., Sgt., 3rd Squadron, FMAF, DOD, October 28, 1918 in France. Mary R. McMahon (Wife) c/o Pittsburgh Lunch, 22 Monroe Ave., Detriot, Michigan [ABMC-Bony] [S2]

McMath, Earl Radle, Sgt., 75th Co., 6th Regt., KIA, October 14, 1918 in the Meuse Argonne. Minie McMath (Mother), RR#1, Hartsburg, Illinois [R] [S2] [SW1]

McMenamy, Charles, Pvt., 67th Co., 5th Regt., KIA, June 6, 1918 in the Chateau-Thierry Sector. Mrs. Sarah G. McMenamy (Mother), 8515 Frankfort Ave., Philadelphia, Pennsylvania [S2] [SW]

McMurray, Hayes Stewart, Pvt., USN Aero Station, San Diego, California, DDS, October 30, 1918 at San Diego, California. Wm. F. McMurray (Father), 420 W. 6th Ave., Spokane, Washington [S3]

McNally, Frank Thomas, Pvt., 83rd Co., 6th Regt., KIA, June 8, 1918 in the Chateau-Thierry Sector. Thomas McNally (Father), 7208 Dobson Ave., Chicago, Illinois [ANC] [S2] [SW]

McNelly, William James, Pvt., 8th Co., 5th Regt., DOW, June 16, 1918 in the Chateau-Thierry Sector. Mrs. Mary A. Tompkins (Mother), RFD#5, Mayville, Michigan [FAG] [S2] [SW]

McPhail, William Percival, Pvt. Co., 5th Regt., DOD, September 30, 1918 in France. William H. McPhail (Father), RFD#5, Box 245, Irendequoit, New York [R] [S2]

Marine Corps Deaths, 1917-1921

McQuiddy, James Erwin, Pvt., 67th Co., 5th Regt., KIA, June 6, 1918 in the Chateau-Thierry Sector. Harden McQuiddy (Mother), RR#7 Lewisburg, Tennessee [ANC] [S2] [SW]

McRoberts, Paul Stine, Pvt., 145th Co., 3rd Replacement Batt., DOD, May7, 1918 in France. Mrs. Elizabeth S. McRoberts (Mother), 18203 Canterbury Rd., Cleveland, Ohio [FAG] [S2]

McSwaim, William Jones, 1st Sgt., Bks. Det., San Diego, California, DDS, May 2, 1921 at San Diego, California. Raymond D. McSwaim (Son), 210 S. Broad St., Winston-Salem, North Carolina [S4]

McSweeney, Gerard Francis, Pvt., 49th Co., 5th Regt., KIA, November 11, 1918 in the Meuse Argonne. Mary McSweeney (Mother), 49 Beverly Road, Buffalo, New York [FAG] [S2] [SW1]

McTaggart, John Wallace, Pvt., 80th Co., 6th Regt., KIA, November 1, 1918 in the Meuse Argonne. James M. McTaggart (Father), 720 W. Marquette Road, Chicago, Illinois [S2] [SW1]

McVay, Ray Henry, Pvt., 79th Co., 6th Regt., DOW, September 16, 1918 in the St. Mihiel Offensive. Vern Thompson (Brother-in-law), Clearwater, Nebraska [R] [S2] [SW]

McWhirter, William Long, Pvt., 20th Co., 5th Regt., DOW, June 12, 1918 in the Chateau-Thierry Sector. Emma Harbin (Sister) RR#2, Glen Allen, Alabama [ABMC- Belleau TOM as W.L.] [S2] [SW1]

Mead, Archie Leroy, Pvt., 76th Co., 6th Regt., KIA, July 19, 1918 in the Aisne Marne. Virginia Mead (Mother), Gen. Del., Sunnyside, Washington [ABMC- Fere] [S2] [SW1 says DOW]

Mead, Leroy Smith, Pvt., 83rd Co., 6th Regt., KIA, June 6, 1918 in the Chateau-Thierry Sector. Thomas A. Mead (Father), RFD#1, Box 39, Mt. Kisco, New York [ABMC- Belleau] [S2] [SW] [SW1 says KOA]

Marine Corps Deaths, 1917-1921

Medley, Edwin Henry, Trumpter, 70th Co., 3rd Provincial Regt., Dominican Republic, KIA, September 11, 1918 near Guayabana, Dominican Republic. William F. Medley (Father), 14 Waterloo Ave., Detroit, Michigan [FAG] [S3]

Meece, James Wesley, Pvt., 8th Co., Newport, Rhode Island, DDS, September 11, 1918 at Newport, Rhode Island. Mrs. Laura Meece (Mother), Mendocino Co., California [S3]

Meehan, John Francis, Sgt., 76th Co., 6th Regt., DOD, April 23, 1919 in France. Mrs. Bridget A. Meehan (Mother), 3555 Southport Ave., Chicago, Illinois [R] [S2] [SW1 says DOW]

Meehan, Thomas G., Pvt., Co. I, Parris Island, South Carolina, DDS, November 22, 1918 at Parris Island, South Carolina. Mrs. Mary Meehan (Mother), 254 Jackson St., Brooklyn, New York [S4]

Meek, John J., Pvt., 1st Prov. Brigade, Haiti, DAS, May 3, 1920 at Hinche, Haiti. Joshua Albert Meek (Father), 2627 Cold Springs Ave., Milwaukee, Michigan [FAG] [S4]

Meeker, Cecil Jewitt, Pvt., Co. B, 7th Sep. Batt, DOD, November 16, 1918 in France. Mrs. Zetta Meeker (Mother), 8½ North Grant St., Chanute, Kansas [R] [S2]

Meighen, Thomas Virgil, Pvt., 49th Co., 5th Regt., DOW, October 19, 1918 in the Meuse Argonne. John F. D. Meighen (Brother), Albert Lee, Minnesota [ABMC- Suresnes] [S2] [SW1]

Meiman, Joseph Edward, Pvt., 82nd Co., 6th Regt., DOD, February 20, 1919 in France. Anthony Meiman (Father), 337 E. 17th St., Covington, Kentucky [FAG] [S2]

Melin, Earl, Pvt., 78th Co., 6th Regt., DOW, September 15, 1918 in the St. Mihiel Offensive. Augusta V. Melin (Mother), 166 N. Leamington Ave., Chicago, Illinois [S2] [SW1]

Marine Corps Deaths, 1917-1921

Melrose, Jack Milton, Cpl., 51st Co., 5th Regt., KIA, June 14, 1918 in the Chateau-Thierry Sector. Daniel H. Kleinman (Friend), Box 56, Mesa, Arizona [ABMC- Belleau] [S2] [SW says Repl. Btln.]

Memmen, Dean Ellsworth, Pvt., 76th Co., 6th Regt., DOW, October 4, 1918 in the Meuse Argonne. Flora Memmen (Mother), Gen. Del., Minonk, Illinois [ABMC- Romagne] [S2] [SW1]

Menefee, Frank C., Sgt., USS *Mississippi*, DOD, December 14, 1918 aboard the USS *Mississippi*. Mrs. Fanny Menefee (Mother), Dudie, Virginia [S4]

Menschel, Paul Hermon, Pvt., 17th Co., 5th Regt., DOW, July 18, 1918 in the Aisne Marne. Emil M. Menschel (Father), Hastings, Iowa [ABMC- Belleau TOM] [S2] [SW1]

Mercer, Gordon McClellan, Cpl., 83rd Co., 6th Regt., KIA, June 8, 1918 in the Chateau-Thierry Sector. Emma Mercer (Mother), Demopolis, Alabama [ABMC- Belleau] [S2] [SW]

Merkel, Charles F., Captain, Santo Domingo, Dominican Republic, DOS, October 2, 1918 at Santo Domingo, Dominican Republic. Miss Hilda Merkel (Sister), 154 N. 3rd St., Paterson, New Jersey [FAG] [S3]

Merkle, Joseph Henry, Pvt., USS *Texas*, DAS, May 8, 1917 killed by a Negro at Norfolk, Virginia. Susan Merkle (Mother), 2325 N. Spaulding Ave., Chicago, Illinois [S3]

Merrill, George Warren, Pvt., 45th Co., 5th Regt., KIA, October 6, 1918 in the Meuse Argonne. Mrs. Jennie Merrill (Wife), 218 W. 13th St., Cincinnati, Ohio [ABMC- Romagne] [S2] [SW says B Co., 2nd Casualty Btln.]

Merryman, George Swan, Sgt., 51st Co., 5th Regt., KIA, October 4, 1918 in the Meuse Argonne. Carlottie A. Merryman (Sister), 148 W. 105th St., New York, New York [FAG] [S2] [SW says Casualty Co.]

Marine Corps Deaths, 1917-1921

Mesplay, Victor Edwin, Pvt., 79th Co., 6th Regt., KIA, June 15, 1918 in the Chateau-Thierry Sector. Elizabeth Wolfe (Grandmother), 6104 Ridge Ave., St. Louis, Missouri [ABMC- Belleau] [S2] [SW]

Messenger, Stuart Francis, Pvt., NP, Navy Yard, Philadelphia, Pennsylvania, DDS, July 10, 1917 at Philadelphia, Pennsylvania. Winthrop Messenger (Father), 15 E. Foster St., Melrose, Massachusetts [S3]

Metcalfe, James Hartford, Pvt., 96th Co., 6th Regt., DOW, April 5, 1918 in the Toulon Sector, Verdun. Mrs. Eva Metcalfe (Mother), 501 E. Market St., Jeffersonville, Indiana [R] [S2] [SW]

Metz, Ivanhoe Kriebel, Cpl., 10th Squadron, Northern Bomb Group, FMAF, DOD, October 14, 1918 in France. Morris U. Metz (Father), 616 Broad St., Quakertown, Pennsylvania [R] [S2]

Metzger, John Virgil, Pvt., 96th Co., 6th Regt., KIA, September 15, 1918 in the St. Mihiel Offensive. Mrs. Addie Metzger (Mother), Georgetown, Ohio [S2]

Metzler, George W., Pvt., 113th Co., 3rd Prov. Regt., Dominican Republic, DDS, June 7, 1919 at Santo Domingo, Dominican Republic. Mrs. Vera Elliot Metzler (Wife), 630 Edwards St., Columbus, Ohio [S4]

Meuren, Joseph P., Pvt., MBks., Parris Island, South Carolina, DOS, September 30, 1919 at Savannah, Georgia. Mrs. Katherine Meuren (Mother), 2313 Vliet St., Milwaukee, Wisconsin [S4]

Meyer, Charles Henry, Sgt., 80th Co., 6th Regt., DOW, June 9, 1918 in the Chateau-Thierry Sector. Mrs. Mary E. Meyer (Mother), 4318 N. Sawyer Ave., Chicago, Illinois [R] [S2] [SW]

Michael, Guy G., Cpl., Hdqtrs., OTC, Quantico, Virginia, DDS, April 10, 1919 at Quantico, Virginia. Dr. Addison Michael (Father), Noblesville, Indiana [FAG] [S4]

Marine Corps Deaths, 1917-1921

Michalski, Frank Joseph, Pvt., 66th Co., 5th Regt., KIA, October 4, 1918 in the Meuse Argonne. Julia Michalski (Mother), 4034 N. Sacramento Blvd., Chicago, Illinois [ABMC- Romagne] [S2] [SW]

Michels, Adrian Joseph, Pvt., 47th Co., 5th Regt., KIA, June 6, 1918 in the Chateau-Thierry Sector. Elisie Michels (Mother), 639 Jackson St., Miwaukee, Wisconsin [ABMC- Belleau] [S2] [SW1]

Mielka, Fred Louis, Cpl., 8th Co., 5th Regt., KIA, October 4, 1918 in the Meuse Argonne. Emma Jonas (Sister), 257 Moselle St., Buffalo, New York [ABMC- Romagne] [S2] [SW1]

Miesch, Alfred George, Pvt., 83rd Co., 6th Regt., DOW, November 5, 1918 in the Meuse Argonne. Susan Miesch (Mother), 3427 Elm St., Indiana, Indiana [R] [S2] [SW1]

Mignacco, Attilio J., Pvt., 55th Co., 5th Regt., KIA, June 8, 1918 in the Aisne Defensive. Marco Mignacco (Father), 38 Laura St., San Francisco, California [ABMC- Belleau] [S2] [SW]

Miles, Ellis Merle, Pvt., 84th Co., 6th Regt., KIA, July 19, 1918 in the Aisne Marne. Lulu Cosgrove (Mother), 701 Fifth Ave., Spokane, Washington [ABMC- Fere] [S2] [SW]

Miles, Thomas H., Jr., 2nd Lieut., 45th Co., 5th Regt., KIA, June 6, 1918 in the Chateau Thierry sector. Mres. Thomas H. Miles, Jr. (widow), 224 Walnut Lane, Germantown, Pennsylvania [FAG] [S1] [SW]

Miles, William Evertt, Pvt., Supply Co., 13th Regt., DOD, September 26, 1918 in France. Mrs. Margaret Miles (Mother), 1112 St. Louis Ave., E. St. Louis, Illinois [VA- Jefferson Barracks] [S2]

Milewski, Joseph John, Pvt., 67th Co., 5th Regt., KIA, October 4, 1918 in the Meuse Argonne. Frank Milewski (Father), Box 661, Crivitz, Wisconsin [R] [S2] [SW1]

Mill, Frederick H., Cpl., Clerical Det., Parris Island, South Carolina, DDS, January 6, 1919 at Parris Island, South

Marine Corps Deaths, 1917-1921

Carolina. Mrs. Eva Mill (Mother), 501 Hamtracmck St., Mt. Vernon, Ohio [S4]

Miller, Adam John, Pvt., 8th Co., 5th Regt., DOW, June 12, 1918 in the Aisne Defensive. Anthony Shasargrgz (Uncle), 128 N. Lehigh Ave., Shenandoah, Pennsylvania [ABMC-Suresnes] [S2] [SW]

Miller, Archibald, Sgt., 51st Co., 5th Regt., DOD, November 8, 1918 in France. Mr. A. Miller (Father), 34 Durston Ave., Ossining, New York [S2]

Miller, Blair Charles, Pvt., 84th Co., 6th Regt., DOW, July 24, 1918 in the Aisne Marne. William H. Miller (Father), 320 S. Union St., Fostoria, Ohio [R] [S2] [SW1 says Clair Charles Miller]

Miller, Brainard William, Pvt., 75th Co., 6th Regt., DOW, October 12, 1918 in the Meuse Argonne. Ella Miller (Mother), RFD#1, Cropseyville, New York [ABMC- Romagne] [S2] [SW1]

Miller, Bryan Verrill, Pvt., 96th Co., 6th Regt., KIA, September 15, 1918 in the St. Mihiel Offensive. Ida Miller (Mother), Desoto, Illinois [FAGM] [ABMC-Thiaucourt] [S2] [SW says Supply Co.]

Miller, Charles Otto, Pvt., 80th Co., 6th Regt., KIA, November 4, 1918 in the Meuse Argonne. Arthur Bishop (Cousin), Route#1, Oronoque, Kansas [ABMC-Romagne] [S2] [SW1]

Miller, Dennis Oliver, Pvt., 43rd Co., 5th Regt., KIA, September 15, 1918 in the St. Mihiel Offensive. Andrew J. Miller (Father), RFD #2, Box 115, Cornellsville, Pennsylvania [ANC] [S2] [SW]

Miller, Ezra Joseph, Cpl., SS *Missanabie*, AEF, DOO, September 10, 1918. Jacob Miller (Father), Tamoroa, Illinois [ABMC- Suresnes TOM] [S2]

Marine Corps Deaths, 1917-1921

Miller, Harry, Sgt., 96th Co., 6th Regt., KIA, October 3, 1918 in the Meuse Argonne. Charles W. Miller (Father), 2 Madison Ave., Silver Creek, New York [S2] [SW1]

Miller, Hudson Irving, Cpl., Sup Co., 6th Regt., DOW, October 8, 1918 in the Meuse Argonne. Justine Miller (Mother), Lacour, Louisiana [FAG] [S2] [SW1]

Miller, Lawrence Blake, Pvt., 75th Co., 6th Regt., KIA, June 16, 1918 in the Chateau-Thierry Sector. Mary Miller (Mother), Box 621, Plaquemine, Louisana [ABMC- Belleau as Laurence] [S2] [SW]

Miller, Louis, Pvt., 181st Co., 15th Regt., Dominican Repbulic, DAS, April 8, 1921 drowned at San Pedro de Macoris, Dominican Republic. Solomon and Martha Miller (Parents), 663 Tinton Ave., Bronx, New York, New York [S4]

Miller, Louis Francis, Pvt., 17th Co., 5th Regt., DOW, July 18, 1918 in the Aisne Marne. Anna Miller (Mother), 855 Fairview Ave., St. Clair Heights, Michigan [ABMC- Belleau TOM] [S2] [SW1]

Miller, Mark M., Pvt., Co. B, 3rd Sep. MG BN, Quantico, Virginia, DDS, November 17, 1918 at Quantico, Virginia. James M. Miller (Father), Eyota, Minnesota [S4]

Miller, Milton Grahl, Pvt., 79th Co., 6th Regt., KIA, June 10, 1918 in the Chateau-Thierry Sector. Helen C. Miller (Mother), 1111 Yale Ave., St. Louis, Missouri [FAG as Milton Grabl Miller] [S2] [SW says 137th Repl. Btln.]

Miller, Nicholas William, Pvt., 144th Co., 3rd Replacement Batt., DOD, May 16, 1918 in France. Amelia Miller (Mother), 1524 Knox St., Cincnnati, Ohio [ABMC- Fere] [S2] [SW] [SW1]

Miller, Otto, Pvt., Naval Prison, Portsmouth, New Hampshire, DDS, February 14, 1917 at Portsmouth, New Hampshire. Mrs. Augusta Miller (Mother), 216 E. 42nd St., New York, New York [S3]

Marine Corps Deaths, 1917-1921

Miller, Paul Hillton, Pvt., Supply Det., Quantico, Virginia, DDS, January 13, 1921 at Quantico, Virginia. Mrs. Susie Miller (Mother), 138 W. Broadway Ave., Mishawaka, Indiana [S4]

Miller, Perry Nelson, Cpl., Supply Co., 4th Regt., Dominian Republic, DOW, October 5, 1921 of a wound inflicted by a Dominican inhabitant at Santo Domingo, Dominican Republic. Mrs. Mary May Miller (Mother), Brooklyn, Michigan [FAG] [S4]

Miller, Raymond Ervin, Pvt., Bks. Det., MB, Portsmouth, New Hampshire, DDS, September 24, 1918 at Chelsea, Massachusetts. Bonnie Miller (Sister), Olive Branch, Illinois [S3]

Miller, Robert Howard, Pvt., 51st Co., 5th Regt., DOW, October 7, 1918 in the Meuse Argonne. Rev. A. C. Miller (Father), 96 Pine St., Yankton, South Dakota [ABMC- Belleau] [S2] [SW says C Co., 5th Sep. Btln.]

Miller, Robert William, Gy. Sgt., 1st Prov. Brigade, Haiti, DAS, April 25, 1919 at Conaives, Haiti. Mr. Vernon Miller (Brother), Georgetown, Ohio [S4]

Miller, William C., Cpl., MBks., Parris Island, South Carolina, DDS, December 23, 1918 at Uitca, New York. Andrew Miller (Father), Hartford, West Virginia [FAG] [S4]

Millerberg, Willard Everett, Pvt., Hdqtrs. Det., 1st Regt., FDF, DDS, October 4, 1918 at Philadelphia, Pennsylvania. Otto F. Millerberg (Guardian), 53 West 5th South, Salt Lake City, Utah [S3]

Mills, John Lincoln, Pvt., 98th Co., Newport, Rhode Island, DDS, September 27, 1918 at Newport, Rhode Island. John and Nora Mills (Parents), Houtzdale, Pennsylvania [S3]

Mills, Joseph Leslie, Pvt., BD, MB, Quantico, Virginia, DDS, November 4, 1918 at Quantico, Virginia. Laura Mills (Mother), Janesburg, Missouri [S3]

Marine Corps Deaths, 1917-1921

Mills, Ralph Thurman, Pvt., MCR, Supply Det., Quantico, Virginia, DDS, October 6, 1918 at Quantico, Virginia. Alexander F. Mills (Father), 150 E. Duval St., Germantown, Philadelphia, Pennsylvania [FAG] [S3]

Mills, Robert A., Pvt., MD, USNH, Fort Lyon, Colorado, DDS, March 26, 1919 at Fort Lyon, Colorado. Mrs. Elizabeth Mills (Wife), 96 Hamburg Ave., Paterson, New Jersey [FAG] [S4]

Milner, Richard H., Gy. Sgt., MB, Nav. Sta., New Orleans, Louisisana, DDS, August 2, 1917 at Marietta, Oklahoma enroute to Fort Lyons, Colorado. Addie Milner (Mother), 713½ Main St., Little Rock, Arkansas [S3]

Milroy, Earl Doak, Pvt., 85th Co., Quantico, Virginia, DDS, February 9, 1918 at Quantico, Virginia. John P. Milroy (Father), Gen. Del., Oneida, Illinois [FAG] [S3]

Mincey, George Alex, Cpl., 55th Co., 5th Regt., KIA, June 5, 1918 in the Aisne Defensive. George Mincey (Father), RFD#1, Ogeechee, Georgia [FAG] [S2] [SW]

Minnemann, Louis, Pvt., B. Det., Puget Sound, Washington, DDS, November 2, 1917 at Puget Sound. Mrs. Louisa Minnemann (Mother), Gen. Del., Bremen, Germany [VA-San Francisco] [S3]

Minnis, John A., Captain, MB, Quantico, Virginia, DAS, September 23, 1921 in an aeroplane accident at Quantico, Virginia. Mrs. Laura W. Minnis (Wife), Greenville, Alabama [S4]

Minstereifel, Louis, Pvt., Parris Island, South Carolina, DDS, June 24, 1921 at Parris Island, South Carolina. Mrs. Louisa Minstereifel (Mother), 400 Frank St., Carrick, Pennsylvania [S4]

Minter, Howard Lee, Sgt., Supply Co., 13th Regt., DOD, September 26, 1918 in France. William R. Minter (Father), Donough, Georgia [FAG] [S2]

Marine Corps Deaths, 1917-1921

Mishler, John H., Pvt., 12th Co., Brooklyn, New York, DDS, January 14, 1919 at Booklyn, New York. Mrs. Delta Mishler (Mother), 107 Spruce St., Chattanooga, Tennessee [S4]

Mitch, Robert, Pvt., 2nd Cas. Det., MB, Philadelphia, Pennsylvania, DDS, May 10, 1919 at Philadelphia, Pennsylvania. Mrs. Hannah Mitch (Mother), Sellersville, Pennsylvania [FAG] [S4]

Mitchell, Clyde, Pvt., 95th Co., 6th Regt., KIA, July 19, 1918 in the Aisne Marne. John Mitchell (Father), RFD #6, Adrian, Michigan [FAG] [S2] [SW1]

Mitchell, Henry Martin, Jr., Pvt., Mar. Det., NPG, Indian Head, Maryland, DDS, October 21, 1918 at Indian Head, Maryland. Henry M. Mitchell (Father), Shelter Island, New York [S3]

Moe, Sigurd Peter, Pvt., 95th Co., 6th Regt., KIA, June 12, 1918 in the Chateau-Thierry Sector. Peter Moe (Father), McKinley, Minnesota [FAG] [S2] [SW]

Moerk, Charles Frederick, 1st Sgt., MB, Charleston, South Carolina, DDS, February 20, 1918 at Charleston, South Carolina. Emma Miller (Sister), 1426 North 24th St., Philadelphia, Pennsylvania [FAG] [S3]

Moffett, Robert Godwin, Pvt., 49th Co., 5th Regt., KIA, November 2, 1918 in the Meuse Argonne. Robert G. Moffett (Father), 3216 Commerce St., Dallas, Texas [FAG] [S2] [SW1]

Mofield, John William, Pvt., 76th Co., 6th Regt., KIA, June 13, 1918 in the Chateau-Thierry Sector. Mrs Mary Mofield (Mother), Box 293, Hondo, Texas [FAG] [S2] [SW]

Mogan, Arthur Vincent, Pvt., 79th Co., 6th Regt., DOW, November 14, 1918 in the Meuse Argonne. Wm. H. Mogan (Father), 21 Lyman Terrace, Wlatha, Massachusetts [R] [S2] [SW1 says Arthur Vincent Morgan]

Marine Corps Deaths, 1917-1921

Moir, Leslie Herbert, Pfc., MBks., New York, DDS, February 15, 1920 at New York, New York. Marie Moir (Sister), Miami, Florida [FAG] [S4]

Moldestad, Harold Lauritz, Pvt., 77th Co., 6th MG Bn., KIA, November 1, 1918 in the Meuse Argonne. John J. Moldestad (Father), Moldestad Ave., St. Louis Park, Minnesota [FAGM] [FAG] [S2] [SW1]

Moles, Jacob Hawthorne, Pvt., 67th Co., 5th Regt., DOW, October 4, 1918 in the Meuse Argonne. Henrietta Moles (Mother), 1416 Vista St., Hollywood, California [R] [S2] [SW1 says KIA]

Molthen, Fred T., 2nd Lieutenant, MB, Parris Island, South Carolina, DAS, June 25, 1920 in an aeroplane accident at Parris Island, South Carolina. Mrs. William Molthen (Mother), Granite St., Butte, Montana [S4]

Monahan, William Henry, Pvt., 47th Co., 5th Regt., KIA, June 17, 1918 in the Chateau-Thierry Sector. Agnes K. Monahan (Sister), 317 E. Magnolia Ave., Louisville, Kentucky [R] [S2] [SW1 says DOW]

Monroe, Frank James, Gy. Sgt., 80th Co., 6th Regt., KIA, June 19, 1918 in the Chateau-Thierry Sector. Mrs. Elizabeth Craigmile (Sister), 3019 N. Ashland Ave., Chicago, Illinois [S2] [SW1]

Montgomery, Claude Henry, Pvt., 16th Co., 5th Regt., KIA, October 5, 1918 in the Meuse Argonne. Mrs. Anna Montgomery (Mother), 1906 South Washington St., Sedalia, Missouri [S2] [SW says Co. A]

Montgomery, James Morris, Gy. Sgt., MB, Boston, Massachusetts, DDS, September 27, 1918 at Chelsea, Massachusetts. Alice Montgomery (Mother), RFD #1, Wesson, Mississippi [S3]

Montgomery, John Thomas, Pvt., 67th Co., 5th Regt., DOW, August 5, 1918 in the Chateau-Thierry Sector. Richard H. Carner (Uncle), Chelsea, Georgia [S2] [SW] [SW]

Marine Corps Deaths, 1917-1921

Moore, Albert Edward, Pvt., 84th Co., 6th Regt., KIA, July 19, 1918 in the Aisne Marne. Thomas Moore (Father), Forest Ave., Riverside, Illinois [ABMC- Fere] [S2] [SW]

Moore, Jack, Pvt., Co. K, 11th Regt., DOD, February 20, 1919 in France. Jeffie Cowels (Sister), 416 Washington St., Wenatchee, Washington [FAG] [S2]

Moore, John Peter, Cpl., 20th Co., 5th Regt., DOW, September 15, 1918 in the St. Mihiel Offensive. Mrs. Anna Moore (Mother), 714 N. Main St., Rochelle, Indiana [S2] [SW]

Moore, John Wilber, Cpl., Bks. Det., Quantico, Virginia, DDS, January 8, 1918 at Minneapolis, Minnesota while on furlough. George W. Moore (Father), Hopkins, Minnesota [S3]

Moore, Morris Dalton, Sgt., 83rd Co., 6th Regt., KIA, June 6, 1918 in the Chateau-Thierry Sector. Ethel A. Rouse (Sister), 317 S. Pine St., Centralia, Illinois [S2] [SW]

Moore, Orlie Earnest, Pvt., 74th Co., 6th Regt., KIA, July 19, 1918 in the Aisne Marne. James W. Moore (Father), 1407 Coit Ave, E. Cleveland, Ohio [ABMC- Fere] [S2] [SW says A Co., Repl. Btln.]

Moore, Oscar Jason, Cpl., 17th Co., 5th Regt., DOW, June 23, 1918 in the Chateau-Thierry Sector. Mrs. Adda Moore (Mother), Oxford, Arkansas [FAG] [S2] [SW]

Moore, Otto, Pvt., 67th Co., 5th Regt., KIA, October 4, 1918 in the Meuse Argonne. Maggie Moore (Mother), Odin, Illinois [R] [S2] [SW1]

Moore, Warren Freemont, Pvt., Co. Z, Parris Island, South Carolina, DAS, October 5, 1918 at Parris Island, South Carolina. John E. Moore (Father), 606 S. Main St., El Dorado, Kansas [S3]

Moore, William Frederick, Pvt., 47th Co., 5th Regt., KIA, June 7, 1918 in the Chateau-Thierry Sector. Mr. James Moore (Father), 4 Waldron St., Corona, Long Island, New York [S2] [SW1]

Marine Corps Deaths, 1917-1921

Moran, John Willard, Pvt., 74th Co., 6th Regt., DOW, June 9, 1918 in the Chateau-Thierry Sector. Joseph F. Moran (Father), 8 Hammond St., Worcester, Massachusetts [R] [S2] [SW]

Moransel, Louis, Pvt., USS *New Orleans*, DAS, April 25, 1921 drowned in the Shangpoo River, Shanghai, China. Mary Soeffler (Sister), 855 South Canal St., Pittsburgh, Pennsylvania [S4]

Moreland, William Albirtus, Pvt., Bks. Det., Quantico, Virginia, DDS, September 22, 1918 at Quantico, Virginia. Henry B. Moreland (Father), Mineral City, Ohio [S3]

Morgan, Arthur Ray, Pvt., 66th Co., 5th Regt., KIA, November 10, 1918 in the Meuse Argonne. James M. Morgan (Father), 520 Mountain Ave., Ashland, Oregon [ABMC-Romagne] [S2] [SW1]

Morgan, David Thomas, Pvt., 76th Co., 6th Regt., KIA, June 13, 1918 in the Chateau-Thierry Sector. J. P. Morgan (Father), 401 N. Fifer St., Bloomington, Illinois [FAG] [S2] [SW]

Morgan, Enos Clifford, Pvt., 84th Co., 6th Regt., DOW, July 19, 1918 in the Aisne Marne. Mrs. Elizabeth Morgan (Mother), Clemont County, Marathon, Ohio [FAG] [S2] [SW1]

Morgan, James Douglas, Pvt., 51st Co., 5th Regt., DOW, July 12, 1918 in the Chateau-Thierry Sector. Charles H. Morgan (Father), Granby, Massachusetts [ABMC- Fere] [S2] [SW]

Morgan, John Edgar, Sgt., 74th Co., 6th Regt., DOW, June 10, 1918 in the Chateau-Thierry Sector. Sarah Hoover (Mother), Gen. Del., Carthage, Illinois [FAG] [S2] [SW]

Morgan, John Hunt, Cpl., Co. C, 13th Regt., DOD, September 29, 1918 in France. Cathrine Morgan (Sister), Austin, Texas [ABMC- Fere] [S2]

Marine Corps Deaths, 1917-1921

Morgan, Maynard, Pvt., MB, Naval Station, Cavite, Philippine Islands, DDS, November 25, 1918 at Cavite, Philippine Islands. John T. Morgan (Father), Moore, Idaho [S4]

Morgan, Robert Darling, Cpl., 49th Co., 5th Regt., DOW, June 6, 1918 in the Chateau-Thierry Sector. Margaret Morgan (Mother), 268 Ogden St., Newark, New Jersey [ABMC- Belleau] [S2] [SW1]

Morgan, Steele William, Pvt., M.G. Co., 11th Regt., DAO, June 9, 1918 in France. Joseph B. Morgan (Father), Gen. Del., Winnett, Montana [R] [S2] [SW1 says KOA]

Moris, Clarence Edward, Pvt., Squadron E, MAF, 15th Regt., Haiti, KIA, November 4, 1919 at Maissado, Haiti by natives. William Moris (Father), 1406 Jefferson St., Buffalo, New York [S4]

Morley, Wallace James, Pvt., Hdqtrs., 10th Regt., Quantico, Virginia, DDS, October 6, 1918 at Quantico, Virginia. Mrs. Nora Morley (Mother), 565 Concord Ave., Detroit, Michigan [FAG] [S3]

Morningstar, George Sleeder, Pvt., 23rd Co., 6th MG Bn., DOW, June 7, 1918 in the Chateau-Thierry Sector. Wm. T. Morningstar (Father), 429 E. North Ave., Baltimore, Maryland [S2] [SW]

Morrel, Daniel Lattimore, Pvt., 76th Co., 6th Regt., KIA, July 19, 1918 in the Aisne Marne. John R. Morrel (Father), Milford, Texas [FAG] [S2] [SW1]

Morris, Charles Downing, Pvt., 96th Co., 6th Regt., KIA, July 19, 1918 in the Aisne Marne. Pearl Fry (Sister), 39 Edgewood Ave., Oakwood, Michigan [ABMC- Fere] [S2] [SW1]

Morris, Frank L., Captain, DDS, February 2, 1919 at New York, New York. John D. Morris (Father), 5861 Plymouth Ave., St. Louis, Missouri [ANC] [S4]

Marine Corps Deaths, 1917-1921

Morris, Wilson Arnold, Pvt., Hdqtrs. Co., 13th Regt., DOD, September 23, 1918 enroute to France. Vera Morris (Sister), Shelby, Iowa [R] [S2]

Morrison, Walter Mathias, Pvt., 79th Co., 6th Regt., KIA, November 11, 1918 in the Meuse Argonne. Peter J. Morrison (Father), 6815 Pear Ave., Cleveland, Ohio [S2] [SW1]

Morse, Clyde Webber, Cpl., Hdqtrs. Co., 5th Regt., DOW, November 4, 1918 in the Meuse Argonne. Elspeth V. Morse (Sister), 42 Hanson St., Boston, Massachusetts [ABMC-Romagne] [S2] [SW1]

Morse, Fred Bates, Pvt., 96th Co., 6th Regt., KIA, June 6, 1918 in the Chateau-Thierry Sector. Edward T. Morse (Father), 339 Central St., East Bridgewater, Massachusettts [S2] [SW]

Moseley, Benjamin Franklin, Pvt., 43rd Co., 5th Regt., KIA, June 12, 1918 in the Chateau-Thierry Sector. Ira L. Mosley (Father), Stockbridge, Georgia [ABMC- Belleau] [S2] [SW]

Moser, Herbert Lewis, Pvt., Co. U, Parris Island, South Carolina, DOS, September 5, 1918 at Parris Island, South Carolina. Louisa Moser (Mother), 574 Central Ave., Brooklyn, New York [VA-Beaufort] [S3]

Mosher, Floyd Charles, Pvt., 23rd Co., 6th MG Bn., DOW, July 29, 1918 in the Aisne Marne. Evelyn J. Mosher (Sister), 408 Beverly Road, Flatbush, Brooklyn, New York [VA-Cypress Hills says U.S. Army] [S2] [SW]

Moskoff, Nicholas, Sgt., Hdqtrs., 1st Brigade, Haiti, DOW, received in action on March 21, 1919 at Haiti. No next of kin given. [S4]

Moskovich, David Abraham, Sgt., 20th Co., 5th Regt., KIA, June 23, 1918 in the Chateau-Thierry Sector. Sadie Moskovich (Mother), 212 Beacon Ave., Jersey City, New Jersey [S2] [SW]

Marine Corps Deaths, 1917-1921

Moss, William Merritt, Pvt., 51st Co., 5th Regt., KIA, June 11, 1918 in the Chateau-Thierry Sector. Angus I. Moses (Father), Mt. Vernon, Illinois [ABMC- Belleau] [S2] [SW]

Mott, Dewey Graydon, Pvt., 82nd Co., 6th Regt., KIA, October 7, 1918 in the Meuse Argonne. Grace Mott (Mother), Waterport, New York [ABMC- Romagne] [S2] [SW1]

Mott, Henry S., 2nd Lieut., MCR, MFF, Miami, Florida, DDS, April 3, 1919 at Key West, Florida. Mrs. Lizzie R. Mott (Mother), 16 Parkway, Goshen, New York [FAG] [S4]

Mount, Leslie Louis, Pvt., Co. C, Parris Island, South Carolina, DDS, February 14, 1918 at Parris Island, South Carolina. George M. Mount (Father), Crothersville, Indiana [FAG] [S3]

Mowry, Ernest Burnside, Pvt., 23rd Co., 6th MG Bn., KIA, November 2, 1918 in the Meuse Argonne. Charles B. Mowry (Father), 29 Central St., South Weymouth, Massachusetts [S2] [SW1]

Mudek, Joseph Stephen, Pvt., 43rd Co., 5th Regt., KIA, June 13, 1918 in the Chateau-Thierry Sector. Mrs. Joe Seck (Sister), Clarissa, Minnesota [S2] [SW]

Mulford, Joseph Allen, Pvt., 95th Co., 6th Regt., DOW, July 19, 1918 in the Aisne Marne. Hattie Mulford (Mother), Route #3, Box 126, Tacoma, Washington [S2] [SW1]

Mullen, Russel Washington, Pvt., 55th Co., 5th Regt., KIA, June 11, 1918 in the Chateau-Thierry Sector. Henry Mullen (Father), 8 Burrows Ave., Bernardsville, New Jersey [ABMC- Belleau] [S2] [SW1]

Mullins, Leslie W., Pvt., Co. D, Parris Island, South Carolina, DDS, January 24, 1919 at Parris Island, South Carolina. Mrs. Georgia Mullins (Mother), RR#6, Dallas, Texas [FAG] [S4]

Mullins, Lester Wane, Pvt., 80th Co., 6th Regt., KIA, June 11, 1918 in the Chateau-Thierry Sector. Mrs. Bessie M.

Marine Corps Deaths, 1917-1921

Mullins (Wife), 701 E. 14th Ave., Apt. 40, Denver, Colorado [ABMC- Belleau] [S2] [SW]

Muncey, Alton Everett, Pvt., 47th Co., 5th Regt., DOW, June 24, 1918 in the Chateau-Thierry Sector. Mrs. Edith M. Muncey (Mother), 50 Central Ave., Providence, Rhode Island [ANC] [S2] [SW]

Munger, Chester Lemuel, Pvt., 20th Co., 5th Regt., KIA, November 2, 1918 Fannie L. Munger (Mother), 86 Fremont St., Somerville, Massachusetts [S2] [SW1]

Munns, Joe Bryan, Pvt., 67th Co., 5th Regt., KIA, June 6, 1918 in the Chateau-Thierry Sector. Laura Munns (Mother), White Haven, Tennessee [ABMC- Belleau] [S2] [SW]

Munroe, Joseph H., Pfc., 37th Co., Cuba, DAS, June 1, 1920 at Camaguey, Cuba. Mrs. Claire Munroe (Mother), Ingersoll, Ontario, Canada [FAG] [S4]

Munsel, Ralph Raymond, Pvt., 78th Co., 6th Regt., KIA, July 19, 1918 in the Aisne Marne. Mrs. Bertha I. Munsel Waite (Former wife), 104 Rural St., Emporia, Kansas [ANC] [S2] [SW]

Munzer, Bernhardt Melvin, Cpl., 99th Co., Newport, Rhode Island, DDS, March 4, 1918 at Newport, Rhode Island. Fank Munzer (Father), 1703 F. St., Bakersfield, California [S3]

Murchison, Byran C., Major, Quantico, Virginia, DDS, October 8, 1918 at Quantico, Virginia. Lillian McDonald Mrchison (Mother), 43 Montague St., Charleston, South Carolina [S3]

Murphy, Emmett James, Pvt., 75th Co., 6th Regt., KIA, September 15, 1918 in the St. Mihiel Offensive. Mary Murphy (Mother), 75 Depot St., Salem, Ohio [S2] [SW says A. Co., 3rd Sep. Btln.]

Murphy, Eugene Francis, Gy. Sgt., 16th Co., 5th Regt., KIA, October 4, 1918 in the Meuse Argonne. Frank Murphy

Marine Corps Deaths, 1917-1921

(Father), 39 Pickering St., Ogdenburg, New Jersey [ABMC- Romagne] [S2] [SW1]

Murphy, George Dallas, Pvt., 76th Co., 6th Regt., KIA, June 3, 1918 in the Aisne Defensive. Mrs. Margaret P. Benton (Mother), 1730 Arlington Ave., Bessemer, Alabama [S2] [SW]

Murphy, John William, Pvt., 79th Co., 6th Regt., KIA, October 7, 1918 in the Meuse Argonne. Lotta M. Allen (Mother), 1184 Latham St., Memphis, Tennessee [S2] [SW1]

Murphy, Leland Maurice, Pvt., 80th Co., 6th Regt., KIA, October 3, 1918 in the Meuse Argonne. James N. Murphy (Father), 701 Roosevelt Ave., Joplin, Missouri [ABMC- Romagne TOM] [S2] [SW says A Co., 5th Sep. Btln.]

Murphy, Martin John, Pvt., Bks. Det., New York, DDS, March 24, 1918 at Hoboken, New Jersey. Margaret Kennedy (Sister), 366 Underclift Ave., Edgewater, New Jersey [S3]

Murphy, Michael James, Sgt., 97th Co., 6th Regt., KIA, July 19, 1918 in the Aisne Marne. Jenie Belmar (Sister), Peshtigo, Wisconsin [ABMC- Fere] [S2] [SW]

Murphy, Moses, Pvt., 80th Co., 6th Regt., KIA, October 3, 1918 in the Meuse Argonne. Alex Murphy (Father), Holdingford, Minnesota [ABMC- Romagne TOM] [S2] [SW says B Co., 5th Sep. Btln.]

Murphy, Richard W., 2nd Lieut., 83rd Co., 6th Regt., DOW, June 26, 1918 in the Chateau Thierry sector. Mrs. Aelaide I. Murphy (Mother), Greensboro, Alabama [S1] [SW]

Murphy, Stephen, Gy. Sgt., Supply Det., Mare Island, California, DDS, December 4, 1918 at Oakland, California. Mrs. Lizzie May Dragamanovich (Daughter), 414 Lakeside Blvd., Oakland, California [S4]

Murray, Claude Charles, Cpl., Hdqtrs., 10th Regt., Quantico, Virginia, DOS, February 19, 1918 at Quantico, Virginia.

Marine Corps Deaths, 1917-1921

William C. Murray (Father), Venice Park, Atlantic City, New Jersey [S3]

Murray, Edward Raymond, Pvt., 96th Co., 6th Regt., DOW, June 14, 1918 in the Chateau-Thierry Sector. Mrs. Marjorie L. Murray (Widow), 5000 Broadway, New York, New York [S2] [SW says Hdqrs. Co., 2nd Repl. Btln.]

Musbach, Carl Fred, Pvt., 66th Co., 5th Regt., KIA, July 18, 1918 in the Aisne Marne. Sophia Neth (Mother), RFD#1, Liberty, Missouri [ABMC- Belleau TOM] [S2] [SW says 115th Co., Repl. Btln.]

Musgrave, Carl, Pvt., 80th Co., 6th Regt., DOW, September 13, 1918 in the St. Mihiel Offensive. Perry Musgrave (Brother), RR#2, Willow Hill, Illinois [FAG] [S2]

Muske, Charles H., Pvt., 80th Co., 6th Regt., KIA, September 15, 1918 in the St. Mihiel Offensive. Mrs. Martha Muske (Mother), 138 Nostrand Ave., Brooklyn, New York [S2] [SW says Charles Herman]

Musson, Scott L., Pvt., Co. E, Parris Island, South Carolina, DDS, January 19, 1919 at Parris Island, South Carolina. Mrs. Gertrude Musson (Mother), Gilbertsville, New York [FAG] [S4]

Mustain, Claud Edward, Pvt., 51st Co., Brooklyn, New York, DDS, May 6, 1919 at Brooklyn, New York. A. P. Mustain (Father), Middleburg, North Carolina [S4]

Mustian, Marion Butler, Pvt., 79th Co., 6th Regt., DOW, October 7, 1918 in the Meuse Argonne. Mrs. Emma L. Mustian (Mother), 2108 Taylor St., Richmond, Virginia [S2]

Muth, Laurence, Sgt., Constable Det., Haiti, KIA, April 4, 1920 by bandits at Haiti. John Muth (Father), Losbanos, Mercer County, California [FAG as Lieut.] [S4]

Myers, Harry Campbell, Pvt., 83rd Co., 6th Regt., DOW, June 13, 1918 in the Chateau-Thierry Sector. Thomas B. Myers (Father), Box #4, McLean, Illinois [ABMC- Belleau] [S2] [SW1]

Marine Corps Deaths, 1917-1921

Myers, Roy Herbert, Cpl., 95th Co., 6th Regt., DOW, July 19, 1918 in the Aisne Marne. Wm. M. Myers (Father), Walnut, Iowa [S2] [SW1]

Mynatt, Burlie Glover, Pvt., 47th Co., 5th Regt., DOW, June 7, 1918 in the Chateau-Thierry Sector. Mary Mynatt (Mother), RFD #4, Fountain City, Tennessee [S2] [SW]

Nachant, Albert, Pvt., 80th Co., 6th Regt., KIA, October 6, 1918 in the Meuse Argonne. Sophia Nachant (Mother), 148 Mary St., Syracuse, New York [ABMC- Romagne] [S2] [SW1]

Naden, Edward, Cpl., 66th Co., 5th Regt., KIA, June 6, 1918 in the Chateau-Thierry Sector. Arthur Naden (Father), 10 Olempic Terrace, Irvington, New Jersey [ABMC- Belleau] [S2] [SW]

Naegelen, Charles Augustus, Pvt., 51st Co., 5th Regt., KIA, June 11, 1918 in the Chateau-Thierry Sector. Mary Naegelen (Mother), 48 W. Rochelle St., Cincinnati, Ohio [ABMC- Belleau] [S2] [SW]

Napp, Jack, Cpl., 15th Co., 6th MG Bn., KIA, June 12, 1918 in the Chateau-Thierry Sector. Mrs. Rebecca Napp (Mother), 424 Reed St., Philadelphia, Pennsylvania [S2] [SW]

Naugher, Robert Leamon, Pvt., 97th Co., 6th Regt., DOW, July 19, 1918 in the Aisne Marne. Thomas Naugher (Brother), Chase, Alabama [ABMC- Fere] [S2] [SW1]

Navarro, Ernest O., Pvt., MBks., Naval Station, Key West, Florida, DDS, January 20, 1919 at Key West, Florida. Chris Navarro (Father), Baldwin, Louisiana [S4]

Neail, Willis Abraham, Pvt., 66th Co., 5th Regt., KIA, November 3, 1918 in the Meuse Argonne. Andrew J. Neail (Father), 4168 Jamaica Ave., Woodhaven, New York [R] [S2] [SW1]

Neary, George, Pvt., MB, Mare Island, California, DDS, January 28, 1920 at Mare Island, California. Lily Culley (Sister), Gen. Del., Maysville, Missouri [S4]

Marine Corps Deaths, 1917-1921

Neary, Patrick James, Pvt., Co. D, 13th Regt., DAO, May 22, 1918 in France. Patrick J. Shannon (Brother-in-law), 116 Lockwood Ave., Buffalo, New York [R] [S2] [SW1 says KOA]

Needell, Benjamin Adolphus, Pvt., 95th Co., 6th Regt., DOW, July 19, 1918 in the Aisne Marne. Ella V. Needell (Mother), RFD#25, Byron, New York [FAG] [S2] [SW1]

Neely, Oliver Lee Mathew, Sgt., 18th Co., 5th Regt., DOD, October 16, 1918 in France. Jeff Neely (Father), Prichard, Alabama [ABMC- Thiaucourt] [S2] [SW1]

Neil, Ernest Arthur, Cpl., 15th Co., 6th MG Bn., KIA, June 10, 1918 in the Chateau-Thierry Sector. Munsel Neil (Mother), 306 Berkshire Ave., San Antonio, Texas [S2] [SW]

Neill, Roy George, Pvt., Western Recruiting Division, District of Montana, Missoula, Montana, DDS, November 4, 1918 at Missoula, Montana. Laura E. Neill (Mother), P O Box 87, Simms, Montana [FAG] [S3]

Nelsan, Orville Albin, Pvt., 20th Co., 5th Regt., KIA, June 7, 1918 in the Chateau-Thierry Sector. John W. Nelsan (Father), Box 445, Litchfield, Minnesota [FAG] [S2] [SW]

Nelson, Charles Emil, Pvt., 51st Co., 5th Regt., DOW, June 9, 1918 in the Chateau-Thierry Sector. Anna C. Nelson (Mother), 1034 W. 2nd St., N. Salt Lake City, Utah [R] [S2] [SW says 2nd Repl. Btln.]

Nelson, Charles Leroy, Pvt., USS *Oklahoma*, DDU, October 21, 1918 aboard the USS *Oklahoma*. Ole M. Nelson, Hector, Minnesota [S3]

Nelson, Everett Lester, Pvt., 67th Co., 5th Regt., KIA, June 6, 1918 in the Chateau-Thierry Sector. Anna Nelson (Mother), Bird City, Kansas [FAG] [S2] [SW]

Nelson, George F., Pvt., Naval Ammunition Depot, Puget Sound, Washington, DDS, November 5, 1919 at Puget Sound,

Marine Corps Deaths, 1917-1921

Washington. Charles A. Nelson (Father), RFD#1, Thief River Falls, Minnesota [S4]

Nelson, Harry Edward, Pvt., MD, USS *Brooklyn*, DDU, March 28, 1918 aboard the USS *Brooklyn*. Mary A. Nelson (Mother), Minden, Nebraska [FAG] [S3]

Nelson, John Carlisle, Pvt., 3rd Squadron, FMAF, DOD, November 2, 1918 in France. Mrs. Isabella O. Nelson (Mother), Main St., Sodus, New York [S2]

Nelson, Lyndon Chalmer, Pvt., 23rd Co., 6th MG Bn., KIA, June 10, 1918 in the Chateau-Thierry Sector. Chalmer Nelson (Father), 103 French Ave., Brockton, Massachusetts [S2] [SW]

Nelson, Otto Christian, Pvt., 18th Co., 5th Regt., DOD, February 13, 1919 in France. Harold E. Nelson (Brother), 3156 Brown Road., West Park, Ohio [ANC] [S2]

Nelson, Solon Albert, Pvt., 51st Co., 5th Regt., KIA, June 11, 1918 in the Chateau-Thierry Sector. Mrs. Della Haskans (Aunt) Fife Lake, Michigan [FAG] [S2] [SW]

Nesbitt, Melvin Allen, Pvt., Co. B, 10th Sep. Batt., Quantico, Virginia, DDS, November 8, 1918 at Quantico, Virginia. Mrs. M. A. Nesbitt (Wife), 12 N. Harvey St., Oklahoma City, Oklahoma [FAG] [S3]

Netherton, James Thomas, Pvt., 84th Co., 6th Regt., KIA, October 3, 1918 in the Meuse Argonne. Etta Netherton (Mother), 1222 Cypress St., Louisville, Kentucky [FAG] [S2] [SW1]

Neuneker, William Edward, Pvt., 45th Co., 5th Regt., DOW, October 4, 1918 in the Meuse Argonne. Josephine Neuneker (Mother), Bushnell, Illinois [ABMC- Romagne TOM] [S2] [SW1]

Neville, Joseph Nicholas, Cpl., MCR, Radio Sta., Tuckerton, New Jersey, DDS, October 25, 1918 at Tuckerton, New Jersey. William Neville (Father), 73 Hooper St., Brooklyn, New York [S3]

Marine Corps Deaths, 1917-1921

Newborg, George Leofred, Pvt., 15th Co., 6th MG Bn., KIA, October 4, 1918 in the Meuse Argonne. Anna S. Newborg (Mother), RFD#1, Granger, Washington [ABMC- Romagne] [S2] [SW]

Newcomb, Ray William, Pvt., 76th Co., 6th Regt., KIA, September 12, 1918 in the St. Mihiel Offensive. Wm. H. Newcomb (Father), Angola, New York [FAG] [S2] [SW]

Newell, Loren Elton, Pvt., 45th Co., 5th Regt., KIA, June 13, 1918 in the Chateau-Thierry Sector. Glenn A. Newell (Brother), 62 Hawley St., Buffalo, New York [ABMC- Belleau as L.E.] [S2] [SW]

Newitt, George Russell, Pvt., 51st Co., 5th Regt., KIA, June 13, 1918 in the Chateau-Thierry Sector. Joseph Newitt (Father), 318 Ridge St., Wilkes Barre, Pennsylvania [S2] [SW]

Newitt, Joseph Francis, Pvt., 76th Co., 6th Regt., KIA, June 13, 1918 in the Chateau-Thierry Sector. Lucie Newitt (Mother), 5323 Magazine St., New Orleans, Louisana [ABMC- Belleau] [S2] [SW]

Newman, Gwenell B., 1st Lieutenant, Washington, D.C., DDS, February 2, 1920 at Washington, D.C. Mrs. Delia Barden (Grandmother), St. Louis, Michigan [S4]

Newman, Kenneth Iver, Pvt., 43rd Co., 5th Regt., KIA, June 11, 1918 in the Chateau-Thierry Sector. Mrs. Helen Newman (Mother), 193 Southern Ave., Pittsburgh, Pennsylvania [ANC] [S2] [SW1 says DOW]

Newton, Valentine Hallock, Pvt., Hdqtrs. Co., 5th Regt., DOO, November 13, 1917 in France. Margaret H. Newton (Mother), Arkville, New York [R] [S2]

Nicely, Benjamin, Pvt., Hdqtrs. Co., 6th Regt., DOD, February 5, 1919 in France. James A. Nicely (Father), RFD#1, Waldron, Indiana [R] [S2]

Marine Corps Deaths, 1917-1921

Nicholas, Arlie Carl, Pvt., 47th Co., 5th Regt., DOW, July 5, 1918 in the Chateau-Thierry Sector. Alice Smith (Mother), Dodge St., Covington, Ohio [ANC] [S2] [SW1]

Nichols, George Stevens, Pvt., Co. A, 13th Regt., DOD, September 27, 1918 in France. Hazel S. Nichols (Wife), Waterman Farm, Harpersville, New York [ABMC- Fere] [S2]

Nichols, Raymond, Pvt., 201st Casual Co., Quantico, Virginia, DAS, August 25, 1919 drowned in the Potomac River. Mrs. Alice B. Nichols (Mother), 156 Main St., Dalton, Massachusetts [S4]

Nicholson, Oscar Evald, Pvt., 66th Co., 5th Regt., KIA, July 18, 1918 in the Aisne Marne. Enoch Nicholson (Father), Carlton, Minnesota [R] [S2] [SW]

Nicol, George Raymond, Pvt., 84th Co., 6th Regt., KIA, July 19, 1918 in the Aisne Marne. Howard M. Nicol (Brother), 240 School St., Cuyahoga Falls, Ohio [S2] [SW1]

Nicolai, Edward Charles, Pvt., Bks. Det., Philadelphia, Pennsylvania, DDS, June 15, 1917 at Philadelphia. Edward Nicholai (Father), 349 E 153rd St., New York, New York [S3]

Niedringhaus, Casper Henry, Pvt., Co. E, 13th Regt., DOD, September 22, 1918 enroute to France. Lena Gutweiler (Mother), 4250 Maffit Ave., St. Louis, Missouri [R] [S2]

Nielson, John Whittaker Taylor, Pvt., 96th Co., 6th Regt., KIA, July 19, 1918 in the Aisne Marne. Andrew Nielson (Father), Manassa, Colorado [FAG] [S2] [SW]

Niesen, Raymond Henry, Pvt., 73rd Co., 6th Regt., KIA, June 5, 1918 in the Chateau-Thierry Sector. Frank Niesen (Father), 817 26th St., Milwaukee, Wisconsin [ABMC-Belleau] [S2] [SW]

Nilan, Michael Aloysius, Pvt., 51st Co., 5th Regt., DOW, July 19, 1918 in the Aisne Marne. Mrs. Saide Doyle (Sister), 219

Marine Corps Deaths, 1917-1921

S. Grove St., E. Orange, New Jersey [ABMC- Belleau TOM] [S2] [SW says Casualty Co., 4th Repl. Btln.]

Niltsche, Roy Alfred, Cpl., 75th Co., 6th Regt., KIA, [R] [SW1]

Noah, Hugo Herman, Sgt. 196th Co., 8th Regt., Haiti, DOS, January 22, 1920 at Calabasa, Haiti. Simon Noah (Father), Loyal, Wisconsin [S4]

Noble, Elbert Percy, Pvt., 74th Co., 6th Regt., KIA, November 1, 1918 in the Meuse Argonne. Frank B. Noble (Father), 8224 Rathbone Ave., Detroit, Michigan [ANC] [S2] [SW1]

Noble, Walter Raymond, Pvt., 76th Co., 6th Regt., DOW, July 19, 1918 in the Aisne Marne. Albert E. Noble (Father), Dundas, Vinton County, Ohio [S2] [SW1]

Noblett, Elmer Anderson, Pvt., 51st Co., 5th Regt., DOW, October 8, 1918 in the Meuse Argonne. Mrs. Mary L. Noblett (Mother), 2253 Horton Ave., Grand Rapids, Michigan [FAG] [S2] [SW]

Nolan, Charles Edmund, Pvt., Bks. Det., Quantico, Virginia, DDS, June 1, 1918 at Washington, D.C. Henry Nolan (Father), 162 Tichener St., New York, New York [S3]

Nolan, William Thomas Jr., Pvt., 51st Co., 5th Regt., KIA, June 11, 1918 in the Chateau-Thierry Sector. Clara Nolan (Mother), 3676 Laclede Ave., St. Louis, Missouri [ABMC- Belleau] [S2] [SW1]

Noonan, William John, Pvt., 75th Co., 6th Regt., KIA, October 9, 1918 in the Meuse Argonne. Patrick Noonan (Father), 54 Canal St., Winchester, Massachusetts [ABMC- Romagne] [S2] [SW1]

Norman, Harvey C., 2nd Lieut., NB Group, FMAF, KIA, October 22, 1918 in the Meuse Argonne. Andrew J. Norman (Father), 2007 Iowa St., Davenport, Iowa [FAG] [S1] [SW]

Marine Corps Deaths, 1917-1921

Norris, David Peter, Pvt., Hdqtrs. Co., 6th Regt., DOW, July 24, 1918 in the Aisne Marne. Catherine Jameson (Sister), 34 Convent Ave., New York, New York [R] [S2] [SW]

North, Albert Lee, Pvt., 14th Co., 9th Regt., Cuba, DDS, January 27, 1918 at Guantanamo Bay, Cuba. Mary North (Mother), Checotah, Oklahoma [FAG] [S3]

North, Homer Willis, Pvt., 74th Co., 6th Regt., DOW, November 2, 1918 in the Meuse Argonne. Archie M. North (Father), 8401 Clark Ave., Cleveland, Ohio [FAG] [S2] [SW1]

Norton, Almer Jean, Cpl., Bks. Det., Norfolk, Virginia, DDS, July 28, 1918 at Norfolk, Virginia. William Norton (Father), Gen. Del., Broderick, California [FAG] [S3]

Norton, John Ferris, Pvt., 83rd Co., 6th Regt., KIA, June 8, 1918 in the Chateau-Thierry Sector. Maggie Norton (Mother), 1024 W. Douglas Ave., East Nashville, Tennessee [VA-Nashville] [S2] [SW1]

Norton, John Lewis, Pvt., Fort Lyons, Colorado, DDS, November 10, 1917 at Fort Lyons, Colorado. Nelly Norton (Mother), Fort Scott, Kansas [VA-Fort Lyon] [S3]

Norton, Walter Victor, Pvt., 51st Co., 5th Regt., KIA, June 11, 1918 in the Chateau-Thierry Sector. Fred Norton (Father), St. Augustine, Florida [ABMC- Belleau] [S2] [SW]

Norwood, Stephen A., 1st Lieut., 15th Regt., 2nd Prov. Brigade, Dominican Republic, KIA, August 9, 1919 at Santo Domingo, Domincan Republic. John R. Norwood (Father), Donna, Texas [FAG] [S4]

Novak, William Rudolph., Pvt., 75th Co., 6th Regt., DOW, July 21, 1918 in the Aisne Marne. Mr. Frank Novak (Father), 116 E. St. Paul Ave., Waukesha, Wisconsin [ANC] [S2] [SW1]

Nowak, Peter, Cpl., 51st Co., 5th Regt., DOW, June 11, 1918 in the Chateau-Thierry Sector. Martin Nowak (Brother), 2809a Elliott Ave., St. Louis, Missouri [S2] [SW] [SW1]

Marine Corps Deaths, 1917-1921

Nunnally, Edward Porter, Sgt., Hdqtrs. Co., 5th Regt., DOW, November 3, 1918 in the Meuse Argonne. Robert F. Nunnally (Brother), 801 N. South St., Petersburg, Virginia [R] [S2] [SW1]

Nutting, Lester Herbert, Pvt., 96th Co., 6th Regt., KIA, September 15, 1918 in the St. Mihiel Offensive. Robert F. Nutting (Father), Rupert, Idaho [FAG] [S2] [SW]

Nye, John Armour, Pvt., 13th Co., 10th Regt., Indian Head, Maryland, DAS, September 26, 1918 of an automobile accident at Winer, Nebraska. Milton Nye (Father), Wisner, Nebraska [FAG] [S3]

O'Banion, Luther Lee, Pvt., 83rd Co., 6th Regt., DOW, June 8, 1918 in the Chateau-Thierry Sector. Andrew O'Banion (Father), Route #1, Mason, Ohio [FAG] [S2] [SW1 says KIA]

O'Boyle, John, Pvt., KIA, Gary, Indiana [S5]

O'Brien, Francis Bernard Joseph, Pvt., Bks. Det., Norfolk, Virginia, DDS, April 17, 1918 at Norfolk, Virginia. J. L. McCarthy (Brother-in-law) Meadowlands, Minnesota [S3]

O'Brien, James Alovsius, Pvt., 96th Co., 6th Regt., DOW, September 15, 1918 in the St. Mihiel Offensive. Mrs. James A. O'Brien (Mother), 906 Morris St., Cincinnati, Ohio [S2] [SW1]

O'Brien, Leo P., Cpl., 43rd Co., 5th Regt., KIA, July 31, 1918 in the Aisne Marne. Patrick P. O'Brien (Father), Route 18, Eureka, Missouri [R] [S2] [SW1]

O'Connell, Daniel Joseph, Pvt., 45th Co., 5th Regt., KIA, June 25, 1918 in the Chateau-Thierry Sector. Johanna O'Connell (Mother), 3821 E. 19th St., Kansas City, Missouri [ABMC- Belleau] [S2] [SW1]

O'Connell, Richard Clement, Pvt., 55th Co., 5th Regt., DOW, October 11, 1918 in the Meuse Argonne. William E.

Marine Corps Deaths, 1917-1921

O'Connell (Father), LeSeuer Center, Minnesota [ABMC-Romagne] [S2] [SW says Co. C, 4th Sep. Btln.]

O'Connor, Charles Arthur, Sgt., 49th Co., 5th Regt., KIA, June 6, 1918 in the Chateau-Thierry Sector. Mrs. Edna Morris (Mother), 42 Parker Ave., Cortland, New York [S2] [SW]

O'Connor, Edwin Francis, Pvt., 77th Co., 6th MG Bn., DOW, November 5, 1918 in the Meuse Argonne. Mrs. Thersa McGarvey (Sister), 11-A Lafferts Pl., Brooklyn, New York [R] [S2] [SW1]

O'Connor, Francis A., Pvt., Co. Z, Parris Island, South Carolina, DDS, March 2, 1919 at Parris Island, South Carolina. Agnes O'Connor (Mother), 2504 M St., N.W., Washington, D.C. [S4]

O'Connor, Joseph F., QM Sgt., Bks. Det., Guantanamo Bay, Cuba, DAS, September 24, 1920 drowned at Guantanamo Bay, Cuba. Anna O'Connor (Mother), 451 48th St., Brooklyn, New York [S4]

O'Connor, William Henry, Cpl., 18th Co., 5th Regt., KIA, July 18, 1918 in the Aisne Marne. Barnard O'Connor (Father), 201 N. First St., Connellsville, Pennsylvania [R] [S2] [SW says 140th Repl. Btln]

O'Donnell, Edward, Cpl., 75th Co., 6th Regt., DOW, October 12, 1918 in the Meuse Argonne. Bridget O'Donnell (Mother), 1507 Butler St., Easton, Pennsylvania [ABMC-Romagne] [S2] [SW1]

O'Donnell, Gordon Sidney, Pvt., 47th Co., 5th Regt., KIA, June 6, 1918 in the Chateau-Thierry Sector. Sidney W. O'Donnell (Father), East Holden, Maine [ABMC-Belleau TOM as G.S.] [S2] [SW]

O'Donoghue, Michael Thomas, Pvt., 67th Co., 5th Regt., KIA, October 4, 1918 in the Meuse Argonne. Katherine H. O'Donoghue (Wife), 270 W. 11th St., New York, New York [ABMC-Romagne] [S2] [SW1]

Marine Corps Deaths, 1917-1921

O'Flinn, James Louis, Pvt., 80th Co., 6th Regt., KIA, June 27, 1918 in the Chateau-Thierry Sector. Pat O'Flinn (Father), 2916 Davis St., Meridian, Mississippi [ABMC- Belleau TOM as J.L.] [S2] [SW1]

O'Hara, Frank Dignan, Pvt., 51st Co., 5th Regt., DOW, November 11, 1918 in the Meuse Argonne. Mrs. Elizabeth O'Hara (Mother), 113 N. Ingalls St., Ann Arbor, Michigan [S2] [SW1]

O'Kelley, Grover Cleveland, Sgt., 80th Co., 6th Regt., KIA [FAG] [SW] [SW1 reported to have been found alive]

O'Leary, Neal, Pvt., 47th Co., 5th Regt., KIA, June 6, 1918 in the Chateau-Thierry Sector. Martin J. O'Leary (Father), 803 Mt. Hope Road, Cincinnati, Ohio [S2] [SW1]

O'Neal, Henry Alvin, Pvt., 55th Co., 5th Regt., KIA, June 3, 1918 in the Aisne Defensive. Mrs. John J. O'Neal (Mother), Concord, Georgia [S2] [SW]

O'Neill, Arthur Cornelius, Pvt., 51st Co., 5th Regt., KIA, October 4, 1918 in the Meuse Argonne. A. S. O'Neill (Father), 5951 Michigan Ave, Chicago, Illinois [FAGM] [S2] [SW]

O'Neill, Owen Eugene, Captain, MB, Philadelphia, Pennsylvania, DDS, March 17, 1920 at Philadelphia, Pennsylvania. Owen E. O'Neill (Father), 27 West St., New London, Connecticut [S4]

O'Neill, Thomas G., Pvt., 100th Co., Guantanamo Bay, Cuba, DDS, February 15, 1919 at Guantanamo Bay, Cuba. Barbara O'Neill (Mother), 2230 N. Kildan Ave., Chicago, Illinois [FAG] [S4]

O'Reilly, Patrick J., Quartermaster Clerk, Philadelphia, Pennsylvania, DDS, October 12, 1918 at Philadelphia, Pennsylvania. Miss Julia O'Reilly (Sister), 19 Pamapo Ave., Jersey City, New Jersey [S3]

Marine Corps Deaths, 1917-1921

O'Reilly, Wallace M., Pvt., 79th Co., 6th Regt., KIA, July 17, 1918 in the Aisne Marne. Kate O'Reilly (Mother), 1528 Kane St., Houston, Texas [FAG] [S2] [SW1]

O'Rourke, Richard John, Pvt., 153rd Co., Quantico, Virginia, DDS, September 24, 1918 at Quantico, Virginia. Mary Burkman (Mother), Matoon, Illinois [S3]

O'Shea, John Bartholomew, Pvt., 97th Co., 6th Regt., DOW, July 19, 1918 in the Aisne Marne. John O'Shea (Father), 2921 1st Ave., South Minneapolis, Minnesota [ABMC- Fere] [S2] [SW1]

Oakes, Oscar B., Pvt., 98th Co., Newport, Rhode Island, DAS, July 14, 1919 at Newport, Rhode Island. Mary E. Oakes (Mother), Maryland, Tennessee [S4]

Oberdoerster, John Wilbur, Jr., Pvt., 36th Co., 8th Regt., Haiti, DDS, December 4, 1920 at Haiti. John W. Oberdoerster (Father), 516 Gordon St., Allentown, Pennsylvania [FAG] [S4]

Odry, Edward, Pvt., 80th Co., 6th Regt., KIA, October 7, 1918 in the Meuse Argonne. Andrew Odry (Father), 1421 Mononic Ave, S Milwaukee, Wisconsin [ABMC- Romagne] [S2] [SW1]

Odum, John R., Pvt., Bks. Det., Quantico, Virginia, DDS, October 15, 1918 at Quantico, Virginia. Donie Odum (Mother), Joaquin, Texas [S3]

Oelschlaeger, Edward Herman, Pvt., 66th Co., 5th Regt., KIA, June 6, 1918 in the Chateau-Thierry Sector. Levenia Oelschlaeger (Mother), 1141 Park Ave., Hoboken, New Jersey [S2] [SW]

Ofenloch, George Felix, Pvt., 80th Co., 6th Regt., KIA, June 10, 1918 in the Chateau-Thierry Sector. Charlotte Ofenloch (Mother), 2723 Magnolia Ave., Chicago, Illinois [S2] [SW1 says Ofenlock]

Marine Corps Deaths, 1917-1921

Olds, Clint, Pvt., 77th Co., 6th MG Bn., KIA, October 4, 1918 in the Meuse Argonne. Lora Olds (Mother), Oakville, Iowa [ABMC- Romagne] [S2] [SW1]

Olin, Russell Walter, Pvt., 75th Co., 6th Regt., KIA, October 14, 1918 in the Meuse Argonne. O. J. Olin (Father), Ada, Minnesota [ANC] [S2] [SW1]

Olive, George Frank, Pvt., Hdqtrs. Co., 5th Regt., KIA, June 6, 1918 in the Chateau-Thierry Sector. Mrs. Mary D. Taylor (Mother), RD#2, Pratt City, Alabama [ANC] [S2] [SW]

Oliver, Augustus Clayton, Pvt., 80th Co., 6th Regt., KIA, September 15, 1918 in the St. Mihiel Offensive. Mrs. Eunice Oliver (Mother), RFD#2, Belton, Texas [FAG] [S2] [SW says Co. B]

Oliver, John Walker, Pvt., 17th Co., 5th Regt., KIA, July 19, 1918 in the Aisne Marne. Mrs. J. W. Oliver (Mother), Jackson, Alabama [ABMC- Fere as John Walter] [S2] [SW]

Oliver, Wendell Holmes, Pvt., 74th Co., 6th Regt., DOW, July 19, 1918 in the Aisne Marne. George Y. Oliver (Father), RFD#1, Nathalie, Virginia [ABMC- Fere] [S2] [SW1]

Olson, Charles Arthur, Pvt., 8th Co., 5th Regt., KIA, September 15, 1918 in the St. Mihiel Offensive. Matilda Hill (Mother), Hutchinson, Minnesota [ABMC- Thiaucourt] [S2] [SW says Repl. Btln.]

Olson, Edward Andrew, Pvt., 23rd Co., 6th MG Bn., KIA, November 2, 1918 in the Meuse Argonne. Isaac Olson (Father), RR#2, Box 236, Toledo, Ohio [S2] [SW1]

Olson, Eskel H., Pvt., MBks., Mare Island, California, DDS, November 18, 1918 at Mare Island, California. Matilda Olson (Mother), Red Ring, Minnesota [FAG] [S4]

Olson, Fred Carl William, Pvt., 75th Co., 6th Regt., DOW, November 4, 1918 in the Meuse Argonne. Charles H. Olson (Father), #6 Glide St., Neponset, Massachusetts [R] [S2] [SW1 says KIA]

Marine Corps Deaths, 1917-1921

Olson, Oscar L., Cpl., Bks. Det., Charleston, South Carolina, DDS, May 17, 1920 at Charleston, South Carolina. Ida Olson (Mother), Odin, Minnesota [S4]

Ommundsen, Abraham L., Pvt., 51st Co., 5th Regt., DOW, June 6, 1918 in the Chateau-Thierry Sector. Mrs. Minnie Ommundsen (Mother), 748 51st St., Brooklyn, New York [VA-Cypress Hills] [S2] [SW]

Opheim, Irving Melvin, Pvt., 18th Co., 5th Regt., KIA, November 4, 1918 in the Meuse Argonne. Nels N. Opheim (Father), Route 3, Williamsburg, Virginia [FAG] [S2] [SW1]

Oring, Alvin Herman, Pvt., Bks. Det., Philadelphia, Pennsylvania, DDS, October 3, 1918 at Philadelphia, Pennsylvania. Lilly Oring (Mother), West Dover, Ohio [S3]

Orr, Joseph Lee, Pvt., 45th Co., 5th Regt., KIA, June 9, 1918 in the Chateau-Thierry Sector. Thomas J. Orr (Father), Matthews, North Carolina [FAG] [S2] [SW]

Orr, Thomas Henry Francis, Pvt., MD, American Legation, Peking, DDS, March 20, 1921 at Peking, China. Angus Orr (Mother), 3102 22nd St., San Francisco, California [VA-San Francisco] [S4]

Orteiger, Edward, Cpl., Constable Det., Haiti, DOS, October 13, 1920 at Haiti. Joseph Orteiger (Father), 2647 W. 18th St., Chicago, Illinois [S4]

Orum, John Robert, Pvt., 18th Co., 5th Regt., KIA, October 9, 1918 in the Meuse Argonne. Hiram Orum (Father), Sherrard, West Virginia [S2] [SW1]

Osborn, Earl Willard, Pvt., Supply Co., Parris Island, South Carolina, DDS, September 24, 1918 at Quantico, Virginia. Angie Osborn (Mother), 2408 Brown St., Alton, Illinois [FAG] [S3]

Osborne, Ernest James, Pvt., 80th Co., 6th Regt., KIA, June 3, 1918 in the Chateau-Thierry Sector. John F. Osborne (Father), 1000 South Washington St., Bloomington, Indiana [S2] [SW]

Marine Corps Deaths, 1917-1921

Osborne, James Ellis, Sgt., 47th Co., 5th Regt., DOW, September 14, 1918 in the Chateau-Thierry Sector. Mr. Mack C. Osborne (Brother), Dante, Virgnia [ANC] [S2] [SW says 138th Co., Repl. Btln.]

Osborne, Vivian Nickalls, Pvt., 18th Co., 5th Regt., KIA, June 12, 1918 in the Chateau-Thierry Sector. Samuel M Osborne (Father), 1525 Wakeling St., Frankford, Philadelphia, Pennsylvania [ANC] [S2] [SW]

Osborne, Wendell H., Jr., Cpl., Hdqtrs., 7th Regt., New York, DDS, January 28, 1919 at New York. Wendell H. Osborne (Father), 51 Lewis Ave., Lansdowne, Pennsylvania [S4]

Otis, Joseph Harvey, Pvt., Casual Det., MB, Navy Yard, Washington, D.C., DDS, August 25, 1919 at Washington, D.C. Margaret Otis (Mother), Yuma, California [ANC] [S4]

Ott, Harvey Ephraim, Pvt., 80th Co., 6th Regt., KIA, September 15, 1918 in the St. Mihiel Offensive. Samuel Ott (Father), 367 Second Ave., Phoenixville, Pennsylvania [FAG] [S2] [SW]

Otto, William Henry, Cpl., 45th Co., 5th Regt., KIA, June 6, 1918 in the Chateau-Thierry Sector. Martha Otto (Mother), 2121 Addison St., Chicago, Illinois [S2] [SW says William Herman]

Ouzts, Joseph Percy, Pvt., 51st Co., 5th Regt., DOW, June 11, 1918 in the Chateau-Thierry Sector. Eva E. Ouzts (Mother), Edgefield, South Carolina [ABMC- Belleau] [S2] [SW1]

Overland, John Albert, Drummer, 15th Co., 6th MG Bn., KIA, June 15, 1918 in the Chateau-Thierry Sector. Albert G. Overland (Father), 517 Barton St., Camden, New Jersey [ABMC- Belleau] [S2] [SW]

Overton, John W., 2nd Lieut., 80th Co., 6th Regt., KIA, July 19, 1918 in the Aisne Marne. Mrs. J. M. Overton (Mother), 901 Stahlman Bldg., Nashville, Tennessee [S1] [SW]

Marine Corps Deaths, 1917-1921

Overton, Macon C., Capt., 76th Co., 6th Regt., KIA, November 1, 1918 in the Meuse Argonne. Mrs. Margaret C. Overton (Mother), 1809 Pike Ave., Ensley, Alabama [ABMC- Romagne] [S1] [SW1]

Owen, Elmer Walton, Pvt., Bks. Det., MB, Portsmouth, New Hamphire, DDS, November 15, 1920 at Portsmouth, New Hampshire. Mary Owen (Mother), Bonham, Texas [FAG] [S4]

Owen, Orville Lathrop, Pvt., USS *Gulfport*, DAS, June 29, 1919 at San Pedro de Macoris, Dominican Republic. Oscar Lee Owen (Father), Dighton, Kansas [S4]

Owens, Frank Robert, Pvt., Bks. Det., Philadelphia, Pennsylvania, DDS, June 7, 1918 at Philadelphia, Pennsylvania. Owen Owens (Father), Sandusky, New York [S3]

Owens, James Edward, Pvt., 97th Co., 6th Regt., KIA, July 19, 1918 in the Aisne Marne. Josephine Owens (Mother), Bennett, Colorado [ABMC- Fere] [S2] [SW says Hdqrs. Co., 1st Repl. Btln.]

Owens, Stephan, Pvt., 74th Co., 6th Regt., KIA, October 8, 1918 in the Meuse Argonne. W. O. Butcher (Friend), 14 New Chambers St., New York, New York [ABMC- Romagne] [S2] [SW1]

Pace, Percy Lefatte, Pvt., 25th Co., 4th Regt., Dominican Republic, DDS, October 7, 1921 at Santo Domingo, Dominican Republic. Miss Claudie Lee Pace (Sister), Grayson, Louisiana [S4]

Pack, Alonzo Gilbert, Pvt., 81st Co., 6th MG Bn., DOW, July 19, 1918 in the Aisne Marne. Dela Pack (Mother), 161 Highland Ave., Winston-Salem, North Carolina [ABMC- Belleau TOM] [S2] [SW1]

Page, Allison Martin, Cpl., 47th Co., 5th Regt., DOW, June 25, 1918 in the Chateau-Thierry Sector. Ella Martin Page (Mother), Aberdeen, North Carolina [ABMC- Belleau] [S2] [SW]

Marine Corps Deaths, 1917-1921

Page, Percy Sherman, Pvt., 83rd Co., 6th Regt., KIA, July 19, 1918 in the Aisne Marne. Daisy E. Page (Mother), Clark, Jefferson County, Kentucky [ABMC- Fere] [S2] [SW]

Paine, Edward Greenman, Pvt., 16th Co., 5th Regt., DOW, October 17, 1918 in the Meuse Argonne. Arthur B. Paine (Father), P O Box 1982, Boston, Massachusetts [FAG] [S2] [SW1]

Paine, Herbert Adams., Sgt., Hdqtrs. Co., 5th Regt., KIA, November 1, 1918 in the Meuse Argonne. Samuel Paine (Uncle), Gen. Del., Bangor, Maine [ABMC- Romagne] [S2] [SW1]

Paisley, John, Pvt. Squadron E, MAF, Haiti, DDS, December 23, 1919 at Port au Prince, Haiti. Lilly Paisley (Mother), West Newton, Pennsylvania [S4]

Palmer, Harold T., 2nd Lieut., 51st Co., 5th Regt., KIA, October 3, 1918 in the Meuse Argonne. Mrs. Abbie C.Palmer (Mother), Willoughby, Ohio [ABMC-Romagne says 1st Lieut.] [S1] [SW]

Palmer, Jesse Adrian, Pvt., 74th Co., 6th Regt., KIA, July 19, 1918 in the Aisne Marne. Jesse Palmer (Mother), Huntsville, Texas [ABMC- Fere] [S2] [SW]

Palmer, Merlin Ellmer, Pvt., 17th Co., 5th Regt., KIA, October 5, 1918 in the Meuse Argonne. Judson A. Palmer (Father), Stamford, Nebraska [ABMC- Romagne] [S2] [SW1]

Pangburn, William Botts, Pvt., 55th Co., 5th Regt., DOW, October 6, 1918 in the Meuse Argonne. Charles G. Pangburn (Father), Mount Sterling, Kentucky [FAG] [S2] [SW1 says KIA]

Pankau, Robert Edward, Pvt., Bks. Det., Philadelphia, Pennsylvania, DDS, January 15, 1918 at Philadelphia, Pennsylvania. Marie R. Weaber (Mother), 219 W. Overland St., El Paso, Texas [S3]

Pankow, Henry, Pvt., 84th Co., 6th Regt., DOW, June 6, 1918 in the Chateau-Thierry Sector. Julius Pankow (Mother), 2718 Keeler Ave., Chicago, Illinois [S2] [SW]

Marine Corps Deaths, 1917-1921

Parent, Ernest Arthur, Cpl., 133rd 1st Replacement Batt., DOD, March 15, 1918 in France. Mr. Henry J. Parent (Father), 20 Newton St., Hoyoke, Massachusetts [R] [S2]

Parfet, Richard W., Captain, MCR, Hdqtrs., USMC, DAS, February 16, 1919 in an automobile accident at Washington, D.C. Mary E. Parfet (Widow), American University Park, Washington, D.C. [ANC] [S4]

Park, James McCalla, Pvt., 67th Co., 5th Regt., KIA, June 6, 1918 in the Chateau-Thierry Sector. Carrie R. Park (Mother), 385 S. Pryor St., Atlanta, Georgia [ABMC-Belleau] [S2] [SW1]

Parke, Frederick John, Pvt., 74th Co., Quantico, Virginia, DDS, June 29, 1921 at Quantico, Virginia. Marina Delgado (Mother), Hyde Park Hotel, Chicago, Illinois [ANC] [S4]

Parker, Donald Martin, Cpl., 80th Co., 6th Regt., KIA, September 15, 1918 in the St. Mihiel Offensive. Esther J. Parker (Mother), 281 Pleasant St., Leominster, Massachusetts [ABMC- Thiaucourt] [S2] [SW1 says DOW]

Parker, Howard LeRoy, Gy. Sgt., 3rd Co., Signal, League Island, DDS, February 11, 1920 at League Island, Pennsylvania. Jane Parker (Mother), E. Morrell St., Streator, Illinois [FAG] [S4]

Parker, Warren Judge, Sgt., QM Sgt., Bks. Det., Philadelphia, Pennsylvania, DDS, October 6, 1918 at Philadelphia, Pennsylvania. Jennie S. Parker (Mother), 38 W. 71st St., Chicago, Illinois [FAG] [S3]

Parkhurst, Andrew William, Pvt., 20th Co., 5th Regt., KIA, June 21, 1918 in the Chateau-Thierry Sector. William Parkhurst (Father), 16 Thomas St., Newark, New Jersey [R] [S2] [SW1]

Parkton, Otis H., Pvt., 96th Co., 6th Regt., DOW, July 19, 1918 in the Aisne Marne. Ernest R. Parkton (Father), Eugene, Oregon [FAG] [S2]

Marine Corps Deaths, 1917-1921

Parmerton, Foster, Pvt., 47th Co., 5th Regt., KIA, October 4, 1918 in the Meuse Argonne. Miss Mary L. Foster (Aunt), 36 Bedford Terrace, Northampton, Massachusetts [R] [S2] [SW says Co. C, Repl. Btln.]

Parmley, William Brackson, Sgt., 18th Co., 5th Regt., KIA, June 6, 1918 in the Chateau-Thierry Sector. N. R. Parmley (Father), Newton, Iowa [FAG] [S2] [SW]

Parr, Charles Earnest, Cpl., Hdqtrs. Co., 13th Regt., DOD, October 3, 1918 in France. Lilly Parr (Mother), 205 East Locust St., San Antonio, Texas [ABMC- Fere] [S2]

Parrott, Earl Leroy, Pvt., 15th Co., 6th MG Bn., KIA, October 4, 1918 in the Meuse Argonne. Charles L. Parrott (Father), 195 E. McMillan St., Cincinnati, Ohio [ABMC-Romagne] [S2] [SW1]

Parrott, Samuel, Pvt., 49th Co., 5th Regt., DOO, November 16, 1917 in France. Mrs. L. B. Byrnum (Mother), 202 Pollock St., New Bern, North Carolina [R] [S2]

Parrott, Stephen Ormsby, Jr., Pvt., 51st Co., 5th Regt., KIA, June 26, 1918 in the Chateau-Thierry Sector. Mrs. Wm. Yankey (Sister), Springfield, Kentucky [ABMC-Romagne] [S2] [SW says Parrett and C Co., Repl. Btln.]

Parsons, Clyde Earl, Pvt., 47th Co., 5th Regt., KIA, October 4, 1918 in the Meuse Argonne. Amy Parsons (Mother), St. George, Tucker Co., West Virginia [R] [S2] [SW1]

Parsons, Frank Harrison, Pvt., NOP, S. Charleston, West Virginia, DDS, October 21, 1918 at South Charleston, West Virginia. Adrian A. Parsons (Mother), RR, Plainfield, Indiana [FAG] [S3]

Parsons, Frank Vinsanhaler, Pvt., Co. E, 11th Regt., Quantico, Virginia, DDS, October 6, 1918 at Quantico, Virginia. Robert H. Parsons (Father), Box 116, Bastrop, Louisiana [S3]

Marine Corps Deaths, 1917-1921

Parsons, John Milton, Cpl., 15th Co., 6th MG Bn., KIA, October 4, 1918 in the Meuse Argonne. Granville Parsons (Mother), Cynthiana, Kentucky [FAG] [S2] [SW]

Partain, Abner Burns, Pvt., Co. A, 13th Regt., DOD, September 24, 1918 enroute to France. Mrs. Ella Partain (Mother), Gonzales, Texas [R] [S2]

Patch, Eckley Erwin, 1st Sgt., MD Sub Base, New London, Connecticut, DDS, February 12, 1920 at New London, Connecticut William J. Patch(Father), Bath, Maine [S4]

Patchin, Leroy Leslie, Pvt., 75th Co., 6th Regt., KIA, July 19, 1918 in the Aisne Marne. Charles A. Patchin (Father), Seneca, Nebraska [FAG] [S2] [SW]

Patient, James Rutley, Pvt., 55th Co., 5th Regt., DOW, June 3, 1918 in the Aisne Defensive. Fannie Patient (Mother), 1202½ Third Ave., Rock Island, Illinois [ABMC-Belleau] [S2] [SW]

Patterson, Chester Arthur, Pvt., Bks. Det., Philadelphia, Pennsylvania, DDS, September 30, 1918 at Philadelphia, Pennsylvania. Emma B. Patterson (Mother), 67 Lincoln Ave., Carbondale, Pennsylvania [S3]

Patterson, Frank G., Pvt., Co. I, 11th Regt., Quantico, Virginia, DDS, September 26, 1918 at Quantico, Virginia. Ellis Patterson (Father), Lincoln, Idaho [FAG] [S3]

Patterson, James Andrew, Sgt., 16th Co., 5th Regt., KIA, June 7, 1918 in the Chateau-Thierry Sector. John Patterson (Father), Goldtown, West Virginia [S2] [SW]

Patterson, James Jenkin, Pvt., 17th Co., 5th Regt., KIA, June 6, 1918 in the Chateau-Thierry Sector. William Patterson (Father), 334 Highland St., DuBois, Pennsylvania [FAG] [S2] [SW]

Patterson, John E., Sgt., Naval Pr. Det., MB, Navy Yard, Mare Island, California, DDS, January 25, 1920 at Mare Island, California. Thomas Patterson (Father), Wilderding, Pennsylvania [S4]

Marine Corps Deaths, 1917-1921

Patterson, Lillian M., (Female), Pvt., RS, New York, DDS, March 27, 1919 at New York, New York. Albert E. Patterson (Husband), 439 Ocean Ave., Woodhaven, New York [S4]

Patterson, Robert Fletcher, Pvt., Co. K, 13th Regt., DOD, October 11, 1918 in France. Millie Patterson (Mother), Verona, Mississippi [R] [S2]

Patterson, Thomas Frederick, Pvt., 83rd Co., 6th Regt., KIA, July 19, 1918 in the Aisne Marne. John Patterson (Father), Eupora, Mississippi [ABMC- Fere] [S2] [SW says 144th Co., Repl.]

Pattison, David Morrison, Pvt., 148th Co., Washington, D.C., DDS, October 4, 1918 at Washington, D.C. Charles and Nancy Pattison (Parents), RFD#2, Newcastle, Pennsylvania [S3]

Patton, Philip E., Cpl., Hdqtrs., 2nd Brigade, Domincan Republic, DDS, January 2, 1919 at Santo Domingo, Dominican Republic. Edward O. Patton (Father), 4437 Whetsel Ave., Madisonville, Ohio [S4]

Payne, Ernest Clearance, Pvt., Hdqtrs., 2nd Regt., Haiti, DOS, August 22, 1921 at Cape Haitien, Haiti. Alice Johnson (Mother), 142 W. 3rd St., Mt. Vernon, New York [S4]

Payton, Thomas Walter, Cpl., Hdqtrs. Co., 6th Regt., DOD, February 14, 1919 in France. Benjamin Payton (Father), Reed Point, Montana [FAG] [S2]

Peake, William P., Captain, MCR, NH, Fort Lyon, Colorado, DDS, October 19, 1919 at Fort Lyon, Colorado. Ethel M. Peake (Widow), 269 East Georgia Ave., Atlanta, Georgia [FAG] [S4]

Peckenpaugh, Loye Bryan, Pvt., 81st Co., 6th MG Bn., KIA, July 19, 1918 in the Aisne Marne. Lee Peckenpaugh (Brother), Skedee, Oklahoma [FAG] [S2] [SW1]

Pedersen, Alfred Joseph, Pvt., 95th Co., 6th Regt., DOW, August 2, 1918 in the Aisne Marne. Neils Pedersen (Father), 917

Marine Corps Deaths, 1917-1921

25th Ave., Tampa, Florida [R] [S2] [SW says Co. A, Repl. Btln.]

Pedersen, Wallace Victor, Pvt., 76th Co., 6th Regt., KIA, July 19, 1918 in the Aisne Marne. Charles H. Pedersen (Father), 2012 W. 2nd St., Duluth, Minnesota [S2] [SW]

Peebles, Edmund Everett, Pvt., 67th Co., 5th Regt., KIA, June 6, 1918 in the Chateau-Thierry Sector. Mrs. Harriet F. Peebles (Mother), 340 McClellan Ave., Detroit, Michigan [S2] [SW]

Peebles, Robert Barclay Jr., Pvt., 80th Co., 6th Regt., KIA, September 12, 1918 in the St. Mihiel Offensive. Robert B. Peebles (Father), 3715 Flora Ave., Kansas City, Missouri [ABMC- Thiaucourt] [S2] [SW1]

Peeler, Benjamin Adis, Pvt., 66th Co., 5th Regt., KIA, June 6, 1918 in the Chateau-Thierry Sector. Mrs. Mary Brooks (Mother), High Shoals, Georgia [FAG] [S2]

Peers, David Kennett, Cpl., 47th Co., 5th Regt., KIA, June 25, 1918 in the Chateau-Thierry Sector. John C. Peers (Father), 1315 Central National Bank, St. Louis, Missouri [ABMC- Belleau] [S2] [SW]

Peggs, John Clayton, Sgt., 17th Co., 5th Regt., KIA, June 15, 1918 in the Chateau-Thierry Sector. Mrs. Mary Peggs (Mother), 18 Buck St., Canton, New York [R] [S2] [SW]

Pellington, Raymond, Cpl., 82nd Co., 6th Regt., KIA, June 8, 1918 in the Chateau-Thierry Sector. Margaret J. Pellington (Mother), 424 Cadillac St., Montreal, Canada [FAG] [S2] [SW]

Peloubet, William Francis, Pvt., 74th Co., 6th Regt., KIA, June 5, 1918 in the Aisne Defensive. Francis W Peloubet (Father), RFD#1, Asheville, North Carolina [ABMC- Belleau] [S2] [SW]

Pence, Fred Leon, Pvt., 45th Co., 5th Regt., KIA, June 26, 1918 in the Chateau-Thierry Sector. Finley Pence (Brother), 503 German St., Erie, Pennsylvania [S2] [SW1 says DOW]

Pence, Walter Raymond, Pvt., 76th Co., 6th Regt., DOD, October 18, 1918 in France. Walter S. Pence (Father), 603 N. Main St., Sidney, Ohio [FAG] [S2]

Pendleton, William R., Cpl., MD, USNH, Fort Lyon, Colorado, DDS, October 18, 1920 at Fort Lyon, Colorado. Disa m. Pendleton (Mother), 107 Ashley St., Jefferson City, Missouri [S4]

Penkal, Joseph, Pvt., 15th Co., 6th MG Bn., KIA, October 4, 1918 in the Meuse Argonne. Mrs Lena Penkal (Mother), 5253 Newland Ave., Chicago, Illinois [ANC] [S2] [SW]

Penney, Henry, Pvt., 49th Co., 5th Regt., KIA, June 6, 1918 in the Chateau-Thierry Sector. Charles A. Penney (Father), RFD #7, Danville, Illinois [S2] [SW says 49th Co. to Repl.]

Pennington, William Earl, Pvt., 80th Co., 6th Regt., KIA, September 15, 1918 in the St. Mihiel Offensive. Mrs. Laura E. Pennington (Mother), Leon St., Gatesville, Texas [FAG] [S2] [SW]

Penwright, Charles Alburn, Pvt., 97th Co., 6th Regt., DOW, June 7, 1918 in the Chateau-Thierry Sector. Mary Penwright (Mother), 115 N. Admire Ave., El Reno, Oklahoma [ABMC- Belleau] [S2] [SW]

Perkins, Clyde Aurelius, Pvt., Co. I, 13th Regt., DOD, September 27, 1918 enroute to France. Aurelius S. Perkins (Father), Elkton, Kentucky [R] [S2]

Perkins, Ernest A., Major, Hdqrs. Co., 5th Brigade, DOD, November 16, 1918 in France. Mrs. Rosalie L. Perkins (Widow), 216 Middle St., Portsmouth, Virginia [R] [S1]

Perkins, Glenn Callan, Pvt., 84th Co., 6th Regt., KIA [SW] [SW1 reported to have been found alive]

Perkins, Luther Allen, Pvt., 95th Co., 6th Regt., KIA, July 19, 1918 in the Aisne Marne. Laura J. Perkins (Mother), 424 South 3rd St., Paducah, Kentucky [VA-Dayton] [S2]

Marine Corps Deaths, 1917-1921

Perkins, Tandy Ross, Pvt., Co. I, 13th Regt., DOD, September 24, 1918 enroute to France. Sallie M. Perkins (Mother), Elkton, Kentucky [R] [S2]

Perkins, Thomas Clifton, Pvt., MD, NPG, Indian Head, Maryland, DDS, October 21, 1918 at Indian Head, Maryland. Frankie Perkins (Mother), Hartsville, Tennessee [S3]

Perrottet, LaVerne Thompson, Pvt., 76th Co., 6th Regt., KIA, June 15, 1918 in the Chateau-Thierry Sector. Arthur Perrottet (Father), 615 N. Wheaton Ave., Wheaton, Illinois [FAG] [S2] [SW]

Perry, Aubrey Hastings, Pvt., 55th Co., 5th Regt., KIA, June 12, 1918 in the Chateau-Thierry Sector. Ester Perry (Mother), 912 Salem Ave., Roanoke, Virginia [ABMC- Belleau] [S2] [SW1]

Perry, Benjamin, Jr., Cpl., 81st Co., 6th MG Bn., DOW, June 13, 1918 in the Chateau-Thierry Sector. Benjamin Perry, Sr. (Father), 365 River Road, Bethesda, Maryland [ANC] [S2] [SW says 6th Regt.]

Perry, Clyde Troy, Pvt., 75th Co., 6th Regt., DOW, December, 7, 1918 in the St. Mihiel Offensive. Hosa Perry (Uncle) Gen. Del., Rayalton, Illinois [ABMC-Suresnes] [S2] [SW says Co. A, 3rd Sep. Btln.]

Perry, Willis F., Pvt., Hdqtrs. Det., MB, Navy Yard, Philadelphia, Pennsylvania, DDS, July 21, 1920 at League Island, Pennsylvania. L. Perry (Uncle), 123 E. Frederick St., Lancaster, Pennsylvania [FAG] [S4]

Peters, Anthony, Pvt., 8th Co., 5th Regt., KIA, November 1, 1918 in the Meuse Argonne. Anthomy Mastropio (Father), 36 Hulin St., Mechanicsville, New York [S2] [SW1]

Petersen, Ludwig Marius, Pvt., Hdqtrs. Co., 6th Regt., KIA, November 2, 1918 in the Meuse Argonne. Mary Petersen (Mother), 948 Adams St., Berlin, Wisconsin [ABMC-Romagne] [S2]

Marine Corps Deaths, 1917-1921

Petersen, Nels Jacob, Pvt., 67th Co., 5th Regt., DOW, August 23, 1918 in the Aisne Marne. Mrs. Caroline A. Petersen (Mother), Dayton, Idaho [FAG] [S2] [SW]

Peterson, Ernest P. J., Pvt., 74th Co., 6th Regt., DOW, April 30, 1918 in the Toulon Sector, Verdun. Christine Peterson (Mother), 6937 South Aberdeen St., Chicago, Illinois [ABMC- Romagne] [S2] [SW says Petersen]

Peterson, Frank Edward, Pvt., 18th Co., 5th Regt., KIA, June 14, 1918 in the Chateau-Thierry Sector. Mary C. Peterson (Mother), Box 272, Park City, Utah [FAG] [S2] [SW]

Peterson, James Christian, Jr., Pvt., Co. F, 11th Regt., Quantico, Virginia, DDS, September 26, 1918 at Quantico, Virginia. James C. Peterson, Sr. (Father), Marmarth, North Dakota [FAG] [S3]

Peterson, Kimball Canute, Pvt., 76th Co., 6th Regt., DOW, July 19, 1918 in the Aisne Marne. Carolina Peterson (Mother), Ephraim, Utah [FAG] [S2] [SW1 says KIA]

Peterson, Lawrence Oscar, Pvt., 96th Co., 6th Regt., DOD, May 13, 1919 in France. Mrs. Wilhelmina Peterson (Mother), 5007 N. Sawyer Ave., Chicago, Illinois [R] [S2]

Peterson, Levi Franklin, Pvt., 84th Co., 6th Regt., KIA, July 19, 1918 in the Aisne Marne. Gunda Peterson (Mother), Monticello, Utah [FAG] [S2] [SW says 139th Co., Repl. Btln.]

Peterson, Louis, Sgt., 67th Co., 5th Regt., DOW, June 8, 1918 in the Chateau-Thierry Sector. Mrs. Lena Lee (Aunt), 1849 W. Chicago Ave., Chicago, Illinois [R] [S2] [SW says Lewis Petersen and Cpl.]

Peterson, Louis, Pvt., 23rd Co., 6th MG Bn., KIA, October 9, 1919 in the Meuse Argonne. Peter Peterson (Father), Little Pine Route, Aitkin, Minnesota [R] [S2] [SW]

Peterson, Martin, Cpl., 96th Co., 6th Regt., DOW, July 19, 1918 in the Aisne Marne. Carey Olson (Mother), Widom, Minnesota [S2] [SW1 says KIA]

Marine Corps Deaths, 1917-1921

Peterson, Olaf Axel, Pvt., Co. D, 13th Regt., DOD, October 2, 1918 in France. Eric A. Peterson (Father), 123 Parker Place, Trenton, New Jersey [FAG] [S2]

Peterson, Swen Harry, Pvt., 96th Co., 6th Regt., KIA, July 19, 1918 in the Aisne Marne. John Peterson (Father), Route 2, Box 45, Craig, Nebraska [FAG] [S2] [SW says B Co., Repl. Btln.]

Petrie, Maitland B., Cpl., Athletic Det., Parris Island, South Carolina, DOS, January 26, 1919 at Newark, New Jersey. Dr. Charles S. Ripley (Stepfather), 56 Livingston St., Brooklyn, New York [S4]

Petticord, Cecil Louis, Cpl., 95th Co., 6th Regt., KIA, July 19, 1918 in the Aisne Marne. Alonzo Petticord (Father), 922 National Road, Wheeling, West Virginia [ANC] [S2] [SW1]

Pfrengle, Walter Edward, Pvt., 8th Co., 5th Regt., DOD, October 16, 1918 in France. John Pfrengle (Father), 217 N. Clark St., Chicago, Illinois [ABMC- Fere] [S2] [SW]

Phalen, James Edward, Pvt., 96th Co., 6th Regt., KIA, November 1, 1918 in the Meuse Argonne. Bridget Phalen (Mother), 2567 Parks Ave., Chicago, Illlinois [ABMC- Romagne] [S2] [SW1]

Pharr, Robert S., Pvt., 25th Co., 4th Prov. Regt., Dominican Republic, DDS, January 8, 1919 at Santo Domingo, Dominican Republic. Alonzo Pharr (Father), RFD#4, Laurel, Mississippi [FAG] [S4]

Phelps, William Ernest, Pvt., 84th Co., 6th Regt., DOW, July 19, 1918 in the Aisne Marne. Minnie Phelps (Mother), Marquand, Missouri [ABMC- Fere] [S2] [SW1 says KIA]

Philblad, Harry William, Cpl., 78th Co., 6th Regt., KIA, October 6, 1918 in the Meuse Argonne. Mrs. Emma Philblad (Mother), Knoxville, Illinois [FAG] [S2] [SW1]

Marine Corps Deaths, 1917-1921

Phillips, Charles Arthur, Pvt., 79th Co., 6th Regt., KIA, July 19, 1918 in the Aisne Marne. Mrs. W. R. Phillips (Mother), 389 Magnolia St., Rochester, New York [S2] [SW1]

Phillips, Gail Oakley, Cpl., 45th Co., 5th Regt., DOW, June 18, 1918 in the Chateau-Thierry Sector. Darius Phillips (Father), 342 Eastern Ave., Herkimer, New York [ABMC- Suresnes] [S2] [SW]

Phillips, Harvey Carlton, Pvt., 18th Co., 5th Regt., KIA, June 12, 1918 in the Chateau-Thierry Sector. Margaret Phillips (Mother), 909 Gramercy Place, Los Angeles, California [ABMC- Belleau] [S2] [SW]

Phillips, John Marcus, Gy. Sgt., Rhine River Patrol, DOO, May 13, 1919 in France. Mrs. Edith Phillips (Mother), 417 Hampton Ave., Wilkinsburg, Pennsylvania [R] [S2]

Phillips, Robert Harold, Pvt., 158th Co. (Signal), Philadelphia, Pennsylvania, DDS, October 6, 1918 at Philadelphia, Pennsylvania. Mrs. Florence Phillips (Wife), 30 Medfield St., Boston, Massachusetts [S3]

Phillips, William Bryan, Pvt., 43rd Co., 5th Regt., DOD, September 19, 1918 in France. Mrs. Sarah Phillips (Mother), Route #2, Prescott, Kansas [R] [S2]

Philo, Leonard Delbert, Pvt., 95th Co., 6th Regt., DOW, July 19, 1918 in the Aisne Marne. Joshua Philo (Father), 1220 New York Ave., Lansing, Michigan [ABMC- Fere] [S2] [SW1]

Pickartz, Walter Bernard, Pvt., 95th Co., 6th Regt., DOW, June 28, 1918 in the Chateau-Thierry Sector. Carrie Pickartz (Mother), 1304 Nelson St., Chicago, Illinois [R] [S2] [SW says Pichartz]

Pickle, James Clarence, Pvt., Co. A, 11th Regt., Quantico, Virginia, DDS, September 28, 1918 at Quantico, Virginia. Mrs. Ellen Pickle (Mother), 432 Sunset St., Dallas, Texas [S3]

Marine Corps Deaths, 1917-1921

Pieper, Bernard P., Pvt., 83rd Co., 6th Regt., KIA, October 10, 1918 in the Meuse Argonne. William Pieper (Father), c/o Bank of Cameron, Cameron, Wisconsin [S2] [SW1]

Pierce, John R., Pvt., OSD, Quantico, Virginia, DDS, November 17, 1918 at Quantico, Virginia. John Pierce (Father), RDD#1, Elizabeth, Pennsylvania [S4]

Piercey, James R., Pvt., Co. D, 10th Sep. Bn., Quantico, Virginia, DDS, November 18, 1918 at Quantico, Virginia. Martha . Piercey (Mother), Olean, Missouri [FAG] [S4]

Pierson, Walter Edwin, Pvt., 74th Co., 6th Regt., KIA, July 19, 1918 in the Aisne Marne. Annette Pierson (Mother), 1645 Olive Ave., Chicago, Illinois [ABMC- Belleau TOM as W.E.] [S2] [SW]

Pietz, John Louis, Pvt., 80th Co., 6th Regt., KIA, October 5, 1918 in the Meuse Argonne. Louis Pietz (Father), Pillager, Minnesota [FAG] [S2] [SW1]

Pigott, Raymond Willard, Pvt., 95th Co., 6th Regt., KIA, July 19, 1918 in the Aisne Marne. Dexter L. Pigott (Father), Long Bottom, Meigs Co., Ohio [ANC] [S2] [SW]

Pihl, Axel, Pvt., Co. B, Mare Island, California, DDS, October 17, 1919 at Mare Island, California. Christine Pihl (Mother), Alder Grove, British Columbia, Canada [FAG] [S4]

Pike, Jesse B., Sgt., 40th Co., Brooklyn, New York, DDS, January 23, 1919 at Brooklyn, New York. James D. Pike (Brother), Dyersburg, Tennessee [S4]

Pilcher, Luther Wade, Sgt., 20th Co., 5th Regt., KIA, June 6, 1918 in the Chateau-Thierry Sector. W. E. Pilcher (Brother), 208 N. Franklin St., Mobile, Alabama [ABMC- Belleau] [S2] [SW]

Pilkington, Robert Edward, Pvt., 23rd Co., 6th MG Bn., KIA, October 9, 1918 in the Meuse Argonne. John Pilkington (Father), 1245 South Emporia St., Wichita, Kansas [FAG] [S2] [SW]

Pinkerton, Raymond Alvin, Pvt., 80th Co., 6th Regt., DOW, July 19, 1918 in the Aisne Marne. Robert W. Pinkerton (Father), 141 N. Broadway, Middletown, Ohio [S2] [SW1]

Pitman, Dewey Lawrence, Pvt., 83rd Co., 6th Regt., KIA, July 19, 1918 in the Aisne Marne. Maude Pittman (Mother), 203 Belmont St., San Antonio, Texas [S2] [SW]

Pizer, Nathan Louis, Pvt., 79th Co., 6th Regt., KIA, June 8, 1918 in the Chateau-Thierry Sector. Sam Pizer (Father), 111 Bryan St., Houston, Texas [FAG] [S2] [SW]

Placek, Joseph Theodore, Pvt., 45th Co., 5th Regt., KIA, June 24, 1918 in the Chateau-Thierry Sector. August Placek (Uncle), 1825 Webster Ave., Chicago, llinois [ABMC-Fere] [S2] [SW1]

Platt, Chester Erastus., Cpl., 45th Co., 5th Regt., KIA, June 6, 1918 in the Chateau-Thierry Sector. Lettie Platt (Mother), 401 N. 24th St., Lafayette, Indiana [FAG] [S2] [SW]

Platt, William Henry, Jr., Sgt., Hdqtrs. Co., 6th Regt., DOW, July 19, 1918 in the Aisne Marne. Hannah Platt (Mother), 936 Lakeside Place, Chicago, Illinois [S2] [SW1]

Pleisch, Cecil Winford, Pvt., 16th Co., 5th Regt., KIA, June 25, 1918 in the Chateau-Thierry Sector. Mary Pleisch (Mother), Gen. Del., Anderson, California [ABMC-Belleau TOM] [S2] [SW]

Plimpton, Robert Scarff, Pfc. 1st Class, 110th Co., 8th Regt., Galveston, Texas, DAS, September 10, 1918 of an accidental gunshot wound at Galveston, Texas. Cora H. Plimpton (Mother), Gen. Del., Modesto, California [S3]

Ploenges, Louis, Pvt., 78th Co., 6th Regt., KIA, September 15, 1918 in the St. Mihiel Offensive. Christ Ploenges (Father), R J2-274, Indianapolis, Indiana [S2] [SW1]

Plummer, Roy St. Valentine, Pvt., Bks. Det., Norfolk, Virginia, DDS, October 15, 1918 at Norfolk, Virginia. Mrs. James

Marine Corps Deaths, 1917-1921

C. Plummer (Mother), 711 Austin St., Houston, Texas [S3]

Poague, Walter S., 1st Lieut., U.S. Naval Base #13, 1st Mar. Aero Co., KOA, November 5, 1918 in the Azores. Charles M. Poague (Father), 1204 E. 63rd St., Chicago, Illinois [FAG] [S1] [SW1]

Poe, William Horace, Pvt., 76th Co., 6th Regt., KIA, November 5, 1918 in the Meuse Argonne. William H. Poe (Father), Chatchee, Alabama [FAG] [S2] [SW1]

Pohnke, Lambert Louis, Pvt., Medical Department, USS *Wyoming*, USMC, DOD, May 6, 1918 enroute to France. Mrs. Mary Pohnke (Mother), Goodells, Michigan [R] [S2]

Pol, Cornelius, Pvt., 49th Co., 5th Regt., DOW, November 12, 1918 in the Meuse Argonne. Jennie Pol (Mother), 1463 W. 73rd Place, Chicago, Illinois [R] [S2] [SW1]

Polhemus, John Cruser, Pvt., 78th Co., 6th Regt., KIA, June 26, 1918 in the Chateau-Thierry Sector. Lida A. Polhemus (Mother), Gen. Del., Flemington, New Jersey [FAG] [S2] [SW1]

Pollock, Frank John, Cpl., MCR, Depot of Supplies, Philadelphia, Pennsylvania, DDS, October 4, 1918 at Philadelphia, Pennsylvania. Rebecca Pollock (Wife), 3464 N. D. St., Philadelphia, Pennsylvania [S3]

Pollock, Norman, Pvt., 8th Co., 5th Regt., KIA, November 1, 1918 in in the Meuse Argonne. Georgiana Pollock (Mother), 1045 Sterling Place, Brooklyn, New York [ABMC-Romagne] [S2] [SW1]

Pomeroy, Albert Stanlely, Pvt., 15th Co., 6th MG Bn., KIA, July 19, 1918 in the Aisne Marne. Mary Przymusiniski (Mother), 527 Austin St., Toledo, Ohio [S2] [SW]

Pomeroy, Robert Owens, Cpl., 51st Co., 5th Regt., KIA, June 6, 1918 in the Chateau-Thierry Sector. Robert J. Pomeroy

Marine Corps Deaths, 1917-1921

(Father), 3608 Cedar Ave., Baltimore, Maryland [FAG] [S2] [SW]

Pond, Philip Marston, Cpl., 67th Co., 5th Regt., DOW, October 16, 1918 in the Meuse Argonne. Louisa Pond (Mother), 1444 22nd Ave., Seattle, Washington [ABMC- Thiaucourt] [S2] [SW1]

Poole, Irving Ray, Pvt., Supply Co., Quantico, Virginia, DAS, December 3, 1918 of an auto accident near Fredericksburg, Virginia. Mrs. Marion D. Poole (Wife), RFD, Oaklawn, Rhode Island [FAG] [S4]

Pope, Ivan L., Pvt., USS *Mississippi*, DDS, January 20, 1919 at Brooklyn, New York. George R. Pope (Father), Lake, Spencer County, Indiana [FAG] [S4]

Porter, Ernest Washington, Pvt., 23rd Co., 6th MG Bn., KIA, September 15, 1918 in the St. Mihiel Offensive. Ernest Porter (Father), 671 Summer Ave., Newark, New Jersey [ABMC- Thiaucourt] [S2] [SW]

Porter, Harvey Wilson, Pvt., Bks. Det., Quantico, Virginia, DDS, November 8, 1918 at Quantico, Virginia. John W. Porter (Father), Marceline, Missouri [S3]

Porter, Joseph E., Pvt., Co. A, 10th Sep. Bn., Quantico, Virginia, DDS, November 16, 1918 at Quantico, Virginia. Mrs. Willard Porter (Mother), RFD#2, Tazewell, Virginia [S4]

Porter, Roy A. Delbert, Pvt., 86th Co., Guantanamo Bay, Cuba, DDS, February 10, 1918 at San Juan, Santiago de Cuba. William Porter (Father), RFD#1, Heyburn, Idaho [S3]

Postlethwait, Randolph Ray, Pvt., Bks. Det., Quantico, Virginia, DDS, September 23, 1918 at Quantico, Virginia. Ellen Postlethwait (Mother), Folsom, West Virginia [S3]

Potter, Carl Orin, Pvt., 67th Co., 5th Regt., DOW, October 8, 1918 in the Meuse Argonne. Nathan C. Potter (Father), RR#2, Hector, Minnesota [R] [S2] [SW1]

Potts, David, Jr., Pvt., 20th Co., 5th Regt., KIA, November 2, 1918 in the Meuse Argonne. David Potts (Father), 29 Jensen

Marine Corps Deaths, 1917-1921

Ave., Mamaroneck, New York [ABMC- Romagne] [S2] [SW1]

Powell, Abe, Pvt., Guard Co. #2, Mare Island, California, DAS, July 8, 1920 drowned at Mare Island, California. Rose Powell (Mother), 515 E. Congress St., St. Paul, Minnesota [S4]

Powell, Walter Ernest, Pvt., 20th Co., 5th Regt., KIA, November 1, 1918 in the Meuse Argonne. Willard W. Powell (Brother), Bement, Illinois [ABMC- Romagne] [S2] [SW1]

Pozdol, John Joseph, Pvt., 81st Co., 6th MG Bn., KIA, June 7, 1918 in the Chateau-Thierry Sector. Hedgewick Pozdol (Mother), 235 Franklin St., Downers Grove, Illinois [ABMC- Belleau] [S2] [SW]

Pratt, Jesse Lounces, Pvt., 51st Co., 5th Regt., KIA, November 2, 1918 in the Meuse Argonne. Gannie Crook (Sister), Gen. Del., Tangier, Oklahoma [ABMC- Romagne] [S2] [SW1]

Prchal, William, Pvt., 76th Co., 6th Regt., KIA, June 16, 1918 in the Chateau-Thierry Sector. Frank Prchal (Father), 2012 S. Troop St., Chicago, Illinois [ABMC-Belleau] [S2] [SW]

Prescott, Argyle, Pvt., Bks. Det., Quantico, Virginia, DDS, October 18, 1918 at Quantico, Virginia. Florence Prescott (Mother), Heyburn, Idaho [FAG] [S3]

Price, Albert Daniel, Sgt., Eastern Recruiting Division, DDS, March 15, 1918 at Chelsea, Massachusetts. Mary B. Price (Wife), 675 Benington St., East, Boston, Massachusetts [S3]

Price, Charles Wesley, Drummer, 8th Co., 5th Regt., KIA, June 4, 1918 in the Aisne Defensive. Samuel Price, Jr. (Father), 16 N. Maine St., Pleasantville, New Jersey [FAG] [S2] [SW]

Price, Clarence W., Pvt., Supply Co., Parris Island, South Carolina, DDS, November 14, 1918 at Parris Island,

Marine Corps Deaths, 1917-1921

South Carolina. Myrtle Price (Mother), Rochelle, Texas [S4]

Price, David Francis, Cpl., 3rd Squadron, FMAF, DOD, November 3, 1918 in France. Lena Price (Mother), Boscobel, Wisconsin [ABMC-Bony] [S2]

Price, Ernest Carlial, Pvt., 51st Co., 5th Regt., KIA, October 4, 1918 in the Meuse Argonne. Erva J. Price (Mother), RFD#4, Hammondsport, New York [ABMC- Romagne] [S2] [SW1 as Ernest Carlisle Price]

Price, Ivan Leo, Pfc, 51st Co., 5th Regt., KIA, November 3, 1918 in the Meuse Argonne. Cora V. Price (Mother), 2021 E. 4th St., Long Beach, California [ABMC- Romagne] [S2] [SW1]

Price, Rusel, Pvt., 67th Co., 5th Regt., DOW, June 18, 1918 in the Chateau-Thierry Sector. Stephen B. Price (Father), Pine Hill, Rockcastle Co., Kentucky [R] [S2] [SW1]

Prichard, Wallace Bruce, Pvt., 76th Co., 6th Regt., KIA, June 12, 1918 in the Chateau-Thierry Sector. Eliza Rice (Mother), RFD#4, Holly, Michigan [ABMC- Belleau] [S2] [SW]

Primeau, Rudolpho J., Pvt., MB, Philadelphia, Pennsylvania, DDS, May 9, 1920 at League Island, Pennsylvania. Mrs. Alice Ludduc (Aunt), 22 Astor St., New Bedford, Massachusetts [S4]

Prindle, Sidney Edwin, Pvt., 83rd Co., 6th Regt., KIA, October 7, 1918 in the Meuse Argonne. Mrs. Maude Prindle (Mother), 519 Park Ave., East Orange, New Jersey [ABMC- Romagne] [S2] [SW1]

Probert, Francis Edgar, Pvt., 97th Co., 6th Regt., KIA, July 19, 1918 in the Aisne Marne. Nellie Probert (Mother), 312 South Whipple St., Chicago, Illinois [ABMC- Belleau] [S2] [SW]

Proctor, David Edward, Pvt., 49th Co., 5th Regt., KIA, June 6, 1918 in the Chateau-Thierry Sector. Catherine Proctor

Marine Corps Deaths, 1917-1921

(Mother), 36 Third St., E. Cambridge, Massachusetts [ABMC- Belleau TOM as D.E.] [S2] [SW]

Prohaska, Frank Boyce, Pvt., 96th Co., 6th Regt., DOW, June 30, 1918 in the Chateau-Thierry Sector. Mrs. Amelia E. Riley (Sister), 1322 Kelly St., Portland, Oregon [R] [S2] [SW says Co. B. Repl. Btln.]

Pross, Gustav Adolph, Pvt., 51st Co., 5th Regt., KIA, November 11, 1918 in the Meuse Argonne. Helen Pross (Mother), 50 Oak St., Gloversville, New York [S2] [SW1]

Prosser, Fred Ellsworth, Pvt., 45th Co., 5th Regt., KIA, June 24, 1918 in the Chateau-Thierry Sector. W. E. Prosser (Father), Newberg, Oregon [ABMC- Belleau] [S2] [SW]

Pruitt, Ballard Lee Edward, Pvt., 55th Co., 5th Regt., DOW, July 24, 1918 in the Chateau-Thierry Sector. Molly Pruitt (Mother), 232 Henry St., Danville, Virginia [FAG] [S2] [SW1]

Pruitt, John Henry, Cpl., 78th Co., 6th Regt., DOW, October 4, 1918 in the Meuse Argonne. Belle Pruitt (Mother), c/o Sec. Service Sta., Red Cross, Phoenix, Arizona [ANC] [S2] [SW says E Co.] [MOH]

Pugh, Arthur Cleo, Cpl., 20th Co., 5th Regt., KIA, June 14, 1918 in the Chateau-Thierry Sector. Miss Myrtle Pugh (Sister), Gowen, Oklahoma [ABMC- Belleau] [S2] [SW says 137th Co., Repl. Btln.]

Pugh, Herschell David, Pvt., 51st Co., 5th Regt., DOW, November 2, 1918 in the Meuse Argonne. Mrs. Catherine Pugh Morris (Mother), 307 Pleasant St., Utica, New York [S2] [SW1]

Pullman, John B., Pvt., MB, Parris Island, South Carolina, DDS, January 8, 1919 at Parris Island, South Carolina. John Pullman (Father), 1408 Clement St., Joliet, Illinois [S4]

Pummill, William Estel, Pvt., 96th Co., 6th Regt., KIA, July 19, 1918 in the Aisne Marne. Hezkiah Pummill (Father), Waynesville, Missouri [FAG] [S2] [SW1]

Marine Corps Deaths, 1917-1921

Pursley, Ernest Raymond, Pvt., 8th Co., 5th Regt., KIA, November 2, 1918 in the Meuse Argonne. Alice A. Pursley (Mother), 316 W. 17th St., Hopkinsville, Kentucky [FAG] [S2] [SW1]

Purtell, Thomas Brierly, Cpl., 77th Co., 6th MG Bn., KIA, October 4, 1918 in the Meuse Argonne. Jennie Purtell (Mother), 200 W. 99th St., New York, New York [ABMC-Romagne] [S2] [SW in "P" section as Thomas Brierly]

Purvis, Rudolph K., Pvt., Central Recruiting Division, DDS, December 1, 1918 at St. Paul, Minnesota. Charles W. Purvis (Father), Route #1, Beach, North Dakota [S4]

Putnam, Charles Lancaster, Cpl., 76th Co., 6th Regt., KIA, October 8, 1918 in the Meuse Argonne. Kate Putnam (Mother), 5120 Constance St., New Orleans, Louisana [ABMC-Romagne] [S2] [SW1]

Pyeatt, Walter James, Cpl., 4th Squadron, FMAF, DOD, September 29, 1918 in Harbor, Liverpool, England. Christopher Pyeatt (Father), 3934 Parnell St., St. Louis, Missouri [R] [S2]

Qualls, Orval Cecil, Pvt., 96th Co., 6th Regt., DOW, June 14, 1918 in the Chateau-Thierry Sector. Mollie Qualls (Mother), 418 E. Gray St., Norman, Oklahoma [S2] [SW says 137th Co., Repl. Btln.]

Quattlander, Paul Jefferson, Pvt., 95th Co., 6th Regt., DOW, July 20, 1918 in the Aisne Marne. Paul Quattlander (Father), 3001 Tennesse Ave., Central Park, Birmingham, Alabama [R] [S2] [SW]

Quilter, James Joseph W., Pvt., 95th Co., 6th Regt., KIA, June 13, 1918 in the Chateau-Thierry Sector. Richard J. Quilter (Brother), 3326 Walnut St., Chicago, Illinois [ABMC-Belleau] [S2] [SW]

Quinlan, Frank Thomas, Pvt., 83rd Co., 6th Regt., DOW, June 14, 1918 in the Chateau-Thierry Sector. Mary Quinlan (Mother), 303 Lake St., Manistique, Michigan [S2] [SW]

Marine Corps Deaths, 1917-1921

Quinlan, John Joseph, Cpl., San Diego, California, DDS, June 17, 1921 at San Diego, California. Mrs. Margaret Sheehan (Sister), Gen. Del., San Francisco, California [VA- Fort Rosecrans] [S4]

Quinn, Eric Dominic, Pvt., 16th Co., 5th Regt., KIA, June 23, 1918 in the Chateau-Thierry Sector. Elizabeth Quinn (Mother), 124 Greenwood Ave., Buffalo, New York [ABMC-Belleau TOM as E.D.] [S2] [SW]

Quinn, Joseph Francis, Pvt., 43rd Co., 5th Regt., DOW, October 4, 1918 in the Meuse Argonne. Thomas F. Quinn (Father), 240 S. 44th St., Philadelphia, Pennsylvania [FAG] [S2] [SW1]

Quinnelly, Charles Wickersham, Pvt., 95th Co., 6th Regt., DOW, October 11, 1918 in the Meuse Argonne. James T. Quinnelly (Father), 1308 Third Ave., N. Columbus, Mississippi [R] [S2] [SW says Co. A, 3rd Sep. Btln.]

Rabczynski, Stanley, Pvt., 6th Co., HA, Quantico, Virginia, DAS, December 2, 1917 accidently drowned at Quantico, Virginia. Kazimierz Rabczynski (Father), 54 Bromley Park, Roxbury, Massachusetts [ANC] [S3]

Racinowski, Stanley, Pvt., 51st Co., 5th Regt., KIA, November 9, 1918 in the Meuse Argonne. Steve Racinowski (Father), 240 Shanley St., Buffalo, New York [S2] [SW1]

Rada, Albert, Jr., Sgt., 74th Co., 6th Regt., DOW, April 16, 1918 in the Toulon Sector, Verdun. Albert Rada (Father), 2239 N. Spalding Ave., Chicago, Illinois [R] [S2] [SW]

Radcliffe, William Henry, Pvt., 96th Co., 6th Regt., KIA, October 3, 1918 in the Meuse Argonne. Mrs. Jennie Radcliffe (Mother), Jackson, Ohio [S2] [SW1]

Raggio, Albert Michael Angelo, Pvt., 78th Co., 6th Regt., KIA, June 25, 1918 in the Chateau-Thierry Sector. Louis Raggio (Father), 863 Amsterdam Ave., New York, New York [R] [S2] [SW says A Co., Repl. Btln.]

Marine Corps Deaths, 1917-1921

Rambath, Charles Elmer, Pvt., USNAD, Hingham, Massachusetts, DDS, September 28, 1918 at Gallops Island, Massachusetts. Sophia Rambath (Mother), 308 Grey St., Buffalo, New York [S3]

Ramold, John, Pvt., 45th Co., 5th Regt., KIA, June 7, 1918 in the Chateau-Thierry Sector. Andrew F. Ramold (Father), RFD#3, Nebraska City, Nebraska [S2] [SW1]

Randolph, Alfred C., Pvt., 31st Co., 2nd Prov. Regt., Dominican Republic, DOS, March 19, 1919 at Puerto Plata, Dominican Republic. Delia Randolph (Mother), 388 Manhattan Ave., New York, New York [S4]

Randolph, Bynum, Pvt., 79th Co., 6th Regt., DOW, July 31, 1918 in the Chateau-Thierry Sector. Mrs. J. B. Randolph (Mother), Cowan, Tennessee [R] [S2] [SW]

Randolph, John, Pvt., 45th Co., 5th Regt., KIA, November 4, 1918 in the Meuse Argonne. Theresa G. Randolph (Mother), 303 W. Euclid Ave., Pittsburg, Kansas [R] [S2] [SW1]

Rankin, Bruce Reyburn, Sgt., 95th Co., 6th Regt., DOW, July 19, 1918 in the Aisne Marne. Elizabeth Rankin (Mother), Media, Illinois [ABMC- Fere] [S2] [SW1]

Ratinski, Walter William, Pvt., 45th Co., 5th Regt., KIA, June 6, 1918 in the Chateau-Thierry Sector. Josephine Ratinski (Mother), 93 Jackson St., Rochester, New York [S2] [SW]

Rausch, John Earl, Pvt., 45th Co., 5th Regt., DOW, June 7, 1918 in the Chateau-Thierry Sector. Mrs. Mabel Harris (Aunt), 113 Northampton St., Easton, Pennsylvania [S2] [SW]

Rawlings, Rexall Joseph, Pvt., 43rd Co., 5th Regt., DOW, June 16, 1918 in the Chateau-Thierry Sector. Cora V. Rawlings Wilkerson (Sister), 1351 E. St., S.E., Washington, D.C. [R] [S2] [SW]

Rawlings, Russell, Pvt., 84th Co., 6th Regt., KIA, June 7, 1918 in the Aisne Defensive. Herchel L. Rawlings (Father), Valley Park, Missouri [ABMC- Belleau] [S2] [SW]

Marine Corps Deaths, 1917-1921

Ray, Earle Wilton, Pvt., 77th Co., 6th MG Bn., DOW, November 8, 1918 in the Meuse Argonne. John Ray (Father), Tracy, Minnesota [ANC] [S2] [SW1]

Raymond, Harry Franklin, Pvt., 96th Co., 6th Regt., DOW, April 19, 1918 in the Toulon Sector, Verdun. Joanna Schofield (Mother), 1472 Hamilton Ave., St. Louis, Missouri [R] [S2] [SW]

Raynor, Roy E., Sgt., 76th Co., 6th Regt., KIA, September 12, 1918 in the St. Mihiel Offensive. Mrs. Sarah L. Watts (Mother), Houston, Missouri [R] [S2]

Rea, Frank Anthony, Pvt., 45th Co., 5th Regt., KIA, June 7, 1918 in the Chateau-Thierry Sector. Daniel Rea (Father), 175 Linden St., Yonkers, New York [ABMC- Belleau] [S2] [SW1]

Read, Walter Lawrence, Pvt., MCR, 1st Co., Philadelphia, Pennsylvania, DDS, September 20, 1918 at Great Lakes, Illinois. Mr. William F. Read (Father), 5404 Park Heights Ave., Baltimore, Maryland [S3]

Reader, Arnold Marshall, Pvt., 49th Co., 5th Regt., KIA, June 6, 1918 in the Chateau-Thierry Sector. H. J. Morris (Admistrator of John Reader's estate), New Cambria, Missouri [ANC] [S2] [SW]

Reamy, Harvey Withrow, Pvt., 7th Co., 5th Regt., DOD, November 29, 1917 in France. Mrs. L. E. Auit (Wife), RD#1, Hickory, Pennsylvania [ABMC- Thiaucourt] [S2]

Reath, Thomas Roberts, Pvt., 43rd Co., 5th Regt., KIA, June 12, 1918 in the Chateau-Thierry Sector. Theodore W. Reath (Father), 1538 Pine St., Philadelphia, Pennsylvania [ABMC- Belleau] [S2] [SW]

Reddick, Howard James, Pvt., 83rd Co., 6th Regt., KIA, October 4, 1918 in the Meuse Argonne. Lonie Reddick (Mother), Perrysvillel, Missouri [FAG] [S2] [SW1]

Marine Corps Deaths, 1917-1921

Redding, Orville A., Pvt., 12th Co., New York, New York, DDS, March 23, 1918 at New York, New York. Sarah J. Redding (Mother), Neligh, Nebraska [S3]

Redford, David A., 1st Lieut., 75th Co., 6th Regt., DOW, July 18, in the Aisne Marne. Mrs. Jane Redford (Mother), 19 Daniels St., Pawtucket, Rhode Island [ABMC-Fere] [S1] [SW1 says KIA]

Redman, Mack Everette, Cpl., Co. C, 1st Tr. MG BN, DOD, September 21, 1918 in France. Charles Redman (Father), RFD#2, Mt. Orab, Ohio [FAG] [S2]

Redmond, Claude Edwin, Pvt., 8th Co., 5th Regt., DAO, January 27, 1919 in France. Mrs. Emma Redmond (Mother), RFD#1, Carbondale, Kansas [R] [S2] [SW1 says KOA]

Redmond, Lee, Pvt., 61st Co., New York, New York, DAS, October 18, 1918 accidently drowned at Brooklyn, New York. Margaret Redmond (Mother), 1373 Lakeview Road, Cleveland, Ohio [VA-Cypress Hills] [S3]

Reed, Andrew Dewey, Cpl., 31st Co., 2nd Brigade, Domincan Republic, DDS, April 24, 1918 at Santa Domingo, Dommican Republic. Mrs. Lizzie Lee (Mother), RFD#1, Heiskell, Tennessee [FAG] [S3]

Reed, Charles Alfred, Sgt., Constable Det., Haiti, DOS, October 28, 1920 at Haiti. Mary Johnson (Mother), 4514 Altgold St., Chicago, Illinois [S4]

Reed, James Miner, Pvt., 97th Co., 6th Regt., KIA, July 19, 1918 in the Aisne Marne. Nellie Reed (Mother), 6028 Michigan Ave., Chicago, Illinios [S2] [SW1]

Reed, Robert Dunlap, Pvt., Co. D, Mare Island, California, DDS, February 22, 1918 at Mare Island, California. Frederick T. Reed (Father), Gen. Del., Windham, Montana [S3]

Reedy, Pete, Cpl., 74th Co., 6th Regt., DOW, July 22, 1918 in the Aisne Marne. Surrieda Reedy (Mother), 2620 Traverse St., Fort Worth, Texas [ABMC- Suresnes] [S2] [SW]

Marine Corps Deaths, 1917-1921

Rees, Hal Bynum, Pvt., Co. X, Parris Island, South Carolina, DDS, November 29, 1918 at Parris Island, South Carolina. Ella Rees (Mother), Fayetteville, Tennessee [FAG] [S4]

Reese, Elmer Addison, Cpl., 80th Co., 6th Regt., KIA, June 8, 1918 in the Chateau-Thierry Sector. Mary J. Jenkins (Mother), 623 E. Washington St., Sandusky, Ohio [R] [S2] [SW1]

Reeves, Keith Royal, Pvt., 74th Co., 6th Regt., DOD, October 6, 1918 in France. Joseph Reeves (Father), 523 E. Maple St., Columbus, Kansas [FAG] [S2]

Regan, Gerald Vincent, Cpl., 16th Co., 5th Regt., DOW, October 4, 1918 in the Meuse Argonne. Frederick Regan (Father), 910 Getty St., Duryea, Pennsylvania [ANC] [S2] [SW]

Reger, Frank Alexander, Pvt., Co. A, 5th Brigade MG Bn, DOD, November 11, 1918 in France. Nettie J. Reger (Mother), Upshur County, Buckhannon, West Virginia [ANC] [S2]

Reichert, Henry D. W., Cpl., 1st Squadron, FMAF, DOD, October 30, 1918 in France. Grace A. Reichert (Wife), Millville, New Jersey [ABMC-Bony] [S2]

Reichle, Edward Julius, Pvt., 55th Co., 5th Regt., KIA, June 12, 1918 in the Chateau-Thierry Sector. Elizabeth Reichle (Mother), 427 Walnut St., Newark, New Jersey [ABMC-Belleau TOM as E.J.] [S2] [SW]

Reilly, Harold Edward, Pvt., 81st Co., 6th MG Bn., KIA, November 2, 1918 in the Meuse Argonne. Alice Reilly (Mother), 628 33rd St., Milwaukee, Wisconsin [ABMC-Romagne] [S2] [SW1]

Reilly, John James, Cpl., 54th Co., 2nd Prov. Regt., Haiti, DDS, December 18, 1920 at Hinche, Haiti. Winifred Bell (Aunt), 2127 Sears St., Philadelphia, Pennsylvania [S4]

Renaud, Henry G., Pfc, Supply Co., Parris Island, South Carolina, DDS, August 11, 1920 at Parris Island, South Carolina. Mary V. Renaud (Mother), 226 Bradhurst Ave., New York, New York [S4]

Renkin, Frederick James, Cpl., 75th Co., 6th Regt., DOW, November 4, 1918 in the Aisne Marne. Sarah Renkin (Mother), Kohler and Walnut Sts., Pittsburg, Pennsylvania [ABMC-Romagne] [S2] [SW1]

Renshaw, John Henry, Pvt., 78th Co., 6th Regt., KIA, September 15, 1918 in the St. Mihiel Offensive. Minnie Reshaw (Step-mother), Coalburg, Alabama [ABMC- Thiaucourt] [S2] [SW as C Co., 2nd Cas. Btln.]

Resendes, William James, Pvt., 47th Co., 5th Regt., KIA, June 25, 1918 in the Chateau-Thierry Sector. Emma Resendes (Mother), Gen. Del. Bodega, California [ABMC- Belleau TOM as W.J.] [S2] [SW]

Reuter, Walter Fritz, Cpl., Co. G, 13th Regt., DOD, October 5, 1918 in France. Carl Reuter (Father), Gonzales, Texas [FAG] [S2]

Reynolds, Earl A., Pvt., Co. B, Mare Island, California, DDS, February 17, 1920 at Mare Island, California. Maude A. Reynolds (Mother), RFD#1, Stanfield, Umatilla Co., Oregon [S4]

Reynolds, Frederick W., Pvt., 10th Sep. Bn., Quantico, Virginia, DDS, November 19, 1918 at Quantico, Virginia. Carrie Smith (Mother), 270 East 161st St., New York, New York [S4]

Reynolds, James Edmund, Cpl., USS *Pueblo*, DAU, March 24, 1918 of poison aboard the USS *Pueblo*. Helen McAlanan (Niece), 902 Gratton St., Los Angeles, California [USN – Portsmouth, N.H.] [S3]

Reynolds, James Forrest, Pvt., 82nd Co., 6th Regt., KIA, June 26, 1918 in the Chateau-Thierry Sector. Nepoleon B. Reynolds (Father), Clare, Ohio [FAG] [S2] [SW]

Reynolds, Leland Merriam, Pvt., 20th Co., 5th Regt., KIA, June 24, 1918 in the Chateau-Thierry Sector. Joseph C. Reynolds (Father), 5439 Page Blvd., St. Louis, Missouri [ABMC-Belleau] [S2] [SW]

Marine Corps Deaths, 1917-1921

Reynolds, Richard S., Jr., Pvt., 45th Co., 5th Regt., KIA, June 13, 1918 in the Chateau-Thierry Sector. Richard S. Reynolds (Father), 305 Beech St., Elmwood Place, Cincinnati, Ohio [ABMC- Belleau] [S2] [SW1]

Reynolds, Walter Cameron, Pvt., 76th Co., 6th Regt., DOW, April 20, 1918 in the Toulon Sector, Verdun. Mrs. Carrie Smith (Mother), 270 E. 16st St., New York, New York [R] [S2] [SW says 120th Co., 1st Repl. Btln.]

Rhines, Merle DeWalt, Pvt., Bks. Det., Quantico, Virginia, DDS, November 6, 1918 at Quantico, Virginia. Grant and Flora Rhines (Parents), 525 6th Ave., New Kensington, Pennsylvania [S3]

Rhoades, Daniel Omer, Pvt., 70th Co., 3rd Prov. Regt., Dominican Republic, DAS, June 21, 1917 of a gunshot wound at Fort Azuma, Dominican Republic [S3]

Rhodes, Clarence David, 1st Sgt., 18th Co., 5th Regt., DOD, December, 3, 1918 in France. Mrs. Minnie Rhodes (Mother), RFD#2, Iowa Ave., Detriot, Michigan [R] [S2]

Rhodes, Robert Jefferson, Pvt., 45th Co., 5th Regt., KIA, June 6, 1918 in the Chateau-Thierry Sector. Thomas J. Rhodes (Father), RFD#1, Hampton, New Jersey [ABMC- Belleau] [S2] [SW1]

Rice, Clarence Richard, Cpl., Hdqtrs. Co., 13th Regt., DOD, October 3, 1918 in France. Mrs. Ella L. Rice (Mother), 360 W. 58th St., New York, New York [ABMC- Fere] [S2]

Richard, Samuel, Sgt., 75th Co., 6th Regt., DOW, October 9, 1918 in the Meuse Argonne. Mrs. Helena Lepon (Sister), 2353 E. 61st St., Cleveland, Ohio [ABMC- Romagne] [S2] [SW1 says KIA]

Richards, Frank, Pvt., 38th Co., Peking, China, DDS, December 13, 1917 at Peking, China. John Richards (Brother), 1023 Parrish St., Philadelphia, Pennsylvania [S3]

Marine Corps Deaths, 1917-1921

Richards, Lowell, Pvt., 69th Co., 4th Regt., Dominican Republic, DDS, November 12, 1918 at Santo Domingo, Dominican Republic. Ellis M. Richards (Father), Pocahontas, Iowa [S4]

Richardson, Charles Savage, Sgt., 95th Co., 6th Regt., KIA, June 9, 1918 in the Chateau-Thierry Sector. Samuel F. Richardson (Father), Urbana, Virginia [ABMC- Belleau] [S2] [SW]

Richardson, Elmo, Pvt., 114th Co., Santo Domingo, Dominican Republic, DOS, September 5, 1919 at Santo Domingo, Dominican Republic. Anna Richardson (Mother), 306 Missouri Ave., Fort Worth, Texas [FAG] [S4]

Richardson, James J., Pvt., 69th Co., 4th Prov. Regt., Dominican Republic, DDS, January 13, 1919 at Santo Domingo, Dominican Republic. Mrs. Lancy Richardson (Mother), Winnsboro, Louisiana [FAG] [S4]

Richardson, Joseph, Pvt., Flt. Sup. Base, Brooklyn, New York, DOS, February 13, 1921 at Brooklyn, New York. Robert Richardson (Father), 143 W. 111th St., New York, New York [VA-Cypress Hills] [S4]

Richardson, Leon Everett, Pvt., 76th Co., 6th Regt., DOD, September 17, 1918 in France. Charles B. Richardson (Father), Naples, Maine [R] [S2] [SW says Co. A., 3rd Repl. Btln.] [SW1]

Richardson, LeRoy, Sgt., Central Receiving Division, DDS, May 22, 1920 at Chicago, Illinois. Donna Richardson (Mother), RR#3, Hartford, Michigan [S4]

Richardson, Lowell Fremont, Pvt., 18th Co., 5th Regt., KIA, June 13, 1918 in the Chateau-Thierry Sector. Mrs. Virginia D. Richardson (Wife), 637 N. 2nd West St., Salt Lake City, Utah [ABMC- Romagne] [S2] [SW]

Richardson, Oard, Pvt., 51st Co., 5th Regt., KIA, June 11, 1918 in the Chateau-Thierry Sector. Thomas E. Richardson (Father), Goreville, Illinois [FAGM] [S2] [SW1]

Marine Corps Deaths, 1917-1921

Richardson, Thomas J., Pvt., 182nd Co., 15th Regt., Dominican Republic, DAS, July 26, 1920 drowned at Santana, Dominican Republic. Mary Richardson (Mother), Sylvia, Tennessee [FAG] [S4]

Ricketts, Langdon Law, Cpl., 18th Co., 5th Regt., KIA, October 4, 1918 in the Meuse Argonne. Elizabeth L. Ricketts (Mother), 2854 Winslow Ave., Cincinnati, Ohio [ABMC- Romagne] [S2] [SW1]

Ridenour, Preston Leroy, Pvt., Mar. Det., Deer Island, Massachusetts, DDS, April 23, 1919 at Deer Island, Massachusetts. William C. Ridenour (Father), RFD#6, Hagerstown, Maryland [FAG] [S4]

Riebold, Frederick Louis, Pvt., 23rd Co., 6th MG Bn., KIA, June 12, 1918 in the Chateau-Thierry Sector. Mary Riebold (Mother), 1637 N. Durhan St., Baltimore, Maryland [ABMC- Belleau] [S2] [SW]

Riegel, Otto Raymond, Pvt., 80th Co., 6th Regt., KIA, November 1, 1918 in the Meuse Argonne. Ethel Bicknell (Sister), R#1, Robinson, Illinois [FAG] [S2] [SW1 says Riegle]

Riehl, Philip Jacob, Pvt., 16th Co., 5th Regt., KIA, June 7, 1918 in the Chateau-Thierry Sector. Mrs. Olive P. Richl (Widow), 619 Mauch Chunk St., Easton, Pennsylvania [S2] [SW]

Riesner, Edmund L., 1st Lieut., 79th Co., 6th Regt., KIA, June 14, 1918 in the Chateau Thierry sector. B. A. Riesner (Father), 61 Young Ave., Houston, Texas [FAG] [S1] [SW says Reisner]

Riester, Benjamin Franklin, Cpl., 49th Co., 5th Regt., DOW, October 9, 1918 in the Meuse Argonne. Mrs. Lena Riester (Mother), 27 Tuxill Square, Auburn, New York [FAG] [S2] [SW1]

Riggs, Russell, Pvt., 55th Co., 5th Regt., KIA, October 5, 1918 in the Meuse Argonne. Mary Riggs (Mother), Ironton, Missouri [FAG] [S2] [SW]

Marine Corps Deaths, 1917-1921

Riker, Harry, Pvt., 66th Co., 5th Regt., KIA, July 18, 1918 in the Aisne Marne. Fred Ricker (Father), box 41, Ledgewood, New Jersey [ABMC- Belleau TOM] [S2] [SW]

Riley, Mark Francis, Cpl., 16th Co., 5th Regt., KIA [SW] [SW1 reported to have been found alive]

Rinaldi, Louis Ignatius, Pvt., 1st Res. Co., Philadelphia, Pennsylvania, DDS, September 22, 1918 at Great Lakes, Illinois. Louis Rinaldi (Father), 23 E. 85th St., New York, New York [S3]

Rindal, Arnold B., Pvt., MD, USNH, Fort Lyon, Colorado, DDS, March 25, 1920 at Fort Lyon, Colorado. Mrs. Carrie Rindal (Mother), 654 E. 4th St., St. Paul, Minnesota [FAG] [S4]

Rindeau, Arthur Joseph, Gy. Sgt., 47th Co., 5th Regt., KIA, June 6, 1918 in the Chateau-Thierry Sector. Mrs. Alma R. Bernier (Sister), 19 Central Ave., Webster, Massachusetts [S2] [SW]

Ring, Henry Grady, Pvt., 82nd Co., 6th Regt., DOW, November 1, 1918 in the Meuse Argonne. Lethia Ring (Mother), 1624 Holly St., Nashville, Tennessee [S2] [SW1]

Ring, John Thomas, Cpl., 97th Co., 6th Regt., KIA, July 19, 1918 in the Aisne Marne. Sanford G. Ring (Father), Kernersville, North Carolina [FAG] [S2] [SW says 145th Co., Repl. Btln.]

Ringer, Stanley Ashton, Sgt., 43rd Co., 5th Regt., KIA, June 11, 1918 in the Chateau-Thierry Sector. Clayton Ringer (Father), Woodman, New Hampshire [ANC] [S2] [SW]

Riordan, George Francis, Pvt., 23rd Co., 6th MG Bn., KIA, November 2, 1918 in the Meuse Argonne. Luke H. Riordan (Father), Killawog, New York [S2] [SW1]

Riordan, Leander Emmett, Pvt., 77th Co., 6th MG Bn., KIA, September 13, 1918 in the St. Mihiel Offensive. Elizabeth Riordan (Mother), 301 N. Lathrop Ave., River Forest, Illinois [R] [S2] [SW]

Marine Corps Deaths, 1917-1921

Rishel, Joseph Lysle, Pvt., 16th Co., 5th Regt., KIA, June 25, 1918 in the Chateau-Thierry Sector. Lillie B. Rishel (Mother), 324 W. 11th St., Hutchinson, Kansas [ABMC- Belleau] [S2] [SW1]

Riska, John Johnson, Pvt., Hdqtrs. Co., 5th Regt., DOW, June 12, 1918 in the Chateau-Thierry Sector. John Riska (Father), c/o N. Mianus Mfg., Co., Coscob, Connecticut [ABMC-Belleau] [S2] [SW1 says KIA]

Ristine, James R., Gy. Sgt., Aviation Det., Miami, Florida, DAS, November 13, 1918 in an aeroplane accident at Miami, Florida. James R. Ristine (Father), 2425Connor Ave., Joplin, Missouri [FAG] [S4]

Ritter, George Clayton, Pvt., Co. D, 13th Regt., DOD, October 5, 1918 in France. Mrs. Ana M. Ritter (Mother), 359 N. Mervin Ave., Philadelphia, Pennsylvania [S2]

Rivard, Rozaire Donald, Pvt., 79th Co., 6th Regt., KIA, June 6, 1918 in the Chateau-Thierry Sector. Joseph H. Rivard (Father), North St. Paul, Minnesota [S2] [SW]

Roan, George Bailey, Sgt., 47th Co., 5th Regt., DOW, June 18, 1918 in the Chateau-Thierry Sector. Mrs. Clara Roan (Mother), Pattison, Mississippi [FAG] [S2] [SW]

Robbins, Garland, Pvt., Hdqtrs. Co., 13th Regt., DOD, October 12, 1918 in France. Mr. James L. Robbins (Father), 1410 Center St., Warsaw, Indiana [FAG] [S2]

Robbins, Thomas Luke, Pvt., Co. D, 13th Regt., DOD, September 21, 1918 enroute to France. William B. Robbins (Father), Equality, Alabama [S2]

Roben, Douglas B., Major, Northern Bomb Group, 9th Sq. FMAF, DOD, October 27, 1918 in France. Lt. Comdr. Douglas Roben, USN (Ret) (Father), Big Rapids, Mich. [FAG] [S1]

Roberts, Archibald Coon, Pvt., Rifle Range Det, Parris Island, South Carolina, DDS, November 8, 1918 at Parris Island,

Marine Corps Deaths, 1917-1921

South Carolina. Herbert W. Roberts (Father), RR#2, Windsor, New York [S3]

Roberts, Claude Aster, Pvt., 96th Co., 6th Regt., KIA, October 3, 1918 in the Meuse Argonne. Jesse M. Roberts (Father), Willacoochee, Georgia [ABMC- Romagne] [S2] [SW says Co. C, 2nd Cas. Btln.]

Roberts, Fred Anderson, Pvt., Co. S, Parris Island, South Carolina, DDS, July 18, 1918 at Parris Island, South Carolina. Virginia Roberts (Mother), Edgerton, Virginia [S3]

Roberts, George Henry, Pfc, Bks. Det., Philadelphia, Pennsylvania, DDS, September 25, 1918 at Philadelphia, Pennsylvania. William Roberts (Father), 3353 W. Madison St,.Chicago, Illinois [S3]

Roberts, Harry Calvin, Pvt., 20th Co., 5th Regt., KIA, November 2, 1918 in the Meuse Argonne. Thomas J. Roberts (Father), P O Box 393, Long Beach, California [ANC] [S2] [SW1]

Roberts, James Henry, Pvt., 51st Co., 5th Regt., KIA, November 10, 1918 in the Meuse Argonne. Elizabeth Roberts (Mother), 127 N. Maderia St., Baltimore, Maryland [ABMC- Romagne says Pfc.] [S2] [SW1]

Roberts, Jay Elmer, Pvt., Co. A, 13th Regt., DOD, September 21, 1918 enroute to France. Elmer Roberts (Father), Glen Elden, Kansas [FAG] [S2]

Roberts, John William, Pvt., 45th Co., 5th Regt., Quantico, Virginia, DAS, May 23, 1921 drowned at Quantico, Virginia. Margaret Roberts (Mother), RFD#2, Morrisville, New York [S4]

Roberts, Leon John, Pvt., 15th Co., 6th MG Bn., DAO, April 29, 1918 in the Toulon Sector, Verdun. Fred L. Roberts (Father), 148 University Ave., Buffalo, New York [ABMC- Romagne] [S2] [SW] [SW1 say KOA]

Roberts, Sidney Cutler, Pvt., 17th Co., 5th Regt., KIA, June 15, 1918 in the Chateau-Thierry Sector. Orin J. Roberts

(Father), 231 Vine St., Toledo, Ohio [ABMC- Belleau] [S2] [SW]

Robertson, Charles J., Pvt., Recruiting Station, Portland, Oregon, DDS, December 4, 1918 at Portland, Oregon. John H. Robertson (Father), RFD#2, Box 44, Wilbur, Lincoln County, Washington [FAG] [S4]

Robertson, Ernest Adam, Pvt., 79th Co., 6th Regt., KIA, June 14, 1918 in the Chateau-Thierry Sector. Frank Robertson (Brother), Jamestown, North Dakota [ABMC- Belleau] [S2] [SW]

Robertson, George Mertan, Pvt., Extra Duty Det., Parris Island, South Carolina, DAS, August 18, 1918 drowned at Parris Island, South Carolina. Joseph E. Robertson (Father), Hermon, New York [FAG] [S3]

Robichon, Alfred C., Pvt., Cas. Det., Navy Yard, Washington, D.C., DDS, February 22, 1920 at Washington, D.C. peter Robichoin (Father), 1427 55th St., Brooklyn, New York [ANC] [S4]

Robins, Howard Vernon, Sgt., 47th Co., 5th Regt., KIA, June 25, 1918 in the Chateau-Thierry Sector. Frank Robins (Father), Lock P O Box 260, Winnemucca, Nevada [ABMC- Belleau] [S2] [SW1]

Robinson, Caldwell C., 2nd Lieut., 82nd Co., 6th Regt., KIA, June 6, 1918 in the Chateau Thierry sector. Mrs. F. H. J. Robinson (Mother), 1161 Prospect Ave., Hartford, Connecticut [ABMC-Belleau as C.C.] [S1] [SW]

Robinson, Cecil Blaine, Pvt., 83rd Co., 6th Regt., KIA, July 19, 1918 in the Aisne Marne. Gilbert W. Robinson (Father), RFD#1, Blandville, West Virginia [VA-Grafton] [S2] [SW]

Robinson, Osco, Pvt., Hdqtrs. Co., 5th Regt., KIA, April 24, 1918 in the Toulon Sector, Verdun. Wm. H. Robinson (Father), RFD#4, Marathon, New York [FAG] [S2] [SW]

Marine Corps Deaths, 1917-1921

Robinson, Phillips B., Captain, Washington, D.C., DAS, November 2, 1918 at Washington, D.C. Mrs. Phillips B. Robinson (Wife), 1812 Riggs Place, Washington, D.C. [ANC] [S3]

Robinson, Tony Loyd, Pvt., 96th Co., 6th Regt., KIA, October 3, 1918 in the Meuse Argonne. Robert Robinson (Father), Jamestown, Ohio [S2] [SW]

Robison, Noal Coral, Pvt., 75th Co., 6th Regt., DOW, October 5, 1918 in the Meuse Argonne. Thomas Robison (Father), R#2, Box 32, DeSota, Illinois [S2] [SW]

Robison, Orra Homer, Pvt., M.G. Co., 13th Regt., DOD, May 14, 1919 in France. Mrs. Norine Robison (Wife), 5420 23rd St., Detroit, Michigan [R] [S2]

Rockwell, Mearl Colin, Cpl., Hdqtrs. Co., 6th Regt., KIA, July 19, 1918 in the Aisne Marne. Katie Rockwell (Mother), Holly, Colorado [FAG] [S2] [SW]

Rodenbo, Hughie Benjamin, Pvt., 74th Co., 6th Regt., DOW, April 16, 1918 in the Toulon Sector, Verdun. William Rodenbo (Father), 146 Jackson St., Pontiac, Michigan [FAG] [S2] [SW]

Rodenburg, John Henry, Pvt., 18th Co., 5th Regt., KIA, June 12, 1918 in the Chateau-Thierry Sector. George Rodenburg (Father), Gen. Del., Marshall, Missouri [S2]

Rodgers, John Wiley, Sgt., 43rd Co., 5th Regt., KIA, June 6, 1918 in the Chateau-Thierry Sector. Elise M. Rodgers (Sister), Equality, Illinois [S2] [SW]

Roehrig, Ralph John, Pvt., 8th Co., 5th Regt., KIA, June 16, 1918 in the Chateau-Thierry Sector. Mrs. Roas Roehrig (Mother), 504 Maple St., Detroit, Michigan [ABMC-Belleau] [S2] [SW]

Rogers, Ben Hadden, Pvt., 95th Co., 6th Regt., KIA, November 5, 1918 in the Meuse Argonne. Rufus H. Rogers (Father), Edna, Texas [ANC] [S2] [SW1]

Marine Corps Deaths, 1917-1921

Rogers, George LaVerne, Pvt., Co. D, 11th Regt., Quantico, Virginia, DDS, September 25, 1918 at Quantico, Virginia. James Rogers (Father), Bearverdale, Pennsylvania [S3]

Rogers, Howard James, Sgt., 79th Co., 6th Regt., KIA, July 19, 1918 in the Aisne Marne. Ellis H. Rogers (Father), 5706 S. Sheridan St., Tacoma, Washington [FAG] [S2] [SW1]

Rogers, John Sim, Pvt., 83rd Co., 6th Regt., DOD, September 20, 1918 in France. Sara O. Rogers (Mother), Pachuta, Michigan [FAG] [S2]

Rogers, Orle Nathan, Pvt., 93rd Co., 7th Regt., Cuba, DDS, December 23, 1917 at San Juan, Santiago, Cuba. Nathan V. Rogers (Father), RD#8, Fulton, New York [S3]

Rolka, Bernard Frank, Pvt., Bks. Det., New York, New York, DDS, October 2, 1918 at New York, New York. Apalenia Rolka (Mother), 919 Carmett St., Dickson City, Pennsylvania [S3]

Rollins, Louis Guy, Pvt., 73rd Co., 6th Regt., DOW, October 13, 1918 in the Meuse Argonne. Mr. W. D. Rollins (Brother), P O Box 1269, New Orleans, Louisana [R] [S2] [SW1]

Rollins, Sidney Edgar, Pvt., 73rd Co., 6th Regt., DOW, November 24, 1918 1918 in the Meuse Argonne. Mr. W. D. Rollins (Brother), P O Box 1269, New Orleans, Louisana [R] [S2] [SW1]

Romans, Ernest, Cpl., 47th Co., 5th Regt., DOW, June 30, 1918 in the Chateau-Thierry Sector. Mary Romans (Mother), Corrigedor, Philippine Islands [VA-Cypress Hills] [S2] [SW1]

Roos, John, Pvt., 73rd Co., 6th Regt., DOD, June 28, 1918 in the Chateau-Thierry Sector. Phillip Roos (Father), RR#1, California, Ohio [R] [S2] [SW1 says DOW]

Root, Harlie T., Jr., Pvt., MBks., Parris Island, South Carolina, DAS, January 3, 1919 of surgical shock following an operation at Parris Island, South Carolina. Harlie Taylor Root (Father), 62 Post St., Rochester, New York [S4]

Roper, William August, Pvt., 49th Co., 5th Regt., KIA, November 6, 1918 in the Meuse Argonne. Olivia Carlson (Sister), Little Woods, Louisiana [R] [S2] [SW1]

Roscoe, Stanley, Sgt., 80th Co., 6th Regt., KIA, October 3, 1918 in the Meuse Argonne. Ada Develin (Friend), 423 Broad St., Newark, New Jersey [ABMC- Romagne TOM] [S2] [SW]

Rose, Richard Wigley P., Cpl., 67th Co., 5th Regt., DOW, June 24, 1918 in the Chateau-Thierry Sector. Charles F. Rose (Father), 1229 N. St., N.W., Washington, D.C. [ABMC-Suresnes] [S2] [SW]

Rosenfeld, Emil, Sgt., 4th Squardron, FMAF, DOD, October 4, 1918 in France. Lela O. Rosenfield (Wife), 604 Cordova Ave., Miami, Florida [VA-Cypress Hills] [S2]

Rosenow, Theodore Carl, Pvt., 95th Co., 6th Regt., KIA, July 19, 1918 in the Aisne Marne. Kate Rosenow (Mother), 410 Naymut St., Menasha, Wisconsin [FAG with date of January 1, 1918, but stone is correct] [S2] [SW] [SW1 says Rogenow]

Rosenquist, George August Richard, Pvt., 67th Co., 5th Regt., KIA, October 4, 1918 in the Meuse Argonne. Arthur Rosenquist (Brother), 3144 N. Oakley Ave., Chicago, Illinois [S2] [SW1]

Rosenspire, Walter, Pvt., 23rd Co., 6th MG Bn., KIA, June 9, 1918 in the Chateau-Thierry Sector. Samuel Rosenspire (Father), 198 Penn St., Brooklyn, New York [ABMC-Belleau] [S2]

Rosenthal, Saul Edward, Pvt., 66th Co., 5th Regt., DOW, October 9, 1918 in the Meuse Argonne. Ada Rosenthal (Mother), 178 Wilkins St., Detroit, Michigan [S2] [SW1]

Rosier, Hoy B., Pvt., 51st Co., 5th Regt., DOW, October 17, 1918 in the Meuse Argonne. Allie F. Deets (Mother), RFD#3,

Marine Corps Deaths, 1917-1921

St. George, West Virginia [ANC] [S2] [SW1 says Roy E. Rosier]

Roska, Joseph Victor, Pvt., 55th Co., 5th Regt., DOW, June 4, 1918 in the Chateau-Thierry Sector. Mrs. Victoria F. Roska (Mother), 12 Gray St., Charlestown, Massachusetts [R] [S2] [SW]

Ross, Henry E., Pvt, 36th Co., 1st Regt., Dominican Republic, DAS, August 27, 1919 drowned at Santo Domingo, Dominican Republic. Miss Pearl Ross (Sister), 2715 2nd Ave., North, Billings, Montana [S4]

Ross, Thomas William, Pvt., MBks., Quantico, Virginia, DDS, November 17, 1918 at Quantico, Virginia. Mrs. Maggie Ross (Mother), Gen. Del., Middletown, Illinois [S4]

Ross, William Keith, Pvt., 55th Co., 5th Regt., KIA, June 12, 1918 in the Chateau-Thierry Sector. William B. Ross (Father), 409 Parke Ave., Aurora, Indiana [ABMC- Belleau] [S2] [SW1]

Ross, William Robert, Pfc, 75th Co., 6th Regt., DOW, September 17, 1918 in the St. Mihiel Offensive. Mrs. Mary S. Ross (Mother), 811 S. Second St., Plainfield, New Jersey [ABMC- Thiaucourt] [S2] [SW]

Roth, John Edward, Sgt., 77th Co., 6th MG Bn., KIA, October 4, 1918 in the Meuse Argonne. Mrs. Henry M. Roth (Mother), 56 Rumboldt Ave., Tonawanda, New York [FAG] [S2] [SW1]

Rouden, Quincy Clarence, Pvt., Bks. Det., Boston, Massachusetts, DOS, October 23, 1921 at Chelsea, Massachusetts. Mr. C. L. Rouden (Brother), Panama City, Florida [FAG] [S4]

Roug[h]ier, William James, Pvt., 8th Co., 5th Regt., DOO, July 17, 1919 in France. Mrs. Mary Rougier (Mother), 12½ E. Harrison St., Saratoga Springs, New York [R] [S2] [SW1 says KOA]

Rounds, William Lawrence, Pvt., 75th Co., 6th Regt., KIA, June 14, 1918 in the Chateau-Thierry Sector. J. M. Rounds

(Father), 250 College St., Wadsworth, Ohio [FAG] [S2] [SW]

Rourke, Arthur Joseph, Pvt., 8th Co., 5th Regt., KIA, November 2, 1918 in the Meuse Argonne. Frank H. Rourke (Father), 9 Bismark St., Worcester, Massachusetts [ABMC-Romagne] [S2] [SW1]

Rowan, Bernard John, Sgt., 80th Co., 6th Regt., DAO, April 17, 1918 in France. Patrick J. Rowan (Brother), 2516 N. Opal St., Philadelphia, Pennsylvania [R] [S2] [SW1 says KIA]

Rowbottom, George Victor, Sgt., Hdqtrs. Co., 5th Regt., DOD, August 8, 1918 in France. Mrs. Alice Rowbottom (Mother), Adsett Westbury on Severn, Gloucestershire, England [ABMC-Fere] [S2]

Rowden, Fritz, Pvt., Bks. Det., Mare Island, California, DDS, May 21, 1917, Mare Island, California. Mrs. Anna Bump (Foster-mother), 326 South Main St., Salt Lake City, Utah [S3]

Rowden, William E., Cpl., 114th Co., 2nd Regt., Dominican Republic, DDS, December 28, 1918 at Santo Domingo, Dominican Republic. Thomas Rowden (Father), 3114 Hickory St., St. Louis, Missouri [FAG] [S4]

Rowe, Edmond Brabrook, Pvt., 81st Co., 6th MG Bn., KIA, July 19, 1918 in the Aisne Marne. Reuben Rowe (Father), Box 276, Wellington St., West Medwa, Massachusetts [S2] [SW]

Rowe, Jerome Cecil, Sgt., MCR, Hdqtrs. USMC, A&I Department, DDS, October 9, 1918 at Washington, D.C. Helen R. Powell (Mother), Sekitan, Ohio [ANC] [S3]

Rowold, Horace Enus, Pvt., 66th Co., 5th Regt., KIA, July 21, 1918 in the Aisne Marne. Emil H. Rowold (Father), Cypress, Texas [FAG] [S2] [SW1 says DOW]

Roy, Charles H., 2nd Lieut., 80th Co., 6th Regt., KIA, July 19, 1918 in the Aisne Marne. Mrs. N. F. Johnson (foster-mother), 105 S. Angus St., Fresno, California [FAG] [S1] [SW]

Marine Corps Deaths, 1917-1921

Rozas, William Joseph, Pvt., Co. B, 2nd Training Batt. DOD, September 18, 1918 in France. Mr. Theone Rozas (Father), Elton, Louisiana [R] [S2]

Rozell, Clarence Otto, Pvt., 74th Co., 6th Regt., DOW, July 27, 1918 in the Aisne Marne. Clara Rozell (Mother), c/o Ehlen and Crote Apartments, Orange California [ABMC-Suresnes] [S2] [SW says Co. A, Repl. Btln.]

Ruble, Harry, Gy. Sgt., Constable Det., Haiti, DAS, September 21, 1919 at Port au Prince, Haiti. Mrs. Harry Ruble (Wife), 332 Olivier St., New Orleans, Louisiana [S4]

Rubinson, Harry, Pvt., 23rd Co., 6th MG Bn., KIA, June 10, 1918 in the Chateau-Thierry Sector. Sarah Rubinson (Mother), 105 Diamond St., Philadelphia, Pennsylvania [S2] [SW]

Rudd, Frederick Ashton, Pvt., 1 Squadron, FMAF, DOD, November 1, 1918 in France. Mary Rudd (Sister), 207 Lincoln Drive, Philadelphia, Pennsylvania [S2]

Ruddick, Charles Lawrence, Pvt., 80th Co., 6th Regt., DOW, September 17, 1918 in the St. Mihiel Offensive. Ella Ruddick (Mother), 655 E. Church St., Elmira, New York [ABMC- Thiaucourt] [S2] [SW says Co. C, 2nd Casualty Btln.]

Ruhnke, Leslie Charles, Pvt., 82nd Co., 6th Regt., KIA, June 8, 1918 in the Chateau-Thierry Sector. Julia Ruhnke (Mother), 4437 Congress St., Chicago, Illlinois [ABMC-Belleau] [S2] [SW]

Rushing, Douglas Gentry, Sgt., 73rd Co., 6th Regt., KIA, November 1, 1918 in the Meuse Argonne. Gentry Rushing (Father), c/o Davids Co., Moskow, Idaho [ANC] [S2] [SW1]

Rusinow, Herman, Pvt., 49th Co., 5th Regt., KIA, June 12, 1918 in the Chateau-Thierry Sector. Bessi Rusinow (Mother), 110 Heddon Terrace, Newark, New Jersey [S2] [SW1]

Marine Corps Deaths, 1917-1921

Russell, Arthur, Sgt., 49th Co., 5th Regt., KIA, June 6, 1918 in the Chateau-Thierry Sector. Delia McNamee (Mother), 308 High St., Oshkosh, Wisconsin [S2] [SW]

Russell, Clement Earl, Pvt., Brigade Signal Co., Haiti, DDS, November 10, 1920 at Haiti. Clement N. Russell (Father), 81½ Green St., Augusta, Maine [S4]

Ruth, Albion Winfred, Pvt., 78th Co., 6th Regt., KIA, July 19, 1918 in the Aisne Marne. G. B. Ruth (Father), DeRidder, Louisiana [ABMC- Belleau TOM] [S2] [SW]

Rutherford, William A., Pay Clerk, Santo Domingo, Dominican Republic, DDS, March 20, 1918 at Santo Domingo, Dominican Republic. Ansen M. Olsen (Cousin), Berkeley Place #110, Brooklyn, New York [VA-Cypress Hills] [S3]

Rutledge, Lance, Pvt., 66th Co., 5th Regt., DOW, November 13, 1918 in the Meuse Argonne. Isabella M. Rutledge (Mother), 1367 7th Ave., San Francisco, California [ABMC-Romagne] [S2] [SW1]

Ryan, John Robert, Pvt., Batt. D, Parris Island, South Carolina, DOS, September 6, 1921 at Parris Island, South Carolina. Mrs. Frances Ryan (Mother), 404 St. Nicholas Ave., New York, New York [S4]

Sacks, Howard, Pfc, 47th Co., 5th Regt., KIA, October 4, 1918 in the Meuse Argonne. Mathew Sacks (Father), 5518 Walnut St., Philadelphia, Pennsylvania [ABMC-Romagne TOM] [S2] [SW1]

Sahm, John Martin, Pvt., 45th Co., 5th Regt., KIA, June 6, 1918 in the Chateau-Thierry Sector. Martin and Anna Sahm (Parents), Box 30, Fair Haven, Pennsylvania [S2] [SW]

Salisbury, Clarence Christian, Pvt., Co. U, Parris Island, South Carolina, DDS, November 8, 1918 at Parris Island, South Carolina. Christian Salisbury (Mother), 37 Arbordale Ave, Rochester, New York [S3]

Marine Corps Deaths, 1917-1921

Sallinger, Lloyd Arthur, Pvt., 79th Co., 6th Regt., DOW, July 19, 1918 in the Aisne Marne. Mrs. L. A. Sallinger (Mother), 121 North Hagan Ave., New Orleans, Louisiana [ABMC-Fere] [S2] [SW1]

Sammon, William Patrick, Sgt., 1st Squadron, FMAF, DOD, October 30, 1918 in France. John R. Sammon (Brother), 6902 Whitney Ave., Cleveland, Ohio [R] [S2]

Sample, Glenn, Pvt., 74th Co., 6th Regt., DOW, April 18, 1918 in the Toulon Sector, Verdun. Mrs. Florence Sample (Mother), 2059 Indiana Ave., Connersville, Indiana [R] [S2] [SW]

Sampson, Frank F., Cpl., Constable Det., 1st Prov. Brigade, Haiti, KIA, September 21, 1919 at Port au Prince, Haiti. Mrs. A. L. Herbert (Sister), 1520 Plymouth Ave., North Mineapolis, Minnesota [S4]

Sanchez, Joachin, Jr., Pvt., 84th Co., 6th Regt., DOW, June 12, 1918 in the Chateau-Thierry Sector. Mrs. Gabriel Sanchez (Mother), 3024 Burgundy St., New Orleans, Louisiana [R] [S2] [SW says Sanches]

Sander, Frederick Edward, Sgt., 45th Co., 5th Regt., KIA, July 19, 1918 in the Aisne Marne. John Sander (Father), Box 90 Pierce Rd., Saratoga, California [VA-San Francisco] [S2] [SW1]

Sanders, John R., Pvt., MD, USNH, Fort Lyon, Colorado, DDS, July 16, 1920 at Fort Lyon, Colorado. Bessie Singleton (Sister), 3109 California Ave., St. Louis, Missouri [S4]

Sanders, Lewis F., Cpl., R.R. Det., Parris Island, South Carolina, DDS, January 29, 1919 at Parris Island, South Carolina. Mrs. Maggie Sanders (Mother), Box 64, Mt. Orab, Ohio [S4]

Sanderson, Joseph, Pvt., 47th Co., 5th Regt., KIA, June 6, 1918 in the Chateau-Thierry Sector. John Sanderson (Father), 129 Crickett Ave., Ardmore, Pennsylvania [FAG] [S2] [SW1]

Marine Corps Deaths, 1917-1921

Sangren, Ray Henry, Pvt., 45th Co., 5th Regt., KIA, June 6, 1918 in the Chateau-Thierry Sector. Edward J. Sangren (Father), 2002 5th Ave., Minneapolis, Minnesota [S2] [SW]

Sarver, Lee Roy, Pvt., 96th Co., 6th Regt., DOW, June 20, 1918 in the Chateau-Thierry Sector. Minnie Sarver (Mother), Henton, Illinois [S2] [SW]

Satterfield, Floyd Dance, Pvt., 8th Co., 5th Regt., DOW, October 8, 1918 in the Meuse Argonne. Minnie Satterfield (Mother), 1913 Oaks Ave., Everett, Washington [R] [S2] [SW1]

Saunders, Franklin Alvos, Pvt., 55th Co., 5th Regt., KIA, November 4, 1918 in the Meuse Argonne. Mrs. J. Darvill (Sister), 3386 E. 117th St., Cleveland, Ohio [ANC] [S2] [SW1 says Franklin Alves Saunders]

Saunders, George Raymond, Trumpeter, 82nd Co., 6th Regt., KIA, July 19, 1918 in the Aisne Marne. Charles E. Saunders (Father), Orlando, Florida [ABMC- Fere] [S2] [SW1 says Pvt.]

Saunders, John Ernest, Pvt., 83rd Co., 6th Regt., KIA, June 8, 1918 in the Chateau-Thierry Sector. Marie Saunders (Mother), 6052 Houston Place, St. Louis, Missouri [FAG] [S2] [SW]

Savercool, David, Pvt., 51st Co., 5th Regt., DOW, June 12, 1918 in the Chateau-Thierry Sector. Frank C. Savercool (Father), 119 Grand Ave., Johnson City, New York [ABMC-Belleau] [S2] [SW1]

Sawyer, Arthur Bates, Pvt., 8th Co., 5th Regt., KIA, June 8, 1918 in the Chateau-Thierry Sector. Charles Sawyer (Father), 326 Williams St., Key West, Florida [R] [S2] [SW]

Sawyer, Harry Roseboom, Pvt., 78th Co., 6th Regt., DOD, September 24, 1918 in France. Mrs. Ruthe Sawyer (Mother), P O, Cherry Valley, New York [ABMC-Romagne] [S2]

Marine Corps Deaths, 1917-1921

Sayles, Claude Elmer, Pvt., 66th Co., 5th Regt., KIA, June 6, 1918 in the Chateau-Thierry Sector. LeRoy E. Sayles (Father), 708 E. Fayette St., Syracuse, New York [ABMC-Belleau] [S2] [SW]

Saylor, William Henry, Pvt., 97th Co., 6th Regt., KIA, June 6, 1918 in the Chateau-Thierry Sector. Mrs. Teresa E. Hain (Mother), 32 North 4th St., Newport, Pennsylvania [S2] [SW]

Scanlan, Joseph John, Pvt., MCR, OTC, Quantico, Virginia, DDS, September 28, 1918 at Quantico, Virginia. Mary Scanlan (Mother), 1939 Waveland Ave., Chicago, Illinois [S3]

Scebold, Theodore Bernie, Cpl., 75th Co., 6th Regt., KIA, October 3, 1918 in the Meuse Argonne. Nellie Scebold (Mother), Holyoke, Colorado [ABMC- Romagne TOM as T.B.] [S2] [SW]

Schaber, Allyn Brice, Cpl., 18th Co., 5th Regt., KIA, October 6, 1918 in the Meuse Argonne. Earl Laswell (Uncle), 314½ East Adams St., Springfield, Illinois [FAG] [S2] [SW1]

Schack, Leon, Trumpeter, 77th Co., 6th MG Bn., DOD, November 15, 1918 in France. Charles Schack (Father), 189 Graham Ave., Paterson, New Jersey [R] [S2]

Schafer, John C., Pvt., MB, Washington, D.C., DDS, January 23, 1919 at Washington, D.C. Mrs. Elizabeth Kolb (Sister), 524 Albina Square, Chicago, Illinois [ANC] [S4]

Schaffer, Roy Joseph, Pvt., 96th Co., 6th Regt., KIA, October 3, 1918 in the Meuse Argonne. Mrs. Pearl D. Berger (Mother), Pedro Miguel, Canal Zone [R] [S2] [SW says 134th Co.]

Schaidt, Gustave, Sgt., 70th Co., 2nd Brigade, Dominican Republic, DOS, May 22, 1919 at Santo Domingo, Dominican Republic. Mrs. Gustave Schaidt (Mother), Lonaconing, Maryland [FAG] [S4]

Marine Corps Deaths, 1917-1921

Schall, James Sherman, Pvt., 49th Co., 5th Regt., KIA, June 5, 1918 in the Chateau-Thierry Sector. James Schall (Father), Templeton, Pennsylvania [R] [S2] [SW says 133rd Co., Repl. Btln.]

Schaufele, Raymond Frederick, Pvt., 43rd Co., 5th Regt., KIA, June 8, 1918 in the Chateau-Thierry Sector. Mrs. Christiana Schaufele (Mother), 3020 E. 78th St., Cleveland, Ohio [ANC] [S2] [SW]

Schell, Howard D., Cpl., Bks. Det., MB, Navy Yard, New York, New York, DDS, September 25, 1919 at White Haven, Pennsylvania. Mrs. Annie L. Schell (Mother), 2181 Bedford Ave., Brooklyn, New York [S4]

Schenk, Edgar G., Pay Clerk, CPM Office, Paris, France. DOC February 9, 1919 in France. Mrs. F. Schenk (widow), 1103 George St., Chicago, Illinois [ABMC-Fere] [S1]

Schindler, Irvin Frank, Cpl., 73rd Co., 6th Regt., KIA, November 1, 1918 in the Meuse Argonne. Mrs. Frederick Schindler (Mother), 4839 Milentz Ave., St. Louis, Missouri [FAG] [S2] [SW1]

Schiro, John, Pvt., Bks. Det., MB, Navy Yard, New York, New York, DDS, February 25, 1920 at Brooklyn, New York. Mrs. Catherine Schiro (Mother), 194 Utica Ave., Brooklyn, New York [S4]

Schlageter, Merle D., Pvt., 20th Co., 5th Regt., KIA, June 6, 1918 in the Chateau-Thierry Sector. Ida Schlageter (Mother), Grimilgi, Colorado [ABMC- Belleau TOM as M.D.] [S2] [SW]

Schlichter, Fred, Pvt., 51st Co., Quantico, Virginia, DDS, April 6, 1921 at Quantico, Virginia. Minnie Schlichter (Mother), 241 N. Howard St., Glendale, California [S4]

Schlieman, Frank Fred, Pvt., 55th Co., 5th Regt., DOW, June 12, 1918 in the Chateau-Thierry Sector. Henry Schlieman (Father), RFD#4, Palmyra, New York [S2] [SW]

Marine Corps Deaths, 1917-1921

Schlumpberger, Alvin Herbert, Pvt., 49th Co., 5th Regt., KIA, June 20, 1918 in the Chateau-Thierry Sector. Alfred A. Schlumpberger (Father), 100 South Franklin St., New Ulm, Minnesota [ABMC- Belleau TOM as A.H.] [S2] [SW1]

Schmidt, Carl Glen, Pvt., Co. H, 11th Regt., Quantico, Virginia, DDS, October 8, 1918 at Quantico, Virginia. Minnie Schmidt (Mother), Beaumont, Texas [S3]

Schmidt, Henry, Pvt., Co. D, 13th Regt., DOD, September 22, 1918 enroute to France. Mrs. Mayme Schmidt (Wife), 815 Livingston St., Cincinnati, Ohio [R] [S2]

Schmidt, John August, Cpl., 51st Co., 5th Regt., KIA, October 4, 1918 in the Meuse Argonne. August K. Schmidt (Father), 206 Balsam St., Liverpool, New York [ABMC-Romagne] [S2] [SW]

Schmidt, William Albert, Sgt., Co. B, OSD, Quantico, Virginia, DDS, September 24, 1918 at Quantico, Virginia. Augusta Schmidt (Mother), 494 Madison St., Buffalo, New York [S3]

Schmidt, William H., Jr., 2nd Lieut., MCR, 47th Co., 5th Regt., KIA, October 4, 1918 in the Meuse Argonne. Sgt. W. G. Schidt (Father), address unknown. [ABMC-Romagne] [S1] [SW]

Schmitt, Leslie Anthony, Pvt., 78th Co., 6th Regt., KIA, June 14, 1918 in the Chateau-Thierry Sector. Mrs. Daniel Schmitt (Mother), 4611 N. Racine Ave., Chicago, Illnois [S2] [SW]

Schnarr, George B. H., Pvt., 18th Co., 5th Regt., DOW, July 20, 1918 in the Aisne Marne. Caroline Schmarr (Mother), 185 N. 4th St., Newark, New Jersey [ABMC- Fere] [S2] [SW1]

Schneider, John G., Jr., 1st Lieut., 80th Co., 6th Regt., DOW, November 3, 1918 in the Meuse Argonne. John G. Schneider (Father), American National Bank, St. Joseph, Missouri [FAG] [S1] [SW1 says KIA]

Marine Corps Deaths, 1917-1921

Schneider, William Joseph, Pvt., 18th Co., 5th Regt., KIA, October 4, 1918 in the Meuse Argonne. Joseph Schneider (Father), 56 F. 36th Place, Chicago, Illlinois [S2] [SW1 says Cpl.]

Schoedel, Alfred Erich, Pvt., 74th Co., 6th Regt., DOW, April 18, 1918 in the Toulon Sector, Verdun. Martha Schoedel (Mother), RR#5, Peoria, Illinois [FAG] [S2] [SW]

Scholler, Harold, Pvt., 51st Co., 5th Regt., KIA, October 4, 1918 in the Meuse Argonne. H. P. Scholler (Father), New Holland, Ohio [R] [S2] [SW says Co. C, 5th Sep. Btln.]

Schoon, John Ben, Pvt., Co. C, 7sep, DOD, November 22, 1918 in France. Ben Schoon (Father), RR#5, Bradford, Iowa [ANC] [S2]

Schott, Alexander, Sgt., Bks. Det., Norfolk, Virginia, DAS, July 15, 1919 of a fractured skull at Norfolk, Virginia. Mrs. Lillie Murray (Sister), 300 East 20th St., New York, New York [S4]

Schramm, Frederick Louis, Cpl., 51st Co., 5th Regt., KIA, June 6, 1918 in the Chateau-Thierry Sector. Wilhelmina Schramm (Mother), 4250 Trumbull St., Bellaire, Ohio [ABMC- Belleau] [S2] [SW]

Schrank, John, Gy. Sgt., 80th Co., 6th Regt., KIA, July 19, 1918 in the Aisne Marne. Mrs. Lillian Schrank (Mother), 615 Palisade Ave., Jersey City Heights, New Jersey [ANC] [S2] [SW]

Schrautemeier, Eugene Stephen, Pvt., 83rd Co., 6th Regt., KIA, June 6, 1918 in the Chateau-Thierry Sector. B. H. Schrautemeier (Father), 1718 Cora Ave, St. Louis, Missouri [S2] [SW1]

Schreiber, Carl Sigmound, Pvt., 51st Co., 5th Regt., DOW, June 24, 1918 in the Chateau-Thierry Sector. Mrs. Elizabeth Schreiber (Mother), 817 Broadway Dormant, South Hill Branch, Pittsburg, Pennsylvania [R] [S2] [SW]

Marine Corps Deaths, 1917-1921

Schroeder, Frank Wesley, Cpl., 49th Co., 5th Regt., DOW, November 2, 1918 in the Meuse Argonne. Nannie E. Schraeder (Mother), North Kansas City, Missouri [FAG] [S2] [SW1]

Schroer, Herman, Sgt., 8th Co., New Orleans, Louisiana, DAS, April 23, 1918 at New Orleans, Louisiana. Miss Margaret Nienaber (Aunt), 2862 Gravois Ave., St. Louis, Missouri [VA-Jefferson Barracks] [S3]

Schuler, LeGrand Edward, Pvt., Co. A, 13th Regt., DOD, September 26, 1918 in France. Frederick Schuler (Father), Wilcox, Pennsylvania [FAG] [S2]

Schuler, Lloyd, Pvt., 95th Co., 6th Regt., DOW, August 12, 1918 in the Aisne Marne. Mrs Bertha Fleming (Mother), 124 Featherbed Lane, Bronx, New York [FAG] [S2] [SW1]

Schulte, Fred William, Pvt., 84th Co., 6th Regt., KIA, June 6, 1918 in the Chateau-Thierry Sector. Anthony Schulte (Father), 935 Ohio St., Quincy, Illinois [ABMC- Belleau TOM] [S2] [SW]

Schultz, Donald David, Pfc, 83rd Co., 6th Regt., KIA, October 10, 1918 in the Meuse Argonne. Mrs. Victoria Schultz (Mother), 407 Lincoln Ave., Council Bluffs, Iowa [ANC] [S2] [SW1]

Schulz, Fred, Pvt., 67th Co., 5th Regt., KIA, June 6, 1918 in the Chateau-Thierry Sector. Matilda Schulz (Sister), 231 South 18th St., St. Louis, Missouri [ABMC- Belleau] [S2] [SW1]

Schulz, Herbert Burt, Pvt., 73rd Co., 6th Regt., KIA, July 19, 1918 in the Aisne Marne. Paul Schulz (Father), 6421 Greenwood Ave., Chicago, Illinois [ABMC- Belleau TOM] [S2] [SW1]

Schwab, Vincent Martin, Sgt., 8th Co., 5th Regt., KIA, June 9, 1918 in the Chateau-Thierry Sector. Tillie Shwab (Cousin) 2511½ Doddier St., St. Louis, Missouri [ABMC- Belleau as V.M.] [S2] [SW]

Marine Corps Deaths, 1917-1921

Schwartz, Bernard Reinhard, Cpl., 49th Co., 5th Regt., KIA, November 1, 1918 in the Meuse Argonne. Joseph Schwars (Brother), 4028 Clayton St., Denver, Colorado [S2] [SW1]

Schweizer, Carl, Cpl., Squadron E, MAF, Haiti, DDS, June 12, 1920 at Haiti. Barbara Schweizer (Mother), 2550 W. 25th St., Cleveland, Ohio [S4]

Scofield, Howard Southerland, Pvt., 8th Co., 5th Regt., KIA, September 14, 1918 in the St. Mihiel Offensive. Mrs. Dorothy Scofield (Mother), P O, St. Johns, Michigan [FAGM] [S2] [SW]

Scolnick, Samuel, Pvt., 182nd Co., 15th Regt., DDS, October 4, 1921 at Washington, D.C. Mrs. Bessie Scolnick (Mother), 133 Lutheran St., Buffalo, New York [S4]

Scott, Leslie Bryan, Pvt., 80th Co., 6th Regt., DOW, September 16, 1918 in the St. Mihiel Offensive. Pearl Scott (Mother), Box 276, League City, Texas [FAG] [S2] [SW] [SW1]

Scott, William Elmer, Sgt., 23rd Co., 6th MG Bn., KIA, June 15, 1918 in the Chateau-Thierry Sector. John Scott (Brother), Tippecanoe City, Ohio [FAG] [S2] [SW]

Scoville, Ernest Jacob, Cpl., 84th Co., 6th Regt., KIA, November 5, 1918 in the Meuse Argonne. Martha E. Buchan (Mother), 300 Ivy St., Portland, Oregon [ANC] [S2] [SW1] [SW1]

Seablom, Conrad Nicholas, Cpl., 74th Co., 6th Regt., DOW, November 5, 1918 in the Meuse Argonne. John A. Seablom (Father), 2508 Kimball Ave., Chicago, Illinois [R] [S2] [SW1 says KIA]

Seal, Max Edwin, Pvt., 97th Co., 6th Regt., KIA, June 6, 1918 in the Chateau-Thierry Sector. Christopher C. Seal (Father), 3873 Isabella Ave., Cincinnati, Ohio [S2] [SW]

Seale, Clyde Wesley, Cpl., 18th Co., 5th Regt., DOW, October 4, 1918 in the Meuse Argonne. Mrs. Elizabeth Seale

Marine Corps Deaths, 1917-1921

(Mother), 227 So. Bunker Hill Ave., Los Angeles, California [FAG] [S2] [SW1]

Seay, Samuel Tellis, Cpl., 75th Co., 6th Regt., KIA, September 15, 1918 in the St. Mihiel Offensive. Samuel J. Seay (Father), Plantersville, Alabama [S2] [SW says 137th Co., Repl. Btln.]

Sebastian, Leo Henry, Pvt., 43rd Co., 5th Regt., KIA, October 5, 1918 in the Meuse Argonne. Mrs. J. H. Sebastian (Mother), 6415 Greenwood Ave., Seattle, Washington [S2]

Seebauer, Joseph Frank, Pvt., Co. F, Parris Island, South Carolina, DDS, October 17, 1917 at Parris Island, South Carolina. Mary Seebauer (Mother), 524 Union St., Columbia, Pennsylvania [S3]

Seib, Herman Conrad, Sgt., 97th Co., 6th Regt., KIA, July 19, 1918 in the Aisne Marne. John Seib (Brother), 40 Bowers St., Jersey City Heights, New Jersey [ABMC- Belleau TOM] [S2] [SW says 145th Co., Repl. Btln.]

Seidel, Theodore Julius, Pvt., Naval Prison, Portsmouth, New Hampshire, DDS, September 23, 1918 at Portsmouth, New Hampshire. Alfred Seidel (Brother), Gen. Del. Logansport, Indiana [S3]

Seifert, Julian Henry, Pvt., Co. D, 13th Regt., DAO, February 12, 1919 in France. Jon Seifert (Father), 2049 E. Monument St., Baltimore, Maryland [R] [S2] [SW1 says KOA]

Seitz, Frederick William, Cpl., 67th Co., 5th Regt., KIA, November 2, 1918 in the Meuse Argonne. Emma Seitz (Mother), Gen. Del., Pomeroy, Ohio [ABMC- Romagne] [S2] [SW1]

Selden, Guy Wentworth, Cpl., 97th Co., 6th Regt., KIA, September 15, 1918 in the St. Mihiel Offensive. Mrs. Eleanore C. Seldon (Mother), 4961 McPeherson Ave., St. Louis, Missouri [S2] [SW says 119th Co., Repl. Btln.]

Marine Corps Deaths, 1917-1921

Sellars, George Durrel, Pvt., 20th Co., 5th Regt., DOW, June 7, 1918 in the Chateau-Thierry Sector. George W. Sellars (Father), Moscow, Texas [S2] [SW says George Burrel]

Selzer, Charles Wilbur, Pvt., Co. A, 13th Regt., DOD, October 9, 1918 in France. Caroline Selzer (Mother), RFD#3, Box 11, Canton, Kansas [S2]

Semian, John, Cpl., 15th Co., 6th MG Bn., KIA, June 12, 1918 in the Chateau-Thierry Sector. Anna Semian (Mother), 538 Thomas Ct., Tayler, Pennsylvania [ABMC- Fere] [S2] [SW]

Servat, Ulysses Rally, Pvt., Co. F, 13th Regt., DOD, September 27, 1918 in France. Jules Servat (Mother), 506 Garfield St., Lafayette, Louisiana [R] [S2]

Severns, Sidney, Pvt., 20th Co., 5th Regt., KIA, June 6, 1918 in the Chateau-Thierry Sector. Ella A. Severns (Mother), Box 211, Martinez, California [ABMC- Belleau] [S2] [SW]

Sewell, John Henry, Cpl., Quantico, Virginia, DAS, August 25, 1919 struck by a train at Cartersville, Georgia. Robert E. Sewell (Father), Marietta, Georgia [S4]

Sexton, Robert F., Pvt., Co. A, MB, Navy Yard, Mare Island, California, DDS, January 29, 1920 at Mare Island, California. F.W. Sexton (relationship not given), Long Beach, California [S4]

Sexton, Sidney Lester, Pvt., 77th Co., 6th MG Bn., DOW, November 4, 1918 in the Meuse Argonne. Joe Sexton (Father), Volney, Virginia [ANC] [S2] [SW1]

Shaar, Luther Adam, Pvt., USS *Vermont*, DDU, September 28, 1917 aboard the USS *Vermont*. H. M. Shaar (Father), 714 E. King St., Lancaster, Pennsylvania [S3]

Shade, John Lewis, Pvt., Hdqtrs. Co., 5th Regt., KIA, April 24, 1918 in the Toulon Sector, Verdun. Jennie Shade (Mother), 515 5th St., Clearfield, Pennsylvania [R] [S2] [SW]

Marine Corps Deaths, 1917-1921

Shadle, Herbert Irvin, Sgt., 79th Co., 6th Regt., KIA, July 19, 1918 in the Aisne Marne. Leon Shadle (Father), 20 Elgin St., W. Chicago, Illinois [ABMC- Belleau TOM] [S2] [SW]

Shaffner, Basil James, Pvt., 76th Co., 6th Regt., KIA, July 19, 1918 in the Aisne Marne. Mrs. Jennie Pfingsten (Mother), c/o Groves, 7255 Calumet Ave., Chicago, Illinois [S2] [SW]

Shalet, Michael, Pvt., MD, USS *Pennsylvania* at Norfolk, Virginia, DDS, April 21, 1917 at Norfolk, Virginia. Dr. Louis Shalet (Brother), Mt. Kiser, Bedford Hills, New York [S3]

Shapton, Leslie Thomas, Cpl., 18th Co., 5th Regt., KIA, July 18, 1918 in the Aisne Marne. Mrs. Elizabeth Shapton (Mother), 112 F. Hurlburt Ave., Charlevoix, Michigan [R] [S2] [SW says 116th Co., Repl. Btln.]

Share, Ralph Cameron, Pvt., 23rd Co., 6th MG Bn., KIA, October 4, 1918 in the Meuse Argonne. Charles L. Share (Father), Main St., Marcellus, New York [FAG] [S2] [SW]

Sharp, Burton, Pvt., 96th Co., 6th Regt., KIA, July 19, 1918 in the Aisne Marne. Herbert Sharp (Father), 307 20th Ave., N. Minneapolis, Minnesota [S2] [SW says Co. B, Repl. Btln.]

Sharpe, Eugene, Pvt., 17th Co., 5th Regt., KIA, August 3, 1918 in the Aisne Marne. Delphia Sharpe (Mother), 512 Lamont St., Johnson City, Tennessee [ABMC- Belleau TOM] [S2] [SW1]

Shatto, Francis E. W., Pvt., Co. B, Mare Island, California, DDS, December 22, 1918 at Mare Island, California, Harvey L. Shatto (Father), Gen. Del., Nashville, Tennessee [S4]

Shauberger, Gale Bryan, Pvt., 16th Co., 5th Regt., KIA, November 2, 1918 in the Meuse Argonne. Mrs. Rebecca Shauberger (Mother), Box 377, Albion, Erie County, Pennsylvania [ANC] [S2] [SW1]

Marine Corps Deaths, 1917-1921

Shaver, John Henry, Pvt., 84th Co., 6th Regt., DOW, October 13, 1918 in the Meuse Argonne. Theodore Shaver (Father), Tioga, West Virgnina [R] [S2] [SW1]

Shaw, Armand George, Pvt., Naval Prison, Portsmouth, New Hampshire, DDS, September 26, 1918 at Portsmouth, New Hampshire. George E. Shaw (Father), 748 Monterey St., Hollister, California [S3]

Shaw, Charles A., Pvt., MB, Navy Yard, New York, New York, DDS, December 23, 1918 at Hartsdale, New York. Mrs. Anna C. Shaw (Mother), Central Ave., Hartsdale, New York [S4]

Shazer, Leslie R., Pvt., Co. Y, Parris Island, South Carolina, DDS, November 15, 1918 at Parris Island, South Carolina. Adam T. Shazer (Father), Newpoint, Indiana [FAG] [S4]

Shea, Willard Cornelius, Sgt., Co. A., OTC, Quantico, Virginia, DDS, September 25, 1918 at Quantico, Virginia. Daniel C. Shea (Father), 706 Jones St., Eveleth, Minnesota [S3]

Shearer, Albert Lee, Sgt., 95th Co., 6th Regt., KIA, July 19, 1918 in the Aisne Marne. Rose B. Shearer (Mother), Monticello, Kentucky [FAG] [S2] [SW1]

Shedden, Clarence Albert, Pvt., 95th Co., 6th Regt., DOW, July 19, 1918 in the Aisne Marne. Katherine Shedden (Mother), 255 Liberty St., Dundee, Kansas [ABMC- Fere] [S2] [SW1 says KIA]

Sheets, Edgar, Pvt., 45th Co., 5th Regt., DOW, October 21, 1918 in the Meuse Argonne. Mrs. Hannah Sheets (Mother), Fairchance, Pennsylvania [FAG] [S2] [SW1]

Sheets, Scott McAllister, Pvt., 23rd Co., 6th MG Bn., KIA, October 9, 1918 in the Meuse Argonne. Ella Sheets (Mother), 520 E. 13th St., South, Salt Lake City, Utah [FAG] [S2] [SW1]

Sheldon, Arthur Louis, Pvt., 45th Co., 5th Regt., KIA, October 4, 1918 in the Meuse Argonne. Mr. John E. Sheldon

Marine Corps Deaths, 1917-1921

(Father), Westmoreland, New Hampshire [R] [S2] [SW1 says Arthur Lewis Sheldon]

Sheller, Arthur Randolph, Pvt., 74th Co., 6th Regt., DOW, November 3, 1918 in the Meuse Argonne. Clark A. McCumber (Mother), Polk, Ohio [VA-Grafton] [S2] [SW1]

Shelton, Elihu, Pvt., 78th Co., 6th Regt., DOW, October 6, 1918 in the Meuse Argonne. Thomas N. Shelton (Father), RR#1, Manchester, Tennessee [ABMC- Belleau] [S2] [SW]

Shelton, Grayson, Pvt., 8th Co., 5th Regt., DOW, October 6, 1918 in the Meuse Argonne. Frank Shelton (Father), 1710 Wagner Place, St. Louis, Missouri [ABMC- Romagne] [S2] [SW1]

Shepard, George Alby, Pvt., 158th Co. (Signal), Philadelphia, Pennsylvania, DDS, September 26, 1918 at Philadelphia, Pennsylvania. William J. Shepard (Uncle), 236 Washington St., Brighton, Massachusetts [S3]

Sherman, Abraham, Pvt., 196th Co., 8th Regt., Haiti, DAS, October 25, 1921 at Port au Prince, Haiti. Mrs. Annie Sherman (Mother), 617 W. 204th St., New York, New York [FAG] [S4]

Sherman, Anthony Michael, Pvt., 96th Co., 6th Regt., DOW, June 21, 1918 in the Chateau-Thierry Sector. Mrs. Elizabeth Sherman (Mother), 809 S. Miami Ave., Sidney, Ohio [R] [S2] [SW]

Sherman, Harold Harvey, Pvt., 77th Co., 6th MG Bn., DOW, October 12, 1918 in the Meuse Argonne. Mrs. Nettie Sherman Smith (Mother), 404 Fisher St., Peoria, Illinois [FAG] [S2] [SW1]

Sherman, Lester, 1st Sgt., 104th Co., 8th Regt., Galveston, Texas, DDS, October 16, 1918 at Galveston, Texas. Marry L. Morse (Cousin), RFD#2, Melrose, New York [S3]

Sherman, Stephen George, Sgt., 20th Co., 5th Regt., KIA, June 6, 1918 in the Chateau-Thierry Sector. George C. Sherman

Marine Corps Deaths, 1917-1921

(Father), 1811 Colfax Ave., Minneapolis, Minnesota [FAG] [S2] [SW]

Shields, Oliver F., 1st Sgt., Co. T, Parris Island, South Carolina, DDS, November 22, 1918 at Parris Island, South Carolina. Cameron Shields (Father), Marietta, Pennsylvania [S4]

Shields, Robert Morris, Pvt., 81st Co., 6th MG Bn., DOW, June 17, 1918 in the Chateau-Thierry Sector. Mrs. Victoria Shields (Mother), 550 Undercliff Ave., Edgewater, New Jersey [R] [S2] [SW 138th Co., Repl. Btln.]

Shields, Terrell Archie, Pvt., 66th Co., 5th Regt., Quantico, Virginia, DDS, March 20, 1921 at Quantico, Virginia. Minerva Shields (Mother), Hampton, Kentucky [S4]

Shilling, Columbus Hiram, Pvt., 13th Co., 10th Regt., Quantico, Virginia, DDS, October 4, 1918 at Quantico, Virginia. Alice Shilling (Mother), Knox, Indiana [FAG] [S3]

Shirk, Milton Richard, Pvt., Bks. Det., Quantico, Virginia, DDS, October 16, 1918 at Quantico, Virginia. Edith Shirk (Mother), Gen. Del., Clearbrook, Washington [FAG] [S3]

Shoemaker, Willis Richard, Pvt., 95th Co., 6th Regt., KIA, June 12, 1918 in the Chateau-Thierry Sector. Delta Shoemaker (Sister), Romney, Hampshire Co., W. Virginia [FAG] [S2] [SW]

Short, Elmer Spencer, Pvt., 84th Co., 6th Regt., DOW, July 23, 1918 in the Aisne Marne. Mrs. Ernest R. Wilson (Sister), 102 N. Second St., Ironton, Ohio [ABMC- Suresnes] [S2] [SW says 139th Co., Repl. Btln.]

Short, Lloyd, Pvt., 96th Co., 6th Regt., KIA, July 19, 1918 in the Aisne Marne. Caroline Short (Mother), Rapid City, South Dakota [ABMC- Fere] [S2] [SW]

Shover, Oscar Earl, Pvt., 18th Co., 5th Regt., KIA, June 10, 1918 in the Chateau-Thierry Sector. Joseph Shaver (Father), 3565 Pennsylvania Ave., Indiana Harbor, Indiana [ABMC- Belleau] [S2] [SW] [SW1]

Marine Corps Deaths, 1917-1921

Showers, James Wayne, Pvt., Hdqtrs. Co., 13th Regt., DOD, September 24, 1918 aboard the USS *Von Steuben* enroute to France. Mrs. Fannie E. Showers (Aunt), Cynthiana, Indiana [R] [S2] [SW says Radio Det.] [SW1 says Radio Detachment]

Shunk, Samuel Henry, Pvt., 96th Co., 6th Regt., KIA, October 3, 1918 in the Meuse Argonne. Mrs. Eva Shunk (Wife), 587 Crawford Ave., Detroit, Michigan [ABMC- Romagne] [S2] [SW1]

Sickinger, John C., Pvt., MBks., Parris Island, South Carolina. DDS, January 16, 1919 at Parris Island, South Carolina. Alice Sickinger (Wife), 426 Wright St., La Salle, Illinois [FAG] [S4]

Sidders, Frank, Cpl., 20th Co., 5th Regt., KIA, June 23, 1918 in the Chateau-Thierry Sector. Mrs. Ida Sidders (Mother), 507 Williams St., Trenton, New Jersey [S2] [SW]

Siefert, Frederick Albert, Cpl., 51st Co., 5th Regt., KIA, November 10, 1918 in the Meuse Argonne. Fred Siefert (Father), Swanton, Ohio [ANC] [S2] [SW1]

Siepker, William Clem, Pvt., 75th Co., 6th Regt., KIA, October 9, 1918 in the Meuse Argonne. Mrs. Minnie Siepker (Mother), 313 Chestnut St., Quincy, Illinois [S2] [SW1]

Silverman, David Granville, Pvt., 75th Co., 6th Regt., DOO, May 26, 1918 in France. Charles Garfinkel (Uncle), 260 Ft. Washington Ave., New York, New York [ABMC-Suresnes] [S2] [SW says DOW, and 139th Co., Repl. Btln.] [SW1]

Silverston, Albert, Pvt., 20th Co., 5th Regt., KIA, June 6, 1918 in the Chateau-Thierry Sector. Mrs. Mary Silverston (Mother), 744 West 8th St., Cincinnati, Ohio [S2] [SW says Silverton]

Simmons, Clarence Leroy, Trumpeter, Aero Co., Advanced Base, Azores, DOD, October 31, 1918 George A. Simmons (Father), 410 East Sixth St., Abilene, Kansas [R] [S2]

Marine Corps Deaths, 1917-1921

Simon, Frank Joe, Sgt., 76th Co., 6th Regt., DOW, December, 11, 1918 in the Meuse Argonne. Margeret Simon (Mother), Lagrange, Illinois [R] [S2]

Simonds, Albert C., 1st Lieut., 80th Co., 6th Regt., KIA, September 15, 1918 in the St. Mihiel offensive. Mrs. Mary C. Simonds (Mother), 726 Garland Ave., Los Angeles, California [ABMC-Thiaucourt] [S1] [SW]

Simonson, Hjalmer Oliver, Sgt., 79th Co., 6th Regt., KIA, July 19, 1918 in the Aisne Marne. Mrs. S. Simonson (Mother), Ada, Minnesota [ANC] [S2] [SW1]

Simonton, Harold F., Pvt., 44th Co. 3rd Prov. Regt., Dominican Republic, DDS, March 4, 1919 at Santo Domingo, Dominican Republic. Mrs. Hazel P. Freeman (Sister), 47 Stevens Ave., Portland, Maine [S4]

Simpson, James Young, Jr., Pvt., 82nd Co., 6th Regt., KIA, June 6, 1918 in the Chateau-Thierry Sector. James Y. Simpson (Father), 3100 Euclid Ave., Kansas City, Kansas [ABMC- Belleau] [S2] [SW]

Sims, Arthur Dudley, Pvt., 84th Co., 6th Regt., DOW, June 10, 1918 in the Chateau-Thierry Sector. Robert B. Sims (Father), 174 Cox Ave., Memphis, Tennessee [ABMC-Suresnes] [S2] [SW]

Singleton, Charles T., Pvt., Co. B, MB, Navy Yard, Mare Island, California, DDS, November 17, 1918 at Mare Island, California. Mrs. Cora Singleton (Mother), Hoyt, Colorado [FAG] [S4]

Sipes, Joshua Earl, Pvt., 83rd Co., 6th Regt., KIA, November 2, 1918 in the Meuse Argonne. Burton Sipes (Father), Curwensville, Pennsylvania [ABMC- Romagne] [S2] [SW1]

Sircy, Sherman, Pvt., 95th Co., 6th Regt., DOW, July 19, 1918 in the Aisne Marne. Mrs. Lassie Sircy (Wife), RFD#1, Oakville, Kentucky [S2] [SW1 says KIA]

Marine Corps Deaths, 1917-1921

Sisco, Charlie C., Pvt., MB, USN Academy, Annapolis, Maryland, DAS, July 3, 1920 drowned at Annapolis, Maryland. Ellen Boyd (Mother), Box 111, RR#1, Cartersville, Oklahoma [S4]

Sissler, Joseph Aloysius, 1st Sgt., 96th Co., 6th Regt., KIA, June 6, 1918 in the Chateau-Thierry Sector. Joseph Sissler (Father), 312 W. 37th St., New York, New York [ABMC-Fere] [S2] [SW]

Sisson, James, Cpl., 82nd Co., 6th Regt., DOD, December, 14, 1918 in the Meuse Argonne. Charles Sisson (Father), Sissonville, West Virginia [R] [S2] [SW1 says DOW]

Six, Ornan Joseph, Pvt., Supply Co., Quantico, Virginia, DDS, October 3, 1918 at Quantico, Virginia. Phillip Six (Father), Gwynneville, Indiana [S3]

Skidmore, Carl Beard, Pvt., 74th Co., 6th Regt., DOW, November 2, 1918 in the Meuse Argonne. Morris W. Skidmore (Father), Jefferson, New York [S2] [SW1]

Skidmore, Herbert Jones, Pvt., 16th Co., 5th Regt., DOW, November 9, 1918 in the Meuse Argonne. Sallie Skidmore (Mother), Harlan, Kentucky [S2] [SW1 says Hobert Jones Skidmore]

Skidmore, Van Rensselear, Pvt., 47th Co., 5th Regt., KIA, June 24, 1918 in the Chateau-Thierry Sector. Mrs. Van Rensselear Skidmore (Wife), 1055 Lincoln Place, Broooklyn, New York [ABMC-Belleau] [S2] [SW1]

Skolba, Linton Clifford, Pvt., 78th Co., 6th Regt., DOW, December, 11, 1918 in the St. Mihiel Offensive. Anund J. Skolba (Father), 3201 Columbus Ave., South Minneapolis, Minnesota [R] [S2] [SW1]

Slider, Clyde Herman, Pvt., 23rd Co., 6th MG Bn., KIA, June 18, 1918 in the Chateau-Thierry Sector. Mrs. Mary Slider (Mother), Davis, West Virginia [FAG] [S2] [SW]

Marine Corps Deaths, 1917-1921

Slone, Harley Hensley, Cpl., 80th Co., 6th Regt., KIA, June 10, 1918 in the Chateau-Thierry Sector. Mrs. Bell Dye (Mother), Mason, Illinois [ABMC- Belleau] [S2] [SW]

Slusser, Glen Dewey, Sgt., 45th Co., 5th Regt., KIA, November 3, 1918 in the Meuse Argonne. Mrs. Lydia E. Slusser (Mother), Ottawa, Ohio [FAG] [S2] [SW1]

Slyke, Alfred George, Sgt., 77th Co., 6th MG Bn., DOD, November 4, 1918 in the Meuse Argonne. William Slyke (Father), 122 North Terrace, Schenectady, New York [ABMC-Romagne] [S2]

Small, Eddie Elonz, Pvt., 95th Co., 6th Regt., DOW, June 14, 1918 in the Chateau-Thierry Sector. Mrs. Susan Small (Mother), 947 Wright Ave., Toledo, Ohio [FAG] [S2] [SW]

Small, Harry Rigney, Pvt., 97th Co., 6th Regt., DOW, July 19, 1918 in the Aisne Marne. Annie Small (Mother), Second St., Aberdeen, Ohio [FAG] [S2] [SW1]

Smalley, Clayton Henry, Pvt., 158th Co., Philadelphia, Pennsylvania, DDS, October 12, 1918 at Philadelphia, Pennsylvania. Anna Faulkner (Mother), 2438 Harrison St., Kansas City, Missouri [S3]

Smart, Henry James, Cpl., 74th Co., 6th Regt., DOW, April 17, 1918 in the Toulon Sector, Verdun. Annie Smart (Mother), Pineville, South Carolina [ABMC- Romagne] [S2] [SW]

Smiley, Dean Franklin, Pvt., 75th Co., 6th Regt., KIA, October 9, 1918 in the Meuse Argonne. Mrs. Jennie Smiley (Mother), 406 S. 5th St., Goshen, Indiana [S2] [SW1]

Smith, Alonzo J., Sgt., Hdqtrs. Det., Navy Yard, Philadelphia, Pennsylvania, DDS, January 31, 1920 at League Island, Pennsylvania. Miss Mary Smith (Sister), 930 Sartain St., Philadelphia, Pennsylvania [FAG] [S4]

Marine Corps Deaths, 1917-1921

Smith, Arnold Coxin, Pvt., 47th Co., 5th Regt., DOD, November 14, 1918 in France. A. F. Smith (Father), 629 Lake St., Lancaster, Pennsylvania [R] [S2]

Smith, Austin Oliver, Pvt., Hdqtrs., 11th Regt., Quantico, Virginia, DDS, October 4, 1918 at Quantico, Virginia. Olive J. Duffy (Mother), RFD#1, Glenwood Springs, Colorado [S3]

Smith, Clarence Elton, Pvt., 8th Co., 5th Regt., DOW, November 2, 1918 in the Meuse Argonne. H. E. Smith (Father), 1325½ North Peak St., Dallas, Texas [ANC] [S2] [SW1 says KIA]

Smith, Clarence W., 1st Lieut., 95th Co., 6th Regt., KIA, June 13, 1918 in the Chateau Thierry sector. Mrs. Martha R. Smith (Mother), 1840 Mintwood Place, Washington, D.C. [ABMC-Belleau] [S1] [SW]

Smith, Edmund Tracy, Pvt., Hdqtrs. Co., 6th Regt., KIA, July 19, 1918 in the Aisne Marne. Julia Smith (Mother), Onarga, Illinois [ABMC- Belleau TOM] [S2] [SW]

Smith, Edward John Evanglist, Pvt., 66th Co., 5th Regt., KIA, November 10, 1918 in the Meuse Argonne. Brother Paul (Friend), St. Mary's Industrial School, Baltimore, Maryland [ABMC- Romagne] [S2] [SW1]

Smith, Ezra Alfred, Pvt., 81st Co., 6th MG Bn., KIA, July 20, 1918 in the Aisne Marne. Pearl Smith (Sister), Otisville, Michigan [FAG] [S2] [SW1]

Smith, Frank George, Pvt., MBks., New London, Connecticut, DAS, June 11, 1919 at New London, Connecticut Miss Florence Smith (Sister), 1621 Prospect Ave., Cleveland, Ohio [S4]

Smith, George Dewey, Sgt., 17th Co., 5th Regt., KIA, October 3, 1918 in the Meuse Argonne. Clara Smith (Mother), 608 W. Auburn Ave., Bellefontaine, Ohio [ABMC-Romagne] [S2] [SW]

Marine Corps Deaths, 1917-1921

Smith, George Elmer, Pvt., Co. K, 11th Regt., Quantico, Virginia, DDS, October 6, 1918 at Quantico, Virginia. Milo W. Smith (Father), RFD#4, Harbor Beach, Michigan [S3]

Smith, Gilbert Grover, Pvt., USNH, Fort Lyon, Colorado, DDS, November 25, 1919 at Fort Lyon, Colorado. Mrs. Martha A. Smith (not given), Sioux Rapids, Iowa [FAG] [S4]

Smith, Harold Jerome, Pvt., Supply Co., Parris Island, South Carolina, DAS, March 6, 1921, drowned in the Johnson River near Parris Island, South Carolina. Benjamin Ball (Uncle), RFD#4, Tunkhannock, Pennsylvania [S4]

Smith, Harry Sidney, Pvt., Co. G, 13th Regt., DOD, September 26, 1918 in France. Sidney Smith (Father), 1113 Troy Road, Edwardsville, Illinois [R] [S2]

Smith, Henry Kunkel, Cpl., 66th Co., 5th Regt., KIA, June 16, 1918 in the Chateau-Thierry Sector. Mrs. Minnie Smith (Mother), 61 Snyder St., Larksville, Pennsylvania [R] [S2] [SW]

Smith, Herbert, Pvt., 8th Co., 5th Regt., KIA, September 15, 1918 in the St. Mihiel Offensive. Floss Smith (Mother), Rockaway, New York [ABMC- Thiaucourt TOM] [S2] [SW says Repl. Btln.]

Smith, James Harry, Pvt., MCR, 1st Res. Co., MB, Philadelphia, Pennsylvania, DDS, September 27, 1918 at Great Lakes, Illinois. Anna Smith (Mother), 1529 Franklyn St., San Francisco, California [S3]

Smith, James LeRoy, Trp, 76th Co., 6th Regt., KIA, September 12, 1918 in the St. Mihiel Offensive. Mrs. Sadie LeBrun (Mother), 257 S. Highland Ave., Baltimore, Maryland [VA-Loudon Park] [S2] [SW says 137th Co., Repl. Btln.]

Smith, James Nicholas, Pvt., MCR, BD, MB, Quantico, Virginia, DDS, October 13, 1918 at Quantico, Virginia. Thomas G. Sawyer (Friend), Carroll, Iowa [FAG] [S3]

Marine Corps Deaths, 1917-1921

Smith, Jesse Leroy, Pvt., Marine Aviation Det., Miami, Florida, DDS, October 26, 1918 at Miami, Florida. Ada Dunn (Sister), Himrods, New York [S3]

Smith, Joe, Pvt., Hdqtrs. Co., 6th Regt., DOW, July 19, 1918 in the Aisne Marne. Mrs. W. W. Smith (Mother), 2015 Avenue G, Birmingham, Alabama [ANC] [S2] [SW1]

Smith, John Allen, Pvt., 210th Co., 2nd Brigade, Dominican Republic, DAS, May 31, 1919 at Santo Domingo, Dominican Republic. John W. Smith (Father), 131 N. College St., Covington, Tennessee [FAG] [S4]

Smith, John David, Pvt., Batt. A, MB, Training Camp, Parris Island, South Carolina. DDS, October 3, 1919 at Parris Island, South Carolina. Miss Anna Smith (Aunt), Box 56, RFD#2, Indiana, Pennsylvania [S4]

Smith, John Francis, Pvt., 8th Co., 5th Regt., DOW, October 4, 1918 in the Meuse Argonne. Mrs. George T. Knox (Adopted Mother), Box 611, Downers Grove, Illinois [ABMC- Belleau] [S2] [SW1 says 8th M.G. Co.]

Smith, John Jesse, Pvt., 95th Co., 6th Regt., DOW, September 14, 1918 in the St. Mihiel Offensive. Anna B. Smith (Mother), 504 South 3rd St., Albia, Iowa [FAG] [S2] [SW]

Smith, John William, Pvt., 70th Co., 3rd Regt., Santo Domingo City, Dominican Republic, DDS, October 25, 1917 at Monte de Palma, Dominican Republic. Charles W. Smith (Father), Cascade, Virginia [S3]

Smith, Kenneth Earl, Cpl., 4 Sq, FMAF, DOD, September 29, 1918 in harbor, Liverpool, England. Jessie Smith (Mother), RR#26, Caldwell, Wisconsin [R] [S2]

Smith, Kirby Roy, Pvt., 66th Co., 5th Regt., KIA, October 4, 1918 in the Meuse Argonne. Frank Smith (Brother), Dallas, Georgia [R] [S2] [SW1 says Kirby Ray Smith and DOW]

Smith, Leon Ralza, Pvt., 73rd Co., 6th Regt., KIA, June 29, 1918 in the Chateau-Thierry Sector. Catherine Smith (Mother),

Marine Corps Deaths, 1917-1921

1426 Cherry St., Detroit, Michigan [ABMC- Belleau] [S2] [SW]

Smith, Leslie Henry, Pvt., 20th Co., 5th Regt., KIA, June 6, 1918 in the Chateau-Thierry Sector. Horace Smith (Father), Monana, Iowa [FAG] [S2] [SW]

Smith, Lester Ernest, QM Sgt., Bks. Det., MB, Philadelphia, Pennsylvania, DOS, June 21, 1917 at Philadelphia, Pennsylvania. Blanche Smith (Wife), 933 G St., Washington, D.C. [ANC] [S3]

Smith, Milton Thomas, Pvt., 83rd Co., 6th Regt., DOD, December 8, 1918 in the Meuse Argonne. Mr. Reuben Smith (Father), RR#3, LaCygne, Kansas [FAG] [S2] [SW1 says DOW]

Smith, Nathan Jarrat, Sgt., Co. I, 13th Regt., DOD, September 25, 1918 enroute to France. No next of kin given. [VA-Cypress Hills] [S2]

Smith, Noble, Pvt., 13th Co., 10th Regt., Quantico, Virginia, DDS, October 10, 1918 at Quantico, Virginia. H. C. Minton (Uncle), Georgetown, Indiana [FAG] [S3]

Smith, Orel Austin, Pvt., 82nd Co., 6th Regt., KIA, November 2, 1918 in the Meuse Argonne. Austin Smith (Father), 925 Kingdon Ave., Danville, Illinois [FAG] [S2] [SW1]

Smith, Paul Vincent, Cpl., MD, USS *Helena*, DDS, June 27, 1921 at Hong Kong, China. Ethel Bearde (Sister), 2 Bouton St., Norwalk, Connecticut [ABMC-Clark] [S4] [Note: The Clark Veterans Cemetery, Philippines was made part of ABMC in January 2013 by an Act of Congress]

Smith, Peter Sterling, Pvt., 67th Co., 5th Regt., DOW, November 5, 1918 in the Meuse Argonne. Andrew M. Smith (Father), Shawnee, Kansas [ABMC- Romagne] [S2] [SW1]

Smith, Ray Xavier, Sgt., 45th Co., 5th Regt., KIA, June 23, 1918 in the Chateau-Thierry Sector. Mary M. Smith (Mother),

Marine Corps Deaths, 1917-1921

Box 445, San Jose, California [ABMC- Belleau TOM] [S2] [SW1 says Ray Zavier Smith]

Smith, Raymond Willard, Pvt., 20th Co., 5th Regt., DOW, June 15, 1918 in the Chateau-Thierry Sector. Minnie Hoffman (Mother), 30 Reed St., Canajoharie, New York [R] [S2] [SW]

Smith, Robert Garner, Pvt., Co. A, MB, Parris Island, South Carolina, DDS, October 25, 1918 at Parris Island, South Carolina. Marcus W. Smith (Father), RFD#5, Staockbridge, Michigan [FAG] [S3]

Smith, Rollie F., Pvt., Guard Co. #2, Mare Island, California, DAS, October 1, 1920 at Mare Island, California. Louise Smith (Mother), 1005 S. Stanislaus St., Stockton, California [FAG] [S4]

Smith, Russell A., Pvt., Co. A, 10th Sep. Bn., Quantico, Virginia, DDS, November 13, 1918 at Quantico, Virginia. J. R. Cooper (Uncle), 2527 Clark Ave., Parsons, Kansas [S4]

Smith, Russell Daniel, Pvt., 15th Co., 6th MG Bn., KIA, October 6, 1918 in the Meuse Argonne. Evelyn Offer (Sister), Elizabethtown, Lancaster County, Pennsylvania [ABMC-Romagne] [S2] [SW]

Smith, William Francis, Pvt., 13th Co., 10th Regt., Indian Head, Maryland, DDS, October 7, 1918 at Quantico, Virginia. Georgia Smith (Mother), Benton Harbor, Michigan [S3]

Smith, William Francis, Pvt., 82nd Co., 6th Regt., KIA, July 19, 1918 in the Aisne Marne. Annie Kane (Guardian), 178 Western Ave., Allston, Massachusetts [S2] [SW]

Snair, Bernard Wesley, Cpl., 49th Co., 5th Regt., KIA, July 18, 1918 in the Aisne Marne. Mrs. Kathryn Reid (Mother), 1036 N. Wells St., Chicago, Illinois [ABMC- Belleau TOM as B.W.] [S2] [SW]

Snedeker, Fred Ray, Pvt., 142 Co., New London, Connecticut, DDS, September 29, 1918 at New London, Connecticut

Marine Corps Deaths, 1917-1921

Clark Snedeker (Father), 4089 S. Acoma St., Denver, Colorado [S3]

Snider, Francis McF., 2nd Lieut., "D" Co., 13th Regt., DOD, September 25, 1918 aboard the *Von Steuben*. Robert J. Snider (Father), 155 14th St., Wheeling, West Virginia [R] [S1]

Snider, Frank, Pvt., 74th Co., 6th Regt., DOW, August 17, 1918 in the Aisne Marne. John P. Snider (Brother), 519 West Washington St., Marquette, Michigan [R] [S2] [SW]

Snider, Henry Clyde, Pvt., 16th Co., 5th Regt., KIA, June 23, 1918 in the Chateau-Thierry Sector. Harry Snider (Father), 413 Stealey Ave., Clarksburg, West Virginia [ABMC-Belleau] [S2] [SW1]

Snider, William Bryan, Pvt., Supply Co., 13th Regt., DOD, September 30, 1918 in France. Alice Roberta Snider (Mother), Fruitland, Missouri [ABMC- Fere as William C.] [S2]

Snidow, George Milner, Pvt., 78th Co., 6th Regt., KIA, September 15, 1918 in the St. Mihiel Offensive. Giles L. Snidow (Father), Willamette, Oregon [ABMC- Thiaucourt] [S2] [SW]

Snover, Oscar, Pvt., 150th Co., 1st MG Replacement Bn, DOD, July 2, 1918 in France. John F. Snaver (Father), Gen. Del., Katy, Texas [ABMC- Fere] [S2]

Snow, Enoch Arvile Jr., Pvt., 75th Co., 6th Regt., DOD, March 22, 1918 in France. Enoch A. Snow (Father), Walton, Kentucky [FAG] [S2]

Snow, Frank Hamiliton, Pvt., 83rd Co., 6th Regt., KIA, June 2, 1918 in the Aisne Defensive. Frank H. Snow (Father), Anniston, Alabama [ABMC- Belleau] [S2] [SW]

Snow, George Dewey, Pvt., 79th Co., 6th Regt., KIA, June 6, 1918 in the Chateau-Thierry Sector. Mrs. Josephine H. Smiley (Sister), 7759 South Carpenter St., Chicago, Illinois [ABMC- Belleau] [S2] [SW says George Dewet]

Marine Corps Deaths, 1917-1921

Snyder, Herbert S., Pvt., Department of Supply, Charleston, South Carolina, DAS, April 5, 1920 in a motorcycle accident at Charleston, South Carolina. Mrs. Marie Snyder (Wife), 657 King St., Charleston, South Carolina [FAG] [S4]

Snyder, James Dwight, Cpl., 95th Co., 6th Regt., DOW, November 5, 1918 in the Meuse Argonne. Mr. Lewis Mc. Snyder (Father), 403 South Clinton St., Syracuse, New York [FAG] [S2] [SW1]

Snyder, James Harold, Pvt., 55th Co., 5th Regt., DOW, June 12, 1918 in the Chateau-Thierry Sector. Annie R. Snyder (Mother), 718 N. Shippen St., Lancaster, Pennsylvania [S2] [SW]

Snyder, Robert Gray, Pvt., 84th Co., 6th Regt., DOW, July 19, 1918 in the Aisne Marne. Mr. and Mrs. Daniel Snyder (Parents), Mardella, New Jersey [ABMC- Belleau TOM as R.G.] [S2] [SW1]

Snyder, Walter M., Pvt., MB, Navy Yard, Washington, D.C., DDS, September 4, 1920 at Washington, D.C. Bertha Snyder (Mother), Box 81, Gnadeuhutten, Ohio [S4]

Snyder, William Henry, Sgt., 158th Co. (Signal), Philadelphia, Pennsylvania, DDS, October 2, 1918 at Philadelphia, Pennsylvania. Mrs. William Snyder (Mother), 607 E. 34th St., Baltimore, Maryland [S3]

Sockel, Frank, Cpl., 47th Co., 5th Regt., KIA, July 19, 1918 in the Aisne Marne. Sarah Kaufman (Mother), 1064 W. 13th St., Chicago, Illinois [ABMC- Fere] [S2] [SW]

Sohl, Rudolph Otto, Pvt., MB, N3, New Orleans, Louisana, DDS, September 28, 1918 at New Orleans, Louisana. Ida Sohl (Mother), 174 Wyana St., Brooklyn, New York [VA- Cypress Hills] [S3]

Sokolowski, Frank, Sgt., 96th Co., 6th Regt., DOW, October 9, 1918 in the Meuse Argonne. Kate Nowitski (Mother), 1104 Person Court, Lansing, Michigan [FAG] [S2] [SW1]

Marine Corps Deaths, 1917-1921

Sokosky, John, Pvt., 95th Co., 6th Regt., DOW, November 2, 1918 in the Meuse Argonne. Miss Helen Sokosky (Sister), Irwin, Pennsylvania [FAG] [S2] [SW1]

Solberg, Percival Harrison, Cpl., 73rd Co., 6th Regt., DOW, December, 13, 1918 in the Meuse Argonne. Lawrence Solburg (Brother), Lake Park Ave., Chicago, Illinois [ABMC-Thiaucourt] [S2] [SW1 says Pvt.]

Solomon, Nathan, Cpl., 77th Co., 6th MG Bn., DOW, October 11, 1918 in the Meuse Argonne. Abraham Solomon (Father), 245 Christopher Ave., Brooklyn, New York [R] [S2] [SW1]

Somers, Vernon L., 2nd Lieut., MCR, 49th Co., 5th Regt., KIA, June 6, 1918 in the Chateau Thierry sector. Mrs. Maggie A. Somers (Mother), Bloxen, Accomac Co., Virginia [FAG] [S1] [SW]

Sone, James Ray, Pvt., 47th Co., 5th Regt., KIA, October 4, 1918 in the Meuse Argonne. Mrs. Lester Sone (Mother), Wagner Place, Jefferson City, Missouri [R] [S2] [SW1]

Sostheim, Vernon Neely, Cpl., 74th Co., 6th Regt., DOW, April 24, 1918 in the Toulon Sector, Verdun. Clare N. Sostheim (Mother), 7412 Princeton Ave., Chicago, Illinois [ABMC- Romagne] [S2] [SW]

Souder, Herbert Hibbs, Pvt., 47th Co., 5th Regt., KIA, June 17, 1918 in the Chateau-Thierry Sector. Paul P. Souder (Father), 19 Pine St., Audubon, New Jersey [ABMC-Belleau] [S2] [SW1]

South, Ira, Sgt., MCR, Bks. Det., MB, Norfolk, Virginia, DDS, October 11, 1918 at Norfolk, Virginia. Mrs. H. W. South (Mother), 3002 Tarvis, Houston, Texas [FAG] [S3]

Southard, Samuel William, Pvt., 49th Co., 5th Regt., KIA, October 4, 1918 in the Meuse Argonne. William K. Southard (Father), Gen. Del., Waitsburg, Washington [FAG] [S2] [SW1]

Southerland *see* Sutherland

Marine Corps Deaths, 1917-1921

Souza, Manuel, Jr., Cpl., 76th Co., 6th Regt., KIA, July 19, 1918 in the Aisne Marne. Manuel Souza (Father), Gen. Del., Cambria, California [FAG] [S2] [SW says Co. A, Repl. Btln.]

Sowell, Vernon Lynn, Cpl., 49th Co., 5th Regt., KIA, November 1, 1918 in the Meuse Argonne. Sophia Sowell (Mother), Gen. Del., Lemoore, California [VA-San Francisco] [S2] [SW1]

Sowerby, Thomas, Jr., Pvt., 197th Co., 2nd Regt., Haiti, DOS, November 23, 1920 at Thomonde, Haiti. Elizabeth Sowerby (Mother), 95 E. Maine St., Bridgeport, Connecticut [S4]

Spake, Jacob Wendel, Jr., Pvt., 96th Co., 6th Regt., DOW, June 21, 1918 in the Chateau-Thierry Sector. Jacob W. Spake (Father), 4703 Bryan St., Dallas, Texas [ABMC- Belleau] [S2] [SW says 138th Co., Repl. Btln.]

Spann, William Rice, Pvt., Supply Co., 13th Regt., DOD, October 13, 1918 in France. Wm. Rice Spann (Father), Morristown, New Jersey [ABMC-Fere] [S2]

Sparks, James Harding, Pvt., Co. I, 13th Regt., DOD, September 24, 1918 enroute to France. William W. Sparks (Father), Route #9, Cynthiana, Kentucky [FAGM] [S2]

Spatz, Charles R., Pvt., Bks. Det., MB, Naval Station, Pearl Harbor, Territory of Hawaii, DDS, January 29, 1920 at Pearl Harbor, Territory of Hawaii. Sarah Anderhalden (Mother), 1117½ L St., Sacramento, California [FAG has a Charles K. Spatz on February 29, 1920] [S4]

Speake, William Leroy, Sgt., 95th Co., 6th Regt., KIA, September 12, 1918 in the St. Mihiel Offensive. Wiliam H. Speake (Father), Bowie, Texas [ANC] [S2] [SW1]

Spearing, Walter Joseph, Pvt., 23rd Co., 6th MG Bn., KIA, June 10, 1918 in the Chateau-Thierry Sector. Ellen Spearing (Mother), 1532 N. 54th St., Philadelphia, Pennsylvania [S2] [SW]

Marine Corps Deaths, 1917-1921

Spence, Jesse G., Sgt., OTC, Quantico, Virginia, DDS, January 26, 1919 at Quantico, Virginia. Bertha Spence (Mother), 1201 Seminary Road, Bloomington, Illinois [S4]

Spencer, Guy Howard, Pvt., 47th Co., 5th Regt., DOW, October 17, 1918 in the Meuse Argonne. Maude E. Spencer (Mother), 218½ 5th Ave., South Jamestown, North Dakota [ANC] [S2] [SW1]

Spencer, Robert Sherman, Pvt., 23rd Co., 6th MG Bn., KIA, June 10, 1918 in the Chateau-Thierry Sector. Harmen A. Spencer (Father), 133 Ross St., Batavia, New York [FAG] [S2] [SW]

Spilmaher, William D., Pvt., 83rd Co., 6th Regt., KIA, November 2, 1918 in the Meuse Argonne. Louise Anderson (Sister), Groton, South Dakota [FAG] [S2] [SW1]

Spire, William J., Jr., Sgt., 49th Co., 5th Regt., KIA, June 16, 1918 in the Chateau-Thierry Sector. Pauline Spire (Mother), 2100 West End Ave., Nashville, Tennessee [ABMC-Belleau TOM as W.J.] [S2] [SW says 137th Co., Repl. Btln.]

Spitzhardt, Gustave, Pvt., 20th Co., 5th Regt., KIA, October 5, 1918 in the Meuse Argonne. Paul Spitzbardt (F 2542 South 5th St., E. Salt Lake City, Utah [S2] [SW says Spitzbardt]

Spotswood, Joseph Frederick, Cpl., 45th Co., 5th Regt., KIA, October 4, 1918 in the Meuse Argonne. Joseph Spotswood (Father), Rising Sun, Maryland [ANC] [S2] [SW1 says DOW]

Spring, Ira Louis, Cpl., 45th Co., 5th Regt., KIA, June 14, 1918 in the Chateau-Thierry Sector. Edward Walton (Father), 406 Lakeview Ave., Jamestown, New York [ABMC- Belleau] [S2] [SW]

Springer, Elva Clifton, Cpl., 83rd Co., 6th Regt., DOW, November 2, 1918 in the Meuse Argonne. John Springer (Father), Famingdale, New Jersey [FAG] [S2] [SW1]

Marine Corps Deaths, 1917-1921

Sprunt, Russell Keane, Pvt., 78th Co., 6th Regt., DOW, July 1, 1918 in the Chateau-Thierry Sector. Laura Sprunt (Mother), Apt. #7, 1034 E. Colfax St., Denver, Colorado [ABMC- Belleau] [S2] [SW says Co. A, Repl. Btln.]

St. Clair, Kenneth L., Pvt., 55th Co., 5th Regt., DOW, June 11, 1918 in the Chateau-Thierry Sector. Mrs. Ada E. St. Clair (Mother), Bane, Virginia [S2] [SW]

St. George, Herbert, Cpl., 16th Co., 5th Regt., KIA, June 7, 1918 in the Chateau-Thierry Sector. Ashley St. George (Father), 175 Beacon St., Worcester, Massachusetts [S2] [SW]

St. George, Stephen E., 1st Lieutenant, MB, Parris Island, South Carolina, DAS, June 25, 1920 n an aeroplane accident at Parris Island, South Carolina. Mrs. Stephen E. St. George (Wife), Box 743, Miami, Florida [S4]

St. John, Alcide Norbert, Gy. Sgt., 96th Co., 6th Regt., DOW, June 24, 1918 in the Chateau-Thierry Sector. Mrs. Dora May St. John (Wife), RFD#1, Selingsgrove, Pennsylvania [R] [S2] [SW1]

St. Louis, Roland Gerry, Sgt., 49th Co., 5th Regt., KIA, July 19, 1918 in the Aisne Marne. Alex St. Louis (Father), 2102 Fred St., Marinette, Wisconsin [ABMC- Fere as St Louis] [S2] [SW] [SW1]

St. Young, Jack F., Pvt., Hdqtrs. Co., 16th Regt., Philadelphia, Pennsylvania, DDS, May 13, 1920 at Philadelphia, Pennsylvania. No next of kin given. [S4]

Stach, Walter Ladislay, Pvt., 55th Co., 5th Regt., DOW, July 18, 1918 in the Aisne Marne. Hattie Stach (Mother), 4304 West 21st Place, Chicago, Illinois [ABMC- Fere] [S2]

Stackhouse, Powell, Pvt., MCR, Bks. Det., MB, Philadelphia, Pennsylvania, DDS, October 9, 1918 at Philadelphia, Pennsylvania. Mrs. Elija B. Stackhouse (Mother), 7135 N. Broad St., Philadelphia, Pennsylvania [FAG] [S3]

Stagg, Malcolm M., Pvt., 95th Co., 6th Regt., KIA, September 13, 1918 in the St. Mihiel Offensive. Ola Stagg (Mother),

Marine Corps Deaths, 1917-1921

Churchpoint, Louisiana [ABMC- Thiaucourt TOM] [S2] [SW says 134th Co., Repl. Btln.]

Stahl, Frank Robert, Pvt., 82nd Co., 6th Regt., DOW, August 1, 1918 in the Aisne Marne. Mrs. Anna Stahl (Mother), Gen. Del., Barnesville, Minnesota [FAG] [S2] [SW1]

Staley, Lloyd Alva, Pvt., 83rd Co., 6th Regt., KIA, June 6, 1918 in the Chateau-Thierry Sector. Nellie Staley (Mother), 1135 South 1st St., Springfield, Illinois [ABMC- Belleau TOM] [S2] [SW]

Stamer, Ernest, Pvt., 16th Co., 5th Regt., DOW, October 23, 1918 in the Meuse Argonne. Helen Stamer (Wife), 1109 Newberry St., Toledo, Ohio [ABMC- Suresnes] [S2] [SW1]

Stamey, Walter Denio, Pvt., USS *Cyclops*, DAU, June 14, 1918 lost at sea aboard the USS *Cyclops*. Jennie Williams (Mother), RFD#8, Topeka, Kansas [S3]

Stankey, Maxamillion, Pvt., 83rd Co., 6th Regt., KIA, October 6, 1918 in the Meuse Argonne. Katherine Stankey (Mother), 5128 Windsor Ave., Chicago, Illinois [R] [S2] [SW1 says DOW]

Stanton, Joseph Aloysius, Pvt., 96th Co., 6th Regt., KIA, October 3, 1918 in the Meuse Argonne. Annie F. Stanton (Mother), 4911 Magazine St., New Orleans [R] [S2] [SW says Co. H]

Stanton, Paul Andrew, Cpl., 80th Co., 6th Regt., KIA, November 1, 1918 in the Meuse Argonne. Edward J. Stanton (Father), 4043 Broad St., Philadelphia, Pennsylvania [ABMC- Romagne] [S2] [SW1]

Stark, Hugo Jacob, Pvt., 84th Co., 6th Regt., DOW, June 7, 1918 in the Chateau-Thierry Sector. Frank Stark (Brother), 304 W. 1st St., Belleville, Illinois [ABMC- Belleau] [S2] [SW]

Stark, John Daniel, Cpl., 81st Co., 6th MG Bn., DOW, July 28, 1918 in the Aisne Marne. Mrs. Mabel D. Stark (Mother),

Marine Corps Deaths, 1917-1921

103 Exetr St., W. Pittston, Pennsylvania [ABMC-Suresnes] [S2] [SW]

Starkey, Floyd Clifford, Pvt., MCR, 81st Co., 6th MG Bn., DOW, July 24, 1918 in the Aisne Marne. Alonzo Starkey (Father), RFD #5, Upper Sandusky, Wyandot County, Ohio [R] [S2]

Starns, Murrell Wellard, Pvt., 43rd Co., 5th Regt., KIA, June 14, 1918 in the Chateau-Thierry Sector. William H. Starnes (Father), 2330 E. Main St., Ottumwa, Iowa [FAG] [S2] [SW]

Start, Charles Worthington, Pvt., Co. Y, Parris Island, South Carolina, DDS, October 30, 1918 at Parris Island, South Carolina. George L. Start (Father), 1814 27th St., Galveston, Texas [S3]

Staton, James Floyd, Pvt., 97th Co., 6th Regt., DOW, July 19, 1918 in the Aisne Marne. Mrs. Cornelius Staton (Mother), Marshville, North Carolina [ABMC- Fere] [S2] [SW1]

Stauffer, Zo David, Pvt., 2nd Co., 1st Regt., Philadelphia, Pennsylvania, DDS, October 4, 1918 at Philadelphia, Pennsylvania. Josiah and Anna Stauffer (Parents), 926 4th Ave., Beaver Falls, Pennsylvania [S3]

Stavely, William Aoysius, Pvt., 95th Co., 6th Regt., KIA, July 19, 1918 in the Aisne Marne. Mr. John P. Stavely (Father), 933 W. 54th Place, Chicago, Illlinois [S2] [SW]

Stearns, John Maxwell, Pvt., 20th Co., 5th Regt., DOW, September 15, 1918 in the St. Mihiel Offensive. John N. Stearns (Father), 215 W. Board Ave., Syracuse, New York [S2] [SW1]

Stearns, Stanley, Cpl., 20th Co., 5th Regt., KIA, July 19, 1918 in the Aisne Marne. Albert L. Stearns (Father), Hecla, South Dakota [FAG] [S2] [SW]

Steckel, Henry Edward, Pvt., Hdqtrs. Co., 5th Regt., KIA, June 6, 1918 in the Chateau-Thierry Sector. Mrs. A.

Marine Corps Deaths, 1917-1921

Witzenberger (Sister), 1722 Decatur St., Brooklyn, New York [VA-Cypress Hills] [S2] [SW]

Steele, Merton Louis, Pvt., MCR, 1st Res. Co., MB, Philadelphia, Pennsylvania, DDS, September 24, 1918 at Great Lakes, Illinois. Mrs. Blanche F. Bozeman (Mother), 250 Kearney St., San Francisco, California [USN-Great Lakes] [S3]

Steeves, John Burton, Pvt., 45th Co., 5th Regt., DOW, June 6, 1918 in the Chateau-Thierry Sector. James I. Steeves (Father), 97 Howard Ave., Dorchester, Massachusetts [S2] [SW1]

Steffen, Frank Herbert, Pvt., Co. B, Overseas Depot, Quantico, Virginia, DDS, September 24, 1918 at Quantico, Virginia. Mary Steffen (Mother), 835 Douglas St., San Francisco, California [S3]

Stegall, Jerry Goldsmith, Pvt., 75th Co., 6th Regt., DAO, June 22, 1919 in France. Robert B. Stegall (Father), Rossville, Georgia [VA-Chattanooga] [S2] [SW1 says KOA]

Steinbach, Henry A., Pvt., 192nd Co., Puget Sound, Washington, DDS, January 25, 1919 at Puget Sound, Washington, D.C. Christian Steinbach (Father), Gen. Del., Stearns Montana [S4]

Steinmetz, Edward Joseph, Pvt., 83rd Co., 6th Regt., KIA, June 24, 1918 in the Chateau-Thierry Sector. Benedict Steinmetz (Father), 631 Forest Ave., Hamilton, Ohio [R] [S2] [SW1]

Stekelenburg, John, Pvt., Hdqtrs. Co., 6th Regt., KIA, April 5, 1918 in the Toulon Sector, Verdun. Mrs. Julia Stekelenburg (Mother), Salix, Iowa [R] [S2] [SW]

Stengel, Frank Joseph, Pvt., 73rd Co., 6th Regt., KIA, November 1, 1918 in the Meuse Argonne. Anthony Stengel (Father), 4557 Edgemont St., Bridesburg, Pennsylvania [S2] [SW1 says Stengle]

Stenkamp, Charles William, Pvt., 49th Co., 5th Regt., KIA, June 20, 1918 in the Chateau-Thierry Sector. Henry Stenkamp

Marine Corps Deaths, 1917-1921

(Father), 829 Columbus Ave, New York, New York [ABMC- Belleau TOM as C.W. Steinkamp] [S2] [SW1 says Steinkamp]

Stenmark, Nels August, Pvt., 67th Co., 5th Regt., DOW, October 5, 1918 in the Meuse Argonne. Erick O. Stenmark (Father), Maidstone, Saskatchewan, Canada [ABMC- Belleau] [S2] [SW1]

Stensson, Carl Hilding, Pvt., 18th Co., 5th Regt., KIA, October 3, 1918 in the Meuse Argonne. Mrs Christine E. Stensson (Mother), RFD#2, Framingham, Massachusetts [R] [S2] [SW says Co. C, 4th Sep. Btln.]

Stephen, Robert Albert, Cpl., 49th Co., 5th Regt., KIA, June 6, 1918 in the Chateau-Thierry Sector. Russell R. S. Stephen (Son), 1343 Montclair Ave., St. Louis, Missouri [S2] [SW]

Stephens, Otto Earl, Pvt., 8th Co., 5th Regt., KIA, July 19, 1918 in the Aisne Marne. Caroline Meinz (Mother), 311 5th Ave., Helena, Montana [FAG] [S2] [SW says Casual Co.]

Stephens, Russell Anthony, Pvt., 47th Co., 5th Regt., DOD, February 19, 1919 in France. Charles C. Stephens (Father), c/o C. F. Ogier, Madeira, Ohio [R] [S2]

Steuer, George Ellwood, Cpl., 67th Co., 5th Regt., KIA, June 6, 1918 in the Chateau-Thierry Sector. Mrs. M. Steuer (Mother), 1011 Achoff Place, Bergen, New Jersey [S2] [SW1]

Steuert, Joseph John Jr., Pvt., 84th Co., 6th Regt., KIA, October 3, 1918 in the Meuse Argonne. Joseph J. Steuert (Father), 25 Van Orden Place, Hackensack, New Jersy [ANC] [S2] [SW1]

Steven, John Julius, Cpl., 47th Co., 5th Regt., KIA, September 15, 1918 in the St. Mihiel Offensive. Mrs. Mary Steven (Mother), c/o C. M Eyser, 1824 E. Baltimore St., Baltimore, Maryland [ABMC- Thiaucourt] [S2] [SW]

Marine Corps Deaths, 1917-1921

Stevens, Charles Lofton, Pvt., 47th Co., 5th Regt., DOW, June 6, 1918 in the Chateau-Thierry Sector. Thomas P. Stevens (Brother), 2506 Blakemore Ave., Nashville, Tennessee [ABMC- Belleau TOM as C.L.] [S2] [SW1 says KIA]

Stevens, Foster Bythan, Pvt., 83rd Co., 6th Regt., KIA, November 2, 1918 in the Meuse Argonne. Henry W. Stevens (Father), RFD#4, Goldsboro, North Carolina [ABMC- Romagne] [S2] [SW1]

Stevens, Ormal Dewey, Cpl., 80th Co., 6th Regt., DOW, July 19, 1918 in the Aisne Marne. Mrs. Sara Stevens (Mother), Warren, Michigan [FAG] [S2] [SW1]

Stevenson, George West, Pvt., 79th Co., 6th Regt., DOW, September 12, 1918 in the St. Mihiel Offensive. Elizabeth Stevenson (Mother), Price, Utah [ABMC- Thiaucourt] [S2] [SW1]

Stevenson, Harold Elmer, Pvt., 74th Co., 6th Regt., DOO, November 23, 1918 in France. Carlie Stevenson (Mother), 150 Lake St., Muskegon, Michigan [ABMC- Suresnes] [S2] [SW1]

Stewart, Albert Dana, Pvt., 51st Co., 5th Regt., DOW, June 11, 1918 in the Chateau-Thierry Sector. Lula Stewart (Mother), RFD#2, Schwenkville, Pennsylvania [ABMC- Belleau] [S2] [SW1]

Stewart, Alphonzo, Pvt., Co. G, Mare Island, California, DDS, November 14, 1918 at Mare Island, California. Sarah E. Stewart (Mother), 819 West 3rd South St., Salt Lake City, Utah [S4]

Stewart, Lester Ehls, Sgt., 80th Co., 6th Regt., KIA, October 6, 1918 in the Meuse Argonne. Anna M. Rogers (Mother), P O Box 402, Walthill, Nebraska [FAG] [S2] [SW1]

Stewart, Myron Franklin, Pfc, NB, Hingham, Massachusetts, DDS, September 28, 1918 at Hingham, Massachusetts. Mrs. Irene Nicholson (Sister), Block St., Abington, Massachusetts [S3]

Marine Corps Deaths, 1917-1921

Stielke, Carl, Pvt., 45th Co., 5th Regt., KIA, June 6, 1918 in the Chateau-Thierry Sector. Mary Weber (Sister), P O Box 112, Cadilac, Michigan [S2] [SW1 says Stieke]

Still, Arthur Chamberlain, Pvt., 55th Co., 5th Regt., KIA, June 5, 1918 in the Aisne Defensive. Mrs. Henry E. Still (Mother), 106 Ansonia Apt., Tacoma, Washington [ABMC- Belleau] [S2] [SW]

Stiller, Michael Joseph, Sgt., 79th Co., 6th Regt., DOW, July 19, 1918 in the Aisne Marne. May Stiller (Mother), 3417 Magnolia St., New Orleans, Louisiana [ABMC- Fere] [S2] [SW1]

Stinar, James Wallace, Pvt., 81st Co., 6th MG Bn., KIA, September 14, 1918 in the St. Mihiel Offensive. Clinton R. Stinar (Father), New York Mills, Minnesota [R] [S2] [SW]

Stine, Fay Edward, Pvt., 17th Co., 5th Regt., KIA, November 2, 1918 in the Meuse Argonne. Charles Stine (Father), c/o First National Bank, New Hampton, Iowa [S2] [SW1]

Stine, George Clarence, Pvt., 79th Co., 6th Regt., DOW, June 4, 1918 in the Aisne Defensive. L. H. Stine (Father), Tower City, North Dakota [ABMC- Belleau] [S2] [SW]

Stinson, Daniel Chase, Pvt., 17th Co., 5th Regt., DOW, June 16, 1918 in the Chateau-Thierry Sector. Ellen F. Stinson (Mother), 7 Copeland St., Roxbury, Massachusetts [ABMC- Belleau] [S2] [SW1]

Stirling, Hugh Alexander, Pvt., 78th Co., 6th Regt., DOW, June 13, 1918 in the Chateau-Thierry Sector. Anie Stirling (Mother), 4403 Osage Ave., Philadelphia, Pennsylvania [ABMC- Suresnes] [S2] [SW]

Stitt, Carl Eugene, Pvt., 95th Co., 6th Regt., DOW, September 15, 1918 in the St. Mihiel Offensive. Ethel Stitt (Mother), 820 Lincoln Ave., Detroit, Michigan [ABMC- Thiaucourt] [S2] [SW says Co. A, 3rd Repl. Btln.]

Stockham, Fred William, Gy. Sgt., 96th Co., 6th Regt., DOW, June 22, 1918 in the Chateau-Thierry Sector. Mrs. Sophy Heinze (Foster-mother), 30 Rich St., Irvington, New Jersey [FAG] [S2] [SW] [MOH] [Note: 1945: USS Stockham (DD-683); 2001:USNS GySgt. Fred W. Stockham (T-AK-3017), Military Sealift Comand]

Stocks, William Edward, Pvt., Hdqtrs. Co., 11th Regt., DOD, January 24, 1919 in France. Mirle A. Stocks (Wife),, 331 S. "D" St., Livingston, Montana [ABMC- Fere] [S2]

Stockwell, Emmons J., 2nd Lt., G Co., 6th Regt., KIA, September 15, 1918 [ABMC-Thiaucourt TOM] [not listed in S1]

Stoddard, Chester Volly, Pvt., Extra Duty, MB, Parris Island, South Carolina, DDS, November 4, 1918 at Parris Island, South Carolina. Mrs. Ola Stoddard (Mother), Planview, Texas [FAG] [S3]

Stoffel, James Floyd, Pvt., 51st Co., 5th Regt., KIA, June 11, 118 in the Chateau-Thierry Sector. Mrs. John H. Stoffel (Mother), Irwin Ave., Pittsburgh, Pennsylvania [R] [S2] [SW]

Stoll, William, Pvt., Bks. Det., MB, San Diego, California, DDS, July 14, 1920 at San Diego, California. Charley Stoll (Brother), New Middletown, Indiania [S4]

Stone, Allen Wesley, Cpl., Supply Co., 5th Regt., DOW, April 23, 1918 in the Toulon Sector, Verdun. John Stone (Father), 736 East 6th St., Stockton, California [ABMC-Thiaucourt] [S2] [SW] [SW1 says Wesley Stone Allen]

Stone, John Franklin, Pvt., 16th Co., 5th Regt., KIA, November 4, 1918 in the Meuse Argonne. Mrs. Mattie Stone (Mother), RFD#4, Jacksonville, Alabama [FAG] [S2] [SW1]

Stonebraker, William, Pvt., 79th Co., 6th Regt., Quantico, Virginia, DAS, July 18, 1917 in a train wreck at Marthaville, Louisiana. Jane Stonebraker (Mother), Cumberland Wyoming [FAG] [S3]

Marine Corps Deaths, 1917-1921

Storey, Adel Moore, Cpl., 83rd Co., 6th Regt., KIA, June 8, 1918 in the Chateau-Thierry Sector. Fred J. Storey (Father), R#1, Palo Alto, California [ABMC- Belleau] [S2] [SW1]

Story, Ralph Raymond, Cpl., Co. C, 13th Regt., DOD, October 8, 1918 in France. Mrs. Florence L. Story (Mother), RFD#13, Dayton, Ohio [R] [S2]

Stout, Paul J., Pvt., Pvt., 76th Co., 6th Regt., July 19, 1918 in the Aisne Marne. Cooper Stout (Father), Murphysboro, Illinois [ABMC- Fere] [S2] [SW says Co. A, Repl. Btln.]

Stover, Isaac Andrew, Cpl., 18th Co., 5th Regt., KIA, June 15, 1918 in the Chateau-Thierry Sector. Catherine Stover (Mother), 742 North 2nd St., Paragould, Arkansas [VA- Little Rock] [S2] [SW]

Stover, John Oscar, Sgt., 80th Co., 6th Regt., KIA, July 19, 1918 in the Aisne Marne. Raymond F. Stover (Brother), Union Deposit, Box 13, Union Deposit, Pennsylvania [FAG] [S2] [SW]

Strain, Benjamin Turner, Cpl., 45th Co., 5th Regt., KIA, June 6, 1918 in the Chateau-Thierry Sector. Mrs. Edna Strain Abbott (Sister), 722 Bosart Ave., Indianapolis, Indiana [FAG] [S2] [SW]

Strain, John Howard, Pvt., 16th Co., 5th Regt., KIA, June 23, 1918 in the Chateau-Thierry Sector. Numa A. Strain (Father), 211 Dalton St., San Gabriel, California [ABMC-Belleau] [S2] [SW1 says DOW]

Stranahan, Guss, Pvt., Co. A, Overseas Depot, Quantico, Virginia, DDS, October 13, 1918 at Quantico, Virginia. Clennie Burnhan (Mother), Middletown, Indiana [FAG] [S3]

Strand, Clarence Henry, Cpl., 75th Co., 6th Regt., KIA, September 14, 1918 in the St. Mihiel Offensive. Sophia A. Strand (Mother), Newman Grove, Nebraska [ABMC-Thiaucourt] [S2] [SW says Co. A, Repl. Btln.]

Marine Corps Deaths, 1917-1921

Strand, Eris W., Pvt., Co. C, MB, Navy Yard, Mare Island, California, DDS, November 29, 1918 at Mare Island, California. Martina Strand (Mother), 607 Columbia St., San Jose, California [S4]

Strand, Walter H., 2nd Lieut., 96th Co., 6th Regt., DOW, October 17, 1918 in the Meuse Argonne. Mrs. Helga Strand (Mother), 125 West 9th St., Mankato, Minnesota [R] [S1] [SW1 says KIA]

Strassburger, Gustave Oscar, Pvt., 135th Co., Quantico, Virginia, DDS, October 1, 1918 at Quantico, Virginia. Sophie Strassburger (Mother), RR#2, Dorchester, Wisconsin [FAG] [S3]

Strasser, Conrad D., Sgt., Co. B, Navy Yard Guard, Philadelphia, Pennsylvania, DDS, May 21, 1920 at League Island, Pennsylvania. Marguerite Strasser (Wife), 5647 Market St., Philadelphia, Pennsylvania [S4]

Strasser, Walter Frank, Pvt., 51st Co., 5th Regt., DOW, July 19, 1918 in the Aisne Marne. Gomasz Strasser (Father), 106 Weimar St., Buffalo, New York [S2] [SW]

Strayer, Dwight Leslie, Pvt., 51st Co., 5th Regt., DOD, November 24, 1918 in France. Paul Strayer (Father), 1309 Grant Ave., Waterloo, Iowa [FAG] [S2]

Streator, Paul Martin, Sgt., 51st Co., 5th Regt., KIA, November 10, 1918 in the Meuse Argonne. Mrs. Dora M. Streator (Mother), 1303 Albert St., New Castle, Pennsylvania [R] [S2] [SW1]

Strehlow, Herbert Albert, Pvt., 17th Co., 5th Regt., KIA, June 7, 1918 in the Chateau-Thierry Sector. Herman Strehlow (Father), 900 4th Ave., West Allis, Wisconsin [ABMC-Belleau] [S2] [SW]

Stretch, Roy C., Sgt., 51st Co., 5th Regt., DOW, July 20, 1918 in the Aisne Marne. Mrs. L. G. Curry (Mother), Hay, Washington [VA-San Francisco] [S2] [SW says Casualty Co.]

Marine Corps Deaths, 1917-1921

Strickland, Charles Alva, Cpl., 80th Co., 6th Regt., DOW, October 12, 1918 in the Meuse Argonne. Netta A. Strickland (Mother), RFD#2, Witt, Virginia [ANC] [S2] [SW1]

Strickland, Chester I., Pvt., Co. W, Parris Island, South Carolina, DDS, November 19, 1918 at Parris Island, South Carolina. E. Farnell Strickland (Father), RFD#1, Akron, New York [S4]

Striegel, Joseph A., Sgt., 48th Co., New York,DDS, January 27, 1919 at Willard Parker Hospital, New York. George C. Striegel (Father), 438 Sherman St., Buffalo, New York [FAG] [S4]

Strine, Charles Jacob, Pvt., Supply Co., 4th Regt., Dominican Republic, DAS, December 8, 1920 drowned at Santiago, Dominican Republic. Charles and Rosa Strine (Parents), New Windsor, Maryland [FAG] [S4]

Strohm, Everett Arthur, Cpl., Co C., Officer Training Camp, Quantico, Virginia, DDS, October 1, 1918 at Quantico, Virginia. Howard A. Strohm (Father), 125 Tennyson Court, Elgin, Illinois [S3]

Strong, Frank John, Pvt., 51st Co., 5th Regt., KIA, October 4, 1918 in the Meuse Argonne. Mrs. Mary Strong (Mother), Box 52, Marion, Pennsylvania [ABMC- Romagne] [S2] [SW says 140th Co., Repl. Btln.]

Stroup, William Leverne, Pvt., 67th Co., 5th Regt., KIA, October 4, 1918 in the Meuse Argonne. Luella Stroup (Mother), 215 Seneca St., Oil City, Pennsylvania [ABMC-Romagne] [S2] [SW1]

Struthers, Charles B., Jr., Pvt., 18th Co., 5th Regt., DOW, November 4, 1918 in the Meuse Argonne. Charles B. Struthers (Father), 172 Franklin Place, Flushing, New York [ABMC-Romagne] [S2] [SW1]

Stuehrk, Ernest Lester, Pvt., 9th Squadron, FMAF, DOD, October 31, 1918 in France. John Stuehrk (Father), Cedar Bluffs, Nebraska [ANC] [S2]

Marine Corps Deaths, 1917-1921

Sturges, Thomas Angelo, Sgt., 82nd Co., 6th Regt., KIA, June 6, 1918 in the Chateau-Thierry Sector. Mrs. Josie S. Lastrapes (Sister), 306 W. Charles St., Hammond, Louisiana [FAG] [S2] [SW]

Stutsman, Charles Otis, Pvt., MB, 22nd Co., Philadelphia, Pennsylvania, DDS, October 1, 1918 at Philadelphia, Pennsylvania. Mrs. Lenore K. Stutsman (Wife), Macon, Macon, Missiouri [S3]

Styer, Charles Benjamin, Pvt., 64th Co., 2nd Regt., Haiti, DDS, April 26, 1921 at Cape Haitien, Haiti. Mrs. Mary Oswald (Mother), Altoona, Pennsylvania [S4]

Suchy, William Otto, Pvt., 96th Co., 6th Regt., KIA, July 19, 1918 in the Aisne Marne. Frank Suchy (Father), RFD#6, Great Bend, Kansas [S2] [SW1]

Suiter, Charles Edwin, Pvt., Hdqtrs. Co., 6th Regt., KIA, June 12, 1918 in the Chateau-Thierry Sector. William C. Suiter (Father), Natchez, Mississippi [ABMC- Belleau] [S2] [SW says 133rd Co., Repl. Btln.]

Sullivan, Arthur G., Sgt., Hdqtrs. Co., 6th Regt., KIA, July 19, 1918 Aisne Marne. Julia Sullivan (Mother), Eureka, Utah [ABMC- Belleau TOM] [S2] [SW]

Sullivan, Daniel Andrew, Pvt., 82nd Co., 6th Regt., KIA, June 8, 1918 in the Chateau-Thierry Sector. Anna Killeen (Sister), 230 Fayette St., Lowell, Massachusetts [ABMC-Belleau] [S2] [ABMC and SW say Sergeant]

Sullivan, Francis Xavier, Cpl., 77th Co., 6th MG Bn., KIA, October 5, 1918 in the Meuse Argonne. James Sullivan (Father), 17 Kane Place, Brooklyn, New York [ABMC-Romagne] [S2] [SW1]

Sullivan, John Joseph, Pvt., 79th Co., 6th Regt., DOW, July 28, 1918 in the Aisne Marne. Michael Sullivan (Father), 2 Carlow St., Roxbury, Massachusetts [R] [S2] [SW says 134th Co., Repl. Btln.]

Marine Corps Deaths, 1917-1921

Sullivan, Melville E., 2nd Lt., 1st Mar. Avia. Force, DAS, May 7, 1918 at Miami, Florida. Mary F. Sullivan (Mother), 1115 Grove Ave., Richmond, Virginia [FAG] [S3] [SW1]

Sullivan, William James, Pvt., 80th Co., 6th Regt., DOW, September 16, 1918 in the St. Mihiel Offensive. Mrs. Mary Murphy (Mother), 1422 Sheridan Ave., Springfield, Ohio [ABMC- Thiaucourt TOM] [S2] [SW1 says KIA]

Summerby, Herbert Connors, Pvt., 79th Co., 6th Regt., DOW, July 22, 1918 in the Aisne Marne. John Summerby (Father), RFD#1, Allenville, Michigan [ANC] [S2] [SW says 134th Co., Repl. Btln.]

Summers, George Willilam, Pvt., Hdqtrs. Co., 11th Regt., DOD, June 4, 1919 in France. Nellie R. Butts (Mother), Gunnison, Colorado [ABMC- Fere] [S2]

Sumner, Allen M., Capt., MCR, 81st Co., 6th MGBn, KIA, July 19, 1918 in the Aisne Marne. Mrs. Mary M. Sumner (widow), 18124 "S" St., N.W., Washington, D.C. [ABMC-Belleau] [S1] [SW]

Suominen, Tuurie Henry, Cpl., 75th Co., 6th Regt., DOW, July 20, 1918 in the Aisne Marne. Robert Suominen (Father), McComber, Minnesota [ABMC- Belleau] [S2] [SW]

Sura, Peter Edward, Pvt., 84th Co., 6th Regt., DOW, July 19, 1918 in the Aisne Marne. Agatha Sura (Mother), Route #1, Independence, Wisconsin [FAG] [S2] [SW1]

Sustin, Benjamin, Pvt., 96th Co., 6th Regt., KIA, July 19, 1918 in the Aisne Marne. Ike Sustin (Father), 330 Roseberry St., Philadelphia, Pennsylvania [S2] [SW1]

Sutherland, Donald James, Cpl., 43rd Co., 5th Regt., DOW, June 18, 1918 in the Chateau-Thierry Sector. Roland E. Sutherland (Father), RFD#4, Hillsboro, Oregon [FAG] [S2] [SW says 140th Co., Repl. Btln.]

Sutherland, George William, Sgt., 78th Co., 6th Regt., DOW, July 23, 1918 in the Aisne Marne. Mrs. Mabel Sutherland (Mother), 1015 E. Cherry St., Olney, Illinois [R] [S2]

Marine Corps Deaths, 1917-1921

[SW says Co. B, Repl. Btln.] [SW1 says George W. Southerland]

Sutkevick, Walter Trofinn, Pfc, 144th Co., 3rd Regt., Dominican Republic, DOS, May 14, 1921 at Santo Domingo, Dominican Republic. George A. Mosher (Friend), Twinsburg, Ohio [FAG] [S4]

Suttles, Maurice Thomas., Pvt., 84th Co., 6th Regt., KIA, June 6, 1918 in the Chateau-Thierry Sector. Thomas E. Suttles (Father), San Marcos, Texas [FAG] [S2] [SW]

Sutton, Bert Thomas, Pvt., 79th Co., 6th Regt., DOW, July 19, 1918 in the Aisne Marne. George Sutton (Father), 476 Frederick Ave., Milwaukee, Wisconsin [ABMC- Fere] [S2] [SW1 says KIA]

Sutton, John Madison, Pvt., Co. C, 13th Regt., DOD, September 24, 1918 enroute to France. Margaret Sutton (Mother), Bell Buckle, Tennessee [R] [S2]

Swaim, Grover Cleveland, Pvt., 16th Co., 5th Regt., KIA, June 23, 1918 in the Chateau-Thierry Sector. Carrie Swaim (Mother), RFD#2, Gleason, Tennessee [FAG] [S2] [SW1 says Swain]

Swan, Oscar A., 1st Lieut., MCR, 23rd Co., 6th MGBn, KIA, November 10, 1918 in the Meuse Argonne. Mrs. Barbara Swan (Mother), 32 East Utica St., Buffalo, New York [FAG] [S1] [SW1]

Swan, Robert, Pvt., 95th Co., 6th Regt., DOW, July 19, 1918 in the Aisne Marne. Mary J. Swan (Mother), Lordsburg, New Mexico [FAG] [S2] [SW1 says KIA]

Swanson, Axel Otto, Pvt., Supply Co., MB, Parris Island, South Carolina, DAS, October 30, 1919 at Parris Island, South Carolina. Miss Agda Swanson (Sister), 1508 E. 26th St., Minneapolis, Minnesota [S4]

Swanson, Leonard Hamilton, Cpl., 124th Co., 9th Regt., Quantico, Virginia, DDU, August 2, 1918 at sea aboard the USS

Marine Corps Deaths, 1917-1921

Hancock. Otto Swanson (Father), Lack City, South Dakota [S3]

Swart, McKinley, Pvt., Hdqtrs. Co., 5th Regt., KIA, June 6, 1918 in the Chateau-Thierry Sector. Jennie Swart (Mother), Lakewood, New York [ABMC- Belleau] [S2] [SW]

Sweeny, Roy Penton, Pvt., L Co., 11th Regt., DOD, in France. Dora Sweeny (Mother), Gen. Del. Ruby, Montana [ABMC-Fere] [S2]

Swenson, Walter Everett, Pvt., 83rd Co., 6th Regt., KIA, June 6, 1918 in the Chateau-Thierry Sector. Sopie Swenson (Mother), 4237 Hartford St., St. Louis, Missouri [VA-Jefferson Barracks] [S2] [SW]

Swingle, Vern Erwin, Cpl., 76th Co., 6th Regt., KIA, June 11, 1918 in the Chateau-Thierry Sector. Charles Swingle (Father), 128 S. Houghton St., Manistique, Michigan [ABMC-Belleau] [S2] [SW]

Sykes, John David, Pvt., 80th Co., 6th Regt., DOD, November 3, 1918 in France. W. Sykes (Father), 262 Kirkwood Ave., Atlanta, Georgia [FAGM] [S2]

Synnott, Joseph A., 2nd Lieut., MCR, 47th Co., 5th Regt., KIA, June 7, 1918 in the Chateau Thierry sector. Mrs. M. S. Reiley (sister), 57 Plymouth St., Montclair, New Jersey [S1] [SW]

Szadach, Leo P., Cpl., 100th Co., 8th Regt., Haiti, DDS, July 21, 1920 at Port au Prince, Haiti, Frances Voss (Sister), 945 E. Kirby Ave., Detroit, Michigan [S4]

Szymonek, Joe, Pvt., Hdqtrs. Det., MB, Parris Island, South Carolina, DAS, August 27, 1918 in an automobile at Savannah, Georgia. Mrs. Frances Szymonek (Wife), 7748 South May St., Chicago, Illinois [S3]

Taflinger, Floyd Layton, Pvt., 75th Co., 6th Regt., KIA, October 9, 1918 in the Meuse Argonne. Lyda Taflinger (Mother), 726 W. Madis St., Paris, Illinois [S2] [SW1]

Marine Corps Deaths, 1917-1921

Taggart, David Alfred, Pvt., 82nd Co., 6th Regt., KIA, June 3, 1918 in the Aisne Defensive. Lucy Taggart (Mother), 1143 Cuyler Ave., Oak Park, Illinois [FAGM] [S2] [SW]

Taggart, Frederick Polk, Sgt., 17th Co., 5th Regt., DOD, July 23, 1918 in the Chateau-Thierry Sector. Eva M. Taggart (Mother), 2545 Regent St., Berkeley, California [ABMC-Romagne] [S2] [SW1]

Talaska, John, Pvt., 20th Co., 5th Regt., DOW, June 24, 1918 in the Chateau-Thierry Sector. Mrs. Teophia Talaska (Mother), 63 Weddale Way, Rochester, New York [R] [S2] [SW]

Talbot, Ralph, 2nd Lieut., MCR, 9th Sq. Northern Bombing Group, FMAF, KOA, October 25, 1918 in France. Mrs. R. J. Talbot (Mother), 310 Park St., S. Weymouth, Massachusetts [FAG] [S1] [SW1]

Talbott, Patrick V., Pvt., Co. B, 3rd Sep. Bn., Quantico, Virginia, DDS, November 18, 1918 at Quantico, Virginia. Julia Talbott (Mother), 202 Main St., Monongah, West Virginia [S4]

Talley, William Edgar, Pvt., 47th Co., 5th Regt., DAO, May 21, 1919 as a result of an accident in France. Mrs. Edith Talley (Mother), 1018 Perry St., Vincennes, Indiana [R] [S2] [SW1 says KOA]

Tarr, Clyde, Pvt., Co. K, 11th Regt., Quantico, Virginia, DDS, October 3, 1918 at Quantico, Virginia. Wlliam M. Tarr (Brother), 802 Long St., Hamilton, Ohio [S3]

Tarr, William Combs, Gy. Sgt., Hdqtrs. Co., 5th Regt., KIA, April 24, 1918 in the Toulon Sector, Verdun. Charles Tarr (Brother), 34 Cobsseese Ave., Gardiner, Maine [R] [S2] [SW]

Tartikoff, David, Pvt., 49th Co., 5th Regt., KIA, June 6, 1918 in the Chateau-Thierry Sector. Samuel Tartikoff (Father), 60 Linwood St., Malden, Massachusetts [S2] [SW]

Marine Corps Deaths, 1917-1921

Tate, James Clark, Pvt., 43rd Co., 5th Regt., KIA, June 11, 1918 in the Chateau-Thierry Sector. James Tate (Father), 1635 16th St., N. E., Canton, Ohio [ABMC- Belleau] [S2] [SW]

Taunt, Clarence, Cpl., 51st Co., 5th Regt., DOW, June 11, 1918 in the Chateau-Thierry Sector. Sydney A. W. Taunt (Father), 2822 N. 12th St., Philadelphia, Pennsylvania [S2] [SW1]

Taylor, Albert Joseph, Pvt., Bks. Det., MB, Guantanamo Bay, Cuba, DAS, July 11, 1917 as a result of a fall from a railway motor car at Guantanamo Bay, Cuba [S3]

Taylor, Albert Lee, Pvt., 66th Co., 5th Regt., KIA, November 10, 1918 in the Meuse Argonne. Maggie E. Taylor (Mother), Fay, Oklahoma [S2] [SW1]

Taylor, Archie Read, 1st Sgt., Rhine River Patrol, DOO, May 13, 1919 in France. Robert W. Taylor (Father), Utica, Missouri [S2]

Taylor, Bert Gary, Pvt., 47th Co., 5th Regt., KIA, June 7, 1918 in the Chateau-Thierry Sector. Adelaide L. Taylor (Mother), Malinta, Ohio [ABMC- Belleau TOM] [S2] [SW1 says DOW]

Taylor, Caleb W., 2nd Lieut., 9th Sq. NB Gr., KIA, October 22, 1918 in the Meuse Argonne. Mrs. Eula Taylor (Mother), Pelahatchie, Mississippi [S1] [SW]

Taylor, Charles Holbert, Pvt., USNH, Las Animas, Colorado, DDS, June 19, 1921 at Las Animas, Colorado. Charles M. Taylor (Father), Shreveport, Louisiana [S4]

Taylor, Corwin Blessing, Sgt., 84th Co., 6th Regt., KIA, July 19, 1918 in the Aisne Marne. Florence Taylor (Mother), 310 Edgewood Rd, Breakline, Pennsylvania [ABMC- Fere] [S2] [SW1 says DOW]

Taylor, Edward Winfield, Cpl., 74th Co., 6th Regt., KIA, June 11, 1918 in the Chateau-Thierry Sector. Mariah L. Taylor (Mother), 101 Raleigh Rd., Oxford, North Carolina [ABMC- Belleau] [S2] [SW1]

Marine Corps Deaths, 1917-1921

Taylor, Ernest L., Pvt., OSD, Quantico, Virginia, DDS, November 12, 1918 at Quantico, Virginia. Fred E. Taylor (Father), RFD #2, Olin, Jones Co., Iowa [FAG] [S4]

Taylor, George Russell, Pvt., 96th Co., 6th Regt., DOW, June 21, 1918 in the Chateau-Thierry Sector. John C. Taylor (Father), 33 Essex St., Cambridge, Massachusetts [ABMC- Belleau] [S2] [SW says 137th Co., Repl. Btln.]

Taylor, James L., Pvt., BD, MB, OSD, Quantico, Virginia, DDS, August 18, 1919 at Washington, D.C. D. J. Taylor (Father), 704 7th St., Temple, Texas [FAG] [S4]

Tebbe, Milo Geoffrey, Cpl., 74th Co., 6th Regt., DOW, July 19, 1918 in the Aisne Marne. Herman Tebbe (Father), 2900 South Jefferson Ave., St. Louis, Missouri [S2] [SW1]

Teeman, Vernon Lee, Pvt., 82nd Co., 6th Regt., KIA, November 3, 1918 in the Meuse Argonne. David Teeman (Father), P O Bergholz, Ohio [R] [S2] [SW1]

Tesson, Joseph Norbeart, Pvt., Bks. Det., MB, Quantico, Virginia, DDS, November 6, 1918 at Quantico, Virginia. Sophie Tesson (Mother), 2111 Barrone St., New Orleans, Louisana [S3]

Thackery, William Waldo, Pvt., 95th Co., 6th Regt., DOD, October 18, 1918 in France. Joseph M. Thackery (Father), Rose Hill, Kansas [R] [S2] [SW1 says DOW]

Tharau, Herman, Gy. Sgt., 55th Co., 5th Regt., KIA, August 8, 1918 in the Marbache Sector. Annie Thereau (Mother), 18 Oberlin St., Buffalo, New York [ABMC- Thiaucourt] [S2] [SW says Tharan]

Tharp, James Pleas, Pvt., 18th Co., 5th Regt., KIA, June 9, 1918 in the Chateau-Thierry Sector. James A. Carroll (Uncle), Walthall, Mississippi [ANC] [S2] [SW says Tharyf] [SW1]

Thatcher, John Raymond, Pvt., Co. A, 4th Sep. Btln. KIA [SW] [SW1 reported to have been found alive]

Marine Corps Deaths, 1917-1921

Thayer, Samuel Harbison, Pvt., 45th Co., 5th Regt., KIA, June 6, 1918 in the Chateau-Thierry Sector. Susan Thayer (Mother), Gen. Del., Bellevue, Pennsylvania [FAG] [S2] [SW]

Theall, Elisha, Colonel, Office of the Secretary of the Navy, Washington, D.C., DDS, January 28, 1921 at Washington, D.C. Mrs. Florence Theall (Wife), 2400 Sixteenth St., N.W., Washington, D.C. [ANC] [S4]

Thezan, Roger A., Pvt., Bks. Det., Philadelphia, Pennsylvania, DDS, December 15, 1918 at Philadelphia, Pennsylvania. Bertha R. Thezan (Mother), 928 Marigny St., New Orleans, Louisana [S4]

Thiele, Frederick Leonard, Pvt., Naval Prison Det., Parris Island, South Carolina, DDS, November 6, 1918 at Parris Island, South Carolina. Catherine Thiele (Wife), 120 E. 119th St., New York, New York [FAG] [S3]

Thomas, Bennie Osker, Pvt., 51st Co., 5th Regt., KIA, October 4, 1918 in the Meuse Argonne. Mrs. Pearl L. Robinson (Sister), Box 113, Shawmut, Alabama [ANC] [S2] [SW1]

Thomas, Charlie James, Pvt., 44th Co., 3rd Regt., Dominican Republic, DAS, September 26, 1921 drowned at Elbotevern District, Dominican Republic. Mrs. Levada Thomas (Mother), 899 Lee St., Danville, Va. [S4]

Thomas, Evan Daniel, Pvt., 81st Co., 6th MG Bn., KIA, September 14, 1918 in the St. Mihiel Offensive. Mary E. Thomas (Mother), RFD#5, Allegan, Michigan [R] [S2] [SW says Repl. Btln.]

Thomas, Edward, Pvt., MB, Parris Island, South Carolina, DDS, January 30, 1920 at Parris Island, South Carolina. Mrs. Dora Thomas (Mother), RFD#6, Brazil, Indiana [S4]

Thomas, Guy, Pvt., 3485803, 16th Co., 5th Regt., DOW, July 25, 1918 in the Chateau-Thierry Sector. Mrs. Lula Thomas (Mother), Price, Utah [FAG] [S2] [SW says 138th Co., Repl. Btln.]

Marine Corps Deaths, 1917-1921

Thomas, John Harman, Pvt., Hdqtrs. Co., 6th Regt., KIA, July 19, 1918 in the Aisne Marne. Edward T. Thomas (Father), 107 Trammel St., Marietta, Georgia [FAG] [S2] [SW1]

Thomas, Parry Alonzo, Pvt., 17th Co., 5th Regt., DOW, November 15, 1918 in the Meuse Argonne. Ann Thomas (Mother), Spanish Folk, Utah [ABMC- Romagne] [S2] [SW1]

Thomas, Thomas Verl, Pvt., 18th Co., 5th Regt., KIA, June 12, 1918 in the Chateau-Thierry Sector. Sylvester F. Thomas (Father), New Lisbon, Indiana [FAG] [S2] [SW]

Thomasson, Willard Wilmer, Cpl., 76th Co., 6th Regt., DOW, November 11, 1918 in the Meuse Argonne. Mary Thomasson (Mother), Fredericktown, Missouri [S2] [SW1]

Thompson, Donald, Pvt., 45th Co., 5th Regt., KIA [SW] [SW1 reported to have been found alive]

Thompson, Daniel Otha, Pvt., 43rd Co., 5th Regt., DOW, June 12, 1918 in the Chateau-Thierry Sector. Martha J. Thompson (Mother), Ivydale, Clay County, West Virginia [ANC] [S2] [SW says Co. F]

Thompson, John Percy Street, Pvt., MCR, 96th Co., 6th Regt., KIA, June 3, 1918 in the Aisne Defensive. Joe H. Thompson (Brother), 1208 Clay Ave., Houston, Texas [S2] [SW says 134th Co., Repl. Btln.]

Thompson, John Wadsworth, Pvt., 76th Co., 6th Regt., DOW, October 15, 1918 in the Meuse Argonne. Robert L. Thompson (Father), RFD#6, Box 118, Charlotte, North Carolina [FAG] [S2] [SW1]

Thompson, Kinney, Pvt., 84th Co., 6th Regt., KIA, September 15, 1918 in the St. Mihiel Offensive. Frank Thompson (Father), Minersville, Ohio [ABMC- Thiaucourt TOM] [S2] [SW]

Thompson, Tommy Alexander, Pvt., 67th Co., 5th Regt., KIA, October 4, 1918 in the Meuse Argonne. Frank W.

Marine Corps Deaths, 1917-1921

Thompson (Father), Gen. Del. Orland, California [R] [S2] [SW1]

Thompson, William G., Sgt., Mountain Receiving Divison, DDS, January 20, 1920 at Mare Island, California. Mary A. Thompson (Mother), Light House Station, Goat Island, California [S4]

Thor, David Lloyd, Pvt., 73rd Co., 6th Regt., KIA, June 11, 1918 in the Chateau-Thierry Sector. Minnie Thor (Mother), 624 N. Humphrey Ave., Chicago, Illinois [S2] [SW]

Thorn, Raymond Stacy, Pvt., 51st Co., 5th Regt., DOW, June 11, 1918 in the Chateau-Thierry Sector. Mrs. Jessie Thorn (Mother), 2001 E. Madison Ave., Philadelphia, Pennsylvania [ABMC- Belleau] [S2] [SW1 says Raymond Stack Thorn]

Thrasher, Dana Bristol, Pvt., Hdqtrs. Co., 6th Regt., DOW, July 19, 1918 in the Aisne Marne. Esther Thrasher (Mother), 4021 Lake Park Ave., Chicago, Illinois [ABMC- Fere] [S2] [SW1]

Tibbitts, Jessup James, Pvt., 84th Co., 6th Regt., DOW, November 1, 1918 in the Meuse Argonne. Mrs. Sarah E. Tibbits (Mother), 99 Third St., Albany, New York [S2] [SW1]

Tice, Byron Anderson, Cpl., 63rd Co., 8th Regt., Haiti, DDS, August 6, 1921 at Port au Prince, Haiti. Lillie Tice (Mother), Tice, Illinois [S4]

Tigan, Walter J., 2nd Lieut., MCR, 81st. Co., 6th MGBn, DOW, July 28, 1918 in the Aisne Marne. Mrs. K. R. Tigan (Mother), 820 Lincoln Hwy., Rochelle, Illinois [FAG] [S1] [SW]

Tignor, Frank Leslie, Sgt., 76th Co., 6th Regt., KIA, July 19, 1918 in the Aisne Marne. Margaret Tignor (Mother), 310 N. Sycamore St., Richmond, Virginia [FAG] [S2] [SW]

Tillman, Luther, Pvt., USS *South Dakota*, DDS, March 5, 1920 at Vladivostok, Russia. James A. Tillman (Father), Gen. Del., Criner, Oklahoma [S4]

Marine Corps Deaths, 1917-1921

Tilson, Glen, Pvt., Bks. Det., Mare Island, California, DDS, August 23, 1917 at Mare Island, California. Mrs. V. Handford (Mother), Bridgeport, Washington [FAG] [S3]

Timberlake, James Whitfield, Pvt., 76th Co., 6th Regt., DOW, July 19, 1918 in the Aisne Marne. Mrs. Hallie M. Timberlake (Mother), Barhamsville, Virginia [ABMC- Fere] [S2] [SW1]

Timothy, James S., 1st Lieut., Hdqtrs. Co., 6th Regt., KIA, June 14, 1918 [not listed in S1] [not listed ABMC] [S5] [Note: MR- This officer was attached from U.S. Army Infantry, serving with the 6th Regt. at the time of his death]

Timrott, Ernest Herman, Pvt., 80th Co., 6th Regt., KIA, June 10, 1918 in the Chateau-Thierry Sector. Godlich Timrott (Father), Gen. Del., Elmhurst, Illinois [ANC] [S2] [SW1]

Tinsley, Melvin Darden, Pvt., 84th Co., 6th Regt., DOW, July 19, 1918 in the Aisne Marne. Fannie Tinsely (Mother), 227 E. 4th St., Atlanta, Georgia [ABMC- Belleau] [S2] [SW1 says KIA]

Tippets, Wallace, Pvt., OTC Det., Quantico, Virginia, DAS, September 14, 1918 of a skull fracture at Quantico, Virginia. Ellen Prescott (Sister), RFD#1, Burley, Idaho [FAG] [S3]

Tischer, William Francis, Pvt., 18th Co., 5th Regt., KIA, June 10, 1918 in the Chateau-Thierry Sector. Mrs. Matilda Tischer (Mother), Gen. Del., Shawano, Wisconsin [S2] [SW]

Titus, Charles Warton, Pvt., 78th Co., 6th Regt., KIA, October 4, 1918 in the Meuse Argonne. Mary Titus (Mother), 3150 N. Park Ave., Philadelphia, Pennsylvania [R] [S2] [SW]

Titus, Rene Joseph, Pvt., 74th Co., 6th Regt., DOW, April 15, 1918 in the Toulon Sector, Verdun. Louis J. Titus (Father), 1807 South Rampart St., New Orleans, Louisiana [FAGM] [S2] [SW]

Tobias, John Michael, Pvt., 96th Co., 6th Regt., KIA, October 3, 1918 in the Meuse Argonne. Andy Tobias (Father),

Clarence, Pennsylvania [ABMC- Romagne] [S2] [SW] says Co. B, 5th Sep. Btln.]

Todd, Harold, Gy. Sgt., 45th Co., 5th Regt., KIA, June 6, 1918 in the Chateau-Thierry Sector. Catherine Todd (Mother), 142 South St., Detroit, Michigan [ABMC- Belleau] [S2] [SW]

Todd, Lee Roy, Pvt., 8th Co., 5th Regt., KIA, June 3, 1918 in the Aisne Defensive. Mrs. Sarah S. Todd (Mother), 115 E. Main St., Manchester, Georgia [FAG] [S2] [SW]

Tollison, Dock M., Gy. Sgt., Fort Lyon, Colorado, DDS, December 5, 1918 at Fort Lyon, Colorado. Noah Tollison (Father), Westminster, South Carolina [S4]

Tomaka, George, Pvt., 17th Co., 5th Regt., KIA, June 15, 1918 in the Chateau-Thierry Sector. Mrs. Mary Tomaka (Mother), Trzebownisko, Past Rzesow, Galicia, Poland [ABMC- Belleau] [S2] [SW]

Tompkins, Lester Olin, Cpl., 153rd Co., 2nd Regt., 1st Prov. Brigade, Haiti, DDS, May 9, 1921 at Maissade, Haiti. Martha A. Tompkins (Mother), Nichols, New York [S4]

Tompkins, Robert William, Pvt., 75th Co., 6th Regt., DOW, September 14, 1918 in the St. Mihiel Offensive. Mrs. A. T. Tompkins (Mother), 408 Hadley Ave., Houston, Texas [R] [S2] [SW1]

Tompkins, Wilbert Neve, Pvt., 49th Co., 5th Regt., KIA, October 4, 1918 in the Meuse Argonne. Mr. Charles Tompkins (Father), 212 E. Winter St., Delaware, Ohio [FAG] [S2] [SW]

Tompkins, William, Pvt., 75th Co., 6th Regt., KIA, October 9, 1918 in the Meuse Argonne. Coleman Tompkins (Father), Preston, Iowa [ABMC- Romagne] [S2] [SW1]

Toner, Elwood Warner, Pvt., 96th Co., 6th Regt., DOW, November 5, 1918 in the Meuse Argonne. 1821 Buckins St., Frankford, Pennsylvania [ABMC- Romagne] [S2] [SW1]

Marine Corps Deaths, 1917-1921

Tonnies, Harry Titus, Sgt., 80th Co., 6th Regt., KIA, November 1, 1918 in the Meuse Argonne. Elizabeth Tonnines (Mother), 15 W. Oakwood Place, Buffalo, New York [ABMC- Romagne] [S2] [SW1]

Toomey, Robert John, Pvt., 49th Co., 5th Regt., KIA, June 15, 1918 in the Chateau-Thierry Sector. Mary Toomey (Mother), 2236 Massachusetts Ave., Cambridge, Massachusetts [ABMC- Belleau] [S2] [SW1 says DOW]

Tooper, Ben Austin, Cpl., 96th Co., 6th Regt., KIA, October 4, 1918 in the Meuse Argonne. Mr. Edward Toooper (Father), 1082 N. Schuyler Ave., Kankakee, Illinois [ANC] [S2] [SW]

Torgerson, James Alvin, Pvt., 43rd Co., 5th Regt., KIA, June 12, 1918 in the Chateau-Thierry Sector. Adolph Torgerson (Father), Gen. Del., Galloway, Wisconsin [ABMC-Belleau TOM] [S2] [SW]

Tormey, Walter Joseph, Pvt., 96th Co., 6th Regt., KIA, July 19, 1918 in the Aisne Marne. Mary Tormey (Mother), RRD Letcher, South Dakota [S2] [SW1]

Torrey, Henry P., Major, "H" Co., 13th Regt., DOD, September 24, 1918 aboard the *Von Steuben*. Mrs. Hannah P. Torrey (widow), Wide Water, Virginia [ANC] [S1]

Toth, Charles K., Cpl., 95th Co., 6th Regt., KIA, April7, 1918 in the Toulon Sector, Verdun. Joseph Toth (Father), Uipest, Hungary [ABMC- Thiaucourt] [S2] [SW]

Toulson, Joseph Clark, Cpl., 49th Co., 5th Regt., KIA, June 6, 1918 in the Chateau-Thierry Sector. Mrs. Margaret Toulson (Mother), 88 5th St., Salem, New Jersey [ABMC-Belleau] [S2] [SW1]

Townsend, Eden Lemial, Pvt., 75th Co., 6th Regt., DOW, October 9, 1918 in the Meuse Argonne. Rosy M. Townsend (Wife), 1518 Draper St., Indianapolis, Indiana [FAG] [S2] [SW1 says KIA]

Marine Corps Deaths, 1917-1921

Towson, Charles Ashby, Pvt., 47th Co., 5th Regt., DOW, June 7, 1918 in the Chateau-Thierry Sector. Lucy Nelson Towson (Mother), 2914 11th St., N.W., Washington, D.C. [ANC] [S2] [SW says 137th Co., Repl. Btln.]

Tracy, William Anthony, Pvt., BD, MB, Navy Yard, Philadelphia, Pennsylvania, DDS, October 3, 1918 at Philadelphia, Pennsylvania. John G. Tracy (Father), 1230 Purcell Ave., St. Louis, Missouri [FAG] [S3]

Trainor, William, 1st Sgt., Bks. Det., New York, New York, DDS, May 13, 1918 at New York, New York. Elizabeth Major (Sister), 93 Front St., Binghamton, New York [S3]

Trapp, Donald Leo, Pvt., 18th Co., 5th Regt., KIA, June 12, 1918 in the Chateau-Thierry Sector. Robert Trapp (Father), Gen. Del., El Toro, California [VA-ANC as June 6, 1918] [S2] [SW1]

Trefry, Willard Homan, Pvt., Naval Station, Pensacola, Florida, DAS, March 25, 1921 drowned at Pensacola, Florida. Mary H. Trefry (Mother), 10½ Sewall St., Salem, Massachusetts [S4]

Trinka, Frank, Pvt., 20th Co., 5th Regt., DOD, November 25, 1918 in France. Emma Trinka (Sister), 144 Hallete St., Astoria, New York [ABMC- Fere] [S2]

Tritt, Walter Jacob, Pvt., 49th Co., 5th Regt., KIA, July 18, 1918 in the Aisne Marne. Jacob Tritt (Father), Guernsey, Wyoming [ABMC- Belleau TOM] [S2] [SW]

Trotter, John Austin, Pvt., Hdqtrs. Co., OSD, Quantico, Virginia, DDS, October 7, 1918 at Quantico, Virginia. Laura E. Trotter (Mother), Scottsburg, Indiana [S3]

Troutman, David Millard, Cpl., 96th Co., 6th R egt., KIA, October 4, 1918 in the Meuse Argonne. Charles F. Troutman (Brother), Shepherdsville, Kentucky [FAG] [S2] [SW]

Trow, Roy Agusta, Pvt., 79th Co., 6th Regt., DOW, June 7, 1918 in the Chateau-Thierry Sector. Edwin Trow (Father), Box 205, Trinity, Texas [R] [S2] [SW]

Marine Corps Deaths, 1917-1921

Trowbridge, James Henry, Cpl., 23rd Co., 6th MG Bn., DOW, November 4, 1918 in the Meuse Argonne. Myron Trowbridge (Father), Bethel, Connecticut [ABMC- Romagne] [S2] [SW1]

Trulock, Philip Sheridan, Pvt., Hdqtrs. Co., 13th Regt., DOD, September 23, 1918 aboard USS *Von Steuben* enroute to France. Mrs. Roberta Trulock (Wife), Cub Run, Kentucky [FAG] [S2]

Truman, Charles J., Pvt., MB, Charleston, South Carolina, DDS, January 21, 1920 at Rochester, Minnesota. Thomas A. Truman (Father), Rochester, Minnesota [S4]

Truppner, Herbert Gerard, Sgt., 18th Co., 5th Regt., KIA, September 15, 1918 in the St. Mihiel Offensive. Mrs. Johanna Truppner (Mother), 126 Dongan St., New Brighton, New York [ABMC- Thiaucourt] [S2] [SW says 34th Co.]

Tuberville, Robert Evert, Sgt., 66th Co., 5th Regt., KIA, July 18, 1918 in the Aisne Marne. Mrs. Ethel Hicks (Sister), Beuna Vista, Tennessee [ANC] [S2] [SW]

Tucker, Frank, Pvt., 75th Co., 6th Regt., KIA, June 13, 1918 in the Chateau-Thierry Sector. Peter Tucker (Father), 408 6th St., Milwaukee, Wisconsin [S2] [SW]

Tucker, Richard Burton, Pvt., 76th Co., 6th Regt., KIA, July 19, 1918 in the Aisne Marne. Adelbert Tucker (Father), Lear, Michigan [ABMC- Fere] [S2] [SW]

Turley, Joseph Otto, Pvt., 8th Co., 5th Regt., DOW, November 12, 1918 in the Meuse Argonne. Mrs. Eva Turley (Mother), Auburn, King Co., Washington [ANC] [S2] [SW1]

Turley, Solomon Stacy, Pvt., Co. A, 13th Regt., DOD, October 3, 1918 in France. Daniel B. Turley (Father), South West City, Missouri [R] [S2]

Turnbow, Ammon, Pvt., 49th Co., 5th Regt., KIA, November 2, 1918 in the Meuse Argonne. James T. Turnbow (Father), Stephenville, Texas [FAG] [S2] [SW1]

Marine Corps Deaths, 1917-1921

Turner, Benjamin Franklin, Cpl., 16th Co., 5th Regt., KIA, June 23, 1918 in the Chateau-Thierry Sector. Lizzie Turner (Mother), Waco, Texas [ABMC- Belleau TOM] [S2] [SW]

Turner, Benjamin T., Pvt., 96th Co., 6th Regt., DOW [R] [SW]

Turner, Burnela Lee, Pvt., 96th Co., 6th Regt., DOW, October 3, 1918 in the Meuse Argonne. Febey J. Turner (Mother), Elmwood, Oklahoma [R] [S2]

Turner, Garland Broooks, Sgt., 18th Co., 5th Regt., DOW, July 19, 1918 in the Aisne Marne. Mrs. Elizabeth M. Shaw (Mother), Box 96, Fouke, Arkansas [S2] [SW1]

Turngren, Gust Andrew, Jr., Pvt., 96th Co., 6th Regt., DOW, June 16, 1918 in the Chateau-Thierry Sector. Gust A Tungren (Father), 5710 Morgan St., Chicago, Illinois [FAGM] [S2] [SW]

Tuskie, John, Pvt., 79th Co., 6th Regt., KIA, June 14, 1918 in the Chateau-Thierry Sector. Amelia Tuskie (Mother), Barnesville, Minnesota [FAG] [S2] [SW1]

Twigg, William Peter, Pvt., Depot Det., Haiti, DDS, April 23, 1921 at Port au Prince, Haiti. Effie Twigg (Mother), 601 W. Madison St., Paris, Illinois [S4]

Tynan, James Gregory, Pvt., Co. S, MB, Parris Island, South Carolina, DDS, November 8, 1918 at Parris Island, South Carolina. Mary J. Tynan (Mother), 401 South 8th Ave., Mt. Vernon, New York [S3]

Tyson, Benjamin Roland, Pvt., Hdqtrs. Co., 5th Regt., DOW, June 25, 1918 in the Chateau-Thierry Sector. Anna Swenson (Cousin), 361 51st St., Brooklyn, New York [ABMC-Belleau] [S2] [SW]

Uhrig, Jake Martin, Pvt., 75th Co., 6th Regt., DOW, July 20, 1918 in the Aisne Marne. John Uhrig (Father), 516 West Main St., Sterling, Ohio [FAG] [S2] [SW]

Ulmer, Charles H., 2nd Lieut., 80th Co., 6th Regt., DOW, June 9, 1918 in the Chateau Thierry sector. Jacob S. Ulmer

(Father), 1407 Mahatenge St., Pottsville, Pennsylvania [FAG] [S1] [SW]

Ulrich, Frank Seldon, Pvt., 8th Co., 5th Regt., KIA, November 10, 1918 in the Meuse Argonne. Frank Ulrich (Father), 410 College St., Pendleton, Oregon [R] [S2] [SW1]

Upton, C. C., Pvt., 78th Co., 6th Regt., DOD, February 17, 1919 in France. Mrs. Lettie Upton (Mother), 128 E. Maple St., Fremont, Michigan [R] [S2] [SW]

Upton, Ulyssus Wilburn, Pvt., 15th Co., 6th MG Bn., KIA, October 4, 1918 in the Meuse Argonne. Mrs. Ada Upton (Stepmother), 811 Oliver St., Cincinnati, Ohio [R] [S2]

Valdez, Thomas, Pvt., MCR, Co. E., MB, Mare Island, California, DDS, February 21, 1918 at Mare Island, California. Isabelle Valdez (Mother), Gen. Del., Campo, California [S3]

Valentine, Fred William Jr., Pvt., Co. B, 9th Sep. Bn. [8th Sep Bn], DOD, November 11, 1918 in France. Fred W. Valentine (Father), 1116 Park Ave., Peckskill, New York [S2]

Van Allen, Clifford William, Sgt., Radio Station, Tuckerton, New Jersey, DDS, November 3, 1918 at Tuckerton, New Jersey. Andrew Van Allen (Father), 400 W. 160th St., New York, New York [S3]

Van Arsdale, Dana Boardman, Pvt. [Pfc.], Co. A, Overseas Depot, Quantico, Virginia, DDS, October 12, 1918 at Quantico, Virginia. Columbus Van Arsdale (Father), RR#17, Anchorage, Kentucky [S3]

Van Camp, George Miller, Sgt., 97th Co., 6th Regt., KIA, October 6, 1918 in the Meuse Argonne. Rev. John Van Camp (Father), West Concord, Minnesota [ABMC- Romagne] [S2] [SW says Co. A and Millner]

Van Cleve, Andrew Jackson, Pvt., 96th Co., 6th Regt., KIA, October 2, 1918 in the Meuse Argonne. Lillie Cooner (Sister), 222 Dallas St., San Antonio, Texas [R] [S2] [SW1]

Marine Corps Deaths, 1917-1921

Van Duesen, Robert Roy, Sgt., 17th Co., 5th Regt., DOW, October 27, 1918 in the Meuse Argonne. Mrs. Robert Van Duesen (Mother), 328 Bontrose St., Vineland, New Jersey [R] [S2] [SW1 says Van Dusen]

Van Dusen *see* Van Duesen

Van Dyke, Thomas John, Pvt., 66th Co., 5th Regt., DOW, November 1, 1918 in the Meuse Argonne. Alletaa Van Dyke (Mother), Box 572, Chico, California [ABMC-Romagne] [S2] [SW1]

Van Eman, Clare Lemont, Cpl., 67th Co., 5th Regt., KIA, June 6, 1918 in the Chateau-Thierry Sector. William Van Eman (Father), 523 South Center St., Grove City, Pennsylvania [ABMC- Belleau] [S2] [SW]

Van Tassell, Theodore R., Pvt., 73rd Co., 6th Regt., KIA, June 13, 1918 in the Chateau-Thierry Sector. Mrs. Anna Van Tassell (Mother), Box 342, Wayland, New York [ABMC-Belleau as T.R.] [S2] [SW1]

Vanderliet, Walter, Pvt., 78th Co., 6th Regt., DOW, November 8, 1918 in the Meuse Argonne. Mrs. Anna Vanderliet (Wife), 732 Market St., Newark, New Jersey [S2] [SW1]

Vandling, George Fredrick, Pvt., 81st Co., 6th MG Bn., DOW, July 20, 1918 in the Aisne Marne. Mrs. Susanne Klingerman (Mother), Station A., Berwick, Pennsylvania [FAG] [S2] [SW1]

Vanwey, Roy Ellsworth, Pvt., 96th Co., 6th Regt., DOW, July 19, 1918 in the Aisne Marne. Lydia Vanwey (Mother), Burlingame, Kansas [S2] [SW1]

Varella, Victor., Pvt., 17th Co., 5th Regt., DOW, October 4, 1918 in the Meuse Argonne. Antonio Varella (Father), 502 South Exeter St., Baltimore, Maryland [VA-Loudon Park] [S2] [SW1]

Varner, Harold, Cpl., Supply Co., 6th Regt., DOD, December, 9, 1917 in France. J. Florence Varner (Father), Belle Rive, Illinois [ABMC- Suresnes] [S2]

Marine Corps Deaths, 1917-1921

Vaughan, Eugene Robbins, Pvt., 96th Co., 6th Regt., KIA, October 3, 1918 in the Meuse Argonne. Fredericka Vaughan (Mother), 2050 N. Broad St., Selma, Alabama [FAG] [S2] [SW says Co. B, 5th Sep. Btln.]

Vaughan, Hazen Amos, Cpl., 76th Co., 6th Regt., KIA, July 19, 1918 in the Aisne Marne. Lillian Vaughan (Mother), 536 S. Wesley St., Oak Park, Illinois [S2] [SW]

Vaught, Joseph Francis, Pvt., MD, US Naval Hospital, Fort Lyons, Colorado, DDS, November 10, 1918 Fort Lyons, Colorado. Nancy Davis (Mother), 824 5th St., Miami, Florida [VA-Fort Lyon][S3]

Veca, Rayman Silvie, Pvt., Co. E, MB, Navy Yard, Mare Island, California, DDS, November 22, 1918 at Mare Island, California. Mary Pena (Mother), Davis, Yolo County, California [S4]

Vegel, James, Pvt., 96th Co., 6th Regt., DOW, October 3, 1918 in the Meuse Argonne. John Viggiani (Father), 80 Romoyn St., Rochester, New York [R] [S2] [SW says Co. B, Repl. Btln.]

Veid, Albert Clarence, Cpl., 83rd Co., 6th Regt., KIA, October 4, 1918 in the Meuse Argonne. Mrs. Mary Veid (Mother), 1248 Gilsey Ave., Cincinnati, Ohio [R] [S2] [SW says 144th Co.]

Veirs, Dyson Sterling, Pvt., 83rd Co., 6th Regt., DOD, December 7, 1918 in France. Mr. J. O.Viers (Father), Vine Grove, Kentucky [FAG] [S2]

Venables, Perry N., Pvt., Vocational School Det., Quantico, Virginia, DAS, July 5, 1920 drowned in the Potomac River near Quantico, Virginia. Anna G. Breston (Mother), Gen. Del., Thomas, Oklahoma [FAG has April 5, 1920 and says USN; tombstone is USMC] [S4]

Venn, Edwin John, Pvt., 97th Co., 6th Regt., KIA, June 7, 1918 in the Chateau-Thierry Sector. Elizabeth Venn (Mother), 625 Crane Ave., Detroit, Michigan [FAG] [S2] [SW]

Marine Corps Deaths, 1917-1921

Veno, George James R., Pvt., 95th Co., 6th Regt., DOW, October 7, 1918 in the Meuse Argonne. James J. Veno (Father), 293 Deerfield St., Greenfield, Massachusetts [ABMC-Belleau] [S2] [SW1]

Venovich, Samuel, Pvt., Co. B, MB, Navy Yard, Mare Island, California, DDS, February 2, 1920 at Mare Island, California. George Venovich (Father), RFD#1, Box 25, Sand Point, Idaho [FAG] [S4]

Verhage, Philip C., 2nd Lieutenant, MCR, Indian Head, Maryland, DDS, December 11, 1918 at Indian Head, Maryland. Mary N. Verhage (Widow), 1118 Superior Ave., Sheboygan, Wisconsin [S4]

Verno, Howard Henry, Cpl., 74th Co., 6th Regt., DOW, June 6, 1918 in the Chateau-Thierry Sector. Hattie Verno (Mother), Box 102, Empire, Michigan [S2] [SW1]

Verplanck, Eldridge, Pvt., Co. B, 10th Sep. Bn., Quantico, Virginia, DDS, November 17, 1918 at Quantico, Virginia. George Verplanck (Father), Hanover, Michigan [FAG] [S4]

Vest, Herbert McKinley, Pvt., 49th Co., 5th Regt., KIA, June 6, 1918 in the Chateau-Thierry Sector. Mrs. Henrietta Vest (Mother), Kerrs Creek, Virginia [FAG] [S2] [SW1]

Vestre, Willard Edwin, Pvt., 49th Co., 5th Regt., KIA, October 4, 1918 in the Meuse Argonne. John Vestre (Father), Drayton, North Dakota [FAG] [S2] [SW1]

Vick, James Aubrey, Cpl., 84th Co., 6th Regt., KIA, September 15, 1918 in the St. Mihiel Offensive. Linton T. Vick (Father), Meigs, Georgia [S2] [SW says 139th Co., Repl. Btln.]

Vierling, Edward Joseph, Pvt., 45th Co., 5th Regt., DOW, November 11, 1918 in the Meuse Argonne. Mrs. Josephine Vierling Wolters (Sister), 1721 Dolman St., St. Louis, Missouri [S2] [SW1]

Vigneau, James Ambrose, Pvt., 84th Co., 6th Regt., DOW, October 6, 1918 in the Meuse Argonne. Miss Delia Vigneau

Marine Corps Deaths, 1917-1921

(Sister), c/o Help's Quarters, Hawthorne Inn, E. Gloucester, Massachusetts [R] [S2] [SW1]

Vincent, David Michael, Sgt., 82nd Co., 6th Regt., KIA, July 19, 1918 in the Aisne Marne. Mrs. Mary Vincent (Mother), 295 Avalon Ave., Detroit, Michigan [S2] [SW]

Vinyard, Howard, Cpl., 51st Co., 5th Regt., DOW, June 11, 1918 in the Chateau-Thierry Sector. Charles Vinyard (Father), Rosiclare, Illinois [ABMC- Belleau] [S2] [SW1]

Vitatoe, Robert, Pvt., 79th Co., 6th Regt., KIA, June 6, 1918 in the Chateau-Thierry Sector. Mary Vitatoe (Mother), Chamberlain, Tennessee [ABMC- Belleau] [S2] [SW]

Voelzow, Elmer Fred, Pvt., 73rd Co., 6th Regt., KIA, November 1, 1918 in the Meuse Argonne. Edward Schiklowski (Father), 3913 Newark Ave., Cleveland, Ohio [S2] [SW1]

Vogt, John Orville, Pvt., 16th Co., 5th Regt., KIA, June 25, 1918 in the Chateau-Thierry Sector. Benjamin Vogt (Brother), RFD#4, Crown Point, Ohio [ABMC- Belleau TOM] [S2] [SW]

Voliva, John Leslie, Pvt., 16th Co., 5th Regt., DOW, October 6, 1918 in the Meuse Argonne. Charlie Voliva (Father), Carmi, Illinois [FAG] [S2] [SW]

Vollrath, Oscar August, Cpl., 81st Co., 6th MG Bn., KIA, June 9, 1918 in the Chateau-Thierry Sector. John Vollrath (Father), Jacksonville, Illinois [ABMC- Belleau] [S2] [SW]

Von Glahn, Herman Henry, Pvt., 96th Co., 6th Regt., DOW, June 17, 1918 in the Chateau-Thierry Sector. Sophie Van Glahn (Mother), 231 Washington Ave., Brooklyn, New York [ABMC- Belleau] [S2] [SW says 137th Co., Repl. Btln.]

Von Lumm, William, Gy. Sgt., 66th Co., 5th Regt., DOW, October 6, 1918 in the Meuse Argonne. Sophia Von Lumm

Marine Corps Deaths, 1917-1921

(Mother), 565 9th Ave., New York, New York [R] [S2] [SW1]

Voorhies, Clyde Clinton, Pvt., 82nd Co., 6th Regt., KIA, June 6, 1918 in the Chateau-Thierry Sector. James I. Voorhies (Brother), Midlothian, Texas [ABMC- Belleau] [S2] [SW]

Vorhauer, Glenwyn Augustus, Sgt., 1 Squadron, FMAF, DOD, November 2, 1918 in France. Mrs. Hazel Vorhauer (Widow), 1822 Pennsylvania Ave., Los Angeles, California [VA-San Francisco] [S2]

Vose, Howard L., 2nd Lieut., 55th Co., 5th Regt., DOW, October 8, 1918 in the Meuse Argonne. Mrs. Ida F. Vose (Mother), 27 Levant St., Dorchester, Massachusetts [ABMC-Belleau] [S1] [SW1 says KIA]

Votaw, Howard Russell, Cpl., 97th Co., 6th Regt., DOW, October 3, 1918 in the Meuse Argonne. Lyman T. Votaw (Father), Gen. Del., Neoga, Illinois [FAG] [S2] [SW says 120th Co.]

Vucic, Jerry, Cpl., 82nd Co., 6th Regt., DOW, June 19, 1918 in the Chateau-Thierry Sector. Mary Vucic (Mother), 5233 South Albany Ave., Chicago, Illinois [S2] [SW]

Wabbersen, Charles Frederick, Pvt., 95th Co., 6th Regt., KIA, June 6, 1918 in the Chateau-Thierry Sector. Henry Wabbersen (Father), Huntington Sta., Long Island, New York [ABMC- Belleau] [S2] [SW] [SW1]

Waddill, Carroll Joseph, Pvt., Co. C, 9th Sep. Bn, DOD, November 10, 1918 of Pneumonia aboard the USS *Henderson* enroute to France. Mrs. Emma C. Waddill (Mother), 602 W. Main St., Madisonville, Kentucky [FAG] [S2]

Wade, Irvin, Cpl., 45th Co., 5th Regt., KIA, June 13, 1918 in the Chateau-Thierry Sector. Maude Whipkie (Sister), 256 Woodlawn Ave., Aurara, Illinois [ABMC- Belleau] [S2] [SW]

Marine Corps Deaths, 1917-1921

Wagner, Fred Calvin, Pvt., 73rd Co., 6th Regt., KIA, July 19, 1918 in the Aisne Marne. Conrad I. F. Wagner (Father), Rollo, North Dakota [ABMC- Belleau TOM] [S2]

Wagner, Harry Eadward., Pvt., BD, MB, Navy Yard, Philadelphia, Pennsylvania, DDS, September 23, 1918 at Philadelphia. Zoah Wagner (Wife), 1820 East 55th St., Cleveland, Ohio [S3]

Wagner, Willard John, Pvt., 47th Co., 5th Regt., KIA, October 4, 1918 in the Meuse Argonne. Mrs. Viola Wagner (Mother), 2925 Cormany Ave., Cincinnati, Ohio [ABMC- Romagne] [S2] [SW1]

Wahlstrom, Frederick, 2nd Lieut., Hdqrs. Co., 5th Regt., KOA August 21, 1917 in France. Harold Wahlstrom (cousin), 333 Prospect Place, Brooklyn, New York [ABMC- Romagne] [S1] [SW1]

Wainwright, Lafayette F., Pvt., 73rd Co., 6th Regt., DOW, October 25, 1918 in the Meuse Argonne. Robert Wainwright (Father), West Point, Georgia [ABMC- Fere as L.F.] [S2]

Waiss, Fred Albert, Pvt., 49th Co., 5th Regt., KIA, November 11, 1918 in the Meuse Argonne. Harold A. Waiss (Brother), 1117 N. Nevada Ave., Colorado Springs, Colorado [S2] [SW1]

Waiter, Joseph, Gy. Sgt., 140th Co., Repl. Btln. KIA [R] [SW]

Wakefield, Russell James, Pvt., 67th Co., 5th Regt., KIA, June 6, 1918 in the Chateau-Thierry Sector. William Wakefield (Father), 185 S. Saginaw St., Pontiac, Michigan [ABMC-Belleau] [S2] [SW]

Walburn, Alfred C., Pvt., 96th Co., 6th Regt., DOW, June 23, 1918 in the Chateau-Thierry Sector. William Walburn (Father), 78 Ewing St., Chillicothe, Ohio [S2] [SW]

Waldo, Philip Sawyer, Pvt., Co. K, 13th Regt., DOO, July 10, 1919 in France. Mrs. Mary Waldo (Mother), 760 Como Blvd., St. Paul, Minnesota [R] [S2] [SW1 say KOA]

Marine Corps Deaths, 1917-1921

Waldran, Raleigh, Pvt., 84th Co., 6th Regt., KIA, June 26, 1918 in the Chateau-Thierry Sector. Mrs. Eliza Bradley (Not Stated), c/o W. S. Hornsky, Millington, Tennessee [R] [S2] [SW]

Wales, James Leo, Pvt., Co. V, 11th Regt., Quantico, Virginia, DDS, September 30, 1918 at Quantico, Virginia. James M. Wales (Father), Glen Rose, Texas [FAG] [S3]

Wales, Thomas Henry, Sgt., 17th Co., 5th Regt., DOW, June 7, 1918 in the Chateau-Thierry Sector. Emma Wales (Mother), Gen. Del., Weston, West Virginia [FAG] [S2] [SW]

Walker, Fay Elza, Pvt., Co. B, 5th Brigade MG Bn, DOD, November 8, 1918 enroute to France. Deford Walker (Father), Green, Kansas [FAG] [S2]

Walker, Ivan Cliffton, Pvt., 47th Co., 5th Regt., DOW, July 28, 1918 in the Aisne Marne. Charles H. Walker (Father), Rockford, Iowa [ABMC- Suresnes] [S2] [SW]

Walker, Sammy Rose, Pvt., 97th Co., 6th Regt., DOW, July 23, 1918 in the Aisne Marne. Naoma Roberts (Sister), RR#1, Box 23, Silver Point, Tennessee [VA-Nashville] [S2] [SW1]

Walker, William John, Pvt., 47th Co., 5th Regt., KIA, June 6, 1918 in the Chateau-Thierry Sector. Maggie Dewart (Aunt), 3608 S. Marschfield Ave., Chicago, Illinois [ABMC-Fere] [S2] [SW1]

Wall, James William Richard, Pvt., 47th Co., 5th Regt., KIA, September 15, 1918 in the St. Mihiel Offensive. Anna M. Wall (Mother), 1204 Ridgeway Ave., Vincennes, Indiana [S2] [SW says Co. R, Overseas Depot]

Wallace, Eugene, Pvt., 15th Co., 6th MG Bn., KIA, June 15, 1918 in the Chateau-Thierry Sector. Anna Wallace (Mother), Fremont, Wisconsin [ABMC- Belleau] [S2] [SW] [SW1]

Marine Corps Deaths, 1917-1921

Wallace, Thomas Joseph, Pvt., 83rd Co., 6th Regt., DOW, November 5, 1918 in the Meuse Argonne. No next of kin given. [ABMC- Romagne] [S2] [SW1]

Wallace, Thomas Orland, Pfc, Bks. Det., MB, Philadelphia, Pennsylvania, DDS, September 19, 1918 at Philadelphia, Pennsylvania. Sarah Wallace (Mother), 307 W. Newton Ave., Greensburg, Pennsylvania [S3]

Wallace, William N., 1st Lieut., 83rd Co., 6th Regt., KIA, October 9, 1918 in the Meuse Argonne. Henry Lane Wallace (Father), 408 E Pike St., Crawfordsville, Ind. [FAG] [S1] [SW1]

Walleigh, Harry Ralph, Pvt., 17th Co., 5th Regt., KIA, July 18, 1918 in the Aisne Marne. Henry B. Walleigh (Grandfather), Chester Springs, Pennsylvania [ABMC- Belleau] [S2] [SW]

Waller, Clifford Orin, Pvt., 73rd Co., 6th Regt., KIA, November 3, 1918 in the Meuse Argonne. Mrs. Susie J. L. Waller (Mother), R#2, Box 71, Rossville, Georgia [R] [S2] [SW1]

Walling, Arthur Nathaniel, Pvt., 79th Co., 6th Regt., DOW, November 3, 1918 in the Meuse Argonne. Benjamin W. Walling (Father), 1330½ Pacific Ave., Tacoma, Washington [ABMC- Romagne] [S2] [SW1]

Walls, Orpheus, Gy. Sgt., MD, USNH, Fort Lyon, Colorado, DDS, August 12, 1920 at Fort Lyon, Colorado. Ethel Noble (Sister), Nora, Indiana [S4]

Walpole, Robert Nichols, Pvt., 81st Co., 6th MG Bn., KIA, July 25, 1918 in the Aisne Marne. Mrs. Nellie L. Walpole (Mother), 453 Vista Ave., Portland, Oregon [FAG] [S2] [SW says 150th Co., Repl. Btln.]

Walsh, William John, Pvt., Co. B, 13th Regt., DOD, September 22, 1918 aboard the USS *Von Steuben* enroute to France. Margaret Walsh (Mother), 6432 S. Loamis St., Chicago, Illinois [FAG] [S2]

Marine Corps Deaths, 1917-1921

Walter, Harry Franklin, Pvt., Co. B, 5th Brigade MG Mn, DOD, February 20, 1919 Louis B. Walter (Father), 128 S. 2nd St., Steelton, Pennsylvania [FAG] [S2]

Walter, William D., Pvt., 27th Co., 4th Prov. Regt., Dominican Republic, DDS, January 19, 1919 at Santo Domingo, Dominican Republic. Margaret E. Walker (Mother), Union City, Tennessee [S4]

Wanberg, Wilfred Richard, Pvt., 45th Co., 5th Regt., KIA, November 2, 1918 in the Meuse Argonne. Josephine Wanberg (Mother), Murray, Utah [ABMC- Romagne] [S2] [SW1]

Wanek, Frank, Pvt., Co. A, 3rd Sep. Bn., Quantico, Virginia, DDS, November 26, 1918 at Quantico, Virginia. Michael Wanek (Father), Ettrick, Virginia [S4]

Wanser, James Dixon, Cpl., Hdqtrs. Co., 5th Regt., DOD, January 25, 1919 om France. Mary Wanser (Mother), 9308 K. Avenue, Brooklyn, New York [FAG] [S2]

Ward, Frank, Pvt., 23rd Co., 6th MG Bn., DOW, October 9, 1918 in the Meuse Argonne. Kate Ward (Mother), 1229 N. Broadway, Baltimore, Maryland [ABMC-Romagne] [S2] [SW1]

Ward, Horace Albert, Pvt., 79th Co., 6th Regt., KIA, June 6, 1918 in the Chateau-Thierry Sector. Mary A. Ward (Mother), Box 178, Plymouth, Ohio [S2] [SW]

Ward, Walter John, Pvt., 74th Co., 6th Regt., DOW, April 15, 1918 in the Toulon Sector, Verdun. Mrs. W.J. Ward (Mother), 83 Maplewood Ave., Detroit, Michigan [ABMC-Romagne] [S2] [SW]

Ware, Arthur Finnel, Sgt., 49th Co., 5th Regt., KIA, June 6, 1918 in the Chateau-Thierry Sector. Libby Riley (Aunt), Mansfield, Missouri [ABMC- Belleau] [S2] [SW]

Ware, Giles Rebon, Pvt., Co. A, Navy Yard Guard, MD, Navy Yard, Philadelphia, Pennsylvania, DDS, February 13,

1920 at League Island, Pennsylvania. Mary A. Ware (Mother), RFD#2, Brighton, Tennessee [S4]

Ware, Harold Bacon, Pvt., MCR, Hdqtrs. Co., 1st FMAF, DOD, November 12, 1918 in France. Mrs. Bessie H. Ware (Mother), 615 Clay Ave., Scranton, Pennsylvania [R] [S2]

Warman, Chester Allison, Pvt., American Legation, Managua, Nicaragua, DOS, August 7, 1917 at Managua, Nicaragua. John H. A. Warman (Brother), Bay Center, Washington [FAG] [S3]

Warner, Frank Barney, Cpl., USS *Pittsburgh*, DDS, October 22, 1918 aboard the USS *Pittsburgh*. Mrs. Frank Fosget (Grandmother), 395 Lawnsdale St., Detroit, Michigan [ANC] [S3]

Warner, Otto James, Pvt., 147th Co. (Signal), Philadelphia, Pennsylvania, DDS,September 25, 1918 at Philadelphia, Pennsylvania. Erie J. Warner (Father), RFD#1, Sunnyside, Washington [FAG] [S3]

Warren, Edward George, Gy. Sgt., 45th Co., 5th Regt., KIA, April 20, 1918 in the Toulon Sector, Verdun. Mrs. Signy E. Warren (Mother), 2968 W. 14th St., Los Angeles, California [ABMC- Thiaucourt] [S2] [SW]

Warren, Joe Baker, Sgt., 79th Co., 6th Regt., KIA, July 19, 1918 in the Aisne Marne. Annie B. Warren (Mother), Spring Hill, Tennessee [ABMC- Fere] [S2] [SW says Loe]

Warren, Joe Malachi, Pvt., Bn. A, MB, Training Camp, Parris Island, South Carolina, DDS, January 3, 1921 at Parris Island, South Carolina. Lillie Warren (Mother), Evergreen, Texas [S4]

Warren, Philip Van Cortland, Pvt., Bks. Det., RD, MB, Navy Yard, Philadelphia, Pennsylvania, DDS, October 11, 1918 at Philadelphia, Pennsylvania. Mrs. Elizabeth Warren (Mother), Croton, New York [S3]

Marine Corps Deaths, 1917-1921

Warren, Samuel, Pvt., 76th Co., 6th Regt., KIA, September 12, 1918 in the St. Mihiel Offensive. Louis Waronoff (Father), 772 Bluchill Ave., Dorchester, Massachusetts [ABMC- Thiaucourt] [S2] [SW says Co. B, 2nd Casualty Rep. Btln.]

Washam, Joe Collins, Pvt., Bks. Det., Brooklyn, New York, DDS, February 23, 1919 at Brooklyn, New York. Lela Washam (Mother), Lillie, Louisana [FAG] [S4]

Washburn, Horace Douglas, Pvt., 55th Co., 5th Regt., DOW, June 11, 1918 in the Chateau-Thierry Sector. Ida Washburn (Mother), Palmer Falls, New York [FAG] [S2] [SW1]

Washington, George Thaddeus, Jr., Cpl., 96th Co., 6th Regt., KIA, October 3, 1918 in the Meuse Argonne. George T. Washington (Father), 440 Clifton Ave., Lexington, Kentucky [R] [S2] [SW1]

Washtock, Peter James, Cpl., 80th Co., 6th Regt., KIA, October 6, 1918 in the Meuse Argonne. Joseph A. Washtack (Father), Main St., Berea, Ohio [FAG] [S2] [SW1 says Wastook]

Wass, Lester S., Capt., 18th Co., 5th Regt., KIA, July 19, 1918 in the Aisne Marne. Lorenzo A. Wass (Father), 28 Cleveland St., Gloucester, Massachusetts [ABMC-Fere] [S1] [SW1]

Waterhouse, Hascall P., 2nd Lieut., 55th Co., 5th Regt., KIA, June 13, 1918 in the Chateau Thierry sector. Mrs. C. J. Waterhouse (Mother), 374 Jayne Ave., Oakland, California [ABMC-Belleau] [S1] [SW]

Watermeier, Leo, Pvt., 74th Co., 6th Regt., DOW, April 15, 1918 in the Toulon Sector, Verdun. Ceceilia B. Watereier (Mother), 4507 Constance St., New Orleans, Louisiana [R] [S2] [SW]

Waters, Robert Albert, Cpl., 47th Co., 5th Regt., DOW, October 8, 1918 in the Meuse Argonne. Mrs. R. J. Franklin (Grandmother), RFD#6, Norwood, Cincinnati, Ohio [FAG] [S2] [SW1 says KIA]

Marine Corps Deaths, 1917-1921

Watson, Edd., Pvt., 78th Co., 6th Regt., DOW, October 4, 1918 in the Meuse Argonne. J. F. Watson (Father), Glasgow, Kentucky [FAG] [S2] [SW says Edward]

Watson, Henry, Sgt., 74th Co., 6th Regt., DOW, October 7, 1918 in the Meuse Argonne. America J. Watson (Mother), 514 E. Forest Ave., Maysville, Kentucky [FAG] [S2] [SW says KIA]

Watson, John Howard, Pvt., 96th Co., 6th Regt., DOW, October 4, 1918 in the Meuse Argonne. John S. Watson (Father), Springfield, Minnesota [ABMC- Romagne] [S2] [SW]

Watson, Marvin, Pvt., 49th Co., 5th Regt., KIA, June 2, 1918 in the Aisne Defensive. John S. Watson (Father), RFD#2, Walnut Ridge, Arkansas [FAG] [S2] [SW]

Waugaman, Lewis, Cpl., 47th Co., 5th Regt., DOW, June 6, 1918 in the Chateau-Thierry Sector. David G. Waugaman (Father), 833 Franklin Ave., Woodlawn, Pennsylvania [S2] [SW]

Waugh, Tom T., Pvt., 73rd Co., 6th Regt., KIA, October 8, 1918 in the Meuse Argonne. Annie B. Waugh (Father), 4309 Wilmer St., Houston, Texas [R] [S2] [SW1]

Wayman, Harry Wostley, Pvt., 78th Co., 6th Regt., DOW, November 1, 1918 in the St. Mihiel Offensive. Mrs. E. M. Lane (Mother), 411 California St., Salinas, California [S2] [SW1]

Wear, Eugene William, Sgt., 49th Co., 5th Regt., DOW, December, 26, 1918 in the Meuse Argonne. Angie P. Wear (Mother), 579 N. Laurel St., Hazleton, Pennsylvania [ABMC-Suresnes] [S2] [SW1]

Weaver, John H., 1st Lieutenant, MB, Parris Island, South Carolina, DAS, August 26, 1920 in an aeroplane accident at Parris Island, South Carolina. Eli W. Weaver (Father), 25 Jefferson Ave., Brooklyn, New York [FAGM] [S4]

Weaver, William B., Sgt., 75th Co., 6th Regt., DOW, June 22, 1918 in the Chateau-Thierry Sector. Mrs. Marie J. Hall

Marine Corps Deaths, 1917-1921

(Mother), 418½ Depot St., Asheville, North Carolina [R] [S2] [SW1]

Weber, Clarence Herbert, Pvt., 84th Co., 6th Regt., KIA, September 15, 1918 in the St. Mihiel Offensive. George Weber (Father), 1145 W. 5th St., Plainfield, New Jersey [ABMC- Thiaucourt TOM] [S2] [SW1 says Webber]

Weber, Joe Conrad, Sgt., 74th Co., 6th Regt., DOW, October 29, 1918 in the United States of wounds received in the Chateau-Thierry Sector. Mrs. Maude Weber (Sister-in-law), 1813 Bell Ave., Houston, Texas [S2]

Webster, Charles Albert, Pvt., 96th Co., 6th Regt., DOD, February 25, 1919 in France. Mrs. Fannie A. Van Honser (Sister), RFD#4, Box 94, McMinville, Tennessee [R] [S2]

Webster, Malcolm F., Pvt., 81st Co., 6th MG Bn., KIA, July 19, 1918 in the Aisne Marne. Ralph J. Webster (Father), 61 Cummings Ave., Wollaston, Massachusetts [S2] [SW1 says Malcom Eugene Webster]

Webster, Robert Lionel, Pvt., 79th Co., 6th Regt., KIA, October 4, 1918 in the Meuse Argonne. Mrs Elizabeth Maze (Mother), Gen. Del., Paso Rables, California [VA-San Francisco] [S2] [SW]

Weed, Sam Leranzo, Pvt., Bks. Det., Navy Yard, Brooklyn, New York, DDS, January 11, 1919 at Brooklyn, New York. Mrs. John Weed (Mother), P O Box 30, Corpus Christi, Texas [S4]

Weed, Thurlow Adelbert, Pvt., 112th Co., 8th Regt., Galveston, Texas, DOS, January 30, 1918 at Galveston, Texas. Kittie A. Weed (Mother), 5606 S. 4th St., St. Joseph, Missouri [VA-San Antonio] [S3]

Weeks, Guy, Pvt., 96th Co., 6th Regt., KIA, October 3, 1918 in the Meuse Argonne. Mrs. Clara Milfs (Mother), 518 Randle St, Edwardsville, Illinois [R] [S2] [SW]

Weeks, William Earl, Pvt., 51st Co., 5th Regt., DOW, June 15, 1918 in the Chateau-Thierry Sector. Mrs. Mildred H.

Marine Corps Deaths, 1917-1921

Weeks (Wife), 136 Grand Ave., Johnson City, New York [ABMC- Belleau] [S2] [SW]

Weems, Hartie Colman, Pvt., Co. H, MB, Parris Island, South Carolina, DDS, July 21, 1918 at Parris Island, South Carolina. Gracie Weems (Sister), Pope, Tennessee [FAG] [S3]

Wegenast, Fred Andrew, Cpl., 18th Co., 5th Regt., DOW, June 9, 1918 in the Chateau-Thierry Sector. Mr. John Rowe (Uncle), RR#20, St. Mathews, Kentucky [FAG] [S2] [SW]

Wegis, Fred William, Pvt., 96th Co., 6th Regt., DOW, October 10, 1918 in the Meuse Argonne. Anton Wegis (Father), RFDA Box 99, Bakersfield, California [ANC] [S2] [SW]

Weigent, William, Pvt., MB, Navy Yard, Boston, Massachusetts, DOS, June 17, 1917 at Orleans, Massachusetts. Lizzie Weigent (Mother), 1713 Pine St., LaCrosse, Wisconsin [R] [S3]

Weiler, Leonard, Cpl., 95th Co., 6th Regt., DOW, November 12, 1918 in the Meuse Argonne. Elmer S. Weiler (Father), 1205 Carson St., Fort Worth, Texas [VA-Lebanon] [S2] [SW1]

Weinberg, Edward, Pvt., 4th Co., Quantico, Virginia, DAS, August 12, 1918 at Baltimore, Maryland. Harris Weinberg (Father), 2205 E. 78th St., Cleveland, Ohio [S3]

Weir, James Patrick, Pvt., Hdqtrs. Co., 6th Regt., DOW, July 19, 1918 in the Aisne Marne. Mrs. James Weir (Mother), 4358 Vincennes Ave., Chicago, Illinois [FAG] [S2] [SW]

Weir, John William, Pvt., 76th Co., 6th Regt., KIA, November 1, 1918 in the Meuse Argonne. Anna Weir (Sister), #8 Lindsley Place, Orange, New Jersey [ABMC- Romagne] [S2] [SW1]

Weisbaker, Alfred Earl, Pvt., 49th Co., 5th Regt., KIA, June 5, 1918 in the Chateau-Thierry Sector. Louisa Weisbaker

Marine Corps Deaths, 1917-1921

(Mother), 121 Chadwick Ave., Newark, New Jersey [ABMC- Belleau] [S2] [SW]

Weiske, George, Cpl., 95th Co., 6th Regt., KIA, July 19, 1918 in the Aisne Marne. Mrs. Amelia Weiske (Mother), Montello, Wisconsin [FAG] [S2] [SW1 says DOW]

Weiss, Samuel, Pvt., 61st Co., New York, New York, DDS, February 13, 1920 at New York, New York. Jacob Weiss (Father), 32 Grand St., Poughkeepsie, New York [R] [S2]

Weitz, John Conrad, Cpl., 96th Co., 6th Regt., KIA, October 3, 1918 in the Meuse Argonne. Mrs. Walter Irwin (Mother), Walla Washington, Washington [FAG] [S2] [SW1]

Wekwert, Louis, Pvt., 47th Co., 5th Regt., KIA, October 5, 1918 in the Meuse Argonne. John Wekwert (Father), 44 Osborne Lane, Bayonne, New Jersey [S2] [SW says Wekert and Co. L]

Welch, Clarence Lester, Pvt., Hdqtrs. Co., 6th Regt., DOW, November 6, 1918 in the Meuse Argonne. George E. Welch (Father), 335 W. 8th St., Elyria, Ohio [FAG] [S2] [SW1]

Welch, Martin Leander Jr., Pvt., 74th Co., 6th Regt., KIA, June 13, 1918 in the Chateau-Thierry Sector. Martin L. Welch (Father), 31 Cleveland St., Gloucester, Massachusetts [ABMC- Belleau TOM] [S2] [SW]

Welch, William Ferdinand, Pvt., 45th Co., 5th Regt., DOW, June 7, 1918 in the Chateau-Thierry Sector. John J. Welch (Father), c/o Mrs. John Timm, 616 Liberty St., Newport, Kentucky [R] [S2] [SW]

Weld, Earl John, Pvt., 8th Co., 5th Regt., DOD, December, 14, 1918 in France. Wirt A. Weld (Father), 3622 Colfax Ave., N. Minneapolis, Minnesota [R] [S2]

Weldon, Roy Lester, Pvt., 96th Co., 6th Regt., KIA, October 3, 1918 in the Meuse Argonne. Orin H. Weldon (Administrator of the estate of Mary E. Fackler (Mother) (Deceased), Minerva, Ohio [FAG] [S2] [SW1]

Weller, Sidney, Pvt., 16th Co., 5th Regt., KIA, June 25, 1918 in the Chateau-Thierry Sector. Abe Weller (Brother), 1195 28th St., Milwaukee, Wisconsin [ABMC- Belleau TOM] [S2] [SW says Supply Co., 5th Regt.]

Wells, Edward Henry, Pvt., 74th Co., 6th Regt., DOW, April 25, 1918 in the Toulon Sector, Verdun. James T. Wells (Father), 5217 E. 28th St., Kansas City, Missouri [ABMC- Romagne] [S2] [SW]

Wells, Even Peace, Pvt., 76th Co., 6th Regt., KIA, July 19, 1918 in the Aisne Marne. Salley Wells (Mother), Bonne Terre, Missouri [FAG] [S2] [SW1]

Wells, William Alfred, Pvt., 45th Co., 5th Regt., KIA, June 6, 1918 in the Chateau-Thierry Sector. Linda Wells (Mother), 1846 Division St., Baltimore, Maryland [ABMC- Belleau] [S2] [SW]

Welsh, John, Pvt., 1208327, 67th Co., 5th Regt., KIA, June 6, 1918 in the Chateau-Thierry Sector. John T. Welsh (Father), Lisbon, Ohio [S2] [SW]

Welsh, Perry Davis, Pvt., Co. H, MB, Parris Island, South Carolina, DDS, November 2, 1918 at Parris Island, South Carolina. Mrs. Kaherine Welsh (Wife), 1323 N. 6th St., W. Cedar Rapids, Iowa [FAG] [S3]

Wempner, Emmett, Pvt., 18th Co., 5th Regt., KIA, June 6, 1918 in the Chateau-Thierry Sector. Ammenda Brown (Grandmother), London, Indiana [S2] [SW]

Wendel, Harry Arthur, Pvt., 96th Co., 6th Regt., DOW, June 28, 1918 in the Chateau-Thierry Sector. Mrs. Carrie Wendel (Mother), 25 N. Mayfield Ave., Chicago, Illinois [R] [S2] [SW]

Wendell, Edward Herman, Pvt., 79th Co., 6th Regt., KIA, June 6, 1918 in the Chateau-Thierry Sector. Minnie Wendell (Mother), Gen. Del., Brule, Missouri [FAG] [S2] [SW]

Marine Corps Deaths, 1917-1921

Wendt, George, Pvt., 153rd Co., Quantico, Virginia, DDS, July 16, 1918 at Quantico, Virginia. Magdalena Wendt (Mother), Victorville, California [FAG] [S3]

Wendt, Otto Julius, Pvt., Co. G, MB, Parris Island, South Carolina, DDS, June 15, 1917 at Parris Island, South Carolina. Armelia Wendt (Mother), 1804 S. Chilsom St., Bay City, Michigan [S3]

Weppler, John Louis, Cpl., 95th Co., 6th Regt., DOW, June 7, 1918 Joseph A. Weppler (Father), 2141 Arcena St., Pittsburgh, Pennsylvania [R] [S2] [SW]

Werner, Bernard, Pvt., 43rd Co., 5th Regt., KIA, June 4, 1918 in the Aisne Defensive. Frederick Ernie (Friend), Binghamton, New York [ABMC- Belleau TOM] [S2] [SW]

Wertz, James Clair, Sgt., 83rd Co., 6th Regt., KIA, June 2, 1918 in the Aisne Defensive. Mrs. Mary Wertz (Mother), 16 Ridge Road, Lewiston, Pennsylvania [FAG] [S2] [SW says Gy. Sgt.]

Weschke, Leo, Pvt., Hdqtrs. Co., 5th Regt., DOD, October 25, 1918 in France. Mrs.Clara Weschke (Mother), 6248 Aspen Ave., Cincinnati, Ohio [FAG] [S2]

West, Chester Thomas, Pvt., Hdqtrs. Co., 5th Regt., DOD, August 26, 1917 in France. Cora Niven (Mother), RFD#30, Carrolton, Ohio [ABMC- Romagne] [S2]

West, Henry, Sgt., 47th Co., 5th Regt., KIA, June 25, 1918 in the Chateau-Thierry Sector. Mrs. Sophie West (Mother), 116 Pleasant St., Ware, Massachusetts [R] [S2] [SW]

West, Ralph O'Neal, Pvt., 80th Co., 6th Regt., KIA, September 15, 1918 in the St. Mihiel Offensive. Mattie R. West (Mother), 1136 Center St., Newton Center, Massachusetts [ABMC- Thiaucourt] [S2] [SW says Hdqrs. Co., 3rd Repl. Btln.]

Marine Corps Deaths, 1917-1921

Westcott, Percy Douane, Pvt., Hdqtrs. Co., 5th Regt., DOD, September 25, 1918 in France. Orville Westcott (Father), #4 Brooklyn St., Eaton, New York [ABMC- Fere] [S2]

Westlund, Conrad John, Pvt., 47th Co., 5th Regt., DOW, November 4, 1918 in the Meuse Argonne. Mary Juveland (Mother), Warren, Minnesota [ANC] [S2] [SW1]

Wethling, Otto H., Pvt., Supply Co., Parris Island, South Carolina, DDS, November 14, 1918 at Parris Island, South Carolina. Louise Wethling (Mother), 7063 Ravenswood Ave., Chicago, Illinois [S4]

Whall, Joseph Haskell, Cpl., 76th Co., 6th Regt., DOW, October 9, 1918 in the Meuse Argonne. Clifford S. Whall (Brother), Colon St., Stop 43½, Santurce, Puerto Rico [S2] [SW1 says KIA]

Wheeler, Albert Ciceroe, Cpl., 80th Co., 6th Regt., DOW, July 19, 1918 in the Aisne Marne. Clara Wheeler (Mother), Gen. Del., Charleston, West Virginia [FAG] [S2] [SW1 says Albert Cicero Wheeler] [Brother of Earnest Doutin Wheeler, below]

Wheeler, Earnest Doutin, Pvt., Navy Yard, Washington, D.C., DDS, October 18, 1918 at Washington, D.C. Clara C. Wheeler (Mother), Charleston, West Virginia [FAG] [S3] [Brother of Albert Ciceroe Wheeler, above]

Wheeler, John Russell, Pvt., Hdqtrs. Co., 6th Regt., KIA, July 19, 1918 in the Aisne Marne. John C. Wheeler (Father), Stiles St., Linden, New Jersey [FAG] [S2] [SW]

Wheeler, Neil Evans, Sgt., 47th Co., 5th Regt., DOW, June 17, 1918 in the Chateau-Thierry Sector. Frank P. Wheeler (Father), 291 W. 2nd St., Oswego, New York [ABMC- Belleau] [S2] [SW1]

Wheeler, Pleasant Eliot, Cpl., 146 Co., 3rd Replacement Bn, KIA, June 6, 1918 in the Chateau-Thierry Sector. William F. Wheeler (Brother), Route #3, Box 103, Bessemer, Alabama [ABMC- Belleau TOM] [S2]

Marine Corps Deaths, 1917-1921

Wheeles, Benjamin Cleo, Pvt., Co. B, 9th Sep. Bn, DOD, December, 31, 1918 in France. Mr. R. F. Wheeles (Father), Swanwick, Illinois [R] [S2]

Whipple, James Bennet, Pvt., 76th Co., 6th Regt., KIA, June 3, 1918 in the Aisne Defensive. Florence Straus (Mother), RFD#57, South Wilton, Connecticut [ABMC- Belleau] [S2] [SW]

Whitbeck, Alden Maben, Cpl., 49th Co., 5th Regt., KIA, July 18, 1918 in the Aisne Marne. William Witbeck (Father), Vernal, Utah [R] [S2]

White, Carleton Burk, Cpl., QM Department, Hdqtrs., Washington, D.C., DDS, January 24, 1919 at Washington, D.C. John Henry White (Father), 108 Woodward St., Camden, Arkansas [S4]

White, Charles Edward, Pvt., 67th Co., 5th Regt., KIA, November 2, 1918 in the Meuse Argonne. Mr. Acelbert E. Clark (Friend), c/o C. B. Shaw, 315-18 Post Standard Bldg., Syracuse, New York [S2] [SW1]

White, Clarence Ray, Pvt., 75th Co., 6th Regt., KIA, June 10, 1918 in the Chateau-Thierry Sector. George R. White (Father), Elnora, Indiana [S2] [SW]

White, Frank James, Cpl., 45th Co., 5th Regt., KIA, June 7, 1918 in the Chateau-Thierry Sector. Ellen White (Mother), 4651 N. Western Ave., Chicago, Illinois [R] [S2]

White, John, Pvt., 16th Co., 5th Regt., DOA, April 4, 1918 in France. Maria White (Mother), 36 Hudson St., N. Tarrytown, New York [S2] [SW1 says KOA]

White, Otis Leo, Pvt., Bks. Det., MB, Quantico, Virginia, DDS, November 6, 1918 at Quantico, Virginia. Mrs. Ruth White (Wife), Flora, Ohio [FAG] [S3]

White, Plymton J., Pvt., Depot Det., Haiti, DAS, January 20, 1921 of injuries received in a truck accident at Haiti. Mrs. George White (Mother), Landover, Maryland [S4]

Marine Corps Deaths, 1917-1921

Whitehead, George R., Pvt., Hdqtrs., MC, A&I Dept., Washington, D.C., DDS, January 25, 1920 at Washington, D.C. Mrs. Ethel Whitehead (Wife), 1539 Broad St., Stratford, Connecticut [S4]

Whiteside, John Ray, 2nd Lieutenant, MCR, Marine Flying Field, Miami, Florida, DAS, January 23, 1919 of multiple injuries received in an aeroplane crash at St. Petersburg, Florida. J. c. Whiteside (Father), Okolona, Mississippi [FAG] [S4]

Whitman, Louis Charles, Cpl., 43rd Co., 5th Regt., KIA, June 11, 1918 in the Chateau-Thierry Sector. Lucy Whitman (Mother), 394 Conkey Ave., Rochester, New York [S2] [SW]

Whitman, Ralph Francis, Pvt., 47th Co., 5th Regt., DOW, June 6, 1918 in the Chateau-Thierry Sector. Jennie Whitman (Mother), 7 Adams St., Mechanicsville, New York [S2] [SW1]

Whitney, Forest Burlett, Pvt., 112th Co., 8th Regt., Galveston, Texas, DDS, October 12, 1918 at Galveston, Texas. Florence Whitney (Mother), Penn Yan, New York [S3]

Whitson, Fred Albert, Pvt., 95th Co., 6th Regt., DOW, July 19, 1918 in the Aisne Marne. George t. Whitson (Father), 3935 South 3rd St., Louisville, Kentucky [ABMC- Fere] [S2] [SW1 says KIA]

Wickwire, Henry John, Pvt., 45th Co., 5th Regt., KIA, October 4, 1918 in the Meuse Argonne. Elizabeth Slater (Sister), RFD, Olean, New York [VA-Woodlawn, NY] [S2] [SW1]

Widmayer, Robert Harold, Pvt., 6th Co., 10th Regt., Quantico, Virginia, DAS, July 15, 1921 of a fractured skull at Quantico, Virginia. Margaret Widmayer (Mother), 2920 5th Ave., Rock Island, Illinois [S4]

Wien, Frank, Pvt., Co. B, 7th Sep. Bn, DOD, November 9, 1918 in France. Fannie Wien (Mother), 1332 Independence Blvd., Chicago, Illinois [FAGM] [FAG] [S2]

Marine Corps Deaths, 1917-1921

Wierman, Benjamin, Pvt., 83rd Co., 6th Regt., KIA, June 6, 1918 in the Chateau-Thierry Sector. Bunion Wierman (Father), RR#2, Lexington, Kentucky [VA-Lexington] [S2] [SW1 says DOW]

Wiertz, Frank, Pvt., 97th Co., 6th Regt., DOW, October 8, 1918 in the Meuse Argonne. Joseph Wiertz (Father), Neillsvill, Wisconsin [R] [S2] [SW1]

Wiesgerber, Michael, Pvt., Bks. Det., MB, Navy Yard, Philadelphia, Pennsylvania, DDS, February 6, 1920 at Philadelphia, Pennsylvania. Annie Bentz (Grandmother), Almont, Michigan [S4]

Wilcox, Monroe Pierce, Pvt., 79th Co., 6th Regt., Quantico, Virginia, DOS, December 30, 1917 at Corsicana, Texas. Nora Wilcox (Mother), RFD#3, Corsicana, Texas [FAG] [S3]

Wilcox, Vernon Arthur, Pvt., 70th Co., Dominican Republic, DAS, October 24, 1920 in Soco River, Dominican Republic. Ida Wilcox (Mother), RFD#1, Robertsdale, Alabama [FAG] [S4]

Wildey, George Edward Jr., Pvt., 76th Co., 6th Regt., KIA, October 6, 1918 in the Meuse Argonne. George E. Wildey (Father), 833 Eastern Parkway, Brooklyn, New York [R] [S2] [SW1]

Wilkerson, Sterling Robert, Pvt., 47th Co., 5th Regt., KIA, September 15, 1918 in the St. Mihiel Offensive. Thomas Wilkerson (Father), 211 E. 20th St., Covington, Kentucky [ABMC- Thiaucourt] [S2] [SW says Oveseas Depot]

Wilkes, Joseph Simmons, Pvt., 79th Co., 6th Regt., KIA, June 8, 1918 in the Chateau-Thierry Sector. Albert Wilkes (Father), 403 7th Ave., Salt Lake City, Utah [R] [S2] [SW] [SW1]

Wilkinson, Alfred, 2nd Lieut., 8th Co., 5th Regt., DOW, October 5, 1918 in the Meuse Argonne. Mrs. James Foulke (sister), 414 E. North Ave., Milwaukee, Wisconsin [ANC] [S1] [SW]

Marine Corps Deaths, 1917-1921

Wilkinson, Claude Luis, Pvt., 74th Co., 6th Regt., DOW, April 20, 1918 in the Toulon Sector, Verdun. Mary F. Wilkinson (Mother), Hillsboro, Indiana [ABMC- Romagne] [S2] [SW]

Wilkinson, Samuel Maris, Pvt., 17th Co., 5th Regt., DOW, June 15, 1918 in the Chateau-Thierry Sector. Della M. Wilkinson (Mother), RFD#2, Hillsboro, North Carolina [FAG] [VA-Raleigh] [S2] [SW1]

Willenbrock, Fred William, Pvt., Hdqtrs. Co., 6th Regt., DOD, March 6, 1918 in France. John Willenbrock (Father), 4461 Chippewa St., St. Louis, Missouri [FAG] [S2]

Willett, Guy Earl, Sgt., MCR, Supply Det., MB, Quantico, Virginia, DDS, September 27, 1918 at Quantico, Virginia. Alfred P. Willett (Father), Indian Head, Maryland [FAG] [S3]

Willi, Arthur James, Pvt., 23rd Co., 6th MG Bn., KIA, November 10, 1918 in the Meuse Argonne. Joseph Willi (Father), 5 Grant Ave., Troy, New York [FAG] [S2] [SW1]

Williams, Alfred, Jr., Pvt., 73rd Co., 6th Regt., KIA, July 19, 1918 in the Aisne Marne. Alfred Williams (Father), Penn Yan, New York [ABMC- Belleau] [S2] [SW]

Williams, Arthur Fisher., Pvt., MCR, 7th Regt., San Juan, Puerto Rico. April 17, 1918 at San Juan, Puerto Rico. Arthur John Williams (Father), 3319 14th St., N.E., Washington, D.C. [ABMC- Thiaucourt] [S3]

Williams, Carl, Pvt., 83rd Co., 6th Regt., KIA, June 6, 1918 in the Chateau-Thierry Sector. James L. Williams (Father), Wyanesville, North Carolina [ABMC- Belleau TOM] [S2 says Carl Clinton and Co. O]

Williams, Carl Oscar, Pvt., 96th Co., 6th Regt., KIA, September 15, 1918 in the St. Mihiel Offensive. Agnette Spangrud (Aunt), Cyrus, Minnesota [ABMC- Thiaucourt] [S2]

Marine Corps Deaths, 1917-1921

Williams, Cecil Augustus, Gy. Sgt., 51st Co., 5th Regt., DOW, July 24, 1918 in the Aisne Marne. George W. Williams (Father), Ahoskie, North Carolina [R] [S2] [SW]

Williams, Charles Ferdinand, Pvt., 96th Co., 6th Regt., DOW, July 19, 1918 in the Aisne Marne. Hannah Williams (Mother), 628a East High St., Jefferson City, Missouri [S2] [SW1]

Williams, Chester Edward, Pvt., 18th Co., 5th Regt., DOW, June 11, 1918 in the Chateau-Thierry Sector. Mary J. Williams (Mother), Hubbell, Michigan [S2] [SW1]

Williams, Elmer Henry, Cpl., Naval Station, Guam, DAS, DAS, May 19, 1919 in an automobile accident at Guam. Ida Wiliams (Mother), Gen. Del., Haines, Oregon [S4]

Williams, Forest Grey, Pvt., 80th Co., 6th Regt., DOW, July 20, 1918 in the Aisne Marne. L. Judson Williams (Father), Charleston, West Virginia [ABMC- Fere] [S2] [SW]

Williams, Francis Edward, Cpl., 49th Co., 5th Regt., KIA, June 6,1918 in the Chateau-Thierry Sector. Thomas E. Williams (Father), 1245 Avalon Ave., Alliance, Ohio [S2] [SW]

Williams, George Edwin, Pvt., 49th Co., 5th Regt., DOW, June 8, 1918 in the Chateau-Thierry Sector. Mrs. Eva Williams (Mother), 1381 Trumbull Ave., Detroit, Michigan [ABMC- Belleau] [S2] [SW]

Williams, George W., Pvt., 17th Co., 5th Regt., DOW, November 3, 1918 in the Meuse Argonne. Dr. W. Carlos Williams (Brother), Gen. Del., Del Monte, California [ABMC- Romagne] [S2] [SW1]

Williams, Harold Morrice, Pvt., 83rd Co., 6th Regt., KIA, June 8, 1918 in the Chateau-Thierry Sector. Mrs. Mary Ayers (Mother), 53 Trowbridge Ave., Detroit, Michigan [R] [S2] [SW1]

Williams, Harry Robert, Pvt., 82nd Co., 6th Regt., DOW, April 2, 1918 in the Toulon Sector, Verdun. Hattie Williams

Marine Corps Deaths, 1917-1921

(Mother), Hillsboro, Indiana [ABMC- Thiaucourt] [S2] [SW]

Williams, Harry Warren, Pvt., 43rd Co., 5th Regt., DAO, April 29, 1919 in France while cleaning rifle. Charles Williams (Father), 2842 48th Court, Portland, Oregon [ANC] [S2] [SW1 says KOA]

Williams, John Patrick, Pvt., 84th Co., 6th Regt., DOW, October 8, 1918 in the Meuse Argonne. George Williams (Father), 602 Mahanoy Ave., Girardville, Pennsylvania [R] [S2] [SW1]

Williams, John Robert, Cpl., 78th Co., 6th Regt., DOW, July 19, 1918 in the Aisne Marne. Mrs. Emma Williams (Mother), 2512 N. 14th St., St. Louis, Missouri [R] [S2] [SW1 says KIA]

Williams, Lloyd W., Capt., 51st Co., 5th Regt., DOW, June 11, 1918 in the Chateau Thierry sector. Mrs. L. W. Williams (Widow), Berryville, Virginia [FAG] [S1] [SW]

Williams, Ollie Pickens, Pvt., 142nd Co., New London, Connecticut, DDS, September 30, 1918 at New London, Connecticut James E. Williams (Father), Grand Cane, Louisiana [S3]

Williams, Oscar, Pvt., 74th Co., 6th Regt., KIA, July 19, 1918 in the Aisne Marne. Tom Williams (Father), Flat Lick, Kentucky [S2] [SW1]

Williams, Paul Roger, Pvt., Co. B, MB, Navy Yard, Mare Island, California, DDS, December 9, 1919 at Mare Island, California. H. E. Williams (Father), 176 RFD, Compton, California [FAG] [S4]

Williamson, Fred E., Pvt., Co. A, MB, Navy Yard, Mare Island, California, DDS, February 4, 1920 at Mare Island, California. Lena Williamson (Mother), 834 Colorado St., Pasadena, California [S4]

Williamson, Thomas Jerome, Pfc, 16th Co., 5th Regt., Quantico, Virginia, DAS, October 28,1920 of burns at Quantico,

Marine Corps Deaths, 1917-1921

Virginia. Stella Williamson (Mother), Dlo, Mississippi [FAG] [S4]

Willis, George Thomas, Pvt., 17th Co., 5th Regt., DOW, June 6, 1918 in the Chateau-Thierry Sector. Florence Willis (Mother), 5510 Poplar St., Philadelphia, Pennsylvania [ABMC- Belleau TOM] [S2] [SW1]

Willis, Henry C., Sgt., 62nd Co., 2nd Regt., Haiti, DOW, March 28, 1919 of wounds received in action at Port au Prince, Haiti. Price Willis (Uncle), Slater, Missouri [S4]

Willis, Jack, Pvt., MB, USNH, Fort Lyon, Colorado, DDS, December 25, 1919 at Las Animas, Colorado. Mrs. Jessie Martin (Sister), Madalay Apts., Seattle, Washington [VA-Fort Lyon] [S4]

Willis, William Sterling, Pvt., BD, MB, Philadelphia, Pennsylvania, DDS, October 16, 1918 at Philadelphia, Pennsylvania. Emma E. Willis (Sister), 106 Academy St., Salem, Virginia [S3]

Willmott, Noah Stark, Pvt., 84th Co., 6th Regt., KIA, October 5, 1918 in the Meuse Argonne. William Tanner Willmott (Father), RFD#3, Finchville, Kentucky [ABMC-Romagne] [S2] [SW]

Wilmot, Harry, Pvt., 18th Co., 5th Regt., KIA, June 10, 1918 in the Chateau-Thierry Sector. Clarence J. Wilmot (Father), Gloversville, New York [S2] [SW]

Wilson, Arthur Shepard, Pvt., 67th Co., 5th Regt., DOW, December, 3, 1918 in the Meuse Argonne. Frank P. Wilson, Jr. (Father), 14317 Darley Ave., N. E., Cleveland, Ohio [R] [S2] [SW1]

Wilson, Edmund Meredith, Pvt. [Pfc], 76th Co., 6th Regt., DOW, June 4, 1918 in the Chateau-Thierry Sector. William Wilson (Brother), 823 Evergreen Ave., Millvale, Pennsylvania [ABMC- Belleau] [S2] [SW]

Marine Corps Deaths, 1917-1921

Wilson, Fred I., Pvt., MB, Key West, Florida, DDS, October 13, 1919 at Key West, Florida. Josephine Beebe (Aunt), 1st St., Scottsville, Michigan [S4]

Wilson, Herman Chambers, Gy. Sgt., 49th Co., 5th Regt., DOW, October 6, 1918 in the Meuse Argonne. Mrs. Harriet E. Wilson (Mother), 169 Cumberland Ave., Ashville, North Carolina [ABMC- Belleau] [S2] [SW1]

Wilson, Herman Lesley, Pvt., 80th Co., 6th Regt., DOD, May 10, 1918 in France. Virginia Wilson (Mother), Franklin Grove, Illinois [R] [S2]

Wilson, James Howard, Pvt., 76th Co., 6th Regt., KIA, November 1, 1918 in the Meuse Argonne. James H. Wilson (Father), 1620 N. Alabama St., Indianapolis, Indiana [FAG] [S2] [SW1 says DOW]

Wilson, Robert D. A., Pvt., 20th Co., 5th Regt., DOW, June 23, 1918 in the Chateau-Thierry Sector. Mrs. Carry Halbert (Mother), 904 13th St., Bakersfield, California [ABMC-Belleau] [S2] [SW1]

Wilson, Robert Harold, Cpl., 84th Co., 6th Regt., KIA, July 19, 1918 in the Aisne Marne. Mrs. Margaret Wilson (Mother), Box K, Norwalk, California [ABMC- Fere] [S2] [SW1]

Wilson, Roicy Dee, Pvt., 49th Co., 5th Regt., DOW, June 17, 1918 in the Chateau-Thierry Sector. May Wilson (Mother), Randolph, Nebraska [ANC] [S2] [SW]

Wilson, Sidney Eugene, Pvt., Co. A, 1st Training Btln., DOW, January 17, 1918 in France. Sidney C. Wilson (Father), New Eagle, Pennsylvania [R] [S2] [SW1]

Wimberly, Robert Hoy, Pvt., 83rd Co., 6th Regt., DOW, June 6, 1918 in the Chateau-Thierry Sector. Jasper L. Wimberly (Father), Gholson, Mississippi [ANC] [S2] [SW1]

Winchell, Judge Earl, Sgt., 84th Co., 6th Regt., DOW, October 6, 1918 in the Meuse Argonne. Richard Winchell (Father), RFD#1, Tell City, Indiana [FAG] [S2] [SW1]

Marine Corps Deaths, 1917-1921

Wingfield, Frank Gordon, Pvt., 82nd Co., 6th Regt., KIA, October 3, 1918 in the Meuse Argonne. Alexander Wingfield (Father), Wilmot, Mississippi [ABMC- Belleau] [S2] [SW]

Winiecki, Edward Leo, Pvt., 67th Co., 5th Regt., KIA, June 6, 1918 in the Chateau-Thierry Sector. Leo J. Winiecki (Father), 4421 Altgeld St., Chicago, Illinois [FAG] [FAGM] [S2] [SW]

Winn, Carl Frances, Gy. Sgt., 67th Co., 5th Regt., KIA, June 6, 1918 in the Chateau-Thierry Sector. Kate Winn (Mother), RFD#4, Portage, Wisconsin [ABMC- Belleau] [S2] [SW1]

Winn, Francis Welliver, Pvt., 79th Co., 6th Regt., Mare Island, California, DDS, January 13, 1918 at Quantico, Virginia. Louisa Winn (Mother), Gen. Del., Wellen, Oregon [FAG] [S3]

Winn, James Kyle, Pvt., 132nd Co., FAB, Quantico, Virginia, DDS, September 29, 1918 at Quantico, Virginia. Mrs. Martha Winn (Mother), Rocksprings, Texas [FAG] [S3]

Winnicki, Stanley, Cpl., 61st Co., New York, New York, DDS, February 1, 1920 at New York, New York. Marion Winnicki (Father), Riverhead, Long Island, New York [VA-Memphis] [S4]

Winston, John Williams, Pvt., 49th Co., 5th Regt., KIA, June 6, 1918 in the Chateau-Thierry Sector. Ada E. Winston (Mother), 668 N. 5th St., Memphis, Tennessee [S2] [SW]

Wintering, Charles, Pvt., 67th Co., 5th Regt., DOD, January 23, 1919 in France. Mr. Henry Wintering (Father), 1544 Pleasant St., Cincinnati, Ohio [R] [S2]

Wise, Guy, Pvt., 95th Co., 6th Regt., DOW, October 10, 1918 in the Meuse Argonne. Margaret Robinson (Sister), Gen. Del., Ipava, Illinois [ABMC- Romagne] [S2] [SW1]

Wise, Simpson Carrol, Cpl., 76th Co., 6th Regt., KIA, October 6, 1918 in the Meuse Argonne. Charity Wise (Mother),

Marine Corps Deaths, 1917-1921

RD#3, Batesburg, South Carolina [ABMC- Romagne TOM] [S2] [SW1]

Wishart, Theophilus Luke, Pvt., 51st Co., 5th Regt., DOW, December, 14, 1918 in the Meuse Argonne. Mabel M. Wishart (Divorced wife), 1148 Brunswick Ave., Trenton, New Jersey [ABMC- Suresnes] [S2] [SW1]

Wisner, James, QM Sgt., 184th Co., 15th Regt., Dominican Republic, DDS, July 29, 1920 at Santo Domingo, Dominican Republic. Margaret Wisner (Wife), 2707 N. 11th St., Philadelphia, Pennsylvania [VA-Philadelphia] [S4]

Wisted, David Gilbert, Pvt., 82nd Co., 6th Regt., KIA, June 3, 1918 in the Aisne Defensive. Marie Rowe (Sister), 1201 E. 4th St., Duluth, Minnesota [ABMC- Belleau] [S2] [SW]

Witbeck, Alden Maben, Cpl., 49th Co., 5th Regt., KIA, July 18, 1918, Utah [ABMC-Belleau] [not listed in S2] [SW]

Wittstein, Eli, Pvt., 74th Co., 6th Regt., DOW, April 21, 1918 in the Toulon Sector, Verdun. Isaac Wittstein (Father), c/o Mrs. Samuel Sery, South Norwood, Ohio [R] [S2] [SW]

Wloch, Barney, Pvt., [unit not stated], DOS, February 20, 1919 at Atlanta, Georgia. Mrs. Frances Wloch (Mother), 1825 Hermitage Ave., Chicago, Illinois [S4]

Wnuk, Joseph Frank, Cpl., 51st Co., 5th Regt., KIA, November 10, 1918 in the Meuse Argonne. John Wnuk (Step-father), Mahaffey, Pennsylvania [R] [S2] [SW1]

Woglom, George Washington, Pfc, MB, Boston, Massachusetts, DDS, September 18, 1918 at Chelsea, Massachusetts. Francis Woglem (Mother), 52 E. 52nd St., Brooklyn, New York [S3]

Wojczynski, Anthony, Sgt., 18th Co., 5th Regt., DOW, June 12, 1918 in the Chateau-Thierry Sector. Joseph Wojczynski (Father), 29 Rother St., Buffalo, New York [ABMC-Belleau TOM] [S2] [SW1]

Marine Corps Deaths, 1917-1921

Wolaver, William Warren, Sgt., 18th Co., 5th Regt., DOW, July 21, 1918 in the Aisne Marne. Elbie Wolaver (Father), Spirit River, Alberta, Canada [R] [S2] [SW1]

Wolfhegel, Charles, Gy. Sgt., 20th Co., 5th Regt., DOW, November 14, 1918 in the Meuse Argonne. Louise Banta (Sister), 76 Walnut St., Tidgewood, New Jersey [ABMC- Thiaucourt] [S2] [SW1]

Wolfkill, Frank Earnest, Pvt., Hdqtrs. Co., 13th Regt., DOD, September 27, 1918 in France. Emma E. Wolfkill (Wife), 269 Rochelle Ave., Philadelphia, Pennsylvania [VA- Philadelphia] [S2]

Wood, Charles, Cpl., 2196270, 78th Co., 6th Regt., KIA, September 15, 1918 in the St. Mihiel Offensive. Mrs. A. O. Breedlove (Sister), 108 Walker St., Durham, North Carolina [ABMC- Thiaucourt TOM] [S2] [SW says Co. B, Repl. Btln.]

Wood, Griffin G., Pvt., Co. C., OT, Quantico, Virginia, DDS, November 15, 1918 at Quantico, Virginia. W. S. Wood (Father), Itasca, Texas [FAG] [S4]

Wood, Howard Bailey, Cpl., 16th Co., 5th Regt., KIA, June 23, 1918 in the Chateau-Thierry Sector. Clarence D. Wood (Father), Elmdale, Kansas [ABMC- Belleau] [S2] [SW1]

Wood, Jeremiah Raymond, Pvt., 47th Co., 5th Regt., KIA, June 6, 1918 in the Chateau-Thierry Sector. Eva Wood (Mother), Agosta, Ohio [ABMC- Belleau] [S2] [SW1]

Wood, Vernon, Cpl., 100th Co., Haiti, DDS, May 8, 1919 at Port au Prince, Haiti. Nancy Wood (Mother), Boxville, Union Co., Kentucky [FAG] [S4]

Woodburn, Robert Lawson, Pvt., 96th Co., 6th Regt., DOW, September 17, 1918 in the St. Mihiel Offensive. Mrs. Margaret M. Woodburn (Mother), Route #3, Plain City, Ohio [FAG] [S2] [SW1]

Woodcock, Hamilton Forbes, Pvt., Co. B, MB, Navy Yard, Mare Island, California, DDS, September 17, 1918 at Oakland,

Marine Corps Deaths, 1917-1921

California. Burgate Woodcock (Father), Camp Cody, Deming, New Mexico [S3]

Woodgrift, Charles Elmer, Cpl., 82nd Co., 6th Regt., KIA, June 16, 1918 in the Chateau-Thierry Sector. Mrs. Birdie L. Woodgrift (Mother), Farmington, Michigan [R] [S2] [SW]

Woodle, Loren H., Pvt., Bks. Det., MB, Navy Yard, Norfolk, Virginia, DDS, February 24, 1919 at Fort Lyon, Colorado. Charles F. Woodle (Father), 508 Baldwin St., Austin, Minnesota [FAG] [S4]

Woodman, Dexter Eugene, Pvt., 96th Co., 6th Regt., DOW, November 2, 1918 in the Meuse Argonne. Chester I. Woodman (Father), 33 Chestnut St., Danvers, Massachusetts [ABMC- Romagne] [S2] [SW1]

Woodruff, George A., Pvt., Marine Barracks, Parris Island, South Carolina, DDS, January 7, 1919 at Parris Island, South Carolina. Aida Woodruff (Wife), RFD#7, Covington, Georgia [FAG] [S4]

Woodruff, Wilbert Albert, Pvt., 51st Co., 5th Regt., DOW, June 7, 1918 in the Chateau-Thierry Sector. Mrs. Mary Whiting (Mother), 609 W. 28th St., Minneapolis, Minnesota [R] [S2] [SW]

Woods, Leland Hartwell, Pvt., 95th Co., 6th Regt., DOD, February 7, 1919 in France. Frank A. Woods (Father), Smith St., Townsend, Massachusetts [R] [S2]

Wootten, Jerome Alexander, Pvt., 51st Co., 5th Regt., KIA, October 4, 1918 in the Meuse Argonne. Mrs. Richard H. Wootten (Mother), Washington, Georgia [ABMC-Romagne] [S2] [SW1 says Wooten]

Workman, James Santford, Pvt., 95th Co., 6th Regt., DOW, November 2, 1918 in the Meuse Argonne. Mrs. Mary Workman (Mother), Paoli, Oklahoma [ANC] [S2] [SW1 says KIA]

Marine Corps Deaths, 1917-1921

Workman, William, Capt., 13th Regt., DOD, September 24, 1918 aboard the USS Henderson. Mrs. Francis Workman (widow), 1529 Waller St., Portsmouth, Ohio [R] [S1]

Worstall, Thurman Edgar, Pvt., 20th Co., 5th Regt., KIA, June 6, 1918 in the Chateau-Thierry Sector. William J. Worstall (Brother), 27½ Madison St., Zanesville, Ohio [S2] [SW]

Wray, James Arthur, Cpl., 82nd Co., 6th Regt., KIA, October 4, 1918 in the Meuse Argonne. Anna Wray (Mother), 390 Poplar St., Topeka, Kansas [R] [S2] [SW]

Wright, Arthur H., 1st Lieut., MCR, 9th Sq. FMAF, Northern Bomb. Gr., DOD, October 31, 1918 in France. Mrs. A. H. Wright (widow), 39 High St., Newburyport, Massachusetts [FAG] [S1] [SW1 says DOA]

Wright, Edward, Pvt., Co. N, MB, Parris Island, South Carolina, DDS, October 23, 1918 at Parris Island, South Carolina. Thomas J. Wright (Father), 200 Wayne St., Jersey City, New Jersey [S3]

Wright, Henry J., Cpl., Extra Duty Detachment, Parris Island, South Carolina, DDS, November 18, 1918 at Parris Island, South Carolina. Attlia Wright (Mother), 372 8th St., Brooklyn, New York [S4]

Wright, James F., Cpl., Co. A, 11th Sep. Bn., Quantico, Virginia, DDS, November 26, 1918 at Quantico, Virginia. Cecil Cora Wright (Wife), Delphos, Kansas [FAG] [S4]

Wright, Leonard Lorenzo, Cpl., 82nd Co., 6th Regt., KIA, June 8, 1918 in the Chateau-Thierry Sector. Mrs. Mary A. Wright (Mother), RFD, Gainesville, New York [ABMC-Belleau] [S2] [SW]

Wrigley, James Francis, Pvt., 66th Co., 5th Regt., DOD, October 16, 1918 in France. Mrs. Eva Wrigley (Mother), 1220 Columbus Terrace, Peoria, Illinois [FAG] [S2]

Wulff, Irving, Pvt., 8th Co., 5th Regt., KIA, October 4, 1918 in the Meuse Argonne. Hannah Wulff (Mother), c/o J. Choyke,

4858 H. Washtenau Ave., Chicago, Illinois [FAGM] [S2] [SW1]

Wunderlich, Arthur Herney, Pvt., 79th Co., 6th Regt., KIA, July 19, 1918 in the Aisne Marne. Clara Wunderlich (Mother), 542 South 9th St., W., Salt Lake City, Utah [FAG] [S2] [SW1]

Wyman, Elmer Claus, Pvt., 43rd Co., 5th Regt., DOW, June 11, 1918 in the Chateau-Thierry Sector. Christine Hambright (Mother), Neffsville, Pennsylvania [FAG] [S2] [SW1]

Wyss, Alfons John, Pvt., 49th Co., 5th Regt., KIA, November 4, 1918 in the Meuse Argonne. Ethel Wyss (Wife), 1107 White Ave., Fremont, Ohio [R] [S2] [SW1]

Yake, Ira Albert, Pvt., 75th Co., 6th Regt., KIA, October 10, 1918 in the Meuse Argonne. Mrs. Albert Yake (Mother), Croswell, Michigan [S2] [SW1]

Yandl, Anthony, Pvt., Co. M, 11th Regt., Quantico, Virginia, DDS, September 26, 1918 at Quantico, Virginia. Rose Weinger (Mother), 713 S. Munsen St., South Bend, Indiana [FAG] [S3]

Yarborough, George H., Jr., 1st Lieut., 45th Co., 5th Regt., DOW, June 26, 1918 in the Chateau Thierry sector. G. H. Yarborough (Father), Mullins, South Caroline [FAG] [S1] [SW]

Yarbrough, James Clifton, Pvt., 67th Co., 5th Regt., KIA, June 6, 1918 in the Chateau-Thierry Sector. Mrs. H. W. Yarbrough (Mother), 742 N. Boulvard, Atlanta, Georgia [VA-Marietta] [S2] [SW]

Yeager, Jennings Bryan, Pvt., 75th Co., 6th Regt., KIA, July 19, 1918 in the Aisne Marne. Mrs. Anna Yeager (Mother), Harrison, Ohio [ABMC- Fere] [S2] [SW1]

Yeaton, Guy Malcolm, Sgt., 66th Co., 5th Regt., KIA, October 4, 1918 in the Meuse Argonne. John Yeaton (Father), Islesboro, Maine [R] [S2] [SW]

Marine Corps Deaths, 1917-1921

Yerger, John Cooper, Cpl., Co. B, Overseas Depot, Quantico, Virginia, DDS, September 25, 1918 at Quantico, Virginia. Nina M. Yerger (Mother), 700 S. McLean St., McLean, Tennessee [S3]

Yerkes, Morris C., Trp, Bks. Det., Brooklyn, New York, DOS, January 23, 1919 at Brooklyn, New York. Rachael Yerkes (Mother), 332 Harrison Ave., Boston, Massachusetts [S4]

York, Asa Claude, Pvt., 51st Co., 5th Regt., DOW, October 21, 1918 in the Meuse Argonne. Dr. W. E. York (Father), Giddings, Texas [S2] [SW1]

York, Daniel Omer, Cpl., Hdqtrs. Co., 13th Regt., DOD, September 27, 1918 in France. Mrs. Cleta Price York (Wife), Shattuc, Illinois [FAGx2] [S2]

Young, Dewey Oliver, Pvt., 67th Co., 5th Regt., KIA, June 6, 1918 in the Chateau-Thierry Sector. Ellen Young (Mother), New Castle, Texas [ABMC- Belleau TOM] [S2]

Young, Francis Leo, Pvt., 97th Co., 6th Regt., DOW, October 14, 1918 in the Meuse Argonne. Edward E. Young (Father), 803 Cheynne St., Alliance, Nebraska [ABMC- Suresnes] [S2] [SW1]

Young, Fred Curtis, Pvt., 47th Co., 5th Regt., DOW, June 25, 1918 in the Chateau-Thierry Sector. Samuel C. Young (Father), 132 Grain Ave., Kent, Ohio [FAG] [S2] [SW1]

Young, George Lindsey, Pvt., 80th Co., 6th Regt., KIA, June 3, 1918 in the Aisne Defensive. Mrs. Maggie Young (Mother), 215 Maggie Young (Mother), 215 N. 6th St., Salt Lake City, Utah [S2] [SW says 139th Repl.]

Young, Gilbert William, Pvt., 16th Co., 5th Regt., KIA, June 7, 1918 in the Chateau-Thierry Sector. Mrs. Dorcas Young (Mother), Springfield, Kentucky [R] [S2] [SW]

Young, James A., Pvt., 7th Co., MB, Quantico, Virginia, DDS, January 14, 1920 at Quantico, Virginia. Mary Young

Marine Corps Deaths, 1917-1921

(Mother), RFD#2, Box 9, Forest, Lewis Co., Washington [FAG] [S4]

Young, James I., Pvt., Co. B, 11th Sep. Bn., Quantico, Virginia, DDS, November 19, 1918 at Quantico, Virginia. Mrs. Lela Young (Mother) R.F.D. #5, Phoenix, Arizona [FAG] [S4]

Young, Robert E., Pvt., Co. B, Mare Island, California, DDS, November 19, 1918 at Mare Island, California. Harriet T. Young (Mother), 244 Calistoga Ave., Napa, Caliornia [S4]

Young, Vearn William, Cpl., 18th Co., 5th Regt., DOW, July 18, 1918 in the Aisne Marne. Ida M. Rutledge (Mother), 1208 W. Ave., Legrande, Oregon [ABMC- Fere] [S2] [SW says 140th Co., Repl. Btln.]

Youngs, Howard Jay, Pvt., 47th Co., 5th Regt., KIA, October 4, 1918 in the Meuse Argonne. Harmon Youngs (Father), Renville, Minnesota [ABMC- Romagne TOM] [S2]

Zane, Randoph T., Major, 79th Co., 6th Regt., DOW, October 24, 1918 in the Chateau Thierry sector. Mrs. R. T. Zane (widow), c/o Gov. W. D. Stephens, Governor's Mansion, Sacramento, California [ABMC-Bony] [S1] [SW1 says KIA]

Zein, Frank Henry, Pvt., 18th Co., 5th Regt., KIA, October 4, 1918 in the Meuse Argonne. Mrs. Robert Skailand (Sister), 108 South 5th St., LaCrosse, Wisconsin [FAG] [S2] [SW1]

Zele, Ferdinand N., Cpl., NAF, Miami, Florida, DAS, February 15, 1919 in an aeroplane accident at Miami, Florida. Joseph Zele (Father), 6502 St. Clair Ave., Cleveland, Ohio [FAG] [S4]

Zemaitis, Mindow Leonard, Pvt., 43rd Co., 5th Regt., KIA, June 13, 1918 in the Chateau-Thierry Sector. Mrs. Teresa Zemaitis (Mother), 714 W. German St., Baltimore, Maryland [ABMC- Belleau] [S2] [SW1 says Minbow Leonard Zenaitis and DOW]

Marine Corps Deaths, 1917-1921

Zender, Jay Edward, Pvt., 74th Co., 6th Regt., KIA, June 10, 1918 in the Chateau-Thierry Sector. Mrs. Lottie F. Zender (Mother), 68 Green St., Fredoinia, New York [R] [S2] [SW1]

Zimmerman, George Ora, Pvt., Supply Co., 7th Regt., Cuba, DAS, August 7, 1919 of a spinal injury at Santiago de Cuba. George R. Zimmerman (Father), Griggsville, Illinois [S4]

Zimmerman, Walter H., Pvt., Marine Detachment, American Legation, Managua, Nicaragua, DOS, December 20, 1919 at Nicaragua. Ida Zimmerman (Mother), 959 Valencia St., San Francisco, California [S4]

Zimmerman, Walter Oscar, Pvt., 55th Co., 5th Regt., DOW, June 30, 1918 in the Chateau-Thierry Sector. Gottlief L. Zimmerman (Father), 2328 Cedar St., Louisville, Kentucky [R] [S2] [SW says Casualty Co.]

Zimmerman, Willis F., Pvt., 68th Co., MB, NS, Guantanamo, Cuba, DDS, July 2, 1920 at Guantanamo, Cuba. John J. Zimmerman (Father), RFD#3, Bellevue, Pennsylvania [S4]

Zinnel, Walter Joseph, Pvt., 79th Co., 6th Regt., KIA, June 25, 1918 in the Chateau-Thierry Sector. Ella Zinnel (Mother), 2321 North 3rd St., Philadelphia, Pennsylvania [R] [S2] [SW1]

Ziolkowski, August Thomas, Gy. Sgt., 79th Co., 6th Regt., DOW, October 4, 1918 in the Meuse Argonne. Mrs. Estell L. Tyran (Sister), 571 Wentworth Ave., Milwaukee, Wisconsin [R] [S2] [SW1]

Zippay, Michael, Pvt., 82nd Co., 6th Regt., KIA, June 3, 1918 in the Aisne Defensive. John Zippay (Father), 1217 McKenn Ave., Charleroi, Pennsylvania [FAG] [S2] [SW says 72nd Co., likely an error]

Zipperer, John Babtist, Pvt., Co. C, Parris Island, South Carolina, DAS, July 12, 1918 of a neck fracture and spinal injuries received when drivng at Parris Island, South Carolina.

Marine Corps Deaths, 1917-1921

Josephine Zipperer (Mother), 321 N. Park Ave., Warren, Ohio [S3]

Zoltowski, William, 2nd Lieut., MCR, 77th Co., 6th MGBn, DOW, October 6, 1918 in the Meuse Argonne. Mrs. Frances Zoltowski (Mother), 676 Livingstone St., Detroit, Michigan [R] [S1] [SW1 says KIA]

Zyglarski, Stanley Paul, Cpl., 77th Co., 6th MG Bn., DOO, May 18, 1918 in France. Mrs. Mary Zyglarski (Mother), 71 Moore St., Albion, New York [ABMC- Romagne] [S2] [SW]

Heritage Books by Craig R. Scott, CG:

Index to the Fairfax County, Virginia Register of Marriages, 1853–1933
Constance K. Ring and Craig R. Scott

*The "Lost" Pensions: Settled Accounts of the Act of 6 April 1838,
Revised Edition*

Marine Corps Deaths, 1917–1921

New Jerusalem Lutheran Church Cemetery
Marty Hiatt and Craig R. Scott, CG

*Preliminary Inventory of the War Department Collection of
Confederate Records (Record Group 109) in the National Archives*
Elizabeth Bethel; indexed by Craig R. Scott, CG

*Records of the Accounting Officers of the
Department of the Treasury: Inventory 14 (Revised)*
William F. Sherman with additions and index by Craig R. Scott, CG

Scott Family Finding Aids, Volume #1: Marriages, 1700–1900

www.ingramcontent.com/pod-product-compliance
Lightning Source LLC
Chambersburg PA
CBHW050830230426
43667CB00012B/1946